THE BANISHED HEART

T&T Clark Studies in **Fundamental Liturgy** offer cutting-edge scholarship from all disciplines related to liturgical study. The books in the series seek to reintegrate biblical, patristic, historical, dogmatic and philosophical questions with liturgical study in ways faithful and sympathetic to classical liturgical enquiry. Volumes in the series include monographs, translations of recent texts and edited collections around very specific themes.

Edited by
Laurence Paul Hemming
Susan Frank Parsons

Forthcoming titles in the series:
Being Liturgical: The Subject of Worship – the Practice of the Love of God
Collects of the Roman Missal: A Study in Liturgical Reform

THE BANISHED HEART

Origins of Heteropraxis in the Catholic Church

Geoffrey Hull

t&t clark

Published by T&T Clark International
A Continuum Imprint
The Tower Building, 11 York Road, London SE1 7NX
80 Maiden Lane, Suite 704, New York, NY 10038

www.continuumbooks.com

British Library Cataloguing-in-Publication Data
A catalogue record for this book is available from the British Library

ISBN 13:   978-0-567-23798-9 (Hardback)
            978-0-567-44220-8 (Paperback)

Typeset by Pindar NZ, Auckland, New Zealand
Printed and bound in Great Britain by the MPG Books Group

CONTENTS

This revolution of an avant-garde clergy is not a manoeuvre affecting the Church alone . . . It affects the whole of civilization, and it is merely the continuation and the completion of a process whose origins it is very important to understand in an objective way.

In every period of crisis and revolution one sees, unfortunately, two parties equally hostile to compromise pitted against each other: extreme progressives interested only in limitless destruction and uprooting; and traditionalists responding with a veneration of the past that excludes all discussion and room for doubt. No dialogue is possible between these two camps, for any movement or progress of the one provokes from the other an immediate and ever stiffer reaction.

Now the first step towards an objective discussion is a proper understanding of the conflict . . .

Marie-Madeleine Martin

The main goal of my life is the unity of the Churches, the unity of people, of God's children . . .

Bl. Andrew Sheptyckyj

FOREWORD

This is both a timely and an untimely book – timely, in that it brings to the case
for traditional liturgy in the Catholic Church a necessary breadth of perspective
and an acuity of analysis which leave no room for the supposition that all was
well in the Church prior to the Second Vatican Council; and untimely, in that it
thereby seeks no accommodation to the entrenched positions of traditionalists
whose perspective is, properly speaking, reactionary; nor to those of the present
'official' Church; nor, far less, to the philosophy and practice of those who, after
the Council, sought to inculturate Catholicism with the antagonistic culture of
modern secular society.

Implicit in this approach to the case in question is a plea for a Catholic restoration – a restoration not envisaged as a blind turning back to a past to which it is
neither possible nor desirable to return, but as a bringing forward into the liturgical
and ecclesial life of Catholicism of all those elements which constitute its authentic
tradition, and hence its patrimony; while enriching the same with the insights,
hard-won over the last forty years, as to the practices, aspirations and assumptions
that have drawn the Church into apostasy from the deepest sources of her life.

The surprising thing in this book – and it is the capacity to surprise that, along
with its scholarship, makes the book convincing – is its exposition of precisely
how the present 'conservative' Catholicism, with its modernistic and secular aura,
grew directly from the 'official traditionalism' that prevailed in the Church until
the death of Pius XII. In this sense, *The Banished Heart* offers, and convincingly
documents, the thesis that the legacies of rationalism and imperialism in the
Church have placed that body in a position of antagonism, always implicit and
frequently overt, to the popular and cultural bases of Catholicism; and that this
has been especially the case since the Counter Reformation and the triumph in the
Church of the mentality represented in the Society of Jesus.

In other words, the mind, or more precisely the will of the Church, has gone into
a species of schism from its body: to be 'Catholic', consciously and with commitment, has tended increasingly to differ from the belonging to Catholicism; and the
focus which this book sets on the phenomenon illuminates it throughout by referring, as if to the very body and life of the Church herself, to the historic liturgies
of Catholicism and their subjection to what were generally *official* undertakings
of reduction, sequestering, or outright abolition.

Consequently, the fate which overtook the traditional Roman liturgy after the
Second Vatican Council had already been foreshadowed in the dealings of the
'Romanizers' with such rites as the Malabarese of India or the Mozarabic of Spain;
and the relative ease of implantation afforded to Paul VI's unauthentic *Novus
Ordo Missæ* may be regarded largely as the outcome of the elimination throughout

Western Christendom of the bonds between liturgy and local culture.

In the pursuit of his thesis, Professor Hull expands upon the notion proposed by the poet T. S. Eliot in respect of literature, that in the seventeenth century a 'dissociation of sensibility' set in among writers – and, by extension, throughout the cultures subjected to the Reformation and the Counter Reformation – and that subsequently the intellect and the emotions, the mind and the body, tended to be conceived of and to function as distinct entities; though always, in the new climate of rationalism, to the detriment of the whole being.

The exploration of this complex historical unfolding is one which, in this work, unites in the central notion of 'culture' and in the defence of traditional worship, both the popular and the hieratic, the witness of the erudite and the urbane with that of the 'dark and opacous hearts' reproved by the Cambridge Platonist John Smith in 1660 for their attachment to the instinctive and spontaneous manifestations of religion. In drawing on the witnesses of history, poetry, anthropology, philosophy and theology, the book adopts what is, properly speaking, a Catholic outlook – one which calls upon the manifestations of intellectual and popular culture and the resources of humanism to elucidate an implicit sense of Western culture as itself fundamentally and inescapably Catholic.

That same sense, I take it, would consider that the wish to ignore or to jettison those witnesses for the sake of a 'pure' Catholicism, in fact participates in Catholicism's marginalization, in the levering of the Church out of her own cultural setting and realm. Outside its natural environment the mind of the Faith has been doomed to sink into inert admiration and feeble imitation of the forms of contemporary secular life – forms which, 'relevant' though they may be to certain assumptions of modern culture, become in the hands of the Church the badge and proclamation of her irrelevance, because they do not proceed from, and cannot address, those deepest human needs to which she is divinely enjoined to respond.

Hence, *The Banished Heart* both seeks to associate for the substantiation of its thesis the faculties which modern intellectual suppositions tend to disjoin, and offers to the traditionalist understanding of liturgy and ecclesiology the disconcerting – but refreshing – insight that immobilism as a consciously entertained posture itself engenders radicalism, and that tradition can remain traditional only so long as it is able to accommodate, within its permanence, growth. For the argument implied throughout Dr Hull's study, and rising now and then to the surface, is that in her need to come to terms with the Reformation, the Church brought into fullness of expression tendencies within her which had always been at odds with such an understanding of tradition as the above. The post-Tridentine Church, it is compellingly argued, was, precisely in her self-conscious, explicit and immobilistic traditionalism, in effect untraditional; and the turning of the Church's attention from this period onwards almost exclusively to the West, and away from the fecund, worship-centred consciousness of Eastern Catholicism and Orthodoxy, confirmed in her the drift of head from heart, the disjunction of a doctrinally orthodox mind from an increasingly heteropractic liturgical body.

In this regard, it may be well said that Protestantism entered the Church through the side-door of rationalism, and proceeded thereafter, beneath the stiff surface of deliberately maintained Catholic forms, to convert into its own substance the life it sought within – that the Church admitted, in both her commitment to progress in the form of political pragmatism, and her espousal of a traditionalism proceeding from merely mental allegiances, the antagonist which, as we see today,

> . . . hath broke ope
> The Lord's anoynted Temple, and stole thence
> The Life o' th' Building.

(Macbeth, II, 3)

The question, then, which *The Banished Heart* urges upon those Catholics committed now to the visible post-conciliar Church and to the artificial, man-centred liturgy by which she worships, is the one that all cultures, if they are to grow and flourish, are bound continually, if tentatively, to answer: by what power, and to what end, do you live, and what is the depth of your life?

Dr Warwick Orr
Anglo-American Institute
Barcelona

INTRODUCTION

Introducing the first edition of this book in 1995, I wrote:

> John Paul II has been called the most loved, and the most disobeyed pope in the history of the Catholic Church. Wherever the 'People's Pope' appears, he is hailed and cheered by throngs of Catholics. Yet it is these same people who practise a religion in which strict observance of the Supreme Pontiff's traditional teachings plays no important part.

Little has changed since the 1990s. Most Catholics today – ordinary believers as well as the theologically literate – have adopted a 'self-service' approach to the beliefs and practices of their Church, accepting some and rejecting others on the basis of private judgement. It is an approach that is quintessentially Protestant. Among those Catholics who unhesitatingly rise to join the Communion queue at a modern Mass are many who rarely fulfil their Sunday obligation, who have not been to confession in years, who deny the existence of Satan and hell, who believe that women no less than men are called to the priesthood, and who scorn official Church teaching on sexual morality.

Since the 1970s conservative Catholics have been deploring this 'anarchical' situation. Yet their strictures ring hollow when they speak of a 'rebellion' in the post-conciliar Church, as if there were a concerted effort on the part of the laity and the clergy to disobey the popes and the immutable teachings they uphold. In reality, what has been happening over the past fifty years is that Catholics have been responding, obediently and conscientiously, to Pope John XXIII's call to *aggiornamento*. They have quite simply implemented the papal command to 'update' (*aggiornare*) and inculturate Catholicism fully into modern civilization. If this inculturation has led inexorably to the compromising of central tenets of the faith and essential principles of its correct practice or 'orthopraxis' (something not intended by Roncalli and his successors), the fault lies with the policy itself, not with the Catholic faithful directed to embrace it.

John XXIII launched this new policy, the central programme of liberal Catholicism, and Paul VI put it into practical effect by dismantling the cumulative orthopraxis of two thousand years. In his revolutionary reform, begun in 1964, the immemorial (i.e. organically evolved) rites and customs that had made up the received culture of Latin Catholicism were abolished or marginalized by papal command. They were officially replaced with arbitrarily devised forms more compatible with, and often directly inspired by, those of contemporary secular society. To this ritual and cultural revolution John Paul I is not known to have made any objection. As for John Paul II and Benedict XVI, not only have they shown themselves to be staunchly committed to it, but they have consistently refused to see any relationship between their own abandonment of integral orthopraxis and the attacks on doctrinal and moral orthodoxy that undermine their authority and have brought about the dramatic dechristianization of two generations.

What the post-conciliar popes have not counted on is the fact that inculturation can never be the sort of half-measure they intended. A culture amounts to much more than mere modes of linguistic, literary and artistic expression. One is struck in hindsight by the ingenuousness of the modern Papacy's belief – the root delusion of liberal Catholicism – that Catholics could embrace the forms and modalities of secularism without at the same time accepting those ideas and standards of behaviour within it that are in conflict with Christianity.

The papal recipe of Catholic orthodoxy and modern secular culture was, from the first, one that could not work. How could a new religious culture based on 'options' in worship and discipline legitimately exclude in the long run options on the doctrinal and moral planes? How could faithful Catholics, told that they needed to develop a more 'mature', 'adult', 'modern' spirituality, be expected to continue in a childlike acceptance of the age-old teachings of the Magisterium? How could practitioners of the new democratic religion of options be blamed for refusing to give a blind obedience to the directives of pope and prelate? And how could a new man-centred, 'ascending' theology not ultimately succumb to the anti-Christian influences of secular humanism? When the post-conciliar catastrophe brusquely presented the faithful with the impossible choice between loyalty to the legitimate Catholic institution and loyalty to the authentic Catholic tradition, most of them, true to their psychological conditioning, chose the former and drifted away from the latter. The result today is the bizarre worldwide phenomenon of Christians who call themselves Catholic and practise a form of Protestantism.

While conservatives have painted themselves into a corner trying to shift the blame for the present crisis from official papal policy to a 'deviant' clergy and laity, or to an erroneous implementation of basically sound reforms, traditionalists have long since identified *aggiornamento* itself as the root cause. The traditionalist position, simply put, is that one cannot change the religious culture in which Catholicism has always been expressed without attacking the bases of faith itself. Traditionalists dissented from Vatican policy during the pontificates of Paul VI and John Paul II above all because they could not reconcile either pope's role as head of the Latin Church with his indifference to a matter that seriously affected its heart, the fate of the immemorial liturgy of Western Catholicism.

The election of Benedict XVI in 2005 brought to the papal throne a man who, unlike his predecessor, was well aware of both the negative aspects of the post-conciliar liturgy and the value of the traditional rite. In 2007 he took the long overdue step of restoring the immemorial Roman liturgy as an official rite of the Church, but readmitted it through the back door, so to speak: merely as an option for those desiring it, by now a very small fraction of Latin Catholics, despised and marginalized by most of the world's bishops. At the same time he remains committed to promoting as normative for the Roman rite a more conservative interpretation of the radical reform inherited from Paul VI. If Pope Benedict has aroused the enmity of those on the extreme left of the post-conciliar revolution, it is because he has emerged as the leader of its right wing. Contrary to what post-Christian journalists believe, this is a dispute of fellow revolutionaries – of ecclesial Jacobins and Orleanists – not of revolutionaries and counter-revolutionaries. Indeed the dissident traditional Catholics whom the new pope has sought to reconcile to the new order remain, like the Catholic mainstream before 1962, completely outside and alien to the revolution in religion that is the post-Vatican II 'renewal'.

Compared with the heteropractic post-conciliar Latin Church, the independent Oriental Churches are today in a remarkably healthy state, even those of formerly Communist states. Contrary to what is so often claimed, there was no pressing need for the Latin Catholic Church to abandon her traditional culture in the 1960s. On the whole, Orthodox and other Eastern Christians (at least those not under the spell of *aggiornamento*) have successfully adapted themselves to a world of rapid change and advanced technology without turning their backs on any essential component of their time-hallowed worship and body of customs.

Why the leaders of the Latin Church did not follow this example is the subject of the present work. *The Banished Heart* aspires to amplify the standard case for traditionalist Catholicism. It has also a corrective dimension. To date, traditionalist recognition and criticism of certain prudential errors of the post-Pacellian Papacy have had as their complement the tendency to idealize the pre-conciliar Church. Disgust for the low moral and cultural standards of our time has reinforced in many minds the rosy vision of a perfectly regulated, all-virtuous institution, one suddenly and wickedly subverted by a Liberal fifth column active within the Church since the anti-Modernist campaign of St Pius X.

The real problem with conspiracy theories of history is not that they are untrue, but that they narrow the truth, obscuring other realities. What this investigation attempts to do is to seek in the history of the pre-conciliar Church the causes of the institutionalized heteropraxis of today and of the crisis it has created. It is a search for inveterate human flaws that have shown themselves to be seeds of destruction and degeneration. Reactionary glorification of the recent past not only blinds us to the possibility that our Church may now be suffering the consequences of her own shortcomings; it prevents us from acknowledging these fatal faults, repenting sincerely of them, and warning posterity not to repeat them in what, God willing, will be a brighter future for Latin Catholicism and for Christendom in general. The historical examination of conscience I propose is the tragic chronicle of the errors and the pride that preceded our fall, a fall that has deprived us of what should be most precious to us as Christians.

My aim in *The Banished Heart* is, then, to raise awareness of the reality and enormity of the recent banishing of the Catholic 'heart'. Some of the argumentation and evidence produced will challenge certain preconceptions of instinctive traditionalists who, never having thought through the implications of their dissidence, espouse positions which are strictly speaking conservative and contradict their actual stance. However, what the following pages reveal and argue should disturb only those who are disinclined to face the fact that the Mystical Body, though divine in origin, is a society of sinners as well as saints. As for Catholics who have wholeheartedly accepted the post-conciliar reforms, the case argued in this study will seem an impertinence to conservative readers, and an irrelevancy to liberal readers for whom Vatican II inaugurated a necessary shift from the supposedly outdated metaphysical approach of Scholasticism to a more 'biblical' and 'personalist' mode of theological discourse. It is hoped, nevertheless, that the book will be of some interest to members of the independent Eastern Churches as well as to other readers curious about the outlook and psychology of Catholic traditionalism which, like any other historical phenomenon, merits objective study.

It needs to be emphasized that if the tone of this quest for the origins of hetero-praxis in the Catholic Church is often pessimistic, it is precisely because the study is a critical assessment of particular historical trends of a negative and destructive nature. In spite of its two thousand-year sweep, this chronicle is *not* a history of the Catholic Church. And since the aim of the work is the identification and diagnosis of a particular *problem*, it is beyond the book's scope to counterbalance the systematic indictment it makes of certain attitudes and deeds with an equally detailed account of contemporary positive developments: the treasures of goodness, wisdom and holiness that have always adorned the Catholic tradition, even in its darkest periods. In the same way, a competent study about the causes of a particular cancer could hardly devote its pages to praise for the powers of the human body free of this disease.

Nor should my use of the Eastern Christian tradition as a reference point and counterpoise be seen as a digressive distraction from the real problem under study, or as an idealization of separated Christian communions which bear no less than ours the scars of human sin and short-sightedness. The problems of Latin and Oriental Christendom are, in fact, intimately connected. It is, above all, a question of restoring a lost balance so that (to borrow a phrase from Pope John Paul II) Catholicism can breathe again with its two lungs, one Western, the other Eastern.

In spite of the critical stance adopted in *The Banished Heart* towards the Vatican's post-conciliar ecumenism, it explores important ecumenical themes in regard to the Eastern Churches not currently in union with Rome. On the other hand, the study is unlikely to resonate with heirs of those Reformation movements which consciously rejected Catholic orthopraxis. Nevertheless, if this book, written from a traditional Catholic perspective, naturally sees the historical phenomenon of Protestantism as essentially problematical, this does not mean that its author is not profoundly moved and edified by such testaments to a Christ-centred life as the religious music of a Bach, the hymnody of a Katharina von Schlegel, a Bishop William How or a Mrs Cecil Alexander, the art of a Eugène Burnand, the drama of a Kaj Munk, or the heroic self-sacrifice of a Sophie Scholl.

In 1924 the German theologian Karl Adam wrote:

> When dark clouds of prejudice and misunderstanding obscure the fair image of our Church, we Catholics often must admit our guilt: *mea culpa, mea maxima culpa*. It is due in no small measure to our imperfections and frailties and sins that those dark clouds arise and conceal the countenance of the Bride of Christ. When God allowed great sections of the Church, containing an abundance of most noble and valuable elements, to separate from us, He punished not only them, but also us Catholics ourselves. And this punishment, this penal permission of God, should, like all His permissions, cause us to look into ourselves and impel us to repentance.[1]

Three decades before these words were written, Pope Leo XIII asserted that Catholics have nothing to fear from the truth. If any part of the evidence and argumentation in this book is found convincing by Catholic readers, no amount of regret for our failings, and for those of our forebears, need shake our loyalty to the Church of our baptism, which is today, yesterday and forever the Mystical

---

[1] Karl Adam, *The Spirit of Catholicism* (Steubenville, 1996), p. 98.

Body of her Founder, and whose greatest need now is to recover the full dimensions of her faith and practice.

Apart from the many individuals whose kind assistance in supplying me with sources, in critiquing the chapter drafts and in providing technical support I acknowledged in the first edition of the work, I wish to own my debt of gratitude to the following, who offered me similar help in preparing the present revised and expanded edition. I thank first of all the Rev'd Dr Laurence Paul Hemming and Dr Susan Parsons, who encouraged me to republish the book and edited this new edition; Rev Fr Bernard de Menthon OSB (Notre-Dame de Bellaigue Abbey), Mr Paul Cavendish and Mr Valentine Gallagher, who undertook a critical reading of the manuscript and suggested many necessary corrections and improvements. I am grateful also to Dr Stephen McInerney and Ms Angela Kolar (Campion College, Sydney), H. G. Bishop Mar Awa Royel (California diocese of the Holy Apostolic Catholic Assyrian Church of the East), Dr Richard Rigby (Australian National University) and Dr Lance Eccles (Macquarie University), who provided references and material. It goes without saying that the opinions expressed in this study are mine alone, and should not be attributed to any of the above-named.

Geoffrey Hull
School of Ancient History
Macquarie University (Sydney)
17 November 2009

1

A NEW LAW OF PRAYER

Destruction takes but a moment. Building takes much longer. Consider the Mass: it took a thousand years for the liturgy to develop to the point where it was codified by the Council of Trent. All of that millennial work was undone in a single generation.

GARRY POTTER (2009)

To tell the truth, it is a different liturgy of the Mass. This needs to be said without ambiguity: the Roman rite as we knew it no longer exists. It has been destroyed.

JOSEPH GELINEAU, SJ (1976)

Breaking the Taboos

One of the few words that the Polynesian languages have given to those of Europe is *taboo*, from the Tongan *tapu*, which originally referred to the pagan custom of setting apart a thing or person considered sacred or accursed. Physically to touch or to have ordinary dealings with the 'tabooed' subject was to attack the very foundations of religion. Taboos are fundamental to all religions. When Christian missionaries to the German tribes of Northern Europe wished to destroy paganism, they went about smashing idols and burning down temples, and on their sites erected churches for Christian worship. Heathen festivals were abolished and replaced by solemnities of the Catholic calendar, and magic wells were christened as places of pilgrimage sacred to saints. There was thus the illusion of continuity, whereas in reality the old religion had been rooted out. The same strategy was employed a thousand years later during the Reformation when radical Protestants destroyed every vestige of Catholic worship in the churches before converting them into conventicles for the preaching of their new doctrines.

Assuming that there was, as some traditionalists insist, a conspiracy at the time of the Second Vatican Council to strike a fatal blow at Catholic orthodoxy, it is obvious that the conspirators would have aimed first at the central cult of the religion by proposing new rites to replace traditional forms and destroying the principal 'taboos' in Catholic worshipping habits. Psychological resistance to change would thus be broken down. Looking objectively at the reform of the Roman liturgy since 1964, it is impossible to avoid the conclusion that a revolution has indeed taken place, and that the cumulative meaning of the new liturgy differs markedly from that of the old.

Worship and Belief

A person completely ignorant of the actual beliefs of Islam cannot fail to comprehend the basic spirit of this religion by watching its adherents at prayer, so vividly does Muslim worship reflect the beliefs of the Koran. The Arabic word *islām* means 'submission', and comes from the verb *aslama* 'to resign oneself', 'to submit peacefully' – appropriate terminology for a fatalistic religion. The repeated prostrations that accompany the prayers of Muslims betoken their total submission of the will to God, and their facing towards Mecca is an acknowledgement of their faith in the revelation they believe to have been received there by Mohammed.

In Latin Catholicism there was the same close correlation between worship and belief until the reforms that followed the Second Vatican Council. The outsider chancing to enter a Catholic church could not fail to notice that most of the activity going on inside was centred around the adoration of what to him might be a piece of bread and a cup of wine, but to the worshippers was the Incarnate God in sacramental form. Everyone in the church, including the officiating priest, would have been facing the high altar on which the Blessed Sacrament was confected during the Mass. The sacramental presence of Jesus Christ on the altar or in the tabernacle was acknowledged with a genuflection; when the faithful came forward to receive their Saviour they knelt in adoration.

While the priest leading his congregation and praying on their behalf faced in the same direction as they, everything about the ritual and the architecture indicated that his role was completely distinct from that of the people.[1] The sanctuary was fenced off from the nave by rails or even a screen, the priest wore special vestments, prayed in a language distinct from that of everyday life, sometimes silently, and only he was permitted to touch the Sacred Species which his consecrated hands alone had the power to make present. Music of a specifically religious character, plainchant, homophony or polyphony, would accompany a solemn celebration of Mass.

For worshippers prepared to make even a minimal effort to enter into its spirit, the liturgy brought closer, through its symbols, realities beyond their normal experience. This transcendence opened a horizontal line of communication with the past ages of Christianity and a vertical communication with the Heavenly Kingdom. While the worshippers remained in the world, for which they prayed, their recollection allowed them to leave it, as if on a journey from time into eternity. Latin Catholic worship, in short, was God-centred, its numinous atmosphere drawing the faithful into the presence of a mysterious yet almost palpable reality. The ethos of the pre-conciliar rites is summed up well by J. D. Davies as the need to

> retire for a time from the secular world and, leaving all that is common behind,
> penetrate another, sacred, world, where we enter the presence of the all-holy God
> and sing His praises in company with the heavenly choir of angels, archangels
> and saints. So worship is a special, religious activity, performed in special holy

---

[1] The celebrant's facing in the same direction as the congregation is known as the 'eastward position' because, in the early Church, sanctuaries were normally oriented towards the east, the direction of Jerusalem and of the rising sun (*sol oriens*), symbol of the Risen Christ.

buildings; it may strengthen us to fulfil the divine purpose within our daily lives but it is, in itself, something separate from our daily lives in the world.[2]

The New Catholic Worship

What impression, by contrast, does a typical celebration of the New Order of Mass make on the casual observer? Except in those cases where a conservative-minded priest and congregation are attempting to perform the new liturgy in the spirit of the old, the rite will appear unmistakably man-centred. The visual impression of a priest leading the faithful in prayer before the throne of God has been demolished by the substitution of a table for the altar, and the celebrant's facing the people as if to turn the congregation in on itself, self-consciously celebrating itself rather than adoring the Divine Presence.

Gone are the altar rails, and with them the last visual distinction between the sanctuary and the nave. The atmosphere of a public meeting or a convivial function is compounded by the execution of the rite in an unstylized form of the vernacular, and the presence of secular music and song (often through electronic recordings) and even dance. In some cases priestly vestments have been minimized or discarded, and members of the congregation may be invited to stand around the altar and hold hands during the Eucharistic Prayer.

The instinctive gravity of demeanour and keeping of silence in a holy place are no longer second nature to the worshipper, having more often than not given way to the whirr of adults chatting in the pews, the squalling of distressed infants and the din and distracting movement of bored, unsupervised children.[3] As for the priest, in celebrating Mass he now makes frequent eye contact with the congregation and speaks through a microphone, interrupting the ritual prayers to dialogue with the people or to inject his own comments – and even pleasantries and jokes – into the proceedings.

But above all the central taboo of the traditional liturgy has been broken: the ban on unconsecrated persons handling the Blessed Sacrament, the ultimate ritual response to faith in the miracle of the Real Presence and in the unique character of the Catholic priesthood. The priest actually places the Sacred Host into the hands of communicants, who then pick it up with their fingers, or else he will hand a ciborium to a layman or to a nun or laywoman to help him with (or take over) the distribution of Holy Communion to practically everyone in the church.[4] The

---

[2] J. G. Davies, ed., *A Dictionary of Liturgy & Worship* (London, 1972), p. 343.

[3] In traditional worship the attitude of the congregation during a service has always been seen as extremely important, not merely a marginal consideration so long as the action unfolding in the sanctuary is orthodox: here the role of a theatre audience – whose demeanour can 'make' or 'break' a performance excellent in itself – provides a relevant analogy.

[4] Touching the Sacred Species is not the same as handling it. Although the distinction may seem trifling, traditional Christian psychology has always recoiled from the idea of unconsecrated persons picking up the Sacred Species with their fingers, now the usual practice in reformed Catholic worship. Indeed, touching the Host was always the privilege of the celebrant, and any priest (even a bishop or the pope himself) communicating at another priest's Mass would receive on the tongue, as would a priest receiving the Viaticum from another. The primitive practice of receiving Holy Communion in the hand required that the Host placed by the priest or deacon onto the communicant's open right palm be directly transferred to the mouth without any touching with the fingers. In the early Roman rite women received with a white cloth, the *dominicale*,

3

other sacred vessels – chalice and paten – may also be freely handled by servers and members of the congregation, the latter no longer being forbidden to enter the sanctuary during Mass.

The overall impression created by such a spectacle is of the gathering of a community for a cosy ritual meal celebrating a common religious sentiment, not of people attending a solemn sacrifice offered by a priest for the living and the dead, and culminating in a sacred banquet in which Jesus Christ Himself is received. The age-old cult of God appears to have been replaced by a new cult of man, even when Christ is made really present upon the tables of the new liturgy. A gulf between the reality of the Eucharist and its image has come into being.

Vatican claims of ritual continuity and doctrinal integrity notwithstanding, it is evident to the unbiased observer that the Roman-rite Mass, as typically celebrated in most Western countries, has been deliberately reshaped to obey the requirements of those who, in all good faith, advocate a radical secularization of Christian worship. According to this latter, Marxist-influenced, school of thought:

> [If] worship today is to have any meaning in the face of secularization, it has to be redefined as an activity which springs out of life in the world; it is a celebration of that life. Instead of involving a divorce from the secular, it takes the secular or common as its basis, and so the cultic action is a means whereby we express the unity of the sacred and the secular. It does not need for its performance holy shrines, and while it is essentially a coming to awareness of and a response to God, this is achieved through what is human and secular.[5]

This was a theme dear to a number of avant-garde French liturgists of the 1960s, especially the Jesuit Pierre Antoine, who unhesitatingly used an analogy with Buddhism to justify the startling trend of desacralization in public worship:

covering their palms, and this custom was current also in the Byzantine rite, apparently for both sexes; see Adrian Fortescue, *The Mass: A Study of the Roman Liturgy* (London, 1912), p. 373 and n. 2, and Hugh Wybrew, 'The Byzantine Liturgy from the Apostolic Constitutions to the Present Day', in C. Jones, G. Wainwright and E. Yarnold, *The Study of Liturgy* (London, 1978), pp. 88–89. One passage attributed to St Cyril of Jerusalem (315–386) describes communicants making a 'throne' for the Sacred Species with their hands and touching the forehead and lips with the Host before consuming it; see J. Quasten, *Patrology*, Vol. III (Utrecht/ Antwerp, 1950; repr. 1963), pp. 364–66. Out of growing reverence for the Real Presence and a deepened appreciation of the priestly ministry, manual communion was abolished in Spain by the Council of Saragossa in 380 and in Rome some time before the reign of Pope St Leo the Great (440–461); in Gaul it was apparently first prohibited by the Council of Rouen in 650. In the Byzantine Empire the custom came to an end after the eighth century, when Communion under both species by intinction using a spoon was first introduced (Wybrew, 'The Byzantine Liturgy', p. 121). The contemporary view in Europe was that the practice had been permitted during the early centuries of persecution, when priests were often unavailable and the faithful had to administer the sacrament to themselves but that the Peace of Constantine had removed this necessity. As Christ's handing the consecrated bread to the Apostles at the Last Supper was seen as part of their ordination, the thought of laymen receiving manually had become unacceptable. Thereafter for the laity – and even deacons, whose role was to administer the chalice – to touch the Host was associated with heresy. Moreover, since for most of Christian history the consecrated Host has universally been placed directly into the communicant's mouth whereas blessed bread (*antídōron* in the Greek rite) is placed or taken into the hands of the faithful (including those who did not communicate) at the end of Mass, the post-conciliar Roman innovation of Communion in the hand has visually and symbolically tended to identify the Body of Christ with ordinary bread.

[5] J. G. Davies, *op. cit.*

Indeed we refuse to consider any place as intrinsically or ontologically sacred in itself, as this would be to localize the divine. Desacralization has a spiritual and mystical dimension which we can scarcely ignore, and which may be perceived outside Christianity. A witness to this is one story, expressive in its crudity, taken from Buddhist literature. It is about a monk who enters a pagoda and pisses on the statue of Buddha. To a bystander who was scandalized by such a sacrilege, the monk replied simply: 'Can you show me a place where I can piss without pissing on a bit of Buddheity?'[6]

Seven years later Fr Antoine's urinary analogy would become a page of Catholic history, when, in the course of a rowdy 'youth celebration' held in Rheims Cathedral, drunk members of the audience used the confessionals and baptismal font as *pissoirs*, and the temple in which the Kings of France used to be anointed had to be reconsecrated by its unvigilant archbishop.[7]

Corporate worship in the numinous mode, as the Christian norm from the birth of the Catholic Church until the Second Vatican Council, always insisted on the performance of sacred rites in specially consecrated buildings. The utilitarian principle that today allows open-air Masses had no place beyond emergency situations in traditional Catholicism, whose instinct in matters of worship has always been profoundly conservative. So strong was this instinct to conserve and shield the sacred in time-hallowed places and forms that it was clear to the post-conciliar reformers that massive changes in the central act of Catholic worship could not be brought about suddenly. Indeed, as Cardinal Heenan of Westminster told the people of his archdiocese in 1969, 'It would have been foolhardy to introduce the changes all at once . . . It was obviously wiser to change gradually and gently. If all the changes had been introduced together you would have been shocked.'[8]

When, in 1549, the English parliament ordered without warning the replacement of the traditional Latin Mass of England with a new liturgy devised by Archbishop Thomas Cranmer, the government had to contend with popular uprisings in several parts of the country. In the 1660s, Patriarch Nikon's comparatively superficial changes to Russian Orthodox worship precipitated the Old Believer schism which has endured to this day.[9] The liturgical reformers of the 1960s were careful not to repeat such tactical errors.

---

[6] Louis Salleron, *La nouvelle messe* (Paris, 1981), pp. 42–43.

[7] This desecration took place on 13 December 1974, during the concert of a visiting German electronic band. The archbishop, Mgr Jacques Ménager, had been a *peritus* at Vatican II and one of the drafters of the pastoral constitution *Gaudium et Spes*.

[8] Michael Davies, *Pope Paul's New Mass: Part Three of Liturgical Revolution* (= PPNM) (Dickinson, Texas, 1980), p. 77.

[9] The reforms introduced by Patriarch Nikon, intended to restore Russian worship to the Byzantine norm, included making the sign of the cross with three rather than two fingers, the placing of five rather than several loaves on the altar at Mass, counter-sunwise rather than sunwise processions, the elimination of certain Lenten prostrations, slight textual changes to the Creed, a triple rather than double Alleluia, and spelling the Holy Name as Иисусъ instead of Iсусъ. On the Old Believer schism, see James H. Billington, *The Icon and the Axe: An Interpretative History of Russian Culture* (New York, 1976), pp. 133–44.

The Liturgical Revolution of the Roman Rite

At the end of 1969, Pope Paul VI (Giovani Battista Montini) imposed on the churches of the Roman rite a new order of Mass. Within six years the French liturgist Fr Joseph Gelineau could state approvingly, and with complete candour: 'the Roman rite as we knew it no longer exists. It has been destroyed.'[10] How was this liturgical revolution engineered?

One thing is certain. *Sacrosanctum Concilium*, the Second Vatican Council's Constitution on the Sacred Liturgy promulgated on 4 December 1963, did not explicitly order the drastic restructuring of the Roman liturgy that actually ensued. The hallowed rites of the Church were to be 'carefully and thoroughly revised' only 'where necessary' and 'in the light of sound tradition'. Furthermore, 'due care' was to be taken 'to preserve their substance'. A 'particular law remaining in force' stipulated that 'the use of the Latin language . . . be preserved in the Latin rites'. Above all, 'there must be no innovations unless the good of the Church genuinely and certainly requires them', and, apart from bishops, 'absolutely no other person, not even a priest, may add, remove, or change anything in the liturgy on his own authority'.[11]

The possibility that this seemingly conservative document could be later exploited as the charter of a liturgical revolution evidently escaped the vast majority of the Council Fathers who appended their signatures to it, Archbishop Marcel Lefebvre among them.[12] What resulted, in any case, was a programme of destruction and the gradual introduction of a new form of worship that bore increasingly less resemblance to the liturgy envisaged by the Council.

The real principles guiding the reform were those of Montini's own philosophy of renewal. The pontiff-elect made it clear that:

> it is not Our intention to say that perfection consists in remaining changeless as regards those external forms that the Church through many centuries has assumed. Nor does it consist in being stubbornly opposed to those new forms and habits that are commonly regarded as acceptable and suited to the character of our times. The word *aggiornamento*, made famous by Our Predecessor of happy memory, John XXIII, should always be kept in mind as our programme of action.[13]

With this futuristic charter announced, the official changes came fast and furious. *Sacram Liturgiam*, issued on 25 January 1964, was the first of a series of documents putting into effect the recommendations of the Liturgy Constitution. At this time the Sacred Congregation of Rites – whose prefect, the Basque Claretian cardinal Arcadio Larraona Saralegui, and whose secretary, Archbishop Enrico Dante, were both conservatives – had in mind little more than permitting the optional use of the vernacular in the readings, chants, proper prayers and dialogues of the Mass, while the Offertory prayers, the canon and the priest's pre-Communion prayers were to remain in Latin.[14]

[10] Joseph Gelineau, SJ, *Demain la liturgie* (Paris, 1976), pp. 9–10.
[11] *Sacrosanctum Concilium*, Preface, 4; II, 50; III, 36, § 1; 23; 22, § 3.
[12] On 7 December 1962, 1,922 Fathers voted in favour of the first chapter of the Constitution, and only 11 against it.
[13] *Ecclesiam Suam*, 6 August 1964.
[14] In 1958 Pius XII had first allowed the reading of the Epistle and Gospel in the vernacular, but this concession had not become widespread in many countries by 1964.

By this time, however, many bishops of the 'Rhine group' countries (France, Belgium, Holland, Germany, Austria and Switzerland) and the United States were avid for far-reaching and rapid changes in public worship. Article 9 of the 1964 motu proprio repeated the conciliar ruling that no vernacular translation of a liturgical text could be put into use unless it had the approval of the Sacred Congregation. When the French and German hierarchies threatened to introduce the vernacular texts they had prepared with or without Rome's approval, Cardinal Giacomo Lercaro, the progressive Archbishop of Bologna, went to Rome to plead their cause with Pope Paul. As a result the article was swiftly revised to concede episcopal conferences the right to approve all translations into the vernacular, the function of the Holy See being henceforth merely to ratify this approval.[15]

Fathers of the Revolution

Pope Paul's next steps were to make Lercaro the president of a new committee named *Consilium ad exsequendam Constitutionem de Sacra Liturgia*,[16] and to appoint the Vincentian priest Annibale Bugnini its secretary. The first general meeting was held on 11 March 1964. Since Montini was personally committed to a liturgical reform far exceeding the directives of the Liturgy Constitution approved by Pope John XXIII, there can be little doubt that his motive in creating this new committee was to remove the process of overseeing the reform from the authority of the insufficiently cooperative Sacred Congregation of Rites.

The Consilium was composed of 58 'members' (bishops and abbots), 149 'consultors' and 74 'advisers'. However, the real authors of the reformed Mass were the following: Fathers Anton Hänggi of Basel (professor of liturgy at the University of Fribourg, Switzerland); Pierre Jounel and Pierre-Marie Gy, OP (director of the Liturgical Institute of Paris), Joseph Gelineau, SJ, Louis Bouyer, Louis Ligier, SJ, G. Gellier (France); José Patino, SJ, Dom Adalberto Franquesa (Spain); Dom Cipriano Vagaggini, Mgr Salvatore Famoso, Dom Anselmo Lentini (Italy); Mgr Theodor Schnitzler, Mgr Johannes Wagner (director of the Liturgical Institute of Trier, Germany); Josef Jungmann, SJ (Austria); Herman Wegman (Holland); Dom Bernard Botte (Belgium); and Frederick McManus (USA). It is to be noted that this sub-committee, known as 'Study Group 10', was top-heavy with French-speaking liturgists, though the most eminent scholar among them was undoubtedly Father Jungmann. The following year Fr Bugnini boldly stated in *L'Osservatore Romano* that the Consilium's task was to remove from the Roman liturgy 'everything that could constitute the slightest risk of a stumbling block or a source of displeasure for our Separated Brethren, that is, for the Protestants'.[17]

It was no exaggeration: this was indeed the mind of the Pope, as Montini's close friend, Jean Guitton, would recall in 1993. In discussing the novelty of Mass facing the people, the French Academician admitted that

the intention of Paul VI . . . in the matter of what is commonly called the Mass, was to reform the Catholic liturgy so that it should approximate as closely as

---

[15] M. Davies, *PPNM*, pp. 22–24.
[16] 'Committee for the Implementation of the Constitution on the Sacred Liturgy'.
[17] *L'Osservatore Romano*, 19 March 1965.

possible to the Protestant Lord's Supper. . . . In other words we see in Paul VI an ecumenical intention to wipe out or at least to correct or soften everything that is too Catholic in the Mass and to bring [it] . . . as close as possible to the Calvinist liturgy.

'Clearly that is a revolution in the Church', commented the interviewer, taken aback.

'Clearly so', Monsieur Guitton happily agreed.[18]

Changing the Mass

Once the Consilium was in charge of directing the liturgical renewal, structural changes to the immemorial rite began to be made. On 25 April the formula for the distribution of Holy Communion (*Corpus Domini nostri Jesu Christi custodiat animam tuam in vitam æternam. Amen.*) was shortened to *Corpus Christi*, to which the communicant was to answer: *'Amen.' Inter Œcumenici*, the 'Instruction on the Proper Implementation of the Constitution of the Sacred Liturgy', signed by Cardinal Lercaro, came out on 26 September 1964. This document ordered the setting up of national and diocesan liturgical commissions, which, as Michael Davies comments, 'were immediately dominated by Liberal liturgists and resulted in the creation of a vast liturgical bureaucracy with a vested interest in the reform, particularly its continual evolution. . . . The role of the bishop [became] reduced to little more than rubber-stamping their decisions.'[19]

The same instruction announced further changes to the Mass. Some of these appeared reasonable and in the spirit of the conciliar decree, but were nonetheless of questionable value. For example, one might doubt the wisdom of suppressing at this point in history the extra-liturgical Leonine Prayers after Low Mass which implored the protection of the Sacred Heart of Jesus and the Archangel St Michael for an embattled Church. The reintroduction of a Prayer of the Faithful after the Creed did not lead to the revival of medieval bidding prayers or of set liturgical litanies like the ekteny of the Byzantine rite but rather opened the door to spontaneous and 'creative' vernacular praying that soon degenerated into inappropriateness and vulgarity. As for the joint recitation of the *Pater noster* by celebrant and congregation, this was a long-established Eastern liturgical practice but contradicted the ancient Roman tradition of its singing by the priest alone while the people responded with the last phrase, as an acclamation.

Other changes were not only unnecessary but destructive of the integrity of the rite, for instance the removal of Psalm 42 (*Judica me Deus*) from the Prayers at the Foot of the Altar, and the dropping of the Last Gospel. Permission for the use of the vernacular in the whole of the Mass except the Preface and canon also destroyed the sound principle of using Latin in those parts of the rite pertaining exclusively to the priest (e.g. the preparatory and Offertory prayers) and the

---

[18] Interview by François-Georges Dreyfus, a Lutheran, on the French national radio programme *Ici Lumière 101*, 13 December 1993. Reported in *The Latin Mass: Chronicle of a Reform*, Vol. 4, No. 1 (Winter, 1995), pp. 11–12.
[19] M. Davies, *PPNM*, p. 30.

vernacular in the public parts. As from 27 April 1965 the Preface, too, could be recited in the vernacular.

With *Attentis Multarum*, issued on 21 November 1964, the existing eucharistic fast of three hours was reduced to one hour. During 1965, priests in the Netherlands began to defy an ancient liturgical law by introducing the practice of Communion in the hand, which had not been mentioned, let alone recommended, in *Sacrosanctum Concilium*. In the following years this abuse spread to Belgium, France and West Germany. The letter *Impetrata Prius* (1965) dealt a blow to the traditional concept of Sabbath observance by introducing the Saturday evening 'Vigil Mass' as an optional substitute for the Sunday Eucharist. As the practice caught on over the following decades, the pastoral advantage for the small number of Catholics unable to hear Mass on the Sunday was overshadowed by the new, convenient social trend of worshipless Sundays.

Tres Abhinc Annos (the 'Second Instruction on the Proper Implementation of the Constitution on the Sacred Liturgy', 4 May 1967) permitted the canon to be recited aloud and in the vernacular, thereby ushering in a wholly vernacular service. Most of the signs of the cross made by the priest during Mass and the kissings of the altar were suppressed, as was his genuflection before elevating each of the Sacred Species at the Consecration.[20] Both clergy and laity were directed not to genuflect during the Creed at the *Incarnatus*.

To this point the reform had consisted of changes in language, the abolition of certain prayers and gestures of the traditional rite, and the introduction of General Intercessions. The Roman missal of 1965 may have enshrined a number of unfortunate novelties, but its texts and rubrics were essentially those of the immemorial rite. However, Pope Paul intended this new missal to be a mere interim measure while more sweeping changes were being planned.

In the meantime, the Consilium's sub-committee had been working on the construction of an artificial order of Mass, including three new canons of their own devising.[21] In their fabrication of this eucharistic rite the members consulted at every stage with six Protestant 'ecumenical observers' who were, however, excluded from the committee's debates.[22] These non-Catholic consultants, approved by

---

[20] Traditionalists viewed this change with suspicion, as it seemed to imply that the bread and wine became the Body and Blood of Christ not through the action of the priest (hence his immediate act of adoration after pronouncing the consecratory formulae), but after their being shown to the people, as if the congregation's ratification were essential.

[21] The oft-repeated charge that the Consilium as a body wanted to scrap the Roman Canon is untrue. Initially, certain members had proposed its restructuring (by grouping together the commemorations after the Consecration, as in liturgies of the Antiochene type), but in 1966 Paul VI endorsed Cardinal Lercaro's view that the traditional anaphora should be left untouched, and ordered the composition of supplementary anaphoras. Dom Botte's proposal of introducing anaphoras from the Oriental rites was rejected by the majority, who favoured the elaboration of modern formulas drawing on ancient sources: Roman (Canon II), Gallican and Mozarabic (Canon III) and Antiochene (Canon IV). See Annibale Bugnini, *The Reform of the Liturgy 1948–1975*, tr. Matthew J. O'Connell (Collegeville, Minnesota, 1990), pp. 449–50.

[22] Bugnini and others later denied that the Protestant observers exercised any influential role in the proceedings. However, Mgr (now Cardinal) William Baum told the *Detroit News* in 1967 that these individuals 'are not simply there as observers, but as consultants as well, and they participate fully in the discussions on Catholic liturgical renewal'. In order to verify this claim Michael Davies wrote to Canon Jasper, one of the six, who in turn assured him that at their 'informal' meetings with the Consilium members there had been 'a very frank exchange of views'. See M. Davies, *PPNM*, Appendix III 'The Participation of the Protestant Observers in the Compilation of the New Catholic Liturgical Texts', pp. 585–88, originally in *The Roman Rite*

the Holy See on 23 August 1966, were the Anglican Canon Ronald Jasper, the Lutheran pastors Wilhelm Künneth and Eugene Brand, Methodist Professor A. Raymond George of the World Council of Churches, American Episcopalian Rev Dr Massey Shepherd, and Brother Max Thurian of the Taizé community. No observer from any of the Eastern Catholic, Orthodox or lesser Oriental Churches was appointed.

From Experiment to Law

The new eucharistic liturgy under the title of *Missa Normativa* was first celebrated entirely in Italian before the Synod of Bishops in the Sistine Chapel on Monday 24 October 1967. The third experimental canon was used at the express wish of the Pope, and a layman read the lessons. (Pope Paul himself was unwell that day and did not attend). After the demonstration 71 bishops gave a *placet* ('yes') vote, as opposed to the 62 who voted *placet juxta modum* ('yes, with reservations'), and the 43 who signified *non placet* ('no') as their response, while four abstained.[23]

In his monumental history of the liturgical reform, Archbishop Bugnini admits: 'It must be said flatly that the experiment was not a success and even that it had an effect contrary to the one intended, and played a part in the negative vote that followed.' But Bugnini this blamed on the Sistine Chapel 'which lends itself to elitist, not popular, celebrations', and on the equally 'elitist' composition of the congregation: prelates and priests.[24] In any case, to many of these 'the changes in the Mass seemed radical', and some felt that they downplayed the dogma of the Real Presence.[25]

Contravening the established principles of authentic liturgical reform, the authors of the *Missa Normativa* had in fact hacked away from the received rite prayers and ceremonies which had been in use since the Middle Ages: the Prayers at the Foot of the Altar, the Offertory and incensation prayers, some of the pre-Communion prayers and most of the final prayers of the Mass. Among the few additions to the now threadbare service was a 'sign of peace' to be made by members of the congregation, and which would become in most Western countries a secular handshake occurring as a noisy disruption to the most solemn part of the rite.

One periodical at the time reported the fear of several bishops that this new rite 'would sweep away the whole theology of the Mass. With it we would, in fact, be approaching Protestant theology, which has destroyed the Sacrifice of the Mass.'[26] Cardinal Heenan, addressing the Synod the following day, took exception to the proposed reform on more pragmatic grounds, protesting that 'the liturgy is not primarily an academic or cultural question. It is above all a pastoral matter for it concerns the spiritual lives of our faithful . . . After studying the so-called

Destroyed (Chawleigh, Devon, 1978), pp. 40–43. For Archbishop Bugnini's side of the story, see Bugnini, *op. cit.*, pp. 199–204 ('Observers at the Consilium').
[23] Bugnini, *op. cit.*, p. 348.
[24] Ibid., p. 349.
[25] Ibid., p. 350.
[26] *Roman Theologians Take a Look at the New Order of the Mass*, tr. Mary Ambrose (Edinburgh, n.d.), p. 3. A new edition of the work, with an introduction, has been published by Rev Anthony Čekada as *The Ottaviani Intervention: Short Critical Study of the New Order of Mass by Alfredo Cardinal Ottaviani – Antonio Cardinal Bacci – A Group of Roman Theologians* (Rockford, Illinois, 1992).

Normative Mass it was clear to me that few [of the members of the Consilium] can have been parish priests.'[27]

Taking note of some of the episcopal objections raised at the Synod to the proposed rite of Mass, Pope Paul watched three distinct celebrations of the *Missa Normativa* in the Cappella Matilde (one Low Mass with singing and one without, and one *missa cantata*) between 11 and 13 January 1968, and then held a discussion after each performance in his private library with Archbishops Cunial and Antonelli, Bishops Manziana and Rovigatti, Dom Rembert Weakland, Father Bugnini and one of the experimental celebrants, Fr Carlo Braga.[28] The Cappella Matilde celebrations were, according to Bugnini, 'one of the many brilliant initiatives marking the pontificate of Pope Paul VI'.[29] A small committee of laity and nuns who had been invited to them submitted to the Pope a list of comments which generally praised the innovations and objected to the retention of various traditional elements.[30]

Pope Paul now became obsessed by the need to persuade the unenthusiastic Roman Curia to accept the schema of the new Mass. 'You know the Roman saying: one Pope approves and another disapproves, and I don't want anyone coming along after me and restoring everything to the present *status quo*', he told Fr Bugnini. 'And if the response is still negative?' pressed the anxious Secretary of the Consilium. 'Don't worry', Montini reassured him. 'I have the final say.'[31] Later that month, Pope Paul suggested the following changes to the existing schema: the Mass was to open with the sign of the cross, a single, truncated *Confiteor* was to be inserted into the new Penitential Rite; the priest's actions at the Offertory were to be accompanied by 'a single set of formulas that will express the idea of an offering of human toil in union with the sacrifice of Christ' (Bugnini accordingly consulted the Jewish *Haggadah* rite for a blessing before a meal and came up with two new prayers);[32] and the Words of Institution in the canon were to be recited as consecratory formulae, not simply as part of the narrative.[33]

---

[27] M. Davies, *PPNM*, p. 111.

[28] Archbishop Ferdinando Antonelli, a Consilium member (and future cardinal), was already alarmed by the direction the reform was taking and repenting of his earlier support of it. In his diary he commented:

> there are few bishop-members of the Consilium who are erudite in specifically liturgical matters and very few who are real theologians. The biggest deficiency in the whole Consilium is the lack of theologians: one might well say that they have been excluded. But what is sad, and a fundamental fact, is that many of those who have been influential in the reform have a particular mind-set . . . while others have no love, no veneration for what has been handed down to us. A negative mentality that is unjust and harmful. Unfortunately Pope Paul VI, too, is pretty much on their side. They may well have all the best intentions, but with this mentality they are driven to demolish, not to restore. (Nicola Gianpietro, OFM. Cap, *Il Card. Ferdinando Antonelli e gli sviluppi della riforma liturgica dal 1948 al 1970* [Rome, 1998], pp. 257–58)

[29] Bugnini, *op. cit.*, pp. 361–67; 368.

[30] Ibid., pp. 367–68.

[31] Ibid., p. 369, n. 20.

[32] The two prayers beginning *Benedictus es Dominus Deus universi . . .* ('Blessed are you, Lord God of all creation: through your goodness we have this bread to offer. It will become for us the bread of life', 'Blessed are you, Lord God of all creation: through your goodness we have this wine to offer, fruit of the vine and the work of human hands. It will become our spiritual drink [!]' The Jewish prototypes would have been identical or similar to prayers used in the Passover ritual preceding the Last Supper.

[33] These recommendations were studied by a new committee consisting of Cardinal Silva Henríquez, Bishops Hurley, Boudon, Spülbeck and Guano, Abbot Weakland and consultors

In the following months the Pope discussed the schema further with the Curial cardinals and the Consilium, at whose general meeting in October 1968 he proposed the insertion of the axed pre-Communion prayer *Domine Jesu Christe* into the 'rite of peace'. He made some further alterations to the Roman Canon, as well as a small number of revisions in a conservative direction, like the return of the *Orate fratres* to the end of the Offertory.[34] After agreement had been reached, Montini gave this new order of Mass his approval on 6 November 1968, and announced its imminent publication on 28 April of the following year. The *Novus Ordo Missæ* was promulgated with the Apostolic Constitution on the Roman missal of Pope Paul VI (*Missale Romanum*) of 3 April 1969, and its use was to become mandatory in churches and chapels of the Roman rite throughout the world from the First Sunday of Advent of that year (30 November).

Sanitizing the 'Work of God'

As a result of its recommendation in the General Instruction prefacing the new missal, the now voguish but anti-traditional practice of celebrating Mass facing the people – with the remodelling (or vandalization) of sanctuaries that this required – became general throughout most of the Western world during 1969 and 1970. Mass in the so-called basilican position was commonly misrepresented as one of the 'conciliar reforms', though, in fact, this practice had absolutely no warrant in *Sacrosanctum Concilium*.[35] Indeed, far from its avowed purpose of democratizing public worship, Mass facing the people created a stiflingly clericalized atmosphere in church, with the priest in the novel and desacralizing role of star of the show.

In regard to the customary gilding of eucharistic vessels, the new missal enjoined this only when they were made of metals that tarnished, and prescribed a single altar cloth instead of the three that were formerly mandatory.[36] It abolished, in favour of standing, the pious Western custom of kneeling to receive the Eucharist. For the priest as well as the people, sitting was recommended as the posture for thanksgiving after Holy Communion.[37] The priest was no longer required to hold together the thumb and forefinger of both hands after the Consecration to avoid all profane contact, and he was freed from the obligation to purify his fingers at the altar during the ablutions.[38] Altar stones containing the relics of saints were merely 'commended', no longer compulsory.[39]

The General Instruction confirmed an earlier decree allowing laymen to read the Epistle and lead the General Intercessions (*Liturgicæ Instaurationes*, 5 September 1970), a logical step after Rome did away, in 1972, with the subdiaconate and the four minor orders, replacing them with the lay 'ministries' of 'lector' and 'acolyte'.[40] Episcopal conferences were empowered to permit women to read the

Agustoni, Gelineau, Jounel, Schnitzler, Vagaggini and Wagner, who accepted some of them and criticized others (Bugnini, *op. cit.*, p. 370).
[34] Ibid., pp. 379–80.
[35] On the anti-traditional nature of this innovation, see Chapter 15, note 64.
[36] *General Instruction on the Roman Missal* (*Principles and Rubrics*) (London, 1973), §§ 268, 294.
[37] Ibid., §§ 146 (b), 131.
[38] Ibid., § 120.
[39] Ibid., § 266.
[40] Ibid., §§ 65, 66. Lay reading of the Epistle had actually been permitted in the 1962 reform

lessons, and provision was made for lay commentators to punctuate the divine service with 'explanations and directions to the people that they may be drawn into the celebration and better understand what is happening'.[41] At the same time, concelebration of Mass by several or large groups of priests was recommended.[42]

Changes were made also in the use of liturgical vestments. The maniple, like the clerical biretta, was consigned to oblivion, and black vestments were no longer to be worn on Good Friday (to be replaced by red, the colour of ordinary martyrs). The customary black in funerals was optionally replaced by violet, the latter colour soon becoming general in conservative churches, while progressive dioceses successfully petitioned Rome for permission to use white.[43] With festive white vestments and the *alleluia* replacing the age-old *Eternal rest grant unto them*, 'the typical funeral, in America at least, was turned into something similar to a canonization ceremony', quips Fr Anthony Čekada.[44]

Discouraging the colour black in requiems was a typical example of the impugning, by experts strongly committed to the inculturation of the liturgy in non-European contexts, of a mourning custom with the deepest roots in European civilization. This cosmetic change was symptomatic of the overhauling of the traditional funeral rites in a sanitizing and euphemizing sense. The Consilium, as Bugnini himself reported:

> got rid of texts that smacked of a negative spirituality inherited from the Middle Ages. Thus they removed such familiar and even beloved texts as the *Libera me, Domine*, the *Dies iræ*, and others that overemphasized judgement, fear and despair. These they replaced with texts urging Christian hope and giving more effective expression to faith in the resurrection.

They also endorsed 'the abandonment of the colour black for another which, in the judgement of the episcopal conferences, will inspire a calmer approach to sorrow and suggest a hope that is illumined by the paschal mystery'.[45]

Regarding the excision of so-called 'negative theology' from the orations (collects, secrets, postcommunions) of the Roman Missal, Fr Čekada has drawn attention to the reformers' horror of 'any language which emphasizes the horrible wickedness of sin as the greatest evil, and its dire consequences for us both in this world and in the next. Contemporary man does not want to hear about such things – and Paul VI's Missal accommodates him'.[46] The old orations were also shorn of references to such undesirable things as the virtue of detachment from the world, the merits of the saints, and miracles.[47]

---

of the Roman missal but had hardly taken root outside arenas of precocious liturgical experimentation.

[41] Ibid., §§ 66, 68 (a). Commentators appointed to read vernacular translations of prayers and texts read in Latin by the priest or other sacred minister had been allowed by Pius XII on 3 September 1958 (one month before his death) in his *Instruction on Sacred Music*, but the practice remained unknown in most places.

[42] Ibid., §§ 153, 154.

[43] Ibid., § 308 (d), (e).

[44] Anthony Čekada, *The Problems with the Prayers of the Modern Mass* (Rockford, Illinois, 1991), p. 20.

[45] Bugnini, *op. cit.*, pp. 773–74.

[46] Čekada, *op. cit.*, p. 17.

[47] Ibid., pp. 17–20, 25–27.

A little-known fact about the liturgical revolution is that one of the earliest official assaults on tradition was the instruction of the Congregation for the Doctrine of the Faith dated 8 May 1963. On this occasion the Holy See disregarded one of the most solemn and ancient taboos in Christendom when it lifted the general ban on cremation of the dead, a practice consistently associated with paganism and atheism, and abhorrent to Catholics as a symbolic denial of the future resurrection of the body.[48] In 1966 Paul VI allowed Catholic priests to officiate at cremations.

From Sacrilege to Option

The no less scandalous abuse of Communion in the hand (at that time mostly confined to the Low Countries and France) meanwhile remained an unsolved problem for the Holy See. The spectacle of lay persons handling the Blessed Sacrament had been deeply shocking to many Catholics, especially since the new practice violated a ban going back a millennium and a half. So negative was popular reaction to it in many places that the Consilium issued a memorandum, dated 30 July 1968, admitting that 'The problem is not exclusively liturgical but has strong pastoral and, even more, psychological consequences. Worship and veneration of the Blessed Sacrament, as well as the very faith in the sacrament, will be not a little affected', but then concluded on an optimistic note, 'unless the transition from the traditional way of receiving to the new one is gradually and carefully prepared for'.[49]

Later that year the episcopal conferences of the world were consulted for their views on the matter. A majority of almost two-thirds were firmly opposed to legalizing what Catholics had long considered a sacrilegious act.[50] The English hierarchy warned that the change would cast doubt on Catholic belief in the Real Presence, and the bishops of Argentina found offensive the prospect of legalizing such a flagrant violation of discipline. The Italian episcopate replied that the innovation would not only give scandal but further sacrileges would result, while the bishops of Congo and Gabon were apprehensive about the introduction of a change that would allow sorcerers and witchdoctors to get their hands on the Blessed Sacrament, a

---

[48] This instruction annulled the ruling of 19 May 1886, which had been incorporated into the Code of Canon Law (canons 1203 and 1240). Needless to say, cremation has since become a common (and economical) 'option' for Catholic funerals in the more secularized Western countries.

[49] Bugnini, *op. cit.*, p. 461.

[50] By the end of the first Christian millennium, manual communion of the laity had disappeared from every apostolic tradition except one, that of the Mesopotamian Nestorians. In their Church, destined to evolve outside the Empire, the ancient practice of Communion in the hand had continued in use, unaffected by the negative attitudes that developed in the Graeco-Roman world. The Nestorians maintained the custom described by Theodore of Mopsuestia (d. 428), a major authority for their Church though himself an Antiochian; see Raymond Tonneau and Robert Devreese, *Les homélies catéchétiques de Théodore de Mopsueste* (Rome, 1949), p. 535. In the modern Assyrian Church of the East this liturgical archaism remains within a thoroughly orthopractic environment: the faithful must fast from the previous midnight, have abstained from fleshmeat on the preceding Wednesday and Friday and from conjugal relations the night before, and be free of serious sin before communicating. Moreover, before receiving the Host in their right palm and transfering it directly to their mouths, they are required to purify their hands symbolically by passing them through the smoke of liturgical incense. The Precious Blood is administered separately. (Some pious laity do opt to receive directly in their mouths, and infants and invalids are communicated under both kinds by intinction.) None of this bears the slightest contextual resemblance to the novelty of Communion in the hand in modern Latin Catholicism, where the model is unequivocally Protestant.

constant danger in Sub-Saharan Africa. Yugoslavia's episcopal conference reminded the Consilium of the great awe and reverence with which members of the Eastern Church approach the Eucharist, married people fasting for some days and also abstaining from the conjugal act before receiving Holy Communion.[51]

Although it would have been possible to condemn and forbid the abuse, the Consilium recommended that legalizing it 'would be in keeping with the line taken by the Council, since the latter allows for a plurality of forms in the area of discipline and relies on the responsibility of the episcopal conferences and the individual bishops'.[52] Subsequently, on 29 May 1969, *Memoriale Domini*, an 'Instruction on the Manner of Distributing Holy Communion', announced Pope Paul's decision to authorize Communion in the hand in those countries where it had come into common use and whose bishops saw fit to approve it.[53]

As each episcopal conference prepared to introduce the sacrilegious innovation, traditionalists could complain of the flurry of 'propaganda tracts, articles and editorials intended to brainwash the faithful' into accepting it.[54] For example, in 1986 one Australian apologist of the abuse made the patently false and sweeping assertion that 'For pastoral reasons the Fathers of the Second Vatican Council decreed that we should return to the earlier custom of receiving Holy Communion in the hand.'[55] These fictitious pastoral reasons have produced the situation prevailing today, where disbelief in the Real Presence is rife among those generations of Catholics brought up entirely with the new rite.

Finishing Touches

The Instruction *Sacramentali Communione* (29 June 1970) authorized episcopal conferences to permit Holy Communion under both species at Mass in certain circumstances (e.g. at ordinations and for the first Communion of catechumens),

---

[51] Ibid., pp. 654–55.

[52] Ibid., p. 656.

[53] The first episcopal conferences to seek permission for Communion in the hand were those of Belgium (May 1969), France and Germany (June 1969), the Netherlands and Czechoslovakia (September 1969), Luxemburg, Monaco, Scandinavia, North Africa, Uruguay and Bolivia (October 1969), Austria, Central Africa and Canada (February 1970), Gabon (March 1970), Japan (June 1970). By 1976 these had been followed by Upper Volta and Niger (February 1971), Indonesia (March 1971), Paraguay (September 1971), Rhodesia (October 1971), Madagascar (May 1972), Mozambique (October 1972), Panama (May 1973), Chile (June 1973), Costa Rica and Angola (September 1973), Korea (January 1974), Zambia (March 1974), New Zealand (April 1974), Mali (July 1974), Scotland (February 1975), Peru and Brazil (March 1975), Portugal (July 1975), Australia (September 1975), Oceania (December 1975), Papua-New Guinea (April 1976), Spain (February 1976), England and Wales (March 1976). In 1977 the abuse was still forbidden in Italy, Malta, Ireland, Poland, Hungary, Romania, Yugoslavia, the Soviet Union, South Africa, India and Ceylon, USA, Argentina, Colombia, Venezuela, Ecuador and other countries, but by 1990 the bishops of all these countries had capitulated except those of Poland, the Soviet Union, Puerto Rico, East Timor and a few other places. Pope John Paul II was initially opposed to giving Communion in the hand but succumbed to a sentimental impulse during his November 1980 visit to Germany when he allowed a boy to receive in this manner, and he gradually conformed to the trend over the following years. He nevertheless forbade the practice in St Peter's Basilica in Rome until 2002, when he authorized the new archpriest, Cardinal Virgilio Noè, to permit it. On Holy Thursday (24 March) 2005, Cardinal Józef Glemp extended the abuse to Poland.

[54] Michael Davies, *On Communion in the Hand and Similar Frauds* (St Paul, n.d.), p. 10.

[55] Paul Stenhouse MSC, 'Why Do We? – Receive Communion in the Hand, Standing?' (*Annals Australia*, March 1986), p. 10.

but not as a general practice. This was among the small number of reforms of an ambivalent nature, arguably traditional but also arguably anti-traditional.[56] Its context, however, suggests the second interpretation, as the contemporary changes were all abusive innovations on which the Holy See had capitulated to pressure from the bishops. Among these were permission for celebrants to extemporize at various points in the order of Mass; for laymen of both sexes to distribute Holy Communion as 'extraordinary ministers'; for the laity to receive Communion twice on the same day; and for the reduction of the eucharistic fast to fifteen minutes for certain communicants. Communion in the hand was formally ratified by *Immensæ Caritatis* (29 January 1973). The composition of new Eucharistic Prayers to meet 'particular needs' was authorized by the Holy See with *Eucharistiæ Participationem* (27 April 1973), and permission for the free composition of special 'children's Masses' followed, with *Pueros Baptizatos* (1 November 1973), a veritable *carte blanche* for innovations of all kinds.

Since the mid-1960s the Congregation for the Clergy had been approving the issuing of local directives to nuns of the Latin rites to simplify their religious habits. Initially the wimple was discarded and veils and dresses were shortened to create a sort of nurse's uniform. But in many First World countries no halt was called to the process of 'adaptation', which by the mid-1970s had already culminated in the complete abandonment of any distinctive religious garb. Sartorially, priests went the same way as the nuns. Where the cassock was abandoned, it gave way either to the Protestant clerical suit of Anglo-Saxon countries or to secular dress with some symbolic concession like a tiny cross worn on the shirt collar.[57] During this period, too, lapsed the custom of women entering a church with their heads covered, a tradition hitherto unbroken since apostolic times. Conversely, at the increasingly common outdoor celebrations of Mass the sight of male worshippers wearing hats would become less and less unusual. Before long, Catholics in Western countries would think nothing of attending Mass dressed in casual clothes instead of the customary Sunday best.

Meanwhile the 'renewal' of the service books was advancing. The revised Roman ordinal of 18 June 1968 (promulgated by the Apostolic Constitution *Pontificalis Romani Recognitio*), though technically valid, disturbed many informed clergy and laity because of its deliberate excision of language alluding to the sacrificial character of the Catholic priesthood.[58] A new Liturgy of the Hours was promulgated by the apostolic constitution *Laudis Canticum* of 1 November 1970, and the reformed *ordo* of baptism, issued in May of the preceding year, did away with ceremonies supposedly 'repulsive' to modern parents, for instance the prayers of exorcism and the use of saliva at the *Ephpheta*.[59] The new *Ordo Pænitentiæ* published on

---

[56] Unlike most of the post-conciliar innovations, Communion under both kinds, still practised in all the Eastern liturgies except the latinized Maronite, Armenian and the Malabarese rites, had been recommended in *Sacrosanctum Concilium* (n. 55).

[57] The Fourteenth Session of the Council of Trent (25 November 1551) had stipulated that

> It is necessary that the clergy always wear clothing suitable to their proper order, so that by the decency of their outward garments they may show forth the interior correctness of their morals. . . . For this reason all ecclesiastical persons in sacred orders, who refuse to wear a suitable clerical dress, may and ought to be compelled to do so by suspension, loss of revenue and deprivation of office.

[58] See Michael Davies, *The Order of Melchisedech: A Defence of the Catholic Priesthood* (Harrison, New York, 1979, 1993), p. 83.

[59] Bugnini, *op. cit.*, p. 608. Imitating the action of Christ when He healed the dumb man, the priest

2 December 1973 changed the prayers and postures of the confessional and authorized 'penitential celebrations' which in some countries led to general absolution
sessions and the virtual disappearance of private (auricular) confession.

Another product of the Consilium was a new rite of extreme unction
(30 November 1972), renamed 'the Anointing of the Sick' and made obligatory at
the beginning of 1974. A casualty of this reform were the six traditional anoint-
ings of great symbolic beauty,[60] henceforth reduced to two (on the forehead and
hands) or even to one (on the forehead), at the discretion of the ministering priest.
An earlier apostolic constitution, *Pænitemini* (23 February 1966), had abolished
compulsory fasting on the weekdays of Lent, on Ember Days and on the vigils
of feasts.[61] It also authorized the substitution of 'other works of penance' for the
customary abstinence from meat on all Fridays and all days of fast.[62] By the mid-
1970s meatless Fridays had become a rarity in most Catholic countries, except
during Lent, and most people ended up performing no Friday penance at all. By
the 1990s Ash Wednesday and Good Friday were the only days of the year when
Catholics had to limit their intake of food, could not eat between meals and were
obliged to abstain from meat. Weddings in Lent and Advent, previously strictly
forbidden, were allowed and became common in many countries after the Second
Vatican Council.

Even in the early phase of these startling innovations it seemed to the tradition-
conscious that 'the whole supernatural atmosphere of the Catholic liturgy as a
reflection of the Heavenly liturgy with the Slain Lamb on the throne, surrounded
day and night by adoring angels and saints, was destroyed'.[63] Yet the reformers
were undeterred. Within a month of the publication of Paul VI's apostolic constitution of 1969, the official bulletin of the Liturgical Institutes of Germany,
Switzerland and Austria responded by advertising its endorsement of the principle
of a permanent liturgical revolution:

> The [new] Latin texts must now be translated into the various vernaculars; the
> 'Roman' style must be adapted to the individual character of the local churches;
> what was conceived out of time must be brought within the changing context
> of concrete situations, the constant flux of the universal Church and its myriad
> congregations.[64]

---

used to wet his finger with saliva, then touch the lips of the infant or person being baptized,
saying the Aramaic word *ephpheta*, 'open'.

[60] On the eyes (for sins of sight), the ears (for sins of hearing), the nose (for sins committed through
the sense of smell), the lips (for sins of taste and speech), the palms of the hands (for sins of
touching or harming), and the feet (for sins committed by walking).

[61] This confirmed existing relaxations made by certain episcopal conferences since 1949 (e.g. that
of England and Wales) abolishing compulsory fast and abstinence on the weekdays of Lent other
than Ash Wednesday and all Fridays.

[62] Children under the age of fourteen were dispensed from abstinence, whereas previously children
aged seven and over had to abstain on the designated days. The wisdom of introducing young
Catholics to abstinence on the threshold of the rebellious adolescent years rather than earlier
(when the habit could be properly inculcated) is highly questionable. The English anthropologist Mary Douglas made the interesting observation that 'the dropping of the prohibition for
Catholics of eating meat on Fridays took away the cohesion of the group' and that 'people who
have become unritualistic in every other way will eventually lose their capacity for responding to
condensed symbols such as that of the Blessed Sacrament' ('The Contempt of Ritual', *Blackfriars*,
Part 1/49 [June 1968], pp. 476–82).

[63] Franz Schmidberger, *The Episcopal Consecrations of 30 June 1988* (London, 1989), p. 17.

[64] *Gottesdienst* (No. 9), 14 May 1969.

In 1975 the French priest Henri Denis, a *peritus* at the Vatican Council, had the honesty to state, in retrospect:

> To claim that everything has changed is quite simply to be honest about what has happened. In some of the debates with traditionalists it has sometimes become the accepted practice to say that nothing has been changed. It would be far better to have the courage to admit that the Church has made important modifications and that she had good reason to do so. Why not acknowledge that religion has changed?[65]

Six years earlier the Lutheran Max Thurian, one of the ecumenical observers at the Consilium, had declared that certain Protestant communities, while rejecting the doctrine of transubstantiation, could now 'celebrate the Lord's Supper with the same prayers as the Catholic Church. This is theologically possible.'[66]

Beginnings of a Resistance

Pope Paul's achievement did not bring joy to the hearts of all, a fact that was to dog him to the end of his days. On 30 November 1969, the day the new missal was implemented in Italy, residents of Rome were surprised to find that the water of several public fountains of the city was running red. During the night a group of traditionalists had tipped dye into the waterworks to symbolize their dissent and their grief over the abolition of the authentic Roman liturgy. Leaflets were distributed in explanation:

> Romans, today, November 30, 1969, the new Reformers have decreed the death of the Holy Mass as celebrated for centuries throughout the world! A cry of indignant protest arises from the City that is the centre of Christianity! The waters of Rome run red just as the waters of Egypt were transformed into blood![67]

Earlier that year, on 16 May, the Italian journal *Lo Specchio* had carried an article by the musicologist and liturgist Mgr Domenico Celada which denounced the liturgical reform in less melodramatic but extremely vigorous terms:

> The gradual destruction of the liturgy is a sad fact already well known. Within less than five years, the thousand year old structure of divine worship which throughout the centuries has been known as the *opus Dei* ['work of God'] has been dismantled. The beginning was the abolition of Latin, perpetrated in a fraudulent manner. . . .
>
> We have seen, during these past years, the abolition of those sublime gestures of devotion and piety such as signs of the cross, kissing of the altar which symbolizes Christ, genuflections, etc., gestures which the secretary of the congregation responsible for liturgical reform, Fr Annibale Bugnini, has dared publicly to describe as 'anachronisms' and 'wearisome externals'. Instead, a puerile form

---

[65] Henri Denis, *Des sacrements et des hommes dix ans après Vatican II* (Lyons, 1975), p. 34.
[66] *La Croix*, 30 May 1969.
[67] Bugnini, *op. cit.*, p. 289.

of rite has been imposed, noisy, uncouth and extremely boring. And hypocriti-
cally, no notice has been taken of the disturbance and disgust of the faithful . . .
Resounding success has been claimed for it because a proportion of the faithful
has been trained to repeat mechanically a succession of phrases which through
repetition have already lost their effect. We have witnessed with horror the introduction into our churches of hideous parodies of the sacred texts, of tunes and
instruments more suited to the tavern.[68]

The Ottaviani Intervention

Over the following years there appeared a spate of publications hostile to the
reform which establishment polemicists found it easier to ignore than to refute.[69]
The most devastating of these was the critical study of the new Mass rite presented
by a group of Roman theologians to Cardinals Alfredo Ottaviani and Antonio
Bacci on the feast of Corpus Christi, 1969. The authors of the *Breve esame critico
del Novus Ordo Missæ* complained that 'it has been said of it that it could be
celebrated with a clear conscience by a priest who no longer believed in either
transubstantiation or the sacrificial nature of the Mass, and hence it would also
lend itself perfectly to celebration by a Protestant minister'.[70]

---

[68] D. Celada, 'La mini-messa contro il dogma', appearing in *Lo Specchio*, according to Bugnini
(*op. cit.*, p. 289) on 29 June 1969. English translation quoted in Michael Davies, *Pope John's
Council: Part Two of Liturgical Revolution* (Chawleigh, Devon, 1977), p. 254.

[69] For an expansion of these arguments see the following publications: Louis Salleron, *La nouvelle
messe* (Paris, 1970); *Why the Tridentine Mass?* (New York, n.d.); James F. Wathen, OSJ, *The
Great Sacrilege* (Rockford, Illinois, 1971); Arnaldo Xavier da Silveira, *La nouvelle messe de Paul
VI: qu'en penser?* (Chiré-en-Montreuil, 1975); Michael Davies, *The Tridentine Mass* (1977),
The New Mass (1977; written in refutation of Mgr Martimort's article mentioned below), *The
Roman Rite Destroyed* (1978), all printed by the Augustine Publishing Co., Chawleigh, Devon,
UK, and his monumental trilogy *Liturgical Revolution* (1976–1980); Daniel Raffard de Brienne,
Lex Orandi – La nouvelle messe et la Foi (Vouillé, 1983) and 'Sacrifice de la messe ou Cène
du Seigneur?' in *L'Église et le monde*, Supplement to *Savoir et Servir*, No. 10 (Paris, 1988),
pp. 18–31; Martin Mosebach, *The Heresy of Formlessness: The Roman Liturgy and its Enemy*
(San Francisco, 2006). Attempts to defend the reform and to demolish the traditionalist case
were made in Bugnini, *op. cit.*, pp. 284–88; and by C. Vagaggini, OSB, 'Il nuovo Ordo Missæ
e l'ortodossia', *Rivista del Clero Italiano*, 50 (1969), pp. 688–99; Peter Coughlan, *The New
Mass: A Timely, Useful and Intelligent Guide to the New Mass* (Washington/Cleveland, 1969);
J. D. Crichton, *Christian Celebration: The Mass* (London, 1971); Carlo Braga, 'Punti qualificanti
della I.G.M.R.' in Pierre Jounel *et al.*, eds, *Liturgia opera divina ed umana: Studi sulla riforma
liturgica offerti a S.E. Mons. Annibale Bugnini in occasione del suo 70 compleanno* (Rome,
n.d. [c. 1972]), pp. 243–61; Adolf Adam, *Die Messe in neuer Gestalt* (Würzburg, 1974); A.-G.
Martimort, 'Mais qu'est-ce que la Messe de S. Pie V?', *La Croix*, 26 August 1976 (reprinted in
L'Osservatore Romano, 30/31 August 1976); Guy Oury, OSB, *La Messe de S. Pie V à Paul VI*
(Solesmes, 1975); R. Renié, 'Le nouvel Ordo Missæ serait-il hérétique?', *Chevalier* (Supplément à
Magistère-Information des Chevaliers de Notre-Dame), Nos 24–25 (1974–1975), pp. 11–15, and
No. 26 (1975), pp. 5–10; A. Richard, *Le mystère de la messe dans le nouvel Ordo* (Paris, 1970);
Edward Matthews, *A Popular Guide to the New Mass* (London, 1970); J. D. Crichton, *Liturgical
Changes: The Background* (London, 1975); James Likoudis and Kenneth D. Whitehead, *The
Pope, the Council and the Mass: Answers to the Questions the 'Traditionalists' are Asking* (W.
Hanover, Massachusetts, 1981), a publication of the extreme ultramontanist but anti-Modernist
organization Catholics United for the Faith; Denis Crouan, *La liturgie confisquée: lettre ouverte
aux évêques et tous ceux qui trahissent la liturgie conciliaire* (Paris°, 1997). One recent publication
attempts to present objectively both the reformist and the traditionalist cases: Thomas M. Kocik,
The Reform of the Reform? A Liturgical Debate: Reform or Return (San Francisco, 2003).

[70] *Roman Theologians*, p. 20. The chief author of the study was the French Dominican theologian
Fr Michel Guérard des Lauriers.

The two cardinals, after considering the charges made in this document and concurring substantially with them, forwarded a copy of it to Pope Paul on the Feast of Saint Pius X (3 September). Cardinal Arcadio Larraona also endorsed the study, but declined to add his signature to the accompanying letter, which stated the conviction of Ottaviani and Bacci that

> the *Novus Ordo Missæ*, considering the new elements, susceptible of widely differing evaluations . . . represents . . . a striking departure from the Catholic theology of the Holy Mass as it was formulated in Session XXII of the Council of Trent, which, by fixing definitively the 'canons' [official prayers] of the rite, erected an insurmountable barrier against any heresy which might attack the integrity of the Mystery.
>
> The pastoral reasons adduced in support of such a grave break – even if they could stand up in the face of doctrinal deficiencies – do not appear sufficient.[71]

The accusations of the *Breve esame critico* were serious and Paul VI is said to have been extremely upset by them. The first objection in the report was to the Protestant rather than Catholic definition of the Eucharist given in Article 7 of the General Instruction ('On the Structure of the Mass'), which ignored the vital distinction between the sacrificial priesthood and the laity:

> The Lord's Supper or the Mass is the sacred assembly or gathering together of the people of God, with a priest presiding, to celebrate the memorial of the Lord. For this reason, the promise of Christ is particularly true of a local congregation of the Church: 'Where two or three are gathered in my name, there am I in their midst.' (Mt. 18.20)

'None of this implies the Real Presence, the reality of the Sacrifice, the sacral character of the officiating priest or the intrinsic worth of the eucharistic Sacrifice independently of the presence of the congregation', commented the authors of the *Esame critico*.[72] Article 8 similarly stressed the supper aspect of the Mass to the detriment of its sacrificial aspect, as did the recommendation that Mass be celebrated facing the people, the suggested relegation of the tabernacle containing the reserved sacrament to a side chapel, and repeated reference to the altar as a 'table' (*mensa*).[73]

The setting out of the consecration formulae as simply part of a narrative, something discouraged by Pope Paul, had become a standard feature of the published drafts of the new ordinary of the Mass. No less alarming were the new 'acclamations' that intruded thoughts of the second coming of Christ at the very moment when He had become substantially present on the altar.[74] As for the replacement of the double series of prayers that had characterized the traditional rite with common ones which priest and people now said together (viz. the *Confiteor*, the pre-Communion prayers), this seemed an obsessive emphasis on the community aspect of the Eucharist. In the new liturgy the celebrant appeared more as the

[71] Ibid., p. 31.
[72] Ibid., p. 6.
[73] Ibid., pp. 7, 12.
[74] Ibid., pp. 13–15.

president of an assembly than as a consecrated priest representing the Church.[75] This whole anti-sacrificial tendency was compounded by the suppression of many other prayers and ceremonies, the absence of which further obscured the Catholic theology of the Mass.[76]

Is Validity Everything?

It must be stressed at this point that the traditionalist case against the liturgical reform did not hinge primarily on the question of validity, as has often been claimed. Since, according to Latin Catholic teaching, the minimum that is required for the validity of the Eucharist is the use of correct matter (wheaten bread and fermented grape wine) and form (the exact Scriptural Words of Institution prescribed in their long or short form) by a validly ordained priest with the correct intention, conscientious objectors were bound to accept the essential validity of the new rite *where these elements remained intact*. What they felt obliged to condemn were its structure and ethos, and the wider implications of the reform itself.[77]

The problems of inauthenticity and decontextualization, the real flaws of the new liturgy, cannot be simply dismissed as a question of externals. For when the reformers undertook a wholesale excision of prayers and gestures that unambiguously expressed the Catholic theology of each rite, the liturgy was stripped of those precise elements which normally guaranteed the correct intention of the celebrant, a fact that Archbishop Lefebvre pointed out on more than one occasion.[78] Thus in the new ordinal and in the new rite of Mass it became possible for a bishop or a priest who no longer believed in Catholic doctrine, or seriously misunderstood it, to celebrate invalidly through defect of intention to offer a sacrifice according to the mind of the Church. It was precisely because of this question mark hanging over the sacraments administered by the products of modern seminaries, where heterodoxy was entrenched, that traditionalist leaders would urge the faithful to avoid the new liturgy altogether, for the sake of 'sacramental security'.

Consequently, a general cause of concern for the authors of the *Breve esame critico* were the numerous ambiguities and desacralizing omissions (for example of silent prayers and of references to the Blessed Virgin and the saints) which brought the new Catholic Mass rite closer to the liturgies of the Reformation. If one of the motives for such changes was ecumenism, it was, the theologians argued, a singularly one-sided one which removed 'all that the Roman liturgy had in common with the Eastern'. Pope Paul's new Mass could only alienate Eastern Catholics and the Orthodox from Latin Christendom:

---

[75] Ibid., pp. 15–20.

[76] Ibid., pp. 11–12 *et passim*.

[77] This fact has been regularly (and sometimes maliciously) misrepresented by opponents of traditionalism. The question of the possible invalidity of the new Mass arose over the mistranslation of the expression *pro multis*, 'for many', in the formula for consecrating the wine as 'for all men' (and today, in 'inclusive language', 'for all'). The problem, admittedly an extremely serious one, therefore concerns English and other vernacular versions of the rite, not the normative Latin text with its orthodox formula. For a clarification of the traditionalist position on the validity or otherwise of the New Order of Mass, see M. Davies, *PPNM*, pp. 623–30.

[78] See, for instance, Marcel Lefebvre, *La messe de toujours: le trésor caché* (Étampes, 2005), p. 374.

Consider, for example – to refer only to the Byzantine rite – the extremely long, urgent and repeated penitential prayers; the solemn rites of clothing the celebrant and the deacon; the preparation, already a complete rite in itself, of the offerings at the *proskomidia*; the constant presence, in the prayers and even in the offerings, of the Blessed Virgin, the Saints and the Angelic Hierarchies . . .; the iconostasis, which clearly separates the sanctuary from the nave, the clergy from the people; the hidden consecration, obvious symbol of the Unknowable to which the whole liturgy alludes; the [general] position of the celebrant 'turned towards God' (*versus ad Deum*) and not towards the people (*versus ad populum*); the administering of Communion only and always by the celebrant; the continual signs of profound adoration towards the Sacred Species; the essentially contemplative attitude of the people. The fact that such liturgies, even in their less solemn form, last for more than an hour, and the repeated references to them as 'awful and ineffable liturgy' and 'awful, celestial, life-giving mysteries' etc., complete the picture for us. It may be noted finally that in both the Divine Liturgy of St John Chrysostom and in that of St Basil the concept of 'supper' and 'banquet' is clearly subordinated to that of Sacrifice, just as it was in the Roman Mass.[79]

The fundamental problem of the incompatibility of the new Roman rites with those of the Eastern Churches would be one that Paul VI and his reformers would ignore at their peril.

[79] Ibid., p. 22.

2

THE HEART OF THE CHURCH

*The whole of Christianity is contained in the sign of the cross; no
theory of the Redemption expresses itself half as much as a simple
crucifix hung on a wall, erected as a wayside shrine, or put on a tomb
or altar. A symbol contains a possibility of total communion, and its
faithful repetition expresses something that escapes all conceptual
analysis. This is why mere believers can transmit the whole of
Tradition, even when they are quite ignorant of the terminology and
subtleties of dogma.*

FR YVES CONGAR (1963)

*You should descend to your heart from your head . . . The life is in the
heart, so you should live there. Do not think that this applies only to
the perfect. No, it applies to everyone who begins to seek out the Lord.*

THEOPHAN THE RECLUSE
(RUSSIAN ORTHODOX SAINT, † 1894)

Missing the Point

In his memoirs, Archbishop Annibale Bugnini, the driving force behind the liturgical revolution, attempted to defend the reform by accusing its opponents, even the most erudite among them, of 'ignorance of theology'. The Italian Vincentian marvelled how an 'intelligent man' like Alfredo Cardinal Ottaviani could have lent public support to the 'one-sided' report of a group of theologians accusing Pope Paul VI's New Order of Mass of compromising the Faith.[1]

Likewise conservative Catholics, aghast that anyone claiming to be orthodox could object to the reforms of a pope, have similarly dismissed the objections of liturgical dissenters on grounds that are purely theological. In their energetic and unquestioning defence of papal policy published in 1981, James Likoudis and Kenneth Whitehead not only stressed the doctrinal sufficiency and validity of the new rite as the only essential considerations, but actually charged the traditional

---

[1] Bugnini, *op. cit.*, pp. 286–87. Presuming that one's opponents in a religious dispute are ignorant of theology can be a counterproductive strategy: Bugnini himself was not considered a brilliant theologian by all and sundry. Fellow Consilium member Archbishop Ferdinando Antonelli noted in his diary that in Bugnini, who was 'always supported by Paul VI . . . the most notable flaw is a lack of scholarly formation and theological sensitivity. I have the impression that he has embraced a Protestant mentality especially in regard to the sacraments' (Gianpietro, *op. cit.*, p. 264).

Roman Mass with having been 'no barrier to the doctrinal deviations that have been the *true* cause of the decline of Catholic faith and practice in the Church in the twentieth century'.[2] (One wonders whether they would level a similar accusation against the Byzantine liturgy for not having been a bulwark against Bolshevism in 1917 . . .)

Practice before Theory

Such use of exclusively rational criteria in dealing with the problem of tradition-alist dissent displays a serious disregard for one of the fundamental realities of religion: its cultural dimension. If the rationalistic approach seems misguided to the tradition-conscious Catholic, it would strike the secular anthropologist as naive in the extreme. When the Cultural Revolution broke out in 1966, most of the four million Catholics of China were simple peasants with an unsophistic-ated understanding of their religion. In his plan to eradicate Christianity from his country, Mao Tse-Tung did not begin the conversion of Catholics to Communism by allowing them free practice of their faith while forcing them to attend courses of Marxist doctrine. Rather, he closed all the churches and sent Catholics to re-education camps where they would imbibe the spirit and ethos of Communist life. In spite of his philosophical idealism, Chairman Mao was enough of a realist to understand that the practice of a way of life always precedes its theory.

Within the Catholic family, children first acquire knowledge about God through learning short prayers and sacred actions like the sign of the cross, accompanied by the explanation of simple truths. Only later do parents or teachers begin to expound to them in detail the doctrines of the Church. For children from non-observant Catholic families whose first experience of religion are occasional catechism lessons outside the home it is very difficult for the faith infused into their souls at baptism to survive. In all cultures, religious knowledge begins *within* religious practice, and praxis is thus anterior to formal theology. Heresies are promoted in a similar way. In 1548, before Cranmer's heterodox first Prayer Book was imposed on the peoples of England, Cornwall and Wales, the faithful were 'softened up' by a vicious campaign in which the most revered and beloved elements of Catholic worship were publicly ridiculed and profaned:

> The sweeping condemnation of the externals of the old faith – 'hallowed candles, hallowed water, hallowed bread, hallowed ashes' – made way for the Protestant emphasis on internal conversion and the devotion of the heart. And by adding to the general bewilderment about belief this furor of invective made at least some in the population doubly eager for the new orthodoxy when it came at last.[3]

A cloud of confusion is the necessary cover for corruptive change. The forces of evil contrive to debase men's morals before they alter their minds, whereas true apostles of Christ strive to inculcate virtue, especially the virtue of humility, in individuals in order to make them receptive to the truth. The French theologian Henri Rondet once remarked that 'outward actions create habits, involving the acceptance by the

[2] Likoudis/Whitehead, *op. cit.*, p. 136.
[3] Carolly Erickson, *Bloody Mary* (New York, 1978), p. 231.

mind of the truths implied by this outward behaviour'. He illustrated this truth with two anecdotes:

'Do you wish to believe?' said Pascal.
   'Humble yourself, take holy water . . .'

One day Abbé Huvelin said to Charles de Foucauld: 'Kneel down, and make your confession.'
   'But I have no faith!'
   'Make your confession.'[4]

Ora ut credas

The Latin saying *ora ut credas*, 'pray that you might believe', makes a similar point. In the natural order, things precede ideas, and in the supernatural order, the divine mystery – the reality of God – is anterior to faith, the response of the individual to contact with this mystery. The Church teaches that while man can arrive at a natural knowledge of God's existence through the use of reason alone,[5] one cannot attain the supernatural knowledge required to believe in such doctrines as the Incarnation and the Trinity without the experience of God's enlightening the intellect and strengthening the will through the infusion of divine grace. St Prosper of Aquitaine, a fifth-century monk from Marseilles who was secretary to Pope Celestine I, argued against the Pelagians that if it was the custom of the Universal Church to pray that unbelievers and enemies of the Cross might receive the light of faith, it was because God had to effect the necessary change of heart by grace before they could truly believe in Him.[6]

It is human beings' experience of the reality of God in the Christian teachings and way of life that leads them to the act of faith, and the strongest presence of God in the world is found in the liturgical mysteries. Indeed it is the sacred liturgy more than anything else that forms true Christians. As Fr Yves Congar put it in 1963:

Nothing is more educative for man in his totality than the liturgy. The Bible is certainly a marvellous teacher of prayer, of the sense of God and of the adult convictions of conscience. Used alone, the Bible might produce a Christian of the Puritan tradition, an individualist and even a visionary. The liturgy, however, is the 'authentic method instituted by the Church to unite souls to Jesus' (Dom Maurice Festugière). The sort of Christian produced by an enlightened and docile participation in the liturgy is a man at peace and unified in every fibre of his human nature, by the secret and powerful penetration of faith and love in his life, throughout a period of prayer and worship, during which he learned, at his mother's knee

---

4   Henri Rondet, SJ, *Do Dogmas Change?* (London, 1961), p. 70.
5   According to the First Vatican Council 'The same Holy Mother Church holds and teaches that God, the beginning and end of all things, may be certainly known by the natural light of human reason, by created things' (Denzinger, par. 3004).
6   See P. De Clerck, '"Lex orandi, lex credendi". Sens originel et avatars historiques d'un adage équivoque', *Questions liturgiques*, 59 (1978), pp. 197–98. Also Karl Lehmann, 'Gottesdienst als Ausdruck des Glaubens: Plaidoyer für ein neues Gespräch zwischen Liturgiewissenschaft und dogmatischer Theologie', *Liturgisches Jahrbuch*, 30 (1980), pp. 197–214.

and without effort, the Church's language: her language of faith, love, hope and fidelity. There is no better way of acquiring 'the mind of the Church' in the widest and most interior interpretation of this expression; it is something quite different from an instinctive obedience.[7]

However, this statement by a modern theologian contrasts sharply with the long-standing tendency among Western Christians to identify orthodoxy with correct doctrinal beliefs and moral ideals, and to regard all other aspects of Catholic life, public worship in particular, as things of secondary or relative importance, or even as *adiaphora* (indifferent things). A corollary of this is the common excuse of people who have given up the formal practice of their religion that one does not need to go to church to know that there is a God, or to tell right from wrong.

What is Orthodoxy?

Such is not the outlook of devout Orthodox Christians of the East, for whom the solemn public worship of God is more than simply a principal duty of believers, but rather a sublime privilege.[8] Following the holistic approach of the Church Fathers, the Easterners refuse to make any practical distinction between the apostolic deposit of faith (Holy Tradition – with a capital T) and the body of individual traditions or immemorial customs (*orthopraxis*) that make up the Christian way of life. Orthopraxis is the culture of Christianity as opposed to secular culture, and for Eastern Christians true orthodoxy implies both the apostolic faith and the traditional practice of it.

In the mind of the Christian East the Church as an institution is completely transcended by its central practices, as Lawrence Cross observes:

> The Orthodox believer, very much like the simple Catholic, knows that the Church is 'the meeting-place of all mysteries' and so . . . will almost never talk about the Church 'from the outside', as a 'thing' to be studied, as an 'object'. To the inexperienced, replies [to questions about the nature of the Church] such as 'in our Church we fast a lot', 'in our Church we have lots of icons', 'in our Church we baptize, chrismate (confirm) and give the Eucharist to our babies all at once', may seem even a little beside the point, a little slow-witted. What they are really saying is, with Jesus, 'Come and see!'

---

[7] Yves Congar, *La tradition et la vie de l'Église* (Paris, 1963); Engl. tr., *Tradition and the Life of the Church* (London, 1964), p. 128.

[8] Attendance at the Sunday Eucharist enjoined by the Third Commandment is frequently not defined as an obligation by the Orthodox Church as it is by the Catholic Church: it is simply assumed that a Christian who loves God will attend Mass regularly, without having to be obliged on pain of sin. 'Participation in the Divine Liturgy is not a duty or obligation, but rather a privilege', writes Fr Michael Soter in his introduction to a bilingual (Albanian and English) Orthodox missal (*The Divine Liturgy according to St John Chrysostom*, Boston, 1988, p. x). This non-juridical approach to the dominical obligation often has the distinct disadvantage of guaranteeing low Sunday attendance among the Orthodox. On the other hand, the Catholic policy of enforcing attendance brought large numbers to Sunday Mass, but many people went for negative rather than positive reasons (fear of mortal sin and hell rather than a disinterested love of God and affection for the liturgy), which explains the catastrophic decline in attendance after Vatican II when many clergy and religion teachers in Catholic schools took it upon themselves to give Catholics the false instruction that going to Sunday Mass was no longer a binding duty.

There is almost an instinct which says that to speculate to no good purpose is dangerous. The instinct is a good one. It stops one from forgetting that we are the Church ourselves; from becoming a spectator at our own prayer, from turning theology into a mental geometry of the divine. For this reason, Christians of the Byzantine churches describe themselves as 'Orthodox' in the Greek language, or as 'Pravoslavnie' in the Slavonic tongue. To be an Orthodox means to be 'right worshipping', to be one who worships God as He desires to be worshipped, which is to say: in Spirit and in Truth through the Eucharist of His Son, Jesus Christ.[9]

Now this statement is no anti-intellectual rejection of speculative theology. It is simply the affirmation of a primacy. The living heart of the Church is the sacred liturgy, in which the grace of God is communicated to the faithful through the sacraments. It is the sacramental life that brings Catholic doctrine alive to us, not the other way round. Oriental Christians are less concerned with *how* a sacramental mystery comes about than with *what* it is.[10] When it is a question of supernatural mysteries, simple acknowledgement of the reality is more important than the most exhaustive understanding of the same reality.

The semantic development of the term 'orthodoxy' in the Christian context is also reflective of the primacy of prayer over understanding. The Classical Greek compound noun ὀρθοδοξία (*orthodoxía*) originally signified 'right opinion'. However, since the second component, *doxa*, had also the secondary meanings of 'glory' and 'praise', the word came, in the usage of Greek-speaking Christians, to mean 'right worship'. Hence the Old Slavonic loan translation *pravoslavie* ('orthodoxy', but literally 'right praise') adapted the secondary (Christian) rather than the primary (classical) meaning of the term.

First Things First

The primacy of worship also belongs to the chronological order, since Christians were hearing the word of God within the framework of the rites of prayer transmitted to them by the Apostles for almost a century before the writing of the New Testament was complete and the first theological treatises appeared. According to J. G. Davies, man's ritual response to the activity of God in the world 'precedes doctrinal [i.e. dogmatic] formulation, so that one may say that worship is primary and theology secondary'. The same writer states that in Christian terms this means that the early Church was worshipping Christ long before its intellectual understanding of His person and work was developed well enough to permit the formulation of official dogmas when basic beliefs came to be contradicted in certain quarters.[11]

Moreover, since the oldest witness to what the Church believes is the tradition of public worship (in which preaching the Faith was from the first an integral element) the teachers of the primitive Church and all the theologians who came after them considered set liturgical formulae as an authoritative guide to the truths of the faith. This does not mean that the liturgy is a sort of quarry from which the

[9] Lawrence Cross, *Eastern Christianity: The Byzantine Tradition* (Sydney, 1988), pp. 33–35.
[10] Ibid., p. 58.
[11] J. G. Davies, ed., *op. cit.*, p. v.

totality of Christian doctrine can be extracted, an equivalent to the Bible in fundamentalist Protestantism. Nevertheless, Pope Leo XIII highlighted the fact that 'the sacred rites, although not instituted specifically for proving the truth of the dogmas of the Catholic Faith incontrovertibly, are effectively the living voice of Catholic truth, the oft-sounded expression of it'.[12]

It is therefore impossible for Christian worship and Christian belief to operate in mutual isolation. Right belief is the guarantee of right worship and vice versa. According to the Russian Orthodox theologian Fr Georges Florovsky:

> in Eastern tradition, the unity of doctrine and worship is strongly stressed. The doctrine itself is here not so much a doctrine taught in the classroom, as a doctrine proclaimed in the temple – theology speaks more from the pulpit than from the desk. It assumes therefore a more existential character. Worship, on the other hand, is free from emotionalism. Sobriety of heart is its first requirement. The fullness of the theological thought of the Church is thrown into the worship. This is possibly the most notable distinctive mark of the Eastern tradition.[13]

In his treatment of the role of worship in the Byzantine Church, Timothy Ware notes that

> [t]he Orthodox approach to religion is fundamentally a liturgical approach, which understands doctrine in the context of divine worship: it is no coincidence that the word 'Orthodoxy' should signify alike right belief and right worship, for the two things are inseparable. It has truly been said of the Byzantines: 'Dogma with them is not only an intellectual system apprehended by the clergy and expounded to the laity, but a field of vision wherein all things on earth are seen in their relation to things in heaven, first and foremost through liturgical celebration.'[14]

Lex orandi, lex credendi

'Christianity is a liturgical religion', writes Fr Florovsky.

> The Church is first of all a worshipping community. Worship comes first, doctrine and discipline second. The *lex orandi* [law of prayer] has a privileged priority in the life of Christians. The *lex credendi* [law of belief] depends upon the devotional experience and vision of the Church. On the other hand, Christian worship is itself to a large extent dogmatic – a worshipping witness to the truth of Revelation. The lyrical element in the worship has a subordinate place.[15]

Fr Florovsky makes use of Latin theological terminology to explain these concepts, which belong equally to Western Christianity and have been summarized in Prosper of Aquitaine's sentence *lex supplicandi legem statuat credendi*, 'let the

---

[12] Encyclical *Orientalium Dignitas* (*On the Churches of the East*), 30 November 1894.
[13] G. Florovsky, 'The Elements of Liturgy' in Constantin G. Patelos, ed., *The Orthodox Church in the Ecumenical Movement: Documents and Statements 1902–1975* (Geneva, 1978), p. 172.
[14] Timothy (Archimandrite Kallistos) Ware, *The Orthodox Church* (Harmondsworth, 1963), p. 271.
[15] Florovsky, *op. cit.*, p. 172.

law of prayer determine the law of belief', and often abbreviated to *lex orandi, lex credendi*.[16] Although St Prosper actually used this sentence in the context of his apology for the doctrine of grace (i.e. 'let our tradition of prayer confirm this particular belief'), it subsequently passed into common theological usage as a general dictum to summarize the teachings that the belief of the Church must be in harmony with its age-old tradition of worship, and that the way in which a congregation worships is the surest indication of what it believes.[17] Prosper's famous sentence, notes Dom Cipriano Vagaggini, 'certainly reflects the thinking of the Roman curia of that era, and has notable theological authority because the Roman See has since then always considered it as the exact expression of its point of view in the matter under discussion and, subsequently, has often appealed to it'.[18]

In his discussion of the Prosperine principle, the American Benedictine Dom Aidan Kavanagh explains that the standard of Christian worship 'establishes' or 'founds' the standard of Christian belief in the sense that prayer, and above all liturgical prayer, actuates belief by bringing us to an encounter with the Source of the grace of faith:

> Christians . . . believe because the One in whose gift faith lies is regularly met in the act of communal worship – not because the assembly conjures up God, but because the initiative lies with the God who has promised to be there always. The *lex credendi* is thus subordinated to the *lex supplicandi* because both standards exist and function only within the worshipping assembly's own subordination of itself to its ever-present Judge, Saviour, and unifying Spirit.[19]

In the Orthodox Church, which has been slower and more hesitant than the Roman Church in defining doctrine, the role of the sacred liturgy as a repository of revealed truth is particularly important:

> Orthodoxy has made few explicit definitions about the Eucharist and the other Sacraments, about the next world, the Mother of God, the saints, and the faithful departed: Orthodox belief on these points is contained mainly in the prayers and hymns used at Orthodox services. Nor is it merely the words of the services which are part of Tradition; the various gestures and actions – immersion in the waters of Baptism, the different anointings with oil, the sign of the Cross, and so on – all have a special meaning, and all express in symbolical or dramatic form the truths of the faith.[20]

It is arguable for this reason that several Roman dogmas officially rejected by

---

[16] Occurring in the eighth chapter (*Capitulum de gratia*) of a text by St Prosper preserved in a collection of theological works from the pontificate of Pope Celestine (422–432) and entitled *Indiculus de gratia* or *Præteritorum Sedis Apostolicæ episcoporum auctoritates de gratia Dei et libero voluntatis arbitrio*.

[17] This is far from meaning that only doctrines expressed in the liturgy are to be believed, as if Holy Scripture were not an equally important source of Tradition. This erroneous idea was condemned by Pius XII in *Mediator Dei* (III, 50, 52).

[18] Cyprian Vagaggini (tr. L. J. Doyle and W. A. Jurgens), *Theological Dimensions of the Liturgy* (Collegeville, Minnesota, 1976), p. 529.

[19] Aidan Kavanagh, *On Liturgical Theology: The Hale Memorial Lectures of Seabury-Western Theological Seminary 1981* (New York, 1984), pp. 91–92.

[20] Ware, *op. cit.*, p. 213.

the Orthodox Church today are materially held by the Orthodox faithful on the strength of their presence, explicit or implicit, in Byzantine liturgical tradition, for instance the Immaculate Conception and the Intermediate State (Purgatory).[21]

Liturgy and Theology

Holy Tradition is bipartite: its rational element consists of the Magisterium (the authoritative teaching of the bishops) and Holy Scripture, while its liturgical element is the principal channel of the divine grace communicated to men. But in this dichotomy the law of prayer has, as already noted, has a chronological primacy over the law of belief; it both founds and transcends it. The liturgy, then, is not something arbitrarily devised by theologians, but *theologia prima*, the ontological condition of theology.[22]

The German Benedictine liturgist Dom Odo Casel once argued that

> the truth of the faith is made accessible not simply in a unique way through the liturgical celebration of the faith of the Church. Rather the liturgical expression of the self-understanding of the Church, while not rendering other modes of expression superfluous, is clearly superior from all points of view. The liturgical traditions are not simply one among many sources of knowledge of faith, but the source and central witness of the life of faith and so of all theology.[23]

Dr Varghese Pathikulangara, a Catholic scholar of the Syro-Malabarese rite, states that 'theology is a search for words and concepts adequate to, and expressive of,

---

[21] Two particular statements should have put paid to lingering but baseless suspicions among Catholic extremists that the theology of the independent Eastern Churches is intrinsically irreconcilable with that of Rome. The decree *Unitatis Redintegratio* (1964, § 17) of the Second Vatican Council declared:

> In the study of revelation East and West have followed different methods, and have developed differently their understanding and confession of God's truth. It is hardly surprising, then, if from time to time one tradition has come nearer to a full appreciation of some aspects of a mystery of revelation than another, or has expressed it to better advantage. In such cases, these various theological expressions are to be considered often as mutually complementary rather than conflicting. Where the authentic theological traditions of the Eastern Church are concerned, we must recognize the admirable way in which they have their roots in Holy Scripture, and how they have nurtured and are given expression in the life of the liturgy. They derive their strength, too, from the living tradition of the apostles and from the works of the Fathers and spiritual writers of the Eastern Churches. Thus they promote the right ordering of Christian life and, indeed, pave the way to a full vision of Christian truth.

A communiqué of the 'Second Non-Official Ecumenical Consultation between Theologians of the Oriental Orthodox and the Roman Catholic Churches' (Vienna, September 1973) similarly stated:

> We recognize the limits of every philosophical and theological attempt to grasp the mystery in concept or express it in words. If the formulas coined by the Fathers and the doctors of the Church have enabled us to obtain an authentic glimpse of the divine truth, we recognize that every formula that we can devise needs further interpretation. We saw that what appears to be the right formulation can be wrongly understood, and how also even behind an apparently wrong formulation there can be a right understanding.

[22] Alexander Schmemann, 'Theology and Liturgical Tradition', in Massey Shepherd, ed., *Worship in Scripture and Tradition* (Oxford, 1963), p. 175.

[23] Rephrased by Edward J. Kilmartin, SJ, *Christian Liturgy: Theology and Practice* (Kansas City, 1988), I, pp. 96–97.

the living experience, i.e. the liturgy of the Church'.[24] In a similar vein, Massey Shepherd, an American liturgist, writes that 'Worship is the experiential foundation of theological reflection', and that the 'practice of worship is the source of rubrical and canonical legislation'. The ministry of clergy and laity, moreover, 'is exhibited most clearly in liturgical assemblies'.[25]

Dom Aidan Kavanagh amplifies this basic definition by stating that 'what emerges most directly from an assembly's liturgical act is not a new species of theology among others. It is *theologia* itself.' The sacred liturgy, he continues,

> is not some thing separate from the Church, but simply the Church caught in the act of being most overtly itself as it stands faithfully in the presence of the One who is both object and source of the faith. The liturgical assembly's stance in faith is vertiginous, on the edge of chaos. Only grace and favour enable it to stand there; only grace and promise brought it there; only grace and a rigorous divine charity permit the assembly, like Moses, to come away from such an encounter, and even then it is with wounds which are as deep as they are salutary. Here is where 'something vastly mysterious' transpires in the Church as it engages in worship worthy of Creation and congruent with the human City within which it abides as witness to God in Christ. As Leo the Great said, those things which were conspicuous in the life of our Redeemer here pass over into the *sacraments*, into the worship of the Church . . .[26]

For Eastern Christians the sacred liturgy is, in the words of Fr Pathikulangara, 'the *epiphany* of the Church's faith', 'the transfiguring experience of the Mystery of the Church' and 'the *locus classicus* of all theological synthesis'. It is the liturgy, moreover, that

> makes the Church what she is and is the fulfilment of her very nature, of her cosmic and eschatological calling. Liturgy for an Oriental is not merely a matter of a few externals and prayers or the sharing of a few ideas; it is the sublime expression of the living traditions of his Church. It sums up his whole Christian life and inspires it. Liturgy is the epiphany of heaven on earth, the passage of the Church from this world into heaven. It is the most perfect expression of the Church.[27]

However, for most professional theologians in the Catholic West the idea of liturgical tradition as primordial theology, the very threshold of Revelation, is now alien. In the main, Latin Catholic theology prefers to identify Revelation with the wisdom living in the 'mind of the Church' and expressing itself in the dynamic interrelationship of Scripture and Tradition, the liturgy being merely one of several forms or witnesses of Tradition. This is a standard outlook nourished by centuries of erudition. It is nevertheless significant, in regard to those dogmatic theologians who have nuanced this general approach with the admission that the sacred liturgy is a very important (or even the most important) form of Tradition, that the overwhelming majority of them made no public objection to the Pauline reforms

[24] Varghese Pathikulangara, 'Liturgy and Theology in Eastern Christian Tradition', in Thomas Vellilamthadam *et al.*, eds, *Ecclesial Identity of the Thomas Christians* (Kottayam, 1985), p. 177.
[25] Quoted in Kavanagh, *op. cit.*, p. 78.
[26] Ibid., pp. 75–76.
[27] Pathikulangara, *op. cit.*

after 1969, and gave not the slightest intellectual (let alone moral) support to the lay movement for the perpetuation and rehabilitation of the banned pre-conciliar rites. A dramatic half-century later, this fact should lead to serious reflection.

Tradition and Liturgical Reform

Given the normative and testimonial nature of the liturgical tradition, whose historical growth has its own dynamic, there can be in Catholicism no question of arbitrarily restructuring received sacred rites to make them reflect new doctrines or new doctrinal emphases. Such a reversal of the Prosperine principle has always been associated with heretical movements in the history of Church, and is especially characteristic of Protestantism: Luther, Zwingli, Calvin and Cranmer all manufactured liturgies reflecting their particular theological preconceptions. On this point the Orthodox East is again in perfect agreement with the pre-conciliar Latin West:

> Because they approach religion in this liturgical way, Orthodox often attribute to minute points of ritual an importance which astonishes Western Christians. But once we have understood the central place of worship in the life of Orthodoxy, an incident like the schism of the Old Believers will no longer appear unintelligible: if worship is the faith in action, then liturgical changes cannot be lightly regarded.[28]

Even when individuals have proposed liturgical innovations which are in harmony with orthodox doctrinal developments, the traditional instinct of the Church has been wary of admitting them by simple reason of the primary nature of the sacred liturgy. On the other hand it is evident that the Christian cult has changed outwardly from the first Eucharist to our own day. The Church's tradition of worship did not 'come from the Lord complete and perfect', as Bossuet said of the apostolic deposit of faith. Development is of the very nature of Catholic worship, which was given to the infant Church as an acorn, not as a full-grown oak. Catholicism is an inculturated religion, and its official cult necessarily varies according to space and time.

Evolution of the Historic Rites

Structurally speaking, seven basic forms of the Catholic liturgical tradition have survived to the present, most of them subdivided into regional variants. They are the Antiochene, Edessene, Byzantine, Alexandrian, Roman, Milanese and Mozarabic rites, all except the last named after important centres of Christianity (mostly patriarchal sees) in the Patristic era. Some of the Christians worshipping in these rites are in communion with Rome, others belong to the independent Orthodox and lesser Eastern Churches. Historians posit the fourth century as the period in which the formal worship of the early Christians crystallized into these distinct parent rites, reflecting the mentality and customs of the different churches.[29]

[28] Ware, *op. cit.*, p. 271.
[29] Fortescue, *op. cit.*, pp. 76–79.

Of all the patriarchal liturgies, it is the Roman one that underwent the greatest development, because, being the rite of the primatial patriarchate, it inevitably absorbed elements from the liturgies of other churches. For instance, two Byzantine influences, the *Kyrie*, originally a litany, and the *Gloria*, enriched the Roman Mass around the time of Pope Gelasius (d. 496) and Pope Symmachus (d. 514) respectively.[30] However, the period of maximum growth was the age of the Saxon emperors (eleventh and twelfth centuries), when prayers and practices from the obsolete Gallican rite (once found in most of Western Christendom outside peninsular Italy) entered the rather jejune Roman order of Mass as a result of the papal court's adoption of German service books containing a mixed Gallicano-Roman liturgy.[31] The so-called modern Roman rite is therefore of central European rather than Italian origin, the original Roman rite having disappeared through this transformation around the end of the first Christian millennium.

Laws of Liturgical Development

While what should in fact be termed the 'Neo-Roman' rite had a more complex development than its sister liturgies, the growth of all of them has been governed by the exact same laws. Liturgical development in any Christian rite is at bottom a dual process, involving two distinct factors of change, one spontaneous, the other legislative. As each church's appreciation of its liturgical treasures deepened over the centuries, the local rite grew organically by the gradual addition of new euchological and ritual elements. Hence the introduction into universal Christian worship of images, lights, incense, vestments and sacral languages, while the Roman Mass developed its Prayers at the Foot of the Altar, its Offertory and Pre-Communion prayers, its Last Gospel – all originally *apologiæ sacerdotis* or private devotions of the celebrant – as well as its substitution of unleavened for leavened bread. The other mode of spontaneous evolution was the abandonment, for various reasons, of certain elements, for example Communion in the hand, Communion under both species and the Bidding Prayers recited after the Creed.

Both types of organic change (addition and omission) grew out of popular piety, were long in developing, and are attributed to the inspiration of the Holy Spirit. In each instance one is dealing either with new customs slipping almost imperceptibly into the existing fabric of the rite, or with old ones gradually disappearing from it: during the actual period of development there was never novel and sudden legislation from above. Before 1969, in the entire history of the Roman Mass the ecclesiastical authorities had intervened only by ratifying or condemning particular customs and normalizing the changes in new official editions of the liturgical books.[32]

In the wider liturgy, additions to the received rites and omissions of particular prayers and ceremonies were rarely made and, in most cases, were minimal and compatible with the spirit of the tradition. In any case, the few official reforms that

---

[30] Joseph Jungmann, SJ, *The Mass of the Roman Rite: Its Origins and Development* (*Missarum Sollemnia*), tr. Francis A. Brunner, CSSSR (1950; Dublin, 1986), I, pp. 336, 356.

[31] Ibid., pp. 92–127. The Milanese and Mozarabic (Old Spanish) liturgies represent local developments of the (never codified) Gallican parent rite suppressed in most places by Charlemagne.

[32] See especially M. Davies, *Cranmer's Godly Order: The Destruction of Catholicism through Liturgical Change* (Chawleigh, Devon, 1976), chapter 9, pp. 63–71; 2nd edn (Fort Collins, 1995), pp. 113–25.

have been criticized as excessive and regrettable – cases in point being Pius X's reordering of the Psalter in the overhauling of the Roman breviary (1911–1913) and Pius XII's changes to the Holy Week ceremonies in 1955 – can hardly compare on a scale of structural and (above all) doctrinal significance with those ordered by Paul VI. The first of them, moreover, did not affect the lives of the laity. Reforms to the *lex orandi* that do not compromise or distort the *lex credendi* have in fact been introduced for disciplinary or pastoral reasons throughout the history of the Church: the Catholic tradition of worship is transmitted but not static, the hierarchy guarding and ordering its development.

While the true Christian cultus is therefore not strictly speaking immobilistic, extreme caution is the constant keynote when it comes to admissible change. Pope Leo XIII highlighted these two facts in stating that because the sacred liturgy is

> the living voice of Catholic truth . . . the true Church of Christ, even as she shows great zeal to guard inviolate those forms of divine worship – since they are hallowed and are not to be changed – sometimes permits something novel in the performance of them in certain instances, especially when they are in conformity with their venerable antiquity.[33]

The process of liturgical development actually parallels that of the canonization of saints: popular cults arise spontaneously and at a later date the hierarchical Church passes authoritative judgement on them. As the Italian canonist Dr Neri Capponi puts it in his study of the juridical status of the Pauline liturgical reform:

> What must be emphasized . . . is the absolute spontaneity of the development of the liturgy – and in particular that of the Eucharist – presided over by various bishops. There was no uniform legislation or imposition from above, but a body of custom developed by free invention of the celebrant and, especially, by imitation of forms in use in the older and more authoritative churches, round the central core of the Eucharist which, as of divine origin, was unchangeable.[34]

In Catholic Christianity the organic growth of the liturgy is not perpetual – at least in its major contours – but has a natural term identifiable with the attainment of structural maturity. Everywhere the guided development of the cultus through the ratification or condemnation of custom by local bishops was brought to an end by definitive legislation through the canonization of service books. This process was complete in all the historical rites of Christendom by the late Middle Ages, providentially before the two historical disasters that were to put the Greek and Latin Churches permanently on the defensive: the fall of Constantinople to the Turks and the Reformation. The so-called 'freezing' or 'fossilization', decried by those for whom evolution is neither limited nor reflective of the rhythm of growth observable in nature, took place relatively early in the Edessene, Antiochene and Alexandrian rites. The Byzantine liturgy was fixed in its present form as late as the fourteenth century, though its basic shape had already solidified in the ninth.[35]

---

[33] Encyclical *Orientalium Dignitas* (*On the Churches of the East*), 30 November 1894.
[34] Neri Capponi, *Some Juridical Considerations on the Reform of the Liturgy* (Edinburgh, 1979), p. 10.
[35] Wybrew, 'The Byzantine Liturgy', pp. 217–18.

Before the Second Vatican Council it was generally accepted that the Roman Mass had achieved the fullness of its spontaneous development with Pope Innocent III's normative edition of the Roman Mass *ordo* around 1195.[36] This evolved Gallicano-Roman form of the eucharistic rite was later codified in perpetuity by Pope St Pius V in 1570. Contrary to what has often been alleged, the Pian missal of 1570 was no arbitrary and radical revision of the immemorial rite fixed in Pope Innocent's *ordo*, but a new edition of the existing service books characterized by the inclusion or exclusion of a small number of recent or variable elements.[37] Subsequent changes to the form of the eucharistic liturgy would be mostly cosmetic, affecting rubrics and such externals as music and ornaments, and the few structural alterations made would be quite insignificant in comparison with what was preserved.

From Evolution to Revolution

Renewal of this kind is evidently a far cry from the veritable liturgical revolution forced on the clergy and faithful of the Roman rite during the pontificate of Paul VI. Unlike the Innocentine and Pian reforms, the Montinian one contravened the principle *lex orandi, lex credendi* by presenting Western Catholics with an order of worship deliberately manufactured to express the modernizing, antiquarianist and ecumenical preoccupations of the apostles of *aggiornamento*. The Consilium experts did to the Roman rite exactly what Archbishop Cranmer and the Anglican reformers had done to the Sarum liturgy in the sixteenth century:

> They knew only too well the intimate bond which unites faith with worship, 'the law of belief' with 'the law of prayer', and so, under the pretext of restoring to it its primitive form, they corrupted the order of the liturgy in many respects to adapt it to the errors of the Innovators.[38]

John Eppstein, an English Catholic writing in 1972, had a clear understanding of the two forces at work in the concoction of the Pauline rites, 'the liturgical purists who were inclined to suppress every prayer and action which was not found in the most primitive post-apostolic texts, and the modernists who were for scrapping everything that was not congenial to contemporary sentiment'.[39]

As reasonable as such reforming projects might have appeared to Catholics of a modern scientific cast of mind or of secular outlook, the fact remains that the idea of an arbitrary restructuring of the sacred liturgy has always been alien to orthodox Catholic instinct and practice. Paul VI's unprecedented attempt to pass off as 'authentic tradition' a reform of this nature was therefore profoundly disturbing

[36] The text of Pope Innocent's ordo will be found in J.-P. Migne, *Patrologia Latina*, Vol. 217, cols 763–74.

[37] This is freely admitted by Paul VI in his apostolic constitution of 1969: '. . . innumerable holy men have abundantly nourished their piety towards God by its [the 1570 missal's] readings from Sacred Scripture or by its prayers, *whose general arrangement goes back, in essence, to St Gregory the Great*' (first paragraph; emphasis added).

[38] The words are those of Pope Leo XIII, expressed in his encyclical *Apostolicæ Curæ* (13 September 1896), which ruled on the invalidity of Anglican orders.

[39] John Eppstein, *Has the Catholic Church Gone Mad?* (London, 1971), p. 58.

to many Catholics.[40] For these it was unthinkable that a committee of liturgists could refashion the patrimonial rites of the Church at will and then foist them on millions of Christians on the ground that their creations were, among other things, theologically sound and sacramentally valid.

Moreover, the consequences of the Montinian revolution are indeed serious if, as Mgr Klaus Gamber has observed, 'To change any of its essential elements is synonymous with the destruction of the rite in its entirety.'[41] As has been shown, received liturgical rites are not mere ecclesiastical conventions of arbitrary devising, but are an integral part of the traditional faith. Referring to the text of the Roman Canon in a letter to the metropolitan of Braga, Pope Vigilius (537–555) described the liturgy itself as 'received, through the kindness of God, from the Apostolic Tradition'.[42]

Quo jure?

The momentous break with tradition ordered by Paul VI also constituted a major innovation from the legal standpoint. Mgr Gamber writes that

> since there is no document that specifically assigns to the Apostolic See the authority to change, let alone to abolish the traditional liturgical rite; and since, furthermore, it can be shown that not a single predecessor of Pope Paul VI has ever introduced major changes to the Roman liturgy, the assertion that the Holy See has the authority to change the liturgical rite would appear to be debatable, to say the least.[43]

It was only after the Council of Trent that the Papacy began to exercise regularly its technical right to oversee diocesan revisions of traditional service books, as indicated in Canon 1257 of the old (1917) *Codex Iuris Canonici* and in Canon 838 of the new (1983) Code.[44] However, the authority to order a radical reform of any rite, even that of Rome, certainly does not come within this competency. Fr Josef Jungmann recalls that the Sacred Congregation of Rites established by Pope Sixtus V after the Council of Trent had as its charter

> to see to it that everywhere in the Latin Church the prescribed manner of celebrating Mass and performing the other functions of the liturgy were carefully followed. . . . On the other hand it was not in the ordinary power of the Congregation to change the rubrics or alter the wording of prayers. Thus the Congregation of Rites was not to be an organ for liturgical evolution.[45]

---

[40] Papal General Audience speech of 19 November 1969, quoted in *The Teachings of Pope Paul VI, 1969* (Vatican City, 1970), p. 288.

[41] Klaus Gamber, *The Reform of the Roman Liturgy: Its Problems and Background* (San Juan Capistrano, California, 1993), pp. 30–31.

[42] ('*quem Deo propitio ex apostolica traditione suscepimus*'), Migne, *Patrologia Latina*, Vol. 69, col. 18, cited in Gamber, *op. cit.*, p. 35.

[43] Gamber, *op. cit.*, p. 39.

[44] Canon 1257 reads: 'The supervision of the sacred liturgy depends solely on the authority of the Church, which resides in the Apostolic See and, in accordance with the law, with the diocesan bishops.'

[45] Jungmann, *op. cit.*, I, p. 139.

The sixteenth-century Jesuit theologian Francisco Suárez, citing Cardinal Cajetan, had already clarified this point by stating that a pope would become a schismatic

> if he rejected his duty and refused to be in full communion with the body of the Church, as, for example, if he were to excommunicate the entire Church, *or if he were to change all the ecclesiastical ceremonies of the Church that have been upheld by apostolic tradition*, as Cajetan remarks.[46] (Emphasis added)

Cardinal John de Torquemada (uncle of the notorious inquisitor) had expressed the same opinion in his *Summa de Ecclesia* of 1489:

> The Pope can separate himself without reason purely by his wilfulness from the body of the Church and from the college of priests by not observing what the universal Church by apostolic tradition observes . . . or by non-observance of what was ordered universally by the universal councils or by the Apostolic See, *especially in respect to the divine cult if he does not want to observe what concerns the universal rite of the Church's worship*.[47] (Emphasis added)

Unhappily, the custodial role of the popes was completely misunderstood by Paul VI, and the reality escaping the erudite vandals of his Consilium was that an historic rite is not something incidental and negotiable, but, as Mar Abraham Mattam reminds us, 'Christianity in concrete, that is to say, the teaching of Christ handed down through the generations by authentic tradition, and involves Christian worship or liturgy, spirituality and ecclesial discipline'.[48] As for the sacred liturgy itself, the *opus Dei* or 'work of God', the part of the human person on which it acts is not only the rational mind, but also that faculty of the immortal soul which Pascal called the 'heart'. The heart, in the thought of the French philosopher, is 'the appropriate channel for intuitive knowledge, for apprehending pre-rational first principles and assenting to supra-rational propositions, as well as for emotional and aesthetic experiences'.[49]

The Magisterium is the mind of the Church, but the sacred liturgy, which is action rather than idea, the celebration of a wisdom beyond human understanding, is the Church's heart. It is this insight that inspired the Latin dictum *tolle missam, tolle ecclesiam*, 'abolish the Mass and you abolish the Church'.

---

[46] ('aut si vellet omnes ecclesiasticas cærimonias apostolica traditione formatas evertere'), *Tract. de Charitate*, Disput. No. 12, p. 1, also cited in Gamber, *op. cit.*, pp. 35–36.

[47] M. Davies, *Apologia pro Marcel Lefebvre* (Dickinson, Texas, 1979), I, pp. 409–10.

[48] A. Mattam, 'Missionary Consciousness of the Thomas Christians', in *Ecclesial Identity*, p. 115.

[49] A. J. Krailsheimer, ed., *Pascal: Pensées* (Harmondsworth, 1966), p. 22. See especially No. 110:

> We know the truth not only through our reason but also through our heart. It is through the latter that we know first principles, and reason . . . tries in vain to refute them. The sceptics have no other object than that, and they work at it to no purpose. . . . That is why those to whom God has given religious faith are very fortunate, and feel quite legitimately convinced, but to those who do not have it we can only give such faith through reasoning, until God gives it by moving their heart, without which faith is only human and useless for salvation.

Validity and Authenticity

One of the most pernicious consequences of the Latin West's downgrading of *theologia secunda* is its concern for validity, the automatic product of doctrinal orthodoxy, to the neglect of authenticity, the natural fruit of orthopraxis. Differently put, this is making *text* all-important and *context* a matter of indifference. Indeed most Catholic debate about the liturgical revolution has centred on the question of whether the new official text makes the Mass and sacraments valid or not; the cultural packaging of the same rites is meanwhile relegated to the realm of relatively unimportant 'externals'.

This problem has been exacerbated by Protestant influence channelled through converts who apply to study for the priesthood and are accepted as ordinands by vocations directors, seminary professors and bishops typically unconcerned to scrutinize the candidates' mentality and cultural outlook which, far too often, are alien and antagonistic to Catholicity. Integral Catholicity is the result of being raised in, and living out, the Faith; it is not the product of education and reasoning alone, and much less the product of a crash course. A veritable 'Trojan horse' phenomenon occurs when such convert-clerics who have recently acquired a Catholic mind but (through no fault of their own) have never had a Catholic heart are recklessly elevated to the episcopate or even the cardinalate.[50] The following remarks made in 2003 by the eminent American convert, Cardinal Avery Dulles, SJ, are in this regard both instructive and disquieting:

> If there be anyone who contends that in order to be converted to the Catholic faith one must be first attracted by the beauty of the liturgy, he will have me to explain away. Filled as I was with a Puritan antipathy toward splendour in religious ritual, I found myself actually repulsed by the elaborate symbolism in which the Holy Sacrifice is clothed.[51]

In stark contrast to this alien *Kirchenanschauung* is the conviction of our Eastern brethren that Christianity stripped of its traditional asceticism is nothing but a sterile and impotent ideology. Oriental Christendom has not forgotten that asceticism, of which participation in the sacred liturgy is the highest expression, is as necessary to the soul as food is to the body. In this life the Christian struggles against the illusions and corruptions that trouble his heart and which spring from the passions. For the Christian, mere faith is not enough: the practice of asceticism is the only way for him to overcome spiritual conflict and to heal the heart.

Catholicism is an incarnational religion, not an abstraction; its teachings are naturally enfleshed in a particular way of life engaging the senses and the emotions – the 'heart' – as much as the mind. Furthermore, if Christianity is a liturgical religion, the Christian is, by virtue of his faith, a liturgical being. This is a reality as ancient as Revelation itself. The Decalogue given to Moses was inscribed on

---

[50] Obviously this truism admits of numerous exceptions (and notably in regard to converts from conservative Anglo-Catholic communities using the traditional Roman liturgy, unaffected by theological modernism and without Freemasonic affiliations), but anyone inclined to reject it out of hand because of the case of Cardinal Newman and other models of orthodoxy should study the connection between heterodox trends and eminent converts in church history since the time of St Augustine.

[51] John Jay Hughes, 'The Mass: No Way Back', *Tablet*, 5 July 2003.

two separate tablets of stone, and the first and most important of these defined man's first duty: the worship of his Creator, without which love of neighbour is meaningless. The disastrous error of modern Western Christianity has been to reverse the hierarchy of the Ten Commandments, and the result in Catholicism is the man-centred cult that now profanes the sanctuaries of the Latin Church.

3

WESTERN WISDOM

In a certain sense Revelation tells us that the world was created
to become a liturgy, a doxology and an adoration. During the liturgy
it is not on himself, but on God, on His splendour, that man focuses
his attention. He is not so much concerned to perfect himself as to
contemplate the life of God, the dazzling beam of His love of mankind.
This is the joy which, in a detached manner, indirectly, reflects on
the nature of man and changes it. Man must not add anything to the
splendour of God, which is self-achieving. There must be times when
man must not search at any price after any sort of aim, moments of
pure adoration when his being blossoms without impediment,
like the attitude of King David who danced in front
of the Ark.

PAUL EVDOKIMOV

Too much light is like too much darkness: it doesn't let you see.

OCTAVIO PAZ

The Dazzling Light of Reason

The revolution in public worship that occurred after the Second Vatican Council was made possible more than anything else by a widespread attitudinal shift among Latin Catholics in regard to their liturgical heritage. This change had been in gestation since the High Middle Ages, beginning when certain Christian thinkers subjected traditional orthopraxis to the same reasoned criticism that they applied to cultural institutions in the secular domain. In other words, at some point in history it seemed to these Western Catholics legitimate first to criticize, and second to change, aspects of the sacred liturgy on the ground that such things, being notionally separate from the revealed dogmas of faith, were less sacrosanct and therefore alterable without any danger to religion.

This hyperanalytical mentality threatening Catholic orthopraxis was the result of a natural rationalism endemic in the West; that is, a strong inclination to derive knowledge from *both* reason and experience (rather than from experience alone), and which must be carefully distinguished from the philosophical and religious rationalism of modern times. However, to the extent that natural rationalism made 'reason' (good sense, logical analysis) the ultimate criterion in liturgical and disciplinary matters, it was arguably the precursor of the synonymous heterodoxy that 'corrected' the infallible teaching of the Church and culminated in the rejection of Revelation itself.

It is generally acknowledged that the Aristotelian revival of the eleventh and twelfth centuries played a large part in the slow drift of the Western mind towards systematic rationalism in philosophy and theology. To be sure, the brilliant synthesis of faith and reason elaborated by St Thomas Aquinas in his *Summa Theologica* was, though Aristotelian in its methodology, a reaction against the rationalism of the Arab translators and commentators of the Greek philosopher. It also served the Latin Church as a powerful weapon against a growing scepticism. Aquinas, moreover, faithfully followed the patristic tradition in treating of the Church not in mere juridical terms, but in the context of his sacramental discourse. Nevertheless, the fact that Aristotle's works on logic were those best known and most appreciated in the West led thinkers lacking St Thomas' deep faith to exaggerate the role of human reason, especially from the Renaissance onwards.

Modern empirical science and modern atheism were offsprings of the same Neo-Aristotelian climate that had produced Scholasticism. The earlier Platonic tradition, stoutly defended by St Bernard of Clairvaux against Abelard and St Albert the Great, may have been, by comparison, a poor stimulus for speculative theology, and there is some truth to the charge that it carried with it a temptation to puritanism. Yet the Platonic emphasis on the mystery of God and His work of redemption, and the dwelling on the divinity of Christ rather than on His humanity had, in shielding Christian truth from the 'profanation' of dialectical analysis, also promoted a climate of traditionalism.[1]

As useful as it was as a philosophical support, St Thomas' teaching never managed to dominate the intellectual scene of the late medieval West, and foundered even in the thought of his followers, especially when they defended Scholastic realism against the Nominalists. In the late sixteenth century, Nominalism influenced the thought of Francisco Suárez, who set the tone for Thomistic studies in the Society of Jesus, and Suarezian 'conceptualism' (a half-way house between nominalism and realism) formed an historical bridge to the rationalism of Descartes (a pupil of the Jesuits), Leibniz, Wolff, Kant and Hegel.[2]

Although the Counter-Reformation Church formally rejected philosophical rationalism, theologians responding to the challenge of Protestantism emphasized dogma – the rational aspect of religion – at the expense of other components of the Catholic tradition. Consequently, the attention paid to the liturgy as a living witness and repository of doctrinal truth was motivated largely by apologetics. Of the post-Tridentine period, Joseph Jungmann has observed that

> [t]hrough the controversy with the Reformers, the whole stress of thought on the Eucharist was directed to and bound down to the Real Presence, almost to

---

[1] Practical traditionalism, the conscious living out of Catholic orthodoxy and orthopraxis, must not be confused with the philosophical error of the same name. A form of fideism, philosophical traditionalism holds that certain knowledge of fundamental truths cannot be achieved by reason, only by the Revelation of God, which Christian society transmits from generation to generation, i.e. by tradition. Félicité de Lamennais and Louis de Bonald were the main exponents of this nineteenth-century philosophy which reacted against the Enlightenment, but which was later condemned by the Church at Vatican I. See Chapter 2, note 5 (p. 25).

[2] The authentic Thomist tradition is that represented by Cardinal Cajetan (1469–1534), St Robert Bellarmine (1542–1621) and their greatest twentieth-century successor, the Dominican Réginald Garrigou-Lagrange.

the neglect of other aspects. Even for the scientific treatment of the liturgy which now began, how much the defence of the eucharistic mysteries stood in the foreground is seen in the fact that Muratori, who issued a careful edition of the older sacramentaries, devoted the greater part of the introductory study to a discussion of this dogma as revealed in the liturgical texts. A detailed re-evaluation of the sacrificial character of the Eucharist resulted from the efforts of a new blossoming of Scholastic study. But these studies were likewise aroused by the Protestants' impugning of the dogma and consequently more or less determined by it.[3]

Towards the Abstract

In the late sixth century St Gregory the Great, reflecting the age, had defined the eucharistic liturgy existentially, in terms of its mystical reality: 'at the hour of Sacrifice, in response to the priest's acclamation, the heavens open up; the choirs of angels are witnessing this Mystery; what is above and what is below unite; heaven and earth are united, matters visible and invisible become united'.[4] By comparison, a thousand years later, when the tendency was to perceive the liturgy as a sacred but functional ritual, a means to an end in God's wonderful work of sanctification, the Catechism of the Council of Trent would prefer to stress the spiritual *value* of the Mass: 'This Sacrament is not only a treasure of heavenly riches, which if turned to good account will obtain for us the grace and love of God; but it also possesses a peculiar character, by which we are enabled to make some return to God for the immense benefits bestowed on us.'[5]

One faith in the Holy Eucharist, two different emphases: for centuries *orthodoxia* 'right worship' had been giving way, in the Western theological hierarchy, to *orthopistis* 'right believing', and *orthodidascalia* 'right teaching'.[6] Ultimately, right worship, instead of being seen as the fruit of man's response to the proclaimed Word of God, became instead:

> a *locus theologicus* in service to correct belief and teaching by church officials and secondary theologians, who were using the liturgy as a quarry for stones set into arguments shaped by increasingly rigorous methodologies worked out in academe. The antithesis of orthodoxy has become heresy rather than heterodoxy, 'wrong worship'. Praxis and belief have grown apart.[7]

Dom Aidan Kavanagh admits that this process of abstraction had one positive result: the refining of the Roman dogmatic tradition. The modern Latin Church might well be proud of its theological sophistication, but the price paid for it has been high, with the sacred liturgy itself the principal casualty:

[3] Jungmann, *op. cit.*, I, p. 142.
[4] Dial. IV, 60, quoted in Gamber, *op. cit.*, p. 12.
[5] John A. McHugh, OP, and Charles Callan, OP, tr., *Catechism of the Council of Trent for Parish Priests, Issued by Order of Pope Pius V* (New York, 1923), pp. 254–55.
[6] Kavanagh, *op. cit.*, p. 82.
[7] Ibid.

As secondary theology [dogmatic theology] moves farther away from the primary theological enterprise of right worship or *orthodoxia*, and as that move becomes a divorce on grounds of incompatibility due to modern academic method and structure, several mutations occur. Ministry changes from consecrated service to communities of faith into first a profession, then a trade, and finally into an avocation for some and a series of options for others. Homiletics becomes less the hearing of the gospel out loud, so to speak, among one's peers in faith than an occasion for the certified to educate the uncertified about 'issues' through argumentation, syllabi, and oratorical tricks. Sacraments diminish as unsettling encounters between presences divine and human in the here and now, to become a rather abstract ritual expression of a pattern set by Christ to give scope to the universal Kingdom.[8]

When taken to its logical extreme, this exclusive emphasis on the rational has always culminated in that heresy which rejects the living components of Catholic tradition in favour of the written records of the early Church, the Bible and patristic writings, and which we have known as classical Protestantism, Jansenism, and the quasi-Protestant movements that have sprung up in latter-day Catholicism.

Necessity and Reason

The characteristically Western eclipse of contemplation by speculation, though occasioned by a series of innovations and reactions in philosophy and theology, was probably cultural in its remote origins. To understand the triumph of secondary theology in the West it is important in the first place to remember that the Roman mentality, in contrast with that of the Greeks, was naturally juridical and administrative and tended to foster a natural rationalism. One needs also to consider the predicament of Latin Christendom after the collapse of the Western Roman Empire. While Christian Roman civilization survived and flourished in the Byzantine Empire, the Latin Church had to cope with one barbarian invasion after the other, living constantly threatened with the collapse of its external structures and its internal tradition. Oriental Christianity was certainly not without its crises, but these were more often the result of prolonged prosperity than of continual misfortune.

As the West looked to the Papacy for social as well as spiritual leadership, its culture, already influenced by the legacy of pagan Roman legalism, intensified its preoccupations with order. Whereas the relatively peace-blessed East could continue 'to establish a worshipping community, in which the celebration of the Holy Mysteries would speak for itself', the traumatized and insecure West, forced by circumstances to be active and practical-minded, 'placed stability and permanence at a premium, focusing upon God's eternal design, of which the Church was the visible expression'.[9] Humiliated by their material losses and a resultant cultural backwardness, Western Christians' thirst for knowledge, reflecting their desire for order, sometimes outstripped their strong appetite for contemplation.

At the same time, while the dynamic of liturgical development continued

[8] Ibid., pp. 82–83.
[9] Cross, *Eastern Christianity*, p. 16.

unhampered in the Western Church, the Platonic legacy and the temporary eclipse of scholarship during the so-called Dark Age had conspired to dim Latin Christians' understanding of the structure of their public worship. By the ninth century, when liturgical treatises were produced again in the West, not even the erudite comprehended any longer the overall relationship and direct meaning of the different components of each rite.[10] To compensate for this, commentators turned to allegorical explanations of the liturgy. Instead of asking what the liturgy *was*, they were asking what it *meant*.[11] Throughout the rest of the Middle Ages the liturgy was commonly explained in allegorical terms, as in the East, in spite of the Aristotelian revival and the new scholarly taste for analysis.[12]

When, around the time of the Reformation, this symbolic approach to ritual reality collapsed, Christian thinkers had no option but to fall back exclusively on secondary theology whenever the liturgy was being considered. There was no monument of liturgiology in the West to match the *Summa Theologica* of the Angelic Doctor, and the consequences were serious according to Dom Aidan Kavanagh. Scholars knew 'little about the liturgy itself; thus they often overcompensated in their attacks on it or defence of it. The liturgy was inexorably brought into disrepute by both sides in the debate between new devotion and learning and the old, between Reformers and Catholics.'[13]

This reaction was especially reflected in the Reformers' erroneous ideas about the shape of the primitive liturgy. Moreover both critical attacks on, and doctrinal defence of, the immemorial rites

> confirmed many on both sides of the schism in a notion of *orthodoxia* not as a sustained life of 'right worship', but as 'correct doctrine' to be maintained by centralized ecclesiastical authority having exclusive power to enforce an absolute standard in liturgical texts by law. This was something unheard of in western Christianity prior to the English Act of Uniformity of 1549, the direct effect of which was to establish as the only liturgy allowed in England that contained in *The Booke of Common Prayer* . . .[14]

Furthermore, during the Counter Reformation the prevalence of secondary theology in the Catholic Church became manifest not only in the growth of rubricism but in the very understanding of the word 'orthodox' in the context of the liturgy. Kavanagh points out that all the twentieth-century translators of the Roman Canon, both pre-conciliar and post-conciliar, concur in changing the originally intended meaning of the phrase *omnibus orthodoxis atque catholicæ et apostolicæ fidei cultoribus* ('all the *right-worshipping* [bishops] and the cultivators of Catholic and apostolic faith') to 'all those *right-believing* teachers who have guardianship of the Catholic and apostolic faith' (1961), and '*all those who hold and teach* the Catholic faith that comes to us from the apostles' (1967).[15]

---

[10] Jungmann, *op. cit.*, I, pp. 87–91.
[11] Kavanagh, *op. cit.*, p. 130.
[12] Jungmann, *op. cit.*, I, pp. 113–18.
[13] Ibid., p. 103.
[14] Ibid., p. 81.
[15] Ibid., pp. 81–82. Dom Aidan's translation 'all the right-worshipping cultivators of catholic and apostolic faith' is not quite accurate, since it does not take into account the differing semantic functions here of the conjunctions *atque* and *et*. On the translation and significance of this

Such an approach ignored attempts by contemporary theologians to correct the prevailing Western emphasis on the didactic and practical value of the liturgy, for instance the clarification made by Yves Congar in 1963:

> The liturgy is not exclusively a form of instruction, even though it is wholly instructive and includes some formal periods of instruction. It is an active memorial, a presence and a realization, in short, a celebration of the Christian mystery itself . . . It is not only taught to us, or merely brought to our notice; it is celebrated, realized, rendered present and communicated, not simply as a doctrine and truth, but as a reality. . . . The liturgy does not theorize on the Redemption, but it ceaselessly brings us into loving communication with Christ our Saviour, with His cross and its fruit, the hope of eternal life.[16]

Foundations of Modernity

In a medieval society where most people were illiterate, sacred images, especially stained glass windows, were the 'Bible of the laity', and giving homilies was not a normal function of pastors but of itinerant preachers licenced by bishops whose own visits to parishes were often rare. To remedy this neglect, the Counter Reformation promoted regular preaching and guided Bible reading in approved translations. Though good in themselves, these activities were also the obsessions of contemporary Protestantism, and they tended in Catholicism to compete with the liturgy instead of harmonizing with it. In spirituality, the Jesuits' new techniques of mental prayer and the thirty-day retreat stressed the rational in that their aim was to press the powers of the mind into the service of faith.

In the meantime, radical change was occurring in the training of aspirants to the priesthood. Originally, clerics had received their formation in the bishop's presbyterium, living there in community with other priests and participating fully in the life of the diocese. However, by the fifteenth century this custom had generally lapsed, and ordinands did an apprenticeship with an experienced pastor while taking lessons in philosophy and theology from a local scholar or at a university.[17] With the decline of the regular life among the secular clergy in a climate of moral decadence, the Council of Trent instituted, as an emergency measure, the system of diocesan seminaries. The seminaries produced a more professional, militant type of priest, better suited to the new social conditions, and 'seminary priests' became as important to the success of the Church's reform as new orders like the Jesuits. However, the products of this system suffered from the consequences of formation in an artificial community separated from the rest of the clergy and from the faithful they were destined to serve.

Another drawback of the seminary system was, from the nineteenth century, the preference for speculative theology of an abstract kind, divorced from the patristic tradition. While Thomism became the standard theology, the teaching of St Thomas was reduced to something approaching an abstract ideology: instead

---

sentence see Enrico Mazza, *The Eucharistic Prayers of the Roman Rite* (Collegeville, Minnesota, 1986), pp. 62–63. Mazza translates *orthodoxis* as 'orthodox believers'.

[16] Congar, *Tradition and the Life of the Church*, pp. 125–26.

[17] See Dom Paul Benoît, *La vie des clercs dans les siècles passés*, Paris, 1915.

of reading Aquinas in the original and thereby benefiting from his constant drawing on the wisdom and examples of the Church Fathers, the minds of the highly
regimented seminarists were nourished on the arid commentaries contained in
manuals.

In Search of the Age of Reason

The Latin inclination to emphasize the rational in religion had been manifesting
itself liturgically ever since the separation of the Eastern and Western Churches.
For instance from the twelfth century, when the apostolic custom of baptismal
communion lapsed, children no longer received their first Eucharist at their
christening, but in a separate ceremony deferred until they were considered men-
tally able to discern the sacrament.[18] In the following century the Fourth Lateran
Council (1215) reacted against the ancient practice of confirming immediately
after baptism, and recommended that chrismation be deferred until the age of
reason (or 'age of discernment') so that this sacrament, like the Eucharist, could
be received 'with knowledge and free will'.[19] The ultimate development in this
direction was the decision in the pontificate of Pius XI to separate confirmation
even further from baptism by conferring the former sacrament *after* a child's First
Communion.[20] This innovation of 1932 subsequently became the norm in the
Latin Church, and consummated the dislocation of confirmation from baptism as
a sacrament of initiation.

The primitive conception of the sealing with chrism blessed by the bishop was
that it completed, with an infusion of the seven gifts of the Holy Ghost, the initiation begun with baptism, bringing the recipient into full union with the Church
(hence the symbolic importance of the bishop being directly or indirectly the minister of the sacrament) and making him a 'soldier of Christ' prepared to fight the
spiritual battles of life. This was as far as the Christian East took the theology of
the sacrament, whereas the West developed the idea that confirmation was also
the 'sacrament of maturity', and hence appropriate only for children who could
already reason and discriminate. In this way what was in the first place a spiritual
gift and help towards sanctification risked being regarded by the less fervent as a
mere rite of passage. For the more devout such an approach also had the disadvantage of creating the expectation that confirmation produced immediate spiritual
maturity in the candidate, whereas in reality its function was to strengthen the
candidate spiritually and its effects were of necessity slow-acting. This tendency

---

[18] Jungmann, *op. cit.*, II, p. 385, n. 81.
[19] John F. Sullivan, *The Externals of the Catholic Church: A Handbook of Catholic Usage* (London,
1955), p. 45. Before this time the administration of this sacrament had been commonly delegated
by bishops to priests because of the sheer impossibility, in the rapidly growing post-Constantinian
Church, of the local ordinary attending every baptism. However, while delegation of the sacrament became the norm in the Greek Church (where, however, the chrism still had to be blessed
by a metropolitan or a patriarch), in the Latin Church bishops continued to confirm wherever
and whenever possible. When this was not possible, confirmation was deferred; in tenth-century
Wales, for example, children were normally chrismated at the age of seven. It should be noted,
however, that in several parts of the Latin patriarchate the old custom of chrismating after
baptism (i.e. confirming infants, as in the East) continued after 1215, notably in England until
the Reformation, and in Spain until the twentieth century.
[20] Instruction of the Sacred Congregation for the Sacraments, 30 June 1932.

to substitute man's finite concept of time for God's time, which is eternity itself, was characteristic of the contemporary rationalizing mentality.

Ritual separation of the three sacraments of initiation for reasons of logic and the deferment (and disordering) of confirmation and the Eucharist would have negative effects in the pastoral sphere, especially during the period of Jansenist influence beginning in the seventeenth century. Pope Pius X was finally obliged to correct these trends in his decree *Quam Singulari* of 1910. This document complained of clerics, 'on the plea of safeguarding the august Sacrament' arbitrarily deciding on separate ages of discernment for the reception of the sacraments of penance and the eucharist, and that children were being prevented from making their first Holy Communion until the age of 14 or older. This was 'the cause of many evils' for

It happened that children in their innocence were forced away from the embrace of Christ and deprived of the food of their interior life; and from this it also happened that in their youth, destitute of this strong help, surrounded by so many temptations, they lost their innocence and fell into vicious habits even before tasting of the Sacred Mysteries. And even if a thorough instruction and a careful sacramental confession should precede Holy Communion, which does not everywhere occur, still the loss of first innocence is always to be deplored and might have been avoided by reception of the Eucharist in more tender years.

The Pope went on to criticize those Jansenistic clerics who prevented children from making sacramental confessions before their first Communion, even though they were old enough to have committed serious sins. Worst of all was the practice of refusing the last sacraments to children dying before being admitted to the Eucharist.

Latin Minimalism

Another result of the West's natural rationalism was the temptation to minimalism in the liturgy. As interest in the liturgy *per se* declined, short cuts which deprived various rites of their full symbolic significance but which could be justified on logical grounds became popular, and many were approved by the Holy See. For example, because of the constant danger of spilling the consecrated wine, Communion under the species of bread alone came to be preferred in some Western European countries in the thirteenth century and was the norm in Latin Christendom by the fifteenth century.[21] This innovation was justified on the techically valid grounds that anyone who received the Eucharist under one species only still received the whole sacrament, but the generalization of a practice that had pre-

---

[21] As an interim measure there obtained at least in England the practice of offering unconsecrated wine to communicants, for example in the decrees of the Council of Lambeth in 1281 (Gian Domenico Mansi, *Sacrorum Conciliorum*, 24, 405). Pope Pius IV allowed some German dioceses influenced by utraquism to retain Communion under both species in 1564 but withdrew permission a year later. However as late as the mid-eighteenth-century Pope Benedict XIV (1740–1758) mentioned that the kings of France retained the privilege of receiving Holy Communion under both kinds at their coronation and on their death bed (*De Missae Sacrif*. II, xxii, n. 32).

viously been exceptional dismayed Eastern Christians.[22] Even more disconcerting to them was the contemporaneous replacement of the apostolic practice of baptism by total immersion with baptism by pouring or sprinkling. This became usual by the beginning of the thirteenth century but the old custom survived in some parts of the West until the Council of Trent.[23]

The complaint of Greek Orthodox theologian Christos Yannaras that Western religious life is 'cut off from daily experience and the direct, empirical utilization of the world' applies not to medieval Latin Catholicism but rather to Protestantism.[24] Nevertheless, he may be right in discerning in medieval Catholicism's innocent reduction of the matter of the two principal sacraments a foreshadowing of that ungracious, puritan response to the created world that would infect the whole Latin Church after Vatican II. For wherever heteropraxis holds sway, Christianity is no longer 'a new utilization of the world, but rather a utilization of symbols, an effort logically and psychologically to relate to the transcendent unknown by means of allegories and ideas'.[25]

Pandora's Box

Is there any truth, then, to the Orthodox jibe that Protestantism was hatched from the egg that Rome had laid? The rationalistic developments of Western Christendom, however Eastern Christians might judge them, were certainly not erosive of right belief and some were necessary developments in their time: in any assessment of liturgical standards the link between faith and culture must not be overlooked. Nevertheless, Eastern thinkers are not entirely wrong in making a correlation between the rationalism-driven heterodoxy of Protestantism and the intellectualism of the Renaissance and its aftermath in Catholic countries, even if the Holy See never made its own the outlook of thinkers like Erasmus who unconsciously paved the way for Luther and Calvin.

In the second half of the sixteenth century the Latin Church recovered, as best it could, from the ravages of the Protestant revolt. But for Catholicism the real tragedy was that four centuries after that fatal egg had been hatched outside the Mystical Body, the doctrinally conservative Pius XII should unwittingly set before the Church a Pandora's box when he endorsed a rationalizing notion by reversing St Prosper's principle and making the *lex credendi* fundamental to the *lex orandi*. In *Mediator Dei* (1947), the encyclical that was to guide the renewal of the Roman liturgy, the Pope stated: 'Indeed if we wanted to state quite clearly the relation existing between the faith and the sacred liturgy we could rightly say that "the law of our faith must establish the law of our prayer".'[26]

Although Pope Pius was undoubtedly blind to the ultimate consequences of this reversal, his pronouncement formally sounded the death knell of what had survived

---

[22] Previously, Communion under the species of bread alone was restricted to the Mass of the Presanctified and the Communion of the sick (the Viaticum). The Eastern Churches similarly have retained till the present day the custom of administering only the Precious Blood to infants.

[23] William H. W. Fanning, 'Baptism', *CE*, III, p. 262.

[24] Christos Yannaras, 'Orthodoxy and the West', in A. J. Philippou, ed., *Orthodoxy: Life & Freedom* (Oxford, 1973), p. 133.

[25] Ibid.

[26] *Mediator Dei*, III, 52.

of primitive *orthodoxia* in the Roman communion.[27] The moment of crisis had arrived for orthopraxis in the West, for, as Kavanagh objects:

> To reverse the maxim, subordinating the standard of worship to the standard of belief, makes a shambles of the dialectic of revelation. It was a Presence, not faith, which drew Moses to the burning bush, and what happened there was a revelation, not a seminar. It was a Presence, not faith, which drew the disciples to Jesus, and what happened there was not an educational program but His revelation to them of Himself as the long-promised Anointed One, the redeeming because reconciling Messiah-Christos.[28]

Moreover,

> To reverse this is to cancel out the meaning of the maxim in its original formulation. The law of belief does *not* constitute the law of worship. Thus the creeds and the reasoning which produced them are not the forces which produced baptism. Baptism gave rise to the trinitarian creeds. So too the eucharist produced, but was not produced by, a scriptural text, the eucharistic prayer, or all the various scholarly theories concerning the eucharistic real presence. Influenced by, yes. Constituted or produced by, no.[29]

---

[27] There is evidence from his dealings with the German hierarchy that Pius XII who, in the Roman tradition, believed strongly in the primacy of doctrine, did not consider liturgical questions important enough to warrant an investigation of the orthodoxy of the liturgical experts he appointed. He was in any case too preoccupied at this time with the Second World War and its aftermath. In a letter of 1943 to Bishop Conrad Gröber, who had complained about questionable liturgical experiments in Germany, the pope had stated that he found it strange that 'as if from outside the world and time the liturgical question should be presented as the problem of the moment'. In the same vein, on 30 April of the same year, he expressed to Archbishop Preysing of Berlin his view that doctrinal matters were of far greater moment than liturgical ones:

> You know that the Holy See has considered the liturgical questions raised in your country important enough to take in hand. We admit nevertheless that we attach infinitely more importance to having Christian consciences protected against all the poisons that threaten them. What would be the point of making the Church's liturgy more beautiful if, outside the Church, the thoughts and deeds of the faithful become, in their lives, alien to the law and love of Christ? (Quoted in Paul Rassinier, *L'Opération vicaire: le rôle de Pie XII devant l'histoire* [Internet, 2002], p. 120)

[28] Kavanagh, *op. cit.*, p. 92.

[29] Ibid. Professor P. De Clerck, of the Centre of Theological and Pastoral Studies in Brussels, also lamented in an article of 1978 how the encyclical, in reacting against the erroneous idea that the liturgical prayers of the Church constitute an absolute rule of faith, 'passe à l'autre extrême et définit ces rapports dans le cadre d'une théologie du Magistère, peu traditionnelle elle aussi, au point de ne pas craindre de retourner la formation de l'adage: c'est maintenant la *lex credendi* qui doit déterminer la *lex orandi*! Voilà le fleuron de la théologie du XXe siècle!' (De Clerck, *op. cit.*, pp. 210–11). On the other hand, the American Jesuit theologian Edward Kilmartin, on the principle of *virtus in medio stat*, tries to balance both approaches when he writes:

> There is no doubt that he [Pius XII] had in mind the problems raised by the reduction of the source of theology to the law of prayer. His solution is to admit that liturgy is a source of the faith of the highest rank, but to accentuate, by reversing the axiom, the unique value of the law of belief, guaranteed by the teaching authority of the Church. Both of these approaches, which tend toward an overdrawn identity between theory and practice, threaten to obscure the unique value of two different kinds of expression of faith. In order to avoid either extreme . . . it seems legitimate to state the axiom in this way: the law of prayer is the law of belief, and vice versa. (Kilmartin, *op. cit.*, p. 197)

However, this solution, in destroying the primacy, nullifies the Prosperine principle.

Without the 'Pacellian reversal', the Montinian revolution of the liturgy would never have been possible. One wonders what that most conservative of modern Roman pontiffs might say today if he returned to contemplate the monstrous offspring of this doctrinal twist.

Getting it Wrong

When the Pauline liturgy was made mandatory in the late 1960s, 'right-believing' Catholics proved to have very short memories. Experience has shown that the protests of the few voices in the West calling their Church back to the true meaning of orthodoxy have been lost on the vast majority of conservative Latin Catholics. Indeed the theological justification of the revolution was not found wanting by the average thinking Catholic. For instance James Likoudis and Kenneth Whitehead did not scruple to denounce in their anti-traditionalist debate

> those who point not to the teaching documents of Pope Paul VI, such as his 1968 Credo of the People of God or his 1965 Encyclical *Mysterium Fidei,* for evidence of the faith he professed about the Mass, but rather to his revisions in the Roman Missal which supposedly prove that this Post-Vatican II pope abandoned orthodoxy. Actually, as Pope Pius XII pointed out, it is the liturgy which is 'subject . . . to the Supreme Teaching Authority of the Church', as expressed in such documents as encyclicals and Pope Paul VI's Credo. It is to these magisterial documents that we must look first, as far as the faith is concerned, and not exclusively and in a spirit of suspicion at the Mass.[30]

There is no escaping the conclusion that this rationalistic approach to the most sacred things is the predominant outlook in the West today, as Dom Aidan Kavanagh frankly admits:

> It would be foolish not to recognize that placing sacramental discourse prior to, above, and in a role which subordinates theology in the modern academic sense is a difficult if not incomprehensible move for many people. We generally think of the two sorts of discourse the other way around, theology coming first and sacramental discourse very much later as a possibly implied excursus off the former. Sacramental discourse in fact is often thought of as theological adiaphora best practised by those with a taste for banners, ceremonial, and arts and crafts. It is regarded as an academically less than disciplined swamp in which Anglican high churchmen, Orthodox bishops, and many . . . Roman Catholics and others are hopelessly mired.[31]

Such a state of affairs is alarming when one considers the essential perspective of the Judaeo-Christian tradition:

> one must not forget that Judaism and Christianity have traditionally set the highest store on divine worship. In fact, most Jews and Christians have for thousands

---

[30] Likoudis/Whitehead, *op. cit.,* p. 133.
[31] Kavanagh, *op. cit.,* p. 46.

of years expressed their religious existence not in books but by participation in assemblies which have met regularly, at least once a week, for worship of the living God. The ordinary, normal Jew or Christian need not be theologically literate or possess a theological degree, and it would surely strike them as odd to suggest that gaining such a degree is somehow more important than the Kiddush meal on Sabbath or Mass on Sunday.[32]

This fact of Christian life was brought home to many churchmen at the time of the Reformation. During the brief reign of Mary I, when great efforts were being made to restore English Catholicism, Cardinal Reginald Pole warned the citizens of London against the dangers of underestimating the role of orthopraxis:

> so the heretykes makythe this the fyrst poynt of theyre schysme and heresyes, to destroye the unyty of the Chyrche by contempte or change of ceremonyes; which seemyth at the begynninge nothinge. As yt seemyd nothinge here amongste you to take awaye holy water, holy breade, candells, ashes, and palme; but what yt came to, you saw, and all felt yt.[33]

The state of public worship today becomes less surprising the more one sees it as the direct consequence of the same error of failing to recognize the primacy of liturgy in the wider framework of orthodoxy. As Dom Aidan laments:

> We today can hardly be expected to understand how liturgy could be considered seriously as the basic condition for doing theology, even less as the law which founds and constitutes the law of belief, so long as we perceive liturgical worship as a pastel endeavour shrunk to forty-five minutes and consisting of some organ music, a choral offering, a few lines of scripture, a short talk on religion, a collection, and perhaps a quick consumption of disks or pellets and a beverage.[34]

Rationalism Rampant

In the 1920s a biritual French Jesuit studying the customs of the Orthodox peasantry in north-eastern Poland reported a revealing exchange of views between a Polish gentleman and a Belorussian parish priest. The Catholic layman advanced the opinion that the really important things in religion were the conversion of sinners, confession, the teaching of catechism, and prayer. The Orthodox, to his mind, were too caught up in ritual, which he saw as secondary to the real ministry of the Church. To this criticism the Orthodox priest replied:

> Among you it is indeed only an accessory. Among us Orthodox (and at these words he blessed himself) it is not so. The liturgy is our common prayer, it initiates our faithful into the mystery of Christ better than all your catechism. It passes before our eyes the life of our Christ, the Russian Christ, and that can be understood only

---

[32] Ibid., p. 56.
[33] Eamon Duffy, *The Stripping of the Altars: Traditional Religion in England c. 1400–c. 1580* (New Haven/London, 1992), p. 531.
[34] Ibid., p. 60.

in common, at our holy rites, in the mystery of our icons. When one sins, one sins alone. But to understand the mystery of the Risen Christ, neither your books nor your sermons are of any help. For that, one must have lived with the Orthodox Church the Joyous Night [of Easter]. (And he blessed himself again).[35]

It was such underestimation of the importance of divine worship that predisposed Latin Catholics to accept the veritable caricature of the Roman liturgy that emerged in the wake of Vatican II. As a consequence the religion of most Catholics today is not a set tradition of worship in which the Faith is lived and reflected upon, but a series of beliefs celebrated in ever-variable patterns and forms.

This state of affairs is a by-product of the Cartesian rationalism that has dominated Western thought since the seventeenth century. Modern man seeks to become the master of all things, arrogating to himself powers which an earlier age attributed to God alone. Catholic reformists, obedient to the *Zeitgeist*, have accordingly subjected the liturgical tradition, the 'work of God', to the human will. Laurence Paul Hemming has observed how modern Catholicism is narcissistically entranced by its mechanical ability to make God suddenly present in public worship, whereas in traditional Christian orthopraxis it is the worshipper, devoid of quasi-magical abilities, who humbly enters the pre-existent divine presence whenever he prays, to be transformed by the power of God:[36]

> Our current age sees everything as an object of manufacture, as something which can be got hold of and improved, or altered, to produce *better* or *more effective* outcomes. This is our present fate, especially in the West, to understand all things in this way – and it is inevitable that we should transfer even to our sacred worship the same outlook. To learn to be entrained to something that precedes and outlasts us, and that, rather than being shaped by us is what shapes us in God, is a task.[37]

Since the so-called Enlightenment of the eighteenth century, man, infatuated by the finite potential of his brain, has tended to make a god of himself and so finds it difficult when not impossible to worship his Creator as befits a creature with a mind encased in a mortal body and animated by an immortal soul. 'Too much light dazzles', wrote Pascal, ideological adversary of Descartes,[38] and Varghese Pathikulangara remarks that whereas Tradition naturally begets traditionalism, 'too much of rationalism and abstraction kill the liturgical spirit. The modern renewals are, in fact, processes of secularization.' A secularization that is quite futile, since 'the ultimate term of reference for Christianity is not this world, but the Kingdom of God'.[39] The fact that post-conciliar Catholicism should agree in so many of its positions with liberal Protestantism against the orthopraxis of the ancient undivided Church is a telling one.

---

[35] Charles Bourgeois, SJ, 'Chez les paysans de la Podlachie et du nord de la Pologne: mai 1924–décembre 1925', *Études* 191 (1927), p. 585. The Belorussian Orthodox in question were the descendants of Uniates forced to join the Russian Orthodox Church in 1839.

[36] L. P. Hemming, *Worship as a Revelation* (London, 2008), pp. 28, 33–36, 46–50.

[37] Ibid., p. 10.

[38] *'Trop de lumière éblouit.'*

[39] V. Pathikulangara, 'Liturgy and Theology in Eastern Catholic Tradition', p. 177.

4

RATIONAL WORSHIP

*If we offend the principles of reason our religion will be absurd and
ridiculous. If we submit everything to reason our religion will be left
with nothing mysterious or supernatural.*

PASCAL, PENSÉES, 173

*Someone was saying: 'At the Latin Mass you can't understand
anything.' And a child replied: 'Yes, but it's lovely.'*

REPORTED IN OPUS SACERDOTALE, OCT.–NOV. 2009

The Rationalist Circle

Philosophical rationalism, which derives all knowledge (including knowledge
about God) from reason, denying the role of the senses and experience, was a
product of societies where Protestantism was the established religion or where the
Catholic puritanism known as Jansenism had a strong presence. Yet it is one of the
great ironies of history that the Reformation, whose rapid ideological development
helped to prepare the ground for the Enlightenment, began as a protest against
what it saw as the Roman Church's idolatry of human reason.

The undivided Church had taught that faith is not opposed to reason, even if
much of the content of faith is beyond our understanding. For Martin Luther, however, human reason was 'the damned whore', 'the greatest enemy that faith has', and
faith, he blustered, 'must trample underfoot all reason, sense and understanding'.[1]
The Renaissance in Northern Europe had held in contempt the established Scholastic
philosophy and theology based on Aristotelian realism and committed to the orthodox teaching that the act of faith requires the assent of the human mind through
the working of the Holy Ghost on the faculties of intellect and will.

Influenced by the voluntarism of John Duns Scotus (1266–1308), which diminished the accessibility of moral truth to natural reason, and by the more radical
Nominalist idea of the inability of the reasoning faculty to grasp the essence of
things, many Christian thinkers of this period disparaged the role of reason in
disposing man to accept supernatural faith. This anti-rational drift had infected
in particular the Franciscan order to which the realist Scotus and the Nominalist
William of Ockham both belonged. It was also reflected in the *Devotio Moderna* of

---

[1] Martin Luther, *Table Talk* [*Dris Martini Lutheri colloquia mensalia, 1569*] (Philadelphia, 1873),
p. 353.

53

the fifteenth century which, with its stress on the life of interior piety, foreshadowed Luther's idea of faith as a kind of graced confidence in Divine Revelation and his conviction that good works were useless to salvation.

By impugning the Scholastic teaching on the relationship between reason and faith, Nominalism undermined the bases of traditional belief, which rests on a firmly objectivist foundation, but it did not act alone. There was another potent cultural factor of revolution at work: humanism. In its historical sense, humanism was the rediscovery of the ancient world by late medieval scholars, and the attempt to reform the society of their day – seen as decadent and inferior – according to the wisdom and outlook of Antiquity, revered as the Golden Age of humanity. While the humanists of southern Europe – Renaissance popes included – flirted with the pagan antiquity of Greece and Rome, the Northern humanists in the main took their inspiration from Christian antiquity, the age of the Apostles and the Fathers of the Church. Professor Owen Chadwick describes how

> All the [Christian] writers of the later Middle Ages saw the primitive Church through rose-coloured glass. In the lives of the saints they read of heroism and apostolic zeal; and seeing the ordinary or worse than ordinary men around them, they looked back wistfully and uncritically. Once there was a golden age. There was devotion, fervour, religion, holy priests, purity of heart. But now that ancient age of gold had degenerated imperceptibly to silver, from silver to wood, from wood to iron. 'There is as much difference between us and the men of the primitive church as there is between muck and gold.'[2]

Belief in the cultural superiority of Christian antiquity naturally implied the reform of the present-day Church. A reform not of her teachings, but of her morals. At the turn of the sixteenth century there may have been widespread moral corruption, but heresy had largely been driven underground and the integrity of faith and practice had hardly been affected. The Reformation exploded upon what was by and large an orthodox, pious Western Christendom. Although Luther's theological deviations predated his first public protest, without such ecclesiastical abuses as the sale of indulgences he would not have been able to launch so powerful an assault on the teachings of the Catholic Church and foment rebellion against her authority.

As he pursued his moral debate with a decadent ecclesiastical system, the German heresiarch found himself rejecting more and more of the Catholic tradition which, before the nailing up of his ninety-five theses, he had so fervently practised. Luther's logic was inexorable. If, because of her profound moral decay, the living, teaching Church of his day could no longer be trusted and obeyed, the pious Christian had no option but to take refuge in the original body of teachings that the latter-day papal 'Antichrist' had debased. Everything taught by the Magisterium of the sixteenth century had, then, to be measured against the teachings of Christian antiquity: the Bible and (to a much lesser degree) the writings of the Fathers. Making reason the ultimate authority in every facet of religion was the only course of action left to Protestantism once it rejected the authority of the living Church and no longer perceived doctrine as a developing thing.

---

[2] Owen Chadwick, *The Reformation* (Harmondsworth, 1964), p. 19.

Scriptural Worship

Along with Catholic philosophy and theology, the Protestant reformers repudiated the immemorial *lex orandi* as yet another medieval corruption. In a system which made Holy Writ the sole rule of faith, Christian worship, no less than Christian belief, had to be scripturally based, and in order to 're-create' (in fact, concoct) a 'scriptural' liturgy, one had to rely on one's own reading of the Bible. For all Protestants (like modern Catholics) the rule of worship had to reflect the rule of faith, though the heretics were divided in their method of excogitating the former from the latter.

The way of the Lutherans was that of 'reasonableness'. Martin Luther took the ideal of a scriptural liturgy to mean that it could not contain anything contrary to biblical teaching (or rather, contrary to his particular interpretation of the sacred texts). Hence his abolition of the ordained priesthood, his excision from the German 'Mass' of everything that 'stank of oblation', and his notion of the Real Presence based on the eucharistic species as a *locus* of the Incarnation realized by the Christian community, rather than the result of a sacrificial act.

At the same time, Luther the social conservative favoured the retention of all other trappings of Catholic liturgy not in conflict with scriptural doctrines and injunctions. Therefore his reformed worship preserved traditional altars and the eastward position, Mass vestments, the elevation of the host, sacred images and kneeling to receive the Eucharistic bread on the tongue. Where the congregation was literate, Latin was an optional liturgical medium. The Lutheran Lord's Supper was a memorial service with the visible shell of the abolished Catholic Mass.[3] This was the approach that Lenin would use to such effect during the Russian Revolution: 'Keep the shell, but empty it of its substance.'

Luther's inclusivist worship was vigorously denounced by the Calvinists and the Zwinglians, for whom a scriptural liturgy was one which strictly excluded any prayer or practice without an explicit warrant in Scripture. In churches taken over by these radical Protestants, the very word 'Mass' was anathema. Stone altars were replaced with tables, the minister stood facing the people wearing lay dress, the merely symbolic bread and cup were received seated and in the hand, all images were removed and destroyed as idols, organs were demolished, and metrical psalms replaced Christian chants and hymns. The order of service itself was founded exclusively on biblical texts and conducted only in the vernacular.[4]

The Prototype of the Pauline Reform

Now while there are certain general parallels between both 'high' and 'low' varieties of classical Protestant worship and the 'renewed' Roman liturgy of Paul VI, the analogy is at best partial, and it would be both inaccurate and unfair to suggest that the Consilium of the 1960s ever entertained a liturgical reform along explicitly Lutheran or Calvinist lines. The new order of Mass may be accused of toning down traditional references to sacrifice, but nowhere in its official Latin

---

[3] Roland H. Bainton. *Here I Stand: A Life of Martin Luther* (New York, 1950), pp. 265–66; O. Chadwick, *op. cit.*, pp. 64–65.
[4] O. Chadwick, *op. cit.*, pp. 77–78.

text does it deny, expressly or by omission, the sacrificial nature of the rite, which is the case with all Protestant liturgies. This is not to say, of course, that Protestant stylistic models were not sometimes used in the elaboration of new forms. Nor can one deny that the New Order of Mass has very often been implemented (or rather reformed) either in part or in full according to a Protestant theology (witness the notorious Article 7 of the General Instruction discussed above) or in a Protestant liturgical mode, for ecumenical reasons.

If the motivations of the Consilium members were rationalistic, but the liturgy they manufactured was neither Lutheran nor Calvinist, is it possible to place their endeavours within the broad tradition of Western reformed worship, or is one dealing with an isolated case of latter-day, *Catholic* rationalism? One does not have to go deeply into the writings of the precursors and apologists of the Pauline reform to see that it has a very definite precedent in the history of Western heterodoxy. To discover the prototype of the *Novus Ordo Missæ* it is not necessary to go as far back as the Reformation; the antiquarianist rather than Protestant ethos of the *official* rite indicates that its ancestry is more recent. The authors and apostles of the new rites did, in fact, readily acknowledge their debt to the ideas and liturgical experiments of a network of eighteenth-century Catholic reformers.

The tendencies of this movement were unequivocally rejected as 'pernicious errors' by Pius XII in *Mediator Dei* (1947). They had culminated in the notorious Synod of Pistoia of 1786 which, writes the same pope, 'the Church, in her capacity of watchful guardian of "the deposit of faith" entrusted to her by her divine Founder, has rightly condemned'.[5] It is worthy of note that many of the leading figures of the same eighteenth-century movement for liturgical reform in France, Germany, Austria and Italy were also partisans of Jansenism, which the teaching Church has always deemed as quasi-Protestant and heretical.

The Jansenist heresy was characterized not merely by an extreme doctrinal Augustinianism, which related it to Calvinism, but also by a contempt for the dogmatic authority of the Holy See. Such an outlook was bound to affect the attitudes of the Jansenists towards the public worship of the Church. Their habit of regarding Saint Augustine as a theological oracle led them to idolize the Church of the era in which he lived, the fifth century. If Catholics ought to follow the teachings of St Augustine (or rather the Jansenists' tendentious interpretation of them), then they should also seek to emulate in their churches the worship of this golden age of Christianity. Hence the heretics' scorn of the theology and liturgy of the Middle Ages. Moreover, since the Holy See was misusing its centralized organization by teaching error (in the Jansenists' view, semi-Pelagianism), more emphasis needed to be placed on the authority of the local church, which as a small unit could be more easily purified in its doctrine and worship.[6] Here Jansenism converged with Gallicanism.

In all these ideas the Jansenists leaned towards the antiquarianist and rationalist ideas of the Hussite, Lutheran and Anglican liturgists of an earlier period. Just as the Protestant Reformers had been supported by secular authorities, so too these reformers who refused to break openly with the Church found powerful allies and avid imitators among the Gallicans of France and the Febronians of Austria and

---

[5] *Mediator Dei*, § 68.
[6] John Parsons, 'The History of the Synod of Pistoia', paper read to Campion Fellowship Conference, Sydney, 1982, pp. 2–3.

the Italian states. In Austria the Emperor, Joseph II, even gave his name to a new form of Erastianism: Josephinism.

'To Joseph II the Church', writes Mgr Philip Hughes, 'was primarily a department of state whose office was the promotion of moral order.'[7] In the 1780s the 'Sacristan Emperor', as he was nicknamed after a remark by Frederick the Great,[8] initiated his reform by placing the Church under strict state surveillance and suppressing the contemplative orders. He then outlawed such traditional practices as the Litany of Loreto, the rosary and novenas, banned sermons expounding Christian dogmas, abolished all prayers and hymns 'offensive' to the state, and forbade certain feasts. Imperial decree fixed the number of masses to be said daily in each church, and even the number of candles to be lit on the high altar.[9] Within a few years Joseph's brother Peter Leopold, ruler of the Grand Duchy of Tuscany, was putting similar reforms into effect with the help of Scipione Ricci, Bishop of Pistoia and Prato.

Rational Worship: Catholic-style

In considering the Jansenist liturgical reform it is important to bear in mind that the partisans of the condemned heresy initially aspired to orthodoxy in their eucharistic theology: their over-scrupulous discouragement of frequent Communion and their insistence on careful preparation through the sacrament of penance are evidence enough of a fervent belief in the Real Presence. Unlike the Protestants, therefore, the Jansenists intended to uphold the Catholic doctrine of the Eucharist, though in their pedantic zeal to be patristic they rejected transubstantiation as an adequate explanation of the eucharistic mystery. Moreover, they stopped short of imitating the public worship of Protestants to the extent that the Reformation liturgies seemed to them unpatristic. They did not, for instance, replace the altar with a table and celebrate facing the people, and most of them retained the use of liturgical Latin. They were not iconoclasts, nor did they place the Eucharist in the hands of standing communicants or abolish the ritual distinction between priest and people.

In Austria and Tuscany, where the Tridentine missal was in common use, the Jansenists tampered little with the existing texts and rubrics of the Mass. By contrast, their French counterparts had more scope for ritual reform because the Mass of Pius V was less widely celebrated in their country: several archdioceses of France, including that of Paris, clung to the indigenous Gallicano-Roman liturgies of the High Middle Ages that had survived the general reform of 1570 by virtue of the indult of St Pius V.[10] In these liturgically non-Roman territories new breviaries, and sometimes new missals, were composed by prominent Jansenist priests and

---

[7] Philip Hughes, *A Popular History of the Catholic Church* (London, 1939), p. 194.
[8] Frederick once mockingly referred to Joseph as 'my brother the sacristan'.
[9] Hughes, *op. cit.*, pp. 194–95.
[10] See Chapter 7. Between 1583 and 1609 all the Occitan-speaking archdioceses (Bordeaux, Auch, Toulouse [except the see of Pamiers], Narbonne, Aix, Avignon, Vienne, Embrun), all the dioceses of Brittany and two French-speaking archdioceses (Rheims and Rouen) gave up their medieval liturgies to adopt the new Roman Missal. The non-Breton dioceses of the province of Tours, and the Francophone archdioceses of Sens (including Paris), Bourges, Besançon and Lyons (except the see of Langres) opted to retain and revise their own missals. See Prosper Guéranger, OSB, *Institutions liturgiques* (Le Mans/Paris, 1840–1851), I, p. 465. It is interesting to note that the

laymen and imposed in place of the traditional ones by local bishops sympathetic to the reformers' ideals. Since in most cases it was the 'revision' of a legitimate local rite, the Holy See did not have any immediate interest in intervening.

Even the venerable liturgy of the primatial see of Lyons was not spared when, in 1759, the Jansenist Antoine de Malvin de Montazet, who had already vandalized the traditional rite of his diocese of Autun, was appointed archbishop. In Lyons Montazet was able to use the power of the Paris Parliament against the cathedral canons who bravely resisted his expurgations.[11] His successor, the juring bishop Mgr Adrien Lamourette, 'Metropolitan of Rhône et Loire', went a step further and tore down the 'archaic' rood screen and high altar of the cathedral.[12] Enthusiasm for reform even reached the monastic Norbertine order. As late as 1787 Jean-Baptiste L'Écuy, the last abbot of Prémontré before the Revolutionary cataclysm, imposed on the French houses of his order a new missal revised along the lines of Charles de Vintimille's Neo-Gallican Parisian liturgy.[13]

Improving on the 'Work of God'

What shape, exactly, did the Jansenist liturgical reform take? Inspired as it was by the prevailing tendency of the age, the attempt to explain the supernatural in a manner consonant with human reason, this movement subjected the traditional liturgical texts to the most relentless criticism. As the work of revision progressed, no element thought to be post-patristic was suffered to survive, so that propers, prayers and hymns composed in the Middle Ages were all replaced by texts from the Bible, especially those thought to favour Jansenist interpretations of dogma.

While not giving formal adherence to the Lutheran doctrine of the priesthood of all baptized believers, the reformers tended to reduce the role of the ordained priest to that of president of the Christian assembly. Consequently, they attacked 'private' Masses (those not attended by members of the laity), discouraged votive Masses and anniversary requiems, and some took a subjectivistic view of the Real Presence in contending that one did not truly receive Christ in Holy Communion administered outside Mass. Attacking the extra-eucharistic cult of the Blessed Sacrament, Joseph II banned the use of the monstrance and Benediction of the Blessed Sacrament in Austria. Meanwhile, in Tuscany, Grand Duke Peter Leopold forbade the laity to hear Mass in monastic (as opposed to parish) churches so as to stress the essentially communitarian nature of the Eucharist.[14]

In France this new approach to the Mass as a communal sacrifice of the Christian people was further emphasized by such reforms as placing a white cloth, cross and lights on the altar only when the Eucharist was to be celebrated. Sanctuaries were not to be encumbered with vases of flowers. Since each church was to have only one altar, side altars were demolished. (One innovation, by contrast, was in fact the

linguistically non-French parts of the country (Occitania, Brittany in part) were less 'Gallican' and more 'Roman' in this regard.

[11] Archdale A. King, *Liturgies of the Primatial Sees* (London, 1957), pp. 24–25. One of the Canons who resisted Montazet was the Abbé Jacquet. In February 1777 the Archbishop had him arrested, and a pamphlet he had written condemning the new Jansenistic liturgy (modelled on that of Paris) was burnt by the public executioner.

[12] Ibid., p. 25.

[13] Lancelot Sheppard, *The Mass in the West* (London, 1962), p. 83.

[14] Guéranger, *op. cit.*, II, pp. 176–88; Parsons, *op. cit.*, pp. 5–6.

revival of an ancient tradition lost in Counter-Reformation times: the practice of the priest singing the *Kyrie, Gloria, Credo, Sanctus* and *Agnus Dei* along with the people instead of reciting them by himself in a low voice while the choir sang.[15])

The role of the people in the offering was highlighted by the revival of various supposedly meaningful acts such as the obsolescent offertory procession and the placing on the altar of seasonal fruits and vegetables for blessing at the end of the Eucharistic Prayer, as in the early Roman rite. Instead of the traditional 'veiling' of the mystery and the deliberate cultivation of a numinous atmosphere, the new rites were to be distinguished by a clarity and openness requiring the abolition of all silent prayers: the canon was now to be recited aloud, the congregation responding with an 'Amen' to each of its prayers. Laymen were allowed to read the Epistle in the vernacular in some places; in one Jansenist parish a woman read the Gospel of the day in French before Vespers.[16]

Orthodoxy on the Defensive

Orthodox churchmen throughout France were alarmed by these developments. Not only were the Jansenists destroying the traditional liturgy, but they had mounted a strong offensive against popular piety as well. At the beginning of the eighteenth century the Parisian Oratorian Pierre-François d'Arères de la Tour complained how:

> They do everything to diminish the cult of the Blessed Virgin, to weaken the respect due to the Pope. They pride themselves on using only Scripture in their liturgies, and in declaring themselves followers of Christian Antiquity, they frequently quote the canons of that age, boldly criticize everything, attack the legends, visions and miracles of the saints, affect elegance of literary style, valuing only their own productions and despising the works of others, and generally set themselves up as reformers . . .
>
> In the liturgical books being produced today they do not attack Catholic dogma, but subtly undermine it, uprooting the tree little by little . . .[17]

Canon de La Tour equally deplored the worldly attitudes of the reformers, whose mania for modernity amounted to an eighteenth-century version of *aggiornamento*, attractive to lovers of novelty and symptomatic of a cultural cringe towards Enlightenment England:

> Such is the frailty of human nature that involuntarily and without even suspecting it, people are taking on the tastes, fashions, language and idiom of the country and age in which they live . . . Our century is the age of Anglomania. It is the dominant strain in the agnostic movement, which rails against the superstition of the populace, the credulity of the devout, the excesses of the cult of the Blessed

[15] This custom was lost when traditional chants were replaced with elaborate baroque settings which only professional musicians could perform. Priests were thus no less silenced than the congregation and so were directed to read silently these prayers that could no longer be sung communally.

[16] Guéranger, *op. cit.*, II, pp. 250–53.

[17] Marie-Madeleine Martin, *Le latin immortel* (Chiré-en-Montreuil, 1971), p. 172.

Virgin and the Saints, the despotism of the Pope, the neglect of Sacred Scripture and the Church Fathers, and so on . . . They would deprive religion of all its flesh if they could, leaving just the skeleton. To this end they abolish, polish, simplify, reduce to nothing the little that has been preserved.[18]

Ironically, the reform-minded bishop who tried to force an antiquarianist missal on the diocese of Troyes in 1736 was the nephew of Jacques-Bénigne Bossuet, and bore the same name. The younger Bossuet's cathedral chapter protested to the Archbishop of Sens, Mgr Jean-Baptiste Languet de Gergy, who issued a condemnation of the Troyes missal in which he remarked that 'If it were necessary to suppress everything in the liturgy that does not go back to the earliest days of the Church, one would have to abolish the *Gloria in excelsis*, which, in the time of Saint Gregory, was recited only by the bishop . . .'[19]

Bishop Bossuet refused to take the condemnation lying down, and in a letter to his metropolitan appealed to a canon of the provincial council of Sens (1528) which gave local bishops the right to 'correct and reform the breviary and the missal'. Archbishop Languet's reply to him is interesting:

The intention of that council was certainly not that each bishop should, on the pretext of acting more wisely than the universal Church, tamper with every part of the Mass, and thereby violate with dubious novelties the uniformity of the liturgy, hallowed by ancient and continuous custom over so many centuries. The council would certainly not have passed such a law if it had been able to foresee how, in the future and in the name of the reform it was prescribing, people would do such things as replace hymns going back to Christian antiquity with texts from Scripture that have been mutilated, altered and twisted so as to take on new meanings, to the great detriment of holy doctrine.[20]

The Archbishop informed his Jansenist suffragan that the provincial council of 1528 had in mind simply the removal from the service books of 'superfluous things injurious to the dignity of the Church'. This was a very far cry from, for instance, 'changing the prayers of the Canon of the Mass, and suppressing a substantial part of the public rites'. On that precedent one could go on to

order the singing of Vespers in the morning or the celebration of Mass at eight in the evening; and abolish the law of Communion under one kind or the rule prescribing the reception of the sacrament fasting. Why not then allow the people to receive Communion after supper, as in the days of Saint Paul?[21]

In 1770, when the canons of Lyons Cathedral were struggling to defend their ritual patrimony against Archbishop Montazet, they appealed to the authority of St Augustine, the idol of the Jansenists, in support of ecclesiastical tradition. The great Bishop of Hippo, the canons reminded the French primate, had said of orthodox Christians that 'What they found in the Church, they retained; what

---

[18] Ibid., p. 173.
[19] Guéranger, *op. cit.*, II, p. 191.
[20] Ibid., II, p. 217.
[21] Ibid., II, pp. 215–16.

they learned, they taught; and what they received from the Fathers they handed down to their children.'[22]

An Exercise in Whitewashing

By 1794, when Pope Pius VI published his bull *Auctorem Fidei*, the mind of the Jansenist reform movement, impoverished by its hard, anxious rationalism and its divorce from living tradition, was moving in an increasingly heterodox direction. One of the five propositions of the Synod of Pistoia condemned in the bull was the classic antiquarianist conviction that 'in these recent centuries there has been a general ignorance about truths of the faith and of the moral teaching of Jesus Christ'.[23] In refuting the Pope's condemnation of their work, the Jansenists insisted that their beliefs, unlike those expressed in the offending bull, were impeccably orthodox. Some of them even refused to believe that the Pope could have freely endorsed such an obviously 'uncatholic' document, and the bishops of the Dutch Jansenist Church lamented that 'this astonishing Bull [is] an injury done to the See of St Peter . . . and dishonours the Pope who has been constrained to adopt it'.[24]

Anticipating the strategy of twentieth-century Modernists, the Jansenists strove to establish their sectarian views as Catholic orthodoxy, and spared no effort to reform the Church from within according to their lights, rather than abandoning it as the Protestants had done. Similarly, just as Catholic progressives today deny the very existence of the Modernist heresy as described by Pope Pius X, the liturgical experts responsible for the post-conciliar reform have done their best to whitewash the eighteenth-century Jansenist liturgies which they readily claim as the blueprint of their own revolutionary programme.

In his introduction to a book on the new liturgy published in 1970, the English liturgiologist Lancelot Sheppard who, like all innovators, takes it for granted that the old order was corrupt or defective, wrote:

> The present reform has obviously been wanted for some time. Its need was felt, for example, in the eighteenth century when some dioceses of France and Germany set about reforming their liturgies along lines that have now become familiar to us in the recent changes. It was unfortunate that the lack of authorization gave them a bad name which probably retarded the eventual reform.[25]

Another prominent liturgist, Fr Louis Bouyer, a convert from Protestantism who had served on the papal committee that manufactured the new rite of Mass between 1964 and 1969, found much to commend in the antiquarianist eucharistic rite invented by Jacques Jubé, the early eighteenth-century parish priest of Asnières, a village near Paris. 'We of today can see in most of [these changes] intelligent and healthy improvements', Bouyer wrote in 1956. They ought, however, to have been 'introduced with the consent of proper authority'.[26]

[22] King, *op. cit.*, p. 24. (*Quod invenerunt in Ecclesia tenuerunt; quod didicerunt docuerunt; quod patribus acceperunt, hoc filiis tradiderunt.*)
[23] Parsons, *op. cit.*, p. 14.
[24] Ibid.
[25] Lancelot Sheppard, ed., *The New Liturgy* (London, 1970), p. 4.
[26] Louis Bouyer, *Life and Liturgy* (London, 1956, tr. of *La vie de la liturgie*, Paris, 1956), p. 54.

In his historical work *The Mass in the West*, Lancelot Sheppard shares Fr Bouyer's admiration of Jubé's experiment, but omits to inform his readers that the French abbé was no ordinary Catholic crank with a penchant for innovation, but a staunch Jansenist.[27] He also fails to mention that this reformed liturgy was not merely Jubé's creation, but the fruit of close collaboration with a certain Nicolas Petitpied, a leading Jansenist theologian who had been banished in 1703 to Holland where he associated himself with the Jansenist Church of Utrecht. Petitpied, incidentally, was later employed as Bishop Bossuet's propagandist in the latter's dispute with Archbishop Languet, while Fr Jubé resigned his parish in 1717 to go to Russia on an ecumenical mission organized by doctors of the Sorbonne working for a reunion of the Roman, Orthodox and Anglican Churches based on a common Jansenistic formula of belief.[28]

The Ecumenical Trap

Fr Petitpied's project of reuniting the Anglican Church as well as Eastern Orthodoxy with the Roman Church stemmed not so much from a utopian dream of Christian unity (other Protestants were excluded *a priori*), as from the Jansenists' awareness of affinities between themselves and High Church Anglicans. What the Jansenists rejected in contemporary Catholicism, the ancestors of the High Churchmen had abandoned at the Reformation, and what the High Anglicans had recovered of the Catholic tradition came close to what the Jansenists deemed the essentials of orthodoxy.

Modern Anglo-Catholic apologists like to regard the anti-Calvinist reforms of Anglican prelates like Hooker, Andrewes, Cosin and Laud as so many stages in the re-catholicizing of the Church of England after the disaster of the Reformation. Likewise, some Catholic ecumenists of our day compare this 'Catholic revival' in early Anglicanism with the increasingly orthodox sacramental theology developing in certain twentieth-century Protestant communities like that of Taizé. The conclusion drawn is that the divisions between Catholics and Protestants will disappear as Catholics shed from their tradition what is non-essential, and Protestants recover what they had lost from their original Catholic heritage.

What reformist Catholics – both the Jansenist originators of the scheme and their modern disciples – have found it possible and expedient to sacrifice in the interests of this ecumenical convergence has already been described. As for the main points of the High Anglican reform, the approach to worship typical of such a churchman as Richard Hooker was, like Luther's, inclusivist. Hooker defended 'the place of reason in religion' in opposition to the Puritan claim that only what was explicitly supported by Scripture could be permitted in church. In his defence of the 'popish' Prayer Book, Hooker contended that

[a]part from that area where God had issued direct commands in the Scripture, there is a wide area where the government of the Church and State must accord with the natural law of God, which may be known by the general reason of mankind and of which ecclesiastical or civil laws must seek to be the practical

[27] Sheppard, *The Mass in the West*, pp. 97–98.
[28] Guéranger, *op. cit.*, II, pp. 251–52.

expression. Human laws do not moderate the details of practice for all time. Human society is changing, and a State or a Church may order whatever practice is edifying and expedient, provided its order obeys the Scripture law or is in harmony with the natural law.[29]

This essentially conservative and utilitarian approach had no need of the full Catholic tradition rejected at the Reformation. Rather, it selected from the past those inoffensive Catholic practices that tended to promote a more dignified order of worship. The joint authority of Church and state, acting on the dictates of reason and common sense, was to determine which practices were to be restored. Thus the Laudians of the reign of Charles I reintroduced crosses, crucifixes and some images, eastward-facing altars fenced off by rails, celebrations of the Lord's Supper in surplice and stole, kneeling for Communion, organs and choirs.[30]

Yet in no way did these reforms amount to a recovery of the real ethos of Catholic tradition, if by this is meant the conservation and cultivation of a received body of ancient beliefs and customs. The Episcopalian reformers were not concerned to restore pre-Reformation English Catholicism. They had no desire, for instance, to revive the embers of the Sarum rite or the use of liturgical Latin. On the contrary, they were generally satisfied with the contents of the *Book of Common Prayer*.

In reality the Caroline Divines, as Christian scholars, were antiquarianists, though sophisticated and unprejudiced enough to see that many of the things rejected by Protestants (the episcopate, the notion of the Eucharist as a sacrifice, confession) had in fact existed in Christian antiquity. Restoring the supposed practices of the primitive Church to the seventeenth-century Church of England was therefore all that the 'Catholic revival' of this period amounted to. Outwardly, it was of exactly the same stuff as continental Jansenist antiquarianism, though inwardly the Jansenist priests possessed valid orders and could administer all the sacraments, whereas Anglican ministers had lost the apostolic succession and a true priesthood. It was precisely this awareness that prompted some Anglo-Catholic revivalists of the nineteenth century to attempt to restore the totality of the lost tradition by seeking orders from Old Catholic and Jansenist bishops.[31]

In the light of these facts, the admiration of the Pauline reformers for their antiquarianist predecessors, Protestant, Jansenist and Anglican, is suspect from a traditionalist standpoint. Louis Bouyer, for instance, admits that the Caroline Divines 'were in their deepest hearts, antiquarians' and failed in their search of the sources of tradition to rediscover all the permanent essentials of a living liturgy, in any case an impossible task outside the communion of an apostolic church.[32] But he does not hesitate, on the other hand, to assert that 'the beginnings of a true liturgical movement . . . are to be found during the sixteenth century', even though

---

[29] O. Chadwick, *op. cit.*, pp. 214–15.

[30] Ibid., pp. 227–28.

[31] Conservative Catholics have seen this as one more example of intellectual dishonesty or bad faith on the part of Anglo-Catholics. This negative view nevertheless overlooks nineteenth- and early twentieth-century Anglo-Catholicism's impressive devotion to liturgical *authenticity*, the indispensable complement of validity. Paradoxically, technically invalid Anglican eucharistic liturgies following the 'English Missal' could often be more authentic in terms of orthopraxis than those celebrated by Latin Catholic priests whose orders were not in doubt. This is important food for thought for those now labouring for a genuine restoration of the Roman liturgy.

[32] Bouyer, *op. cit.*, p. 47.

'sad to say, it was among the adherents of this nascent liturgical movement that the Protestant Reformation found its promoters'.[33] For Fr Bouyer, then, certain Jansenists and Protestants have been the modern Church's best teachers in matters liturgical, and indeed 'the worst of heretics may sometimes have very useful truths to tell us, truths which need only to be put back in a Catholic setting to take on their full value'.[34] So much for context and authenticity.

The Pruning Theory

According to the French liturgist all that was necessary to bring the Latin Catholic cult back to its pristine purity was for 'the true [i.e. Patristic] tradition [to] be disengaged from all spurious and unhealthy additions, and thus be renewed in its primitive freshness, in order to be re-expressed in a frame which should make it accessible to the people of [to]day'.[35] Now the root error of Bouyer's thought on this question is a false distinction between the outright antiquarianism condemned by the Church and reformist programmes so destructive of living tradition that they amount to the same thing. Yet those who thought like him on the eve of Vatican II were convinced that they could avoid the pitfall of the 'dead' archaeologism of schismatics of the past simply by restoring the ancient liturgical canons within the *living* communion of the Catholic Church.

What the pre-conciliar reformers hoped for was a return to ancient tradition under the guidance of the Holy Spirit and within the framework of an official reform ordered by a pope. Giovanni Battista Montini was the answer to their prayers. Significantly, in justifying his liturgical legislation to Archbishop Lefebvre in 1976, Pope Paul VI stated that 'the present reform derived its *raison d'être* and its guidelines from the Council and from the historical sources of the Liturgy',[36] and on another occasion he actually described his anti-historical innovations as 'a step forward in the Church's authentic tradition'.[37]

Fr Josef Jungmann was another scholar who advocated an indirect return to Antiquity through a thorough pruning of the inherited Romano-Gallican liturgy: this, in his view, was the acceptable 'Catholic' alternative to a direct return through the creation of artificial rites based on ancient euchological texts. Jungmann did not see the essentials of the Catholic liturgy as having grown organically for over a millennium. Rather, he believed that the ritual tradition, like the apostolic deposit of faith, had been passed on perfect by the inspired Church Fathers who had fashioned it. In the following centuries it suffered gradual degeneration, and it was the constant duty of the official Church to strip away periodically the foreign matter that had crept into it.

The Jesuit scholar went so far as to claim that the primary aim of Pius V's revision, as expressed in the bull *Quo Primum Tempore* of 1570, was to restore the primitive Roman rite by removing medieval accretions, and that 'the self-evident idea that the development which had taken place meanwhile, separating the present from the *pristina sanctorum Patrum norma* ['the ancient norm and rite of the holy

---

[33] Ibid., p. 41.
[34] Ibid., p. 44.
[35] Ibid., p. 46.
[36] M. Davies, *Apologia*, I, p. 330.
[37] M. Davies, *PPNM*, p. 557.

Fathers'] should not be put aside as long as it did not disturb the ground plan but rather unfolded it – that idea was never once expressed'.[38]

Now while it is undoubtedly true that Pius V had no idea of liturgical development as we understand it today, the fact is that the commission entrusted with the revision of the Roman Missal codified a rite that was still essentially medieval. Jungmann, however, suggests that their failure to restore the primitive Roman rite was due largely to a superficial and undeveloped liturgical scholarship unable to distinguish clearly between medieval and ancient elements.[39] It is precisely here that the antiquarianist argument falls down, for if the liturgists of the sixteenth century did actually have an historically inaccurate idea of the Mass rite of the Patristic age, one can hardly argue that St Pius envisaged an exhumation of such unknown quantities as the Eucharist of Saint Hippolytus or the Mass of Saint Leo.

Furthermore, there is good reason to suppose that what the pontiff meant by 'the ancient norm and rite of the Holy Fathers' was not indeed the ordinary of the Mass, that is, its basic structure, but the propers or changeable prayers that went with it, since the most ancient sacramentary extant in his day (the so-called *Sacramentarium Leonianum* of the seventh century) did not contain the ordinary.[40] The excisions from the Roman rite in 1570 were thus particular examples of standard variable elements like introits, prefaces and sequences.

In his time Fr Jungmann (who died in 1975) was hailed as the greatest authority on the history of the Roman liturgy, but his formidable scholarship was vitiated by the subjective assumption that the analysis of a thing necessarily implies its reform. In this error, which was to wreak such havoc in the Latin Church, he resembled those nineteenth-century theorists who, not content with contemporary scientific analysis of English as a hybrid language, went on to advocate its 'purification' through the elimination of all its French, Latin and Greek 'accretions'. The 'Saxonism' promoted by the poet-philologist William Barnes (1801–1886) and the Anglo-Catholic Oxford historian Edward Augustus Freeman (1823–1892) was doomed to failure, for language, no less than liturgy, is a living organism that cannot be radically reshaped by those whose special knowledge leads them to pass particular judgements on history. Prescriptive grammarians can influence to some extent the evolution of a language, but they can never alter its historical course.

The very idea of returning to the ancient form of the Mass is in fact a delusion: since it is obvious that the structure of the rite grew from the days of the Apostles until the time of the Crusades, and that there was never in the Patristic period a liturgical codification with the same permanence and juridical force as that of St Pius V, what precise phase in the development of the liturgy is the Church to canonize as the ideal form of the Roman Mass? The obvious result of such a wild goose chase is to give up the search altogether and 'return' to the ritual of the Last Supper, a logical conclusion that has inspired the coffee table eucharists of our day.

---

[38] Jungmann, *op. cit.*, I, p. 137.
[39] Ibid.
[40] Fortescue, *The Mass*, p. 118.

Chasing the Wild Goose

It must be admitted in the last analysis that it is impossible to hold up as a permanent paradigm one particular phase in the growth of the liturgical tradition and not succumb to the temptation of an anachronistic imitation of it. In the first decade of the twenty-first century one may legitimately ask what, in fact, is the substantial difference between a 'living return to the sources of the liturgy' that dismisses a millennium of growth as so much corruption, and 'the perennial mistake of archeologism' which Bouyer, one of the authors of the Pauline rites, censured in 1956.[41]

A case in point during the period in which the new liturgy was concocted was the reformed pontifical or rite for the consecration of bishops. The traditional Roman pontifical originated in the Patristic age, in the fifth century, and developed gradually until its perfection at the end of the thirteenth century. Like the traditional Mass, this rite had an ancient Roman core and a Gallican superstructure. For this reason, the Belgian Benedictine Dom Bernard Botte, a member of Pope Paul's Consilium, complained that 'The essential element, that is, the laying on of hands, was somewhat buried under a pile of secondary rites. Furthermore, certain formulas were inspired by medieval theology and needed correction.'[42]

The solution Botte presented in 1965 was the complete ditching of the Roman pontifical and its replacement by an ancient Roman text dating from at least AD 218, the *Apostolic Tradition* of St Hippolytus, which had become obsolete in the West but had been adopted by the Antiochene and Alexandrian rites. The Belgian monk's proposal won over the Consilium members because of its timely ecumenical merits, and it was repackaged as the new pontifical that was imposed on the Roman rite in 1968.[43] Questions of validity apart, Botte's pontifical was an egregious example of rationalistic antiquarianism's contempt for the principle of organic liturgical development.

Not only did the Consilium scholars succumb to this age-old error, but another of the dangers of idealizing the Patristic age, 'the no less fatal error of projecting into an imagined antiquity some of the most unfortunate fashions of our time', has now become a standard feature of Western Catholic liturgy.[44] Today it is evident from its fruits that the whole Pauline reform lacked the inspiration claimed for it, precisely because its basic method was anti-traditional. The history of Christianity shows that the Holy Ghost, the promoter of all authentic change in the Church, works through the institutions of human culture, not in spite of them. Yet the creators of the new rites were scathingly critical of contemporary traditionalists who, in their opinion, wrongly viewed the existing Roman liturgy as a sacred cow. Seven years before the Council, Louis Bouyer made it clear that 'There is no longer any question of considering the liturgy as something set once and for all in the forms now established.'[45] The mentality that excludes the possibility of liturgical change on a sound rational and theological basis was, in his view, essentially pagan, since

---

[41] Bouyer, *op. cit.*, p. 56.
[42] Bernard Botte, OSB, *From Silence to Participation* (Washington, DC, 1988), p. 134.
[43] It is noteworthy that the new pontifical was intended to appeal to Eastern Christians whereas the new ordinal had been designed to please Protestants, but of course neither could be attractive to members of the Roman rite who knew and appreciated their own tradition.
[44] Ibid.
[45] Ibid., p. 68.

only to the pagan mind 'sacred means untouchable, something to be preserved intact at any price'.[46]

A Forgotten Charter

In one of the boldest admissions of his pontificate, Paul VI informed the Church in 1969 that his new Mass was a manufactured product, 'a law thought out by authoritative experts of sacred liturgy'.[47] To Catholic 'pagans' Montini's reform was all the more scandalous in that many of the innovations he attempted to pass off as 'a step forward in the Church's authentic tradition' were repackagings of the Jansenist principles of Pistoia. These had been condemned outright by Pope Pius XII in 1947 as symptoms of 'archeologism' in the encyclical *Mediator Dei*, the official charter for the renewal of Catholic public worship. Only two decades before the appearance of the *Novus Ordo*, Pope Pius had written:

> It is true that the Church is a living organism and therefore grows and develops in her liturgical worship; it is also true that, always preserving the integrity of her doctrine, she accommodates herself to the needs and conditions of the times. But deliberately to introduce new liturgical customs, or to revive obsolete rites inconsistent with existing laws and rubrics, is an irresponsible act which We must condemn. . . .
>
> The liturgy of the early ages is worthy of veneration; but an ancient custom is not to be considered better, either in itself or in relation to times and circumstances, just because it has the flavour of antiquity. More recent liturgical rites are also worthy of reverence and respect, because they too have been introduced under the guidance of the Holy Ghost . . .
>
> . . . the desire to restore everything indiscriminately to its ancient condition is neither wise nor praiseworthy. It would be wrong, for example, to want the altar restored to its ancient form of a table, to want black removed from the liturgical colours, and pictures and statues excluded from our churches; to require crucifixes that do not represent the bitter sufferings of the divine Redeemer . . .[48]

Thus the Pope criticized as simplistic and destructive of living tradition that mentality which considers worthless or detrimental the historical growth of the liturgy, in odious comparison with an ecclesiastical golden age proposed for perpetual emulation. A century before *Mediator Dei*, Dom Guéranger had drawn up a syllabus of such tendencies and denounced them collectively as 'the anti-liturgical heresy'.[49] What is significant is that Pius XII did not simply censure liturgical antiquarianism as misguided, but actually passed a moral judgement on it as 'a wicked movement, that tends to paralyse the sanctifying and salutary action by which the liturgy leads the children of adoption on the path to their heavenly Father'.[50]

---

[46] Ibid., p. 52.
[47] *Teachings of Pope Paul VI*, p. 288.
[48] *Mediator Dei*, §§ 63, 65, 66.
[49] Guéranger, *op. cit.*, I, pp. 405–23; II, pp. 252–55.
[50] *Mediator Dei*, § 68.

5

THE PRIMACY OF PETER

*And I tell thee, thou art Peter, and on this rock I will build My Church,
and the powers of death shall not prevail against it. I will give thee the
keys of the kingdom of heaven, and whatever thou bindest on earth
shall be bound in heaven, and whatever thou loosest on earth shall be
loosed in heaven.*

(*MATT. 16.17-19*)

*A second time He said to him, 'Simon, son of John, lovest thou Me?'
He said to him, 'Yes, Lord, Thou knowest that I love Thee.' He said to
him, 'Tend my sheep.'*

(*JN 21.16*)

Post-conciliar Irony

If anyone shall say that Blessed Peter the Apostle was not constituted by Christ
our Lord as chief of all the Apostles and the visible head of the whole Church
militant, or that he did not receive directly and immediately from the same Lord
Jesus Christ a primacy of true and proper jurisdiction, but one of honour only,
let him be anathema.[1]

In 1870, when this canon of the First Vatican Council was framed, the Roman
Church, with its glorious liturgical tradition intact and flourishing (whatever the
human flaws and contemporary tribulations of the Bark of Peter) could afford the
luxury of looking down on the Eastern Orthodox, whose inability to accept this
new dogma of faith made them targets of the associated anathema.

However, almost a century and a half later in 2007, when the Congregation for
the Doctrine of the Faith elaborated, in reference to the dissident Eastern Churches,
that 'these venerable Christian communities lack something in their condition as
particular churches',[2] the truth of the dogma identifying the true Church of Christ

---

[1] Denzinger/Bannwart, *Enchiridion*, n. 1823.
[2] *Clarification of the Doctrine of the Church from the Congregation for the Doctrine of the Faith*,
10 July 2007. The complete statement was:

> Because these Churches, although separated, have true sacraments and above all – because of
> the apostolic succession – the priesthood and the Eucharist, by means of which they remain
> linked to us by very close bonds, they merit the title of 'particular or local Churches', and are
> called sister Churches of the particular Catholic Churches. It is through the celebration of

with the Roman communion alone seemed tragically ironical. For in the period following the Second Vatican Council the *opus Dei* had been all but destroyed in the Latin Church, replaced – directly through papal diktat and indirectly through papal indulgence or weakness – by protestantized travesties of the Roman and other Western liturgies, not infrequently including eucharistic celebrations and sacramental rites of doubtful validity. Yet meanwhile, in most of the ecclesially deficient Oriental bodies of apostolic foundation formally outside the Catholic communion, the Catholic liturgy had been preserved in all its vigour, beauty and integrity. How is this paradox to be accounted for? The question is a complex one, and can be explained only by revisiting some milestones in the bimillenary relations between the Latin Church and the Christian East.

The Church as Communion

If liturgical revolution has never been a real possibility in the Eastern Churches, it is not simply because of the absence of strong rationalist currents, but also because of the normative role which these bodies, unlike the modern Roman Church, assign to traditional worship in Christian life. Such liturgical conservatism is due to the fact that the Orientals have preserved the earliest Catholic ecclesiology, which views the Church as a communion of local churches united in their celebration of the same sacraments. The primacy of the Bishop of Rome is in full harmony with this scheme, and if the Eastern Orthodox and certain modern Catholics have formed the opposite impression the fault lies with distortions in the presentation and the application of the doctrine, not with the primacy itself, which is of divine institution.

'My Kingdom is not of this world' (Jn 18.36): the Gospels make it clear that Christ intended His Church to be the antithesis of the Roman Empire into which it was born. Far from being a compulsory union held together by law and force, it was in the first place a voluntary communion founded on grace and charity. The structure and laws necessary to a human institution were secondary to this.

The polity of the early Church is summed up by the world 'Catholicity'. Grigorij Protopopov, a Russian Catholic writer, relates how

> in ancient times the Church of believers was constituted as a unity in diversity: unity of faith, sacraments and ecclesiastical administration; diversity of rites, as an expression of the national and cultural peculiarity of local Churches. This characteristic has taken the name of 'Catholicity' (in its Old Church Slavonic translation, *sobornost'*), and the first and basic definition that the Christian Church made of itself was expressed in the adjective 'catholic', from the Greek word *katholikós*, meaning 'universal', 'which is established everywhere'. Catholicity is one of the most important and fundamental characteristics of the Church: on the one hand it reflects faith in universality, in the human 'globality' of the Christian mission; on the other it reflects the conviction that in practice this universality is incarnated

the Eucharist of the Lord in each of these Churches that the Church of God is built up and grows in stature. However, since communion with the Catholic Church, the visible head of which is the Bishop of Rome and the Successor of Peter, is not some external complement to a particular Church but rather one of its internal constitutive principles, these venerable Christian communities lack something in their condition as particular churches.

in the specificity of the spiritual life of this or that people. In a structure of this kind each parish, each diocese, each local Church, following its own traditions and way of life, and constituting in itself a sort of 'little church', was also aware of being part of the unitary organism of the Catholic Church which extended from the Atlantic Ocean in the West to the 'frontiers of India' in the East.[3]

Although the local churches comprising the Universal Church were considered complete in themselves, they adhered for practical reasons to regional centres of unity determined by the accidents of history: the three apostolic patriarchates of Alexandria, Antioch and Rome. In the early Church the title *Papa* came to denote a patriarch, but if the 'Pope of Rome' was greater in honour and authority than the 'Pope of Antioch' and the 'Pope of Alexandria', it was because, as bishop of the centre of the civilized world, he was also the successor of Saint Peter, the 'rock' upon whom Christ had built His Church,[4] and Rome was the See of Peter.[5] The growth of the two historic patriarchates of the East was, in any case, gradual. Alexandria and Antioch did not come into their own as centres of authority until the age of Constantine.[6] The primacy of the Bishop of Rome was, by contrast, an apostolic tradition. If the material cause of the Catholic Church was orthodox faith and practice, its formal cause was communion with the Roman See.

In the first Christian centuries this unquestioned primacy in the Church was manifested in the special responsibility which the Pope assumed – outside his immediate duties as Bishop of Rome – of aiding his brother bishops everywhere in their work of upholding tradition, by his presiding over ecumenical councils and by his authoritative arbitration in the disputes of other churches. The Roman See was thus the Church's supreme court of appeal, and the norms and limits of ordinary papal authority outside the Western Patriarchate were set by the third, fourth and fifth canons of the Council of Sardica (modern Sofia), held in (or around) 343.

Even today there are Eastern Orthodox theologians who grant in theory to the Successor of Peter a primacy of ultimate authority, responsibility and care. According to Alexander Schmemann

> the essence and purpose of this primacy is to express and preserve the unity of the Church in faith and life; to express and preserve the unanimity of all Churches; to keep them from isolating themselves from the unity of life. It means ultimately to assume the care, the *solicitude* of the Churches so that each one of them can abide in that fullness which is always the *whole* catholic tradition and not any 'part' of it.[7]

---

[3] Grigorij Protopopov, 'La Chiesa greco-cattolica ucraina: origini e caratteristiche', in A. Judin and G. Protopopov, *Cattolici in Russia e Ucraina* (Rome, 1992), pp. 143–44.

[4] Matt. 16.18-19, Lk. 22.32; Jn 21.15-17.

[5] The Greek noun πάππας (*páppas*) 'daddy', later, 'father', was originally applied to any priest, and this is still the case in certain European languages, cf. modern Greek παπάς (*papás*), Russian, Serbian and Bulgarian *pop*, German *Pfaffe*, Finnish *pappi*, 'priest'. In these languages the Latin *papa* (from the Greek) was later borrowed to denote the Pope (i.e. Patriarch) of Rome. The Coptic patriarchs still style themselves 'popes'.

[6] Louis Duchesne, *The Churches Separated from Rome* (London, 1907), p. 113.

[7] Alexander Schmemann, 'The Idea of Primacy in Orthodox Ecclesiology', in J. Meyendorff, A. Schmemann, N. Afanassieff and N. Koulomzine, *The Primacy of Peter in the Orthodox Church* (Leighton Buzzard, 1963), 2nd edn 1973, p. 49.

The Bishop Who Presides in Love

The office of the Roman Patriarch as Universal Shepherd of Christians is therefore, according to the eucharistic ecclesiology of the Easterners, a ministry in the Church rather than a power over the Church.[8] As Mgr Pierre Batiffol showed long ago, this view of papal authority is no medieval Byzantine innovation, but characterized the Latin Church of the early centuries: 'The papacy of the first centuries is the authority exercised by the Church of Rome *among* other Churches, authority which consists in caring after their conformity with the authentic tradition of faith . . . and which is claimed by no other church but the Church of Rome'[9] (emphasis added).

Authority among the Churches and authority *over* the Churches are not mutually exclusive when one makes the requisite distinction between the ordinary and the absolute and between the actual and the potential in government. For like doctrine, ecclesial government has developed over the centuries with things implicit in the original constitutions gradually becoming explicit, often through testing in particular disputes. In any case it is clear from historical evidence that while the style of the early Papacy was not autocratic, its authority was nonetheless supreme in the Church. When, about the year 96 AD, Pope St Clement I intervened in a dispute between the Christian laity of Corinth and their clergy by sending three legates to arbitrate, the service aspect of his primatial role was evident from the mild and respectful tone of his apostolic letter:

> You will cause us great joy if, complying with what we have written to you in the Holy Spirit, you at once set aside the unjust excess of your anger, as we have exhorted you to do in recommending to you peace and concord by this letter. We have sent faithful and prudent men, who, from their youth up until their old age, have lived among us without reproach; they will be witnesses between you and us. If we act thus, it is because our only anxiety has been, and still is, to see your speedy return to peace.[10]

---

[8] Ibid., p. 39. Since, according to early Catholic teaching, each orthodox bishop has the fullness of apostolic authority, the Orthodox reject the later Latin notion of the Roman Pope as a 'super-bishop' from whom all other bishops derive their authority in the same way that priests derive their powers from the bishop who ordains them. However, of 'eucharistic ecclesiology' Schmemann writes:

> It must be stated emphatically that this type of ecclesiology does not transform the local Church into a self-sufficient monad, without any 'organic' link with other similar monads. There is no 'congregationalism' here. The organic unity of the Church universal is not less real than the organic unity of the local Church. But if universal ecclesiology [that of Rome] interprets it in terms of 'parts' and 'whole', for eucharistic ecclesiology the adequate term is that of *identity*: 'the Church of God abiding in . . .' The Church of God is the one and indivisible Body of Christ, wholly and indivisibly present in each Church, i.e. in the visible unity of the people of God, the Bishop and the Eucharist. And if universal unity is indeed *unity of the Church* and not merely *unity of Churches*, its essence is not that all churches together constitute one vast, unique organism, but that each Church – in the identity of order, faith and the gifts of the Holy Spirit – is the same Church, the same Body of Christ, indivisibly present wherever is the 'ecclesia'. It is thus the same organic unity of the Church herself, the 'Churches' being not complementary to each other, as parts or members, but each one and all of them together being nothing else, but the One, Holy, Catholic, and Apostolic Church. (Ibid., p. 40)

[9] Pierre Batiffol, *L'Église naissante et le catholicisme* (Paris, 1927), p. 28.

[10] Duchesne, *op. cit.*, p. 84. This occurred some two and a half centuries before the establishment of the historic patriarchates.

Nevertheless, St Clement asserted his authority by warning of the consequences of non-compliance with a directive of Christ's representative on earth: 'If any man should be disobedient unto the words spoken by God through us, let him understand that he will entangle himself in no slight transgression or danger.'[11] A decade later St Ignatius of Antioch would write of Rome that 'with this church, because of its superior authority, every church must agree – that is, the faithful everywhere – in communion with which church the tradition of the Apostles has always been preserved by those who are everywhere'.[12]

The Roman primacy performed a most important role in Christendom, since doctrinal orthodoxy would always be the prime mark of the Roman See. In post-apostolic times Rome was distinguished by the purity of her faith and teaching when the Christian East was rocked by a succession of destructive theological controversies: Arianism, Nestorianism, Monophysitism, Iconoclasm. By comparison, papal wanderings from orthodoxy were few indeed.[13] With Constantine's transfer of the imperial seat from Rome to Byzantium in 330 and the definitive division of the Empire at the death of Theodosius (395), the East found itself dominated by Christian emperors who, while styling themselves defenders of the faith, in practice persecuted the orthodox whenever they chose to promote heresy for political reasons, usually to achieve a rapid religious consensus within the state. As the problem of heterodoxy in the Church grew, the guiding role of the Roman popes from a theological principle came to be more and more a practical necessity.

A New Consciousness

The Papacy is often blamed for destroying the early 'communion model' of unity by attempting to impose on Christendom an imperially inspired monarchy alien to its nature, but in fact the 'juridical model' of the Church first arose in the East, as a direct consequence of the shift of the Empire's capital from Rome to Constantinople in 330. While it is true that St Peter's choice of Rome as his seat was an accommodation to the political reality of his day, this decision was made within the providential context of the Incarnation, which took place precisely when the whole known world was united under Roman rule.

In the early days of the Papacy the pagan Rome-centred Empire was the chief persecutor of the Church, but with the conversion of Constantine the relationship between Church and Empire not only changed radically but was complicated by the new role of emperors as protectors of the Church after the Edict of Milan (AD 313). The baneful effects of imperial domination of the Church (caesaropapism), especially in the East after 330, manifested themselves in a particular way at the Council of Chalcedon (451), whose mainly Oriental Fathers unwittingly planted the seeds of division in Christendom by seeking to adapt the growing organization of the Church to the changed political structure of the Empire.[14]

---

[11] Epistola, n. 59.
[12] Adversus Haereses, III, iii, 2.
[13] See below, Chapter 9, pp. 143–45.
[14] Before 451 only the Church of East Syria (Mesopotamia) was cut off from Catholic unity, for political reasons: the Zoroastrian Persian rulers of this region forced the East Syrian hierarchy at the Council of Seleucia-Ctesiphon (424) to sever relations with their co-religionists in the Roman Empire. No less politically motivated was this Church's official adoption after 431 of the

In 325 the Council of Nicaea had confirmed the patriarchal status of the three apostolic sees, but after the foundation of Constantinople five years later, it was natural that the bishop of the new imperial capital should also aspire to the title of patriarch. The First Council of Constantinople (381) had accorded the imperial see a primacy of honour after Rome 'because Constantinople is the new Rome', while omitting due acknowledgement of the apostolic character of the Roman See, whose bishop was the successor of the Prince of the Apostles.[15] Pope St Damasus I consequently refused to sanction the canon in question.

Furthermore, when the Council of Chalcedon seventy years later upgraded Constantinople's primacy of honour to one of jurisdiction over the churches of Thrace and Asia Minor, areas originally subject to the patriarchate of Antioch,[16] and confirmed Constantinople's precedence over Antioch and Alexandria, the bishops of these two apostolic sees joined the Roman Pope (St Leo I) in protest.[17] At this time the anti-imperial feeling widespread in the East brought pejorative senses to the words *Rome* and *Roman* because Constantinople styled itself the 'Second Rome' and the Byzantines called themselves Ρωμαῖοι (*Rōmaîoi*), i.e. 'Romans'. On the popular level the so-called Monophysite schism, which sundered most of Egypt and Syria from Catholic unity after 451, was provoked more by indignation over successive imperial assaults on local culture than by any rational commitment to the heresy in question which the Council of Chalcedon had met to condemn.[18] The Church of Constantinople against which the Monophysites rebelled had become compromised by its direct link with the Byzantine government and it was this same bond that complicated its relationship with the West and produced the paradox of Greek-speaking Christians calling themselves Romans coming into

---

Nestorian heresy condemned by the Council of Ephesus, seen by the Persians as an instrument of Byzantine power.

[15] Francis Dvornik, 'Byzantium and the Roman Primacy', *American Catholic Review*, 1961, p. 299.

[16] It should be recalled that the rest of Greece, and the Greek-speaking parts of southern Italy and Sicily, then belonged to the Roman province of the Western Patriarchate and remained in that jurisdiction until the eighth century. On the other hand, all the pagan territories of Eastern Europe and Asia were assigned to Byzantine missionaries, making Constantinople an actual rival of Rome.

[17] Rome did not recognize the new status of Constantinople until the ninth century. The Council of Chalcedon also granted patriarchal status to the See of Jerusalem. It was only at the end of the seventh century that the Byzantines began to claim St Andrew as the apostolic founder of their see; the Apostle previously claimed St John the Evangelist, reputed founder of the See of Ephesus to which Constantinople was heir.

[18] Indeed the so-called Monophysite or Jacobite Churches of West Syria, Armenia, Coptic Egypt and Ethiopia never embraced extreme Monophysitism, and their official Christology, Miaphysitism (or Henophysitism), reveals itself, upon analysis, to be orthodox, since they do not actually deny the two natures of Christ and they reject the teaching of Eutyches. This fact was conceded by the Eastern Orthodox after an ecumenical meeting with theologians of the Armenian, Jacobite, Coptic and Ethiopian Churches at Aarhus, Denmark in 1964, and by Rome in April 1991 by a Joint International Commission between the Coptic Orthodox Church and the Catholic Church. Since the Aarhus meeting these Churches have adopted the epithet 'Orthodox'. As for the reputedly Nestorian faithful of the East Syrian Church, though Nestorian doctrines have been preserved to the present day, there is evidence from the early thirteenth century that the heresy of Nestorius did not form part of their ordinary beliefs, at least in Antioch. The crusader-chronicler Roger of Wendover mentions the East Syrians of that city who 'say that they believe that the two natures are united in the person of Christ. They confess that the Blessed Virgin is the mother of God and of man, and that she bore both God and man, which Nestorius denied' (Edward Peters, ed., *Christian Society and the Crusades 1198–1229* (Philadelphia, 1971), p. 121).

conflict with the original Rome.[19] Nevertheless, according to Dr Francis Dvornik there is no convincing evidence of any theoretical or substantial rejection of the supreme authority of the Roman See on the part of the Greeks until the thirteenth century.[20]

All these threats to the unity of the Church slowly brought the Papacy to a deeper understanding of its guiding role in Christendom. While fraternal supervision of the living out of apostolic tradition remained the main concern of the Eastern patriarchs, the Roman popes were increasingly conscious of having received the fullness of power which Christ had bestowed on Saint Peter: supreme authority in both the spiritual and the temporal spheres. The Bishop of Rome's supremacy in the spiritual sphere was already evident from the tradition of his (so far circumscribed) role as universal arbiter of the disputes of otherwise autonomous churches, and from the fact that the decisions of general councils were held to be invalid unless ratified by him.

Likewise, since the conversion of Constantine, the pope's privilege of anointing Roman emperors showed that the latters' right to rule was derived not directly from God, but indirectly, through Saint Peter's successors. The polity of early Christendom necessitated the existence of an emperor to govern the secular sphere, and in normal circumstances the pope should not have to intervene in affairs of state. But since as a Christian the emperor was subject to the pope, the Universal Shepherd retained in theory the right to guide, admonish and, if necessary, depose an unworthy monarch.

The Frankish Adventure

For as long as the diarchy of pope and emperor remained intact, the full implication of this theory of government was ignored, especially in the East, where imperial rule survived the fall of the Western Empire to the Ostrogoths in 476. However, the traditional arrangements were upset in 756 when the popes threw off the political authority of the Byzantine Emperor, as whose vicars they had been ruling over Latium since the creation of the Duchy of Rome around 711. This was the only imperial territory that remained free after the Byzantine Exarchate of Ravenna was seized by the Lombards in 751. Lombard expansion owed much to the Emperor Leo IV's failure in his duty to defend his North Italian dominions, urgent appeals from Pope Stephen II to send troops to protect Rome against impending Teutonic attack meeting with no response.

At this time the Papacy had an additional reason to question the value of its bond with Constantinople, for the Emperor Leo was actively pursuing the iconoclast policies of his predecessors. In 754 Rome was confronted with the deplorable

---

[19] Until the twentieth century the modern Greeks were still calling their language ρωμάϊκα, 'Roman'. The Arabic term for 'Eastern Orthodox' is *rūmi*, literally 'Roman', in contradistinction to *yunāni*, 'Greek', lit. 'Ionian'.

[20] Dvornik, 'Byzantium and the Roman Primacy', p. 300.

One thing is securely established, namely, that the Byzantine Church did not intend to question the primacy of Rome in the Church. In spite of what happened, Rome continued to be regarded as the superior of Constantinople and as the first See in the Church. The conflict can be explained by the clash of two principles in the organization of the Church – accommodation to the secular situation and the apostolic origin. (Ibid., p. 300)

spectacle of the Greek episcopate condemning the veneration of images in an almost plenary assembly, meekly bowing to the dictates of the Emperor.[21] No doubt to Stephen's mind the Papacy had more to gain than to lose from being independent of monarchs who had so often favoured or tried to impose heresy.[22]

On the feast of the Epiphany, 753, the King of the Franks had responded to Pope Stephen's personal appeal for help, and after Pepin's defeat of the Lombards three years later, the Pope named him 'Patrician of the Romans'. The Frankish king in turn established the Pope as temporal ruler of all the regions of Italy that had previously comprised the Byzantine Exarchate (Latium, Umbria, the Marches and Romagna). Pope Stephen authorized this apparent usurpation of imperial authority by appealing to the *Donation of Constantine*, the famous forgery composed by some member of his chancery.[23] The *Donation* alleged that the Emperor Constantine had invested the Bishop of Rome with imperial power and dignity, and affirmed his right to rule over the Empire's lands in Italy and the West.[24]

This was a claim never made by any of this pope's predecessors. Nevertheless, since the local temporal power of the Papacy was considered a pragmatic measure rather than an ideal, Stephen II and his successors were content to exercise their technical right to rule over the West through the agency of their protectors, the Frankish kings. As one historian puts it, Pepin 'was not yet an emperor in his own right; but he was already an emperor *in petto* to be produced as and when the Papacy required him'.[25] When Pope Leo III placed the imperial crown on the head of Pepin's son Charlemagne a generation later in 800, he did so in the expectation that the Frankish monarch, unlike the Byzantine emperors of old, would acknowledge the ultimate supremacy of the Roman pontiffs in the temporal sphere.

Although these events unfolded without any prejudice to the theory of the 'two swords' (the principle that spiritual and secular authority were in practice discrete), the new political role of the Pope, exercised simultaneously with his more important spiritual one, introduced a serious imbalance into the papal institution and, ultimately, into the social order of Latin Christendom itself. While in the East imperial and Muslim domination of the Catholic hierarchy increasingly made local churches agencies of government power, the Papacy, in ruling directly or indirectly over the feudal barbarian West, was inevitably absorbed by it, and came to embrace many of its values.

Filioque

While the psyche of the Catholic West was being transformed by the tendency to conceive of the Church in increasingly juridical terms, the Catholic East, despite the passing crisis of iconoclasm and the enduring problem of secular domination, was less tempted to abandon the patristic vision of Church and Tradition as one

[21] Duchesne, *op. cit.*, p. 48.
[22] In 729, the iconoclast emperor Constantine V, in his capacity as defender of the faith, had commanded Pope St Gregory II to remove images of saints from the churches of his patriarchate. Constantine the Great himself had favoured Arianism in the fourth century.
[23] Stephen was probably unaware that the document was a fabrication; David Knowles and Dimitri Obolensky, *The Middle Ages* (London, 1969), p. 76.
[24] This in turn had been based on an earlier, fifth-century forgery, the *Legenda Sancti Silvestri*.
[25] Richard Southern, *Western Society and the Church in the Middle Ages* (Harmondsworth, 1970), p. 60.

and the same thing. For the Easterners, as for the Church Fathers, the rule of faith was Tradition itself 'as the measure of Christian reality both doctrinally and sacramentally'. Hence 'to be a member of the Church, whether bishop, monk, layman or priest, is to be immersed in Tradition and to be responsible for it as a bishop, and responsive to it as one of the baptized'.[26]

Given that for Christians ecclesiastical authority and faith cannot be mutually opposed, real friction between Rome and the Eastern patriarchates was inevitable when popes under Frankish domination tolerated or initiated actions which seemed to the Orientals to be not only arbitrary but untraditional. The first liturgical controversy to test the unity of the Church was the *filioque* affair. In the light of past events, a new inter-ecclesial dispute involving the doctrine of the Holy Trinity augured badly.

The anti-Arian Nicaean Creed completed by the First Council of Constantinople (381) had stated that the Holy Ghost proceeds (ἐκπορευόμενον) 'from the Father'. The Greek participle used here connotes not just a coming forth (like the Latin *procedit*), but the action of flowing or proceding from a source.[27] According to the Catholic teaching the relationships of the Father with the Son, and of the Father with the Holy Spirit, are distinct. While the Son is begotten (γεννηθέντα, *genitum*) of the Father, the Spirit proceeds from the Father (ἐκπορευόμενον, *procedit*). There is only one single principle or cause of procession common to the Father and the Son, but whereas Greek theologians inferred from this that the Holy Ghost proceeds from the Father '*through* the Son', the preferred Latin explanation was that the Holy Ghost proceeds 'from the Father *and* the Son' (*ex Patre Filioque procedit*). In the latter formula, however, the Latin verb *procedit* corresponded in meaning not to the Greek ἐκπορεύεσθαι, which referred strictly to the Spirit's non-generational mode of procession from the Father, but to the verb προϊέναι. This verb signified 'proceed' in a broader sense, its primary meaning being 'to be sent'. For this reason it was chosen by the Greek Fathers of Alexandria and St Gregory Nazianzen († c. 390) to describe jointly the distinct modes in which the Son and the Holy Ghost come from the Father.[28]

The two views were complementary and enriched the theology of the Universal Church. In the main the Greek tendency was to stress the character of the Father as the first origin of the Spirit whereas the Latin approach emphasized the consubstantial communion between Father and Son.[29] Nevertheless, the Eastern idea had been expressed by Tertullian († c. 220) and St Hilary of Poitiers († c. 368),[30] while St Cyril of Alexandria († 444) had espoused the prevailing Western view. In the seventh century the Greek monk St Maximus the Confessor not only recognized that there was no doctrinal conflict between the two explanations but remarked that resultant misunderstandings between Greeks and Latins had been due to linguistic differences, since the semantic range of the Latin verb *procedere* included both ἐκπορεύεσθαι and προϊέναι.[31] In the fourteenth century Gregory Palamas

---

[26] Cross, *Eastern Christianity*, p. 47.
[27] Avery Dulles, SJ, 'The Filioque: What is at Stake?', *Concordia Theological Quarterly*, January/April 1995, pp. 43–44.
[28] Cyril of Alexandria, *Thesaurus de Sancta Consubstantiali Trinitate*, 75.585; Gregory of Nazianzus, *Oration*, 39.12.
[29] *Catechism of the Catholic Church*, p. 248.
[30] Tertullian, *Adversus Praxean*, 4,5; Hilary, *De Trinitate*, 12.56.
[31] Dulles, 'The Filioque', pp. 32, 40.

explained that while the Holy Ghost proceeds from the Father alone according to the essence of God, the Holy Ghost proceeds as 'divine energy' 'from the Father through the Son – and if one wishes, from the Son'.[32]

Towards a Divisive Creed

Doctrinal elaborations of phrases in the historical creeds are a natural part of the Church's theological life. In this spirit St Tarasius, Patriarch of Constantinople from 784 to 806, would expand the Nicene statement to read: 'the Holy Ghost, the Lord and Giver of Life, who proceeds from the Father through the Son'.[33] Similarly, Spanish divines of the fifth century had developed the same passage to read 'who proceeds from the Father and the Son' in reaction to the Arianism of the Visigothic kings, which taught that Christ was not divine but only the 'adopted son' of God the Father. This interpolation was already present in the so-called Athanasian Creed, a Gaulish text composed some time before AD 500, and in the Rule of St Benedict († 547).

However, such expansions, salutary measures to safeguard orthodoxy in both East and West, belonged to the realm of the *lex credendi*. Conflict arose when the Third Council of Toledo (589) inserted the exegetical *Filioque* interpolation into the *liturgical* form of the Nicene Creed, and the addition was judged orthodox by Pope St Gregory I the following year. The chanting of the altered Creed became widespread (though not universal) in western and northern Europe during the course of the seventh century: at the Council of Gentilly, held in 767, some French theologians were still protesting against the interpolation, which in their view compromised the *lex orandi*.[34] Meanwhile in Rome the *filioque* was not used, on the same conservative ground that, while differences of exegesis were perfectly admissible within the Church's broad theological tradition, Catholic practice considered established liturgical formulations sacrosanct.

In 794 Charlemagne, a strong supporter of the *filioque*, called the Council of Frankfurt, whose canons were of dubious orthodoxy because of their semi-iconoclast slant. Not only did the Fathers of this Frankish council sanction the addition of the *filioque* to the liturgical Creed, but they made a specific condemnation of Greek Catholics who adhered to the Symbol of Faith in its original form and held to the doctrine of the Holy Ghost's procession through the Son. The aggressive thrust of Frankfurt must, of course, be viewed against the background of growing political and cultural hostility between the old Christian civilization of Byzantium and an expanding Frankish state with imperial aspirations in Western Europe.

The Western liturgical innovation was problematical to the Greeks because the *filioque*, unlike the phrase ὁμοούσιον τῷ Πατρί 'consubstantial with the Father', added to the Creed by the First Council of Nicea, had not been accepted by the Universal Church and hence was illicit as well as strange and suspect. The Oriental

---

[32] . . . διὰ τοῦ Υἱοῦ, εἰ βούλει, καὶ ἐκ τοῦ Υἱοῦ. Knowles/Obolensky, *op. cit.*, p. 328.

[33] Mansi, XII, 1122D. See also the Pontifical Council for Promoting Christian Unity's 1995 statement 'The Greek and Latin Traditions regarding the Procession of the Holy Spirit', printed in *L'Ossservatore Romano*, 20 September 1995, pp. 3ff.

[34] The strongholds of the *filioque* were at that time Spain, where it originated, and Germany. Its introduction was resisted longer in Italy and France, and in the thirteenth century the original text of the Creed was still being sung in Paris.

Catholics of Jerusalem were therefore disturbed when, in 808, news reached the Greek monastery of St Sabas that the Latin monks of Mount Olivet had added the *filioque* to their singing of the liturgical Creed. The year before, two of these Latin monks had travelled to Aix-la-Chapelle to the court of Charlemagne, whom the Caliph Harūn al-Rashīd had recently made honorary suzerain of the Christians of Jerusalem. After hearing the interpolated Creed sung in the imperial chapel, the monks had returned to Jerusalem with the intention of introducing the same novelty into their own church. So on Christmas Day 808 the Byzantine Catholics of the city gathered to denounce the Latin monks as heterodox, and to demand that their faith be examined by the local Greek hierarchy.

The reaction of Pope St Leo III was exemplary. In the 'Creed of the Orthodox Faith' which he sent to the monks of Mount Olivet, he upheld the *filioque* as a theological truth, but not as an admissible addition to a liturgical text which was also a dogmatic monument. For Charlemagne, however, a question of imperial prestige was involved, and he intervened by calling theologians favourable to the teaching to the Council of Aix-la-Chapelle in 809. The emperor then sent to Rome his council's conclusions endorsing the insertion of the *filioque*. However, Leo simply reaffirmed his earlier ruling, pointing out to Charlemagne's legates that previous councils had expressly forbidden tampering with the text of the liturgical Creed and that the innovation moreover threatened to divide Eastern and Western Catholics. Informing them that the Roman Church did not in any case chant the Nicene Creed at Mass, Pope Leo counselled the suppression of the new custom in the imperial chapel. Then, in spite of Charlemagne's ignoring of his decision, the Pope pressed his point by having the Greek and Latin texts of the Nicene Creed engraved in silver on the wall of St Peter's Basilica, without the *filioque*, as a token of Catholic unity.[35]

St Leo's action would remain, however, a symbolic gesture out of step with the sentiment of most of his patriarchate, a church largely dominated by the Frankish Empire. Should the day come when a Roman pope endorsed the heteropraxis of certain of his subjects against the orthopraxis of the Eastern patriarchates, the scene would be set for schism . . .

The First Papal Autocrat?

St Nicholas I (858–867), a native of Rome, was the first pope to attempt to give practical effect in the spiritual sphere to the implications of earlier assertions of papal authority by Stephen II and Leo III. He set to work in his own patriarchate, where the Frankish church, under imperial tutelage, showed a considerable degree of independence in relation to the Holy See. When Rothad, the deposed Bishop of Soissons, appealed to Rome against the action of his metropolitan, Nicholas forced the Archbishop of Rheims, Hincmar, to retract his claim that the Pope had no right to review the decision of a provincial council.[36]

Next Nicholas turned his attention to the Greek Church, finding in the patriarchal dispute settled by the Constantinopolitan council of 861 a golden opportunity to make a similar show of strength. This council, to which the Pope had sent legates,

---

[35] Jeremiah J. Smith, OFM.Conv., 'Filioque Controversy', *CESH*, IV, pp. 291–92.
[36] Leonard Mahoney, 'St Nicholas I', *CESH*, VII, p. 626.

had confirmed the distinguished scholar Photius as successor to Patriarch Ignatius, who had resigned from office under pressure from Emperor Michael III following the fall of his patroness, the Empress Theodora, in 856.[37] Pope Nicholas, however, supported the Ignatian party's claim that the deposition of the former patriarch was canonically invalid, and accordingly annulled the decisions of his legates. In 863 he convoked a new council in Rome which declared Photius deposed and reinstated St Ignatius as rightful Patriarch of Constantinople.[38]

Now the majority of the Byzantine bishops, who knew only the canons of Sardica, protested that the decisions of 861 were binding and that the recent papal actions were *ultra vires*.[39] Nicholas' claiming of power 'over all the earth, that is, over every church' did not seem to the Greeks to justify the ignoring of traditional rules of procedure which required the Pope to order any retrial in the territory of the dispute, not in Rome.[40] But Nicholas insisted, plausibly enough, that he was responding to a request to intervene from aggrieved Byzantine Christians, in this case the Ignatian party.

As the dispute worsened, the Greeks claimed to have difficulty in recognizing in Pope Nicholas 'the Bishop who presides in love', as St Ignatius of Antioch had described the successor of Peter at the end of the second century. Nicholas' dismay at the insubordination and arrogance of the Byzantine litigants peaked in 867, when an equally indignant Photius summoned another council in Constantinople which declared Nicholas excommunicate and gave proof of its anti-Western sentiments by denouncing the *filioque* as heretical.[41] In the eyes of the Pope, the Patriarch of Constantinople had now clearly exceeded his authority. Later that same year Photius was deposed by the Emperor Basil I and condemned by a new council of Eastern bishops. Finally, the wheel turned full circle when Ignatius died in 877 and Photius was again elected patriarch, then formally reconciled with Pope John VIII at the Constantinopolitan council of 879.[42]

A century later Photius, whom the Greeks now considered fully vindicated, was canonized by the Church of Constantinople, and in the inter-ecclesial controversies to come the Byzantines would make no practical distinction between monarchy and autocracy. Their understanding of the role of the Papacy in the Church suffered as a result.

The Duel of Theory and Practice

Rome had won the day in this dispute, but the fundamental questions had not been resolved. Had St Nicholas gone beyond his powers, as the Byzantines alleged? In fact, depositions and rehabilitations of Eastern bishops and patriarchs by Roman popes were nothing new in the history of the Church. In 346 Pope Julius I had reversed the deposition, by the Council of Tyre, of St Athanasius, and Pope St

---

[37] Ignatius fell into disfavour because, as a rigorist, he recommended harsh treatment of former Iconoclast clergy who had returned to orthodoxy. Knowles/Obolensky, *op. cit.*, p. 98.

[38] Knowles/Obolensky, *op. cit.*, pp. 98–99; Ware, *op. cit.*, pp. 61–63.

[39] Knowles/Obolensky, *op. cit.*, p. 100.

[40] Ware, *op. cit.*, p. 62.

[41] This council, which excluded the Latins, was subsequently reckoned uncanonical by both the Roman and Byzantine Churches.

[42] Ibid., p. 64.

Innocent I (401–417) similarly reinstated St John Chrysostom, who had been banished from his patriarchal see of Constantinople by the Empress Eudoxia. Pope Leo I annulled the decree of the Eutychian 'Robber Synod' of Ephesus (449) which had deposed St Flavian of Constantinople, Bishop Eusebius of Doryleum and Bishop Theodoret of Cyr. In 536 Pope Agapitus I personally deposed Anthimius, the crypto-Monophysite Byzantine patriarch.[43]

All of these were cases of papal support for orthodox Eastern bishops against their heretical or immoral adversaries, the pontiffs in question responding to direct appeals from the Eastern Churches for them to adjudicate personally or to send out Roman legates to arbitrate in accordance with the canons of Sardica. In the year 483, when Felix III excommunicated Acacius, Patriarch of Constantinople, for having promoted an imperially sponsored compromise favouring Monophysite error, the papal action on this occasion resulted in a schism lasting three and a half decades. Pope Felix had summoned Acacius to Rome to account for his actions, but the patriarch refused to go, on the legitimate grounds that no appeal had been lodged in Rome by any Eastern bishop and that any trial should take place in Constantinople. Nevertheless, since a serious question of heresy was involved and since the Greek clergy and faithful as a whole regretted the break with Rome, on Maundy Thursday 519 their leaders acknowledged the justness of Pope Felix's extraordinary action against Acacius. This reconciliation confirmed Pope Hormisdas' *Formula*, which declared that the Apostolic See had never erred in its dogmatic teaching, and that the final test of orthodox belief was full agreement with Rome in doctrinal matters.[44]

The Acacian schism had been an isolated event, and three centuries later, when Nicholas I and Patriarch Photius were locked in conflict, the Easterners had not yet thought out the logical consequences of the Pope's primacy as manifested by the Formula of St Hormisdas. They were aware, moreover, that there was no question of heresy in the current dispute. For his part, in claiming universal ordinary jurisdiction St Nicholas was simply applying the declaration of Pope Gelasius I (492–496) that 'the see of Blessed Peter has the right to loose what has been bound by the decisions of any bishop whatever'.[45] The position that the Roman pontiff has an ordinary, immediate and universal jurisdiction in the Church would become a *de fide* dogma of Catholicism.[46] At the same time, the constitution of the Church, reflecting the nature of all social bodies, had from the beginning recognized the existence and the importance of intermediary communities between the members and their head, that is to say, the reality that the Universal Church is made up of churches: the dioceses and patriarchates of apostolic institution. The *usual* manner of exercising the ordinary universal jurisdiction of the Roman Pope was through the patriarchs and bishops, episcopal power being founded on that of the Supreme Pontiff.

---

[43] Duchesne, *op. cit.*, pp. 134–35.
[44] Bernard Reilly, 'St Hormisdas', *CESH*, V, p. 284.
[45] Henry Chadwick, *The Early Church* (Harmondsworth, 1967), p. 245.
[46] DS 3060–61.

Pious Mother or Mistress of Slaves?

From the Roman perspective this ecclesiology was a legitimate doctrinal development, even if other Churches had not realized the full implications of the primacy
of Peter. But on the Roman side there was a tendency to forget that it ran counter
to the constitution of the Church for the Papacy to reduce patriarchates and dioceses to the rank of administrative circumscriptions, and to turn the patriarchs and
bishops themselves into mere functionaries of a central power without any real
relationship with the local communities they serve. Occasional failures to respect
these twin realities were dangerous lapses, and proved to be factors of schism in
the Catholic East.

The root problem was the fact that the dogma of the universal jurisdiction
had not yet been defined by a general council and hence formally accepted by the
whole Church. As for the position of the Greeks, it was archaic and incomplete
rather than culpably heretical. However, since ecumenical councils had always
been convoked principally to define doctrine in the context of condemnations of
heresy, and since the the actual dispute had been settled and the Greeks had not
rejected supreme Roman authority in principle, there seemed to be no good reason
to assemble the bishops of the world again in 863. Nevertheless, had St Nicholas
called an ecumenical council to dispel all doubts during the conflict with Photius,
the future course of history might have been very different.

Unhappily, whereas the law of charity and concern for the unity of the Church
counselled some form of theological discussion respectful of the traditions and
mentality of the other patriarchates, Pope Nicholas I opted on this occasion to
exercise his office in a heavy-handed way that recalled the iron rule of the recently
deceased Emperor Charlemagne.[47] Behind this act of papal imperiousness the
Greeks perceived – rightly or wrongly – a despotic conviction that the Supreme
Pontiff was free to act at his pleasure, an impression lamented three centuries later
in the much-quoted letter of Nicetas, Orthodox Archbishop of Nicodemia, to the
German bishop Anselm of Havelberg, in 1136:

> My dearest brother, we do not deny to the Roman Church the primacy amongst
> the five sister Patriarchates; and we recognize her right to the most honourable
> seat at an Ecumenical Council. But she has separated herself from us by her own
> deeds, when through pride she assumed a monarchy which does not belong to
> her office . . . How shall we accept from her decrees that have been issued with-
> out consulting us and even without our knowledge? If the Roman Pontiff, seated
> on the lofty throne of his glory, wishes to thunder at us and, so to speak, hurl his
> mandates at us from on high, and if he wishes to judge us and even to rule us and
> our Churches, not by taking counsel from us but at his own arbitrary pleasure,
> what kind of brotherhood, or even what kind of parenthood can this be? We
> should be the slaves, not the sons, of such a Church, and the Roman See would
> not be the pious mother but a hard and imperious mistress of slaves.[48]

---

[47] Dom David Knowles writes that 'the language of the pope's letters is at times drastic, almost
brutal, in its remorseless logic' (Knowles/Obolensky, *op. cit.*, p. 78).

[48] S. Runciman, *The Eastern Schism* (Oxford, 1955), p. 116, and repeated in Ware, *op. cit.*, p. 58,
and in Knowles/Obolensky, *op. cit.*, p. 101. Lothair III, the Holy Roman Emperor, had sent
Anselm to Constantinople to secure a Byzantine alliance and there he had debated publicly with
the Greek metropolitan.

In the evolving dispute between East and West everything would now turn on the definition of the term 'monarchy' which, as the above passage demonstrates, had come to mean different things for Latins and Greeks. In fairness to St Nicholas, one might perhaps measure his need to assert the Pope's ordinary universal jurisdiction against Constantinople's comparatively poorer record of doctrinal orthodoxy. However, from the realization that the Orient needed the guidance of Rome in doctrinal matters and in clerical disputes it was a short leap to the erroneous idea that their internal affairs, liturgical matters included, needed to be regulated directly and without consultation by the Roman pontiff.

6

PIETY AND POWER

> *But when tradition is not listened to any more, when the Pope is the
> only guide proposed, and he has been taken unawares, and when the
> true source of truth, that is, tradition, is excluded, truth is no longer
> free to appear . . .*
>
> PASCAL, PENSÉES, 865

There is a certain poetic justice in the recent destruction of the Roman liturgy by its very custodians when one considers the past behaviour, both official and unofficial, of Roman-rite Catholics towards Catholics of other traditions. As for the Orthodox, they see, rightly or wrongly, a cause-and-effect relationship between papal claims of universal ordinary jurisdiction and the sorry history of repeated 'Frankish' attacks on the liturgical and cultural traditions of Eastern Christians who came under Latin rule, attacks which in many cases destroyed communion with the Holy See. Roman-rite traditionalist dissidents today might well draw the analogy of their own anomalous situation *vis-à-vis* their lawful patriarch. And yet full papal authority does not necessarily imply the cultural imperialism it has so often engendered.

Unity and Uniformity

The Roman Patriarch's universal jurisdiction, enjoyed by divine right, in fact imposes a limit on papal power, a limit which, given the natural law and the obligations of charity, ensures that the Supreme Pontiff upholds the Apostolic Faith and never impugns any immemorial custom constitutive of orthopraxis. On this one point of the problematical papal claims ecumenical agreement is, in fact, possible, for while Catholics accord the Pope a plenary power which Orthodox deny him beyond his own patriarchate,[1] both Catholics and Orthodox concur that the Bishop of Rome is morally bound to respect the legitimate and orthodox customs of his own and every other apostolic church.

    The whole question of cultural imperialism in the Church hinges on the two principles of unity and uniformity, which though unequal and mutually exclusive, were often equated and allowed to become a factor of division among Christians.

---

[1] The Orthodox grant the Pope, as metropolitan and patriarch, the technical authority to order a liturgical reform in the West, just as they uphold the ritual reforms of Russian Patriarch Nikon which, in the seventeenth century, provoked the schism of the Old Believers.

Apostolic tradition has always insisted on absolute unity in matters of faith and morals, and the historical role of Rome, as the first See, has been that of responsibility for the dogmatic integrity of the Universal Church. By contrast, the discipline and worship animating the life of each church (i.e. diocese) of Christendom was not originally intended to be the object of universal legislation, but rather the outcome of an authentic synthesis of Catholic faith and local culture. Thus there is a synergy here of the two distinct but complementary ecclesial models: the 'communion model' functioning at the local level and the 'juridical model' working above it. Within this synergy there has always been pluralism, not uniformity, in non-doctrinal matters.

In the light of these fundamentals, truisms like 'rite follows patriarchate' need to be treated with great caution, for the fact that all the churches of a given province or patriarchate may present a picture of relative uniformity in liturgical matters is no proof that this cultural consensus was not achieved by natural and equitable means. The dynamic of ritual development dictated that change in custom and worship be effected by the ruling class of a given society: it was always the higher clergy and the scholars of the local church who decided, in periods of cultural crisis, whether local tradition would be maintained, modified, or abandoned. Where the decision was taken to imitate or adopt more prestigious foreign forms, usually those of the metropolitan or patriarchal see, the change was, in the polity of the early Church, a completely voluntary one.

The replacement of this centripetal process based on natural development by a centrifugal one realized by intrusive legislation was an innovation of the Roman Church, and is clearly linked with the growth of monarchical government described in the previous chapter. While there was wide agreement throughout the Universal Church that a certain degree of ritual uniformity was desirable for practical reasons, Rome's growing predilection for a compulsory uniformity allegedly consonant with her primacy was strenuously resisted by her sister churches during the first Christian millennium.

Liturgical Absolutism

What might be aptly termed liturgical absolutism, the placing of local liturgical and disciplinary matters (of relative importance) on the same level as universal doctrinal prescriptions (of absolute importance), began early in the Church of Rome. Those pontiffs initially guilty of this error were, however, concerned only with the forms of individual Christian rituals, not with local rites in themselves.

The first recorded case of a contested papal intervention arose over the Easter controversy. In the second century the churches of Asia Minor were accustomed to celebrating Easter three days after the Jewish Passover (14 Nisan), which might fall on any day of the week. In Rome and the West, on the other hand, the custom was to celebrate the Lord's resurrection on the Sunday following the Passover. Now there was a growing consensus throughout the Church that the latter custom was preferable, and Pope Anicetus (d. 166) supported those Oriental bishops who believed that the Judaic tradition ought to be discontinued wherever it was still in use.[2]

---

[2] Miroslav Turek, 'Easter Controversy', *CESH*, III, p. 622.

However, when Pope Victor I took the unprecedented step of excommunicating those 'Quartodeciman' churches refusing to conform to the majority practice, he was reproached by St Irenaeus, Bishop of Lyons (who himself followed the Roman custom), for using force in what was essentially an optional matter. In his letter to the Pope, Irenaeus pleaded that an immemorial custom which had previously caused no difficulty should not be impugned. The inefficacy of Pope Victor's intervention is evident from the fact that the question was not settled until the First Council of Nicaea (325), when the Asian churches finally agreed to give up their controversial usage.[3]

Papal preoccupation with liturgical uniformity reappears with St Innocent I, who in 416 complained that the diocese of Iguvium (Gubbio) in Umbria had not yet adopted the Roman liturgy.[4] A few decades later, the Sicilian bishops were admonished by Pope St Leo I (440–461) for following the local Greek custom of baptizing at the Epiphany instead of at Easter and Pentecost. The Sicilians seem nevertheless to have ignored their patriarch, since the same reproach was made to them and to their fellow bishops of Calabria and Lucania by Pope St Gelasius I (492–496). The latter also tried to impose on the Italiots the Saturday fast and the Roman custom of ordaining priests and deacons on Ember Days.[5]

The Cultural Schism

From the fifth century papal interference in the liturgical life of local churches was perhaps compensation for Rome's feelings of inadequacy since Constantine's transfer of the imperial capital to Byzantium, whose bishops soon rose to patriarchal status. During the seventh century Greek replaced Latin as the official language of the Byzantine Empire, and as Latin was gradually forgotten by educated Easterners, so too was much of the religious culture of the West. Since the Greek East was the richest and most cultured section of Christendom, it was inevitable that the Greeks should begin to look down on the Latin West, dominated as it was by men they deemed uncouth and illiterate barbarians. Ritual and disciplinary differences also gave rise, in the minds of arrogant Greeks and ignorant Latins, to mutual suspicions of an underlying heterodoxy. In 668, when Pope St Vitalian appointed the Greek Theodore of Tarsus Archbishop of Canterbury, he also sent the Roman-rite abbot Hadrian with instructions to see that Theodore 'introduced no Greek customs contrary to the true Faith into England'.[6]

The re-evangelization of the European continent by Irish monks in the seventh and eighth centuries spread a brand of Western Christianity to which the Greek tradition had little relevance. At bottom the difference between Eastern and Western culture was a philosophical one:

---

[3] St Victor wrote to several churches of Europe and Asia advising them to adopt the Roman custom, and several did, but of their own volition.

[4] Fortescue, *The Mass*, p. 98, n. 3.

[5] 'You would not have fallen into this fault if you had taken the rule of your observance from that place where you received the honour of consecration; if the See of blessed Peter, which is the mother of your sacerdotal dignity, had been the teacher of your ecclesiastical custom' (Adrian Fortescue, *Uniate Eastern Churches: The Byzantine Rite in Italy, Sicily, Syria and Egypt* [London, 1923], p. 71).

[6] Southern, *op. cit.*, p. 56. Admittedly, Pope Vitalian was concerned about the spread of Monotheletism, which Peter, the former Patriarch of Constantinople (654–666), was favouring.

From the very beginning the Christian culture of the West differed from those of the East by greater emphasis on man, suggested by certain strands of Hellenistic philosophy, and by a well-developed practical spirit inherited from ancient Rome. Whereas in the East Christians liked to speculate about God and, under the influence of Platonism, stressed the seeking of mystical union with God, the West, swayed more by Roman pragmatism and by Stoic doctrine (with all that this implied of naturalism), concentrated on man, on his problems, and on the organization of society, both ecclesiastical and civil.[7]

The first significant strain in East–West relations came in 692, when the Synod in Trullo (or Quinisext Synod, called by Emperor Justinian II to clarify points of discipline not settled by the Third Council of Constantinople in 680) condemned those liturgical customs of other churches that did not agree with Greek usages. This synod, whose decrees show that liturgical absolutism had also become a vice of the ambitious Byzantine patriarchate, censured the Armenians for eating eggs and cheese on the Sundays in Lent and for not mixing water with wine in the eucharistic chalice. The African Christians were reproved for celebrating the Eucharist immediately after the Maundy Thursday repast in simulation of the Last Supper. But the strongest strictures were reserved for the Roman Church, which celebrated Mass on the weekdays of Lent, fasted on Saturdays during the penitential seasons, limited the number of Roman deacons to seven and, above all, preferred a celibate parish clergy.[8]

This last institution of the Latins most disturbed the Greeks, whose bishops wanted to oblige the West to abandon it as a heterodox innovation. Here the Easterners smelt puritanism, a defect derived, ironically enough, from Greek Stoic and Neo-Platonic strands in early Roman Christianity, and no doubt compounded by a dose of barbarian simplism. Other puritan customs of the West that shocked the more sophisticated (and so more easy-going) Greeks were the discouraging of frequent communion, refusal to accept widows as nuns, the keeping of slaves by Latin monks, and permission for clerics to bear arms and to take part in warfare.[9]

Since Rome formed the bridge to the East in the barbarian West, the greatest wound to the sense of intercultural religious brotherhood was inflicted in 756, when Pope Stephen II threw off the political authority of the Byzantine Empire. Seeing himself as the ruler and protector of all Christians, it was natural for the East Roman emperor to view the now independent Latins as less than Catholic. Before the foundation of the Papal States, the truly ecumenical character of the papal office had been evident from the many nationalities of its incumbents who, though bishops of Rome and Latin patriarchs, were also shepherds of the Universal Church. Thus in the hundred years preceding the pontificate of Stephen II, eleven out of seventeen popes had been of Greek ethnic or cultural background. Stephen was the first of a new line of Latin popes which was not broken until the election of the Greek Franciscan, Alexander V, seven centuries later.[10]

If Eastern Catholics were becoming increasingly indifferent to their co-religionists in the West, Germanic and German-dominated Christians, strongly attached as

---

[7] Neri Capponi, 'La nevrosi dell'Occidente', unpublished article (Florence, 1991), p. 4.
[8] Duchesne, *op. cit.*, p. 141.
[9] Southern, *op. cit.*, p. 57.
[10] Elected by the Council of Pisa in 1409 to bring an end to the Great Schism of the West, Alexander V is considered an antipope by some historians.

they were to the Papacy, were growing impatient of the Pope's relations with the Greek Church. Behaving like jealous sons of a previous marriage, the barbarian rulers of the West did not want to share their great Father in Rome, who had brought them the precious gifts of the true Faith and Roman civilization, with those they considered mere half-brothers. During a visit to the Holy See in 704, the English bishop St Wilfrid felt slighted when, after addressing Pope John VI (a native of Greece) in Latin, the latter turned to his advisers and conversed with them in Greek, a language Wilfrid did not understand.[11]

The Barbarian Challenge

After Pope Leo III's fateful crowning of Charlemagne in Rome on Christmas Day, 800, the Frankish monarch with the title 'Emperor of all Christians' showed the same inclination as his Byzantine rival to equate Catholicism and imperial citizenship. Already, six years before the foundation of the Holy Roman Empire, the pro-iconoclastic stance of the Council of Frankfurt had been intended as a direct challenge to the Pope, whose support of the anti-iconoclastic Greeks in this matter was simple-mindedly interpreted by Charles as disloyalty to his state and to the Catholic West in general.

Charlemagne's interference in religious matters, which at times brought the Church within his realm to the brink of heterodoxy, was continued after his death by the Frankish bishops in the Eastern Kingdom of Lewis the German. But whereas Leo III had bravely confronted the Franks in the Iconoclast controversy and the *filioque* affair, his successor, Pope John VIII, though even more anti-German by disposition, wavered during the Moravian liturgical dispute.

In 862 ambassadors of Prince Ratislav, ruler of Moravia (then including present-day Slovakia) arrived in Constantinople requesting Slavonic-speaking priests to replace the Frankish clergy who had recently brought the Faith to his realm. The political motive behind Ratislav's request was to weaken Frankish cultural influence at home. The Emperor Michael III entrusted the Moravian mission to two deacons, the brothers Constantine (later Cyril) and Methodius. The latter had invented the Glagolitic alphabet for the Slavonic language, at that time spoken in the neighbourhood of his native Thessalonica.

Since Moravia belonged to the Roman patriarchate, celebration of the Byzantine rite in Slavonic by the priests of the Greek mission offended the local Frankish missionaries on the two counts of ritual impropriety and linguistic innovation. When, in 864, Lewis the German defeated Ratislav and Greater Moravia became a vassal state of the East Franks, the hostility of the Latin clergy became formidable, and Constantine and Methodius judged it prudent to adopt the so-called Liturgy of St Peter, a Greek Mass rite containing the Roman Canon, which they translated into Slavonic.[12] Such a concession could hardly satisfy the Franks, who protested

---

[11] Southern, *op. cit.*, p. 57.

[12] Cyril Korolevsky, *Living Languages in Catholic Worship: An Historical Inquiry*, tr. Donald Attwater (London, 1957), p. 74. This ritual usage recalled a time when the dioceses of Athens, Patras and Thessalonica had belonged to the Roman province. The other churches of Greece developed liturgies of the Antiochene type (one of which was that of Byzantium), but the bishoprics subject to Rome followed Milan and other liturgically non-Roman sees in adopting the anaphora of the Papal Church. In Greece the Roman Canon was naturally translated into

to Rome about the missionaries' use of a barbarian tongue in the sacred liturgy.

The eclipse of liturgical Latin, the Byzantine culture of the newcomers, and the welcome given them by Kocel, the Slavic prince of neighbouring Pannonia (modern Hungary), were all a provocation to their Frankish rivals, who had powerful friends in Rome. In 867, during a stay in Venice, where Constantine and Methodius had over fifty of their Moravian and Pannonian disciples priested, the brothers were obliged to defend their liturgical use of Slavonic against proponents of the so-called 'trilingual heresy', the opinion that only the three languages of Holy Scripture, Hebrew,[13] Greek and Latin, were permissible in divine worship.

Catholic Language Policy

That same year, Pope Adrian II called the two brothers to Rome to discuss their difficulties. Enthusiastic at the prospect of gaining another missionary church directly subject to the Holy See rather than to the Frankish bishops, the Pope gave wholehearted support to the linguistic policy of the Greek missionaries. In the bull *Gloria in Excelsis* Adrian based his ruling on what might be conveniently termed the *literary principle*, the custom allowing the celebration of the sacred mysteries in any vernacular tongue into which the Bible (or at least substantial portions of it) had already been translated.

The literary principle had already permitted the introduction of (Western) Syriac, Coptic, Armenian and Georgian as liturgical languages in various Oriental churches alongside the original Greek. Moreover, if Latin had hitherto been the only other ritual medium in the Roman patriarchate, it was because no-one in the culturally Latin West had so far thought to create religious literatures from any of the welter of Celtic, Germanic or emerging Romance vernaculars spoken there. No-one except the Arian Goths, whose use of their East Germanic native tongue as a scriptural and liturgical language served to associate 'barbarian' languages with heresy in black-and-white Western minds. If the West Germans, overawed by Roman greatness, had opted not to cultivate their own language, that was their prerogative, but they had no right to impose their solution on the Slavs, the Pope evidently reasoned.

In authorizing the ritual use of the Slavonic language, Pope Adrian insisted at the same time that in celebrations of the Eucharist the Epistle and Gospel be sung in Latin before being chanted in Slavonic. By this ruling the pontiff was confirming another Catholic liturgical principle, that of *linguistic continuity*. This required that whenever the literary principle justified a change from an ancient liturgical language to a vernacular, some vestiges of the former should remain as a tradition of the church in question. Thus the Roman rite, celebrated principally in Latin

---

Greek. While Sts Constantine and Methodius took the Liturgy of St Peter to Greater Moravia, in the ninth century other Greek missionaries took it across the Black Sea to Georgia where, however, the liturgy of Byzantium had been dominant since the Council of Chalcedon (451) when the Georgians, breaking with the Miaphysite Armenians, abandoned the Syriac rite of St James.

[13] Medieval Christians constantly confused Hebrew with its sister language Aramaic (the ecclesiastical variant of which is termed Syriac), the actual vernacular of Our Lord. Both Hebrew and Aramaic were languages of the Old Testament, but the 'Hebrew' inscription placed (with the Latin and Greek ones) on the Cross (Jn 19.20), was in fact in Aramaic. Similarly the normal liturgical language of the judaizing Hebrew church of the first century was Aramaic, not Hebrew.

by Adrian's time, had retained some vestiges of the earlier Greek: the *Kyrie* and *Trisagion* chants, and the custom of singing the Gospel in both Greek and Latin at papal Masses. Likewise the West Syrian and Egyptian Churches interspersed their Syriac and Coptic liturgies with Greek formulas, as did the Armenians. And all Catholic rites preserved isolated Hebrew words forming a direct link to the religion of the Old Covenant: *alleluia, hosanna, Sabaoth, amen.*

Franks versus Catholicity

To press these two points, Pope Adrian ordained Methodius priest and invited him and four of his followers to sing Mass in Slavonic in various Roman churches. Constantine and Methodius then returned to their mission fully vindicated.[14] A few months after the death of Constantine in 869, the Pope appointed Methodius Archbishop of Sirmium (modern Srijem), a city on the Danube designated to be the seat of a large missionary diocese including both Pannonia and Greater Moravia. The setting up of this new jurisdiction effectively forced the Frankish clergy out of the region. However, the latter, determined to win the day, exerted their influence on Prince Svatopluk, who had recently deposed his uncle Ratislav, and was now a pawn of Lewis the German.

Foremost among Methodius' enemies was Bishop Hermanrich, out of whose Bavarian diocese of Passau the Pope had carved the new metropolitan see. In 870 Svatopluk allowed this prelate to have Methodius arrested and tried by a synod of Frankish bishops in Regensburg. Condemned as a usurper, Methodius was imprisoned at the Swabian monastery of Ellwangen.[15] It was only four years later that the Pope, hearing of the new archbishop's fate, ordered his release and restored him to his see.

Adrian II died soon after, and before the end of 874 the Frankish party had managed to bully the new Pope, John VIII, into prohibiting the Slavonic liturgy in the archdiocese of Sirmium. Deeming the papal ban illicit, Methodius and his clergy ignored it and laboured on regardless, braving the constant harassment of Frankish priests. In 880 the Archbishop had an opportunity to travel to Rome, where he persuaded the Pope to rescind his earlier prohibition. The resultant bull, *Industriæ Tuæ*, clearly restated the literary principle:

> It is certainly not against faith or doctrine to sing the Mass in the Slavonic language, or to read the Holy Gospel or the divine lessons of the New and Old Testaments well translated and interpreted, or to chant the other offices of the hours, for He who made the three principal languages, Hebrew, Greek and Latin, also created all the others for His own glory and praise.[16]

Unfortunately for St Methodius, one of the members of his Moravian delegation was a Frankish priest called Wiching who, apart from having episcopal ambitions, was secretly a member of the anti-Slavonic party. Complying with the wishes of

[14] Knowles/Obolensky, *op. cit.*, p. 23.
[15] Vittorio Peri, *Lo scambio fraterno tra le chiese: Componenti storiche della comunione* (Vatican City, 1993), p. 153.
[16] Migne, *Patrologia latina*, Vol. 126, col. 906.

the Moravian king, Pope John appointed this favoured cleric Bishop of Nitra in Slovakia, the most important suffragan see of Methodius' archdiocese. But Wiching was not satisfied with his promotion. While in Rome, he obtained through bribery a forged papal letter which claimed that John VIII had strictly forbidden the liturgical use of Slavonic and that Methodius had vowed at the tomb of St Peter to discontinue the practice. Back in Moravia, Svatopluk gave credence to Wiching's forgery rather than to the letter presented by Methodius, and the Slavonic liturgy came under attack once again.[17] The diocese of Nitra thus became the linchpin of the liturgical relatinization of Greater Moravia.

Meanwhile in Rome the partisans of the aspirant pope Formosus (then Bishop of Oporto in Portugal and a principal target of John's purges of 876), took advantage of the pontiff's death in 882 to remove all the *regesta* of the papal archives referring to the period following 1 September 875.[18] Thus Pope John's legislation in favour of Old Slavonic was permanently lost. When St Methodius died in 885, Bishop Wiching made an appeal to the current Pope, Stephen V who, being ignorant of his predecessor's ruling, was easily taken in by Wiching's deception and outlawed what remained of the Slavonic liturgy.[19] Armed now with a legal pretext, the Franks lost no time banishing the Slavonic clergy from Pannonia and Moravia and reclaiming the See of Sirmium for the Latin language.

The Battle for Bulgaria

In the 860s, at the same time that Sts Constantine and Methodius were launching their mission in Moravia, a major dispute between the patriarchates arose over the evangelization of Bulgaria, another zone of Slavonic speech. In late imperial times the greater part of this region had been the province of Moesia, culturally Latin and ecclesiastically subject to the Roman patriarchate, even though it belonged administratively to the Eastern Empire. Christianity was virtually extinguished there by two successive waves of sixth- and seventh-century pagan invaders, the Slavs and the Asiatic Bulgars.

After the foundation of the Bulgar khanate in 681, the local church revived through the presence of Christian slaves, then under the care of missionaries from Constantinople. In spite of its Latin origins, and the legal claim of Rome to what had been Moesia, the Church in Bulgaria was therefore Greek in rite and *de facto* jurisdiction. Around 790 Pope Adrian I demanded in vain that the Byzantine emperor Constantine VI detach the bishops of Moesia from the obedience of Constantinople and transfer them to that of Rome, naturally without any expectation of a change of rite.

When the Khan Boris received Greek baptism in 865 and decided to make Christianity the official religion of his kingdom, his plan was to secure an autonomous Bulgarian hierarchy under a patriarch, but the Byzantine metropolitan, at that time Photius, would not even grant him a bishop. Boris then turned to Lewis

---

[17] Korolevsky, *op. cit.*, pp. 77–79. It is thought that Wiching obtained the forged letter from a papal notary called Gregory (ibid., pp. 82–83).

[18] Ibid., p. 80–81. Formosus was actually elected pope in 891 and reigned for five years. The documentation of the year following 01/09/875 was destroyed and the successive sections were hidden in the monastery of Monte Cassino.

[19] Ibid., p. 84.

the German, stating his willingness to subject his church to the Roman patriarchate should the Pope accede to his wishes. Aware that Bulgaria was technically subject to his jurisdiction, Nicholas I offered the Khan an archbishop, and in 866 the whole region was confirmed as belonging to the Roman patriarchate.

Anxious as the Greek Church was to keep neighbouring Bulgaria within its orbit, it had no choice but to accept the new situation. However, relations soured between Rome and Constantinople when St Nicholas, instead of sending Greek priests from Southern Italy or Latin ones under instruction to adopt the local Byzantine rite, opened the territory to Latin-rite missionaries from Aquileia and Greater Bavaria. The existing Byzantine clergy were not expelled, but the new bishops, in reorganizing the Bulgarian Church along Western lines, went about putting down Greek customs that differed from Latin ones. Greek parish priests were not only ordered to drive their wives and children out of their houses but even forbidden to continue supporting them, and the sacrament of confirmation, administered directly after baptism in the Byzantine rite, was systematically repeated in the case of Bulgarians who changed over to the Roman rite. The Latin use of the *filioque* in the liturgies of the Eucharist and baptism was another source of scandal to the Greek Christians.[20]

Complaints of Latin persecution in Bulgaria soon reached Constantinople. Patriarch Photius, already hostile to Rome because of his excommunication by Nicholas I in 863, denounced these 'irreligious men who dare to call themselves bishops', who had 'sprung out of the darkness', hailing as they did from 'the western lands where the sun, instead of shining, goes down, giving way to the night', and whose misdeeds in Bulgaria were like 'a thunderbolt, a thick hailstorm, or the unleashing of some wild boar sent to lay waste the Lord's vineyard'.[21] Meanwhile Photius' diplomats successfully persuaded the Bulgarian king to change his allegiance back to Constantinople, promising him this time a semi-autonomous archbishop. So in 870 the Latin bishops and priests were dismissed by Patriarch Ignatius (who had succeeded Photius), and Bulgaria was restored forever to Byzantine Christianity.

Constantinople was appeased, and within twelve years Photius had been rehabilitated after his deposition in 867 and communion with Rome restored. Among other things the Constantinopolitan Council of 879/880 made the following solemn declaration:

> each Throne has handed down to it by tradition several ancient customs, and these should cause no-one to enter into conflict or argument. Indeed the Church of the Romans observes her own usages, and that is as should be. Likewise the Church of the Constantinopolitans observes several customs which she has received from the distant past, as do the Eastern Thrones [Antioch, Jerusalem and Alexandria].[22]

When the Slavonic clergy were expelled from Moravia and Pannonia in 885, Rome's loss – this time the result of her inability to maintain her Catholic principles against the pretensions of an aggressive Frankish episcopate – became Constantinople's gain. The disciples of Sts Constantine and Methodius found refuge in Bulgaria,

[20] Peri, *op. cit.*, p. 56.
[21] Ibid., pp. 55–56.
[22] Mansi, *SCNAC*, XVII, 489.

whose king was naturally delighted to find his dream of a vernacular Christianity suddenly coming true. With the blessing of Constantinople, the refugees replaced Greek with Slavonic in the rites of the local church and, abandoning the complicated Glagolitic script they had been using in the Roman patriarchate,[23] fashioned a new ('Cyrillic') alphabet from Greek and Hebrew characters. Bulgaria benefited from the flowering of a vigorous Slavic Christian culture which, a century later, played a pivotal role in the evangelization of the Kievan Rus by Byzantine-rite missionaries.[24]

Storm Clouds

In the collective consciousness of the Church, papal vindication of the (nevertheless ill-fated) Slavonic liturgy against the claims of the Frankish trilingualists, as well as the victory scored by Greek Christianity over Latin Christianity in Bulgaria, confirmed the Catholic principle that the cultural integrity of a people must, under the law of charity, take precedence over the juridical powers of hierarchs to enforce liturgical uniformity. Moreover, at the conference held in Constantinople in 870 to settle the question of Bulgaria's juridical status, the legates of Pope Adrian II had simultaneously confirmed the *local principle*, which asserted that the traditional usages of a church should be respected and preserved, and the *pluralist principle*, according to which any number of local ritual uses might be tolerated within the one ecclesiastical jurisdiction:

> Diversity of languages [read, rites] does not disturb the ecclesiastical order. For the Apostolic See, though she herself is Latin, nevertheless in many places has always until the present day set up priests [read, bishops] who, on account of their nationality, are of the Greek rite. Nor does she, or has she ever, felt this to be detrimental to her privileges.[25]

Nevertheless, in view of the Latin doings in Bulgaria, the admission had come rather late. The logic of this vindication of the local and pluralist principles was all too clear to the Byzantines: Rome had deserved to lose Bulgaria. Moreover, the spirit of Latin expansionism that had fuelled the Bulgarian adventure was not exorcised, and would endure in Christendom as a bad example to the Oriental Churches themselves and as a future factor of schism.[26]

---

[23] The Glagolitic alphabet continued in use among the Croatians until the 1920s, when it definitively gave way to Latin characters in their service books.

[24] It is worth noting in this connexion that it was precisely the same Frankish hierarchy that had destroyed the Slavonic religious culture of Moravia that oversaw the conversion of the Polish state from 967. The introduction of Latin Christianity brought into being a Slav political power that would always be uncompromisingly western in outlook, and predestined to sharp conflicts with its eastern Slav neighbours of Byzantine rite whose civilization would evolve along vernacular lines.

[25] Peri, *op. cit.*, p. 87. ['Linguarum diversitas ecclesiasticum ordinem non confundit. Nam Sedes Apostolica, cum ipsa latina sit, in multis tamen locis pro ratione patriæ græcos sacerdotes et semper et nunc usque constituens, privilegii sui detrimenta sentire nec debet nec debuit.']

[26] The Franks' sundering of the Czechs from their Slavonic Christianity left a long legacy of bitterness that found outlets in a succession of religious protest movements among this intellectually precocious people at the crossroads of East and West: the Utraquist and the Hussite movements, Protestantism, the fideistic Pan-Slavism of nineteenth-century Prague, the

Charity among the Churches cooled after the Council of 880. Constantinople may have got the better of Frankish bigotry and papal weakness, but memories of the Roman intervention in Bulgaria under Nicholas I remained bitter in the minds of Greek patriarchs who – whatever their anti-Roman prejudices – had always respected the right of their Dalmatian subjects to their Roman liturgy. Thereafter Constantinople would be convinced of a papal plot to expand the Roman domain at its expense. At this time hostility to the Holy See was fomented, especially by the Byzantine emperors, who, ever since the 'treacherous' alliance of the Papacy with the 'barbarian' Frankish Empire, were determined to claim for the See of Constantinople the primacy that Rome, in their view, no longer deserved.[27] A new theory of 'pentarchy', rightly considered heretical by Rome, was now asserting that the five historical patriarchates were all equal in status and authority, Christ alone being the head of the Church. The consequences for Catholicity were sinister.

The Law of Talion

In the ninth century, attempts were made to force the Greek liturgy on the Latin churches of Byzantine Italy, whose bishops, remaining loyal to the Pope, their rightful metropolitan, were deemed a subversive element in this semi-Greek province of the Empire.[28] During the pontificate of Stephen V (885–891), there were civil disturbances in Taranto when the Byzantine governor attempted to prevent the newly elected Latin bishop from going to Rome to be ordained, and tried to install as bishop a Byzantine-rite cleric ordained in Constantinople.[29] The following century, Italian-speaking Taranto was finally made a Greek see, as was Brindisi.[30] But John, the Latin Bishop of Bari (951–978), defied the Emperor Nicephorus Phocas by recognizing the Pope as his patriarch and refused, together with the bishops of Cosenza, Bisignano, Cassano and Anglona, to conform to the Byzantine rite.[31] Then, in 1009, when Pope Sergius IV declined to sanction the title of 'Ecumenical Patriarch' coveted by his rival and namesake Sergius II, this pontiff's name was removed from the Constantinopolitan diptychs.[32]

---

schismatic Czechoslovak National Church of 1920, and the strong tendency towards secularism that alienated the Czechs from the Slovaks in recent times and contributed to the break-up of Czechoslovakia in 1992.

[27] Emperor Leo the Isaurian (717–740) removed the Byzantine lands of Southern Italy (including Malta), Illyria and Greece from the Roman patriarchate and attached them to Constantinople to punish Pope Gregory II (715–731) for having refused to implement his iconoclastic decrees and for leading the opposition to them. The Greek nationality of most of the population was made to justify this administrative innovation. In 883 the Emperor Leo the Wise published a list of Greek provinces and dioceses which described the sees of Thessalonica, Syracuse, Corinth, Reggio, Nicopolis/Sancta Severina, Athens, Patras and New Patras as 'from the Roman diocese detached and now subject to the throne of Constantinople . . . since the Pope of ancient Rome is held by Gentiles' (Fortescue, *Uniate Eastern Churches*, pp. 87–88).

[28] The northern part of Byzantine Italy (Campania, northern and central Apulia, Lucania and northern Calabria) were Italian in speech and Latin in rite; the south of Calabria and the Salento peninsula (Terra d'Ótranto), were, like Sicily, Greek in both senses. From the ninth century, Arabic began to displace vernacular Greek in Sicily and Malta, now occupied by the Tunisian Aghlabids.

[29] Fortescue, *Uniate Eastern Churches*, p. 86.

[30] Ibid., p. 89.

[31] Ibid., p., 87.

[32] However, in 1089 a Constantinopolitan synod claimed that the omission of the pope's name had not been deliberate, but an oversight (Knowles/Obolensky, *op. cit.*, p. 322).

The Norman presence in Southern Italy in the first half of the eleventh century brought matters to a head. First appearing on the scene as pilgrims to the shrine of St Michael the Archangel on Mount Gargano, some of these French-speaking descendants of Vikings lingered in the region, where they found employment as mercenaries of the local Lombard dukes and Byzantine governors. By 1053 their leader, Robert Guiscard, was planning to oust the Byzantines and carve a great Norman state out of their Italian possessions. Threatened by the ascent of a warrior people feared for their brutality and rapacity, Pope Leo IX joined forces against the Normans with the Byzantine emperor Constantine IX, but Guiscard dealt the allies a crushing defeat. Taken prisoner by the Normans, the Pope had no choice but to come to terms with his respectful captors.

Pope Leo was an avid reformer, and during the war against the Normans a reforming synod held at Siponto in Apulia sought to abolish – quite legitimately – a number of Greek usages that had crept into the liturgy of the local Latin churches.[33] This reassertion of Latin tradition was resented by the Greek clergy of the region, who had been trying for some time to hellenize the Apulian Latin churches in Byzantine-ruled territory. Attempts by the Pope to enforce celibacy among the local Latin clergy also unsettled their Byzantine-rite brothers in the priesthood.[34] In the meantime reports had reached Constantinople that the Normans, Latin Catholics, were forcing the Greek clergy of Greater Calabria to adopt the Roman rite.[35] This attack on Byzantine custom was not sanctioned by the Pope who, in any case, was in no position to exercise control over the troublesome Normans.

To make matters worse, the Byzantine Patriarch at the time was the ambitious Michael Cerularius, a man strongly prejudiced not only against the Roman Church, but against the non-Byzantine traditions of the East as well. Territorially, the Greek Church was now at its greatest extent, and the Patriarch aimed, among other things, to byzantinize liturgically the Armenian and Syrian dioceses of the Middle Eastern territories recently recovered from the Saracens. The Patriarch of Antioch, Peter III, rejected Cerularius' proposal that the churches of his jurisdiction adopt the Byzantine rite, but when the Latin clergy of Constantinople refused to give up certain of their Roman customs, Cerularius ordered the closure of their churches.[36]

Exploiting the tense situation in Southern Italy, the Patriarch justified his action as retaliation for Latin encroachments there. The following year his ally the Archbishop of Ochrid wrote to John, the Latin Bishop of Trani in Apulia, condemning Roman liturgical customs such as the interpolated Creed, the use of unleavened bread, celibacy of the secular clergy, and clean-shaven priests.[37] The ensuing quarrel, resulting in the mutual excommunication and anathematization of the fractious papal legate Cardinal Humbert and the equally hot-headed Byzantine Patriarch in 1054, drew from the Pope a number of hard sayings about Rome's disobedient and insolent daughter of Constantinople who 'mocked her Mother's old age and her body worn out by long labours, claiming the Mother's primacy . . .'

---

[33] Francis Dvornik, 'Eastern Schism', *NCE*, V, p. 24.
[34] Kenneth M. Setton, ed., *A History of the Crusades*, (Philadelphia, 1955), I, pp. 20–29.
[35] Ware, *op. cit.*, p. 66.
[36] Steven Runciman, *A History of the Crusades*, (Cambridge, 1951), I, p. 96. The Latin churches in Constantinople were maintained for Western merchants, pilgrims and Scandinavian members of the Varangian Guard.
[37] Ludvik Nemec, 'Michael Cerularius', *CESH*, VII, p. 136.

Any church that dared to dissent from Rome, stated the papal letter (drafted according to some by Humbert), was a 'confabulation of heretics, a conventicle of schismatics, a synagogue of Satan'.[38] In reference to Cerularius' closure of Latin churches in Constantinople, Leo IX furthermore recalled the classic Catholic position on the question of ritual pluralism:

> See how much more reasonable, moderate and clement the Roman Church is than you on this point! Although there are in and around Rome a great number of churches and monasteries of the Greeks, to this day none of them has been disturbed, nor has anyone forbidden them to follow the tradition of their fathers or their own customs; if anything they are persuaded and admonished to observe them . . . Your Fraternity should know that different customs according to places and times are in no way an obstacle to the salvation of souls when a single faith, producing through charity the good works of which it is capable, commends all to the one God.[39]

Breaking with the Past

Michael Cerularius' attack on the Latin liturgy was to be expected of a Byzantine patriarch who, aspiring to obtain for himself the authority that the Pope claimed over the churches of the East, had striven to destroy the alliance between the Emperor Constantine IX and Pope Leo IX.[40] His qualifying as heretical various Western customs was the strongest Byzantine expression of liturgical absolutism so far, and directly contradicted the Catholic principle of pluralism clearly re-enunciated by Patriarch Photius at the time of his reconciliation with Rome in 879.

In making liturgical uniformity as essential to communion as doctrinal unity, Cerularius violated the apostolic tradition of pluralism cementing the communion of the churches of God, and set a dangerous precedent for every section of Christendom. Historically, this led to the tragic situation whereby, as Vittorio Peri has remarked,

> The sacred seasons of liturgical life and of fasts, the celibacy of the lower clergy and their habit of wearing or of shaving their beards, the use of unleavened or leavened bread in the Eucharist, the single or triple baptismal immersion: all of these were considered intolerable manifestations of deviation from apostolic Tradition and of culpable dogmatic dissent. By both sides they served as sufficient motive to interrupt eucharistic communion between the Churches.[41]

Furthermore, in renewing the *filioque* controversy, the quarrelsome patriarch was ignoring Photius' closure of the question with the admission that since the theological formula had been used by Sts Ambrose, Augustine and Jerome,

---

[38] Quoted in Southern, *op. cit.*, p. 71. The three other Eastern patriarchs did not join in the quarrel, and their relations with Rome remained unimpaired throughout this episode.

[39] *Epistola ad Michaelem Constantinopolitanum patriarcham*, cited in Peri, *op. cit.*, p. 89.

[40] In 1024 the Byzantine Patriarch Eustathius had offered to restore relations with Rome on the condition that the pope recognize him as head of all the Catholic churches of the East.

[41] Ibid., pp. 35–36.

all acknowledged as Fathers by the Eastern Church, it was capable of interpretation in an orthodox sense.[42] Yet one significant event had intervened to cause the Greeks to harden their stance. In the ninth century, when Photius had made this exegetical concession to the Latins, the contentious use of the *filioque* in the liturgical Creed was still an aberration of the Frankish and Spanish churches which the Roman Pope (like most French bishops) emphatically refused to sanction, even if he lacked the power to eradicate it.

The ominous prelude to the destructive events of 1054 had been Pope Benedict VIII's decision in 1014 to introduce the singing of the Creed in its interpolated form into the churches of Rome for the coronation of Emperor Henry II. By this act Pope Benedict added to Pope Nicholas I's sin of cultural imperialism and to Stephen V's sin of trilingualism the new sin of reversing, in defiance of tradition, the dictum *lex orandi, lex credendi*. It was hardly the Easterners' fault if, thinking with the mind of the Fathers, they were convinced thereafter that a formal change in public prayer denoted a substantial change in belief.

---

[42] Ibid., p. 57.

7

THE IDOL OF UNIFORMITY

Variety is the mother and beginning of discord.
HUMBERT DE ROMANS[1]

Politics has no heart, only a head.
NAPOLEON BONAPARTE

One Church, One Rite

In 1060, only six years after the Cerularian schism, Pope Nicholas II made a political alliance with the Papacy's erstwhile Norman enemies. In return for the Pope's recognition of Robert Guiscard as lawful ruler of the former imperial lands of Southern Italy, the Norman count separated the Greek churches of his new realm from the Byzantine patriarchate (which had usurped them three centuries earlier) and restored them to the See of Rome.[2] Then, in 1098, after the conquest of Islamic Sicily and the foundation of a Norman state there, Roger I negotiated with Pope Urban II a concordat that made him apostolic legate for the whole of Southern Italy. As a result, the geographical extent of the Western patriarchate was suddenly increased to include the whole region from Naples to Malta. From that time forward, the Papacy tacitly encouraged the Normans' policy of latinizing the local churches, whose Greek faithful now found themselves subject to Latin bishops.[3] Thereafter the fate of Byzantine institutions in the former Magna Græcia was sealed.

Because of the abolitionism of Charlemagne, the rest of the Roman patriarchate was similarly moving towards greater uniformity in liturgical matters. In the ninth and early tenth centuries the fusion of the old Roman and obsolescent Gallican

---

[1] '*Varietas mater est et initium discordiæ*'. Humbert de Romans was fifth Master General of the Dominicans and a *peritus* at the reunion council of Lyons (1274).

[2] For the time being, the Pope tolerated the presence of Greek bishops willing to break with the Patriarch of Constantinople and to acknowledge him as their metropolitan, but he replaced with a Latin the Bishop of Reggio Calabria, who refused to conform. Peri, *op. cit.*, p. 108; Fortescue, *Uniate Eastern Churches*, p. 98.

[3] In a few dioceses the Normans allowed a Greek bishop to co-exist with a Latin one, viz. in Gallipoli (Apulia) and in Rossano (Calabria), where there was a Greek metropolitan until the fifteenth century. As for the other Calabrian sees that were made Latin, some retained a Greek ordinary after the reign of Roger I: Gerace (until the fifteenth century), Santa Severina (until the thirteenth century), Gerace and Oppido (until the fifteenth century), Bova (until the sixteenth century). The metropolitan See of Reggio still had Greek suffragan bishops in the thirteenth century.

rites became complete north of the Alps. Then, from the accession of Otto, the first Saxon Roman emperor, in 963, the evolved Gallicano-Roman liturgy was introduced into Rome.[4] Becoming the liturgical norm of the papal church, this hybrid rite spread throughout most of the Roman patriarchate, though local variations would long continue to be a fact of life in the West.

Abolitionist Offensives

There is irony in the fact that the rite which the contemporary pontiffs were soon striving to impose on the whole Church was not a product of papal Rome, but of its rival the Frankish Empire. Significantly, too, the new liturgical centralism marked the temporary eclipse in the papal mind of apostolic traditionalism by rationalist pragmatism, at least in matters of praxis. The opening gun was fired during the pontificate of John X (914–928), who saw fit to interfere in the cultic affairs of a ritually diverse church of his patriarchate.

In 923, when Zanelo, the papal legate assigned to Sisuando, Archbishop of Santiago de Compostela, informed the Pope about the distinct liturgical customs of his native church, John sent him back to Galicia to examine the doctrinal orthodoxy of the local service books. Zanelo's report was favourable, and Pope John sanctioned its use, ordering, however, that the Institution Narrative in the Eucharistic Prayer of the Mass be altered to conform with the Roman one.[5] Although the point of this exercise was to assert papal authority rather than to interfere with legitimate local customs, the Joannine intervention was a significant innovation and, in historical terms, a revival of the interventionism earlier practised by Victor I, Leo I and Gelasius I. It meant that in liturgical matters the function of the Pope was no longer merely consultative, and that responsibility for the regulation of divine worship no longer ended with local bishops or metropolitans.

The liturgy of Galicia at that time was a variant of the old Gallican-based Hispanic rite still in use throughout the Iberian Peninsula. In Galicia and the other independent Christian kingdoms (Leon, Castile, and Aragon), where the turmoil of centuries of war against the Moors of the south had made communication with Rome difficult, the so-called Mozarabic liturgy had escaped the centripetal influences of the Carolingian reform. Pope John X's intervention of 923 left the liturgical order of Iberia undisturbed, but memories of it boded increasingly ill in an age of disciplinary reform.

A direct papal challenge to Spanish tradition came over a century later from Pope Alexander II (1061–1073). Before his election this pontiff was the monk Anselm, a Milanese trained at the Benedictine abbey of Bec in Normandy, then an important centre of reform. Returning to Milan during the pontificate of Leo IX, he headed the local reformist faction and opposed Archbishop Guido who, aligned with the Saxon Emperor, was encouraging various ecclesiastical abuses. In Anselm's tidy mind any custom at variance with that of the Church in Rome was suspect, and he associated the distinct Ambrosian rite of his native archdiocese with simony and the other deviant practices he found there. So in 1060 he backed

---

[4] Jungmann, op. cit., I, p. 95.
[5] Antonio Cabrera Delgado y Silveira, Ordo missæ pontificalis ritu hispano mozarabico peragendæ: Esquema general, rúbricas, notas e introducciones (Toledo, 1975), p. vi.

the unsuccessful attempt of Pope Nicholas II to suppress the Milanese liturgy. Anselm was elected Pope the following year; in 1069 he appointed his old ally, Peter Damian, legate for Lombardy and charged him with the task of enforcing liturgical conformity. St Peter Damian's high-handed and uncanonical campaign to make the Milanese abandon a tradition they ascribed to St Ambrose himself was strenuously resisted by the clergy of the great archdiocese, with the result that the 'reform' could not be implemented.[6]

Alexander's decision to leave the Ambrosian Catholics in peace followed a similar failure to achieve the abolition of the Old Spanish rite. In 1064 he had despatched his legate, Hugo Candido, to Spain with orders to suppress liturgical diversity. Hugo's insinuations that the Mozarabic texts were infected with the Adoptionist heresy incensed the Bishops of Castile and Leon, who sent their liturgical books to Rome to be examined by the Pope.[7] Finding them perfectly orthodox, and daunted by the resistance he was encountering from the Milanese, Alexander II was obliged to approve the Hispanic rite, subject to minor revisions, at the Council of Mantua in 1066.[8]

Nevertheless, this conciliar 'concession' (in reality the confirmation of a right) had been made only to the churches of Castile and Leon. Determined to force his liturgical policy elsewhere in Spain, Alexander immediately targeted the churches of the other kingdoms. Hugo Candido returned to Spain in 1067 and pursued a different approach: that of convincing the reformist monasteries of Aragon of the need to worship in the same manner as the Holy See. The prestigious abbey of San Juan de la Peña succumbed to this propaganda in the Lent of 1071, and all the other Aragonese churches followed suit. Within five years Navarre and Catalonia had taken the same step.[9]

Laws Go Where Kings Will

Meanwhile Alfonso VI, King of Castile, had also been won over by Cluniac promoters of the Roman rite, and in 1072 he permitted two French legates of Alexander II to convoke a council in Burgos for the purpose of imposing the reform. However, the Castilian episcopate defended its rights so effectively that the status quo could not be altered. The legates were forced to leave Burgos, but not before excommunicating and deposing from their sees those bishops who had shown them the most vigorous opposition. Appeals were lodged in Rome, and the new Pope, Gregory VII, vindicated the Castilian bishops, without, however, deviating from the abolitionist policy of his predecessor as far as the Hispanic liturgy was concerned. (St Gregory, who had been the principal adviser of Alexander II, was equally adamant that the Milanese abandon their distinct rite). In a letter to the King of Aragon, the Pope actually referred to the venerable rite of Spain as 'the Toledan superstition', and associated himself with the erroneous view of it as

---

[6] King, op. cit., p. 305.
[7] The Adoptionism mentioned here was the eighth-century Spanish revival of an earlier heresy that denied the real human nature of Jesus Christ. One of its principal proponents was Elipando, Archbishop of Toledo (717–816), hence the later, erroneous tendency to associate the heresy with the Spanish liturgy.
[8] Cabrera Delgado y Silveira, op. cit., p. vii.
[9] Ibid., p. vii.

the unorthodox product of a past age when Spain was ruled by Visigothic kings addicted to the Arian heresy.[10]

Alfonso of Castile, courted by Gregory and still partial to the reform, decided to settle the matter in the year 1078. In what must be the most colourful episode in Catholic liturgical history, the fate of the Hispanic liturgy was determined by two trials by ordeal. In the first a Castilian knight defending the national rite vanquished his Toledan opponent who was made to represent the Roman liturgy. In the second trial the rival books were placed on a bonfire. According to one contemporary account the Roman Missal burned, while the flames ejected the Hispanic Mass book intact. But then King Alfonso, who was standing by, kicked the Hispanic missal back into the fire with the words: 'Laws go where kings will' (Allá van leyes do quieren reyes).[11]

And so at a second council held in Burgos in 1080, this time presided over by Cardinal Ricardo as papal legate, the lex hispana was formally abolished in Castile, Leon and Galicia, and replaced forever by the lex romana. Only the free city of Toledo clung to its ancient heritage, but by the time Alfonso conquered it in 1085, his enthusiasm for liturgical change must have cooled, for he allowed the six Toledan parishes the distinction of remaining the last bastion of what had been the pride of Iberian Christianity.[12]

In the self-confident communes of Lombardy, by contrast, there was no king to police papal abolitionism, and in the middle of the following century two bulls addressed to the provost of the cathedral church of St Thecla in Milan (those of Eugenius III in 1145 and of Anastasius IV in 1153) confirmed the legitimacy of the Ambrosian liturgy.[13]

Gothic Ghosts

Yet another target of the reform movement of the eleventh century was the Slavonic liturgy of the Roman patriarchate, a tradition that had managed to outlive the destructive legislation of Stephen V two hundred years earlier. By the end of the ninth century the ritual use of Slavonic had disappeared in Moravia, Slovakia and Pannonia, this last region occupied by the Hungarians who would soon be converted to pure Latin Catholicism. However, in three former dependencies of Greater Moravia, the peripheral regions of Croatia, Bohemia and south-eastern Poland (the See of Cracow), liturgical Slavonic continued to co-exist with Latin during the tenth and eleventh centuries, in spite of bans renewed by those popes most concerned with the consolidation of Roman power: John X (914–928), John XIII (965–972), Alexander II (1061–1073), and St Gregory VII (1073–1085).[14]

In Croatia, attachment to the Slavonic liturgy was particularly strong. Ecclesiastically the Croats were under the metropolitans ('patriarchs') of Aquileia in Friuli, who had proved less hostile to the ritual diversity of the Slavs than the Frankish hierarchy. But when the Pannonian Croats united against the Magyars with the Croats of Dalmatia under King Tomislav (910–928), the Latin bishops of

---

[10] Ibid., p. vii.
[11] Ibid.
[12] Ibid., p. viii.
[13] King, op. cit., p. 305.
[14] Peri, op. cit., p. 290, n. 79.

the Adriatic coastal cities, threatened culturally by this expanding Slav state, began to discourage the Slavonic rites in their dioceses. The Synod of Spalato (Split), convoked by Pope John X in 925, proclaimed the Archbishop of that Latin city Metropolitan of All Croatia and voted to suppress the entirely Croatian diocese of Nin. The synodal acts also banned the use of Slavonic in the Roman liturgy. Since the decrees of Spalato were widely ignored by the Croatians, another synod was convened in 1060 to renew them. This second synod also attempted to outlaw in Croatia established Oriental customs such as clerical marriage and the wearing of long hair and beards by priests. In order to justify their rulings, the Latin bishops denounced St Methodius as a heretic who had used the Slavonic language to spread errors against the Catholic faith.[15]

The antipope Honorius II's upholding of the anti-Slavonic prohibitions three years later led to a temporary schism in Croatia, the events of which make a curious tale.[16] In 1063 the Croatian nobility sent the priest Vuk to Rome to beg the anti-pope to rescind the offending synodal decrees. Honorius agreed to an investigation of the dispute and gave Vuk a letter to the Croatian king and the Dalmatian hierarchy demanding that two bishops come to Rome to present their case. However, the papal letter was never delivered by Vuk, who falsified what had happened in Rome, claiming that Honorius sided with the Croatian party and was willing to consecrate a suitable candidate bishop. Vuk then returned to Rome with Zdeda, an old priest chosen by the Croatian clergy. Honorius received the delegation unfavourably, not only because the required bishops had not been sent, but because Zdeda was bearded, in contradiction to the current Latin custom. As an expression of his displeasure, the antipope personally cut off a piece of the old priest's beard and ordered him to be shaved clean and tonsured. Confusing the ethnic identity of the Slavs, Honorius dismissed the Croatian delegation with a refusal to grant any concessions to 'Goths' tainted by the Arian heresy.

Unwilling to concede defeat, the crafty Vuk convinced Zdeda that in having him shaved Honorius had actually ordained him bishop. The Croatians then drove the Latin Bishop of Veglia (Krk) out of his see, installing Zdeda in his place. The new 'bishop' lost no time in creating a rival Slavonic clergy and hierarchy, and the schism escalated until the antipope's legate, Cardinal John, arrived in Croatia with news that Zdeda's episcopal consecration was a fiction and all his ordinations were invalid. Zdeda was then excommunicated, Vuk was convicted and imprisoned, and a new Spalato Synod of 1075 eventually healed the rift by lifting the ban on the Slavonic liturgy.[17]

This expedient concession was confirmed by the same Pope Gregory VII who was supervising the destruction of the Slavonic liturgy in Bohemia, where resistance to latinization was less violent than in Croatia. The attack on Church Slavonic in the north had intensified during the preceding century. In granting King Boleslav II a bishop for the city of Prague in 973, Pope John XIII specified that 'not according to the rite or sect of the Bulgarian or Russian nation, or of the Slavonic language, but, following rather the institution and decrees of the Apostles, you should choose

---

[15] Francis Dvornik, *Byzantine Missions among the Slavs: SS. Constantine-Cyril and Methodius* (New Brunswick/New Jersey, 1970), pp. 237–40.
[16] Honorius (Peter Cadalous of Parma) withheld the papal throne from the validly elected pope, Alexander II, until 1064.
[17] Dvornik, *Byzantine Missions*, pp. 241–43.

rather, according to your will, for this work a cleric who would be well trained in Latin letters'.[18]

After 1038 the Polish king Casimir I, unopposed by Pope Benedict IX, obliged the Slavonic See of Cracow to conform to the pure Latin liturgy already established in the neighbouring archdiocese of Gniezno.[19] By contrast, Vratislav II, the Bohemian monarch who ruled between 1061 and 1092, was a zealous defender of the Slavonic liturgy. Around 1080 he wrote to Gregory VII asking permission to restore Church Slavonic throughout his realm, but received a characteristic rebuke from the authoritarian pontiff. 'Certain religious men had patiently tolerated this use and left it uncorrected' only because, St Gregory argued, 'the primitive Church left in darkness many things which, after Christianity had been firmly established and the religion was growing, were corrected after a profound examination by the holy fathers.'[20] After Vratislav's death in 1096, what Francis Dvornik has described as the 'mortal blow to Slavonic letters and liturgy in Bohemia' was dealt when the Slavonic monks were expelled from the monastery of Sázava. By the middle decades of the twelfth century only Latin was heard in the sanctuaries of the Czech Church.[21]

Casus belli

In 1098, only two years after Slavonic worship in Bohemia was doomed to temporary extinction, the warriors of the First Crusade entered Syria and captured the patriarchal city of Antioch. The Melkite Patriarch, John VII the Oxite, compliantly consecrated Peter of Narbonne as Latin Patriarch, and both sees coexisted for two years. However, Bohemund, the Latin Prince of Antioch, had a record of hostility to the Byzantines and, showing lofty contempt for the dignity and rights of the local Eastern Christians, abolished the Orthodox jurisdiction. The mistreated patriarch fled to Constantinople in 1100.[22] With the new Latin Patriarch, Bernard of Valence, now ruling alone, a usurper Latin patriarchate of Antioch was established, while the legitimate Melkite patriarchs remained in exile for the next two hundred years. The same fate also befell the Orthodox Patriarch of Jerusalem.

Oppression bred hatred, and in 1182 an enraged mob massacred the Latin colony in Constantinople. Three years later the Normans embarked on a rampage of murder against the Greek population of Thessalonica.[23] The new tide of violence culminated in the disgraceful sacking of the imperial capital in 1204 by the soldiers of the Fourth Crusade. Already irritated by the Crusaders' dashing of his hopes of placing on the Byzantine throne a pretender who had promised to heal the rift between the two Churches, Pope Innocent III severely condemned this outrage and excommunicated its perpetrators, writing:

---

[18] Ibid., p. 214.
[19] Ibid., p. 204.
[20] Ibid., p. 228.
[21] Ibid.
[22] Fortescue, *Uniate Eastern Churches*, p. 191. Patriarch John had already been tortured by the Turkish governor during the siege of 1097 on suspicion of siding with the Crusaders. In exile he would become a noted writer of anti-Latin tracts.
[23] Dvornik, 'Eastern Schism', p. 25.

How, indeed, is the Greek Church to be brought back into ecclesiastical union and to a devotion for the Apostolic See when she has been beset with so many afflictions and persecutions that she sees in the Latins only an example of perdition and the works of darkness, so that she now, and with reason, detests the Latins more than dogs? As for those who were supposed to be seeking the ends of Jesus Christ, not their own ends, whose swords, which they were supposed to use against the pagans, are now dripping with Christian blood – they have spared neither age nor sex. They have committed incest, adultery, and fornication before the eyes of men. They have exposed both matrons and virgins, even those dedicated to God, to the sordid lusts of boys. Not satisfied with breaking open the imperial treasury and plundering the goods of princes and lesser men, they also laid their hands on the treasures of the churches and, what is more serious, on their very possessions. They have even ripped silver plates from the altars and have hacked them to pieces among themselves. They violated the holy places and have carried off crosses and relics . . .[24]

However, barely had the ink dried on Innocent's solemn condemnation of the Crusaders' destructive and sacrilegious conduct in Constantinople than he acknowledged Baldwin of Flanders as the new 'Latin Emperor' of Byzantium and, taking advantage of the dethronement of the legitimate Greek Patriarch, he installed in his place a Latin patriarch, the Venetian bishop Tomaso Morosini. In the Greek churches priests were forced to use unleavened bread and to insert the *filioque* into the Creed.[25] If the invasion itself consummated the emotional estrangement of the Greeks from their Western co-religionists, it was this, arguably most cynical act of the Papacy, that justified their practical (as opposed to theoretical) rejection of the Roman primacy from that time forward.

From Communion to Integration

Papal claims of universal ordinary jurisdiction were thus translated into grim fact as the Latin hierarchy, setting at nought immemorial traditions of the See of Constantinople, attempted to absorb by force an 'errant' sister church of Christendom into the Roman patriarchate. While most Orthodox theologians continued thereafter to accept the Roman primacy in theory, their justification of the breach with Rome was the contention that the contemporary incumbent of the throne of St Peter had forfeited his authority by breaking so radically with Catholic tradition.[26] In the fifteenth century the theologian and liturgiologist, Symeon of Thessalonica, expressed it this way:

---

[24] Peters, *op. cit.*, pp. 23–24. According to the Byzantine chronicler Nicetas, the Crusaders' desecration of the Hagia Sophia went so far that 'a certain harlot, a sharer in their guilt . . . insulting Christ, sat in the patriarch's seat, singing an obscene song and dancing frequently' (ibid., p. 17). Two centuries later, as the Turks closed in on the imperial city, the Grand Duke Loukas Notarâs would remark: 'I would rather see the Muslim turban in the midst of the city than the Latin mitre' (Ware, *op. cit.*, p. 81).

[25] Deno John Geanakoplos, *Byzantine East and Latin West* (New York, 1966), p. 103.

[26] As to the Byzantine attribution of heresy to the Holy See, Patriarch Michael of Anchialous (1170–1177) contended that the Roman primacy had actually been transferred to Constantinople, the 'new Rome'; see Meyendorff, 'St. Peter in Byzantine Theology', in *The Primacy of Peter*, p. 15.

One should not contradict the Latins when they say that the Bishop of Rome is the first. This primacy is not harmful to the Church. Let them only prove his faithfulness to the faith of Peter and to that of the successors of Peter. If it is so, let him enjoy all the privileges of Peter, let him be the first, the head, the chief of all and the Supreme Pontiff . . . Let the Bishop of Rome be successor of the orthodoxy of Sylvester and Agatho, of Leo, Liberius, Martin and Gregory, then we also will call him Apostolic and the first among the other bishops; then we will obey him, not only as Peter, but as the Saviour Himself. . . .

By no means do we reject the Pope; it is not with the Pope that we refuse to enter into communion. We are bound to him, as to Christ, and we recognize him as father and shepherd . . . In Christ, we are in communion and in an indissoluble communion with the Pope, with Peter, with Linus, with Clement . . . But in as much as he [the present Bishop of Rome] is no longer their successor in the faith, he is no more the inheritor of the throne. The one whom one calls Pope will not be Pope as long as he has not the faith of Peter.[27]

The usurpation of 1204 was given juridical legitimacy at the Fourth Lateran Council, convoked by Innocent III in 1215. To add insult to injury, only now when a *Latin* bishop sat on the throne of Byzantium's patriarchs did Rome choose to endorse Canon 28 of the Council of Chalcedon (held seven and a half centuries earlier) which styled Constantinople the most important see in the East.[28] The Lateran Council also proclaimed the uncatholic principle of unity of jurisdiction (i.e. the ban on two or more bishops of different rites residing in the same city). The obvious model was the situation that had obtained in Greater Calabria and Sicily since the foundation of the Norman Kingdom, whereby Byzantine-rite parishes and monasteries were placed under the rule of Latin bishops. Applied in the Latin-occupied patriarchates of Byzantium, Antioch and Jerusalem, unity of jurisdiction had the two practical effects of obstructing the functioning of Oriental canon law, and of facilitating the latinization of the lower clergy and laity.[29]

Not that the systematic latinization of non-Roman rites was an official desideratum of the Papacy at this time. Indeed, the Fourth Lateran Council commanded that all the different rites, customs and languages co-existing in various places be respected, and Latin ordinaries of ritually mixed dioceses were directed to provide the non-Roman faithful with churches and clergy of their own rite.[30] However, conscious as she now was of her role as universal custodian of orthodoxy, Rome insisted on her right to guide her sister churches in theological matters, a prerogative that led – because of the warped ecclesiology then current – to interference in the discipline and liturgical arrangements of ritually diverse communities both inside and outside the Roman patriarchate.

In reality the respect which the Papacy accorded other ecclesiastical traditions was not absolute, but relative to their perceived degree of doctrinal orthodoxy. Characteristic of this trend was the ground on which approval was finally granted, in 1247, for the Slavonic liturgy, the *de facto* ritual tradition of Croatia. Pope Innocent IV acceded to the age-old demands of the Croatian clergy not in deference

[27] Ibid., pp. 25–26.
[28] Dvornik, 'Byzantium and the Roman Primacy', p. 301.
[29] Elias El-Hayek, 'Maronite Rite', *NCE*, IX, p. 249.
[30] Dvornik, *Byzantine Missions*, p. 244.

to their rights but because he had been convinced by their spurious claim that St Jerome, the Dalmatian doctor of the Church (but a Latin living four hundred years before the conversion of the Croats!) had invented the Glagolitic alphabet and established the Slavonic liturgy.[31] Thanks to this same concession Charles I of Bohemia was able, 99 years later in 1346, to persuade Pope Clement VI to permit the celebration of Slavonic rites in the new abbey of Emaus in Prague. This foundation was served by Benedictine monks from Dalmatia.[32]

The First Uniates[33]

The Byzantine patriarchate, restored to its rightful incumbent when the Latin rulers were expelled by the Emperor Michael Palaeologus in 1261, emerged unscathed from the 'Latinocracy', but in the patriarchate of Antioch, already weakened by schism and centuries of Islamic domination, the damage done would be great. The first Antiochene victims of latinization were the Maronites. Isolated from the Roman Church since the pontificate of Pope Agatho (678–681), these Lebanese mountaineers re-established their links with the West during the First Crusade. In 1098, the year after the Crusaders' arrival in Syria, Maronite bishop Thomas Kephartab had informed the ill-fated Patriarch John of Antioch that his people were 'united in faith with the Franks'.[34] The union of this community with Rome was consolidated in 1216, when Innocent III, who had recently closed the Fourth Lateran Council, sent a bull to the Maronites and placed their patriarch, Jeremias Amchitti, under the obedience of the Latin Patriarch of Antioch, whose predecessors had usurped the throne of the legitimate Melkite patriarchs.

Quia Divinæ Sapientiæ clarified the faith of the Catholic Church and listed a

---

[31] Ibid., pp. 244–45. Pope Innocent actually made this concession only to the diocese of Senj, but it was extended in fact to all the Croatian bishoprics of the provinces of Spalato and Aquileia. The wording of the pope's rescript to Bishop Philip of Senj, whom he met at Lyons, was the following:

> In the petition you presented to us, it is said that in Sclavonia there existed a special alphabet which the clerics of that land were using in the celebration of the divine office, affirming that they had it from St Jerome. Therefore you asked and prayed our permission to celebrate the divine office in the said letters, in order to conform to these priests and to the custom of the land where you are acting as bishop. Thus, we give you through the authority of this letter the permission asked for, well aware of the principle that the letter is subject to the matter and not the matter to the letter, but only in those parts where, according to the above-mentioned custom, it is observed, on condition that the meaning shall not be disturbed because of the use of different letters.

[32] Dvornik, *Byzantine Missions*, p. 229. Interestingly (and doubtless ammunition for the contemporary enemies of liturgical pluralism), the Czech Utraquists invoked this privilege of 1346 when, a century later, they petitioned the Council of Basel for permission to celebrate Mass in the vernacular.

[33] The controversial term 'Uniate' (though often used disparagingly by the Orthodox and disliked by Eastern-rite Catholics themselves) is employed in the present work (as it was by Adrian Fortescue) simply as a convenient synonym for 'Eastern Catholic', 'Oriental Catholic'. 'Uniate' and 'Eastern Catholic' are not absolutely interchangeable, however, since one Eastern Catholic group, the Italo-Greeks, was never out of union with Roman and hence 'reunited'. For the independent Eastern Churches Uniatism has always been an ecumenical stumbling block because although the avowed intention of individual corporate reconciliations was to restore pre-schism Catholic unity, the unions were in fact achieved without consultation of the (now estranged) Mother Churches in question, and the result was integration and partial assimilation rather than a simple restoration of communion. It is with the problems of integration and assimilation that the present study is principally concerned.

[34] El-Hayek, *op. cit.*, p. 248.

number of Antiochene liturgical practices which the Pope directed the reconciled Maronites to abandon in favour of Roman ones. They should stop giving Holy Communion to infants; bishops and not priests should confer the sacrament of confirmation; Roman liturgical vestments were to replace the oriental ones; they should make holy chrism out of balm and oil and not out of aromatic substances; they should replace their glass and wooden chalices with metal ones; and their churches were to be fitted with bells.[35] The disinclination of the Maronites to give up so many of their immemorial customs moved Pope Alexander IV to write to Patriarch Simon in 1256, repeating the prescriptions of Innocent III, to which he added the substitution of azyme for leavened bread in the Eucharist.[36]

These thirteenth-century dealings with the Maronites provided future popes with a blueprint for the reconciliation of other Eastern Christians separated from the Holy See. In the main the policy was to tolerate the ancient rites and the traditional liturgical languages, but to impose as much uniformity as practicable in individual customs. The adoption of this programme of assimilation instead of the total abolitionism that must have seemed preferable was, however, a practical measure. Here the cultural and social differences between East and West were decisive. Whereas the absence of a strong body of educated laymen in Spain had allowed the papal legates and the regional kings to destroy the Hispanic rite, in the East a more cultured and influential laity in many places presented a strong challenge to the Roman-rite hierarchs and rulers committed to latinization. Indeed, the ultimate failure of attempts to reunite the Oriental Churches at the Second Council of Lyons (1274) and the Council of Ferrara-Florence (1438–1445) were principally due to the antagonism of the Greek lower clergy and laity, who believed that the true motive behind these imperially sponsored endeavours was not religious but political: in both cases, the need to secure Western military aid against the Turkish menace.[37]

The initial reunion of the Maronites with Rome had been followed by that of the Jacobite Armenians in 1198, at the time of the Fourth Crusade. In that year a vassal kingdom of the Holy See and Germany was founded in 'Lesser Armenia' (Cilicia): the region of south-eastern Asia Minor where many Armenians had taken refuge from the invading Turks. During the union, a number of latinisms found their way into the worship of the Armenians. The innovations, mostly imitations of the liturgical practices of Dominican missionaries, were imposed on the entire Armenian Church by the various Councils of Sis (1204, 1246, 1307, 1342). Thus the Roman Prayers at the Foot of the Altar and the Last Gospel became part of the Armenian Mass, and azyme hosts replaced unleavened bread. Apparelled collars came to adorn the *shoochar*, the cope-like eucharistic vestment worn by Armenian priests, and Latin mitres appeared on the heads of the bishops, who also began to carry Latin-style croziers.[38] Superficial as these novelties were, they provoked at least one schism: among the Gregorian monks of Jerusalem, who elected a patriarch of their own in 1311.[39]

---

[35] Ibid.
[36] Ibid., p. 249.
[37] The Orthodox delegates who attended the Second Council of Lyons were appointed not by their patriarchs, but by the Emperor.
[38] These latinisms persisted as part of the rite when the Armenians later went back into schism, and remain customs of the Gregorian (Armenian Apostolic) Church today.
[39] Joseph Kaftandjian, 'Armenian Rite', NCE, I, p. 836.

Then, early in the fourteenth century, the Blackfriars gained admittance into Greater Armenia and established there the Brothers of Unity, a special branch of the Dominican order to foster the work of reconciling the dissidents. In 1330 a Uniate archbishopric was founded at Nakhichevan, a town situated north of Lake Urmi, with an Italian, Bartolomeo di Bologna, as its first metropolitan.[40] Having already won the goodwill of the Cilician Armenians, the Blackfriars confidently pursued a policy of direct latinization. Archbishop Bartolomeo translated the Dominican missal and breviary into Classical Armenian. After the collapse of the union in 1375, this Western liturgy became the ritual norm of the few Catholic churches left inside Armenia until their last faithful were dispersed by Muslim oppression in the mid-eighteenth century.[41] Fortunately, the Miaphysite Armenians (Gregorians) had remained faithful to their immemorial rite, so that when a Uniate church was reorganized among the exiled Armenians of Syria in 1740, it was still possible for the Catholics to worship according to the ancient tradition that the Dominicans had interrupted.

Towards a Tidy Church

Latin influence in the East at this time was not limited to the small groups of Oriental Christians who united, voluntarily or under duress, with Rome. Perhaps its most destructive effect on the Eastern patriarchates was the adoption of a characteristic Roman concern for liturgical conformity by their persecuted leaders themselves. From the twelfth century this attitude, previously in evidence at the Trullan Synod and manifested by Patriarch Cerularius, increasingly coloured the outlook of Orthodox patriarchs aware of the importance of strengthening their churches' defences against Latin aggression.

During their exile in Constantinople after the First Crusade, the exiled Orthodox patriarchs of Antioch and Jerusalem naturally became familiar with the Byzantine liturgy. Already in 1194, a decade before the Latin sack of Constantinople, Theodore Balsamon, the absentee Patriarch of Antioch and foremost Orthodox canonist of the time, was urging the suppression of the ancient liturgies of St James and St Mark in the patriarchates of Antioch, Jerusalem and Alexandria, going so far as to declare them unlawful: 'All the churches of God ought to follow the custom of New Rome, that is, Constantinople.'[42] When the hated Latinocracy was over, and the Patriarchs of Antioch and Jerusalem returned to their sees in 1268, they brought home with them the rite of their Greek hosts, which they proceeded to make mandatory in their churches, though allowing its translation into Syriac. In Egypt the Melkite Patriarch eventually ordered the same reform, and the Byzantine liturgy replaced the ancient Alexandrian rite. The latter continued to nourish the spiritual lives of the separated Copts, but in Syria the liturgy of Antioch, abandoned by the Melkites and latinized among the Maronites, became henceforth the preserve of the Jacobites.

Such a centripetal process of change inevitably led to the conviction among

---

[40] Korolevsky, *op. cit.*, pp. 93–94.
[41] Ibid., p. 94. All the Uniates of Cilicia had reverted to Monophysitism in 1375, after the Turkish invasion and the decimation of the Dominican missions.
[42] Wybrew, *op. cit.*, p. 209.

the Orthodox that there could be no real Christianity beyond the beliefs and practices of the Greek Church. In the Patriarchate of Moscow, made independent of Constantinople in 1458, this exclusivism became even narrower than that of imperialist Rome at her worst. According to Grigorij Protopopov, the newly auto-cephalous Russian Church

> increased her isolation from the rest of the Christian world; the slightest diver-gences from the liturgical and canonical praxis that she herself had adopted began to be considered heresies, deviations from genuine Christianity. In its extreme form this tendency culminated in the belief, widespread in Russia in the sixteenth and seventeenth centuries, that authentic orthodoxy had been preserved only in Rus', and that the rest of the Christian world (including the other Orthodox patriarchates), had strayed from the truth, a conviction firmer for the fact that it was usually supported by arguments on the basis of ritual practice.[43]

The Romanization of Magna Graecia

The auto-byzantinization of the Melkite churches was doubtless seen by Constantinople as compensation for the decline of Hellenic Christianity across the Ionian Sea. After the establishment of Aragonese rule in Sicily (1282), the hereditary Byzantine rite of the dependency of Malta was eradicated by Carmelite and Franciscan missionaries who imposed the Roman rite on the population of this small and still Arabic-speaking archipelago during the first half of the fourteenth century.[44] The Byzantine rite was restored by the Knights of St John in 1530, but only for the benefit of the Greek and Graeco-Venetian retainers who had followed them from Rhodes.[45]

At a time when a southern variety of Italian was becoming the common language of Sicily and the extreme south of Italy, the Byzantine rite maintained itself best in those areas where the population remained Greek in speech, namely the diocese of Otranto in southern Apulia, and the archdioceses of Reggio in southern Calabria and Messina in north-eastern Sicily. Here, unlike in Malta, Greek parish priests and monks still outnumbered those of the Roman rite throughout the fourteenth century, but over the following 200 years two factors – the dwindling numbers of Byzantine-rite clergy proficient in Greek, and the hostility of many Latin ordinaries to the older tradition – sped its decline. A number of venal Greek clerics aspiring to the office of bishop proved their loyalty to Latin authorities willing to promote them by embracing the Roman rite after their elevation and abolishing the ancestral rite of their new sees. Such was the case with Athanasios Kalkeophilos, the former abbot of the Basilian monastery of Santa Maria del Patire, who was appointed Bishop of Gerace (the see of the celebrated Barlaam) in 1467, and with Ioulios Staurienos, a Cypriot who became Bishop of Bova (the last stronghold of Greek speech in Calabria) in 1571.[46] By the turn of the sixteenth century practically all

---

[43] Protopopov, op. cit., p. 147.
[44] Geoffrey Hull, The Malta Language Question: A Case Study in Cultural Imperialism (Valletta, 1993), p. 327.
[45] Ibid., p. 330.
[46] Fortescue, Uniate Eastern Churches, p. 109. Bova and its environs are still Greek-speaking today.

the Greek Catholics of Messina had become Roman in rite, and the Greek dialect of the local peasantry was also on the verge of extinction.

From the year 1595 the Archbishop of Reggio, Annibale D'Afflitto, began the work of suppressing what had survived of the Byzantine rite in his province, inspired less by the Counter-Reformation spirit of disciplinary reform than by resentment of the exemptions and privileges enjoyed by his Greek clergy.[47] D'Afflitto finally achieved his objective in 1628, when the last Byzantine priest of his archdiocese went over to the Roman rite.[48] Throughout the sixteenth century the Franciscans of the diocese of Otranto strove to stamp out the remaining vestiges of its Greek liturgy, but in some Greek-speaking villages Byzantine worship lingered on until the late 1600s.[49] As for the archdiocese of Rossano in northern Calabria, the claim to fame of its Franciscan ordinary, Matteo Saraceni, was, judging from the pompous inscription on his tomb, his abolition of the Byzantine rite in 1461:

> *Hanc quam cernis ille cuius laus est perennis*
> *Transtulit in latinum, ecclesiam, de græco ad cultum divinum.*[50]

It would be easy to characterize the Holy See as the natural accomplice in these attacks on liturgical tradition in Greater Calabria and Sicily, but in fact the situation was rather more complex. Certainly Pope Gregory XIII may be blamed for supporting the turncoat Bishop of Bova in 1571 and ignoring the protests of a laity being deprived of their religious patrimony. But far more numerous were cases of popes and curial officials rejecting the requests of local Latin bishops to abolish the Byzantine rite in the parish churches and monasteries of their jurisdictions. Indeed, when Byzantine-rite Albanian refugees from the Turkish invasion of the Peloponnese (Morea) began settling in these regions from the fifteenth century,[51] a succession of popes (Paul III, Pius IV, Clement XII, Benedict XIV) enacted laws to protect the new Uniates, whose arrival had rekindled the embers of the Greek tradition, from the depredations of the surrounding Latin clergy and laity suspicious and scornful of their strange customs.[52] Typical was Pius IV's constitution of 1564, which stipulated that while the Albanians were to be placed under the jurisdiction of local Latin bishops, 'by this we do not mean that the Greeks [= Albanians] themselves are to be taken away from their Greek rite, or that they are to be in any way hindered by the ordinaries or by others'.[53]

---

[47] Ibid., p. 106.
[48] Ibid., p. 107.
[49] Ibid., pp. 111–12.
[50] Ibid., p. 109, n. 9. 'He, whose praise is eternal, transferred this church which you see from Greek divine worship to the Latin.' Dr Fortescue describes Mgr Saraceni as 'an absurd person'.
[51] By this time there were numerous settlements of Byzantine-rite Tosk Albanians (Arvanites) throughout peninsular Greece. Even the neighbourhood of Athens became Albanian-speaking.
[52] For instance they were attacked for not observing Roman fasts, for giving Holy Communion to newly baptized infants, and for having married priests. Their Italian neighbours also falsely accused them of rejecting the authority of the pope, of clinging to the 'errors of the schismatics', and even of digging up the bodies of their dead and cremating them! See Fortescue, *Uniate Eastern Churches*, p. 121.
[53] Ibid., p. 123. Pope Pius V confirmed this policy in 1566.

Latina fides

Nevertheless, papal support for the right to ritual diversity in Southern Italy was seriously undermined by the decision to subject Eastern Christians to Latin jurisdiction. The consequences of this were all too evident to Orthodox observers. After 1054 truly effective papal interventions on the side of common justice in the Oriental sphere were, on balance, the exception rather than the rule. If the Greek Church has, as a whole, repudiated the union of 1439, the real reason was that the Easterners remained unconvinced of the sincerity of the Roman overtures and guarantees. And they had good grounds for this attitude of suspicion.

The Greeks, unlike certain Latins, had long memories. For them, Florence's approach to reconciliation left much to be desired. The Council had made no apologies for past wrongs, especially the outrage of 1204, nor had it anathematized Latin fanatics like the Dominican Burchard of Mount Sion. This German friar advocated the conversion of all Byzantine-rite churches into Latin ones, the suppression of Oriental monasticism, the burning of 'heretical' Greek books, and the discouragement of the Greek language. He even conceived an ingenious plan to send one male child from every patrician Greek family to the West to be brought up in the Latin faith and culture.[54]

Easterners recalled how, in 1339, the Avignon pope Benedict XII had made light of Barlaam the Calabrian, sent by the Byzantine emperor Andronicus III to sue for reunion. Barlaam had informed the Pope that 'what separates the Greeks from you is not so much a difference in dogma as the hatred of the Greeks for the Latins provoked by the wrongs they have suffered'. He had also advised Benedict that the only possible way forward was to accede to Byzantine demands for a general council to effect the reunion.[55]

When Pope Eugenius IV agreed to such a council exactly a hundred years later, he immediately forfeited the goodwill of the Orthodox faithful by insisting that the bishops of the Church meet in the West. And, far from showing a desire to appease his estranged brethren, he sought to humiliate Patriarch Joseph of Constantinople by demanding that he genuflect and kiss the papal foot.[56] In any case, Eugenius' policy of pursuing liturgical uniformity within his own patriarchate doubtless seemed ominous to the Easterners: in 1439 the Pope encouraged King Afonso V of Portugal to substitute the Roman rite for the traditional Portuguese use in the royal chapel, and three years later he sent his legate Giovanni Castiglione to Milan with orders to abolish the Ambrosian liturgy. The citizens of Milan answered the papal diktat with a successful public revolt.[57]

This recrudescence of Roman imperialism in the West must have made the assurances made at Florence sound hollow to Eastern Christians, who found it more and

---

[54] Geanakoplos, op. cit., p. 2, n. 3; p. 103, n. 74. Did this Catholic friar inspire the Turkish Janissary system?

[55] Ibid., p. 91.

[56] Ibid., pp. 94–96. The patriarch's response was: 'This is an innovation and I will not follow it . . . If the Pope wants a brotherly embrace in accordance with ancient ecclesiastical custom, I will be happy to embrace him, but if he refuses, I will abandon everything and return to Constantinople.' Eugenius gave in, but insisted on a private reception of Joseph in order to save the papal face. This episode did nothing to mitigate the Orientals' resentment of what they perceived as Roman arrogance.

[57] King, op. cit., p. 197. Margaret Yeo, A Prince of Pastors: St Charles Borromeo (London, 1938), p. 123. In 1497 Alexander VI renewed the twelfth-century papal approval of the Ambrosian rite.

more difficult to see the Good Shepherd, meek and humble of heart, in the bishop who called himself Vicar of Christ. The tragedy was compounded by the hardening of Eastern hearts not simply towards the individuals who flouted the laws of the Church and oppressed them, but towards all their Western brethren in faith.

8

PETER'S ROME OR CAESAR'S?

He [the Pope] rules and disposes all things, orders and governs
everything as he pleases . . . He can deprive anyone of his right, as it
pleases him . . . for with him his will is right and reason; whatever
pleases him has the force of law.

FRAY ÁLVAREZ PELAYO (1332)

And if a man consider the originall of this great Ecclesiasticall
Dominion, he will easily perceive that the Papacy *is no other, than*
the Ghost *of the deceased* Romane Empire, *sitting crowned upon the*
grave thereof.

THOMAS HOBBES (1651)

Going it Alone

Though there had clearly been fault on both sides, the slow mutual estrangement of Rome and the Byzantine East, which was definitive and irrevocable by the thirteenth century, could hardly have been more disastrous for both communions. While the union of European Christendom had lasted, however precariously, Latin thought and practice were fertilized and modified in a Catholic sense by those of the Greeks, and this valuable counterbalance applied a brake to the absolutist tendencies of the Papacy, constantly recalling it to the ecclesiology of the Fathers. After the separation of the Churches, there was nothing to halt the most energetic and dangerous trend in the Latin tradition: that of rationalism.

Meanwhile the loss of the Latin West to the Greek East gradually locked the Orthodox and other Oriental Churches in an attitude of immobilism excluding the possibility of true doctrinal development. Henceforth, Greek theologians and Byzantine emperors who took an authentically Catholic approach to the question of union with Rome would be outnumbered and defeated by unenlightened co-religionists who, motivated by blind cultural prejudice or the hard-heartedness of a schismatic spirit, were 'content with denunciations of the "Latin heresy"'.[1] At the same time the absence of a strong central authority for the churches that remained in communion with Constantinople made it difficult for the independent Orthodox Church to speak with one voice on points of faith and morals that had not been

---

[1] Dimitri Obolensky, 'The Eastern View: Schism between Eastern and Western Christendom', in Knowles/Obolensky, *op. cit.*, p. 326.

fully defined before 1054. But most alarming of all for the Greeks and their fellow Orthodox, the resultant isolation of the Byzantine Empire exposed it to the attacks of the latest enemies of Christendom, the Muslim Seljuk Turks who had gained a strong foothold in central Anatolia in the late eleventh century.

If universal ordinary jurisdiction, as the full expression of papal authority, seemed an innovation to most Greek theologians it was because they remained under the influence of the old Hellenistic political philosophy which made the emperors, not the patriarchs, God's chief representatives on earth. Ever since Constantine had declared Christianity the state religion the Roman emperor had both the right and the duty to ensure the purity of doctrine and the authenticity of divine worship in the interests of civil unity and peace, though the imperial bishops always claimed the privilege of defining Christian doctrine.[2] This polity, against which the Roman popes reacted in the assertion of their authority, had produced catastrophic results in the past, for example when Constantine favoured the Arian heresy and when Leo the Isaurian promoted iconoclasm, errors which it fell to the Papacy to correct.

In the area of Christian morality the most troubling of imperial influences on the Greek Church was the practice of remarrying divorced persons, albeit with ceremonies of a penitential character. Following the Gospel of St Matthew (5.31-32; 19.3-9) the Catholic Church tolerated legal separations on the grounds of adultery (πορνεία), but given the indissolubility of Christian marriage, divorced men and women were required to remain single until the death of their legal spouses. This position had been staunchly maintained by the Roman Church since apostolic times but in the mid-sixth century the Emperor Justinian, who notoriously treated the Church as a department of state, enacted without papal sanction legislation allowing the divorced to remarry. The Greek Church passively accepted these laws, made in the spirit of a paganism whose embers were not yet extinguished and which contradicted the teachings of most of the Eastern and Western Fathers. On the eve of the Cerularian Schism this moral aberration was given canonical sanction by Patriarch Alexius the Studite (1025–1043), and the divorce laws were retained and developed, however reluctantly, by the Orthodox Church.[3]

Towards a Centralized Latin Church

In 861 Pope Nicholas' statement to the Byzantine Emperor that 'without the Church of Rome there is no Christianity' had seemed not only to discredit the Eastern tradition, but to imply that 'true' Catholicism was an Occidental thing.[4] Indeed, St Nicholas could 'not remember that the western countries . . . have ever disagreed with the See of Saint Peter in questions of this kind', and he regretted that the chaotic social conditions in the West, then plagued by the Viking invasions, prevented his calling all the archbishops of his patriarchate to Rome to discuss the Greeks' hostility 'to every church that uses the Latin language, especially our own'.[5]

From this time forward the popes strove to tighten the bonds between the bishops of the West and their patriarch, bonds until then based more on a unity

---

[2] Dvornik, 'Byzantium and the Roman Primacy', p. 305.
[3] John A. Hardon, SJ, 'Mixed Marriages: A Theological Analysis', *Église et Théologie*, I (1970), pp. 229–60.
[4] Knowles/Obolensky, *op. cit.*, p. 78.
[5] Southern, *op. cit.*, p. 98.

of faith and cult than of jurisdiction, and enlivened by intense feelings of loyalty aroused by the cult of St Peter, venerated in the person of the Pope:

> It was a unity compatible with the very slightest exercise of administrative authority. The affairs of the church received little direction from Rome. Monasteries and bishoprics were founded, and bishops and abbots were appointed by lay rulers without hindrance or objection; councils were summoned by kings; kings and bishops legislated for their local churches about tithes, ordeals, Sunday observance, penance; saints were raised to the altars – all without reference to Rome. Each bishop acted as an independent repository of faith and discipline. They sought whatever advice was available from scholars and neighbouring bishops, but in the last resort they had to act on their own initiative. The legal compilations that were made for their guidance were the work of local compilers. The majority of papal letters during this period simply confirmed and approved what others had done.[6]

Until the mid-twelfth century theological and moral leadership in the Latin Church was given more often by monks, such as St Bernard of Clairvaux, than by popes.[7] This was another reason why Nicholas I had looked forward to a full 'restoration' of the power of the Papacy which he considered to have been unjustly eclipsed by Germanic kings in the West and Byzantine emperors in the East. In fact, since the Constantinian settlement the Church had always depended on a partnership with the prevailing secular power, and in the real world the authority of popes over kings and emperors had rarely been more than technical.

In the West at least Nicholas could count on the cooperation of the semi-barbarian faithful in his effort to assert papal authority. He also commanded the loyalty of the missionary church of England which (ironically, when one considers the future history of that country) was then unsurpassed in its devotion to the Bishop of Rome. The papal mission to the Anglo-Saxons in the sixth century had created a church as directly subject to the Roman see as the Suburbicarian dioceses of central Italy. When the English missionary St Boniface embarked on the evangelization of Germany, he first swore in Rome an oath of obedience to St Peter and his vicar. Indeed, the custom of Western archbishops-elect journeying to the Papal See to receive the pallium was apparently initiated by the English.[8]

In the Carolingian state and its royal church Pope Nicholas found an excellent model of government for his reform. The Germanic feudalism of Pepin and his son Charles had been cross-fertilized by the Roman legal positivism still practised by the Byzantine emperors, and which equated law and the will of the prince. Frankish government was thus weighted strongly in favour of the central power. Whereas the early popes' contacts with their patriarchate were principally through the Western archbishops, in his own church Charlemagne weakened the authority of the metropolitans and strengthened that of the local bishops. The latter he made directly responsible to himself, with royal agents or plenipotentiaries (*missi dominici*) travelling through his realm in pairs and policing his capitularies or religious decrees, which he issued in the same manner as the Byzantine emperor.[9]

---

[6] Ibid., pp. 96–97.
[7] Friedrich Heer, *The Medieval World* (New York, 1961), p. 61.
[8] Southern, *op. cit.*, pp. 95–96, 97.
[9] Knowles/Obolensky, *op. cit.*, p. 32.

Charlemagne's obsession with uniformity – a strange blend of barbarian simple-mindedness and Byzantine caesaropapism – caused the general decline of the pre-Frankish Gallican rite in favour of the Roman, which, as the liturgy of the See of Peter, the Holy Roman Emperor considered more prestigious than the traditional cult of his realm. Yet when Charles obtained for his Gallic and Frankish archbishops the honour of receiving the pallium from the Pope,[10] he unwittingly paved the way for the replacement of royal power over the local church by papal supremacy. In the decades following the Emperor's death, metropolitans were struggling to assert their customary authority over suffragan bishops ever more determined to be answerable only to the Pope.[11]

The Need for Reform

The papal authoritarianism of St Nicholas I, maintained by his successor Adrian II, was short-lived. The murder of the next pope, John VIII, by a Roman mob in 882 ushered in the most dismal period in the history of the Papacy, its so-called 'Iron Age', when scandal and corruption were rife, and pontificates mostly brief. The institution itself was appropriated and manipulated by a Roman nobility free to act independently of the emperor against the backdrop of a disintegrating Carolingian state. During the tenth century, social life in parts of Western Europe was paralysed by the incursions of the Magyars and the Arabs. Nevertheless, the example of Nicholas I was not forgotten. John X (914–928), whose reign of fourteen years was the longest in the tenth century, strove to make papal leadership respected outside Rome. In 915 he headed the combined forces of Italian princes which expelled the Arabs from mainland Italy. John made good use of his papal legates, and took a direct interest in the affairs of the Western metropolitans.

One of the bright spots in the life of the tenth-century Church was the Cluniac revival, which spread the desire for moral and disciplinary reform. This reflowering of Benedictine monasticism produced St Leo IX (1049–1054), the pope in whom most of St Nicholas' long-dormant dreams were suddenly realized. An Alsatian by birth, Bruno of Egesheim understood the administrative machinery of the Empire and knew how to apply its workings to the Church. In his bid to call the clergy of his vast patriarchate to order by enforcing clerical celibacy and wiping out the vice of simony, he travelled through Italy, Germany and France, calling councils over which he personally presided. The synod Leo convoked in Rome in 1050 to condemn the eucharistic heresy of Berengarius did much to rehabilitate the dogmatic role of the Papacy.

The background to widespread corruption and sporadic heresy was a feudal society in which bishoprics were commonly given as rewards for services to military men thoroughly unsuited to the episcopal office. Many such bishops were, like most parish priests, married, and transmitted their benefices to their sons. Clerics who were secular in a literal sense were little inclined to follow instructions from Rome, but bent readily to the wills of their feudal masters. Abuses were most entrenched in cities and towns untouched by monastic influence, and the secularization of the clergy tended to be worst in the imperial territories. Nor had the

---

[10] This hieratic garment was first placed on tomb of St Peter.
[11] Knowles/Obolensky, *op. cit.*, p. 35.

eleventh-century popes forgotten about the trouble that a Frankish episcopate under the imperial thumb had caused two hundred years earlier, when the Papacy had sought to uphold the cultural rights of Slavonic Christians.

The high standards of the reformist popes are well reflected in their attitude towards the marriage of the higher clergy or 'nicolaism' and their zealous promotion of clerical celibacy, which had been an ideal since apostolic times but not an official requirement anywhere until the late third century. In attacking the abuse of married bishops (most common in the remoter areas of Europe), they were simply applying the existing laws of the Universal Church, in force in the West since the decree of Pope Siricius (386) and in the East since the Trullan Synod of 692. However, Siricius had allowed married priests and deacons to retain their wives though forbidding continued conjugal relations between them. In 747 Pope Zachary had ruled that marriage could not be contracted after a man was ordained subdeacon but married men who received the subdiaconate could still progress to the priesthood. In seeking to eradicate the firmly established custom of licit clerical marriage (where the required chastity depended on the virtue of individuals), the reformers were reviving the rigorist spirit of the Spanish Council of Elvira (295–302), which had ordered the deposition of any bishop, priest or deacon who continued to live with his wife and beget children after ordination.[12]

Rigorism in this area was emblematic of a wider reaction to the breakdown of ecclesiastical discipline throughout the Roman patriarchate. What particularly rankled with the popes was that this chaos was tolerated by emperors whom they themselves anointed, monarchs who had the responsibility to protect the Faith and enforce the laws of the Church in their domains. St Peter Damian who, like Dante Alighieri after him, was a strong believer in the 'two powers', took an idealized view of the Christian Empire which had a very imperfect relationship with reality. Peter wanted an emperor and a pope who, being 'two for men, but one for God, shall be enflamed by the divine mysteries'.[13] Around this time Megingaud of Eichstätt, a Bavarian bishop appointed by his relative Emperor Henry II (1002–1024) and confirmed in office by the Pope, was displaying certain liturgical attitudes hardly unusual for the age:

> In every divine service he was a lover of brevity, preferring a short Mass to a short meal. Thus, there was one occasion when he was publicly singing Mass on Easter Day. He had at last got to the point at which the Sequence should be sung, and the precentor solemnly started it in the usual way. Angrily the bishop called to the archdeacon and ordered him to read the Gospel as quickly as possible. 'These fellows', he said, 'are mad, and by singing for such a dreadfully long time they are making me die of hunger and thirst!'[14]

If in combating the wordliness of the contemporary clergy Leo IX limited his journeys to the lands of the Holy Roman Empire, it was largely because the Papacy

---

[12] The majority of secular priests in Western Europe who took wives and had families after ordination came to be accused of concubinage because they were not continent, but technically they had contracted valid marriages because at this time holy orders was not yet a canonical impediment to matrimony (ibid., p. 170).

[13] Quoted in R. H. C. Davis, *A History of Medieval Europe from Constantine to Saint Louis* (London, 1957; repr. 1970), p. 235.

[14] Ibid., p. 240.

already had the Spanish and English churches at its command, and because the refractory Celtic church of western Britain and Ireland had, under English pressure, grudgingly but definitively conformed to Roman practices. The task at hand for Rome was to reverse the stranglehold of the Saxon emperors who, since 963, had empowered themselves to control papal elections as well as controlling the appointment of bishops through lay investiture.

The Imperial Papacy

The Church's struggle against the Empire and other political units was centripetal as well as centrifugal: the popes were moved to action and emboldened by constant complaints from conscientious bishops all over Western Europe whose apostolic work was impeded in various ways by secular interference, especially in episcopal appointments. Contending with imperial recalcitance and arrogance was thus foremost among the problems that Hildebrand of Tusculum set about correcting upon his elevation to the papal throne as Gregory VII. By 1077 Pope Gregory had won the first round of his bitter struggle against the Emperor Henry IV, going so far as to excommunicate him and declare him deposed. By the end of the eleventh century the right of the Church to control her own affairs was generally acknowledged, even if tensions between church and state would continue to be a normal feature of European life.

In the sphere of internal government St Gregory advanced the work of centralization initiated by Leo IX and resumed by Nicholas II. The latter had decreed in 1059 that henceforth only cardinals (six of whom were bishops, the majority priests and deacons) could elect the Bishop of Rome, formerly chosen in a public meeting of the clergy and laity of the city, a custom so abused in the past by the Roman nobility.[15] In 1163 Pope Alexander III took a further step in this direction by allowing the Archbishop of Mainz, whom he had made cardinal, to reside in his German diocese while retaining a titular church in Rome.[16] This precedent broadened the base of curial power, spreading it more evenly throughout the Latin Church. However, the eclipse of Western metropolitans by cardinal bishops and papal legates affected also those Eastern patriarchs who later came into union with Rome and who, nine centuries later, were still protesting that their rightful precedence in the Church hierarchy was directly after the Roman Pope and *before* his cardinal bishops, not after them.[17]

The rational basis for the mode of papal autocracy exemplified by St Gregory VII and his successors was the so-called descending concept of government, according to which all power was concentrated in the Bishop of Rome as visible head of the Church on earth. According to this ecclesiology, the Supreme Pontiff stood outside and above the Church since he had no earthly superior; consequently there could

---

[15] Kevin O'Rourke, OP, 'Cardinals, Sacred College of', *CESH*, II, p. 276. Cardinals, 'hinge men' of the pope, were a creation of the Roman Church dating from the sixth century, when the pastors of certain city parishes and deacons charged with the collection and distribution of alms received this title. In the eighth century the bishops of the Latian sees bordering on Rome (Ostia, Frascati, Velletri, Palestrina etc.) were given the title of cardinal bishop. The college of cardinals (in which the bishops were always a minority) became an advisory body of the pope, and increasingly involved in papal elections, which remained public until 1059.

[16] O'Rourke, *op. cit.*, p. 276.

[17] See also Chapter 16, p. 296.

be no appeal against the judgement of a pope: *Prima sedes a nemine judicatur*.[18] In the years following Gregory's death Cardinal Deusdedit drew up the document *Dictatus Papæ*, a summary of the late Pope's thoughts on the question of papal supremacy in both the spiritual and the temporal spheres.[19] One of the Gregorian sentences, stating that 'whosoever does not agree in all things with the Roman Church is not to be considered a Catholic', not only justified Rome's current estrangement from the Greek Church, but also consecrated the ecclesiological aberration that made the will of the Pope, and not ecclesiastical tradition, the norm for liturgy and discipline in local churches. The same document admonished anyone who might baulk at such absolutism with the statement that 'a duly ordained pope is undoubtedly made a saint by the merits of St Peter'.[20]

Pyrrhic Victory?

Once the Papacy had identified the Empire as the prime obstacle to its freedom of action and to the fulfilment of its mission, this tutelary institution was doomed to marginalization. The popes now pursued a foreign policy which courted as allies or client states the numerous Catholic kingdoms that lay outside the borders of the Empire: Norman Sicily, France, England, Spain, Portugal, Denmark, Sweden and Poland. At the same time the communes of northern and central Italy were encouraged to rebel against imperial rule. The second excommunication of the dubiously Christian emperor Frederick II in 1245 marked the apogee of a long and bitter propaganda war in which the twelfth- and early thirteenth-century Papacy sought relentlessly to discredit the imperial 'brood of vipers', as Innocent IV called them. Soon afterwards the Empire of the Hohenstaufens was a spent force in Europe, shrinking to the dimensions of modern Germany, Austria, Switzerland and the Low Countries. At the turn of the fourteenth century the power of the Pope as 'father of princes and of kings, guide of the world, and vicar upon earth of Christ our Saviour' seemed unsurpassed and unsurpassable.

From the papal point of view, winning the liberty of Holy Church more than justified the humbling and displacement of an enlarged Frankish feudal kingdom pathetically posturing as the 'Holy Roman Empire' when powerful states in the West lay outside its borders. But it has not escaped the notice of historians that when Charles of Anjou, leader of the anti-imperial papal crusade called by Clement IV, captured Conradin, Frederick's sixteen-year old grandson, in 1268 and had him beheaded in a Naples marketplace, future European idealists were provided with a model of 'righteous' tyrannicide which would make possible the judicial murder of Charles I in England and Louis XVI in France, both Christian monarchs perceived by their high-principled subjects as the foes of liberty.[21]

Moreover, once imperial authority was fatally weakened, centuries of civil strife

---

[18] Walter Ullmann, 'Conciliarism', *CESH*, III, p. 105. The Latin dictum meaning 'The First See is judged by no-one' simply states a hierarchical fact; it does not mean that the pope has unlimited power. See Cardinal Joseph Ratzinger and Archbishop Tarcisio Bertone, 'The Primacy of the Successor of Peter in the Mystery of the Church: Reflections of the Congregation for the Doctrine of the Faith', *Osservatore Romano*, 18 November 1998, pp. 5–6.

[19] Arthur Murphy, 'Dictatus Papæ', *CESH*, III, pp. 496–97.

[20] *Gregorii VII Registrum, M.G.H. Epistolæ Selectæ*, ii, cited in Southern, *op. cit.*, p. 102.

[21] Heer, *op. cit.*, p. 331.

ensued, with no possibility of strong central government for Germany. It was for this reason that the German states could not be united politically until the nineteenth century (a fate shared by Italy, which the temporal Papacy was committed to keeping divided).[22] Another consequence was a current of religious cynicism, which hardened when German and Northern Italian states that defied the Papacy were placed under interdict and Mass, preaching and all sacraments except baptism and extreme unction were unavailable for long periods.[23] With such precedents, a future emperor, Charles V, would fail to prevent many of his regional electors from opting for Protestantism in the 1520s. As for Martin Luther, like the numerous Germans among the imperial troops who sacked the Eternal City in 1527, desecrating its sanctuaries and indiscriminately slaughtering its citizens, he fed on a German legacy of anti-Roman sentiment sharpened by the general exclusion of Germans from the Curia during the Avignon Papacy.[24] In modern times Bismarck and Hitler would breathe this same anti-Roman air.

Ironically, the vacuum left after 1245 by the Holy Roman Empire as partner and protector of papal Rome was filled within half a century by the France of the ruthless Philip IV, who turned on Pope Boniface VIII, and kept his successors under royal supervision in their luxurious Provençal exile.

Western Ways

The ill-omened Roman victory over the Hohenstaufens, which the popes achieved as politicians rather than as pontiffs, was a source of scandal to a Greek Church inured to submission to a strong imperial power. That Innocent III, Honorius III, Gregory IX and Innocent IV should have made a wide use of spiritual sanctions such as interdict and excommunication to achieve political ends only made it worse.[25] The militarism at the heart of Western feudal society was always a stumbling block for the Greeks, whose clergy did not join the ranks of civil armies, let alone lead them, an aberration that would have horrified the Fathers of the Church, Western no less than Eastern. Widespread by now in Byzantine society was a low opinion of violent and rapacious 'Franks', whose only virtue seemed to be physical courage. Such attitudes were coloured by the population's familiarity with the Normans of Sicily and their regular raids on Greece which appeared to have the tacit support of their papal patrons.

As for the eight Crusades called by the Papacy (1095–1270) – the parting shot of the first of which was a general massacre of Jews in the Rhineland – Eastern Christians did not share the Western ideal of the holy war. The only battles their religious tradition recognized were those of the spirit; wars waged by the Christian state were considered secular affairs. For the Byzantines the rapine, bloodshed and wanton cruelty of the Crusaders' assaults on the Muslims occupying the Holy Land, in which Oriental Christians as well as Jews were often unwillingly caught up, seemed directed solely at conquering territories which by right belonged to the Eastern Empire.[26] Indeed, when the Emperor Alexius I Comnenus had first

---

[22] Davis, *op. cit.*, pp. 256–57.
[23] Heer, *op. cit.*, p. 220.
[24] Ibid., p. 338.
[25] Knowles/Obolensky, *op. cit.*, p. 299.
[26] Heer, *op. cit.*, pp. 126–30.

appealed to Pope Urban II for military aid against the Muslims in Palestine and Syria (which the Byzantines had temporarily recovered in 969) it was his expectation that the forces of the First Crusade would restore these lands to him in return for military assistance. Instead, Latin kingdoms were set up in the Levant, where the Eastern Church was marginalized, and where, strangely, the new Frankish overlords made no attempt to convert the infidels.

The rift with the East was not helped in 1123 when Pope Calixtus II called the first general council of the Latin Church, which he termed ecumenical in spite of the fact that the bishops of the Eastern churches were not represented. There would be six more such Latin councils over the following two hundred years. Their principal function was not to define dogmas of faith (unlike the seven ecumenical councils held in the East in the first millennium), but to impose the papal will in disciplinary matters. The unilateral character of these councils implied that the traditions of the wayward Easterners were unimportant, and indeed when Oriental Christians came under Latin rule during the Crusades, they were expected to give assent to the disciplinary laws of the four Lateran Councils (held in 1123, 1139, 1170 and 1215) in which their leaders had played no part. The Second Council of Lyons (1274) was concerned with the reunion of the Churches, but instead of being invited to discuss doctrinal and other differences, the few Eastern delegates were simply expected to submit unceremoniously to the Roman claims, which they did by singing the Nicene Creed with a thrice-repeated *filioque*.[27]

A controversial reform for Eastern Christians – and for many in the West – had been the legal measures of eleventh-century popes against clerical marriage, contradicting the decisions of contemporary diocesan councils that upheld the institution.[28] The Synod of Pavia (1018), approved by Benedict VIII, stigmatized as concubines the wives of priests (*presbyteræ*) and deacons (*diaconissæ*) and declared their children not only illegitimate but slaves of the Church without any prospect of enfranchisement. In 1075 Gregory VII interdicted married priests from saying Mass and forbade the faithful to attend their services and receive their ministrations. Finally, the First Lateran Council (1123), institutionalized universal clerical celibacy, declaring all marriages contracted by subdeacons, deacons and priests not only illegal but also invalid, and making holy orders an impediment to matrimony.[29]

Henceforth only celibate men could be ordained as secular priests, and they had to make a tacit vow of chastity (*votum annexum*). Ordained men already married were required to separate from their wives and children – a decree that was widely resented and in some places ignored.[30] As for Greek Christians – especially those of Southern Italy, Sicily and Malta recently reintegrated into the Roman patriarchate – they were scandalized and intimidated by the new legislation. For the Easterners (as for many in the West who were not necessarily opposed to Church reform) it was a *lex iniqua* not only because of its harshness but by virtue of the apostolic law forbidding spouses to separate.[31]

---

[27] Knowles/Obolensky, *op. cit.*, p. 321.

[28] For instance the Councils of Lisieux (1064), Rouen (1063, 1072) and Winchester (1072).

[29] In Greek canon law married men could receive the sacrament of orders but marriage could not be subsequently contracted by men ordained as celibates.

[30] The whole legislation continued to be disregarded in peripheral countries like Iceland, whose last Catholic bishop, Jón Arason, martyred by Lutherans in 1550, was married with children.

[31] In 1 Cor. 7.10, 1 Cor. 7.5, 1 Tim. 3.3 and 4.1-5. The Eastern Trullan (Quinisext) Synod of 692 had actually condemned the Roman demand of continence for married clergy:

However, as well as the old spiritually motivated desire for parish priests of a higher calibre undistracted by wives and children,[32] the reformists were aware that a secular clergy 'monasticized' by compulsory celibacy would be more amenable to the commands of their superiors and less of a drain on diocesan financial resources than married priests with dependants and strong social and local loyalties. Thereafter the man-made law of compulsory celibacy in the Latin West would divide Catholic opinion until the present day. For opponents, especially those inclined to naturalism, it was wrong because it imposed on clerics a way of life properly sustained by a charism granted by God, rather than by human will.[33] Unquestionably compulsory celibacy was a blessing for the Church when it was willingly observed in the framework of a strong life of prayer and spirit of pastoral sacrifice fortified by the 'grace of state'. On the other hand it became a terrible liability when imposed on individuals psychologically unsuited to it.

There is an uncomfortable connection between the rule of celibacy and the epidemic of defections from the priesthood during the Reformation, as well as the plague of clerical fornication and sexual abuse of minors that struck a modern Latin Church in rapid spiritual decline after Vatican II, a long-term consequence, in part, of making the priestly life an unattractive one for most men. Moreover, after the ordination of married men ceased to be an option in the Latin Church, secular priests, none of whom was barred by his state from potential advancement to the episcopate, lost their natural protection against clerical ambition and all its attendant vices.

A New Age of Faith

Whatever the short- and long-term results of these specifically Western measures and contemporary papal *Realpolitik*, it is certain that the motives of practically every pontiff from Leo IX to Gregory IX, men who believed themselves to have been placed by God over all peoples and nations, were high-minded, intentions 'primarily . . . of a spiritual father with great prestige and wide interests and responsibilities rather than those of an authoritarian autocrat' according to Dom David Knowles. The same historian describes the Papacy of this age as an institution 'of great benefit to Europe' which 'worked almost solely for the benefit of those who acknowledged its authority'.[34] Innocent III's replacement of the old papal title of 'Vicar of St Peter' with 'Vicar of Christ', whereby he proclaimed himself a power in his own right rather than a mere link in a tradition, was sym-

---

> Since we have learnt that in the Church of the Romans it is handed down as a law that deacons and priests have to promise restraint from intercourse with their wives, we wish, following the old law observed and prescribed by the apostles, that the legal marriages of ordained men shall continue to be valid in that we in no way put an end to their cohabitation. They shall not be forced to promise at the time of their ordination that they will have to restrain themselves . . .

[32] Cf. 1 Cor. 7.32: 'The unmarried man is anxious about the affairs of the Lord; but the married man is anxious about worldly affairs, how to please his wife, and so his interests are divided.'

[33] Heinz-Jürgen Vogels, *Celibacy – Gift or Law? A Critical Investigation*, tr. G. A. Kon (Tunbridge Wells, 1992), pp. 23–36. This book summarizes the standard case against universal celibacy from a modern viewpoint unappreciative of the value of this Latin institution and more impressed by its failures than its successes.

[34] Knowles/Obolensky, *op. cit.*, pp. 332, 333.

bolic of this heightened sense of universal responsibility.[35] In any case there was a general belief among Western Christians in the superiority of the spiritual power to the temporal power derived from it, which is precisely why the papal victory had been possible.

The spiritual priorities of this line of reforming pontiffs were reflected in the Fourth Lateran Council, which Innocent III called in 1215 to remedy, among other things, the alarming rise of irreligion among the laity during the previous century. The age of the great Gothic cathedrals was also a period of rapid urbanization, when local dioceses had been unable (or had neglected) to expand parochial networks to keep up with the population explosion. In many places a hierarchy recruited mainly from the nobility, often preferring lives of comfort to the rigours of apostolic labour, had allowed new generations to grow up in ignorance of the Faith and as strangers to the sacraments. In Northern Italy, France and Germany especially, the spiritual vacuum was quickly filled by pietistic and charismatic movements of dubious orthodoxy which were spread by traders and lay preachers and gained great popularity.[36]

Responding to this situation the Council decreed that all adult Christians must confess their sins to their parish priest at least once a year and receive Holy Communion during Eastertide. Pope Innocent renewed prohibitions on pluralism and on the buying and selling of benefices, clerics were forbidden to hunt, frequent taverns and go to war, and they were ordered to wear black clerical dress and the tonsure.[37] Innocent gave his blessing to two new orders of itinerant friars, the Franciscans and the Dominicans, who came to be a powerful force for rechristianization as well as for civilization in general.

Church Business

Nevertheless, the thirteenth-century ascendancy of the Church was not without its negative side. From the pontificates of Innocent IV (1243–1254) and his successors the Church was effectively run by canon lawyers who gradually bureaucratized the Papacy through their reform of the Curia. This enabled the popes to tighten their control over the Latin clergy through a variety of measures and strategies. Maximum use was made of papal legates, who established an effective communication network, opening the channels by which Rome could impose her will in the affairs of local churches.

Growing centralism led to the clericalization of the Church and the gradual exclusion of laymen from its government. Liturgically this trend was reflected in the clergy's monopolizing of actions traditionally shared by the laity, such as vocal participation in the sacred rites (in which the people's parts were now performed exclusively by servers and choirs) and the withholding of the chalice from the laity in Holy Communion. One particularly unfortunate development during the fourteenth century was the shifting of the time for the celebration of the Easter

---

[35] Southern, *op. cit.*, p. 105. Innocent's words were: 'We are the successor of the Prince of the Apostles, but we are not his vicar, nor the vicar of any man or Apostle, but the vicar of Jesus Christ Himself' (ibid).

[36] Davis, *op. cit.*, pp. 349–50.

[37] Ibid., pp. 343–44.

Vigil from its already anomalous mid-afternoon slot to the very early morning.[38] As a result of this change, relatively few of the laity would henceforth attend this service, seen as a mainly clerical affair but which in fact was the most important liturgical function of the Christian year.[39]

The model for centralization were the canons of Roman imperial law rediscovered in the eleventh century and later systematized by the Bolognese jurist-monk Gratian. Patronage became the main method by which the eleventh-century popes consolidated their political supremacy. Clerical and lay clients from all over the West were encouraged to come to Rome, not simply to pray at the tomb of St Peter as in the past, but also for the practical purpose of having their litigations settled by the papal court. These legal proceedings poured into the papal coffers huge sums of money which were then used to pay rewards, mostly benefices, to those most loyal to the Supreme Pontiff, who had now replaced the emperor in more ways than one.[40]

As business boomed, the scramble for indulgences offered by the Holy See in return for almsgiving and good works began to affect the outlook of Latin Christians. The traditional view of a God whose ways are largely unknown to man tended to give way to the crude popular notion of a 'banker God' prepared to negotiate with his human clients, the currency in the transactions being the merits of Christ and His saints. One repercussion on orthopraxis was the custom of dispensing laymen from abstinence from eggs and dairy foods (*lacticinia*) in Lent if they participated in certain crusading activities or contributed funds to some church project. Rouen Cathedral's *Tour de Beurre* (Butter Tower), begun in 1488, was built this way, and in contemporary Germany similar dispensations became known as *Butterbriefe* 'butter letters'.

The Price of Order

The corruptive effects of what often became a cynical traffic in dispensations from religious duties and in commutations of the punishment due to absolved sins, as well as the frequent misdemeanours of 'pardoners' licensed by Rome, were favourite themes of contemporary writers like the Englishmen William Langland

---

[38] Adolf Adam, *The Liturgical Year: Its History and its Meaning after the Reform of the Liturgy* (New York, 1981), p. 76. The bizarre anticipation of the Paschal Vigil, a night service in the first seven centuries of the Roman Church (and always such in the Eastern rites), was not corrected until 1951. In the mid-eighth century the custom arose of beginning the Vigil in the evening, after the first star had appeared, evidently because of a widespread desire to bring the exhaustingly rigorous fast of Holy Week to as early an end as possible. During the following century it became permissible to begin the Vigil Mass at the hour of None around 3pm (None marking the end of the daily Lenten fast from the previous midnight) and this meant that the ceremonies preceding the Vigil Mass began around midday. A fourteenth-century reform allowed None to be sung around dawn on fast days, so that an early morning Mass could be celebrated on fast days. The semantic shift whereby the English word *noon* and the Flemish *noen* (from Latin *nona* [*hora*]) came to denote midday rather than 3pm reflects this historical anticipation of the ninth liturgical hour.

[39] The night vigil, preserved in some places, disappeared after the bull *Sanctissimus* of Pius V (1566) forbade all afternoon and evening Masses. The Pian missal of 1570 prescribed the morning celebration of the Vigil.

[40] Southern, *op. cit.*, pp. 109–15.

and Geoffrey Chaucer.[41] At the same time, the clericalism used to exploit the uneducated faithful was given a powerful impulse by medieval legislators like Gratian, who despised the lay state enough to describe it as 'a concession to human weakness'.[42] Nevertheless, religious sentiment in Western Europe at this time was sincere and deep enough to prevent the new clericalism from engendering a widescale anti-clericalism, at least for the time being. The position of the Roman Church had never been more secure. Moreover, as Richard Southern concedes, the 'flow of business' to and from Rome

> had one great positive result. It was responsible for tidying up large areas of ordinary life. The papal court protected parish priests against eviction and gave them a minimum income that could not easily be plundered; it gave laymen a discipline that was clear-cut and not very onerous; it laid down rules and conditions for all the main occasions and areas of Christian life – baptism, confirmation, confession, communion, penance, marriage, religious instruction and religious duties, alms, usury, last wills and testaments, the last rites, burial, graveyards, prayers and masses for the dead. With similar clarity and completeness it dealt with all the incidents of clerical life – dress, education, ordination, duties, status, crimes and punishments. It drew into one intricate but coherent system the vast complex of religious Orders that grew up in the twelfth century . . .[43]

Unhappily the great age of the Papacy was also one in which pontiffs often ignored their spiritual obligations in order to devote themselves to the daily business that had become necessary to maintain their leadership of Western Christendom. In the previous century St Bernard of Clairvaux, reading the signs of the times, had warned his former protegé Pope Eugenius III (1145–1153) about the dangers of this concentration of papal power, especially the temptation to materialism in religion.[44] But a century and a half later Pope Clement V was considering the advantages of transfering the papal court from turbulent Rome to peaceful Provence so that the now all-important church business could be conducted from a more central location, easily accessible to all parts of the West. The move to Avignon in 1309 underscored the Papacy's alienation from Eastern Christendom. It also marked another step in the abstraction of the papal office, when the new Gascon successor of St Peter, physically prevented from taking possession of his Italian see, could convince himself that he no longer needed to breathe the memory-laden air of Rome to be truly pope.

The Heterodox Challenge

In the Latin West the heterodox movements that would soon make possible the great religious upheaval of the sixteenth century had been, like Bogomilism in the East, largely social in motivation. Yet unlike this Bulgarian heresy, Catharism and the Proto-Protestantism of the Waldensians, Patarines and other sectaries began

---

[41] See, for instance, Langland, *Piers Plowman*, Prologue, 69–82, and Chaucer, *The Canterbury Tales*, General Prologue, 669–714.
[42] Yves Congar, *Lay People in the Church*, tr. D. Attwater (Paramus, 1956), p. 9.
[43] Southern, *op. cit.*, pp. 116–17.
[44] Ibid., p. 111.

not as peasant revolts against secular lords, but as an urban protest against the materialism and corruption of certain sections of the Latin clergy.[45] In Languedoc this movement soon assumed the form of a hierarchical counter-Church, outwardly Christian but essentially Manichean; elsewhere Proto-Protestantism grew out of reformist lay movements that were initially orthodox, that of the Lyonese merchant Peter Waldo and his followers being a case in point.

Common to all the Western heretics was deep resentment of priests judged – fairly or unfairly – to be more interested in worldly pursuits than in their spiritual calling. Such anti-clericalism was the root cause of the anti-sacramentalism of the Waldensians and other Proto-Protestant groups: spurning power-mongering Catholic clerics, the heretics went on to reject the very things that set the 'proud' (or demonized) priesthood above the 'humble' laity: the sacraments which the priests alone were empowered to administer and the teaching of the Church which it was the privileged role of the clergy to impart.[46]

In such a disastrous divorce of faith from traditional orthopraxis there was a large element of rationalism. But whereas the 'orthodox' rationalism of Charlemagne and Pope Gregory VII had sought to transform the traditional Church in pursuing an ideal of unity which they were incapable of distinguishing from uniformity, the Proto-Presbyterians of the High Middle Ages rejected the real Church and replaced it with an ideal one of their own devising. And significantly, fourteenth-century Lombard Waldensians targeted the temporal power of the Papacy as the prime cause of the corruption of the 'ungodly' Roman Church which they had abandoned.[47]

Hunting the Heretic

The Church was not slow in reacting to this challenge. But in the new, fervid climate of reform the practical necessity of directing the minds and behaviour of Christians for the sake of order and orthodoxy could easily conflict with the evangelical precept of charity. The Catharism in reaction to which the Inquisition made its appearance on the stage of history was unquestionably the greatest threat to Christian faith and civilization since the rise of Islam. Medieval society, Eastern and Western, unanimously regarded heresy as treason, and since the Council of Tours in 1163, Latin bishops had been acting on their duty to investigate reported cases of heresy, to condemn the culprits, and to hand the obdurate over to the secular authorities for punishment, initially only imprisonment and the confiscation of their property.

While modern liberal objections to 'intolerance' may have little relevance to the medieval reality, in which most people regarded heretics as the very worst of criminals, it is legitimate to regret the socio-cultural consequences of turning the

---

[45] Bogomilism was founded by a priest (named Bogumil or Jeremiah), not a layman, and stemmed directly from puritan tendencies in ninth- and tenth-century Bulgarian monasticism that opened the door to Manichean influences, kept alive in the East by Paulicianism. The heresy spread among a Slavophone peasantry alienated from the byzantinized upper classes of Bulgaria, and was characterized from the first by a spirit of contempt for secular authorities no less than for the Catholic hierarchy.

[46] Giorgio Tourn, *I valdesi: La singolare vicenda di un popolo-chiesa* (Turin, 1977, 1993), pp. 16–17.

[47] Ibid., pp. 40–43.

Inquisition into an instrument of totalitarian government within the Church. In the West the cruelty involved in the discovery and punishment of deliberate heresy by the religious and secular authorities – the use of torture and barbaric executions by burning alive – was an innovation of the late twelfth century, a direct outcome of the contemporary revival of Roman law and its standard penalties.[48] Only one generation earlier St Bernard had insisted, like most of the Church Fathers before him, that faith must be 'the result of conviction and not be imposed by force'.[49] In this he was in agreement with Tertullian, Origen, Lactantius, St Hilary, St Cyprian and St John Chrysostom who, while recommending the excommunication of heretics, condemned the use of corporal punishment and the death penalty which the early Christian emperors were keen to impose. The principal exception to this patristic tradition was St Augustine who, after initial hesitation, finally approved of the fining and flogging of the troublesome Donatist heretics of his day.

The prestige of Augustinian thought in the West allowed Pope Innocent III, alarmed by the spectre of quasi-institutionalized heresy in Languedoc, to launch a crusade against the Albigensians in 1208. This resulted in the French invasion and conquest of Languedoc on the pretext of stamping out Catharism. There followed mass killings of Occitan Catholics alongside the targeted heretics, and the destruction of the most brilliant Western culture since the Roman Empire.[50] The same Pope, at the Fourth Lateran Council of 1215, universally sanctioned the burning of unrepentant heretics, and in 1229 Gregory IX centralized the investigation of heresy by instituting the Papal Inquisition at the Council of Toulouse. Two years later Pope Gregory would approve and introduce into universal canon law the current secular processes of prosecution.

Nevertheless, there was considerable resistance from local bishops to the papal command to set up diocesan inquisitions, as well as from ordinary Christians who abhorred heresy but also feared and hated the (mainly Dominican) policemen of orthodoxy.[51] The excesses and abuses of the Inquisition would provide the future enemies of the Catholic faith with powerful ammunition. And Dom David Knowles deplores how, after its introduction into the Latin Church, the inquisitorial process became a mechanical force which the popes themselves could no longer control:

> Throughout the proceedings the dice were loaded against the accused, and what protection he had in the earliest times – an advocate, the inadmissibility of evidence obtained by violence, protection from torture and from its repetition – were gradually whittled away by legislation and by casuistry and by open and direct equivocation, and the attempts of popes such as Clement V to restore equitable treatment were ignored. We of the present century have some knowledge of the seeming inevitability by which the machinery of the law becomes a snare when used by a sovereign authority for a political end, or indeed by any who hold that

[48] Ibid., pp. 373–74. The burning of heretics was also prescribed by Byzantine laws of an earlier era, though never applied as widely as in the West. Burning was favoured by the Church as a form of execution because it did not involve the spilling of blood.

[49] Richard E. Trame, SJ, 'Inquisition, The', *CESH*, V, p. 475.

[50] The Albigensian Crusade led to the cultural colonization of Occitania by France and sent the Occitan language, once more prestigious than French, into permanent decline. It is no coincidence that anti-clericalism and a disposition towards both Protestantism (the Camisards) and Jacobinism (Danton, Combes etc.) would henceforth be a characteristic of this humiliated Latin nation.

[51] Trame, *op. cit.*, pp. 477–78; Knowles/Obolensky, *op. cit.*, p. 372.

a reason of state or ideology or of religion can be invoked against truth and just judgment.[52]

The worst result, however, was a certain blunting of the Catholic conscience, since 'justice and Christian charity were often strangely neglected by men acting in a public capacity when as private individuals they showed themselves both just and humane'.[53] Meanwhile the victims of this papally directed drive for conformity would become, in Cathar and Waldensian lore, 'martyrs of conscience' waiting to be avenged in the cataclysmic revolt of the sixteenth century.

The Conciliarists against the Emperor-popes

By the late fourteenth century the culmination of so many negative trends in the Latin Church was precipitating a deep crisis. As the Papacy teetered on the brink of ruin during the Great Western Schism the conciliarist movement paradoxically presented itself as the only way out of the impasse. Suddenly in the balance were the evolved papal claims. While the Eastern Churches vigorously rejected them, many in the West were troubled by the unqualified contention of papal absolutists since the time of Innocent IV that the Roman pontiff was not subject to the laws of the Church (as opposed to the laws of God), following the principle of imperial Roman jurisprudence that the prince stands above the law (*princeps legibus solutus*).[54] The problem was compounded by the question of papal infallibility since, as Fr Brian Tierney remarks:

> The circumstances in which a pope's pronouncements could be regarded as infallible had been neither defined nor much discussed. It was generally accepted that a pope could err in faith and it seemed intolerable that the whole Church should be thrown into confusion as a result. There was a need to find norms that might set proper limits to the powers of a pope.[55]

Certain canonists of the twelfth and thirteenth centuries had seen the Pope and the Church as forming a corporation, subject to the common laws governing any human guild. In such a system the Pope was merely a 'proctor' of the corporation with his brother bishops. This corporation theory was quite distinct from the 'parliament theory' of Bartolo de Sassoferrato (1314–1357) and the Postglossators, who, in making the episcopal 'proctors' representatives of the people, were advocating the popular-democratic model of the Church that paved the way for Protestantism. Both theories were, however, opposed to the constitution of the Church, which is strictly monarchical.

[52] Knowles/Obolensky, *op. cit.*, pp. 372–73.
[53] Ibid., p. 374. The justice-based culture of the Middle Ages, when life was hard and short and physical suffering was the common lot, accepted as fair many severe corporal punishments which seem horrendous and wantonly cruel to the comfort-based society of today. It has been well said that every age accepts things that scandalize the men and women of other periods: in the eighteenth century decent Christians made no objection to slavery, just as today decent secular people refuse to be shocked by the widespread institutionalized murder of the unborn.
[54] Klaus Schatz, *Papal Primacy: From Its Origins to the Present* (Collegeville, Minnesota, 1996), pp. 93–94.
[55] Brian Tierney, 'Conciliarism, History of', *NCE*, III, p. 109.

Most prominent Conciliarists, moreover, trod a dangerous path by taking an 'ascending' view of power which subordinated the authority of the Pope to that of a general council, an impossibility in orthodox theology because the collective power of bishops is realized only when they assemble and act in communion with the Pope as divinely appointed head of the Church (his presence alone making a council ecumenical).[56] The more heterodox conciliarists, like Marsilius of Padua and William of Ockham, actually denied the divine origin of the Papacy and argued for imperial supremacy.[57]

On the other hand it was possible in orthodox Catholic theology to subject the exercise of full papal power to a series of checks and balances determined by the natural law and, especially, by the Christian law of charity. The moderate Conciliarists influenced by the thought of the Dominican Thomist John Quidort of Paris (c. 1240–1306), adhered to tradition in eschewing any false opposition of conciliar and papal authority. This party sought not to deny the Pope's supreme authority in principle, but rather to limit it in practice, so that the power exercised by the Roman pontiff normally devolved to the bishops, whose office, too, was of divine institution.

John of Paris had clearly distinguished the divinely instituted office and the human person of the pope, elected by the college of cardinals as a steward (*dispensator*) to guard the Catholic faith and the property of the Church. The papal office itself could never be abolished because it had been created by Christ, but a pope who sinned against the Faith, attacked tradition or otherwise abused his privileges could be deposed by the same electors who had chosen him.[58] Hence when, in times of crisis, the Pope did invoke his full juridical powers, he would do so not alone and arbitrarily, but within the context of a general council, in consultation with his fellow orthodox bishops, and with respect for the legitimate customs and institutions of every Christian church.[59] In theory this new outlook guaranteed Christian unity; in practice it also brought its proponents closer to the Eastern tradition. It was, nevertheless, a challenge to the concept of papal supremacy that placed the Pope under no obligation to govern through councils of bishops.

Before the Western Schism, clerics and laymen alike were accustomed to conforming their thinking to that of the Pope in all matters, not just in what was *de fide*. But faith in the spiritual and moral authority of the Vicar of Christ had been widely undermined by the scandals surrounding the Avignon Papacy (1309–1377), notably the nepotism and heterodoxy of John XXII (1316–1334), the extravagant living of Clement VI (1342–1352), and the servile attitude of all seven exiled pontiffs towards the French crown.[60] Dissident voices indignantly accused of simony a papal bureaucracy that taxed the faithful for spiritual services and trafficked in benefices and indulgences.

Against this background, sincere Catholics of the fourteenth century began to search the history of the Church and the writings of the early Fathers for better models of church government. Instead of ignoring the dissident Christians of the

---

[56] Ladislas Örsy, 'Conciliarism (Theological Aspect)', NCE, IV, p. 111.
[57] Ibid.
[58] Ibid.
[59] Walter Ullmann, *op. cit.*, p. 108; Philip Hughes, *A History of the Church*, III (London, 1947), p. 274.
[60] H. A. Rommen, 'Avignon Papacy', CESH, I, pp. 516–17. Regarding the heterodoxy of John XXII, see Chapter 8, p. 144.

East, various thinkers came to the realization that the Roman communion had been disadvantaged by the estrangement of so important a part of it, and so had everything to gain from the recovery of its earlier unity.[61] As the end of the century drew near, demands for administrative reform became more urgent. Yet the late medieval popes were resolute in rejecting any qualification of what they considered their absolute authority. From 1378 the 'Babylonian Captivity' of the Church was followed by the disconcerting spectacle of three rival claimants to the papal throne. The Conciliarist movement consequently gained strength as the obvious remedy for the breakdown of central government in the Latin Church.

In 1414 the Holy Roman Emperor Sigismund called the Council of Constance, which deposed the three rival popes, and elected a new one, Martin V (1417–1431). However, Martin refused to approve the heterodox decree *Sacrosancta*, which asserted that popes were subject to the rulings of general councils deriving their authority directly from Christ and acting independently of the Roman pontiff. Throughout his pontificate, Martin, a notorious nepotist, strove to exalt the powers of the Papacy, though he thought the better of publishing his decree banning appeals against papal decisions to a general council. On the other hand, he bowed to Conciliarist pressure and issued the decree *Frequens*, which bound the Pope to call frequent councils to assist him in his government of the Church. Unhappily, the vehemence of Pope Martin's justified and necessary reaction against extreme Conciliarism doomed to failure his efforts, in 1422, to reconcile a Greek Church instinctively uneasy with any display of papal imperialism. This was all the more unfortunate in that the contemporary Byzantine emperor, John VIII Palaiologos, was extremely anxious to bring about the reunion of the Churches in order to present the Ottomans poised to attack Constantinople with the opposition of an undivided Christendom.

An Opportunity Lost

The reign of the next pontiff, Eugenius IV (1431–1447), was marred by acrimonious conflict with the rebellious Council of Basel (1431–1437) which the Pope, after initial objections to its aggressive conciliarism, recognized as lawful in 1433.[62] Eugenius' capitulation may have been a temporary setback to the cause of papal autocracy, but it was pregnant with ecumenical potential. At a new council opened in Ferrara in 1438 and concluded in Florence in 1445, moderate conciliarist principles and an understanding that the reconciliation of the Greeks, Armenians, Copts, Syrian Jacobites and (Cypriot) Nestorians could be brought about only by conciliar deliberation, were proposed as substitutes for the papal imperialism of recent centuries.

Much of the theoretical groundwork for this reunion council had been the work of Jean Charlier de Gerson, chancellor of the University of Paris. In 1410, during the brief pontificate of the Greek pope Alexander V, Gerson had preached a sermon before King Charles VI in which he averred that the differing liturgical

---

[61] Ibid., p. 79. The English heresiarch John Wycliffe, in his *De Christo et Antichristo*, indulged his anti-papal prejudice by contending that 'the schism had been caused by the greed and cupidity of the Roman pontiff, and that the Greeks alone were faithful to Christ' (ibid., p. 84).

[62] In its final phase, from 1437 to 1449, the Council lacked papal approval and was formally schismatic.

and ecclesiastical customs of the Byzantines were legitimate traditions and no impediment to full corporate reunion with the Roman Church. As for the problem of papal authority, in the French theologian's opinion:

> No papal decision even in a General Council was binding (he declared) except on matters directly affecting the truth of the Faith and the Gospel. All those matters of local usages which caused so much trouble – the use of unleavened bread, the marriage of priests, the differing practices with regard to confession, and so on – lay outside the scope of papal authority.[63]

Admittedly, Eugenius' qualified support for this plan was in the ambit of his struggle against the Conciliarists of Basel: a reunion of the Orientals achieved directly by a pope would mean the triumph of papal power over both the schismatic Easterners and the Conciliarists. But once the reunion council was under way, Eugenius felt sufficiently secure in his position to publish the bull *Lætentur Cœli*, which asserted his full and unlimited authority over the Universal Church.

At the same time, the success of the Pope's reunion scheme depended on his meeting the Easterners as far as possible on their own terms. The acts of the Council did characterize the Pope as 'successor to the blessed Peter first of the Apostles, true vicar of Christ, head of the entire Church, and father and teacher of all Christians, with complete power received from our Lord Jesus Christ through Peter to teach, rule and govern the universal Church'. However, this full definition of papal power was qualified by a clause adding that 'all the rights and privileges of the Patriarchs of the East are excepted'.[64] Because the Primacy of Peter was now defined in more moderate terms, the relevant formula proved acceptable to most of the Greeks and other Easterners attending the reunion council.[65] Moreover, in diametrical opposition to the tendencies of St Gregory VII, the union was based on the dual principle of 'unanimity in matters of doctrine; respect for the legitimate rites and traditions peculiar to each Church'.[66]

But no sooner had the Council of Florence done its work of putting an end to the schisms of West and East than Eugenius launched another attack against the Conciliarists by condemning, in 1446, the anti-papal conciliar decrees of Constance and Basel. This act of triumphalism brought about the collapse of the Conciliarist movement, but it also served to erode the confidence of the reconciled Greeks, who eventually repudiated the union which, in any case, had failed to win popular support in the East, where popular dislike of the 'Franks' was as strong as ever. The bishops who had attended the council in Italy were deposed and fanatical monks stirred up the population of Constantinople against any reconciliation with the Roman Church.

It boded ill that the failure of the reunion council coincided with the definitive victory of the Papacy, now confirmed in its inveterate absolutism, over all who sought to limit the arbitrary exercise of its power. According to Professor Southern:

---

[63] Southern, *op. cit.*, pp. 85–86.
[64] Geanakoplos, *op. cit.*, pp. 107–09, and n. 99.
[65] Only the intransigently anti-Latin archbishop Mark Eugenikos of Ephesus refused to sign the final decree. He was canonized by the Orthodox Church in 1734.
[66] Ware, *op. cit.*, p. 80.

In 1453 the papal view of Christendom had triumphed. More than any other force it had been responsible for giving western Christendom an independent existence in the eighth century, and for providing the doctrinal basis for western supremacy from the eleventh century onwards. The movement towards Conciliar government in the church, which might have offered a new path to unity, had in the end collapsed, not least because of the strength of the papacy. So, from the point of view of Christendom as a whole, the papacy was the great divisive force throughout the Middle Ages.[67]

A divisive force at least to the extent that the papal supremacists drew on the pagan legacy of Roman law, with its absolutist concept of imperial power, at the expense of traditional Catholicity. For papal monarchy, while not constitutional in the modern sense, was nonetheless not absolute, since (as the First Vatican Council would later declare) the power of the Pope was full and supreme merely 'in the sense that it cannot be limited by any greater human power but only by the natural and divine law'.[68]

Seeds of the Reformation

Papal absolutism not only undermined the inter-ecclesial reconciliation made possible by the Conciliarist movement, but in seeking to increase its material wealth and political power in the High Middle Ages, the Papacy sowed the seeds of its own destruction, a fate from which it would be saved only by the promise of immortality made to it by its Divine Founder. The spirit of the Renaissance had much to do with the moral decline of the fifteenth century. As Mgr Philip Hughes writes:

> Gradually, inevitably, the amoral spirit of the revived Paganism gained a hold in the Church, halting effectively the whole reform movement and divorcing the papacy from it. For the final achievement of the neo-Pagans was the most unexpected thing of all, namely to bring about the moral collapse of the very centre of the Christian world. Pope Nicholas VI (1447–1455) had desired to see Rome the centre of the new learning, the new culture, the new art. Fifty years after his time it was all this, and it was also the centre of all the new vices, and the popes were foremost among its practitioners. And this continued for some forty years, so that Pope Adrian VI (1521–1523), who lived all through the period, could preface his reform with the deliberate statement that the Roman Church had been the first source of evils which good men everywhere were lamenting.[69]

Few bishops of the Latin Church bothered to act on the reform decrees of the Fifth Lateran Council; in the year that council closed – 1517 – Luther opened fire on what he considered a hopelessly corrupt ecclesiastical system. Yet the Protestant revolt owed its success not to widespread corruption in the Church, to the Renaissance spirit, nor indeed to the heresy itself. Most medieval Christians were too realistic, too deeply attached to the practice of their faith, to let the

---

[67] Southern, *op. cit.*, pp. 89–90.
[68] Declaration of Bishop Zinelli of the Deputation of the Faith, Mansi, 52: 1108 D-1109.
[69] Hughes, *A Popular History of the Catholic Church*, p. 138.

shortcomings and misdemeanours of their spiritual lords scandalize them to the point of rejecting the Church.

Nor did the sophisticated criticisms of Erasmus and other thinkers cut much ice with the unlettered mass of believers, or for that matter with many educated ones: the thoroughly orthodox Thomas More was a friend of the Dutch humanist but remained at heart a conservative churchman. As for heresy, it was as old and as familiar as Christianity itself; the fact that every age had seen individuals willing to believe and propagate the most extravagant notions deadened the impact of successive waves of heterodoxy. The immediate trigger of the Reformation was in fact the political eclipse of the Papacy by the Western monarchs after the Schism of the West.

Devised to secure for the popes a loyal clergy throughout the Roman patriarchate, the business of papal patronage had also made the kings of the West emulate Rome in the expansion of their own bureaucracies and legal systems. The Papacy's satellite states patronized the Roman Curia until, inevitably, they themselves became strong enough to challenge its power. At the end of the thirteenth century Boniface VIII was locked in conflict with English and French monarchs who were claiming the right to tax the Church directly in order to finance their wars. Boniface's bull *Unam Sanctam* (1303), which asserted once again the principle of the pope's supreme authority in both the spiritual and the temporal spheres, could not alter the fact that henceforth the Papacy would be at the mercy of secular governments that were to some extent its own creatures.

Much convincing historical evidence today confirms the view that the Reformation was not essentially a popular movement, but in most cases the ruthless forcing of heresy on unwilling Catholic populations by secular governments.[70] As for the Germans, they already had ambivalent attitudes towards Rome; the secret of Luther's success was his timing. His rebellion came precisely at the moment when the secular authorities of the West were fully able to throw off the papal yoke. If the southern kingdoms decided against this option, it was in part because Spain and Portugal, newly rich from their overseas empires, now had greater economic power than the Papacy, while the French crown had long since enacted a series of effective legal reforms that gave it supremacy over the Church. By contrast, in the contemporary race for political and economic supremacy, the German and Scandinavian states, like England, could make good use of the money the appropriation of church property would bring.

The great sorrow of the sixteenth-century Papacy was to look on helpless as the Catholic princes of the West imposed by law the same heresy that they had formerly been so energetic in repressing. But even had it occurred to the popes of that era that the calamity that had befallen them was the consequence of their straying in certain ways from the polity of the undivided Catholic Church, and of the monarchs' imitation of the Papacy's own pursuit of absolute power, it was by now too late to undo the damage. The 'sacramental' ecclesiology of the early Church was still alive, but remembered mainly in an Eastern branch of Christendom

---

[70] For the widespread hostility of the English to the changes in religion, see especially J. J. Scarisbrick, *The Reformation and the English People*, Oxford, 1984, and Eamon Duffy, *The Stripping of the Altars, op. cit.* That the people of northern Germany and Scandinavia wanted continuity, not change, in religion is evident from the fact that so many Lutheran reformers did not allow the vandalization of churches and kept their Protestant rites as outwardly similar as possible to the old Catholic ones.

confirmed in dissidence and in its hostility to a permanently centralized Roman communion. The lessons of Constance and Florence were all but forgotten when the Latin Fathers gathered at Trent in 1545 to plan the recovery of what remained of Western orthodoxy.

9

FROM TRADITION TO OBEDIENCE

Would the Pope be dishonoured for being enlightened by God and tradition? Is it not dishonouring him to separate him from this holy alliance?

PASCAL, PENSÉES, 867

Anything with the signature of Pope Paul VI appended to it, I kiss; and then I say: 'This is an inspiration of the Holy Spirit to me, N.N.'

AN AUSTRALIAN VINCENTIAN PRIEST (1973)

A *New* Sensus Fidelium

Whatever their attitude towards Eastern Christendom, the Renaissance popes showed, as patriarchs of the West, little interest in the liturgical centralism that had characterized some of their predecessors. After the time of Gregory VII most of the archdioceses of the Latin patriarchate fostered their own Gallicano-Roman liturgical uses without the slightest pressure on them to conform to the ritual norm of the Holy See. The Old Spanish rite survived in five parishes of the archdiocese of Toledo; the province of Milan remained faithful to its Ambrosian liturgy; and in 1346 Pope Clement VI had lifted the existing ban on the Slavonic liturgy in Bohemia. The only temporary deviation from this policy of cultural laissez-faire was the pontificate of Eugenius IV (1431–1447), whose castigation by the Milanese revolt of 1442 deterred subsequent popes from repeating his mistakes.

Whereas the great liturgical disruptions of the past had occurred more often than not on the prompting of some over-zealous pontiff, this new passive traditionalism of the Renaissance Papacy – even if due in part to a certain worldly indifference – disinclined it to view with sympathy attacks on ecclesiastical traditions by the reform-minded Catholics and Protestant sympathizers of the early sixteenth century. As for the concession made by the Council of Basel to the Utraquists in 1433 (permission for the laity to receive the chalice in Holy Communion), this had been a pragmatic measure calculated to avert a schism among the restive Czechs rather than the general endorsement of an apparent innovation.

Protestantism exploded, then, onto a Catholic scene remarkable for its conservatism in matters of worship. Of the various Protestant liturgical reforms, the one of greatest interest to us today is undoubtedly that of the new Church of England. Writers have commented on the similarity in composition and manner of implementation between the new Mass of Paul VI and Archbishop Cranmer's first Holy Communion service of 1549.[1] Pope Paul may not have intended, like Thomas Cranmer, to destroy the Eucharistic Sacrifice, but the artificial nature of his reform made it no less a break with tradition externally, and no less shocking to the faithful. However, whereas in sixteenth-century England the abrupt changes in traditional worship had provoked popular uprisings which were savagely repressed, the imposition of the Pauline missal more than four centuries later drew an entirely different reaction from Roman-rite Catholics.

While the more secular-minded faithful enthusiastically welcomed the new Pauline liturgy with its modernistic aura, very few of those who resented the demolition of the time-hallowed forms reacted by demanding back the old Latin Mass as had the English and Cornish rebels who marched on Exeter in the summer of 1549. In the 1970s and 80s, the vast majority of dissatisfied Catholics either meekly accepted the reform, or voted with their feet by gradually giving up the formal practice of their religion. One of the few things that did appal many pious Catholics at this time was the 'schismatic' career of Archbishop Lefebvre and his followers, persons who had the effrontery to disobey and even criticize the Pope. But in sixteenth-century England it had been the opposite. The Act of Supremacy repudiating papal authority (1534) had drawn few martyrs: the bulk of the nation could take the unpopular attack on the Pope in its stride, but not, fifteen years later, the abolition of the immemorial liturgy.[2]

Clearly the Catholics of the 1970s were of a very different mettle from those of 1549. Whereas the latter had no inhibitions about rebelling against what they considered unlawful interference with their religious patrimony, it generally went against the grain for twentieth-century Catholics to take a stand against an ecclesiastical establishment bent on the destruction of that same ritual heritage. Indeed, most of them believed that it was their sacred duty to accept the reform. To them it was inconceivable that reforms commanded by a pope could be harmful to the Faith. And the clergy imposing the changes, from the Pontiff down, quelled the complaints (if not the anxieties) of the faithful by solemnly reminding them of the need to practise the Catholic moral virtue of obedience.

In reality, from the sixteenth century until the 1960s, the *sensus fidelium* of the West had been undergoing a transformation so profound that the same psychological gulf separating Latin Catholics from Eastern Orthodox today also separates modern Catholics from their pre-Reformation ancestors. This gulf is the cultural rupture caused by the emergence of Protestantism and the birth of the modern world, with both of which the Counter Reformation had to contend. While rationalist and antiquarianist currents in our past inspired the official project for the Pauline liturgical reform, and a certain theological subjectivism provided its rational basis, the new psychological orientation set by the Counter Reformation would ensure its acceptance by most of the Latin Catholic faithful.

---

[1] See especially M. Davies, *Cranmer's Godly Order*.
[2] When Mary Tudor succeeded Edward VI in August 1553, her first concern was to restore Catholic orthopraxis; only at the end of 1554 did it become possible for her to achieve the desideratum of restored communion with Rome.

Adapt or *Perish*

When Luther issued his bold challenge to Rome in 1517, the monarchs of Western Europe were free enough of papal tutelage to decide the religious future of their subjects. The Protestant revolt swept away Latin Christendom as it had been known. There was now only the Papacy and a patchwork of voluntarily Catholic states where the survival of the traditional faith was completely dependent on the sovereign's goodwill towards the Holy See. *Cujus elector, ejus religio*. With such massive losses to her ranks, the Church could hardly afford to antagonize the Catholic princes, however much the popes would have liked to rule them as they had in the Middle Ages. It was the beginning of a modern dilemma for the Church: how to adapt herself to a new age without betraying her apostolic mandate.

The Fathers of the Council of Trent had one further problem in common with the Pope and bishops who assembled for Vatican II: how to ensure the survival of the Church in a new age that repudiated the customs and values of the immediate past. The Counter Reformation had to cope with the aggressive advance of a Protestantism aided and abetted by a humanistic culture indifferent to Catholic truth. And in their struggle, Catholic leaders could no longer draw on the wisdom and insights of a Christian East long since alienated from Rome.

Complicating the situation were structural changes that had transformed the Catholic states. In the feudal monarchies of the Middle Ages, sovereigns had ruled in concert with the landed nobility, and royal powers were limited by custom and the law. However, by the sixteenth century these devolutionary kingdoms had been superseded by increasingly centralized states where political power was concentrated in the hands of an autocratic monarch who ruled through a strong army, civil service and judiciary. Dispensing with parliaments, allowing few other checks and balances, and in effect tolerating no higher authority, political absolutism rested on a pessimistic (and extreme Augustinian) philosophy that stressed the fundamental depravity of mankind. This view of man as 'a creature so debilitated by sin that his salvation could be achieved only by coercion' had already been expressed by Pope Innocent III in his tract *De Contemptu Mundi*, which had been a strong influence on Western Catholic thinkers since the thirteenth century.[3]

If the wounds of original sin made human beings so weak and prone to corruption that harsh and even tyrannical rule was imposed on them by divine ordinance, it followed that public order and social security depended on the absolute obedience of citizens to a single will. There could be only one authority, one law. For Innocent III that authority was the Roman Pope; by the sixteeth century that role had devolved to kings, who believed they received their right to rule directly from God. For the absolutists the greatest of crimes was high treason, punishable with the cruellest penalties. The philosophy of absolutism is eloquently expressed in John Milton's *Paradise Lost*, where the Puritan poet puts in the mouth of the Archangel Michael these words:

> Since thy original lapse, true Libertie
> Is lost, which alwayes with right Reason dwells
> Twinn'd, and from her hath no dividual being:
> Reason in man obscur'd, or not obeyd,

---

[3] Heer, *op. cit.*, p. 335.

Immediately inordinate desires
And upstart Passions catch the Government
From Reason, and to servitude reduce
Man till then. Therefore since hee permits
Within himself unworthie Powers to reign
Over free Reason, God in Judgement just
Subjects him from without to violent Lords;
Who oft as undeservedly enthrall
His outward freedom: Tyrannie must be,
Though to the Tyrant thereby no excuse.[4]

The Jesuits to the Rescue

It was this bleak world that produced the man who would do so much to restore the dignity and authority of the Latin Church: Ignatius Loyola (1491–1556). The religious order he founded in 1534 was not only the driving force of the Catholic reform movement, but the Church's principal weapon against the encroachments of Protestantism and, later, of the anti-Christian Enlightenment.

It is impossible to understand the Counter Reformation without studying the rise of the Society of Jesus. As the shock troops of the Vatican, a militia of disciplined and single-minded men personally devoted to Christ and ready to devote their lives to the defence of His Church 'to the shedding of their blood' (*usque ad effusionem sanguinis*), the Jesuits contributed more than any other order to the revitalization of Latin Catholicism in the Reformation period. They were also the spearhead of the Church's intrepid missionary enterprises that brought the light of faith to millions in the New World and Asia. During the Enlightenment, when the forces of international Freemasonry and their royal dupes and accomplices cooperated to undermine the very foundations of Christianity in Western Europe, these priestly strategists led the Church's counterattack, and paid for their loyalty in 1773 with the dissolution of their society by a pontiff who had been elected to the See of Peter on the strength of a promise to the Bourbons to disband the Jesuits.

The Catholic Church's debt to the Jesuits can hardly be exaggerated. Yet at the same time one must examine the debit side of the Jesuit contribution and the weaknesses of the Counter Reformation in general. It will be seen how, with the admirable intention of defending the Faith, the Society of Jesus introduced (or rather confirmed) in Latin Catholicism certain attitudes and tendencies which, in the light of subsequent developments, were actually seeds of destruction, even though before the 1960s it was no doubt impossible to recognize them as such.

Power and Obedience

Iñigo López de Oñaz y Loyola was a man of his time. When states and individuals everywhere were abandoning Catholic belief and practices, and when Catholic monarchs exercised a stranglehold over the Church, this devout convert to the Christian life understood that the only way to save the Bark of Peter was to beat

---

[4] John Milton, *Paradise Lost*, Book XII, 83–96.

its enemies at their own game. The Ignatian solution was to use the methods of contemporary absolutism to defend and strengthen the Catholic faith.

Militarism was the order of the day, and Loyola was quick to see its usefulness to the Catholic cause. A Basque nobleman who had been a professional soldier, Ignatius deliberately gave his order a military title: the Company of Jesus. If men had been taking advantage of the freedoms and particularisms of the old religious climate to forsake the true faith, they would now have to be taught to believe in the Church's teachings absolutely, to obey her precepts to the letter, and to fear the dreadful consequences, in this world and in the next, of irreligion. No less than in secular society, the most necessary moral virtue of Christians in these turbulent times was obedience.

Loyola erected the traditional trinity of evangelical counsels into a pyramid, enumerating them unequally as 'the religious vows of chastity, poverty and perpetual obedience'.[5] The emphasis St Ignatius placed on obedience was far from novel, and part of an ascetic tradition going back to the early Church. In his famous *Letter on Obedience*, composed in Rome in 1553, Ignatius drew on the sayings of St Paul, St Gregory the Great, St Leo I, Daniel the Abbot, Cassian, St Bernard and others. The primacy of obedience in the religious life had its origins in the Desert Fathers, and in the West was elaborated in the Rule of St Benedict. It is important not to caricature Loyola's concept of holy obedience as the mindless acceptance of tyranny, as the following quotation from the saint's writings makes clear:

> As to their [one's Superiors'] conduct, although there may not always be the uprightness of conduct that there ought to be, yet to attack or revile them in private or in public tends to scandal and disorder. Such attacks set the people against their princes and pastors; we must avoid such reproaches and never attack superiors before inferiors. The best course is to make private approach to those who have power to remedy the evil.[6]

Jesuits were permitted to make three 'representations' or objections to a superior before submitting to his judgement, and the art of 'discerning spirits' and making sense of commands was an integral part of Jesuit obedience. Nevertheless, while St Ignatius always admitted the possibility of a superior commanding things against divine precepts or the natural law (which commands no subject could obey without sin), following the Christian ascetic tradition he made it clear that allowing reasoning to come between an order and compliance with it was to be the exception rather than the rule.[7]

What did constitute a real innovation in Catholicism was the Jesuits' systematizing, and popularizing through retreats given to both clergy and laity, of a monastic custom previously confined to the cloister. The Jesuits' safety valves of 'representing', 'discerning' and 'manifesting' were not normally available to parish clergy, religious and laymen when informed consciences conflicted with an arbitrary order from above. In time, the partial monasticization of lay life brought about by the Counter Reformation instituted a culture of obedience which failed to make many requisite distinctions and paid little heed to the counsel of St Thomas Aquinas

---

[5] *Spiritual Exercises*, part ii, § 5.
[6] Ibid., 'Rules for Thinking with the Church', No. 10.
[7] Ibid., 'Representation in the Life of Obedience'.

that 'sometimes the things commanded by a superior are against God. Therefore superiors are not to be obeyed in all things.'[8]

One finds the same approach in contemporary religious orders, especially those under the influence of the Jesuits, like the Discalced Carmelites. The advice of St John of the Cross to his monks was:

> Never look upon your Superior, be he who he may, otherwise than if you were looking upon God, for he stands in his place. If you reflect upon the character, ways . . . or habits of your Superior, you will change your obedience from divine into human . . . and obedience influenced by human considerations is almost worthless in the eyes of God.[9]

The combination of monastic forms of obedience and attitudes of secular absolutism had its greatest impact in the seventeenth century, when the Jesuits established themselves throughout the Catholic world as educators of the children of the powerful and the rich. Now that the Church had much less control over the Catholic rulers, Jesuit champions of the Faith contrived to instil an authentically Catholic conscience into the princes and kings to whom they acted as tutors and counsellors. Unfortunately, the direction of influence was often reversed, and the spirit of the world of power and wealth made inroads into the Society of Jesus. Whenever this occurred, the Jesuits not only lost much of their moral authority (witness Pascal's campaign against them in seventeenth-century France), but weakened their own resolve to prevent the Catholic princes from converting the sovereign Universal Church into a network of complaisant national chaplaincies.

From Privilege to Duty

St Ignatius' passionate commitment to the preservation of traditional Catholicism is evident from his *Rules for Thinking with the Church*. Loyola believed that the true Catholic should be always ready:

> To commend the confession of sins to a priest as is practised in the Church; the reception of the Holy Eucharist once a year, or better still every week, or at least every month, with the necessary preparation.
>
> To commend to the faithful frequent and devout assistance at the holy sacrifice of the Mass, the ecclesiastical hymns, the divine office, and in general the prayers and devotions practised at stated times, whether in public churches or in private.
>
> To praise relics, the veneration and invocation of Saints: also the stations, and pious pilgrimages, indulgences, jubilees, the custom of lighting candles in the churches, and other such aids to piety and devotion.
>
> To praise the use of abstinence and fasts as those of Lent, of Ember Days, of Vigils, of Friday, of Saturday, and of others undertaken out of pure devotion: also voluntary mortifications, which we call penances, not merely interior, but exterior also.

---

[8] *Summa Theologica*, II-II, Q. CIV, art. V, ad 3.
[9] Monica Baldwin, *I Leap over the Wall* (London, 1951), p. 100.

.   To commend moreover the construction of churches, and ornaments; also images, to be venerated with the fullest right, for the sake of what they represent.[10]

However, the Ignatian means of upholding this orthopraxis constituted another innovation. Ignatius was still medieval enough to see the liturgical life as a joyful privilege of the baptized. But he deemed it no less important to present Christian piety as a round of duties to be fulfilled on pain of sin. Moreover, his counsel of total subordination of will and mind seemed revolutionary when placed in apparent competition with traditional ascetical practices: 'The other religious leaders may surpass us in fastings, all-night vigils of prayer, and other austerities in food and clothing. Our members must excel in true and perfect obedience, in the voluntary renunciation of private judgment.'[11]

Ignatius wrote that the rules of his *Spiritual Exercises*

are to be observed in order that we may hold the opinions we should hold in the Church Militant. We should put away completely our own opinion and give our entire obedience to our holy Mother the hierarchical Church, Christ our Lord's undoubted Spouse . . . should openly approve of the frequent hearing of Mass . . . speak with particular approval of religious orders and the states of virginity and celibacy, not rating matrimony as high as any of these . . . approve of relics of the saints, pilgrimages, indulgences, the lighting of candles . . . church decoration and statues.[12]

The content and forms of the traditional Faith remained the same, but the spontaneous religiosity of the Middle Ages was giving way to the regimented and self-conscious Catholicism of the Counter Reformation.[13] New socio-cultural conditions may well have necessitated this change of approach, but that it was in the long term a healthy development is a matter of opinion.

Follow the Leader

In absolutist states, obedience was due not simply to the law but to the monarch as the living principle and embodiment of the law. Similarly, in the Counter-Reformation Catholicism pioneered by the Jesuits, the all-important moral virtue of obedience was directed towards the person of the Roman Pontiff. What St Ignatius recommended to all Catholics amounted to 'the complete subjugation of all a man thinks, feels, and does to a practical ideal achievable in the world

---

[10] *Spiritual Exercises*, part ii, §§ 2, 3, 6, 7, 8.
[11] Malachi Martin, *The Jesuits: The Society of Jesus and the Betrayal of the Roman Catholic Church* (New York, 1987), p. 196.
[12] Peter Mitchell, *The Jesuits: A History* (London, 1980), p. 35.
[13] Ignatius' ideal of the obedient Jesuit:

Altogether, I must not desire to belong to myself, but to my Creator and to His Representative. I must let myself be led and moved as a lump of wax lets itself be kneaded. I must be as a dead man's corpse without will or judgement; as a little crucifix which lets itself be moved without difficulty from one place to another; as a staff in the hand of an old man, to be placed where he wishes and where he can best make use of me. Thus, I must always be ready to hand, so that the Order may use me and apply me in the way that to Him seems good. (Malachi Martin, *op. cit.*, p. 197)

around him, in absolute obedience and submission to the mind and decisions of the Roman Pope, the Vicar of Christ.'[14] This special regard for the Pope was no Ignatian novelty, being a common feature of the other orders of clerks regular founded between 1524 and 1533. Nevertheless, the Jesuits refined it far beyond anything envisaged by the Theatines, Barnabites or Somaschi.

No less than his concepts of piety and obedience, Loyola's cult of the Pope had a distinctly military flavour. In a war situation, he reasoned, a disciplined *esprit de corps* and absolute obedience to the commander are imperative if victory is to be achieved. Seeing the Papacy as the only guarantee of orthodoxy in an age of spiritual insubordination and heresy, the former soldier taught his disciples that 'the more precise and closer one's bond with the Pope, the closer would be one's bond with the leader, Christ, and the more effective one's actions in this universal, perpetual warfare'.[15]

The cult of the Pope promoted by the Jesuits, and Ignatius' willingness to obey to the letter every papal command, attributed to the visible head of the Church a personal sanctity and wisdom never in fact guaranteed by the *Tu es Petrus* ('Thou art Peter': Christ's affirmation of Peter's potential charism of infallibility). Loyola went so far as to aver that 'if the Holy Father were to order me to abandon myself to the sea without a mast, without sails, oars or rudder . . . I would obey not only with alacrity but without anxiety or repugnance, and even with great internal satisfaction'.[16]

Binding the Mind

In Counter-Reformation Catholicism the obedience of lay members of the Church Militant must be unquestioning, too. The first of St Ignatius' *Rules for Thinking with the Church* admonished Catholics: 'Always to be ready to obey with mind and heart, setting aside all judgements of one's own, the true spouse of Jesus Christ, our holy Mother, our infallible and orthodox mistress, the Catholic Church, whose authority is exercised over us by the hierarchy.'[17]

Such an approach ran the risk of fostering a politically motivated anti-intellectualism hardly appropriate to an institution whose very reason for existence was the propagation of truth. The pre-Reformation Church had checked the spread of error by burning heretical books and obliging preachers to obtain licences from local bishops. In post-Tridentine Catholicism, intellectual surveillance was tightened and systematized with a variety of new measures such as the publication of the first Index of Prohibited Books in 1559. As for the saint whose apostolate did so much to promote the regulation of thought, the following famous passage from his *Spiritual Exercises* would give scandal not only to the enemies of Christianity, but to many orthodox Catholics as well: 'That we may be altogether of the same mind and in conformity with the Church herself, if she shall have defined anything to be black which to our eyes appears to be white, we ought in like manner to pronounce it to be black.'[18]

---

[14] Malachi Martin, *op. cit.*, p. 162.
[15] Ibid., p. 160.
[16] Mitchell, *op. cit.*, p. 65.
[17] *Rules for Thinking with the Church*, 1.
[18] Ibid., 13.

Here everything turns on one's interpretation of the verb 'defined'. The counsel is perfectly acceptable if it is used to urge unquestioning acceptance of dogmas infallibly defined by the Pope as head of the Church. However, it would be over three centuries before the dogma of papal infallibility would be promulgated by the First Vatican Council, and in the meantime the Society of Jesus popularized the counsel by interpreting the verb in the loosest possible sense. For many this meant that the Church, and more precisely the Pope, could never be wrong in any decree or command. The Jesuits' fourth vow, to accept any mission entrusted to them by the Pope, strengthened them in this conviction.

Such concepts of absolute and mindless obedience were to become a permanent feature of modern Latin Catholicism, as can be seen from the following testimony of Monica Baldwin, who once consulted the well-known English Dominican, Bede Jarrett, on the matter. Fr Jarrett related how he had once taken to his novice master this very problem of whether or not to comply with the unwise and unjust command of a superior:

> He asked me to re-read *The Charge of the Light Brigade*. The idea, you see, is that you do what you're told, no matter how certain you feel that someone has blundered. To ride fearlessly into the jaws of death without reasoning adds splendour to your obedience.
>
> 'Even', I [Monica Baldwin] persisted, 'if you feel convinced that what you've been told to do is sheerest lunacy?'
>
> He smiled.
>
> 'Ah, but don't you see? – that's just where the heroism comes in.'[19]

That Counter-Reformation absolutism could, and did, lead to a paradoxical relativization of the truth, was noted over a century ago by Lord Acton, in reference to the Jesuits' manipulation of the teaching of St Thomas Aquinas. St Ignatius, John Acton wrote,

> suppressed independence of mind, discouraged original thinking and unrestrained research, recommended commonly accepted opinions, and required all to hold without question the theology of St Thomas. . . .
>
> [The Jesuits] were conservatives, advocates of authority and submission, opponents of insubordination and resistance. Accordingly, they became the habitual confessors of absolute monarchs, in Austria, and in France under the Bourbons, and were intimately associated with great conservative forces of society. At the same time they were required to be disciples of St Thomas Aquinas, and St Thomas had a very large element of political liberalism. He believed in the Higher Law, in conditional allegiance, in the illegitimacy of all governments that do not act in the interests of the commonwealth. This was convenient doctrine in the endeavour to repress the forces of Protestantism, and for a time the Jesuits were revolutionists.[20]

---

[19] Baldwin, *op. cit.*, p. 100.
[20] Lord Acton, 'The Counter Reformation', in *Lectures on Modern History* (London, 1960), pp. 118, 119.

While encouraging rebellion against heretic governments the Jesuits promoted in Catholic lands a contrasting culture of obedience which ignored most of the checks and balances central to the Thomist ethic. Their attempt to regiment the whole Church Militant was a knee-jerk reaction to the shock of the Protestant revolt, but in demanding monastic obedience and attitudes of people not bound by religious vows the Counter-Reformation Church was inviting a major reaction, and this would come before long in the form of Catholic liberalism.

The Fog of Ultramontanism

'Ultramontanism' is an historical term, referring originally to seventeenth-century French churchmen whose allegiance was to papal Rome *ultra montes* ('beyond the mountains') rather than to the Gallican Church and the King of France. Later it was the label applied to the theologians and Council Fathers of 1869–1870 who favoured the promulgation of the dogma of papal infallibility, and in this latter sense it denotes a wholly orthodox position. What is nowadays termed ultramontanism, by contrast, is the tendency to exaggerate beyond the bounds of tradition and sound reason the authority of the Roman Pontiff. As a general attribution of inerrancy or impeccability to the Pope, this modern mindset, however popular and institutionalized, is also undoubtedly heterodox.[21]

Papal infallibility, as expounded in the dogmatic constitution of 1870, *Pastor Aeternus*, must be carefully distinguished from papal infallibilism. The First Vatican Council taught that the occasions on which the Roman Pontiff was preserved from error by the Holy Ghost were limited to solemn (*ex cathedra*) definitions of dogmas of faith or morals. The Council Fathers recognized that outside these strict conditions every pope was subject to error, a fact confirmed by the history of the Papacy itself, which offers abundant evidence of pontiffs not only making disastrous prudential judgements in church government, but even of erring in their dogmatic teaching.

Cases of popes straying from justice and truth – providentially always outside the set limits of infallibility – are not difficult to find. Indeed the very first papal error was made by St Peter himself, who was rebuked by St Paul for insisting on the imposition of Jewish practices on Gentile converts. 'But when Cephas [= Peter] came to Antioch I opposed him to his face, because he stood condemned', wrote the Apostle of the Gentiles to the Galatians.[22]

Pope Liberius (352–366) offended against justice and against the Faith itself when, harassed by Arian heretics and by the Emperor Constantius, he excommunicated St Athanasius and added his signature to the Arian creed drawn up at Sirmium.[23] Though Liberius was personally orthodox and signed under coercion, this betrayal caused him to be excluded from the Roman Martyrology. When he entered into communion with heretical Eastern bishops, St Ambrose's dictum *ubi*

---

[21] It should be noted that in recent years Neo-Modernists have used the label 'ultramontanist' as a term of disparagement for Catholics obedient to the Roman Magisterium. By contrast, the use of the term in the present study implies no doctrinal stance other than an exaggerated and unorthodox view of papal authority.

[22] Galatians, 2: 11: Ὅτε δὲ ἦλθεν Κηφᾶς εἰς Ἀντιόχειαν, κατὰ πρόσωπον αὐτῷ ἀντέστην, ὅτι κατεγνωσμένος ἦν.

[23] M. Davies, *Apologia*, I, pp. 369–71.

Petrus ibi Ecclesia ('where Peter is, there is the Church') ceased temporarily to apply, and the true Church became the small band of Christians gathered around the persecuted and excommunicated Bishop of Alexandria.

In 680 Pope Leo II and the Third Council of Constantinople posthumously anathematized Pope Honorius I (625–628) who, in order to please the Emperor Heraclius, had written letters capable of interpretation in a sense favourable to the Monothelite heresy: 'we excommunicate . . . Honorius, who did not enlighten this apostolic Church with the doctrine of apostolic tradition, but allowed it to be contaminated through his sacrilegious treachery'.[24]

John XXII shocked the Church by his claim in 1331 that the souls of the just did not enjoy the Beatific Vision until the day of judgement. A commission of theologians ruled that the papal teaching was heretical and the Pontiff later made a public retraction of his error.[25] So great was the scandal caused by John that his successor, Benedict XII, had to issue the corrective constitution *Benedictus Deus*.[26]

Pope Sixtus V (1585–1590) was personally responsible for a number of errors and omissions in the revision of the Vulgate undertaken during his pontificate, mistakes which had to be corrected after his death by Pope Urban VII.[27] As for the numerous tactical blunders of the Papacy in the areas of politics and government, the one readily admitted by all ultramontanists was Clement XIV's suppression of the Jesuits in 1773.

Cardinal Cajetan (Tommaso de Vio), who had lived through the scandalous pontificate of Alexander VI (1492–1503), summed up Peter's ability to err like Simon with the saying: 'the person of the Pope can reject the duties and the office of pope' (*Persona papae potest renuere subesse officio papae*).[28] Four centuries later, the Fathers of Vatican I were thus conscious of the fact that the security which the Pope normally offers the faithful could fail, precisely because inerrancy was not one of the guarantees of infallibility. Indeed, without the 'chrism' of an *ex cathedra* definition the Pope 'speaks as Peter' only conditionally. Accordingly, whereas the Church demands of Christians an absolute assent to *ex cathedra* teaching on the grounds of God's promise of infallibility, in the case of non-infallible papal teachings and directives the Church requires only a 'prudent and relative assent', relative to the fidelity of the Pope himself to tradition.[29]

Calling Popes to Order

Whatever the defects of the pre-Reformation Church, ultramontanism was not among them. Not only were medieval Catholics well aware that popes were capable of error, but the sages and saints of this age did not hesitate to call to order pontiffs who offended against morality or strayed beyond the bounds of tradition. In 1253, when Pope Innocent IV arrived in Assisi to attend the funeral

[24] Denzinger, Sch. 563; M. Davies, *Apologia*, p. 399.
[25] M. Davies, *Apologia*, I, p. 320.
[26] John XXII's heterodoxy in this matter eroded much confidence in the Papacy and added fuel to the fire of contemporary Conciliarism.
[27] M. Davies, *Apologia*, I, p. 413.
[28] Cited in 'Tu es Petrus', *Sì sì, no no*, XVI, No. 12 (30 June 1990), p. 2.
[29] J. Salaverri, SJ, 'De Ecclesia Christi', in *Sacræ Theologiæ Summa* (Madrid, 1952, 2nd edn), art. III, thesis 15.

of St Clare, whom he revered as a saint, he was displeased to find the Franciscan friars singing the Office of the Dead. Innocent wished the Office of Virgins to be sung instead, since he considered Clare fit to be canonized on the spot. However, Cardinal Rainaldo (the future Alexander IV) intervened, reminding the Pope of his obligation to respect the liturgical tradition of the Church, and the prescribed mourning rites went ahead.[30]

This same pontiff crossed swords with Robert Grosseteste, Bishop of Lincoln, over an abuse of power. Though a staunch upholder of papal authority, Bishop Grosseteste refused to obey the command to hand over a vacant benefice in his diocese to Innocent's nephew, who he knew had no intention of coming to England and performing the duties attached to that office.[31] That a pope could betray his charge was not beyond the realm of possibility for the Bishop of Lincoln, who had written in 1237: 'But God forbid, God forbid that this most Holy See [of Rome] and those who preside in it, who are commonly to be obeyed in all their commands, by commanding anything contrary to Christ's precepts and will, should be the cause of a falling away.'[32]

Better known are the strictures of Jacopone da Todi and Dante Alighieri against avaricious contemporary popes. To the damned shade of Nicholas III (1277–1280), the great Florentine poet delivered the following apostrophe in his *Inferno*:

> Our Lord required of Peter, ere that He
> Committed the great keys into his hand;
> Certes He nothing asked, save 'Follow Me.'
> Nor Peter nor the others made demand
> Of silver or gold when, in the lost soul's room,
> They chose Matthias to complete their band.
> Then bide thou there; thou hast deserved thy doom;
> Do thou keep well those riches foully gained
> That against Charles made thee so venturesome.
> And were it not that I am still constrained
> By veneration for the most high Keys
> Thou barest in glad life, I had not refrained
> My tongue from yet more grievous words than these;
> Your avarice saddens the world, trampling on worth,
> Exalting the workers of iniquities.
> Pastors like you the Evangelist shewed forth,
> Seeing her that sitteth on the floods committing
> Fornication with the kings of the earth . . .[33]

There is also the celebrated case of St Catherine of Siena who, convinced of the iniquity of the 'Babylonian Captivity', travelled to Avignon in 1376 to remind Pope Gregory XI of his duty to return the papal court to Rome.

---

[30] Nesta de Robeck, *St Clare of Assisi* (Milwaukee, 1951), p. 135.
[31] M. Davies, *Apologia*, I, pp. 387–89.
[32] Ibid., p. 383.
[33] *Inferno*, XIX, 91–106 (Dorothy L. Sayers' translation, Harmondsworth, 1949).

Papal Authority Unlimited?

Even after the Reformation, the Italian theologian St Robert Bellarmine spelt out with abundant clarity the duty of informed members of the faithful to disobey the illicit command of a pope:

> Just as it is licit to resist the Pontiff who attacks the body, so also is it licit to resist him who attacks souls or destroys the civil order, or above all tries to destroy the Church. I say that it is licit to resist him by not doing what he orders and by impeding the execution of his will; it is not licit, however, to judge him, to punish him, or depose him, for these are acts proper to a superior.[34]

Bellarmine was a member of the Society of Jesus, but on the question of papal authority many of his confrères preferred to make no distinction between theory and practice. In its early phase (sixteenth–eighteenth centuries), ultramontanism was largely a partisan phenomenon in the West: that is to say, a special trait of the Jesuits and other orders influenced by them, and by no means typical of the entire Roman Church. It was only after the restoration of the Society (1801–1814), and especially during the pontificate of Pius IX, that ultramontanism was popularized, and the cult of the person of the pope so familiar to us today became part and parcel of Catholicism.[35] It is interesting to note in this connexion that the modern papal cult was contemporary with the efforts of the House of Hanover and other European dynasties to win the affection of the common people in an age of revolutions by shedding some of their traditional aloofness. As temporal ruler of the Papal States, Pio Nono was a member of this same monarchical network.

Before the First Vatican Council Pius IX not only favoured the definition of papal infallibility as a dogma of faith, but seriously entertained the notion of papal inerrancy in matters of church policy and discipline. In this he was encouraged by the strident French ultramontanist, Louis Veuillot, editor of the Catholic newspaper *L'Univers Religieux*. Veuillot and those who thought like him attributed infallibility not merely to the Pope's solemn dogmatic definitions, but to all of his encyclicals and speeches as a private doctor.[36] When Mgr Georges Darboy, Archbishop of Paris, and Bishop Félix Dupanloup of Orleans condemned *L'Univers* in 1853, Veuillot appealed directly to the Pope. His patron promptly responded with the encyclical *Inter Multiplices*, rightly calling French Catholics to vigilance against all thought opposed to the official teaching of the Church but which also contained passages that could be, and were, interpreted in an ultamontanistic sense, for instance the unqualified statement that 'all honour and obedience must be offered' to the Chair of Peter.

One of Pius IX's most dangerous extravagances was his equation of Catholic tradition itself with the authority of the successors of Peter, a claim that stripped the

---

[34] *De Summo Pontifice*, n. 30, lib. II, cap. 30.
[35] R. Aubert writes that 'the decisive element in the rapid and conclusive triumph of ultramontanism was the personality itself of Pius IX and the immense prestige, surpassing by far that of any of his predecessors over centuries, which the Pontiff enjoyed with the great mass of Catholics and of the clergy during more than a quarter of a century' (*Le pontificat de Pie IX* [Paris, 1952], p. 289).
[36] E. E. Y. Hales, *Pio Nono: A Study in European Politics and Religion in the Nineteenth Century* (London, 1956), p. 308.

bases of belief and practice of all objective reality outside the will (or whim) of the reigning pontiff. When, during the First Vatican Council, the Dominican Cardinal Filippo Guidi questioned the conciliar schema's description of the Roman Pontiff's infallibility as 'personal' and 'separate', and proposed that a reference to the infallibility of his teaching office would be theologically more correct, the Pope angrily reminded him that 'I am Tradition!' (*La tradizione son'io!*) – a chilling example of papal megalomania, and later providentially checked by the Holy Spirit.[37]

Vatican I vindicated Catholic orthodoxy on this point. The 'inopportunist' minority at the Council worked hard to ensure that the limited nature of infallibility be clearly explained: 'The Holy Ghost was promised to the Successors of Peter not so that they might reveal any new doctrine, but so that, with His assistance, they might keep it in its purity and faithfully teach the Revelation transmitted by the Apostles, that is, the deposit of faith.'[38]

Custodian or Arbiter of Tradition?

As the complement of the *Tu es Petrus*, the *Pasce agnos* ('Feed My lambs') taught that popes are bound by the moral law to uphold everything integral to Tradition. Unfortunately, the *Pasce agnos* was merely implicit in the conciliar documents, and the constitution *Pastor Æternus*, which dealt with infallibility itself, glossed over the indirect way in which the Pope normally exercised his universal jurisdiction. Instead, the document stated in a forthright manner that

> the shepherds of whatever rite and dignity and the faithful, individually and collectively, are bound by a duty of hierarchical subjection and of sincere obedience; and this not only in matters that pertain to faith and morals, but also in matters that pertain to the discipline and government of the Church throughout the whole world.[39]

From the point of view of the Eastern patriarchates especially, this omission was a serious weakness, for it seemed to paint the picture of an irremediably centralized Universal Church. Nevertheless, it was contextually clear from the cumulative theological tradition of the Church that papal authority was indeed limited by the fact that Christ had given St Peter fullness of power to build up the Church, but not to destroy it. This immemorial ban on arbitrary papal innovations covers every ecclesiastical tradition of apostolic origin. Fr Joseph Steiger explains that 'the Pope's power is not unlimited: not only may he not change anything of divine institution (for example, abolish episcopal jurisdiction), but, since his role is to build up and not destroy (cf. St Paul, 2 Cor., 10), he is bound by the natural law not to sow confusion in the flock of Christ'.[40]

Papal authority is actually limited by divine right. Christ did not forfeit His sovereign authority in passing it on to Peter as His representative on earth. The Pope may be the supreme legislator of the Church, but he is not absolutely above

---

[37] R. Aubert, 'Guidi (Filippo Maria)', *DHGE*, XXII, cols 791–92; John C. Dwyer, *Church History: Twenty Centuries of Catholic Christianity* (New York, 1985), p. 345.
[38] Dogmatic constitution *De Ecclesia Christi*, Denzinger, 1836.
[39] Denzinger, 1827.
[40] J. Steiger, SJ, 'Causes majeures', *DTC*, II, cols 2039–40.

its laws, insofar as he is obliged to employ due process in changing them. Moreover, if he flouts an existing law without having formally altered it, he is subject to the pertinent penalty. Indeed, at the Vatican Council the idea that the Pope could govern the Church arbitrarily was dismissed as an absurdity by the majority of Fathers. Fr Cuthbert Butler, the historian of Vatican I, relates that when Bishop Verot of Savanna (USA) proposed a canon to the effect: 'If anyone says that the authority of the Pope in the Church is so full that he may dispose of everything by his mere whim, let him be anathema', the response was that the Council Fathers had not assembled in Rome 'to hear buffooneries'.[41]

During the sessions discussing the Pope's power of jurisdiction, Mgr Freppel of Angers stated that

> Absolutism is the principle of Ulpian in the Roman law, that the mere will of the prince is law. But who has ever said that the Roman pontiff should govern the Church according to his sweet will, by his nod, by arbitrary power, by fancy, that is without the laws and canons? We all exclude mere arbitrary power; but we all assert full and perfect power. Is power arbitrary because it is supreme? . . . Let the genuine teaching of the schema be accepted in its true, proper, genuine sense, without preposterous interpretations.[42]

Bishop Zinelli, Relator of the Deputation of the Faith at the Council, reassured the Melkite Patriarch of Antioch, Gregory II, that 'papal power was not absolutely monarchical because the form of Church government had been instituted by Christ and could not be abolished even by an ecumenical council'. Indeed, 'no one who is sane can say that either the Pope or the Ecumenical Council can destroy the episcopate or other things determined by divine law in the Church'.[43]

Finally, to put an end to popular misconceptions, after the Council Joseph Cardinal Hergenröther, a prelate in the confidence of Pius IX, issued a clarification to set forth the actual limits of papal power in the light of the *Pasce agnos*:

> The Pope is circumscribed by the necessity of making a righteous and beneficent use of the duties attached to his privileges . . . He is also circumscribed by the respect due to General Councils and to ancient statutes and customs, by the rights of bishops, by his relation with civil powers, by the traditional mild tone of government indicated by the aim of the institution of the papacy – to 'feed' . . .[44]

As for *Pastor Æternus* itself, Cardinal Guidi, considered a theological moderate at the Council, was also responsible for ensuring that papal authority was not defined

---

[41] M. Davies, *Apologia*, I, p. 405. A. Similarly, in 1875 the bishops of Germany explained to Bismarck that 'The title of absolute monarch cannot be rightly applied to the Pope even in purely ecclesiastical affairs, for he is subject to divine law and bound by the dispositions made by Christ for his Church' (DS 3114). In other words, bound by Tradition. At Vatican I, Mgr Iosif Papp-Szilágyi, the Greek Catholic Bishop of Oradea Mare in Transylvania, reminded the Council that Eastern Orthodoxy considered heretical the notion that papal power was absolute and unrestricted. See Patrick Granfield, 'The Possibility of Limitation', in Gerard Mannion *et al.*, eds, *Readings in Church Authority: Gifts and Challenges for Contemporary Catholicism* (Aldershot, 2003), p. 250.
[42] Ibid.
[43] Ibid., p. 405.
[44] Ibid., p. 409.

in absolutist terms. In the speech he delivered on 18 June 1870, the Dominican prelate reminded the Fathers that the Pope was obliged, before defining any dogma *ex cathedra*, to consult with the bishops and theologians of the Church. Guidi recommended that the constitution include the following canon:

> If anyone says that the Roman Pontiff, when he issues these decrees or constitutions, acts according to his own judgement and alone, independently from the Church, that is, separately and not in consultation with the bishops who set forth the tradition of their churches, let him be anathema.[45]

The ultramontane majority reacted by accusing Cardinal Guidi of Gallicanism, the traditional rivalry of Jesuits and Dominicans embittering the dispute. However, during his heated interview with Pope Pius that evening, Guidi was able to draw from the Pope the admission that he himself had not defined the dogma of the Immaculate Conception in 1854 without first consulting the Catholic episcopate (even though a general council had not been called).[46]

Eventually, Cardinal Guidi's views were taken into account, and Chapter IV of *Pastor Æternus* was revised to include a long paragraph qualifying the infallibility of the Pope in the sense that he is always obliged to inform himself first of the authentic tradition of the Church.[47] In the final draft the original title of the chapter, 'Of the Infallibility of the Roman Pontiff' was accordingly changed to 'Of the Infallible Teaching Office (*Magisterium*) of the Roman Pontiff'.[48]

Roma locuta, causa finita

The vagaries of Pius IX and of the ultramontane extremists defeated at the Council remained nonetheless alive long after the Pontiff's death and coloured the thinking of ordinary Catholics, especially in the period between 1870 and 1914 and in the interwar years, when the Church had its back to the wall in many parts of Europe. Given that the Church is always influenced by the age in which she finds herself, it was easy to forget at this time that authentic Catholicism is the very antithesis of totalitarianism. The chauvinistic style of national governments, encouraging a fervent patriotism little given to reflection and self-criticism, percolated into ecclesiastical structures where, in spite of the liberalizing efforts of Leo XIII, the emphasis was on an unthinking obedience. Recognizing the cohesive potential of popular ultramontanism, the embattled Church's analogue of nationalism, the hierarchy fomented rather than discouraged an uncritical fidelity to the Pope. This approach was not, in the last analysis, Catholic, but at the time it seemed not only harmless but necessary.

The same St Pius X who was praised by his admirers as the defender of doctrinal

---

[45] Aubert, 'Guidi (Filippo Maria)', col. 791.

[46] Ibid., col. 792.

[47] '. . . explorata Ecclesiæ per orbem dispersæ sententia' (ibid., col. 793). In the actual definition of papal infallibility, Vatican I asserted that the Pope 'by the divine assistance promised him in Blessed Peter, is possessed of that infallibility with which the divine Redeemer willed that His Church should be endowed for defining doctrine regarding faith and morals, and therefore such definitions of the Roman Pontiff are irreformable of themselves and not from the consent of the Church' (First Dogmatic Constitution on the Church of Christ, Ch. 4, Denzinger, 3074).

[48] Aubert, *op. cit.*, col. 792.

purity and the promoter of liturgical renewal was deplored by his enemies as the pope of anti-intellectualism. There is certainly evidence that Giuseppe Sarto, while still Bishop of Mantua, gave little thought to the limited nature of papal authority. Addressing his flock concerning their attitude to all matters of Church teaching and discipline once the Pope had spoken, Mgr Sarto stressed that 'there should be no questions, no subtleties, no opposing of personal rights, but only obedience'.[49]

Now whereas the future Pius X and countless other bishops saw ultramontanism as a guarantee of orthodoxy, it must be admitted that the essential subjectivism of the ultramontanist position made it an apt instrument of subversion in the hands of groups determined to corrupt the Faith. In other words, absolute loyalty to the Pope could be encouraged on the one hand, and the Pope himself could conceivably be persuaded to preside over the destruction of tradition on the other: anything was possible in the absence of objective standards. It is no coincidence that nineteenth-century liberal Catholics like Félicité de Lamennais ardently preached ultramontanism long before Vatican I. Vincenzo Gioberti, who wanted Italy united under the political rule of the Pope, was also of the opinion that 'the Church will have to reconcile herself with the spirit of the age . . . and with modern times . . .'[50] Incipient Modernism saw in ultramontanism an ideal climate in which to flourish, and in the normally fallible Roman Pontiff a perfect puppet for its aims.

The nineteenth-century popes were soon alerted to the dangers of religious liberalism and took steps to dissociate themselves from a movement exploiting their adulation for its own ends. But their successors of the next century, influenced by the nationalisms of the *belle époque* and the authoritarianism of the interwar period and of the postwar years before Vatican II, had little motivation to disavow ultramontanism.

A Model for Totalitarianism?

It will be clear by now that there was a direct cause-and-effect relationship between the spirit of ultramontanism and the general acquiescence of Latin Catholics in the Pauline liturgical revolution. Or, put another way, ultramontanism is the difference betwen the rebellious, strong-minded Catholics of 1549 England and the conformist, unthinking ones of the decades following the Second Vatican Council.

Although from the early 1970s there existed in many places the alternative of 'Tridentine' Masses celebrated outside churches and in open defiance of the bishops, few conservative Catholics could in conscience commit the disobedience of attending these. In the last analysis the instinct of blind obedience to ecclesiastical authority proved stronger than the moral dictate of fidelity to the truth or patrimonial loyalties. In any case the possibility of papal error was by now a fact ably suppressed in ordinary Catholic education. If the average man in the pew knew nothing of the occasions when past popes had erred dogmatically outside the *Tu es Petrus*, it is understandable how a mere prudential judgement on the part of the reigning Pontiff could have been claimed as an 'infallible' (and hence irreformable) act of the Papacy.

---

[49] D. O'Connor, SJ., *What's Wrong with the Catholic Church Today?* (Melbourne, 1975), pp. 5–6.
[50] Malachi Martin, *op. cit.*, p. 266.

Qualitatively, the dutiful obedience of Catholics in this circumstance is little different from the unquestioning obedience of 'good' citizens of Communist Russia, Fascist Italy or Nazi Germany to the state and its leader. Shocking as it may seem, the analogy is a valid one, and the Church's militaristic ideal of an absolute obedience ever ready to give lawful superiors the benefit of the doubt in practical questions would provide the proponents of twentieth-century totalitarianism with millions of docile and even cooperative subjects in countries where Catholic authoritarianism was already strong. The Bolshevik revolutionary cadres used methods of training akin to those of the Society of Jesus, though obviously for radically different ends:

> What Loyola and Lenin both understood . . . was that you must reach out by means of alluring images to possess the minds and imaginations of individuals; for it is through their minds that you grip and control their wills. With that tight union of wills at your disposal, history is yours for the making.
>
> Even in the basic lines of the organization each man founded – Lenin with his Communist Party; Iñigo with his Society – the similarities are so obvious that one is tempted to accuse the self-made twentieth-century Dictator of all the Russias with having plagiarized the sixteenth-century Saint.[51]

Indeed, Heinrich Himmler (whose uncle was a Jesuit and whom Hitler nicknamed 'my Ignatius Loyola') actually toyed with the blasphemous idea of adapting St Ignatius' *Spiritual Exercises* to Nazi neo-paganism as a method of training SS officers of the Third Reich.[52] Where the saint had used his rule of complete submission of mind and will for the salvation of immortal souls and the promotion of the common good, the dictators of the twentieth century used the same technique to create their hellish earthly paradises. With the Jesuits there was nothing of the Marxists' wicked presentation of known falsehoods as sacred truths, nor of the overt cynicism of the Italian Fascists with their slogan 'The Leader is always right' (*Il Duce ha sempre ragione*).

Certainly, the historic charge that the Pope's militia subscribed to the Machiavellian-like notion that an immoral means can be justified by a good end is without foundation.[53] Nevertheless, to the extent that the Jesuits and others, in stressing obedience, tended to discourage their subjects from making their own moral judgements with a properly informed conscience, they did merit criticism, even if the strictures of Pascal and others were often misdirected and unfair. With the motive of promoting man's wellbeing in this life and the next, one can have no possible quarrel; it is the means – encouraging people always to give to human superiors the unlimited obedience due only to God – that worries the traditional Christian.[54]

---

[51] Ibid., p. 185.

[52] Ibid., p. 183.

[53] Two public challenges were made in Germany (in 1852 and 1903), offering a monetary reward to anyone who could prove that any Jesuit document contained, formally or materially, the proposition 'the end justifies the means', but no-one was able to produce the necessary damning evidence. See Bertrand Conway, *The Question Box* (New York, 1929), p. 295.

[54] One is dealing here with an imbalance in Jesuit policy, *not* with a principle of the Society of Jesus. In the *Modern Catholic Dictionary* (New York, 1980, p. 384), Fr John Hardon, SJ writes:

> Obedience is a moral virtue that inclines the will to comply with the will of another who has the right to command. . . . The extent of obedience is as wide as the authority of the person who commands. Thus obedience to God is without limit, whereas obedience to human

The Voluntarist Snare

From the moral point of view political absolutism, and the Catholic ultramontanism distilled from it, is not only disordered; it is founded on a serious philosophical
error: that of voluntarism. This error, taught by Duns Scotus in the thirteenth century, William of Ockham in the fourteenth, and later by Martin Luther, certain
Jesuit Molinists and the Jesuit-educated René Descartes, asserts that the goodness
and badness of actions is not intrinsic to their nature, but dependent upon the
will of God. In the voluntarism of Arthur Schopenhauer (1788–1860), will was
made prior to intelligence in both the metaphysical and physical orders, and it
was on this idea that Friedrich Nietzsche (1844–1900), a potent influence on the
Nazi ideologues, built his theory of the 'will to power', a philosophy which, two
decades before the rise of Hitler, one Catholic scholar described as 'breath[ing]
at once tyranny and revolt: tyranny against the weak in body and in mind; revolt
against the supremacy of the State, of the Church, and of convention'.[55]

The logical conclusion of the voluntarist position is that God, should He so
choose, could will an evil action, whereas sound Christian philosophy has consistently taught that actions are good or bad by virtue of their intrinsic nature, and
that God cannot possibly command anything contrary to His own nature, which
is goodness itself.[56] Translated into political theory, voluntarism means that when
a ruler issues a command, it is the act of exercising his authority rather than the
moral value of the order itself that gives it validity.

Voluntarism was not explicit in the teaching of St Ignatius, and the Ignatian
subordination of mind and will seemed to present no danger to the Catholic faith
in an age when ecclesiastical authority had the upholding of objective tradition
as its *raison d'être*. But when Vatican II brought the Counter-Reformation era to
its end, Loyola's counsel meant subordinating the Catholic mind to an authority
indifferent and sometimes even hostile to the right opinions listed by the saint.

Ultra vires

It could be argued that the actual trigger of liturgical revolution which followed
the Second Vatican Council was a single assertion of the First Vatican Council, the
dangerously unqualified statement in *Pastor Æternus* (quoted above) that unquestioning obedience was due to papal decisions on disciplinary matters. That this was
misunderstood by the faithful to mean that such rulings excluded the possibility of
error is not surprising, given the mentality of the time. What is disconcerting, on
the other hand, is the fact that the hierarchy, including Pope St Pius X, appears to
have concluded that the sacred liturgy belonged to the area of discipline mentioned
in the conciliar statement.

beings is limited by higher laws that must not be transgressed, and by the competency or
authority of the one who gives the order. As a virtue it is pleasing to God because it means
the sacrifice of one's will out of love of God.

[55] L. Walker, 'Voluntarism', CE, XV, p. 506.

[56] See for instance J. S. Hickey, O.Cist., *Summula Philosophiæ Scholasticæ in Usum Adolescentium*,
III: Theodicæa et Ethica (Dublin, 1919): 'Discrimen inter bonum et malum morale non provenit a
libera Dei voluntate . . . quia si nulla datur actio ex seipsa bona, nulla ex seipsa mala, sequitur nul-
lam esse actionem adeo turpem et inhonestam, quin ex libero divinæ voluntatis decreto decora et
honesta fieri potuerit, et vicissim; quod sane manifeste repugnat ipsi divinæ naturæ . . .' (288. III).

In 1911 the reforming Pope, responding to numerous requests from bishops, promulgated the bull *Divino Afflatu* inaugurating a reform of the Roman breviary intended to lighten the spiritual burden of parish clergy. The commission appointed to undertake this work was concerned to restore the ancient custom of reciting the whole Psalter each week and to free the temporal cycle from encroachments of the sanctoral cycle. However, in the opinion of many contemporary (and later) liturgical scholars, among them Anton Baumstark and Pierre Batiffol, the reform went too far and amounted to a mutilation of the ancient office, whose basic elements were nevertheless, preserved.[57]

Even if Pius X's well-intentioned reform of the breviary did not constitute the grave wound to tradition that is sometimes alleged, a serious precedent was nonetheless set, one which effectively gave the Pope the role of arbiter – not merely regulator – of the Church's liturgical patrimony. Such a relegation of the objective ritual tradition to the semi-subjective realm of hierarchical authority was highly problematic, since historically the role of the Papacy had been merely to supervise minimalistic revisions of traditional liturgical books and to approve similar revisions undertaken by local bishops. Moreover, as has been seen in the cases of papal abolitionism directed, in full or in part, at the Milanese and various Eastern rites, when popes arrogated this power to themselves in the past and it was strenuously opposed by local churches on grounds of immemorial custom, the offending pontiff in question usually backed down.

In the 1970s, when the inevitable cleavage between traditionalist and conservative Catholicism was not yet complete, Catholics struggling to come to grips with an apparently legal liturgical reform, which instinct disinclined them to accept, felt able to reject it on what, in the last analysis, were solely moral grounds.[58] As Michael Davies put it: 'that Pope Paul VI had a legal right to make a substantial reform of the Missal cannot be disputed; that he had a moral right to do so certainly can'.[59] However, the liturgical scholar Mgr Klaus Gamber, in a later study endorsed by Cardinal Joseph Ratzinger, prefect of the Congregation for the Doctrine of the Faith, pointed out, in reference to papal authority in ritual matters:

> The argument could be made that the pope's authority to introduce a new liturgical rite . . . can be derived from the 'full and highest power' (*plena et suprema potestas*) he has in the Church, as cited by the First Vatican Council, i.e. power over matters *quæ ad disciplinam et regimen ecclesiæ per totum orbem diffusæ pertinent* ('that pertain to the discipline and rule of the Church spread out over all the world') (Denzinger, 1831).
>
> However, the term *disciplina* in no way applies to the liturgical rite of the Mass, particularly in light of the fact that the popes have repeatedly observed that the rite is founded on apostolic tradition. For this reason alone, the rite cannot fall into the category of 'discipline and rule of the Church'. To this we can add that there is not

---

[57] Reid, *The Organic Development of the Liturgy* (Farnborough, 2004), pp. 75–78. Among the innovations that drew strong criticism were the suppression of the twelve psalms at Matins going back beyond the Rule of St Benedict to the Desert Fathers; and the abolition of the 'Laudate Psalms' (148, 149 and 150) at the end of Lauds, a custom of the Universal Church which had been inherited from the Jewish synagogue and was part of a daily commemoration of the Resurrection.

[58] Some also tried to argue that the reform was legal but not licit.

[59] M. Davies, *PPNM*, pp. 52–53.

a single document, including the *Codex Iuris Canonici*, in which there is a specific statement that the pope, in his function as supreme pastor of the Church, has the authority to abolish the traditional liturgical rite. In fact, nowhere is it mentioned that the pope has the authority to change even a single local tradition.[60]

Hence the liberties that Pius XII took when defining papal power in the liturgical sphere bode particularly ill, especially his broad statement in *Mediator Dei* that the Roman Pontiff 'alone has the right to permit or establish any liturgical practice, to introduce or approve new rites, or to make any changes in them he considers necessary'.[61] Pacelli put this assertion into practice in 1955 with the reform of the Holy Week ceremonies, designed this time not by clumsy if conservative revisers, but by antiquarianist innovators using the minor ceremonial changes on this occasion as a trial run for the liturgical revolution they were planning.

Contextually it is clear that Pius XII made this affirmation of what he considered his full authority with the intention of safeguarding the Roman liturgical inheritance from the wanton vandalism of irresponsible reformists. No doubt he made it also in the innocent belief that none of his successors would ever dream of using his supreme authority to promote ritual forms and practices opposed to tradition. It is nevertheless true that the above-quoted declaration of 1947 provided the rational basis for the future reformist policies of Popes Paul VI and John Paul II. The former's presiding over the destruction of the immemorial Roman rite and the latter's continuing consent to its marginalization would introduce into the Latin Church a new era of heteropractic pontiffs who considered themselves the inerrant arbiters of disciplinary and liturgical tradition rather than its respectful custodians.

Subversion by Obedience

By the 1960s and 1970s the potentially subversive authoritarianism of papal Rome was ripe for exploitation by the reformist party in the Church: the clerical revolutionaries were only too well aware that obedience to current Vatican policy, to 'the system', had become more important than the living tradition which Catholic leaders had the duty to foster and defend. And so in 1969 the immemorial Roman liturgy was consigned to the scrapheap of history with a minimum of fuss. The radically different nature of the cult that replaced it was evident to anyone with eyes to see, but the change in rationale was not so obvious: whereas the pre-conciliar rites had been authenticated by traditional usage, the new ones had clerical authority as their foundation and justification.

Timothy Williams, an American academic, has remarked of the Pauline liturgy that

it is only as reverent as the celebrant. It never transcends the priest, on whose personal holiness the faithful must rely to transcend the earthbound liturgy. In this respect the new Mass is far more clerical than the traditional Mass. The personality of the priest dominates the entire proceeding. Defenders of the Novus Ordo

---

[60] Gamber, *op. cit.*, p. 34.
[61] *Mediator Dei*, V, 62.

tacitly admit this, by interpreting every criticism of the liturgy as a personal attack on the sanctity of the celebrant, be he pope or parish priest.[62]

In the last analysis the value of the new liturgy was a subjective one, and the trump card of the revolutionaries was a classically voluntarist argument: the reform was to be accepted not because it was good or bad in itself, but because the Vicar of Christ willed it. The Pope, however, is not Christ, and can therefore will something that is not good. Significantly, there was a conspicuous voluntarist element in the philosophy of John Paul II, according to whom 'the will of God is the absolute determinant between good and evil'.[63]

Faced with a full-frontal assault on the heart of their faith, ordinary twentieth-century Catholics, rendered anti-intellectual and uncritical by their religious education, were totally helpless. Professor Marcel de Corte of the University of Liége complained in 1977 that for most members of the Latin faithful:

> it is as if the person of the Pope were, as such, infallible, and as if all of his words, all his directives, all his judgements in all matters, even those foreign to religion, could never be subject to error, though the whole history of the Church protests against that conviction which is close to idolatry.[64]

In such a heady mental climate the solemn admonitions of theologians and saints to question and, if necessary, disobey unlawful or immoral commands of legitimate superiors were disregarded, except by a scorned minority of traditionalist 'rebels'. Instead, while tradition was attacked with impunity, clergy and laity disobeyed the church authorities whenever these dared to interfere with the free exercise of their new secularistic outlook or 'lifestyle', as Paul VI was to learn to his grief when he issued *Humanæ Vitæ*.

The binomium of papolatry and theological liberalism (with its implied moral relativism) might seem at first glance a most bizarre product of the post-conciliar era, but an analysis of the pairing reveals it to be a natural one, given the subjectivism common to both phenomena. At any rate the Roman Church was being undermined by the same virtue of obedience that had once been its strength; the dangerous weapon designed by St Ignatius Loyola for the use of the champions of Catholic tradition was now, in the wrong hands, being turned on those for whose protection it had been fashioned.

Looking back on the destruction of the past fifty years it is difficult to disagree with Archbishop Marcel Lefebvre's paradoxical observation that 'Satan's masterstroke is to have succeeded in sowing disobedience to all Tradition through obedience.'[65]

---

[62] *The Latin Mass*, Vol. 4, No. 1 (Winter 1995), p. 6.
[63] Pope John Paul II, 'Why Read the Bible?', in *Catholic One Year Bible: Arranged in 365 Daily Readings* (Wheaton, Illinois, 1978), p. i. The error was repeated in the encyclical *Veritatis Splendor* (1. Freedom and law, 35): '. . . Revelation teaches that *the power to decide what is good and what is evil does not belong to man, but to God alone*' (emphasis in text). In reality, things are not wrong because God forbids them: God forbids them because they are wrong.
[64] *Courrier de Rome*, March 1977; quoted in M. Davies, *Apologia*, I, p. 396.
[65] M. Lefebvre, *Un évêque parle* (Jarzé, 1974), pp. 148–49.

10

REFORMED CATHOLICISM

*One is sometimes amazed that in France the eighteenth century, the
century of unbelief, should have followed the seventeenth, which is
still styled the religious century par excellence. What is overlooked
is how that very religious century had its particular ideas, tastes,
preferences, and biases on everything in opposition to Rome and to the
rest of Catholicity.*

MELCHIOR DU LAC (1846)

Codifying Immemorial Custom

Strange and startling as they were, the changes in religion that unsettled the
Catholic scene in the 1960s were not bolts from the blue: their seeds had been
growing out of the Church's own life, unperceived, for centuries. Although socially privileged in Catholic states during the post-Tridentine era, the Latin Church
suffered a certain interior decline through the transformation of its praxis during
this period, an ill perhaps no less serious than latinization in the subjugated Eastern
Churches. Largely responsible for this was one of the themes of the Counter
Reformation: the revival of earlier centralistic trends in all domains of ecclesiastical
life, including that of public prayer.

When it was promulgated on 14 July 1570, there was nothing very novel about
the missal of Pope Pius V. Its structure and texts were practically identical with the
Missale ad usum Curiæ Romanæ of 1474, which in turn had reproduced practically unaltered the rite codified by Innocent III at the end of the twelfth century.[1]
What *was* novel about Ghisleri's liturgical legislation was the force with which it
was enacted. For the first time in the history of the Roman patriarchate a pope
was fixing a particular liturgical order both in space and in time. Not only was
the new missal potentially obligatory for the entire Latin Church, but the bull
Quo Primum Tempore stated explicitly the Pope's intention of perpetuating the
immemorial rite, warning that 'should any person venture to tamper with it, let him
know that he will occur the wrath of Almighty God and of the blessed Apostles
Peter and Paul'.[2]

---

[1] This twelfth-century form of Mass was adopted by the Franciscans and used in their houses all
over Europe. See Jungmann, *op. cit.*, I, pp. 101–02.
[2] 'Si quis autem hoc attentare præsumpserit, indignationem omnipotentis Dei, ac beatorum Petri
et Pauli Apostolorum ejus se noverit incursurum.'

The essential thrust of *Quo Primum* has been widely misunderstood in recent years. Contrary to those who suggest that Saint Pius' intention was to bind all his successors forever, forbidding them to make the slightest change to the public worship of the Roman Church, it is contextually clear that the Pope was standardizing not the exact text and rubrics of his 1570 edition of the missal, but the immemorial liturgy itself. Minor textual and rubrical details of the Roman Missal were altered on several occasions by subsequent popes,[3] but until the pontificate of Paul VI no-one presumed to make radical changes to a rite universally considered mature and fixed in its essentials.

Nor was Pius V imposing the principle of absolute liturgical uniformity in the sense of 'rite follows patriarchate'. *Quo Primum* gave all dioceses and religious orders of the West the option of retaining liturgical uses going back at least two hundred years.[4] Thus the historic rites of Milan and Toledo survived the reform, as did the variants of the Gallicano-Roman liturgy peculiar to numerous French dioceses, the archbishopric of Braga in Portugal, and the Carthusian, Calced Carmelite and Dominican orders. One may safely assume that Pope Pius, as a former Dominican, had a healthy respect for legitimate ritual diversity in the Church.

Furthermore, the Council of Trent's confirmation of Latin as the predominant liturgical language of the Roman rite did not imply the rigid exclusion of vernacular worship so often attributed to the Counter-Reformation Church. The practice of Old Slavonic continued as before in parts of Croatia, and the Holy See authorized the liturgical use of at least three literary vernaculars in the foreign missions: Chinese (1615), Persian (1624) and Georgian (1631).[5] Early in the eighteenth century, Jesuit missionaries in Quebec obtained from Rome permission to teach their Indian converts to sing the choir's part of the Mass in the Iroquois tongue.[6]

On the other hand, there was an implicit abolitionism in the pontiff's legislation, since the possibility of retaining local liturgies was presented as a legal option, not as an explicit command or even a desideratum. Indeed St Pius actively encouraged the abandonment of immemorial local traditions by any diocese or religious order desirous of adopting the new Roman Missal when he stated: 'Nevertheless, if this Missal which We have seen fit to publish be more agreeable to these last, We hereby permit them to celebrate Mass according to its rite, subject to the consent of their bishop or prelate, and of their whole Chapter, all else to the contrary notwithstanding.'[7]

---

[3] Jungmann, *op. cit.*, I, p. 139.

[4] '. . . nisi ab ipsa prima institutione a Sede Apostolica adprobata, vel consuetudine, quæ, vel ipsa institutio super ducentos annos Missarum celebrandarum in eisdem Ecclesiis assidue observata sit: a quibus, ut præfatam celebrandi constitutionem, vel consuetudinem nequaquam auferimus . . .'

[5] Permission to celebrate parts of the Mass in Chinese was granted by Pope Paul V, but was not made public because of its controversial nature, and it was finally withdrawn in 1631. Jungmann, *op. cit.*, I, p. 166, n. 28. During the late Middle Ages the Holy See had authorized the use of Armenian (fourteenth century) and Greek (1398, 1406) in the Latin rites then being abusively spread among converts from dissident Eastern Churches.

[6] Gerard Ellard, SJ, *The Mass of the Future* (Milwaukee, 1948), p. 155.

[7] From the bull *Quo Primum Tempore*: '. . . sic si Missale hoc, quod nunc in lucem edi curavimus, iisdem magis placeret, de Episcopi, vel Prælati, Capitulique universi consensu, ut, quibusvis non obstantibus, juxta illud Missas celebrare possint, permittimus . . .'

Absolutism and the Counter-Reformation Church

This flaw in an otherwise reasonable and traditionalist approach to public worship betrayed the spirit of the age, which was that of absolutism. The same desire for uniformity in all things that had motivated the reforming popes of the Middle Ages characterized the Catholic princes and enlightened despots of the pre-revolutionary period. The Age of Absolutism had a selective respect for tradition. Official traditions associated with political power were respectable, whereas heteronomous ones had to be eliminated in the interests of public order. Everywhere in Europe local customs and institutions considered obstacles to the unity of an authoritarian state and the smooth operation of central power were under attack.

As early as 1527 Francis I had abolished the official use of all languages other than French throughout his realm, thus dealing the majority Occitan language of the south a blow from which it would never recover. Nine years later the part-Welsh Henry VIII would impose English as the official language of Wales. Under the Spanish Bourbons who succeeded the old Hapsburg dynasty in 1700, the autonomous institutions of Catalonia were abolished and the Catalan language was gradually proscribed in public life. Already, since the sixteenth century, the Mudéjares and Marranos of Andalusia, Christians of Muslim and Jewish descent, had been under heavy pressure to abandon the remaining vestiges of their ethnicity. In the French, Spanish and Portuguese colonies of Asia and the Americas, the cultures of the indigenous peoples, however advanced, were usually ignored and despised, and a 'good' native subject of the king in Europe was one who spoke his language as well as practising his religion.

The Church could hardly remain unaffected in such an environment. A guiding principle which equated cultural diversity with political disloyalty likewise interpreted ritual differences as so many doctrinal and moral aberrations. Wherever reforming fervour was strong, the need for order and visible unity with the Holy See was translated into hostility towards relics of liturgical diversity against which Rome herself often had no quarrel. New reform-minded orders like the Jesuits and Theatines naturally made the missal of Pius V their liturgical norm, and other congregations of a similar bent followed their example. In 1586 Nicola Doria, vicar general of the Discalced Carmelites, forced his province to abandon the Rite of the Holy Sepulchre still observed by the unreformed and ancient branch of the order, from which he wanted complete independence.[8] The Cistercians abolished their own liturgical use in 1618, and four years later the Premonstratensians followed suit and conformed to the Pian missal, albeit with a small number of euchological and ceremonial concessions to the traditional rite.[9]

During this period when everything coming from Rome was held up for emulation and liturgical diversity was unfashionable when not suspect, clerical and popular affection for ancient traditions cooled in many places. In 1566, when the provincial council of Braga recommended that each Portuguese diocese should retain its historic liturgy, the use of the contemporary Roman Missal and breviary was already a reality everywhere except in the metropolitan see.[10] Similarly, an

---

[8] Sheppard, *The Mass in the West*, pp. 68, 88–89.
[9] Ibid., p. 83. Sheppard notes that in 1660 the general chapter of the Norbertines took this reform a step further by scrapping all the medieval sequences apart from the Christmas sequence *Lætabundus* and the five others contained in the Roman Missal.
[10] King, *op. cit.*, p. 198.

attempt to revive Old Slavonic in Bohemia was doomed to failure. In 1593 some Dalmatian monks moved to the monastery of Emaus, but when the last of them died in 1635, current Czech indifference to tradition caused the foundation to be handed over to Latin Benedictines from Montserrat in Catalonia.[11]

At the beginning of the century the old Mozarabic rite would have died out altogether had Cardinal Cisneros, Archbishop of Toledo, not re-edited the ancient service books and built in 1504 a new chapel in his cathedral church where Mass and the Divine Office could be celebrated daily, a measure ratified by Pope Julius II four years later.[12] Nevertheless, the Old Spanish liturgy was not restored in any of the Mozarabic parishes of the city apart from the churches of Sts Justa and Rufina and St Mark where its celebration was, in any case, confined to titular feasts. Then, in 1842, the four Mozarabic parishes where the ancient rite had lapsed were suppressed, and from 1851 the Roman rite became normal in the two where it had maintained a residual presence.[13] Similarly the revived use of the Mozarabic rite in the chapel of the old cathedral of Salamanca since 1517 was discontinued indefinitely in the 1830s during the turmoil of the First Carlist War.[14]

Even the venerable rite of Milan, which had been so successfully defended against papal aggression during the Middle Ages, had to fight for survival during the Counter Reformation. In 1575 a brief of Gregory XIII approved the Ambrosian liturgy 'in perpetuity' and the Archbishop, St Charles Borromeo, was permitted to introduce the old rite into various monasteries under his jurisdiction. Nevertheless, the upholders of Milanese tradition had to contend with the opposition of the Spanish governor, who insisted that the Roman liturgy to which he was accustomed be celebrated at all the religious functions he attended. Pressure on Rome brought forth another papal brief 'authorizing' Borromeo to use the Roman rite on such occasions. The Archbishop protested vehemently to Mgr Cesare Speciano, protonotary apostolic at the Vatican: 'Indeed, if the existence of our rite is called into question, I should consider this one of the gravest concerns of the Universal Church.'[15] Thanks to the prestige and moral authority of St Charles, Milan was spared any further attempts by Rome to interfere with its liturgical traditions for the next four centuries.

By comparison, the Sarum use (originating in the diocese of Salisbury but common to much of England by the end of the Middle Ages) found no such powerful defender. Since the accession of Queen Elizabeth I in 1558, the Sarum missal had been used at the English College in Douai by Jesuits training for the mission in their native land. But in 1576 the superiors of the College saw fit to adopt instead the Roman Missal of Pius V, and the Jesuits working in England subsequently promoted its use there at the expense of the traditional liturgy to which the surviving Marian clergy had remained loyal.[16]

This centralism also took its toll on the distinct customs of Roman-rite Croatia. From the early seventeenth century the use of Latin made considerable headway

---

[11] Korolevsky, *op. cit.*, p. 86.
[12] Cabrera Delgado y Silveira, *op. cit.*, p. viii; King, *op. cit.*, p. 519. The *Capilla Mozárabe* was named 'Corpus Christi' and equipped with thirteen chaplains, a sacristan and two altar boys. Pope Julius described the Old Spanish rite as 'antiquissimum et magnæ devotionis'.
[13] King, *op. cit.*, pp. 520–21.
[14] Ibid., pp. 519–20.
[15] Ibid., p. 309.
[16] Sheppard, *The Mass in the West*, p. 102.

among the Croatian clergy, and the printing of service books in Glagolitic script was increasingly neglected. The consequent shortage of Old Slavonic missals and breviaries led to a decline in the knowledge and use of the language and its Western alphabet. Thus, by the nineteenth century, the Latin Mass had become the norm in many parts of Croatia and only one local branch of the Franciscans was still using the Slavonic version of the Roman breviary.[17]

Banishing Gothic

Writings on the baroque period of Catholic history make much of the self-conscious conservatism of the Counter Reformation. This was a time when liturgists and architects deliberately exulted in, and emphasized, everything in Catholicism that was attacked by the Protestants: worship of the Blessed Sacrament, the cult of the Blessed Virgin and the saints, the use of sacramentals and so on. But conservatism of this kind was different from the healthy traditionalism of the medieval Church, for in reaction to the Protestant Reformation's wholesale assault on tradition, the leaders of the Catholic Reformation sought to preserve this heritage by abstracting and absolutizing it. The contemporary rush for uniformity and the suspicion of legitimate diversity betrayed an underlying rationalism with its typical reversal of the *lex orandi, lex credendi*: for each Catholic sacramental doctrine there must be an illustrative ritual, identical throughout the Universal Church.

The same Counter-Reformation confidence and self-assurance that renewed men's faith in all that was Catholic also convinced them that the ways of the immediate past, a corrupt age that had culminated in heresy and revolt, were inferior to those of the present. With few exceptions the revised Roman rite was dominant in the Western Church by 1600, but uniformity of worship now went far beyond text and rubrics. In their ardent devotion to *romanità* the Jesuits and other centralists promoted a disdain of everything that smacked not only of local particularism, but also of the now suspect Middle Ages. Everywhere, ample 'Gothic' chasubles were cut down to resemble the pinafore-like Mass vestments worn in Rome. The worldly lace so popular with the Roman clergy became a regular embellishment of albs and surplices. Medieval furnishings (especially rood screens) and ornaments were removed from churches and replaced with baroque statuary and decorations, so that today, in a country like Germany, one often has to visit Lutheran churches to admire the art of the Catholic Middle Ages.

Dazzling the Throngs

This turning away from medieval Catholicism involved, however, much more than simple cultural centralism. In the absolutist civilization of the age, autocratic monarchs were using the splendour of their courts as much as their fearsome armies of mercenaries as means of imposing direct rule throughout their realms and new conquests. Inevitably this political triumphalism affected the worship of the national churches, whose clergy made the fullest use of a new method of affirmation and conversion: dazzling people with the splendour of God and of His

---

[17] Ibid., p. 105.

Church. In the baroque era features of court life tended to set the liturgical tone in Rome, too: the Vatican was, after all, one of the courts of Europe. Louis Bouyer describes well the rationale of this trend:

> An earthly king must be honoured daily by the pageant of court ceremonial, and so also the heavenly King. The courtly atmosphere around Him was to be provided by the liturgy. The liturgy, as many handbooks of the period actually say, was considered to be 'the etiquette of the great King'. The most obvious features of it were those embodying the external pomp, decorum and grandeur so befitting a Prince.[18]

Referring to the eighteenth century, Bouyer also points to the influence of opera, as the great artistic creation of the period, on pre-revolutionary worship:

> the faithful of the same period sought to find a religious equivalent of the Opera in the liturgy. . . . The liturgical pomps displayed in . . . churches tended to smother the traditional text of the liturgy under an increasingly profane kind of polyphony, the text itself having little more importance either for the performers or the onlookers than did Da Ponte's poems for devotees of Mozart. And, in the end, liturgy was embalmed in productions which treated it as reverently and as indifferently as the King's corpse at a royal funeral . . .[19]

Did not French Rationalism in the eighteenth century mock the High Mass as 'the grand opera of the poor' (Voltaire)?

While the baroque and rococo periods were not without liturgical growth (producing for instance the beautiful ceremony of Benediction of the Blessed Sacrament), so much aping of worldly court ceremonial inevitably led to the secularizing not of the structure of the liturgy (which the intensely conservative mood of the age insisted on keeping unchanged), but of its performance. One has only to listen to a Mass by Mozart or Haydn to realize how little different church music of this era must have sounded from that of the concert hall. All kinds of secular instruments were now being used in church, while the organ itself was played in a bombastic manner that drowned out the singing of the liturgical texts. The ceremonial, too, tended to be stiff, gaudy and exhibitionistic, those in the sanctuary often looking and acting more like obsequious courtiers than recollected sacred ministers.

As for the churches themselves, their appearance was inevitably affected by this new orientation. The typical baroque church was built to resemble a theatre or a concert hall in plan and decoration.[20] As the sanctuary increasingly assumed the appearance of a stage, the now gigantic altar came to look like its principal property, and the mensa, the most important part of the altar symbolically, was dwarfed in a swirl of lapidary ornament. Pews and seats for the pious spectators of liturgical performances appeared everywhere, and the choir moved from the recess between the sanctuary and the nave to the organ loft at the back of the church. In baroque temples the atmosphere of sacred darkness and 'dim religious

---

[18] Bouyer, *op. cit.*, p. 4.
[19] Ibid., p. 7.
[20] Ibid.

light' from stained glass windows and candles gave way to the hard brightness of whitewashed walls and huge chandeliers.

Divine Protocol

The Counter Reformation approached its liturgical heritage less as a living tradition than as 'the official form for the external worship of the Church' – so Fr Bouyer found it being described in a handbook on liturgy still circulating in 1956.[21] With the sacred rites equated to civil protocol, often more energy went into ensuring a punctilious performance of them than into the consideration of their meaning. Contemporary courses on liturgy in seminaries were thus largely instruction in rubrics. Dom Bernard Botte recalled from the early years of the twentieth century how liturgy, even at the Catholic University of Louvain,

> was the ceremonial part of worship emptied of its real content. The goal was to prepare clerics for correctly carrying out ritual acts, and this was very good. Only it is regrettable that no one ever thought of explaining the liturgical texts and showing the spiritual riches they contain. From the way these texts were read it was apparent that most priests devoted only indirect attention to their meaning. The texts were neither food for clerical piety nor a source for sermons. These are reasons, I think, for the poor preaching at the beginning of the twentieth century.[22]

To many in the Church the connection between public worship and spirituality was not even obvious, as Bouyer relates of a prominent French liturgist of the pre-conciliar period:

> He had just finished instructing some candidates for the priesthood in the ceremonies of the Mass, when one of his young and, we hope, candid students asked: 'But, Father, when we are saying Mass, at what moments can we pray?' 'What? Pray?' answered the sage, 'But, my boy, this is not the time for that!'[23]

That this astonishing desacralization was a by-product of baroque culture is also suggested by art historians and musicologists. Concerning the Catholicism of the Mozart family in the eighteenth century, Arthur Hutchings writes:

> nothing written by the Mozarts (and little written by other people of their time) suggests that Catholic worship *impressed* them. Confession and communion, fasting and feasting, observance of days of obligation – the duties of the Catholic are mentioned often enough; but they do not write with delight about the high masses and vespers for which their grand music was purveyed. When daily dress and manners were ceremonious, there may have been more of convention and pomp than of awe and mystery in church . . . However much the paintings and sculptures of Baroque and Rococo churches depict the anthropomorphic deity and the saints,

[21] Ibid., p. 1.
[22] Botte, *op. cit.*, pp. 6–7.
[23] Bouyer, *op. cit.*, p. 3.

patriarchs and angels, these grand theatrical buildings do not suggest mystery as medieval churches do; instead they are like the finest halls of royal palaces, conceived for the Supreme Prince.[24]

Mathematical Worship

When legitimate concern for the correct execution of prescribed ritual acts, narrowed in scope to become mere rubricism and the cultivation of liturgical spirituality, was neglected, there arose the danger of a rationalist approach to the sacraments that made validity a more important consideration than authenticity. The work of the priest at the altar was to perform the Eucharistic Sacrifice, thereby applying its fruits to those for whom it was being offered; the concept of the Mass as the most sublime celebration of the cosmic mystery of Redemption often made less of an impression on the minds of that age.

As has been seen, this change of emphasis, typical of the Latin Church, had earlier manifested itself liturgically in the general tendency towards a minimized symbolism in the administration of the sacraments: to baptism by sprinkling and Communion under one kind was now added the distribution of Communion to the faithful outside its proper place in the rite of Mass, the general rule by the end of the eighteenth century.[25]

One particularly potent long-term factor of change had been the multiplication of votive Masses – celebrations of the Eucharist offered for particular intentions – from the seventh century onwards. The early multiple votive Masses were requiems sung for deceased members of pious confraternities, and the offering of a hundred Masses for each soul was not uncommon during the High Middle Ages.[26] As votive Masses (which could be offered only on weekdays) became more popular, the primitive custom of celebrating the Eucharist only once a week gave way, by the ninth century, to a situation whereby the average priest celebrated every day, some even doing so several times a day.[27] With the decline of concelebration in the West, and growing numbers of Masses sung in a given church on any day, side altars and separate chapels began to be constructed in churches.[28]

Votive Masses were originally celebrated with small groups of the faithful present, but their numerical increase led to the so-called private Mass, with the priest assisted only by a server making the responses. Now in the early Christian centuries the Eucharist was always sung, a tradition since faithfully maintained in the independent Eastern Churches. But as the sheer number of votive Masses made sung services increasingly impractical, a new form of celebration, the *missa lecta* or Low Mass, emerged, as did the *missa solitaria*, said by the priest alone, without even a server present.

---

[24] Arthur Hutchings, *Mozart: The Man* (London, 1976), p. 98.
[25] The Orthodox continue to view these developments with strong misgivings; see, for instance, Nicholas Zernov, *Eastern Christendom: A Study of the Origin and Development of the Eastern Orthodox Church* (London, 1961), p. 263. On the development of Holy Communion outside Mass, see Jungmann, *op. cit.*, II, pp. 409–11.
[26] Jungmann, *op. cit.*, I, p. 218.
[27] Ibid., pp. 221–22.
[28] Ibid., pp. 223–24.

For the rest of the Middle Ages these developments had little effect on the principal Sunday liturgies of Latin Catholic churches, which continued to be sung services. However, the revision of the liturgy after the Council of Trent included two measures prejudicial to the public or communitarian nature of divine worship. The missal of St Pius V formally permitted the 'solitary Mass', in the face of earlier legislation to the contrary by numerous provincial councils.[29] It also treated the Low Mass as the standard form of the eucharistic liturgy. Henceforth, the sung High Mass and *missa cantata* were seen more and more as solemn, but optional, embellishments of a service normally reduced to its simplest and shortest form. Since a twenty-minute Low Mass was, from the theological standpoint, just as efficacious as a two-hour High Mass, rationalistic Catholics of early modern times inclined towards the merits of the former. By the nineteenth century it was not unusual to find parishes where the main Sunday Mass itself was rarely if ever sung, a situation that has endured to the present day, especially in English-speaking countries.

All this was the logical outcome of a perfunctory approach to worship. As well as being reduced to its simplest terms, the communal Eucharist often became a private Mass at which a congregation was required to be present but need not follow the ritual intelligently as long as its members recollected themselves and prayed in some form or other. A parallel aspect of the Tridentine reform, this time concerning the Divine Office, also compromised the celebratory nature of the sacred liturgy. Made compulsory for all clerics, the breviary had to be recited in full each day under pain of sin, but the appointed hours did not have to be observed literally: a priest could, for instance, recite Matins, Lauds, Prime and Terce, all morning offices, late in the evening. With numerical considerations and obligation thus prevailing, the Prayer of the Church was increasingly removed from its ritual context.

Out of Context

Counter-Reformation piety was, as Owen Chadwick has remarked, 'more personal than liturgical'.[30] This personalism had not only brought about the 'privatization' of the Divine Office, but caused confessionals to appear in churches. In medieval Catholicism the liturgical nature of the sacramental acts of confession and absolution had been manifested in the custom of penitents kneeling beside a priest somewhere in the body of the church (just as in the Byzantine rite they stand with him before the iconostasis). In post-Tridentine Catholicism, the visual impression was, by contrast, that of a private affair between confessor and penitent, not a penitential act witnessed by a priest before the altar of the God Who forgives sin.

The revival of preaching and Bible reading were other reforms promoted more for their own sake than cultivated in their proper liturgical context. Trent's general ban on the vernacular in the set liturgy had deprived the proclamation of the Word of its full intended effect and, before the advent of lay missals, created a situation whereby laymen who read the Scriptures did so separately from their experience of divine worship. The erection of high, impressive pulpits far away

---

[29] Ibid., p. 227.
[30] O. Chadwick, *op. cit.*, p. 293.

from the sanctuary also tended to emphasize the separateness of the sermon from the rest of the sacred liturgy.[31]

Similarly decontextualized were the ascetic customs of the Latin Church, gradually eroded throughout the post-Tridentine period. In the early Church it was the universal custom for Christians to abstain from meat, eggs, milk, butter and cheese during Lent. Although there was much flouting of this rule in Northern Europe (where nutritious vegetable substitutes like olive oil were less available than in Mediterranean countries), the Papacy continued to enforce it until the sixteenth century.[32] After the Council of Trent a series of papal dispensations allowed one provincial council after another to relax this ancient discipline to which the Christian East would continue to remain attached. These dispensations enjoined the performance of an alternative act of penance, often left to the discretion of the individual.[33] It was the same rationalistic process that had abolished the traditional Friday abstinence outside Lent in Spain, whose bishops continued to appeal to a medieval indult granted at the time of the Iberian Crusades.[34]

By the eighteenth century the consumption of dairy foods in Lent was common, but the prohibition concerning eggs and meat was maintained longer in many dioceses. Finally, the decree *Indulto Sacro*, Pope Pius X's concession to modern living in 1904, lifted all remaining local bans on the Latin faithful partaking of eggs and dairy products during the penitential season and allowed meat to be eaten at the main meal alone on all days of Lent except Fridays, Ash Wednesday, the Ember Days, the vigils of St Joseph and the Annunciation (18 and 24 March) and the Easter Triduum.[35] Abolishing abstinence on most Lenten weekdays while retaining the fast not only confused fasting and abstinence in people's minds, but also deprived abstinence of its liturgical character, turning what had once been a sacrosanct immemorial custom enjoined by tradition into a simple disciplinary regulation determined by legislation. The ever decreasing number of Latin Christians who would continue to observe the ancient abstinence customs would do so as a private devotion, rather than as a liturgical act in union with the Universal Church.[36]

---

[31] In recent times this trend has appeared in Eastern Orthodoxy as well. Fr Georges Florovsky complains that

> Unfortunately there is a tendency to develop preaching along non-liturgical lines. Sermons very often have little connection with the rite itself, and usually it is done deliberately in order to make the sermon more actual [sic] and to bear on contemporary topics and interests. At the Liturgy the sermon is, most unfortunately, shifted towards the end of the service, and becomes rather an addition to the service, instead of being its integral part, closely related to the scriptural lessons. (*Op. cit.*, pp. 63–64.)

[32] E. Vacandard, 'Carême (Jeûne du)', *DTC*, II, Part 2, col. 1736.

[33] Ibid., §§ 1745–47.

[34] In 1089 Pope Urban II had granted the dispensation to Spanish counties whose leaders had fought the Moors. Pius V extended the privilege to the whole Hispanic world after the Battle of Lepanto (1571). Apart from Ash Wednesday and Lenten Fridays, abstinence was still required on the vigils of four major feasts (Christmas, Pentecost, the Assumption and All Saints' Day). In a bid to make what remained of the law of abstinence uniform throughout the Latin Church, Pope Pius XII withdrew the exemption from Latin American countries (but not from Spain) in 1950; the United States' dioceses of El Paso and Gallup, with large Hispanic populations, were also affected the following year.

[35] Ibid., §§ 1747–48. It is interesting to note that Lenten abstinence was so firmly rooted a tradition in the life of the English people that it was at first retained by the Anglican Church, and the ban on consuming meat, eggs, milk and cheese in Lent was enforced by civil as well as ecclesiastical law until the reign of William III (1694–1702).

[36] In the Orthodox Church it is admitted that many people nowadays cannot keep the ancient

Public Worship: Jesuit-style

It was natural that all these Counter-Reformation attitudes towards liturgical custom should have been closely associated with the Society of Jesus, the most dynamic and influential order of the period. The active virtues loomed large in the Jesuit cosmos, and from the first St Ignatius wanted his priests, though clerks regular, to be freed from the traditional choir duties in order to enjoy greater mobility: 'All priests of our Society are bound to recite the office, but not in choir lest they be withdrawn from those works of charity to which we have wholly dedicated ourselves.' Cardinal Ghinucci was not the only churchman of the day to look askance at this 'Lutheran' innovation.[37]

Such liturgical minimalism, it should be pointed out in fairness to the Jesuits, was in fact the development of a late medieval trend already set in motion by the friars. Louis Bouyer noted how the Franciscans and Dominicans had been

> too deeply immersed in the civilization of their time to be able to satisfy themselves with the traditional prayer and worship of the Church. They held to it as closely as they could – the Franciscans with drastic abbreviations, the Dominicans by systematically reducing it to a position of honourable but distinctly secondary importance in their life.[38]

Piety, mysticism and intellectualism had filled the partial liturgical vacuum in these two orders, and would later form the groundwork of Jesuit spirituality.[39]

In their pastoral work some Jesuits were enthusiastic promoters of congregational singing, but of edifying hymns similar to those popular with Protestants, not of the liturgical texts themselves. As for the Society's main tool of conversion, mental prayer, i.e. structured meditation:

> The old orders, especially the Dominicans, loudly condemned the *Exercises*, a spiritual crash-course with memory, reason and will as its Trinity. Designed for the laity as much as for the priest and the postulant, they brought an element of hustle into religion – Benedictines complained of a coercive, parade-ground attitude to prayer.[40]

There can be no doubt that the *Exercises* had been designed as an adjunct of the liturgical life, certainly not as a rival to it. Nevertheless, according to Dom Maurice Festugière the Jesuit recipe of liturgical minimalism, mental prayer and new sentimental devotions amounted to a Catholic individualism created to compete with contemporary Protestantism.[41] There was a danger that such new approaches to prayer could cause the ordinary faithful to lose their taste for the liturgy in its full form – where it was still available. When this occurred, compulsory public worship

---

abstinence with full rigour, but the custom has not been degraded by official legislation and therefore retains its liturgical character.
[37] Mitchell, *op. cit.*, p. 45.
[38] Bouyer, *op. cit.*, p. 245.
[39] Ibid.
[40] Ibid., p. 37.
[41] Maurice Festugière, OSB, 'La liturgie catholique: essai de synthèse', *Revue de Philosophie*, I (1913), pp. 692–886.

could easily be seen as something to be got over as quickly as possible for one to get on with private prayer and good works. Two new contemplative orders, the Discalced Carmelites and the Capuchins, modified a basic Jesuit principle when they took up the modern custom of singing all their offices *recto tono* in order to allow more time for mental prayer.

Today, attachment to the conveniently short Low Mass has as its unfortunate complement – even among traditionalists – an impatience with the sung Mass and with long, elaborate ceremonies in general. Consequently, it is natural for the average 'unliturgical' Latin Catholic to find the lengthy and solemn Eastern liturgies a penance, as did the Polish-American Jesuit missionary Walter Ciszek while a student at the Russian College in Rome:

> The greatest hardship for me, in fact, during those years of study was the Oriental liturgy. Those of us assigned to the Russicum had Mass every morning in the Oriental rite, and I couldn't stand it. But since I had made up my mind to work in Russia, I hung on grimly, trying to learn and appreciate it.[42]

Within Catholic ranks the aliturgical (and sometimes anti-liturgical) reputation of the sons of St Ignatius would also give rise to the facetious expression 'as lost as a Jesuit in Holy Week'. In the first decade of this century it actually led one of their number, Fr Jean-Joseph Navatel, to make the extraordinary assertion that the sacred liturgy was marginal to true piety, and merely 'the sensible, ceremonial and decorative part of Catholic worship'.[43] The French Jesuit, in defending Ignatian spirituality as more effective than liturgical spirituality, also challenged the Benedictine claim that the liturgy had played a central role in the building up of Christian civilization in the past and that it could serve as an excellent means of evangelizing the secularized sections of society in modern times.[44]

There were, of course, members of the Society of Jesus (like the Englishman Herbert Thurston) who recognized the importance of the liturgical life and made valuable contributions to its study.[45] However, that the general Jesuit ethos was to an appreciable degree responsible for 'implanting an anti-liturgical and anti-social spirituality in the Church' is admitted by one of the order's apologists, Fr Joseph de Guibert:

> But have not the Jesuits at least contributed towards distorting the tendencies of Catholic piety? In their churches and amid the groups of the faithful whom

---

[42] Walter J. Ciszek, SJ with Daniel L. Flaherty, SJ, *With God in Russia* (New York, 1966), p. 26. Fr Ciszek eventually learned to love Russian worship and suffered heroically for the Faith in Communist Russia, but his initial revulsion says a lot about his formation, both as a Latin-rite Catholic and as a Jesuit scholastic.

[43] J.-J. Navatel, SJ, 'L'Apostolat liturgique et la piété personnelle', *Études*, 137 (1913), p. 452.

[44] Navatel, *op. cit.*, pp. 450–53. It surely would have been preferable (and orthodox) to recommend mental prayer as an important complement of liturgical prayer within Catholic spirituality, than to oppose the two.

[45] The Society of Jesus may be well known for certain tendencies, but the individualism of its members is also proverbial. The Jesuits who commissioned the building of that architectural gem, London's Farm Street Church of the Immaculate Conception, in the 1840s can hardly be accused of insensitivity to sound liturgical principles, and one of the leading apologists of traditionalist resistance to the Pauline liturgical revolution was another English Jesuit, the late Fr Paul Crane. In the twentieth century, numerous priests of the Society would also participate in the building up of the strongly liturgical Byzantine-rite mission which Fr Ciszek joined.

they directed they developed exercises and ceremonies which might be termed paraliturgical. Did they not by these developments take away from souls the taste and the feeling for true liturgical ceremonies and for their rich and beautiful simplicity?

To the detriment of the Mass and the Divine Office did they not multiply solemnities which had a somewhat gorgeous splendour and were sustained by a kind of music too far removed from the profound religious sentiment of the true Gregorian chant?[46]

The reason that Fr de Guibert gives for these departures from the norm is somewhat damning: the fact that 'In the matter of exercises of prayer in common and of public ceremonies, the Jesuits also largely adapted themselves to the habits and tastes of their contemporaries.'[47]

Jesuit 'modernism' may have been detrimental in the liturgical sphere, but according to Marie-Madeleine Martin it had even more disastrous consequences for the Catholic faith of the new generations:

Filled with an infatuation for their time, something quite compatible with their desire for a rapid impact on society, they [the Jesuits] were prisoners of the fashions and errors of an era; they were ignorant of the Middle Ages and despised them, *because their own Order was modern*. They flattered themselves moreover that they were able to promote simultaneously the teaching of religion and the progress of culture, *but in distinguishing the two totally, they implicitly cast discredit upon religion*. There was on the one hand a domain for free, strong minds, and on the other an ever less justifiable piety, more and more reduced to practices unconnected with the rest of intellectual life. *They separated, imperceptibly and increasingly, reason and faith: the triumphal synthesis of the Christian Middle Ages.*

One should not forget that Voltaire had been a pupil of the Jesuits (which shows how at that time one could be a brilliant pupil of the Jesuits and an enemy of the Christian religion). Nor should it be forgotten that all the speakers of the Revolutionary Assemblies were products of religious colleges: from Robespierre to Danton, from Saint-Just to Fouquier-Tinville. It was in these colleges that they had all learned to quote Cato and Brutus, to love Roman pagan Antiquity, even in its idolatrous cult of the State and in its cruel harshness towards individuals.[48]

Secularizing the Worship of God

Secularization to varying degrees was the natural result of a new Catholicism that belittled the Christian culture of the immediate past in order to embrace – and baptize – modernity. Baroque architecture, for instance, proves on analysis to have been as contemporary and secular in spirit as the functionalist Bauhaus monstrosities

---

[46] Joseph de Guibert, *The Jesuits – Their Spiritual Doctrine and Practice: A Historical Study* (St Louis, 1972), p. 557. However, the Jesuits did pioneer a useful correlation of private and public prayer. For instance St Francis Borgia adapted schemes of mental prayer to the framework of the daily liturgy (ibid., p. 554).

[47] Ibid., p. 558.

[48] Marie-Madeleine Martin, *op. cit.*, pp. 143–44.

that traditional Christians find so alienating today. Regarding the rites celebrated within baroque edifices, a further analogy which Louis Bouyer draws with the profane liturgical ethos of our own day is more real than might at first appear:

> The men of the seventeenth century were sure that the short-cut formulae of their theological and controversial handbooks were enough to hold all the pith and marrow of Christian tradition concerning the Eucharist. Therefore so long as they retained somewhere in the background of a ceremony the substance of the rites and the texts of the traditional liturgy, they believed themselves to be perfectly Catholic, and felt quite entitled to dress up these rites and texts to resemble as closely as possible the profane performances of that period, paying no attention at all to the ways in which the Eucharistic doctrine had traditionally been expressed in the rites and texts themselves. But do not many people today do exactly the same kind of thing when they try to disguise a rubrically correct Low Mass by reading and singing in the vernacular, to make it resemble as closely as possible the style of public meeting now popular, endeavouring also to give to the performance of the sacred rite itself a setting resembling that of the stadium, of the factory, or of the movie-theatre? Is it not of the very essence of the Baroque spirit to transpose into a worldly setting a liturgy envisioned merely as an external formality?[49]

One of the bad fruits of the post-Tridentine Church was indeed a liturgical indifferentism which separated the ethos and the doctrine of the *lex orandi*. In other words, provided that the validity and integrity of the rite itself were preserved, it might be performed in whichever way the Church saw fit at that particular time. Hence the same Mass of St Pius V might be celebrated in the style of grand opera in the seventeenth and eighteenth centuries, in an entirely artificial mock-Gothic style in the nineteenth, and, on the eve of the Pauline revolution, with electric guitars and pop tunes blasted through microphones.

Romanità *versus Local Tradition*

The end result of ritual minimalism and secularization was, inevitably, to divorce the faithful even further from the liturgical rites themselves, which they neither knew in full nor followed comprehendingly. Yet it would be unjust to blame this ill on the Jesuits and other instructors of the laity: clearly, pastors were responding to the needs of the day and working within the limits set them. The root cause of liturgical alienation was, in fact, the general centralization of Catholic life and worship, especially since the liturgical reform of 1570, which in most places had broken the bond between the faithful and their proper ritual patrimony. One outcome of the Counter Reformation was that the majority of Latin Christians were made to worship according to new forms which, though traditional in themselves, were foreign in that they were imported from the capital of the Catholic world and had not grown organically out of the culture and spirituality of each people.

Latin Catholic worship had become almost completely centralized by the second half of the nineteenth century, and the new situation was in perfect harmony with the ultramontanist spirit of the pontificate of Pope Pius IX, who 'was ready to

---

[49] Bouyer, *op. cit.*, pp. 8–9.

summon Bishops more frequently to Rome *ad limina*, to distribute Roman titles – and particularly that of Monsignor – more widely, to encourage the general adoption in the Church of Roman rites, liturgy and clerical costume . . .'[50]

It is from this period, too, that dates the attempt to make the pronunciation of liturgical Latin (traditionally reflecting the speech habits of local churches) conform to the contemporary Italian-influenced norm of papal Rome, the 'chees-and-chaws', as the new fashion was contemptuously dubbed by the more old-fashioned English clergy.[51]

The successful spread of *romanità* in France, in spite of vigorous Neo-Gallican resistance, was closely tied to the Catholic revival of the last decades of the century. Significantly, this was largely an urban-based, middle-class affair involving converts with no direct experience of the immemorial religious traditions of their country. Louis Veuillot, editor of *L'Univers religieux*, was the moral leader of this new bourgeois Catholicism distinguished by an ultramontanism that was cultural as well as doctrinal.

One of the reforms aggressively promoted by *L'Univers* was the replacement of the so-called Neo-Gallican uses of France with the modern Roman rite. Liturgical abolitionism at this time was closely associated with the Jesuits and, especially, with the liberal Catholic movement to which Dom Prosper Guéranger had belonged until its condemnation by Pope Gregory XVI in 1832 and 1834.[52] That the liberal Catholics were concerned to christianize rather than to repudiate the Enlightenment legacy is evident from the antiquarianism of Dom Guéranger (otherwise so anti-revolutionary and anti-rationalist), in his case an 'orthodox' antiquarianism substituted for the classicist antiquarianism of the Jansenists. In his energetic liturgical campaign of the 1840s, Guéranger pressed not for the adoption of the 'pure' Roman liturgy as something admittedly new, but for a 'return' to it. The underlying – and quite erroneous – supposition was that

> Christianity had been brought to Gaul by missionaries sent personally by Saint Peter and the second Pope, Saint Clement, and Gaul had thus depended on Rome for ritual as well as doctrine from the very earliest centuries. In that simple age of austere uniformity before local variants and impurities had appeared, all the scattered Gaulish dioceses had followed an original Roman liturgy; it was the plain duty of modern bishops to return to it.[53]

Bourgeois Catholicism owed a greater debt than it cared to acknowledge to the legacy of Napoleon: Article 39 of the 1801 Concordat had prescribed 'Only one liturgy and one catechism' for the whole of France.[54] Cardinal Consalvi had, however,

---

[50] E. E. Y. Hales, *op. cit.*, p. 280.

[51] On 25 July 1912 Mgr Louis Dubois, Archbishop of Bourges, made public a letter from Pope Pius X encouraging the spread of the Italian pronunciation of Latin in France (at least in liturgical singing); see *Acta Apostolicæ Sedis*, IV, 577.

[52] Encyclicals *Mirari Vos*, condemning Lamennais' newspaper *L'Avenir* in 1832, and *Singulari Nos* (1834), condemning the same writer's *Paroles d'un croyant*.

[53] Austin Gough, *Paris and Rome: The Gallican Church and the Ultramontane Campaign 1848–1853* (Oxford, 1986), p. 122. Pope Gregory obviously subscribed to this misreading of history, for in 1846 he told the vicar general of the bishopric of Nevers that he 'would be very pleased, certainly, to see all the dioceses return successively to the unity of the Roman liturgy . . .' (ibid., p. 126).

[54] Ibid., p. 119.

rejected as imprudent the proposal of Mgr Bernier, Bishop of Orleans, that the Roman rite of 1570 be imposed throughout the country, and at first Guéranger and his allies received only lukewarm support from the Holy See. Popes Gregory XVI and Pius IX were both favourable to the spread of the modern Roman liturgy in France but they considered this a desideratum rather than a real necessity, and they were moreover reluctant to force a change that would be resented by the majority of French Catholics.[55] As for the Congregation of Rites, it was so indolent during the 1840s that letters from French bishops requesting clarifications of liturgical law were rarely answered.[56]

The Baby and the Bathwater

The abolitionists nevertheless had a powerful weapon in their arsenal: the fact that most of the extant diocesan liturgies bore the scars of eighteenth-century Jansenist revisionism. True as this may have been in general, Dom Guéranger was not disposed to check the finer details, and his anti-Gallican offensive targeted equally liturgies like that of Paris (which was indeed deformed) and others which still preserved the substance of the old Gallicano-Roman tradition. For instance, in many of its features the liturgy of Tours, Austin Gough writes, 'could be traced back to St Gregory of Tours, and [it] was so beautiful and historically interesting, the [local] archbishop claimed, that even the sceptical bourgeoisie of the city came to Mass for aesthetic reasons'.[57] The uses of Chartres and Saint-Denis even retained the very ancient custom of singing the Maundy Thursday Mass in Greek.[58]

Though reviled by the French higher clergy as 'an arsonist' forever 'altering, falsifying, and exaggerating the facts in order to arrive at his goal of discrediting the French episcopate', Dom Prosper refused to be deterred.[59] The anti-Gallican campaign whipped up by *L'Univers* had considerable impact on the lower clergy, who were happy to trade loyalty to their often autocratic local bishops for obedience to a more distant Vatican authority. Accepting the rites of the Holy Father in Rome was part of the deal.

A minority in the national episcopate also embraced the ultramontane cause in the mid-1840s. By 1851 twenty-nine bishoprics had opted to go over to the modern Roman rite and most of the provincial councils decided to implement the same reform sooner or later.[60] The last ritual vestiges of Jansenism were thus cleaned away, but at the same time what was genuinely medieval and French in

---

[55] Ibid., p. 126. Pope Gregory actually counselled Archbishop Gousset against abolishing the use of Rheims in 1842:

> the Popes, he said, had always accepted any local liturgy which had been used for more than two hundred years, and 'it would be in any case a difficult and awkward task to uproot these customs implanted in your region for so long a time'. Three years later the same Pope stated: 'I understand the difficulties in the way [of a "return" to the Roman liturgy] and I would never order it; I will never order it.' As for Pius IX, he told Guéranger in the 1840s that he had 'no wish at all that rites and prayers consecrated by long practice should be proscribed'.

[56] Ibid., pp. 127–28.
[57] Ibid., p. 123.
[58] Ibid., p. 121, n. 3.
[59] Ibid., p. 124.
[60] Ibid., p. 168.

the received rites was lost forever as one diocese after another adopted the Roman service books.

The fate of the 'Neo-Gallican' uses was sealed in 1852 when Guéranger was appointed a consultor to the Congregation of Rites. Dom Prosper's monastery of Solesmes was situated within the diocese of Le Mans, and the steadfast refusal of its ordinary, Mgr Jean-Baptiste Bouvier, to introduce the modern Roman liturgy had especially rankled with the Benedictine abbot. Following his Roman appointment, Guéranger encouraged his allies in the diocesan synod to write to the Vatican and press their case for the abolition of the old liturgy. The official reply they received not only condemned the use of Le Mans, but made this particular judgement normative for the whole of France.[61] Pope Pius IX's encyclical of 1853 to the French bishops, *Inter Multiplices*, though written primarily to vindicate Veuillot from the condemnation of the French bishops, manifested a new centralistic outlook in expressing satisfaction that 'by your special zeal the liturgy of the Roman Church has been restored according to Our desires in many of your dioceses'.[62]

In the 1860s Cardinal de Bonald's proposal to reinstate the old Lyonese use (which Mgr de Montazet had abolished in 1777 in favour of the new Jansenistic service books of Paris) was opposed by both the Gallican conservatives and the ultramontanists of his archdiocese. The latter triumphed when, in 1864, Pius IX decided to impose the Roman Missal and breviary on the primatial See of Lyons, albeit with a few superficial concessions to local usage; it was not until 1902 that Pope Leo XIII would eventually reinstate the genuine Lyonese *ordo missæ*.[63] Meanwhile, the staunchly Neo-Gallican Archbishop of Paris, Mgr Georges Darboy, resisted Pope Pius and the French Jesuits by delaying as long as possible the introduction of the Roman liturgical books, as did Bishop Ginoulhiac of Grenoble and Mgr Mathieu of Besançon.[64] The last diocese to adopt the Roman Missal was Mgr Dupanloup's see of Orleans, which held out until 1875.[65]

---

[61] Ibid., pp. 174–76. Gough describes (p. 179) the French hierarchy's pathetic response to this ruling,

> Letters flowed in to the Nunciature from bishops who had been 'moved by the recent decision of the Congregation of Rites . . . to express our feelings of filial piety towards the Sacred Person': their diocesan liturgies were ancient and distinguished, they said, they were understood and cherished by the laity in the parishes, but nevertheless they would be changed at the first opportune moment. Some dioceses asked plaintively if they could keep one small devotion to a popular saint, adding that of course they would not insist.

On 28 October 1852 Mgr Jean-Baptiste Bouvier of Le Mans issued a pastoral letter stating with sorrow that 'although the liturgy of this diocese was perhaps one of the most irreproachable of the liturgies of the last century . . . in spite of its genuine beauty and the remarkable balance of its component parts, we have taken the decision to replace it with the Roman liturgy' (ibid., p. 178).

[62] Par. 2. See also Hales, *op. cit.*, p. 283. Guéranger's victims had the last laugh when, in 1856, the Congregation of Rites rejected a special liturgical order he had drawn up for his monastery based on medieval Cluniac and Benedictine texts. Guéranger was apparently furious not to have got his way, for Gough records that he 'vowed never to return to Rome in the lifetime of Pius IX, and refused a personal invitation to attend the Vatican Council in 1869' (Gough, *op. cit.*, p. 180).

[63] King, *op. cit.*, pp. 28–29; Sheppard, *The Mass in the West*, pp. 51–52. Attempts to restore the old liturgy had begun during the reign of Bonald's predecessors Mgr de Pins and Cardinal Fesch. Pius IX allowed the Lyonese to retain in their celebration of the Roman liturgy the medieval ceremonial that had survived Montazet's reform. After the revival of 1902 Lyons was the only diocese in France to retain its patrimonial use.

[64] Hales, *op. cit.*, p. 283; Gough, *op. cit.*, p. 180.

[65] Gough, *op. cit.*

Loyalist romanization was not, however, confined to France. In contemporary England efforts by traditionalists to revive the Sarum liturgy after the restoration of the Catholic hierarchy in 1850 were similarly defeated by ultramontanist pressure.[66] Throughout Latin Christendom, clergy and faithful were moving towards a new perception of the liturgy as a thing provided and regulated by an international hierarchy, and not something inherited through the local church.

Rarefying the 'Work of God'

The bull *Quo Primum* (1570) may have foreshadowed this gradual liturgical unification of the Roman patriarchate, but the ritual centralism of the Counter Reformation was set in motion by Pope Sixtus V in 1588 when he created the new Congregation of Rites and Ceremonies. This new curial organ deprived the local bishops and provincial councils of most of their authority and initiative in cultic matters and became the instrument of what many metropolitans resented as the Vatican's usurpation of their prerogatives.[67]

The charter of the Congregation of Rites, presided over by five cardinals, was to

> see to it that the old sacred rites are exactly observed in all places and by all persons, in the churches of Rome and of the whole world, including our pontifical chapel, in everything concerning the Mass, the Divine Office, the administration of the sacraments and, in general, other functions related to worship.[68]

In the doctrinal sphere greater central control was undoubtedly a salutary measure in the face of Protestantism and Jansenism, but it could also be deadly to local tradition (as the experience of nineteenth-century France has shown), and would later be the principal channel of liturgical subversion in the pontificate of Paul VI.

Liturgical centralization affected not only the form of public worship, but its cultural accidents as well. In its early years, the Congregation of Rites was so vigilant about the threat of Protestant influences that it was judged prudent to subordinate the liturgical life of the faithful to the supposed dictates of doctrinal orthodoxy. The Congregation's language policy is a good illustration of this bid to control the natural development of worship. Since the 'veil of mystery' that Latin cast over the Catholic cultus was especially prized as a shield against heresy, all initiatives to introduce the vernacular into the services of Western countries were strictly forbidden, in keeping with the recent rulings of the Council of Trent.

Certainly the Protestant case against liturgical Latin was not fully compelling: in Italy, France, Spain and Portugal the traditional sacral language had not lost its place in popular culture, not least because the Romance languages remained

---

[66] Lancelot Sheppard, a staunch defender of the Pauline revolution, records with satisfaction the failure of a laudable proposal to revive the Sarum rite for use in London's new Westminster Cathedral; see *The Mass in the West*, p. 102. It is interesting to note that the High Church Anglicans who were busily imitating Catholic rites and ceremonies at that time also slavishly followed the general centripetal trend in the Roman Church. The 'English Missal' that would become the staple of Anglo-Catholic worship was not a revival of the Sarum use, as one would expect of a Church separated from Rome, but an English translation of the Mass of St Pius V!

[67] A. Bride, 'Rite', *DTC*, XIII (1937), col. 2738.

[68] Pierre Loret, CSSR, *The Story of the Mass: From the Last Supper to the Present Day* (Missouri, 1982), p. 102.

relatively close, in vocabulary if not in structure, to the parent Latin. But in Northern Europe a different situation obtained. Holland, Germany, Austria, Hungary, Poland, England and Ireland had Catholic populations that were doubly distanced from liturgical Latin, not merely because the local vernaculars were non-Romance, but because the Reformation had broken cultural continuity from medieval times: many of the people who were won back to the Faith during the Wars of Religion could recall, positively enough, the experience of liturgical worship in their native tongues.

In ordinary circumstances the Holy See might have authorized the use of Dutch, German, Hungarian, Polish, English, Welsh and Gaelic as liturgical languages, in keeping with the literary principle. Indeed, in the Tridentine debates held between 11 and 24 August 1562, several Fathers pronounced themselves in favour of conceding, for pastoral reasons, a partial use of the vernacular in the liturgy; only one, the Bishop of the Slavonic See of Krk in Dalmatia, was completely opposed to Latin.[69] That the ban on the vernacular was a safety measure rather than the application of a principle is clear from the nuanced wording of the relevant canon of the Council of Trent, which decreed that: 'If anyone shall say . . . that the Mass ought to be celebrated in the vernacular tongue only . . . let him be anathema.'[70]

There were undoubtedly cogent pastoral reasons for Rome to break with a questionable medieval development and allow the proclamation of the Word of God in the vernacular during the Mass rite. While Protestants had services built entirely on the Bible, and most of the Eastern Churches using hieratic languages switched to the vernacular for the Liturgy of the Word, Catholics prayed their private devotions at Mass while the officiating priest read the Latin Epistle and Gospel in a low voice facing the altar. The sole concession the Congregation of Rites was prepared to make in this matter was to allow the priest, if he so desired, to read a translation of one or both readings during his homily, if he preached one. The effect of all this was to make the faithful identify the Scripture readings with the sermon rather than with the Sacrifice of the Mass.

Even if the traditional rights of Latin posed an obstacle to the full application of the literary principle in Northern Europe, the obvious solution to the linguistic problem of the sixteenth century was the admission of a partial use of the vernacular at Mass (primarily in the Liturgy of the Word) and in the administration of the sacraments. The principle of linguistic continuity could then have been invoked to ensure that the most sacred parts of the Mass and those services pertaining directly to the clergy remained in the hieratic language, Latin. This would later be the tenor of a Propaganda ruling of 1631 concerning the use of Georgian in the Caucasian missions: 'that part of the Mass called "of the Catechumens", being instructional, can be allowed to all peoples in their own tongue, if Latin and Greek be not in use among them'.[71] The same linguistic compromise was already in use in many Eastern Churches, and was given its first formal Catholic expression at the Maronite Synod of the Lebanon, held in 1736 to decide the respective uses of Syriac and vernacular Arabic in the local Antiochene rite.[72]

---

[69] Korolevsky, op. cit., p. 98.
[70] Canons on the Sacrifice of the Mass, 9 (Denzinger 956).
[71] Korolevsky, op. cit., p. 100.
[72] Ibid., pp. 19–20. In Lebanon, Syriac had only recently become extinct as a spoken tongue, replaced everywhere by Arabic. The synodal decrees, which closely resemble the initial scheme for mixing Latin and the vernacular in the liturgical reforms immediately issuing from the Second

Unfortunately, the current association of vernacular worship with heresy and the general reaction against Protestantism defeated all moves towards implementing such a compromise in the Latin rites. Indeed, to add to this baneful veiling of the Liturgy of the Word and the absence of any popular liturgical exegesis, in 1661 Alexander VII proscribed all vernacular translations of the texts of the Mass, a ban that was renewed without policing in 1857 and would not be officially lifted until 1897.[73] A number of French bishops (especially Jansenists) defied the prohibition, which was also ignored in England and other European countries (Bishop Richard Challoner's *Garden of the Soul*, first published in 1740, contained the Ordinary of the Mass in Latin and English). Nevertheless, the possibility of following the sacred rites with a bilingual or vernacular missal did not become an option for Catholics in many places until the twentieth century.

The Counter Reformation's Counter-liturgy

In the aftermath of Trent, there remained only two solutions to this cultural problem of language, both of them proposed and pursued by the Jesuits, and both of them hinging on the celebration of Low Mass. The first was to let the vernacular in through the back door by encouraging the singing of vernacular hymns (rather than direct translations of the sacred texts themselves) during Mass. St Peter Canisius, the Jesuit apostle of Germany, did much to popularize the so-called *Singmesse* in that country, and this practice also caught on in Poland. The second was to engage the faithful at Mass with devotional practices in their native tongue such as the Rosary, litanies and (in the case of the literate) meditations read from prayer books. While vernacular hymn singing remained a special trait of church life in Northern Europe, the new extra-liturgical devotions – most of them modern rather than traditional – spread throughout the Latin Church and became enormously popular.

No doubt the most deplorable lacuna in the religious experience of most of the Roman-rite laity (and one quite incomprehensible to Eastern Christians) was their lack of familiarity with the great and dramatic climax of the liturgical year: the Sacred Triduum, including the solemn Easter Vigil which St Augustine had called 'the mother of all vigils'.[74] In 1642 under Pope Urban VIII, Maundy Thursday,

Vatican Council, stipulated that all liturgical books be printed bilingually (Syriac and Arabic), that in more solemn celebrations the Epistle and Gospel be sung in Syriac before being read in Arabic, and that extempore translation of Syriac prayers be strictly forbidden. The Syrian Catholic Synod of Sharfeh (1888), the Coptic Synod of Cairo (1898) and the Armenian plenary council of 1911 (Rome) all enacted parallel legislation (ibid., pp. 20–22).

[73] Jungmann, *op. cit.*, I, p. 161.
[74] Almost a century ago, Fr Herbert Thurston, SJ, could complain that this office

gradually, through the increasing infirmity and apathy of the clergy and the faithful, has come to be celebrated at a more and more early hour, until it is now an early service for Saturday morning instead of a night-watch upon Easter-eve. . . . It is, I think, something of a reproach to modern English Catholics that the attendance at the service of Holy Saturday morning is usually so scanty. Of course it is easy to understand that the length of the ceremonies and the dreariness of the prophecies [then twelve in number and sung in Latin] act rather as a deterrent, but when we come to remember that this function represents what was for many ages almost the very greatest celebration of the year, it seems that a mere feeling of *ennui* ought not to frighten us away from a rite both historically and devotionally so interesting. (*Lent and Holy Week: Chapters on Catholic Observance and Ritual* [London, 1914], pp. 412, 404).

Good Friday and Holy Saturday officially ceased to be holy days of obligation for the Roman rite. Small wonder then that by the twentieth century, while the Mass may have commanded the loyalty of the faithful, it was not the liturgy in all its richness but the popular devotions, practised in virtual competition with the *opus Dei*, that held their affection. It was this situation that caused Mgr Giuseppe Sarto, Bishop of Mantua and the future Pope Pius X, to sigh:

> Oh, if we could only bring it about that all the faithful would sing the ordinary parts of the Mass, the *Kyrie*, the *Gloria*, the *Credo*, the *Sanctus*, and the *Agnus Dei*, as they now sing the Litany of Loreto and the *Tantum Ergo*! This would be the most wonderful triumph of sacred music. For then the faithful would nurture their piety and their devotion by taking a real part in the sacred liturgy![75]

But a Church in which such dreams would remain generally unfulfilled was also one ripe for liturgical revolution: it is no coincidence that in the early twenty-first century, when the traditional Roman Mass is now the treasure of only a small remnant of Western Christians, the principal devotions of the Counter Reformation have weathered the storm of Vatican II with remarkable resilience. By and large, those Catholics who continued to practise their religion during and after the Pauline liturgical revolution were those sentimentally attached to some private devotion – daily prayer, eucharistic or Marian piety, the cult of the saints, intercession for the Holy Souls, penitential practices – or other. For the far greater number of Catholics who went to Mass regularly but were not particularly pious at other times, no comparably potent inoculation was available to help their faith survive the epidemic of heteropraxis. For what is sound in the new order survives only by drawing on the capital of the old order it wishes to forget.

Indeed, of the millions of Latin Catholics who have quietly given up the practice of their faith since the Second Vatican Council, most have done so in the context of the official liturgical reform, emblematic of a novel religion of 'options' with a God of modern devising who makes few demands and refuses to condemn. These are the same souls who, in the last decades of the regimented post-Tridentine era, were attending Mass regularly and receiving the sacraments perhaps more for fear of losing their immortal souls than out of an instinctive and disinterested love of the sacred liturgy, that wonderful place where the human soul encounters the life of the Divine.

[75] Ellard, *Mass of the Future*, p. 161.

11

RESPECTABLE RELIGION

*Archaic societies envisage their existence and survival as being
dependent on exchanges between the world of the living and the
world of the dead, the latter contributing to the fertility and renewal
of the former. In France, as elsewhere, exchanges of this kind were
symbolized by seasonal ceremonies that had been taken over by the
Church . . . As supernatural interpretations crumbled under the impact
of materialism, and even more before the puritanical expurgations of
the clergy, the basis for the belief itself . . . also crumbled.*

EUGEN WEBER

The Assault on Popular Catholicism

After Trent, Catholicism did not merely risk metamorphosing into a sterile religion
of compulsory practices whenever and wherever it lost touch with its traditional
roots. Even more seriously, to the extent that the modernization of the Church
involved the uprooting of popular Catholicism, it led to the erosion and loss of
the Faith itself, given that folk religion was the fertile soil in which the liturgical
traditions of centuries had grown and flourished. The ancient links between faith,
worship and popular culture could not be broken without also shattering the delicate synthesis that Catholicism is by its very nature.

Histories of the Church rightly highlight the destructive effects of the French
Revolution on the practice of religion in France and other countries. It is true that
the events of 1789 spawned a militant atheism determined to entice or force people
away from religious belief and practice. Nevertheless, one might question whether
anti-clerical continental liberalism was solely responsible for the paganization of
much of France, Spain, Portugal, Italy, Austria and other historically Catholic
countries. What is often not considered is that the same degree of dechristianization came also to characterize England and the Protestant countries of Northern
Europe, all areas where there were state churches and no government hostility to
religious practice.

It is not unreasonable to suggest that one of the main causes of the decline of
Protestant Christianity in the North equally affected Catholic Christianity in the
South: the attack, in both religions, on popular religion. That ordinary Northern
Europeans have, since the Reformation, been repelled and alienated by the coldness
and harshness of iconoclastic Protestantism is well known. Less appreciated is the
extent to which a similar spirit of puritanism undermined the faith of Catholics.

In some cases the transformation led to complete dechristianization; in others it helped to create the 'modern' Catholicism described in the last chapter, one quite insensitive to the past and therefore open to radical change.

In a Church of exclusively celibate clergy, parish priests could, for all their virtues and pastoral zeal, easily fall out of touch culturally with the people they served, especially after the Council of Trent, when they were normally trained, secluded from the laity, in seminaries. By comparison, in the first millennium of Christian history, when emphasis was on the local church, candidates for the priesthood were normally recruited from, and recommended by, the faithful among whom they were destined to live and work. In these earlier times a vocation was not seen simply as a private call of God to the individual. Rather, it was believed that God simultaneously inspired a young man to desire the priestly life, and the community that had produced him to present him to the bishop for ordination.

In the Malabarese Church of India this integrated approach to vocation was maintained by the traditional parish councils (*palliyogam*) made up of priests and parishioners.[1] Promoting overall fidelity to tradition – rather than simply policing church law – was the principal function of these typically Oriental councils, whose existence inhibited the growth of clericalism. Here, candidates for the priesthood 'were taught by learned priests called Malpans, who were very careful to train them in the traditions of the Church'.[2] The role of the ordaining bishop in such a system was to confirm, where possible, the community's choice of candidate. It was as unthinkable for a bishop to ordain a deacon or priest without reference to the latter's home community as it was for a bishop to impose on a parish an incumbent unacceptable to it.

By contrast, in the Counter-Reformation Church there could be no place for such lay 'interference'. And the real threat of heretical presbyterianism merely confirmed the rightness of the new clericalist order.

The Puritan Leaven

Clericalism affected not only the administrative aspects of the Latin Church, but its cultural institutions as well. It seems a self-contradictory aspect of the Counter-Reformation period that the strongest offensive against the traditional forms of popular religion was carried on by both the Jansenists and the Jesuits. At first sight these two mutually hostile clerical groups might seem to have had little in common, and certainly the emphases of their reformism differed considerably. The Jansenists, like Protestants, were deadly foes of 'superstition', by which they meant any non-scriptural or non-patristic religious custom. Apart from the liturgical destruction perpetrated by Jansenist reformism in France, Italy, Austria and Germany, war was declared on the 'pagan' aspects of Catholic life: festivals of saints, seasonal processions, confraternities, carnival celebrations, and pilgrimages to ancient shrines and holy wells. The festive side of these customs especially

---

[1] P. Podipara, CMI, *The Rise and Decline of the Indian Church of the Thomas Christians* (Kottayam, 1979), p. 18; Xavier Koodapuzha, 'The Ecclesiology of the Thomas Christians of India', in Vellilamthadam *et al.*, eds, *Ecclesial Identity*, pp. 78–83. The Jesuits naturally abolished *palliyogam* among the Uniates in the seventeenth century, but it has survived as an institution of the Malabar Jacobite Church.

[2] Ibid., p. 18; see also Koodapuzha, *op. cit.*

worried the Jansenist bishops and parish priests, who did all they could to stamp out the attendant moral 'perils' – not just drinking, feasting and carousing, but also dancing and public sports.[3]

There is, at least in France, a close correlation between the regional incidence of religious indifference and dioceses that were dominated by Jansenistic clergy before the Revolution. In provinces such as Burgundy, Berry and Champagne, generations of parishioners were driven away from formal religious practice not only because of clerical hostility to 'superstitious' traditions but also because of the abuse of the confessional by puritanical pastors who habitually refused absolution on petty grounds, and alienated penitents by unnecessary and sometimes prurient interrogations. Writing of the nineteenth century, Eugen Weber relates how husbands, in particular,

> evinced a growing resentment toward confessors who wrung every last detail of intimate practice from their wives. There had always been some objection . . . to confessors prying into private affairs – the profits of merchants, the small peculations of traders, the indiscretions of untoward talk or reading. Now, confession was attacked as an interference in marital relations, 'probing the conjugal bed', and an invasion of privacy that excited minors to debauchery by suggesting motions they would not themselves have thought of.[4]

It has been plausibly suggested by sociologists that it was precisely this sort of clerical intrusion that helped to promote the irreligious behaviour so common among men in Latin countries. Emmanuel Le Roy Ladurie has remarked that since in sexual matters such as contraception men, rather than women, were at that time normally the guilty party, 'this subtle distinction would become the basis of French theological and confessional practice, hence of the country's religious dichotomy: men = sinners, and as such are excluded or self-excluded [from the Church]; women = resigned, innocent, and passive, and remain within the Church'.[5]

That the most censorious priests were not all paragons of virtue furthermore tended to raise the old spectre of clerical hypocrisy. Miraculously, pious Catholics could live with the eternal paradox of priests being so often morally worse than the lay folk they led, and given to the most bitter fraternal jealousies: *clericus clerico lupissimus*. But in a civilization where temperamental anti-clericalism was widespread even among the devout, serious clerical shortcomings could be for lukewarm Christians the last nail in the coffin of their estrangement from the Church.

---

[3] In this they were hardly different from Protestants, for example the Anglican bishop Hugh Latimer who, towards the end of Henry VIII's reign (i.e. before he was able to declare his heresy), had preached a sermon to the Convocation of the Clergy in which he said:

> Do ye see nothing in our holidays? Of which very few were made at first, and they to set forth goodness, virtue, and honesty: but sithens, in some places, there is neither mean nor measure in making new holidays, as who should say, this one thing is serving of God, to make this law, that no man may work. But what doth the people on these holidays? Do they give themselves to godliness, or else ungodliness? See ye nothing, brethren? If you see not, yet God seeth. God seeth all the whole holidays to be spent miserably in drunkenness, in glossing, in strife, in envy, in dancing, dicing, idleness, and gluttony. He seeth all this, and threateneth punishment for it. (George Elwes Corrie, ed., *Sermons by Hugh Latimer, Sometime Bishop of Worcester, Martyr, 1555* [Cambridge, 1844], p. 52)

[4] Eugen Weber, *Peasants into Frenchmen: The Modernization of Rural France 1870–1914* (London, 1979), p. 365.

[5] Emmanuel Le Roy Ladurie, *Le territoire de l'historien* (Paris, 1973), pp. 314–15.

The Shadow of Neo-Platonism

The moral rigour and near Calvinism of the Jansenists was justly deplored by the Jesuits, yet they themselves could be morbidly moralistic. A particularly potent influence on the Jesuits were the Neo-Platonic ideas permeating the Renaissance classicism to which they were so zealously devoted. According to Fr J. P. Kenny, SJ, the Ignatian tradition bears a large responsibility for transmitting to modern Catholicism

> Greek philosophy's systematic contempt for the body and the concomitant stressing of the ideal: liberation of the soul from the shackles and burden of the flesh. This notion has dictated much Roman Catholic thinking about sex and marriage, and has helped build up certain inhibitions. It keeps reappearing in Roman Catholic spiritual writers, even those of the highest eminence and irreproachable orthodoxy. Thus St Francis of Assisi urges mortifying the body in terms which betray their Greek provenance: 'beat brother ass into subjection'. St Ignatius of Loyola echoes a favourite neoplatonic expression when, in his meditation on sin, he describes the soul as 'imprisoned in a corruptible body'. It is no easy task for any man to educate himself to a serene, mature, balanced outlook on sex. Perhaps the constant drip of hellenization has made it still harder for Roman Catholics.[6]

This unhealthy pagan undercurrent became unfortunately so bound up with the Catholic way of life that it tended to bring the whole Judaeo-Christian moral code into disrepute with individuals and groups already alienated by the puritan excesses of the post-Tridentine Church.

David Mitchell observes that in colleges run by the Society of Jesus, 'Every minute of the day was filled with prescribed activity and as far as possible children were never left alone; for the acceptance of sexual curiosity so general in medieval society was now being replaced by the ideal of respectability which the Jesuits did much to foster.'[7] Naturalness and spontaneity were not desirable traits of Jesuit pupils, as St Ignatius' thirteen *Rules of Modesty* show:

> As regards the conversation of Ours let it be said in general that in all outward actions there should appear modesty and humility joined with religious maturity . . . For the most part let the eyes be downcast . . . When speaking, especially with men of authority, let not the gaze be fixed full upon the face but rather a little between the eyes . . . Wrinkles on the forehead and much more on the nose are to be avoided so that outward serenity may appear as a testimony to inner serenity . . . The hands, if not engaged in holding one's cloak, should be kept decently quiet . . . The gait should be moderate without notable haste unless necessity requires it; in which case care of decorum should be had . . . All gestures and movements should be such as to give edification to all.[8]

The Ignatian system of training was too sophisticated not to make ample provision

---

[6] J. P. Kenny, SJ, *Roman Catholicism, Christianity and Anonymous Christianity – The Role of the Christian Today* (*Theology Today* No. 44) (Hales Corners, Wisconsin, 1973), p. 59.
[7] Mitchell, *op. cit.*, pp. 60–61.
[8] Ibid., p. 62.

for the expression of human emotion. But this expression was a guided one and, most significantly, largely independent of the received cultural forms. The Jesuits were pioneers of the baroque art of theatrical effects calculated to capture and fire the imagination, all in the interests of rapid sanctification. The Lutheran scholar Heinrich Boehmer unfavourably contrasts this artificial and unrealistic mode of formation with the 'childish simplicity, joy, vivacity and the simple love of nature' of the Franciscan spirit and of the Catholic popular tradition generally:

> The Jesuits' pupils are far too clerical, devout, absorbed to preserve these qualities. They are taken up with ecstatic visions and images; they literally intoxicate themselves with the paintings of frightful mortifications and the martyrs' atrocious torments; they need pomp, and all that is glittering and theatrical. From the end of the sixteenth century onwards, Italian art and literature reproduce faithfully this moral transformation . . . The restlessness, the ostentation, the shocking display which characterize the creations of that period promote a feeling of revulsion instead of sympathy for the beliefs they are supposed to interpret and glorify.[9]

Jesuit devotion to the baroque culture of Counter-Reformation Rome was in keeping with their Society's ultramontanism. In France the Jesuits' middle-class enemies (and not all of them Jansenists) especially deplored the new religious devotions and customs they were introducing from Spain and Italy as substitutes (so it was alleged) for national moral traditions. Antoine Adam relates how:

> Since the beginning of the [seventeenth] century the French had been able to watch the growing ascendancy of ultramontane Catholicism. They knew that the policy of equilibrium practised by Henry IV had been long since abandoned, that Anne of Austria, a devout Spaniard, was entirely devoted to the religious party, that the papal nuncio was intervening in every detail of French affairs, and that the episcopate had for the most part lost its independence. Of this Catholicism imported from Rome and Madrid they formed a picture, unfair perhaps, but one about which they had no illusions. A religion of exterior pomp, rites and devotions. A Christianity emptied of what, in the eyes of the French, was its essence: its moral virtues.[10]

The 'Barrier' of Latin

Ironically, one of the victims of the classical Catholicism cultivated by the Jesuits and Jansenists was the sacral language of the Western Church itself. The case can be made that the manner in which Latin was used in Counter-Reformation liturgy contributed to its decline and marginalization in our own day. This post-Tridentine 'abuse' of Latin consisted precisely in altering its traditional functions in Christian culture, unnaturally opposing it to the living vernaculars as a 'dead' language, so as to create a lapidary, clerical style of worship which the laity needed only attend, not follow intelligently. In time the Church would have to reckon with the negative pastoral consequences of this development.

[9] Heinrich Boehmer, *Les Jésuites* (Paris, 1910), p. 83.
[10] Antoine Adam, ed., *Blaise Pascal: Lettres écrites à un provincial* (Paris, 1981), p. 17.

Nevertheless, if there was in baroque Catholicism a barrier between the worshippers and the liturgy they attended, it did not lie between the laity and Latin. The Middle Ages had known no such barrier. Given the partly mantric nature of liturgical worship, only the literal-minded will object to the use in church of a language 'not understanden of the people' and insist that the worshipper must rationally comprehend every word being sung or said. That is a Protestant position which has no place in either Catholicism or Eastern Orthodoxy.

Certainly there is great variation of intelligibility among the liturgical languages used in the Universal Church. Intelligibility ranges from *nil to low* (Latin in most countries; Coptic in Egypt; Ge'ez in Ethiopia; Syriac in Lebanon and Kerala; Greek among the Italo-Albanians) to *medium* (Classical Greek in Greece; Old Slavonic in Russia, Ukraine, Croatia, Serbia, Macedonia and Bulgaria; Syriac among some West Syrians and all the East Syrians of Iraq and Iran; Classical Armenian among the Armenians; Latin among the Italians, Spanish and Portuguese); to *high* (Arabic among the Melkites and Maronites; Romanian in Romania; Malayalam among the Malabarese and Malankarese).[11]

However, it would be wrong to conclude from these facts that worshipping Christians in the high-intelligibility bracket have always enjoyed an absolute advantage over those in the nil to low groups. Each of the historic liturgies is structured in such a way that the basic prayers and invocations are repeated with such regularity that the frequent worshipper becomes familiar with their meaning simply through immersion in his religious culture. Just as no worshipping Christian today is ignorant of the general import of the Hebrew words *amen* (voicing assent) and *alleluia* (expressing joyful praise), there were few devout pre-conciliar Latin Catholics for whom the phrases *In nomine Patris . . ., Dominus vobiscum, Gloria in excelsis Deo, Sanctus, Pater noster* and *Agnus Dei* meant nothing at all. What the wisdom of the Church has always understood is man's obligation to address and praise God in the finest and most elevated language available to him. Sacral language, whether it be Latin or a Cranmerian English readily comprehensible to the literate Anglo-Saxon, is essentially an idiom as far removed as possible from the banalities and profanities of everyday life.

In regard to the use of Latin in public worship, the 'problem' of rational comprehension is largely the projection of a modern obsession into a cultural context where the question was rarely, if ever, posed. The real problem with liturgical Latin after the Council of Trent was not its existence, but Rome's unwillingness to allow 'the language of the Church' to share its domain with its traditional partner, the vernacular. In medieval Catholicism Latin had not been an obstacle to active participation in the liturgy precisely because the laity, who knew their *Pater, Ave* and *Gloria* in that language were – in many places at least – taught to sing the common chants of the Mass. Latin and the local vernacular lived, in fact, in a fruitful symbiosis: the popular hymns that flourished before the Reformation were frequently macaronic compositions (like the Christmas carol *In Dulci Jubilo*) in which vernacular verses alternated with, and often glossed, Latin ones.

---

[11] The most accurate and comprehensive work on Catholic liturgical languages is Korolevsky, *Living Languages in Catholic Worship, op. cit.*

In any case the modern caricature of medieval Latin as a caste language of the educated clergy, an idiom utterly removed from the lives of the illiterate laity, is one that the cultural historian would reject. The 'death' of Latin was not consummated until early modern times. It is true that when the structural gap between literary Latin and spoken Latin had reached its peak around the fifth century after Christ, the classical language ceased to be spoken from the cradle by any member of society, and was technically extinct. Nevertheless, knowledge and use of Latin continued alongside the emerging Romance vernaculars as the medium of learning and international communication as well as of public worship. At the same time, because of its widespread use by people of all levels of instruction, medieval Latin cast off the restraints of the artificial, castigated idiom of the ancient Roman authors and was nourished and enriched by the mother tongues of the Christians who used it.[12] The death of Latin as an important cultural presence in the West took place when the Counter Reformation unwittingly killed it by changing its received form and function.

Killing Christian Latin

Catholic culture's simplification and amplification of Classical Latin were praiseworthy activities according to St Augustine ('it is better that the grammarians should reproach us than that the people should not understand us'),[13] but amounted to a barbarous degeneration not only for Erasmus and his Renaissance contemporaries, but for the Jesuits who dominated Catholic higher education after the Council of Trent. In their teaching of the language, the schoolmasters of the Society of Jesus cast aside the works of medieval authors written in an easy, accessible Latin, and imposed on their pupils the gruelling study (in suitably expurgated editions) of the gems of Roman pagan literature.[14]

Whereas the teaching of Latin should have served to deepen the student's understanding and appreciation of the rites and writings of the Christian civilization to which he was heir, the effect of this new Jesuit pedagogy was to turn the study of Latin into an esoteric academic pursuit. The Jesuits' desire to reform the language of the Church in the directions of artificiality and pomp prolonged the traditions of the Renaissance Papacy which, for instance, had endorsed the substitution of allegorical classical terms for traditional ones in a new edition of the Roman breviary: *Deus deorum maxime*, 'Greatest God of gods', for *Deus omnipotens*; *Numen triforme Olympi*, 'threefold Spirit of Olympus', for *Sancta Trinitas*; and *Felix Dea*, 'Happy Goddess', or *Nympha Candidissima*, 'Most bright Nymph', for *Beata Virgo Maria*.[15]

Western Christians of the Middle Ages cherished Latin because it was one of the highest expressions of their culture; now Counter-Reformation Catholics defended the language, ever more divorced from their ordinary experience, as a sign of loyalty to the Church. As literary vernaculars took over the traditional functions of Latin in most departments of modern life, the language of Catholic culture came

---

[12] On Christian Latin see Christine Mohrmann, *Liturgical Latin: Its Origin and Character* (Washington, DC, 1957).
[13] Tract. in Ps. 138: '*Melius est reprehendant nos grammatici, quam non intelligant populi*'.
[14] Marie-Madeleine Martin, *op. cit.*, p. 145.
[15] Mitchell, *op. cit.*, p. 40.

to be seen as merely the official language of the Church, yet another of the prescriptions of orthopraxis. Concerning this exculturation (and absolutization) of liturgical Latin, Owen Chadwick makes the interesting observation that

> [i]n 1500 a man would have been more likely to assume that the liturgy should be in Latin because the liturgy should be in the highest prose available, and Latin was that highest form. In 1650 a defender of Latin would have been more likely to declare that Latin was the sacred language of the liturgy.[16]

It was liturgical Latin's less-than-attractive association with duty and obligation in post-Tridentine Catholicism that sealed its doom. When the day came that Latin would no longer be decreed the normal language of the liturgy, it would disappear, and with it other vital but unsanctioned constituents of orthopraxis.

Polite Religion

Part and parcel of the classicism vowed to the destruction of Christian Latin was the progressive clergy's disdain of local forms of Catholicism, and their promotion of all that was Roman, modern and respectable. In Elizabethan and Jacobite England (where, as has been seen, the Jesuits discontinued the use of the Sarum missal), the mission priests found themselves on a collision course with surviving Marian clergy anxious to preserve continuity with the pre-Reformation English Church, and who 'rejected many of the innovations of the Counter Reformation, especially the widening of the religious ideal epitomized by the Jesuits'.[17]

In his study of English recusancy, Alan Dures draws attention to the fervour with which the Jesuits set about trying to change the religion of a populace that 'was certainly traditional rather than Tridentine'.[18] Fr Robert Parsons criticized the more old-fashioned English Catholics for ignoring the spirit of religion while 'they relied on such external practices as living on bread and water on Fridays, vigils and most of Lent and things like that'.[19] Discouraged by the reluctance of their medieval-minded charges to confess and communicate more frequently, the Jesuits blamed their old-fashioned religiosity and 'thought the celebrations of feasts, especially Christmas, too boisterous'.[20]

Local traditions fell victim to this same cultural reformism in the absolutist Catholic states of the continent where, however, the Jesuits and their allies made social conformity a virtue equal to religious conformity. This bourgeois devotion to national orthodoxy, already encouraged under the Ancien Régime, would become a hallmark of the post-revolutionary French Church. Everywhere in the centralized but polyglot state of France it was believed that

> [t]he language of prayer, when it was not Latin, was French. One spoke French to gents of the upper classes; it followed that one used it when addressing God

[16] O. Chadwick, *op. cit.*, p. 299.
[17] A. Dures, *English Catholicism 1558–1642: Continuity and Change* (Harlow, Essex, 1983), pp. 38–39.
[18] Dures, *op. cit.*, p. 39.
[19] Ibid., p. 62.
[20] Ibid., p. 63.

or saints. . . . Most of the bishops, like prefects, came from outside their diocese. They had no understanding and little sympathy for popular religious practices that the Church generally associated with paganism or folklore, or a mixture of both. Students were prohibited from speaking patois in seminaries, as in normal schools [teachers' colleges]. The teaching orders were notoriously opposed to local dialects, and most of all the Jesuits, inventors of the infamous 'symbols', borne in evidence of linguistic lapses. It comes as no surprise to hear a Breton nationalist criticizing them as well-meaning strangers only interested in the spread of French.[21]

Champions of Occitan civilization in the so-called *Midi* found the attitudes of the Catholic clergy no less inimical to the degraded language of the Troubadours than those of local Protestant ministers or the secular authorities. The vernacular poet and novelist Joan Bodon, a practising Catholic from the 'white' Rouergue, wrote in 1948:

Let us not forget that the Church has killed our language here. It is the Church that forbids the convent nuns to speak 'patois', even when they return to their homes; it is the Church that has abolished preaching in Occitan. In the free [Catholic] schools the *signal* [= shaming symbol] is still used.[22]

In nineteenth-century Ireland the reform-minded clergy of the reign of Cardinal Paul Cullen (1849–1878) were no less energetic in destroying what remained of the Gaelic language and the rich vernacular Catholicism of the country, spreading everywhere more 'acceptable' practices imported from Rome and the continent. English, the language of respectability in Great Britain, became the preferred language of the Irish Church and it is reported that in certain *Gaeltacht* districts confessors actually expected children to confess the speaking of Irish as a sin. In some places precious Gaelic manuscripts were thrown out of libraries and used by peasants as kindling or as stuffing for walls.[23] Parallel examples of cultural icono-clasm could be produced for most of the Catholic countries of Western Europe for the period from 1850 to the First World War. In colonial lands scorn for local cultures had begun earlier and would persist longer.

---

[21] Weber, *op. cit.*, p. 362. The 'symbol' was an object, often a wooden clog with a string tied to it, which pupils caught speaking their mother tongue had to wear until they could find another child guilty of the same 'sin' to whom to pass on the symbol. The pupil found wearing it at the end of the day was caned. A similar device (the tally-stick: *bata scóir* or *scóirín*) was used in the Irish National Schools; in Wales it was called the 'Welsh not'.

[22] 'Cal pas oblidar que la Gleisa a tuada nòstra lenga aicí. Es ela que defend a las sòrs dels convents de parlar "patés", mèmes quand tornan al lor ostal, es ela que a pas manteguts los presics en lenga d'òc. Dins las escòlas lo "signal" existís encara' (Ramon Chatbèrt, ed., *Letras de Joan Bodon a Enric Mouly* [Naucelle, 1986], p. 108). Similar anti-vernacular attitudes reigned in Italian and Spanish convents, nuns being foremost among the promoters of linguistic 'respectability'.

[23] Seán de Fréine, *The Great Silence: The Study of a Relationship between Language and Nationality* (Dublin/Cork, 1965), p. 73.

The Road to Dechristianization

Eugen Weber has documented how, like puritanism, clerical contempt for local religious traditions contributed to the dechristianization of rural France during the nineteenth century. Everywhere over-zealous curés were troubled by

> the whole popular cult of relics, processions, ostensions, rogations, statues, rocks, caves, and healing springs, successively routed out as excrescences. . . . At Allanches (Cantal) one of the major local feasts – Saint John's, in midsummer – waned during the 1830s when local priests ceased to take part in 'ceremonies outside religious worship' and restricted themselves to purely religious ceremonies. About the same time in Gers a miraculous fountain of Saint John the Baptist at Nougarolet was put out of commission by a priest intent on scotching superstition, who simply filled its basin in. . . .
>
> A new priest assigned to Breuilaufa (Haute-Vienne) in 1880 tried to put an end to the traditional practice of ringing the church bells on All Hallows eve and throughout the morning of All Souls. He locked the church doors, but the indignant peasants threatened to break them down, crying 'that no one could prevent them from ringing for their dead'. A few years later another Limousin village rose to defend its right to ring the church bells in a storm.[24]

Historical evidence belies the oft-made assertion that the Catholic clergy in France and other countries with anti-clerical governments were always the valiant defenders of local tradition against Jacobin centralism. In linguistically non-French regions of France like Lower Brittany, Flanders, Alsace, Roussillon, the Basque Country and Corsica many priests did preach and teach catechism in the local language, but this was primarily a pragmatic measure. The fact that these minority languages and their literatures were excluded from the curricula of most Catholic schools, and the lack of real hierarchical support for linguistic activists like Fr Yann-Vari Perrot in Brittany, are clear indicators of the cultural loyalties of the French clergy as a whole.[25] Indeed,

> Far from sustaining 'retrograde' ideas, the priest seems to have collaborated with the schoolteacher to stamp them [popular customs] out. The scorn that teachers showed for rustic superstitions was often shared by priests . . . The peasants 'are very stick-in-the-mud and want essentially to keep their ancient practices' – shades of the village schoolteachers' decrying of routine! Reformist priests, on the other hand, were bent on renovation. Even familiar statues were sacrificed for posher urban plaster, and at Landivisiau (Finistère) in 1906 an English traveller noted so many old saints for sale for a few francs that one could have furnished a Breton paradise.[26]

Breton traditionalists lamented the romanization of the local liturgical calendars and the demise of old Celtic saints and feasts, but similar developments were

---

[24] Weber, *op. cit.*, pp. 366–67.
[25] The attitude of the hierarchy towards this saintly apostle of Breton Catholic culture murdered by the Maquis in 1943 is very revealing. See Henri Poisson, *L'Abbé Jean-Marie Perrot, fondateur du Bleun-Brug*, Rennes, 1955.
[26] Weber, *op. cit.*, pp. 369–70.

taking place all over France. For the 'Gallican' clergy and laity all this was merely the continuation, under a different guise, of the iconoclasm unleashed by the Revolution:

> Any national church, the Gallicans said, had to have roots deep in the national history, and its liturgical practices should reflect the national character. Guéranger and the ultramontanes were inclined to laugh at the diocesan liturgies because they contained devotions to local saints, 'a tribute to the supernatural fertility of the soil of Artois', as one priest remarked; 'we have only to stoop to gather a rich harvest of saints'.[27]

As old forms were discarded, more 'respectable' ones rushed in to fill the vacuum. With the increase of anti-clericalism under the Third Republic, Catholics grew more militant, and a new calendar of international and 'politically correct' saints and a whole repertoire of triumphalistic French hymns and 'reparatory' devotions was popularized, naturally to the detriment of old pieties.[28] A similarly prestigious counter-culture, expressing itself exclusively in the official language, emerged in Germany during the Kulturkampf, as well as in the newly united Italy.

By the time the last vestiges of the national liturgical tradition had disappeared in France, the bulk of the peasantry in the central-northern and south-eastern regions were already lost to the Faith. Many Frenchmen had drifted away from the Church during the nineteenth century not because of the anti-religious propaganda of the government, but because in a situation where Catholicism no longer held a privileged status, ordinary people were disinclined to patronize a clergy who had become culturally alien to them. Priests were vilified by anti-clericals as reactionary and avaricious, but 'the priest's immediate problem', Weber remarks, 'was not that he was too absolutist, but that he was less retrograde than the villagers he sought to direct. Venality lost friends, but attempted reform lost more.'[29]

What keeps a religion integrated and healthy is, according to Émile Durkheim, the holding in common of a set of beliefs and practices which, being traditional, are accepted as obligatory: 'The essential is that they should be such as to keep up a collective life of sufficient intensity.'[30] What too many of the nineteenth-century French clergy failed to comprehend was that the 'attachment of the popular masses to ancient things that the Church wanted to leave behind was even greater than their attachment to the Church. Eliminating the practices helped to estrange the people.'[31] A fatal mistake repeated in our own time, but all over the world.

---

[27] Gough, op. cit., p. 123.
[28] Weber, op. cit., pp. 363–64.
[29] Ibid., p. 364.
[30] Émile Durkheim, Le suicide (1897, repr. Paris, 1960), p. 173.
[31] Weber, op. cit., p. 370.

12

THE COST OF BELONGING

*Neither the Roman Catholics, the Orthodox nor historical
circumstances have treated these [Uniate] churches very kindly. The
Romans have more or less constantly interfered with their customary
style of life and with their liturgical traditions; while the Orthodox
heartily dislike them, seeing them as dupes of Roman imperialism,
created to lure away the Orthodox faithful to Roman obedience.*

LAWRENCE CROSS

The Politics of Assimilation

'Auto-demolition' was Pope Paul VI's description of the suicidal movement rav-
aging the Roman Church in the 1970s. An uncharacteristic moment of lucidity, one
might think, since Montini – whom his predecessor had once likened to Hamlet
– never had eyes to see that his own liturgical reform had led to the weakening
of the Catholic Faith: a faith for centuries enshrined in, and nourished by, the
'outmoded' cultural forms he was determined to destroy. Yet Paul VI, reckless
innovator that he was, should not be viewed in isolation from the institution to
which he belonged, for in the inexorable logic of history it was inevitable that a
Roman-rite clergy so ready in the past to scorn other people's religious traditions
would ultimately scorn their own.

In the policies of Montini's pontificate, Western alienation from a tradition no
longer properly understood merged with another live current in Latin Catholicism:
disregard for the customs and rights of Eastern Christians. The latter was an old
vice, but two historic events had been decisive in its growth in modern times. The
first was the fall of Constantinople to the Muslim Turks in 1453, which consummated the schism of East and West. The second was Columbus' arrival in America
thirty-nine years later, which confirmed militant Latin Catholics in certain aggressive and intolerant attitudes that had already manifested themselves in the Crusades
and the Inquisition.

Few historic acts of the Papacy have been as morally dubious as the issuing, by
Nicholas V (1447–1455), of bulls authorizing Prince Henry the Navigator and the
Portuguese nation to reduce Moors and pagans to perpetual slavery, and approving
his trade in Black Africans on the supposition that this would lead to their conversion to Christianity.[1] Pius II was soon confronted with the sinister results of his

---

[1] Acton, *op. cit.*, p. 62.

predecessor's rash optimism, yet it was not until 1537 that another pope, Paul III, globally condemned 'the enslavement of fellow human beings by anyone, under any pretext, or for any profit or gains' – a prohibition coming too late to have any effect on the conscience of Catholic monarchs who had enriched themselves by the obscene trade in human lives.[2]

With a new world to evangelize and organize along Roman lines, the Western Church could now happily forget the estranged Christians of the East, dismissing them as obdurate schismatics. But this new, constantly expanding Church was no longer integrally Catholic in outlook, if by Catholic is meant universal. Catholicity had shrivelled to the dimensions of Latinity, an idiosyncratic Latinity no longer tempered and fertilized by Hellenity, and a polity in which the supernatural mission of the Church was compromised by the earthbound ambitions of its secular arm. In the age of the great Catholic princes the duty to evangelize could become a justification for imperialism of the most brutal and rapacious kind. The extermination of virtually the entire indigenous populations of Hispaniola and Cuba by the Spanish is just one example of this.

In the overseas empires of the Catholic states, Counter-Reformation Rome had a free rein. The generous missionary endeavours of this age brought the Faith to millions, but the methods employed were frequently vitiated by Western prejudice and ignorance. Heathens were to be converted outright to Latin Catholicism, and no distinction was made between the primitive pagan cultures of America and Sub-Saharan Africa and the sophisticated civilizations of Asia.[3] It was characteristic of the age that enlightened Jesuit attempts to inculturate the Faith in India and China were eventually condemned by the Vatican authorities.[4]

The esteem for classical pagan cultures typical of Jesuits like Roberto De Nobili and Matteo Ricci contrasted strangely with the disdain shown by other members of the Society, and by Latin priests generally, for the institutions of dissident Eastern Christians. Wherever these latter came under Latin political rule in the Old World, they were considered not subjects for reconciliation with Rome, but, like their pagan and Muslim neighbours, objects of conversion to Latin Catholicism, now conceived as the only valid form of Christianity. From the mid-sixteenth century, Roman curial documents no longer describe Eastern Christians as members of 'Churches' but as special groups whose proper place was within a Latin jurisdiction.[5]

In all these attempts to assimilate the Orientals through latinization, the Western religious orders would play an important role: Jesuits (everywhere), Discalced Carmelites (in Malabar), Dominicans (in Armenia and Mesopotamia), Vincentians

---

[2] Albert Foley, SJ, 'Slavery', *CESH*, X, pp. 152–53.
[3] There were some notable exceptions to the general disdain of non-Christian New World cultures, for example the brilliant initiatives of the Franciscan linguist-anthropologists of the Royal College of Santa Cruz de Tlatelolco in Mexico (Bernardino de Sahagún, Andrés de Olmos and Alonso de Molina), sixteenth-century scholars who turned the Nauatl vernacular into a modern literary language, and used it as a teaching medium alongside Spanish and Latin.
[4] Tamil customs not in conflict with Catholicism were initially approved by Gregory XV in 1623, but subsequently banned by Vatican decrees of 1706, 1727, 1739 and 1744. However, in 1940 Pope Pius XII once again approved a prudent policy of cultural adaptation of the Faith in India. The Jesuits' toleration of non-religious honours paid to Confucius and to the ancestors of their Chinese converts was forbidden by Innocent X in 1645 and again by Clement XI in 1704, with catastrophic consequences for the Chinese missions. In 1939 Pius XII authorized – again with counsels of caution – the principle of cultural adaptation along the lines developed four centuries earlier by Fr Ricci.
[5] Peri, *op. cit.*, p. 385.

(in Ethiopia) and Redemptorists (in Ukraine). The Latin regular clergy were in fact the chief promoters of ritual hybridism in the Eastern Catholic Churches, according to Fr Geevarghese Chediath:

> The various religious orders working among the Oriental Catholics spread their own peculiar mode of piety at the expense of genuine Eastern liturgical tradition; thus there grew hybridism and amalgamation and no organic growth; it was neither Eastern nor Western, but a mixture.[6]

'Reducing' the Greeks

Since 1564 the Italo-Greeks and Italo-Albanians had been deprived, by papal decree, of bishops of their own Byzantine rite and subjected to Latin ordinaries. As for the Greek Christians living under Turkish rule, Pope Gregory XIII spoke of the need to 'reduce' or bring them back to the Catholic way of life.[7] The mind of this pope on the question of Oriental Catholics was reflected in the regime of the Greek College, which he established in Rome in 1577. Entrusted to the Jesuits, this institution had as its charter the training of Byzantine-rite Catholic clergy to be sent out as missionaries among the Orthodox. Not only were all the rectors of the college Latins, but the Greek and Ruthenian students being trained as priests of the Byzantine rite were obliged to hear daily Mass in the Roman rite. Even when a token Byzantine Mass was introduced for certain occasions, the students had to communicate in the Latin manner, i.e. under one species only and with unleavened bread.[8]

Surely the most grotesque rule in force at the Greek College was the imposition of *both* the Roman and the Byzantine fasts on the seminarists. Ordained in the Roman rite, the missionaries were then expected to celebrate the Byzantine rite for the rest of their priestly lives. The inevitable result of this dubious formation was ignorance of the spirituality and culture of the Eastern Church and the consequent tendency of these priests to latinize the rites and customs of the Uniates to whom they ministered. As if this were not enough, the Jesuits took advantage of their direction of the Greek College to siphon off into their own order the most talented students, circumventing the canonical impediments by securing, through their influence in the Roman Curia, the necessary dispensations for a change of rite.[9]

Cleaning up the Maronites

Another Roman foundation of Gregory XIII, the Maronite College of 1584, was likewise placed under Jesuit rule and became an instrument for the latinization of the Lebanese clergy. 'At this time', writes Fr J. Murtagh,

---

[6] G. Chediath and T. Vellilamthadam, eds, *Ecumenism in Danger* (Kottayam, 1986), p. 24.
[7] Peri, *op. cit.*, p. 398.
[8] Fortescue, *Uniate Eastern Churches*, pp. 157–58.
[9] Ibid.

the idea seems to have been held that 'Catholic' and 'Latin' were synonymous, that the customs of the East were concessions to the Orientals in order to keep them in touch with Rome but that the Easterners would never be proper Catholics until they were completely latinised. The Maronite students in Rome seem to have shared this false idea which is today almost universally reprobated. They even went beyond the desires of the authorities in Rome in their zeal to latinise their particular corner of the Near East.[10]

From the first the Jesuits set about implementing at the College the various papal directives for latinization, hitherto dead letters in Lebanon, in the well-founded hope that the graduate priests, once home in the Middle East, would enforce them among their 'unenlightened' compatriots. To this end a new and highly latinized edition of the Maronite missal was prepared and printed in Rome in 1592.[11] A pontifical delegation of Jesuits despatched to Lebanon four years later held a synod which enjoined the use of this new missal and prohibited many traditional practices of the Antiochene rite: confirmation administered by priests, Communion under both kinds, the use of leavened bread in the Eucharist, and joint monasteries and convents under a common rule.[12] In 1606 Patriarch Joseph Al-Rizi ordered the Julian calendar to be given up in favour of the new Gregorian one and attempted – unsuccessfully – to modify the Eastern rules of fast and abstinence, in particular the ban on bishops eating meat and the prohibition of fish and wine during Lent.[13]

This wave of latinization reached its peak at the Synod of Mount Lebanon (1734), which ratified all the innovations to date and introduced others, for instance the substitution of Latin for Oriental marriage legislation, and the optional use of the Roman rites of baptism, confirmation and extreme unction.[14] In 1792 Pope Pius VI condemned the Synod of Ain Shaqiq, which Patriarch Istefan had called three years earlier to reverse some of the prescriptions of 1734 and restore a number of Maronite customs, such as the residence of suffragan bishops with the patriarch.[15] At another synod, held at El Louaize in 1818, a whole series of unwelcome Latin customs were again enforced, but these were so widely resented that in 1856 Patriarch Boulos Mas'ad deemed it prudent to decline the offer of the Apostolic Delegate in Syria to send Latin 'experts' to guide the regulation of liturgical matters at the upcoming Synod of Bkerke.[16]

[10] J. Murtagh, SMA, *The Maronite Church* (Dublin, 1965), pp. 11–12.
[11] El-Hayek, *op. cit.*, p. 250.
[12] Ibid., pp. 246, 250.
[13] Ibid., pp. 246, 250–51. The Gregorian calendar was accepted in Lebanon, but not by the Maronite colony of Cyprus. The Syrian Catholics were obliged to abandon the Julian calendar in 1836, the Chaldeans in 1837 and the Melkites in 1858. In the latter case, a six-year schism ensued, after which Rome thought the better of forcing the same reform on other Byzantine Catholics such as the Greeks, Romanians and Ukrainians. See Robert J. Taft, SJ, 'Between East and West: The Eastern Catholic ("Uniate") Churches', in Sheridan Gilley and Brian Stanley, eds, *The Cambridge History of Christianity: World Christianities c. 1815–c. 1914* (Cambridge, 2006), p. 423.
[14] El-Hayek, *op. cit.*, p. 251.
[15] Ibid., p. 252.
[16] Taft, *op. cit.*, pp. 417–18.

Ostpolitik

Rome's tightening of her hold over the Maronites was achieved without having to demote or remove the traditionally complaisant patriarchs of this Uniate church which lacked a dissident counterpart. By contrast, the Greek Catholics of Southern Italy were deprived of Byzantine-rite bishops because of the threat, more imagined than real, of schism. The problem of ordaining priests for their bishopless churches was solved in 1595 by Clement VIII's appointment of an 'ordaining bishop': a travelling Latin prelate without proper jurisdiction but with faculties to celebrate in the Byzantine rite.

That same year the obliteration of a distinct Eastern Catholic identity was institutionalized in Rome when the pontifical congregation set up in 1588 to publish the documents of all the ecumenical councils made the Council of Florence (the only one at which Eastern bishops were present since Nicaea II in 787) not the eighth but the *sixteenth* ecumenical council. This effectively made the decisions of the intervening Latin councils from Constantinople IV to Trent binding on the Universal Church.[17]

In 1596 Clement VIII formally launched the *Ostpolitik* of the Counter Reformation with his *Perbrevis Instructio*, addressed to Italian Latin bishops with Greek Catholics within their jurisdiction. This instruction ordered the indefinite toleration of non-Roman ritual traditions in the Church and expressly forbade the forcible latinization of Eastern Catholics. Nevertheless, as Vittorio Peri remarks:

> This tolerance, dictated by considerations of a pastoral nature, still did not eliminate the deeply rooted conviction that the adhesion of all men to the Roman Church and to her rite, which was held to be the most perfect and safe for the purpose of eternal salvation, remained the ideal and desirable goal, one towards which every single member of the faith and every community was required to strive. [Rome] was nonetheless willing to postpone this acceptance of the Roman rite in order to encourage without traumas the desired process of complete assimilation and homogenization of all Christians in the one Catholic Church, identified on the visible plane with that of Rome.[18]

Any idea that the Uniate Churches were bridges to a dissident East – whose reunion remained a prime duty and goal of Catholics – was demolished in 1729, when the Propaganda Congregation forbade 'in terms of the utmost strictness' intercommunion (*communicatio in sacris*) between Catholics and Orthodox, which had been tolerated, especially for practical reasons, until then.[19] The lowering of this

---

[17] Peri, *op. cit.*, p. 397.

[18] Ibid., p. 383.

[19] Aidan Nichols, OP, *Rome and the Eastern Churches: A Study in Schism* (Edinburgh, 1992), p. 285. Before the 1729 ruling, the policy advocated in 1661 by the Greek Catholic scholar Fr Leo Allatius had been widely followed in relation to dissident Orthodox Christians:

> Individual persons, although holding office in the Greek Church, do not constitute the Greek Church. Nor, because various heresies have arisen and spread within that Church, is she herself to be considered heretical ... The Greek Church as a whole, whether in her professions of faith or in the service-books read continually in her public worship, has never professed any heresy condemned by the councils and the Church of Rome ... Because certain individual Greeks have endeavoured to spread some ancient or freshly invented heresy, and have inveighed against the Papacy in their published writings, it does

'iron curtain' would confirm the image of the Uniate communities as substitutes for the larger, dissident Oriental Churches now disowned by an ever less ecumenical Rome.

Light from the West

The logical application of the Clementine policy was the gradual assimilation of the rites practised by Uniates to the 'true Catholic', i.e. Roman liturgy. Having given general approval to this policy, the Holy See could hardly hope to temper the enthusiasm for it displayed by the clergy of the various Latin empires, the Portuguese in particular. Reacting against the Moorish component in their recent past, many Portuguese of this era had a pathological hatred of Islam and a fear and loathing of everything that was not European. The physical distance of Portugal and Spain from Eastern Europe and the Middle East also inclined them to view Eastern-rite Christians as aliens rather than co-religionists.

When Vasco da Gama and his crew reached the Malabar (Kerala) coast in 1498, they discovered a thriving church of some two hundred thousand Christians in communion with the East Syrian katholikos (patriarch) in Kurdistan. In their fifteen hundred sanctuaries the priests of this community, which claimed Saint Thomas the Apostle as its founder, celebrated the Holy Eucharist according to the ancient rite of Edessa in the Syriac tongue, though the local vernacular was Malayalam, a Dravidian language related to Tamil. They had one bishop, the Metropolitan Mar Joseph, whose seat was at Angamale.[20]

Although the East Syrians were supposed to be both a schismatical and a heretical (Nestorian) body, the Portuguese clergy coming to India were surprised to find that the local Christians readily acknowledged papal supremacy as a tradition of their Church and seemed blissfully ignorant of the erroneous christological doctrines condemned at the Council of Ephesus (431).[21] Yet the attitude of the Latin newcomers was already poisoned by their native suspicion of non-Roman Christianity. When a certain Fr Penteado spent some time among the Thomas Christians in 1516, he wrote unfavourably of them in a letter to his Portuguese sovereign: 'As regards their national customs, their will is corrupted by their priests

---

not therefore follow that the Greek Church is separated from the Church of Rome: this would only be the case if the heresy in question were universally adopted and outwardly professed by all alike; and this, you will find, has never happened on the occasions when certain individuals have launched attacks against the Roman Church. (Quoted in Nichols, *op. cit.*, pp. 283–84)

[20] Adrian Fortescue, *The Lesser Eastern Churches* (London, 1913), p. 363. The East Syrian Church had once been a mighty missionary enterprise with as many as eighty million faithful scattered over a vast area of Asia bounded by Mesopotamia and Socotra in the west, Mongolia in the north, Manchuria in the east and Ceylon in the south. But the sudden and bloody persecution launched by the Muslim rebel-emperor Timur Leng, whose Turkic hordes swept Central Asia in the late fourteenth century, had reduced this great (but fatally, largely urban-based) Church to a few small remnants.

[21] In 1122 one Malabarese bishop had travelled to Rome and received the pallium from Pope Calixtus II, and there were further contacts between this Church and the Holy See in the fourteenth century. See D. Attwater, *Christian Churches of the East* (Milwaukee, 1961–1962), II, p. 280. On the papal question and the supposed Nestorianism of the Malabarese, see Podipara, *Rise and Decline*, pp. 13–14.

who say that just as there were twelve Apostles, even so, they founded twelve customs.'[22] An insult to the supremacy of Peter!

Unaware of such reservations, the 'Thomas Christians' welcomed the Portuguese as brothers in faith, and intercommunion with the Latin missionaries was immediately established. In 1553, five decades after the reunion of the Malabar Christians, half of their former Nestorian co-religionists in north-western Mesopotamia and Kurdistan also returned to Catholic unity, thanks to an internal dispute and the mediation of the Franciscans.[23] The new Catholics were henceforth known as 'Chaldeans'. Pope Julius III confirmed the Chaldean katholikos, John Sulaqa (Simon VIII), as rightful patriarch of the Malabarese.[24]

In India, however, Counter-Reformation rigorism brought the honeymoon to an end. Trouble began in 1558, when the Portuguese prevented the new bishop sent out by the Chaldean Patriarch from entering Malabar, claiming that the Latin Archbishop of Goa alone had jurisdiction over the Syrian Catholics. Then, when Pope Pius V obliged the Portuguese to admit a new Chaldean Metropolitan in 1567, the Latin missionaries, who were now determined to convert all the Malabarese, Christian and pagan alike, to Latin Catholicism, imprisoned Mar Abraham for a year on trumped-up charges of heresy. Hard pressed by the aggressive secular clergy working under the patronage of the King of Portugal (the *Padroado*), the Metropolitan was forced to turn for support to the Jesuits, who began preaching in Syrian churches and spreading Latin customs.[25]

At the Goan Synod that Mar Abraham was obliged to attend in 1585, it was decided that all future Chaldean bishops appointed for India would have to be approved by the King of Portugal and the Archbishop of Goa. The Portuguese Jesuits then turned on the Syrian Metropolitan who was now opposing their policies, and in 1594 obtained a papal brief to have him tried for heresy. This threat forced Mar Abraham to resume his earlier cooperation. He died three years later.[26]

Once the Metropolitan was out of the way and a docile Malabarese archdeacon had been appointed as administrator of the Church, the Portuguese Archbishop of Goa, Aleixo de Menezes, went to Kerala in February 1599 to assert his authority over the Syrians. Rome's doubts about the orthodoxy of the Malabarese hardened Menezes in his resolve to force the assimilation of East Syrian customs to those of the Latins. At the Synod of Udayamperur (Diamper), Menezes accused the Uniates of Nestorianism and forced them to anathematize their Chaldean Catholic Patriarch in Mesopotamia and break off all relations with him.

The Inquisition was then set up and drastic penalties enforced for all acts of

---

[22] Varghese Pathikulangara, *Church in India* (Kottayam, 1986), p. 59.
[23] Patriarch Simon IV (1437–1493) had made the office of katholikos hereditary, passing from uncle to nephew. This was the essence of the dispute of 1551–1552, when the northern metropolitans (of Amid and Salmas) demanded the revival of the electoral system after the death (or, according to some accounts, the deposition) of Simon VII (bar Mama). The bishops supporting Sa'ud bar Daniel (John Sulaqa) as the non-hereditary candidate suggested that he enlist the support of the Pope, and this was facilitated by Franciscans based in the Holy Land. In 1616, Mar Elias II, of the rival Nestorian patriarchal line in Alqosh (near Mosul) also entered into union with Rome in reaction to Franciscan accusations of heresy. This precarious union formally lapsed in the second half of the seventeenth century, though for the next hundred years or so several of Mar Elias' successors would consider themselves Catholic.
[24] Attwater, *op. cit.*, II, p. 280.
[25] Placid Podipara, CMI, 'Malabar Rite', in *NCE*, p. 93.
[26] Ibid.

schism and heresy. In violation of Chaldean canon law, celibacy was imposed on the entire clergy; married priests were ordered to dismiss their wives and children. As if to add insult to injury, the Holy See immediately appointed a Catalan Jesuit bishop, Francesc Ros (Francisco Roz), as successor to Mar Abraham, and Malabar was placed directly under Padroado jurisdiction. Even when the main Malabarese see (now Cranganore) regained its metropolitan status in 1608, it remained firmly in Latin hands.[27]

Policing the 'Law of Peter'

The violence done to the Keralan Church with the consent of Rome was not simply political and social. Mgr Ros, a Syriac scholar, immediately took it upon himself to 'correct' Malabarese public worship as a first step towards the complete imposition of Latin liturgy and discipline. The Jesuit bishop embarked on a rampage of vandalism quite without precedent in the history of Roman liturgical imperialism. All Syriac books found (or thought) to contain Nestorian errors were burnt, and the Malabarese liturgical calendar was abolished for honouring 'Nestorian' saints. Most of the Portuguese Braga ritual was translated into Syriac and imposed in place of the received sacramental rites, while all ordinations had to be performed using the Roman pontifical in Latin.[28]

Only the Malabarese Mass (*Qurbana*) remained, and Ros was not satisfied to replace occasional Nestorian phrases with orthodox ones. Although its continued celebration in Syriac was tolerated, the entire eucharistic rite was overhauled. The preparation of the bread and wine, traditionally performed at two side altars (*bethgaze* or 'treasure houses') before Mass, was now transferred to the Offertory, as in the Roman rite, and the use of leavened bread was forbidden. The sanctuary veil, formerly closed and opened at various points in the liturgy, disappeared and the *Qurbana* was now to begin with the sign of the Cross.

Latin positions had to be observed during the prayers, genuflections were substituted for profound bows, and oriental Mass vestments were destroyed and replaced with Roman ones. The server was no longer allowed to read the Epistle; the Creed was shifted from the end of the Offertory to after the Gospel. Two of the East Syrian anaphoras were abolished, and the remaining one was restructured on the Roman model, so that the intercessions, anamnesis and epiclesis would occur before the Consecration, at which Latin-style elevations were introduced. The *Agnus Dei* and *Domine non sum dignus* were inserted into the pre-Communion prayers; Holy Communion itself had to be distributed under one kind only and with the standard Roman formula.[29]

Not content with all this, the Europeans altered the appearance of Malabarese churches. Western furnishings took the place of oriental ones, and new churches were built in the Latin style with Latin altars and tabernacles. Western statues and images appeared everywhere, and all the devotions currently popular in Europe were taught to the Syrian faithful, while their own more liturgically oriented forms of piety were discouraged. Even the traditional laws of fast and abstinence were

---

[27] Ibid.; Podipara, *Rise and Decline*, pp. 24–25.
[28] Charles K. Von Euw, 'Malabar Rite, Liturgy of', *NCE*, IX, p. 96.
[29] Podipara, 'Malabar Rite', pp. 96–97; *Rise and Decline*, p. 25.

replaced by the contemporary Latin regulations: when the Portuguese missionaries first tried to oblige the people to eat fish and eggs and drink wine during Lent, many of them fled the European settlements rather than break the 'law of Thomas'.[30] At the same time individual conversions to the Roman rite were accepted when not actively encouraged, and since all Malabarese converts from Hinduism were automatically baptized in the Roman rite, a favoured rival church soon appeared in Syrian territory.[31]

Cracks in the Monolith

The seventeenth century ought to have brought about a change in Roman think-ing on the Eastern question, for the violence done to the immemorial traditions of the subject Churches was proving disastrous for the promotion of Catholic unity among non-European Orientals less passive than the Malabarese. A fresh conflict arose when Latin advisers to the older Chaldean Uniate Church based in Diyarbekir began pressuring the East Syrians to abandon various of their ancient customs for Roman ones. In 1670 this prompted the new katholikos, Simon XIII, to send a profession of Catholic faith to Rome in which he explicitly requested Pope Clement X to honour the promises of the union of 1553 and to leave the Edessene liturgy intact.[32] When no assurance was received, the patriarch severed the links with Rome and moved his seat east into the Hakkari mountains, eventually settling at Qudshanes. Fortunately for the East Syrian Catholic movement, in 1672 Capuchin missionaries succeeded in reconciling Joseph, dissident Metropolitan of Diyarbekir, and sent him to Rome in 1680 to be made patriarch.[33]

If the peacemaking missionaries in Mesopotamia were able to undo the dam-age of Latin imperialism and salvage the unionist movement among the East Syrians, the Jesuits who set out to make Ethiopia Catholic again failed miser-ably in their objective. Before Portuguese adventurers appeared on the Eritrean coast in the 1490s, the Christian church of Ethiopia was in communion with the Coptic Patriarch of Alexandria, who provided the only bishop (*abuna*) resident in the country. In 1520 King Manoel I responded favourably to an appeal from the Ethiopian negus, Lebna Danghel, for military aid against the Muslims, and a Portuguese garrison protected the Abyssinian coast for the next seven years. During this initial period of European contact, the Negus handed the Portuguese chaplain a letter of submission to Pope Clement VII. This was, however, a mere political gesture, and nothing concrete was done to normalize relations between the dissident Ethiopian Church and the Holy See until 1541, when King John III sent out another expedition under Cristóvão da Gama to ward off renewed Muslim attacks.[34]

---

[30] Podipara, *Rise and Decline*, p. 61, n. 4.
[31] See P. Podipara, *The Latin Rite Christians of Malabar*, Kottayam, 1986.
[32] Raphael Rabban, 'Chaldean Rite', *NCE*, III, p. 428.
[33] Mar Joseph was a suffragan of Elias IX, who had tried unsuccessfully to renew the union with Rome. In 1804 John Hormizd, the hereditary Nestorian katholikos of Alqosh, became Catholic, and his church joined the Chaldean Uniates of Diyarbekir. The two patriarchates merged in 1830. We thus have today the odd situation whereby the Catholic Chaldeans are descended from the sixteenth-century Nestorians, whereas the Assyrian Church of the East continues that of the original Uniates. See Fortescue, *Lesser Eastern Churches*, pp. 102–03.
[34] Korolevsky, *op. cit.*, p. 141.

A priest-physician accompanying this second expedition, João Bermudez, exploited current disaffection with Coptic rule by making the false claim that he had been appointed Patriarch of Ethiopia by Pope Paul III, but he failed to assert his authority. Finally, the Society of Jesus was entrusted with the Abyssinian mission, and in 1557 Bishop Andrés de Oviedo and several other Jesuits set out for Ethiopia. Meanwhile João Nunez Barreto, the priest chosen by St Ignatius Loyola to head the Abyssinian mission, was confirmed as Latin Patriarch by Pope Paul IV. This action caused the impostor Bermudez to flee the country – unnecessarily as it turned out, because Nunez Barreto died in Goa before reaching his destination.[35]

After initial hesitations, the reigning negus, Galadewos (Claudius), permitted the Jesuits to commence their missionary activity. Impressed by the Latin priests' works of charity, their construction of new churches, public buildings, roads and bridges, the native Christians inclined increasingly towards union with Rome. Under the guidance of the energetic Spaniard Pedro Paez, the negus Susenyos (Sisinnius) III became a Catholic in 1614, and in 1626 (five years after making his conversion public) he proclaimed the union of the Ethiopian Church with Rome.[36]

Unhappily, this joyful event brought not peace but a sword to Abyssinia because of the Jesuits' 'inveterate conviction that everything eastern is bad'.[37] Afonso Mendes, the new Latin Patriarch who had arrived in 1625, immediately put into action a plan for the latinization of the national Church. Not content to set right a number of abuses and irregularities in ecclesiastical discipline and in the administration of the sacraments, the Portuguese bishop aimed at no less than the imposition of the Roman rite on the country, with the linguistic concession of its translation into Ge'ez, the liturgical language of the Abyssinians. This objective could obviously not be realized immediately, but other reforms, like the introduction of the Gregorian calendar and of Roman rules of fast and abstinence – innovations foisted upon the people with military aid – aroused widespread opposition. Popular discontent only increased when the Negus, acting on the advice of the Jesuits, prohibited various practices of the Abyssinian Church and demanded celibacy of the local married clergy.[38]

Susenyos' harsh persecution of those who resisted these reforms sparked off rioting in many districts, and culminated in a general revolt.[39] The growing civil strife was such that in 1632, shortly before his death, Susenyos was obliged to grant toleration to the Miaphysites. His son and successor, Fasiladas (Basilides), who had taken the side of the native clergy and faithful, immediately banished Mendes and all the Jesuits from his kingdom. 'The sheep of Ethiopia are now delivered from the hyenas from the West', the native clergy exulted.[40] For the next two hundred years any Latin priest caught setting foot on Ethiopian soil was put to death.

---

[35] Ibid., pp. 141–42.
[36] Ibid., p. 142.
[37] Ibid., p. 145.
[38] Ibid., pp. 142–43. Some of the practices put down were legitimate customs of the Coptic Church; others were local abuses due to pagan or Jewish influence, for example polygamy and sabbatarianism (Sabbath observance on Saturday instead of Sunday).
[39] D. F. Bourke, CM, St Justin De Jacobis, Hero of Ethiopia (Rockhampton, 1975), p. 6.
[40] Sir Charles Fernand Rey, 'Abyssinia', in Encyclopedia Britannica, I (1961), p. 68.

Architects of Disunity

In Kerala the same arrogant bullying of Oriental Christians led not to one schism, but to a succession of them. Malabarese resentment of Latin oppression and interference finally exploded into open rebellion in 1653 when Mar Aithallaha, a Syrian bishop who arrived in Kerala bearing papal credentials, was seized by the Portuguese authorities, turned over to the Inquisition and reportedly put to death. Thousands of Malabarese, led by members of their clergy, gathered around the Coonan Cross near Cochin and took an oath renouncing the authority of the Portuguese Metropolitan of Cranganore. Thomas Pakalomattam was chosen archdeacon to lead the Church until such time as they could obtain a new East Syrian bishop.[41]

At this point the Holy See intervened and the Propaganda Congregation sent out a group of Italian Discalced Carmelites with the mission of reconciling the Syrians with their Latin archbishop. When this proved impossible, Rome created a Propaganda jurisdiction alongside the Padroado one in Malabar: the Syrian Christians outside Cochin were now to be governed by the former. Giuseppe Sebastiani, the Carmelite superior in Kerala, was made apostolic administrator of Cranganore. Through the efforts of the Discalced Carmelites about half of the dissidents made their peace with Rome. These reconciled Uniates became known as the *Pazhayakuttukar* or 'old party'. The rest, becoming the 'new party' (*Puthankuttukar*) drifted into permanent schism, and in 1665 joined up with the West Syrian Jacobite Church after Thomas Pakalomattam failed to obtain episcopal ordination from the Nestorian katholikos.[42]

In spite of their new status as Miaphysites (a shift in theological allegiance which shows how little importance the Kerala Christians attached to the ancient christological controversies), the New Party (*Malankars*) recovered their old East Syrian customs. However, in 1846 the Antiochene rite of their patriarch was introduced into Kerala, and by the late 1870s had completely superseded the traditional Edessene liturgy among them.[43] The formation of this rival non-Uniate church had been favoured by the Dutch conquest of 1662 and only three centuries later, in 1930, did some Malankars return to Catholic unity. Before the new Calvinist rulers expelled the Latin clergy from Kerala, Fr Sebastiani consecrated a native Christian, Alexander Parampil, as vicar apostolic to ensure the survival of the Uniate Old Party. However, after the death of Bishop Parampil in 1700, the Carmelites returned to Malabar and re-established Latin control of the Malabarese Church.

From that year until 1896, the Vicar Apostolic and the Archbishop of Cranganore were all Latin-rite Europeans. In the meantime the Thomas Christians would have a great deal to suffer under the 'protection' of the Carmelites, who resumed the earlier Western tampering with local social and ecclesial customs. All Malabarese candidates for the priesthood now had to be trained in Latin seminaries, where they were subjected to Western discipline.[44] The Propaganda Congregation in Rome received repeated complaints from Kerala, and in 1774 it was obliged to deliver a stern reprimand to one Carmelite vicar apostolic too fond of 'keeping

---

[41] Fortescue, *Lesser Eastern Churches*, p. 364; Attwater, *Christian Churches*, I, p. 282.
[42] Podipara, 'Malabar Rite', p. 93. Mar Gregorius, Jacobite Bishop of Jerusalem, consecrated Pakalomattam as Thomas I.
[43] Attwater, *Christian Churches*, I, p. 283.
[44] Podipara, *Rise and Decline*, pp. 26–27.

order' among the restless Malabarese by chaining, flogging, and imprisoning their priests without trial.[45]

The independent Malankar Church, far from Syria and increasingly turned in on itself, lost many members of its flock to Protestantism as a result of nineteenth-century Anglican proselytism, one result being the Church of South India.[46] As the eminent Malabarese scholar, Fr Placid Podipara laments:

> All the misfortunes, divisions and schisms that took place in the Indian Church of the Thomas Christians and caused its decline under the Latin rule had their root cause in the violence done to its traditions and in the denial of the legitimate demands of the Thomas Christians for bishops of their own rite.[47]

Union and Uniatism

Latin oppression of the Chaldean, Malabarese and Ethiopian Uniates implied a racial discrimination against Christians who were not European but 'natives', and hence 'uncivilized'. It was impossible to apply these prejudices fully to the Byzantine-rite Catholics of Europe who, though certainly treated as second-class members of the Church, nonetheless represented strong Greek and Slavonic cultures which the Latins were obliged to respect, however much they disliked them. Even if Rome had despaired of bringing the Orthodox churches of the East back to her obedience, Russia was politically a force to contend with, and bad treatment of Greek Catholics could only aggravate tensions between the powerful Tsarist Empire and the Latin West.[48]

The Polish domination of Western Belorussia and Western Ukraine, and Hapsburg rule in Transylvania, facilitated the reunion with Rome of millions of Belorussian, Ukrainian, Ruthenian and Romanian Orthodox in 1596 (Union of Brest-Litovsk) and 1700 (Union of Alba Julia) respectively. However, these two unions were not merely the result of political pressures. They followed upon the assimilation to Western civilization of East Slavonic and Transylvanian Romanian laity who, for over a century, had been educated in Latin schools and universities. Whereas theological studies had languished in the Orthodox Church since the Turkish conquest of the Byzantine Empire and the violent Tatar invasions of Russia, the Latin Church had experienced the great intellectual revival of the Renaissance. Furthermore, the reflowering of Hellenic studies in the West, bolstered after 1453 by the contributions of Greek scholars fleeing the Turks, made the Latin Church the *de facto* heir to the theological tradition of the Eastern Fathers. Consequently, the Ukrainian Orthodox bishops planning to submit to the Holy See saw in union with Rome an opportunity to save and strengthen the inheritance of their own church.[49]

---

[45] Ibid., p. 62, n. 12.
[46] Fortescue, *Lesser Eastern Churches*, pp. 367, 369–70.
[47] Podipara, *Rise and Decline*, p. 37.
[48] The widened use of the term 'Greek Catholic' as a synonym for a Byzantine-rite Catholic of any nationality is relatively recent, popularized by the administration of Empress Maria Theresa (1740–1780).
[49] Sophia Senyk, 'The Ukrainian Church and Latinization', *Orientalia Christiana Periodica*, 56 (1990), pp. 167–70.

Unfortunately this unionist movement inspired at first by sound motives eventually led to a general cultural cringe towards the 'progressive' Latin West, increasingly viewed in unfavourable contrast with a 'backward', 'ignorant' East. In the case of the Ukrainian Uniates, the Cossack Rebellion beginning in 1654, which aimed to destroy the Union of 1596 and was backed by a fiercely anti-Catholic Muscovy, drove a psychological wedge between the Greek Catholics, who now threw in their lot definitively with Poland and the West, and their Orthodox co-ritualists. Henceforth, the Catholic Ukrainians would foster their Byzantine identity without reference to the contemporary Orthodox Church and within a purely Latin context.[50]

If the Greek Catholic Church of Eastern ('Left Bank') Ukraine was destroyed by the Muscovites in the 1650s, the surviving Uniates west of the Dnieper were barely tolerated by the Latin secular and ecclesiastical authorities in Polish Galicia, Ruthenia and Transylvania, who pressed in innumerable ways for their gradual latinization. Restrictions against the Uniates in Poland included forbidding their priests to administer the Eastern sacraments to Latin Catholics without episcopal authorization, whereas Latin priests were free to minister to Greek Catholics.[51]

In 1744 Pope Benedict XIV authorized the Theatine rector of the Pontifical Seminary for Armenians and 'Ruthenians' (i.e. Galicians) in Lviv to make the Eastern-rite students conform to Latin discipline, in accordance with the custom of the Greek College in Rome.[52] And in the view of Mgr Mario Filonardi, papal nuncio to Warsaw in 1642, prohibiting Greek Catholics from transfering to the Roman rite 'would be very prejudicial to the Catholic religion and to the salvation of those souls'. On this, Sophia Senyk, a Ukrainian scholar, comments: 'The conclusion can only be that the nuncio did not consider an Eastern Catholic Church really Catholic.'[53]

Nevertheless, unlike the Maronite and Malabarese rites, the Byzantine liturgy of the Greek, Ukrainian, Ruthenian and Romanian Uniates remained essentially intact thanks to the valiant resistance of their bishops. (The same cannot be said of the Armenian diocese of Lviv whose priests, two centuries later, were quietly reading a highly latinized form of the Armenian Mass while the people sang Polish hymns).[54] Indeed, in the early days of union the Uniate hierarchy had been anxious to maintain their ritual oneness with the Orthodox. In 1605, ten years after the Union of Brest-Litovsk, Ipatij Potij, the Greek Catholic metropolitan of Kiev, could boast:

---

[50] Ibid., pp. 172–74.
[51] Ibid., p. 176.
[52] Ibid., p. 180. Galicians and Ruthenians (Rusyns) are linguistically and culturally diverse, in part because the former were long under Polish influence whereas the latter belonged to the Hungarian cultural sphere and were mostly citizens of Czechoslavakia between the world wars. When both Eastern Galicia and Ruthenia were integrated into the Ukrainian Soviet Socialist Republic at the end of the Second World War, the government policy of considering the Ruthenians to be Ukrainian began. However, in North America the two ethnic groups remained separate. In early modern times (and in many Church documents) the three westernmost East Slavonic groups (Belorussians, Ukrainians and Ruthenians/Rusyns) were jointly termed 'Ruthenians'.
[53] Ibid., p. 179.
[54] Korolevsky, op. cit., p. 22. This situation still obtained in the years following the Second World War, when the Armenian Catholic diocese was liquidated by the Soviets. Its faithful were the descendants of Armenians who had settled in Galicia during the period of Austrian rule (1772–1919).

> They [the Orthodox] say that we corrupt the orthodox faith and the ceremonies of the Holy Eastern Church. . . . As regards the ceremonies and rites of the Holy Eastern Church, those people must be blind if they refuse to see how these are celebrated, in which no change has occurred and will not for all ages . . .[55]

On the feast of the Epiphany in 1629 Archbishop Rutskyj celebrated the Divine Liturgy in Kiev and the numerous Orthodox present in the congregation were amazed to find no difference between the Uniate service and their own. Nevertheless, for more astute Orthodox observers there lurked behind this impressive façade of pure Byzantine ritual the inadmissible reality of a Church that was becoming Latin in mentality and spirituality, the inevitable consequence of intellectual and religious formation in a Western milieu. This was for the Eastern Orthodox the essence of Uniatism.

In any case, it proved impossible in the long run to keep the door tightly shut to Latin influences in the sphere of worship. The misgivings of the Orthodox were confirmed with the gradual admission – especially after the 1720 Synod of Zamość – of Western devotions like the rosary, novenas and Benediction of the Blessed Sacrament, the introduction of certain Western feasts and cults of saints. Even more distasteful to the Orthodox were the practice of kneeling for Holy Communion (sometimes given in one kind only),[56] the insertion of the *filioque* into the liturgical Creed, the evolution of a form of Low Mass, and the vogue for pulling down icon screens and setting up side altars in Uniate churches.[57] The elements most addicted to these latinisms were members of the Basilian order, who were in close touch with the Latin clergy and laymen educated in Western institutions.[58] By comparison the Byzantine-rite churches of the Romanians, Aegean Greeks and Antiochene Melkites (Uniate since 1720) resisted the infiltration of Latin influences more strongly.

Hybridism was an even graver problem in the numerically smaller (and culturally more insecure) Uniate churches of the Middle East, especially those of the Armenian Catholic patriarchate of Cilicia erected in 1740 and the Coptic Catholic Church created the following year. In the early seventeenth century a group of West Syrian Jacobites in Aleppo had also reunited with Rome as a result of Capuchin and Jesuit missionary endeavour. The gradual latinization of this church reached crisis point during the patriarchate of Mar Anthony Semhairy (1853–1864), whose enthusiasm for things Latin was such that he wanted to undertake a complete reform of the Antiochene liturgy to bring it into closer conformity with the Roman rite. Fortunately, however, Mar Anthony's scheme was abandoned thanks to the pleadings of Fr George Shelhot, his future successor.[59] A similar predilection

---

[55] Senyk, *op. cit.*, p. 170.
[56] In the Orthodox Byzantine rite kneeling is reserved for penitential services and standing is considered the appropriate stance for Sunday worship, the upright posture being a symbol of resurrection.
[57] Louis Aloys Tautu, 'Rumanian Rite', NCE, XII, p. 720. Some Catholics of the Byzantine rite admit the *filioque* (e.g. the Ukrainians until very recently), others (e.g. the Romanians and Melkites) do not. When the Ruthenian Uniates (formerly Czechoslovak citizens) were forced to rejoin the Orthodox Church by the occupying Soviets in 1947, the new hierarchy abolished the custom of Low Mass.
[58] Senyk, *op. cit.*, pp. 174–80.
[59] Gabriel Khouri-Sarkis, 'Syrian Rite', NCE, XIII, p. 903. However, several latinisms, among them universal clerical celibacy, were later made obligatory by the Synod of Sharfeh (1888). See Taft, *op. cit.*, p. 418.

for Italianate statuary and modern Latin devotions was a weakness of the first Malankarese Patriarch, Mar Ivanios, who died in 1954.[60]

Variety of Rites: A Hindrance in the Church?

In no Oriental land were Latin imperialists more convinced of the inequality of East and West than in Ethiopia, where after two centuries of total exclusion, Catholic missionaries were able to penetrate from 1837 onwards. In that year an Italian Vincentian, Giuseppe Sapeto, managed to tour the country as the Arabic interpreter of two explorers from France. This prompted Pope Gregory XVI to erect a prefecture apostolic for Abyssinia in 1839, with Fr Sapeto as the first prefect.[61]

The undeniable corruption of traditional Christian doctrine and practice in Ethiopia was a daunting problem for the Vincentian, Capuchin and Franciscan missionaries of the nineteenth century. Apart from the recrudescence of polygamy and sabbatarianism since the short-lived reforms of the mid-seventeenth century, there were the great social evils of general illiteracy, superstition and institutionalized slavery. The service books of the Church, never printed, were badly organized and often inaccurate. Because of many irregular and ignorant practices of the clergy, the validity of certain sacramental acts was also doubtful.[62] The particular problems of the Abyssinian Church were in a different category from the perceived irregularities of another isolated church, that of the Nestorians in Kurdistan, whose idiosyncrasies were mainly archaisms (e.g. lack of image veneration, Communion in the hand, absence of private confession but not of absolution) or the result of isolation and decline (for instance the loss of monasticism).[63]

---

[60] George A. Maloney, 'Malankar Rite, Liturgy of', *NCE*, IX, p. 106.

[61] Korolevsky, *op. cit.*, p. 152.

[62] Ibid., pp. 152–53. For instance, the eucharistic wine was actually the juice of raisins steeped in water; in baptism the correct form was often not uttered at the moment of immersion, and in other cases the form itself was distorted; the chrism used in confirmation was not consecrated by a bishop but common oil blessed by priests with a simple sign of the cross; confession and absolution were more often a paraliturgical act than a sacramental rite; and in many places Holy Communion was given only to children at Mass, never to adults. Some of these practices have apparently persisted to the present day. In Egypt the Coptic Church also displayed certain irregularities in the nineteenth century, especially in regard to baptism (see Attwater, *Christian Churches*, II, p. 191).

[63] True irregularities of the Nestorian Church included the introduction of a hereditary patriarchate (passing from uncle to nephew) in the fifteenth century and not abandoned until the 1970s, and the absence of the Institution Narrative from the eucharistic anaphora of Sts Addai and Mari (but not from the two other anaphoras). The latter remains one of the thorniest problems of Catholic liturgiology because of the question of validity. Scholarly opinion is divided on whether the original anaphora simply did not contain the Words of Institution (plausible on structural grounds according to some, since clear alternative references to transubstantiation are dispersed through the prayer), or whether the formula, originally included but traditionally left out of liturgical texts through *disciplina arcani*, disappeared in early modern times when ill-educated priests neglected to recite it from memory. This was apparently a problem only in Kurdistan and not in Malabar, since the acts of the 1599 Synod of Udayamperur did not mention it. In the twentieth century it was common for Nestorian priests under High Anglican missionary influence to reinsert the missing phrases, but a highly controversial Vatican ruling of 2001 (the Pontifical Council for Promoting Christian Unity's 'Guidelines for Admission to the Eucharist between the Chaldean Church and the Assyrian Church of the East') that their omission did not affect the validity of the Mass (based on the really unprovable thesis that the original anaphora did not contain the Words of Institution) has encouraged the Nestorian clergy to overcome any scruples. However, many Chaldean and other Catholics remain sceptical on this point.

In such a situation it was clearly impossible for even the best-intentioned Western missionaries in Ethiopia to adopt the rites and ceremonies of the dissidents *en bloc*, with one or two corrections and alterations. What *was* possible and, indeed incumbent upon them, was to revise the existing liturgical books along the lines of the Coptic rites, of which they were, substantially, Ge'ez redactions. This work of restoration had as its obvious model the Catholic editions of the Coptic service books published in Rome between 1761 and 1763. With this end in view, the Neapolitan Vincentian Giustino De Jacobis, who worked in Abyssinia from 1842 to 1860, becoming its first vicar apostolic and Catholic bishop, was given the faculty to adopt the local rite. However, the task of revision proved to be beyond him, in spite of his knowledge of Ge'ez, and to the end of his days he celebrated according to the Roman rite and in Latin.[64]

Guglielmo Massaia, the Piedmontese Capuchin (and future cardinal) placed in charge of the prefecture apostolic of the Gallas erected in 1846, lacked even the goodwill of De Jacobis in this matter. Any inclination to restore the current Ethiopian liturgy was precluded by his general contempt for it as

> arbitrarily introduced, and . . . provisionally tolerated by the Church to avoid worse evils. . . . Liturgical unity is more to be desired than variety. . . . National pride, the begetter and guardian of all these different rites, which are an obstacle and a very great difficulty in the way of apostleship in the unfortunate East, is equally the unhappy origin of the misshapen Ethiopic rite. . . . Variety of rites . . . is not a beauty but, today anyway, a hindrance in the Church. She accepts them as a lesser evil, lest a poor people be lost. . . . The prohibitions of passing to the Latin rite and of conferring orders according to that rite are unnecessary measures. It would be much better to leave everything to the prudent discretion of the vicars apostolic.[65]

Massaia's answer to the liturgical problem was to have the Roman Mass translated into Ge'ez, and he authorized the native priests working with him to celebrate this liturgy privately within the sanctuary while the people sang the traditional Ethiopian chants in the nave, blissfully unaware that their immemorial eucharistic rite had been taken away from them.[66]

Mgr Marcel Touvier, the Vincentian vicar apostolic in 1892, was in full agreement with Fr Massaia's solution, and therefore recommended the making of a Ge'ez version of the Roman ritual. With the customary Ethiopic rite, the vicar apostolic opined, it was

> impossible to form souls in the ways of piety, to produce saints; we shall never have sincere and solid Catholics; for everything in this rite draws people away from the Roman Church, from religion and from God . . . Will not the time come when it should be considered whether, in order to restore this Ethiopian nation to Catholicity, it would not be better and even necessary to give it the Roman rite, purely and simply?[67]

---

[64] Korolevsky, *op. cit.*, p. 147.
[65] Ibid., pp. 145–46.
[66] Ibid., p. 146.
[67] Ibid., p. 147.

As a prelude to this desirable romanization, the Italian Capuchins in Eritrea imposed the use of unleavened bread at Mass, prohibited Communion under both kinds at all but solemn celebrations of the Eucharist, and removed sanctuary veils from churches. Their French Vincentian colleagues working inland also put a stop to priests chrismating children immediately after baptism.[68] Although a truncated Ethiopic order of Mass was finally printed in Keren in 1890 by Fr Jean-Baptiste Coulbeaux, CM, the romanization scheme went ahead. Even in the pseudo-Ethiopic rite the wearing of Roman vestments was encouraged, Latin genuflections and elevations were prescribed, and the *filioque* was introduced into the Creed. In 1895 Pope Leo XIII formally approved the principle of spreading the Roman liturgy in Ge'ez as the normal form of Catholic worship in Ethiopia.[69]

The Land of Liberty

It is a shameful fact that the progressive latinization of the Eastern Catholic Churches was finally brought to a halt by the Holy See only because of new threats of schism in the late nineteenth century. The first loss of faithful to the Roman obedience began in Malabar after 1860, when the Chaldean Patriarch, Joseph Audo VI, granted the request of the Uniates of Trichur to send them a bishop of their own rite. This was done without the approval of Rome and precipitated him into a long and bitter dispute with Pope Pius IX, but Mar Joseph was unwilling to forget the responsibility for the Church in India traditionally attached to his office.[70] Mar Thomas Rokkos, the bishop sent out from Mesopotamia, was expelled by the Latin authorities, but Anthony Thondanatta, leader of the Trichur group, meanwhile persuaded the Nestorian katholikos in Kurdistan to ordain him bishop for Malabar. Thondanatta later returned to the Roman obedience, but the schism revived when Mar Joseph sent another Chaldean eparch, Mar Elias Mellos, to Kerala in 1874. The small party that gathered around Mar Elias at Trichur eventually severed its ties with Ernakulam and Rome, and in 1908 formally established communion with the Nestorian katholikos, from whom they obtained a bishop.[71] Their church still thrives today.

If this small haemorrhage in India was of slight concern to the Vatican authorities, rumblings in North America in the last two decades of the century moved them to swift action. At this time, large numbers of Galician and Ruthenian Uniates were migrating to the United States, where they found themselves without the services of priests of their rite. The trouble began in 1886, when the first Greek Catholic church was opened in Shenandoah, Pennsylvania. Its Galician pastor, Father Ivan Volans'kyj, was subjected to harassment by the Latin clergy and hierarchy because he was married, and he was unable to exercise his ministry unhampered until

[68] Ibid., pp. 148–49.
[69] Ibid., pp. 150, 155.
[70] To this day Rome has kept the Malabarese Church juridically separated from its Mother Church in Iraq and no Malabarese patriarchate has been established to compensate for this violation of tradition.
[71] Attwater, *Christian Churches*, II, pp. 232–33. After Mellos returned to Mesopotamia in 1882, his place was taken by Thondanatta (Mar Abdisho) who had tired of his reconciliation with the Roman authorities. In 1872 Pope Pius IX gave his own side of the story to date in the encyclical *Quæ in Patriarchatu* (On the Church in Chaldea).

Cardinal Sylvester Sembratowicz, the Greek Catholic Archbishop of Lviv, intervened on his behalf with the Holy See.[72]

Indeed, it could hardly be plain sailing for Uniates in a country whose bishops, tainted to varying degrees by what would later be classified as the Americanist heresy,[73] were determined to force the linguistic and cultural assimilation of non-Anglo-Celtic Catholics of all rites. Most of the American ordinaries gave a chilly reception to the Uniates, who, as well as being aliens, were in their view at best dubiously Catholic. Some bishops even refused to tolerate the celebration of Oriental rites in their Latin dioceses. During the 1880s and 1890s the worst offender in this regard was Archbishop John Ireland. His treatment of Father Alexis Toth, a Ruthenian from Hungary sent out to minister to the priestless Uniates of Minnesota, is an especially deplorable page in the annals of Latin Catholic bigotry. It is worth quoting at length from the memoirs of the sorely tried Greek Catholic missionary:

I came to America as a Uniate. As a former professor of Church Law, I knew that here in America, as a Uniate priest, I must respectfully obey that Latin bishop in whose diocese it shall be my pleasure to serve – this is demanded by the Unia, Papal briefs and decrees, because there is no Uniate bishop here and never was. This was written in my resolution and certificate of assignment. The place of my assignment was Minneapolis, Minnesota, diocese of Archbishop Ireland. As a loyal Uniate, by order of my former Bishop John Valyi, I personally appeared before Archbishop Ireland, December 19, 1889, as customary kissed his hand (but did not kneel and bow down – and this was my biggest mistake as I found out later) and presented my credentials. I well remember, scarcely had he read that I was a 'greco-kaftolic', his hands began to tremble! It took him nearly fifteen minutes to complete the reading. He then sharply asked me: (The conversation was in Latin)

'Do you have a wife?'

'No!' I answered.

'But did you have?'

'I am a widower . . .'

When he heard my answer, he threw the papers on the table and loudly exclaimed:

'I already sent a protest to Rome not to send me such priests . . .'

'What kind do you mean?'

'Such as you . . .'

'But I am a Catholic priest of Greek rite! I am a Uniate! I was ordained by a lawful Catholic bishop . . .'

'I do not consider you or that bishop a Catholic; furthermore I have no need for Greek Catholic priests; it is sufficient that in Minneapolis there is a Polish priest; he can be priest for the Greek Catholics . . .'

'But he is of the Latin rite; our people cannot understand him; they will not go to him for service – it is for that reason that they built themselves a separate church . . .'[74]

[72] Joseph F. Marbach, 'Eastern Churches, United States', CESH, III, p. 628.
[73] Even Archbishop Corrigan of New York, the leader of the anti-Americanist faction in the US hierarchy, was unsympathetic towards Eastern-rite Catholics.
[74] Ireland the xenophobe was typically ignorant of the fact that Polish was the second language of

'I gave them no permission to build, and give you no jurisdiction to act in any capacity here . . .'

Extremely distressed by such remarks and action of this high church dignitary, I answered, sharply:

'In that case I do not need your jurisdiction, or your permission. I know the rules of my Church, and I know under what conditions the Unia was established; therefore I shall act accordingly.'

The Archbishop flew into a rage . . . It went so far that it is not worthwhile to repeat the conversation.[75]

Second-class Citizens

Completely blocked in his duty to minister to his flock, Fr Toth eventually entered into negotiations with the Russian Orthodox Bishop of San Francisco and joined the Orthodox Church with most of his congregation in 1891.[76] This drastic step was taken in the absence of any effective support either from the Greek Catholic hierarchy in Europe or from Rome. As James Jorgenson observes:

> Father Toth undoubtedly came to realize quite soon that he was in a totally impossible situation. The Uniate hierarchy was ill-disposed to assert the rights which were legitimately theirs under the provisions of the *unia*. They felt and acted as the inferiors of the Latin prelates – they had, ironically, never attained the equal rights which they so ardently desired and for which they originally accepted the terms of the union. Their whole history was and is to this day characterized by a humiliating second-class citizenship in the Roman Catholic Church. In their path-etic attempts to be as Catholic as the Romans, the higher Uniate clergy were the main instigators in the progressive latinization of the Greek Catholic Church.[77]

The Ukrainians and Ruthenians who defected from the Catholic Church because of this persecution soon became the backbone of the Russian Orthodox Church in the United States.

In 1994, a century later, two events would bring home the extent of this wound inflicted on the unity of the Church by American bishops and create a further obstacle to Catholic–Orthodox reconciliation: the canonization of Alexis Toth by the Russian Orthodox Church of America, and of Maxim Sandovich by the Polish Orthodox Church. The latter was a Lemko-Ruthenian Greek Catholic in Austrian Poland who converted to Russian Orthodoxy, fled to nearby Russian-ruled Volhynia to become a priest, returned home to pursue his mission of 'reconciliation' and was executed by the Hapsburg authorities as an alleged Russian spy on 6 August 1914, the same day that Austria-Hungary declared war on Russia. A

Galicians, *not* of the Hungarian-dominated Ruthenians: the 'all foreigners are the same' school of thought.

[75] Quoted in James Jorgenson, 'Father Alexis Toth and the Transition of the Greek Catholic Community in Minneapolis to the Russian Orthodox Church', *St Vladimir's Theological Quarterly*, 32 (1988), pp. 126–28.

[76] Ibid., p. 132. See also Konstantin Simon, SJ, 'Alexis Toth and the Beginnings of the Orthodox Movement among the Ruthenians in America (1891)', *Orientalia Christiana Periodica*, 54 (1988), pp. 387–428.

[77] Jorgenson, *op. cit.*, pp. 129–30.

fact usually glossed over by Orthodox hagiographers is that it was the proselytizing influence of ex-Uniate Orthodox returning to Lemkoland from the United States that created the circumstances for the conversion, mission and martyrdom of Maxim Sandovich. But Catholics scandalized by this episode need also to be reminded that without the fanaticism and ignorance of Bishop Ireland and Latin Catholic leaders who thought and behaved like him this bilateral tragedy would not have been possible.

It was particularly disgraceful that after the Minneapolis episode of December 1889 the Vatican, instead of disciplining Ireland, acceded to his demands, and those of his fellow hierarchs, to curtail the rights and activities of Eastern-rite Catholics in the United States. Accordingly, on 1 October 1890 the Propaganda Congregation sent a stern directive to the Greek Catholic bishops of Austria-Hungary, forbidding them to send married priests to America and stressing that prospective celibate chaplains had to be accepted by the ordinaries of the Latin dioceses in which they would serve. Communicated to the United States hierarchy in May 1892, these regulations, though intended exclusively for Ukrainian and Ruthenian Uniates, were soon extended to all other Oriental Catholics settling in America.[78]

A second instruction of the Congregation for the Propagation of the Faith of 1 May 1897 directed American bishops to provide Byzantine-rite pastors for Ukrainian and Ruthenian Catholics, but at the same time gave general permission to Uniates in America to conform to the Latin rite, while retaining their status as Eastern Catholics. This concession, made by the Holy See as an interim measure to ease the religious difficulties of Uniates cut off from the facilities of their rite, became for many of them in the aggressively assimilationist American situation a first step along the road to complete latinization.

On the whole, Vatican attempts to improve the lot of Eastern Catholics in the United States at this time were far from satisfactory. For instance Kyr Stefan Ortyns'kyj, the Ukrainian bishop appointed by Pope Pius X in 1907, was obliged to receive delegated jurisdiction from local Latin ordinaries, which was tantamount to a mere vicarial status. In 1913, Uniate dissatisfaction and fears of systematic latinization finally prompted Rome to grant the resident Uniate prelate full ordinary jurisdiction over Greek Catholics wherever they resided in the United States.[79]

Frankish Diplomacy

Rome's half-hearted support of the American Uniates was due in part to a new wave of anti-Orthodox feeling that had arisen as a by-product of ultramontanism during the pontificate of Pius IX. There was a general awareness that the Orthodox were bitterly hostile to Rome, and this generated the opinion that the Uniates, who held so much in common with the schismatics, were not quite trustworthy Catholics.[80] At a time when inerrancy was popularly attributed to the Pope, few

---

[78] Marbach, *op. cit.*, pp. 628–29.
[79] Ibid., p. 629.
[80] Already in 1837 *Propaganda Fide* had made it mandatory for Eastern Catholic patriarchs-elect to seek papal confirmation, and all synodal acts had to be approved by Rome before being promulgated. In his bull *Reversurus* (1867) Pius IX reserved the right to choose all Armenian Catholic bishops; and while the existing hierarchy could put forward three names for each vacant

Latin Catholics were inclined to question whether the offensive enmity of the Orthodox was in any way justified. The standard view was that the Holy Father's generous and tireless outreach to the ungracious and ungrateful Orientals was really a wasted effort.

In 1848, answering an appeal from the recently founded Society for the Union of All the Christians of the East, the Pope had addressed to the Orthodox an encyclical, *In Suprema Petri Apostolici Sede*, appealing to them to return to the Roman Communion. In this letter the dissidents' rights to their proper liturgies and customs were expressly guaranteed, but with what Fr Aidan Nichols has described as 'an extraordinary tactlessness, which was to hamper all Pius' relations with the Orthodox', the Pope had the text distributed directly to the Orthodox faithful, ignoring their bishops. It is hardly surprising that the four Eastern patriarchs responded in hostile terms.[81]

Pius attempted to undo the damage in 1868. Now, on the eve of Vatican I, he composed another letter to the Orthodox eparchs (*Arcano Divinæ Providentiæ Consilio*) inviting them to attend the Council, and used the occasion to entreat them again to submit to the Roman See. Unfortunately, the 'Commission for Missions and Eastern Churches', set up in 1867 in preparation for the Council, placed Orthodox Christians on the same footing as pagans, and its members included Archbishop Giuseppe Valerga, the same Latin Patriarch of Jerusalem who governed a flock made up mainly of converts from Orthodoxy and who had recommended that the Eastern Catholic Churches be compelled to give up their codes of canon law for the Roman one.[82]

In these circumstances the papal letter could only give offence to the Orthodox hierarchy, who feared that their presence at the Council would be interpreted as an acceptance of papal claims of universal jurisdiction. The two main reasons which the Ecumenical Patriarch Gregorios VI gave for his inability to accept it were 'that the Pope had called the Council without consulting his brother patriarchs' and 'the known personal attachment of the Pope to extreme theories of both primacy and infallibility'.[83] After Vatican I the constitution *Pastor Æternus* would be viewed by most Orthodox commentators as a major stumbling block to the cause of reunion. Eastern Catholic bishops, for their part, had much to complain about at the Council, and often found the Pope rigid and unsympathetic both in the sessions and in private.[84]

---

see, the lower clergy were henceforth excluded from patriarchal elections. See Taft, *op. cit.*, p. 423.

[81] Nichols, *op. cit.*, p. 306. The encyclical of the Orthodox hierarchy, published in May 1848, was signed by the patriarchs of Constantinople, Alexandria, Antioch and Jerusalem and the members of the Holy Synod.

[82] Bernhard Stasiewski, 'Papal Hopes for Unification: The Independent Eastern Churches', in Hubert Jedin, ed., *History of the Church, Vol. IX: The Church in the Industrial Age* (New York, 1981), p. 335.

[83] Nichols, *op. cit.*, pp. 306–07. The fact that protocol was violated when the invitation was leaked to the press before the Orthodox hierarchy received it was the immediate motive for declining the invitation.

[84] See Taft, *op. cit.*, pp. 423–24.

Trial Run?

The papal view that the more Eastern Christians were assimilated to Latin ways the more truly Catholic they would become is well reflected in the encyclicals Gregory XVI and Pius IX addressed to the Armenian and Ukrainian Catholic bishops, and which make painful reading because of their patronizing tone.[85] The constant complaint of both popes was that Uniates were taking it upon themselves to narrow the gap between themselves and their non-Catholic counterparts by purifying their deformed rites of latinizing innovations promoted by Western missionaries and approved by the Holy See. The culprits, Pius IX complained in 1854, 'want to eliminate many practices which were justly introduced' into the Oriental rites 'to show how strongly you abhor heresy and schism and adhere to Catholic unity'.[86] In other words, these latinisms (which went far beyond mere corrections of problematical doctrinal formulations) were seen as a test of loyalty to Rome.

Yet the same Roman pontiffs who affected to know what was best for the liturgical and disciplinary lives of these ancient Churches were on the whole personally ignorant of the languages, customs and psychology of the peoples they sought to reform. The blame attaching to the pre-Leonine papacy is not lessened by the fact that those chiefly responsible for these latinizing trends were often the Uniates themselves, especially those burdened with an inferiority complex.

Ironically, the humiliation of the Catholic East at this time was merely the prelude to the far greater degradation of the Catholic West that would follow in the middle of the next century. The terrible conclusion to be drawn from the history of Latin cultural vandalism in the East is that Rome's commitment to the principle of liturgical revolution began not in the 1960s, as most people think, but during the Counter Reformation. The damage inflicted, in varying decrees, on the Oriental Churches under Roman rule was, historically, an unwitting trial run for the destruction of the Latin rites in our own time, for the imperialism and rationalism involved in the post-Tridentine offensive against Eastern Christianity reflect the idea that authority alone made the Roman liturgy universally valid. Once that authority lost its hold on Western Catholics, the privileged liturgy itself would be fair game for the vandals.

---

[85] See, for instance, Gregory XVI's *Inter Gravissimas*, addressed to the Armenian Catholics in 1832, Pius IX's *Neminem Vestrum* (1854, to the Armenians), and *Omnem Sollicitudinem* (1874). It should be recalled, however, that the last-named encyclical, addressed to the Ukrainian bishops, was written in reaction to a delatinization campaign in the Russian-administered but culturally very polonized eparchy of Cholm. This drive was led by its new, russophile ordinary, Myxajlo Kuzems'kyj, who was not a local cleric but a citizen of Austrian Galicia, where there was considerably less affection for Latin influences in the liturgy. The sudden reforms had been unpopular with the clergy and people and had been brutally enforced by the Tsarist police, who killed a number of protesters. As Russian subjects, the Uniates of Cholm saw the innovations as ominous because a similar process of ritual delatinization had preceeded the forced suppression of the Greek Catholic Church in Volhynia, Belorussia and Central Ukraine when these regions had come after Tsarist rule after the Partitions of Poland. See John-Paul Hinka, *Religion and Nationality in Western Ukraine* (Montreal, 1999), pp. 35–39.

[86] *Neminem Vestrum*, 15.

13

A NEW LAW OF BELIEF?

*On the basis of a whole series of research, questionings and significant
works, the explanation of these things has been sought – and often
found – not above, in heaven, but below, in the things themselves and
in Man. Yes, Man has become the centre and the reference point for
everything.*

YVES CONGAR, OP (1976)

What is Tradition?

Western disdain for an Eastern Christianity supposedly doomed by its inveterate
dissidence to intellectual and cultural inertia conveniently overlooks the extent
to which the schism of 1054 sentenced the West to the consequences of its own
rationalist tendencies. The most serious of these was the Reformation, and for all
Rome's efforts to maintain her purity of faith, the cultural environment in which
a great part of the Latin Church would henceforth be anchored was one in which
Protestant and, later, liberal thought loomed ominously large. Henceforth the great
concern of Occidental minds would be not what united Christian East and West,
but what divided Catholics from the heirs of the Reformation. For Catholics, the
twin sources of Revelation were Scripture and Tradition: since the root error of
Protestantism was its rejection of the latter, Catholic thinkers, especially those of
the Northern countries, devoted their energies to seeking a better understanding
of this component of Catholicism which their fellow Western Europeans had
repudiated.

From Patristic times until the Second Vatican Council, the Church saw tradition primarily (though not exclusively) as *content*, a set of beliefs and teachings
founded on Divine Revelation, accepted and passed on substantially unchanged.
According to the relevant entry in the 1931 *Catholic Encyclopaedic Dictionary*,
Tradition is

> The sum of revealed doctrine which has not been committed to Sacred Scripture
> . . . but which has been handed down by a series of legitimate shepherds of the
> Church from age to age. As revelation it must have come directly from the lips of
> Christ or been handed down by the Apostles at the dictation of the Holy Ghost.
> More broadly the term is used of the sum of doctrine revealed either in Scripture

or by word of mouth, so in 2 Thessalonians ii, 15: 'Hold by the traditions you have learned, in word and in writing, from us.'[1]

This is also the teaching of the Second Vatican Council. *Dei Verbum*, the dogmatic constitution on Divine Revelation, states that God intended

> the apostolic teaching, which is expressed in a special way in the inspired books, . . . to be preserved by a continuous succession of preachers until the end of time. Therefore the apostles, handing on what they themselves had received, warn the faithful to hold fast to the traditions which they have learned either by word of mouth or by letter (cf. 2 Th. 2.15), and to fight in defence of the faith handed on once and for all (cf. Jude 3). Now what was handed on by the apostles includes everything which contributes to the holiness of life, and the increase in faith of the People of God; and so of the Church, in her teaching, life, and worship, perpetuates and hands on to all generations all that she herself is, all that she believes.
>
> This tradition which comes from the apostles develops in the Church with the help of the Holy Spirit.[2]

Jewish tradition, 'the discipline which establishes the correct practice and interpretation of the Torah', is also, as Rabbi Leon Yagod explains, content in the first place and process only in the second: 'Generally, it refers to the beliefs, doctrines, customs, ethical and moral standards, and cultural values and attitudes which are transmitted orally or by personal example. Under this designation, the process of transmission itself is included.'[3]

In Catholicism, Tradition in the theological sense ('Tradition' with a capital T) is, as the deposit of faith, likewise distinguished from the progressive growth of the Church's understanding of her beliefs through explanation and interpretation (exegesis). However, the authentic development of doctrine can never involve a fundamental change in any part of the original content of belief, as St Vincent of Lérins made clear in the fifth century:

> Let that which formerly was believed, though imperfectly apprehended, as expounded by you be clearly understood. Let posterity welcome, understood through your exposition, what antiquity venerated without understanding. Yet teach still the same truths which you have learnt, so that though you speak after a new fashion, what you say may not be new. . . .
>
> But someone will say perhaps, 'Shall there be no progress in Christ's Church?' Certainly; all possible progress. . . . Yet on condition that it be real progress, not

---

[1] Donald Attwater, ed., *The Catholic Encyclopaedic Dictionary* (London, 1931), p. 498.

[2] *Dei Verbum*, II, 8. A good definition of Tradition in its objective aspects is also given by Yves Congar, OP:

> In the objective sense it [Tradition] is the unanimous belief common to the whole Church, considered not only from the aspect of present-day Catholicity, but from that of its continuity, and identity even, throughout the ages; it is the practice of the faith common to the faithful today, to the preceding generations from whom they inherited it, and through them, to the apostles and first Christians themselves. It is the heritage of the Catholic Communion, a heritage that is truly 'catholic' and total, which greatly surpasses the part that is recorded, and even more the part that we have understood and are capable of explaining. (*Tradition and the Life of the Church*, p. 35)

[3] Yagod, 'Tradition', *Encyclopedia Judaica*, XV, col. 1308.

alteration of the faith. For progress requires that the subject be enlarged in itself, alteration that it be transformed into something else. The intelligence, then, the knowledge, the wisdom, as well of individuals as of all, as well of one man as of the whole Church, ought, in the course of ages and centuries, to increase and make much and vigorous progress; but yet only in its own kind; that is to say, in the same doctrine, or the same sense, and in the same meaning.[4]

In striking contrast with the received Judaeo-Christian teaching, the Rahner–Vorgrimler theological dictionary of 1965 defines Tradition no longer primarily as content, but as the *process* of handing down this content, the 'progress' spoken of by St Vincent:

> Tradition for Catholic theology is the process whereby revealed truth (Dogma), ultimately derived by oral preaching from the original bearers of Christian revelation (particularly Jesus Christ and the Apostles) is transmitted by the Church, with the assistance of the Holy Spirit, and thereby developed; and the truth thus transmitted.[5]

Content or Process?

It may seem possible to invoke linguistic facts to support this novel notion of Tradition as primarily process, given that the Latin noun *traditio* referred in the first place to the action of transmitting a thing, not to the thing transmitted. *Traditio* derives from the transitive verb *trádere*, which in turn comes from an earlier *transdere*, 'to give across'. Lewis and Short's *Latin Dictionary* glosses *tradere* (*trado*) as 'to give up, hand over, deliver, transmit, surrender, consign' (pp. 1883–84). Consequently, the primary meaning of the deverbal noun *traditio* is indeed 'giving up, delivering up, surrender'.[6] Cassell's *New Latin Dictionary* (p. 609), citing Quintilianus and Tacitus, gives the related deverbal meaning of 'a giving over by means of words', which introduces in turn a series of secondary, metaphorical meanings: 'a teaching, instruction' and 'a saying [or custom] handed down from former times, a tradition'. Lewis and Short's *Latin Dictionary* (p. 1883) adds 'livery, a delivery of possession' as a standard Roman legal term (Lewis and Short). Significantly, it was in the first of these transfered concrete senses that the word was used by early Christians as a religious term. A semantic analysis of biblical and patristic Latin usage shows that for the Church Fathers, 'tradition' generally meant things handed down, *not* the act of handing them down.[7]

---

[4] *Commonitorium*, chs 22, 23.
[5] K. Rahner and H. Vorgrimler, *Concise Theological Dictionary* (London, 1966), p. 507.
[6] This semantic usage was perpetuated in the Romance languages: Spanish *traición*, Portuguese *traição*, French *trahison*, 'betrayal' (whence English *treason*) and (with different suffixes) Italian *tradimento* and Romanian *trădare*.
[7] Rainer Kampling notes that

> When *traditio* did not refer strictly to the transmission of property, it assumed a metaphorical usage which, however, is rarely met in non-Christian [Latin] authors. Christian authors used the word *traditio* early and explicitly in a metaphorical sense, qualifying it more precisely with adjectives and genitives. Thus we find Tertullian using *traditio evangelica* (Adv. Marc., V, 19, 1), *traditio apostolorum* (De Praescript. haer. 21, 6), and *traditio catholica* (De Monog., 2, 1), all in the sense of a teaching received by tradition. Tertullian

The verb *tradere* and the noun *traditio* correspond formally to the Welsh *traddodi* and *traddodiad*, and to the Greek παραδίδομαι and παράδοσις, which had the same range of meanings. However, in the Gospels of St Matthew and St Mark, *parádosis* always refers to the rabbinical customs of the Jews (ἡ παράδοσις τῶν πρεσβυτέρων), and it is to these that the reproach 'You leave the commandments of God, and hold fast the tradition of men' (Mk 7.8) refers.[8] As theological terms, the Greek *parádosis* and the Latin *traditio* were approximations of older Semitic concepts.

The Syriac (Aramaic) word for 'tradition' is *mašlmānuthā*, from the root ŠLM meaning 'to hand over, deliver' (cf. Arabic *salima* 'to hand over (safely)'), whence *salām* 'peace'[9] and *islām* 'submission' are derived. According to R. Payne Smith's *Compendious Syriac Dictionary* (p. 307), the primary meaning of *mašlmānuthā* is 'handing down, handing over, delivery . . .', the word's semantics thus paralleling closely those of Latin *traditio*. However, in the lexical group to which it belongs there was also a strong sense of finishing or completion, cf. *ašlem* 'to finish' and *šallem* 'to achieve'. This suggests that the original transfered meaning of *mašlmānuthā* was something handed down in a definitive way, i.e. a set tradition. Other Syriac words used for 'tradition' in a Christian sense were *yulpānā* (in Gal. 1.14), literally 'teaching, doctrine' and *puqdānā*, lit. 'commandment, precept' (2 Thess. 2.15), both with concrete meanings.

Hebrew had two distinct words corresponding to the Christian concrete notion of tradition: *masōreth*, which denoted religious tradition generally, and *qabāla*, the name given to the mystical tradition. According to Feyerabend's dictionary of biblical Hebrew (p. 185), *masōreth* originally meant 'bond, fetter' and thence 'obligation, duty'. Since the root of this noun is the verb *māsar*, 'to give, commit', God is the agent of the action: He imposes on mankind a law of tradition. The Latin word corresponding semantically to *masōreth* is not *traditio* but *religio*, 'binding, obligation: to God, hence religion', and indeed the Jews, like orthodox Catholics, do not force a rational distinction between religion and tradition. The Jewish or Catholic religion *is* tradition. The other word, *qabāla*, derives from the verb *qabal*, 'to take, receive, accept; to admit, adopt' (Feyerabend, p. 293), the latter stemming in turn from the adverb *qobel*, 'before'. A *qabāla* in its fullest sense was therefore a teaching or practice received from an anterior source, which in Judaism is Divine Revelation. In this word, man is the agent, receiving from God the tradition by which he must regulate his life.

Both Hebrew terms point unequivocally to a deposit, a content given by God and received by man. Moreover, the emphasis is strongly theocentric: tradition, as religion, is ultimately the work of God, not of man. This theocentricism is even stronger in the religious terminology of Arabic-speaking Christians and Muslims, for whom 'tradition' is *taqlīd*, from *qilada* 'to adorn, invest, confer', and glossed in Wehr's Arabic-English dictionary as 'imitation, copying; blind, unquestioning adoption (of concepts and ideas); uncritical faith (e.g. in a source's authoritativeness); adoption of the legal decision of a *madhab* (Isl. Law); tradition; convention, custom, usage' (p. 786). Again, the root idea is God's endowing or 'adorning'

---

also used *traditio*, or its plural, in the sense of 'transmitted customs'. ('Tradition', in Peter Eicher, ed., *Dictionnaire de théologie* [Paris, 1988], p. 795)

8 Ἀφέντες τὴν ἐντολὴν τοῦ Θεοῦ κρατεῖτε τὴν παράδοσιν τῶν ἀνθρώπων. Coptic borrowed the Greek word directly: παραδοcιc.

9 Eastern Aramaic *šlāmā*, Western Aramaic *šlomo* 'peace' and Masoretic Hebrew *šālôm*.

213

man with a religion. The Semites, then, conceived tradition principally as man's response to Divine Revelation. However, the Greeks, like the Romans, had no words in their language corresponding exactly to the Hebrew *masōreth* and *qabāla*, and adapted the basic concept in the form of their deverbal noun for 'handing over, delivering' (*parádosis*). The religious idea was dedivinized and mechanized in the translation, so that 'tradition' could be seen by the literal-minded of a later age as referring in the first place to man's work of transmitting.

That most of the Semitic terms for 'tradition' clearly indicate content rather than process is not surprising when one considers that most European vernaculars also lacked specific nouns denoting exclusively the handing down of religious traditions. For medieval Europeans a tradition in the concrete sense was simply a custom, and all languages had native terms for this. The Latin *traditio* itself passed into European languages with initially concrete meanings, for instance the Old French *tradiccion*: 'delivery, transmission' in both a general and a juridical sense.[10] It was only during the Renaissance that efforts were made to coin vernacular terms to translate the Latin religious term more exactly. The English word *tradition* dates from the fifteenth century, when its meaning was 'that which is handed down as a belief or practice in a community'. In English texts of the following century the secondary (if etymologically primary) meaning of 'delivery, transmission' appeared in literature.[11] The German loan translation *Überlieferung* ('delivering over', the second element borrowed from Latin *liberare*) dates from the same period.[12]

European languages that did not simply borrow the Latin word invented terms for 'tradition' applicable in both religious senses but with semantically concrete primary meanings. Russian adapted its word предание (which could also mean 'legend'), a calque on the Greek παράδοσις.[13] In Irish, *traditio* was rendered *seanchas* (from *sean* 'old') which also means 'traditional law', this word surviving alongside the more modern loanword *traidisiún*. The Finno-Ugrian vernaculars translated the religious concept with words meaning 'bequest, inheritance' (Hungarian *hagyomány* and Finnish *perinne*) as did Icelandic *arvalæring*, literally 'inheritance lore'. In these languages, 'law' and 'bequest' were the closest possible adaptations of *traditio* in its concrete sense. That tradition is something essentially old, and therefore inherited rather than partly created in the present, is also the tenor of the Breton term *hengoun*, literally 'old memory'.

What this linguistic evidence indicates is that for most of Christian history the idea of tradition foremost in people's minds was the concrete one: were this not the case, one would expect in the newer literary languages a whole series of coinages based on deverbal nouns like the original *traditio* itself. It was this pre-existent objective approach to the concept, a cultural reality transparent in so many word histories, that modern theology set out to challenge.

---

[10] A. Q. J. Greimas, *Dictionnaire de l'ancien français jusqu'au milieu du XIVe siècle* (Paris, 1968), p. 636.

[11] *The Oxford Dictionary of English Etymology*, 1966, p. 935.

[12] *Duden Etymologie: Herkunftswörterbuch der deutschen Sprache* (Mannheim, 1997), p. 421. The German word was the model for Dutch and Danish *overlevering*; Swedish *överföring* literally means 'carrying over'. All these languages now have as synonyms the Latin term: Ger. *Tradition*, Du.Dan.Sw. *tradition*.

[13] Modern Russian, following other Slavonic languages, also uses the latinism традиция.

Living Tradition

While Catholic Tradition is primarily content and not process, it is in no sense dead. The dogmas and pious beliefs that constitute theological tradition are guarded and transmitted by the Church which teaches, preaches, professes and practises them in her daily life. The doctrinal tradition comes alive when reasonable propositions are, by the grace of the Holy Spirit, believed by human beings and become faith. Individual disciplinary and liturgical traditions are also living. Although the rite of Mass is basically an assemblage of prayers and rubrics, its forms become a living reality when validly celebrated by an ordained priest on behalf of the Christian people. It is thus the constant actuation of the Church's worship since the time of Christ that gives the liturgical tradition its living character. A similar concept of living tradition is found in the Orthodox Church. Fr Georges Florovsky writes that

> [t]he main distinctive mark of the Eastern Orthodox Church is its traditional character. Devotional forms and manners of the Early Church are preserved, or rather have been continuously used for centuries, without any major changes. For an outsider they may seem obsolete and archaic, and the whole system of worship can be mistaken for a lifeless piece of antiquity. Nonetheless, *in the process of its continuous use the rite was kept alive, and is still a natural means of a spontaneous expression of the religious life*. It is felt, within the tradition, to be the most adequate vehicle of the spiritual experience.[14] (Emphasis added)

Tradition is a 'living continuity' with the apostolic past. However, in a higher and more real sense, the life of tradition is perpetual contemplation of the Eternal Truth and love of the Eternal Good. This teaching of the Latin Church is echoed in Eastern Orthodox theology: 'In order to live within Tradition, it is not enough simply to give intellectual assent to a system of doctrine; for Tradition is far more than a set of abstract propositions – it is a life, a personal encounter with Christ in the Holy Spirit.'[15]

Hence sudden or constant changes to the set forms of the Church's contemplative life (such as Catholics have experienced since Vatican II) would appear to be the very antithesis of the life of Tradition. Change is not a divine attribute. 'The Divine Perfection is eternal and immutable', writes Fr François Laisney, drawing on Plato. 'In heaven the saints "rest" in God, living without change, sharing divine eternity. On the contrary, in hell the damned will be tormented by unrest: the unceasing succession and change of torments . . .'[16]

This religious truth, apprehended by men of wisdom even before the dawning of Christianity, was given a solid moral basis by Aristotle, who wrote that

---

[14] Florovsky, *op. cit.*, p. 182.
[15] Ware, *op. cit.*, p. 206.
[16] François Laisney, *Archbishop Lefebvre and the Vatican 1987–1988* (Dickinson, Texas, 1989), p. 153. According to Plato (Laws, VII, 7973):

> Change – except when it is change from what is bad – is always, we shall find, highly perilous, whether it be change of seasons, of prevailing winds, of bodily regimen, of mental habit, or, in a word, change of anything whatever without exception, except in the case I have just mentioned, change from bad.

God, whose nature is one, enjoys one simple pleasure for ever. For there is an activity not only of movement but of immobility, like that of thought, and there is in rest a more real pleasure than in motion. Yet, as the poet says, 'in all things change is sweet'. It is sweet to us because of some badness in us. For a nature that needs change is bad, just as a changeable person is bad, and it is bad because it is not simple or good.[17]

Enter Johann Adam Möhler

A radically different idea of the living character of Tradition was the contribution of Fr Johann Adam Möhler (1796–1838), a leading light of the nineteenth-century Tübingen school, and a powerful influence on twentieth-century Catholic theology. Möhler's Germanness is of capital importance in any attempt to assess his work, for this young scholar, fired with the nationalism of his Romantic contemporaries and pained by the spectacle of a people divided by religion, determined to integrate contemporary German idealist thought and the Neo-Kantian liberal Protestantism of Friedrich Schleiermacher into what he deemed the inferior and atrophied Catholic theology of his day.[18]

Möhler's close study of the Church Fathers convinced him that Christian doctrine had progressed according to what amounted to a Hegelian dialectic. In history the 'thesis' of Catholic faith had been repeatedly stimulated into further self-awareness by the challenge of its antithesis, heresy. Consequently, it should be possible to heal the divisions between Catholics and Protestants by a frank confrontation of the two traditions. This would produce a new and higher synthesis of orthodoxy.[19] Johann Möhler was thus a forerunner of modern horizontalizing ecumenism.

Fr Henry Nienaltowski has observed that while under the influence of the Protestant theologian August Neander, Möhler

> came as close as orthodoxy could possibly allow to the fundamental thesis of Protestantism in regard to the internal Church and the mystical, internal principle acting so powerfully on the faithful. On this basis of mysticism, Möhler begins to build the structure of his ecclesiology and his theological system for his great debate with Protestantism, and what perhaps in his mind was meant to serve the purpose of the reunion of the Churches.[20]

Classical Protestantism, of course, conceived of the Church not as a structured communion with a hierarchy invested with divine authority to teach, but as a

---

[17] *Ethics*, VII, Ch. 14.
[18] In line with the British empiricist philosophers John Locke (1632–1704) and David Hume (1711–1776), Immanuel Kant (1724–1804) had taught that the essence of things is unknowable, and that only their sensible appearances or external manifestations could be apprehended by the human mind. Theology which dealt with the nature of God was therefore to him a pseudo-science and an irrelevancy; what counted was the religious experience of man. Similarly, for Schleiermacher (1763–1834) religion was not synonymous with knowledge about God, but a mode of subjectivity, a certain way of experiencing the world.
[19] Rondet, *op. cit.*, pp. 103–04.
[20] Henry Raphael Nienaltowski, OFM.Cap, *Johann Adam Möhler's Theory of Doctrinal Development: Its Genesis and Formulation* (Washington, DC, 1959), p. 70.

community of individual believers who acknowledged the Scriptures as their sole authority. Schleiermacher's system, moreover, shifted the emphasis in Christianity from the knowableness of God to the experience of believers. In spite of his subjectivist approach, Möhler was concerned not to deny the reality of Divine Revelation and the divine foundation of the Catholic Church. But, conscious that all heresies err in exaggerating certain elements of the one Truth, he attempted to reconcile these alien concepts with orthodoxy by introducing them as new emphases which, he hoped, would fertilize contemporary Catholic doctrine and promote its progress.

Within the confines of conventional orthodoxy, Möhler thus stressed certain realities and de-emphasized others.[21] In his ecclesiology, the Church was above all 'an effect of Christian faith, the outcome of the living love of the faithful united by the Holy Spirit'. The 'feeling' of the faithful was all-important, the Church itself having taken shape when 'round a single centre [the Apostles preaching the Gospel] gathered all those who shared the same feelings'.[22]

Fr Nienaltowski admits that in this mystical and essentially subjective conception of the Church: 'there is too much emphasis given to God (the Holy Spirit) and to His action as *causa prima*. As a result, *causæ secundæ* (hierarchy, Magisterium) are very much in the background and quite obscure.'[23]

'Subjective Tradition'

More meaningful than the Counter Reformation's emphasis on the visible, juridical, hierarchical Church, was, in Möhler's view, the vision of the Mystical Body as a church of the Spirit and of charity, a communion of grace. Such a playing down of the objective aspects of the Church betrayed a characteristically Romantic disdain of 'mechanistic' conceptions in favour of 'organic' ones. What mattered above all was the vital principle, the notion of a living, ever-growing organism. The Church was a dynamic communion of believers, albeit one committed to an infallible deposit of faith and to a definite hierarchy. What made the Church grow was her members' practical experience of the Faith under the inspiration of the Holy Ghost.[24]

While Möhler accepted the historical meaning of Tradition as the received rule of faith, he introduced into his theology the abstract notion of tradition as process, which he termed 'subjective tradition' in contradistinction to the content, 'objective

---

[21] Möhler's thought, best expressed in *Die Einheit in der Kirche* (1825) and *Symbolik* (1832), became more conservative as it matured. Nienaltowski notes in his article 'Möhler, Johann Adam' for the *New Catholic Encyclopedia* (IX, p. 1005) that Möhler 'exhibited an ideological metamorphosis in his later works, gradually retreating from a mystical and immanent approach to Christian doctrine into an objective evaluation of Christian revelation' – hence his respectability with modern Rome. See also the reservations of an otherwise favourable Fr Congar in *Tradition and the Life of the Church*, pp. 76–77.

[22] Rondet, *op. cit.*, p. 103.

[23] Nienaltowski, *Möhler's Theory*, p. 72.

[24] It is interesting to find a reflection of this idea of Möhler's in the writings of the nineteenth-century Russian Orthodox theologian Alexei Khomiakov (1804–1860). Khomiakov, too, exalted the *sensus fidelium* (*sobornost*) above the Magisterium and, on the ground that the Christian people as a whole rejected the Council of Florence, opposed Greek theologians inclined to accept it as ecumenical. Khomiakov's ecclesiology, while appealing to certain liberal currents in modern Eastern Orthodoxy, is treated with reserve by the traditionalist majority of that Church.

tradition'.[25] For him subjective tradition was 'the ecclesiastical consciousness, the general sense of Christ's revelations, of Christ's promises and of His gifts. Tradition is the living word perpetuated in the heart of believers.'[26]

Möhler's constant emphasis on the process, helped by a literalistic interpretation of *parádosis/traditio*, served to obscure the theocentric character of 'objective' tradition (*masōreth/qabāla*), and to favour an alternative anthropocentrism.

Man as Reference Point

The subjectivist thrust of Möhler's thought was one of the foundations of the 'New Theology' of today, in which man, and not God, is the point of depature in all speculation. According to Dr David Coffey, one of the principal Australian proponents of this methodology:

> [U]ntil recent decades the Christology of the Church, Catholic, Protestant and Orthodox, and in regard to both doctrine and theology, has been grasped and expressed in the 'descending' mode, that is, according to an intellectual process which has its starting point in God and moves from there to humankind. Thus, the event of Christ is expressed in terms of 'incarnation', that is to say, the pre-existent and divine Word of God is said to come down to earth and assume a human nature in Jesus of Nazareth. Implied in this approach, and made explicit in the history of theology, is also a 'descending' theology of the Trinity, of Grace, of the Church, and of all else that comprises the subject matter of theology. . . .
>
> Recent decades have, however, witnessed a revolution in the methodology of Christology. Descending Christology has given way, first in Protestant thought, and now in Catholic, to an 'ascending' Christology, in which the starting point is the humanity of Jesus; and all that we know of God, including Jesus' unity with him, is read off from the history of his life (which includes the history of the people who produced him) and especially from his passion and Resurrection. This ascending Christology, already firmly ensconced in catechetics, is now extending its influence into other fields, the Trinity, Grace, and finally ecclesiology. This is the rightful domain of the *communio* theology, and thus is explained the congeniality with which it fits into the present mode of theologizing, for in *communio* theology the direction of the sacramental movement is clearly from human beings to God. Ordinary inter-personal relations among people, set on the foundation of a shared faith, constitute the point of departure for leading them (us) into a saving relationship with God.[27]

---

[25] Cardinal Newman made a similar distinction in his *Via Media* (t. 1, pp. 249–51) where he speaks of the 'episcopal (= objective) tradition' and the 'prophetic (= subjective) tradition'. The latter is 'the mind of the spirit, the thoughts, the principles which are like the breathing of the Church, the way in which habitually and, as it were, unconsciously, she looks at things, rather than any set of dogmas, static and systematic'. Modern theology also uses the contrast 'active tradition' (= process) and 'passive tradition' (= form).

[26] Nienaltowski, *Möhler's Theory*, p. 30, citing *Symbolik*, pp. 356–57. The translation is that of J. B. Robertson, *Symbolism or Exposition of the Doctrinal Differences between Catholics and Protestants as evidenced by their Symbolic Writings*; 2nd edn, 2 vols (London, 1834), pp. 49–50.

[27] David Coffey, 'The Church as Community', in *Gospel in Word and Action* (*Faith and Culture* No. 17) (Sydney, 1990), p. 47.

This was precisely the position of Dom Lambert Beauduin, one of the prophets of the Roman liturgical revolution. In the latter half of his career the Belgian Benedictine's *bête noire* was the 'Monophysite' orientation of contemporary Catholic theology, by which he meant the tendency to emphasize Christ's divinity at the expense of His humanity. 'We are not Nestorian enough', he liked to tell priests on retreat, tongue in cheek.[28] To a disciple who bemoaned the modern inclination to see in Christ 'only the man, the perfect model for humanity', Beauduin replied, indignant:

> But it's by that that we must begin! The apostles at first saw only a man; by following him they saw his wisdom, his goodness and his miracles, and finally, after a good many hesitations, they concluded to his divinity . . . Man first, who leads us to God: in short, the incarnation.[29]

However useful this 'ascending' Christology may have been as a theological working method or as a reflection for preachers of the social gospel, its effects in the liturgical sphere would be disastrous. When, in 1953, Beauduin criticized 'the somewhat Monophysite character of the Byzantine liturgy',[30] he was being true to an earlier principle of his which asserted that the effectiveness of the Catholic liturgy depended 'not on its becoming better understood but rather more human'.[31] In other words the cultic action should reflect man's search for faith and his efforts to enliven that faith, once found, in union with his brothers and sisters. The customary 'monophysite' approach to worship was, in stark contrast, one that laid the emphasis on mystery and adoration – a 'descending' liturgy, as it were.

Towards a Darwinian Liturgy

The practical difficulty for liturgical reformers like Beauduin was how to invert the axis without departing from the essential practices of Catholicism. A century earlier, Möhler had been wrestling with this very problem. Crucial to it were one's understanding and treatment of the principles and shape of constitutive ecclesiastical tradition. For the German theologian the solution was to think in terms of the immutable principle of each sacramental rite of the Church, for instance the Eucharist's being the sacrifice of the New Covenant, or that Holy Orders was the setting apart of an individual with a special priestly character. Catholicism had bound every such principle to a definite and equally immutable matter and form. Hence for the Eucharistic principle to be realized in the Latin Church there must be correct matter (bread and wine) and form (the Words of Institution) as well as the ministration of a validly ordained priest with the intention of doing what the Church intends by this rite.

Now Möhler (unlike his master Schleiermacher, who celebrated the Lord's Supper on his deathbed with water instead of the wine his doctor had forbidden

---

[28] Sonya A. Quitslund, *Beauduin: A Prophet Vindicated* (New York, 1973), p. 364. This was a rather strange criticism at a time when devotion to the Sacred Heart of Jesus and meditations on His human sufferings loomed so large in Catholic piety.
[29] Ibid., p. 252.
[30] Ibid., p. 253.
[31] Ibid., p. 266.

him to drink)[32] nowhere attacked the established matter and form of individual sacramental traditions. However, he introduced the notion that the general shape of Tradition, no less than the understanding and transmission of doctrine, is subject to evolution. The outward shape of Tradition changed, in fact, according to the spirit and needs of each age: 'Tradition often hands down to later generations the original deposit in another form, because that deposit has been entrusted to the care of men, whose conduct must be guided by the circumstances in which they are placed.'[33]

Simply by virtue of the fact that humanity was the object and recipient of Divine Revelation, the latter's transmission and life in the Church must obey the evolutive processes of the human mind. The Divine Word had to be given human dress, and the human aspects of Tradition (words, terms, practices, customs) accordingly had only a relative value since 'they correspond to the period in which they have been formed, and they change with the changing historical setting'.[34] Indeed Tradition was 'not a fixed set of fossilized statements, but the Word of God living in the faithful. It is constantly developing and has constantly to be rethought in the light of the total movement of human culture.'[35]

In the long run this dynamic 'vitalist' view of doctrine could not leave untouched the received principles of orthopraxis. In the Tübingen school we find the seeds of the twentieth-century *aggiornamento* mentality, the view that nothing in the liturgical tradition posterior to its apostolic foundations should have any permanent value in the Church unless the current Christian mind and the spirit of each age required it.

There was at least one Council Father at Vatican II, Bishop Wilhelm Duschak SVD of Calapan in the Philippines, who openly advocated the logical liturgical consequences of Möhlerian vitalism. During the debates on the Liturgy Constitution, the German missionary spoke in favour of

> an ecumenical Mass, stripped wherever possible of historical accretions, one that is based on the essence of the Holy Sacrifice, one that is deeply rooted in Holy Scripture. By this I mean that it should contain all the essential elements of the Last Supper, using language and gestures that are understandable, adopting the method and spirit of the prayers and words that were used then. . . .
>
> If men in centuries gone by were able to choose and create Mass rites, why should not the greatest of all ecumenical Councils [!] be able to do so? Why should it not be possible to ordain that a new Mass formula be drawn up with all due reverence, one that is suited to, desired and understood by modern man, who lives in a world which is daily becoming smaller and more uniform?[36]

The modern age of ascending theology required a frankly minimalistic approach to worship, made possible by a practical application of the theologian's splitting of Tradition into its component parts. In other words, the actual deposit of faith

---

[32] Alec R. Vidler. *The Church in an Age of Revolution: 1789 to the Present Day* (Harmondsworth, 1961), p. 27.

[33] Nienaltowski, *Möhler's Theory*, p. 31.

[34] G. Voss, 'Johann Adam Möhler and the Development of Dogma', *Theological Studies*, IV (1943), p. 430.

[35] Vidler, *op. cit.*, p. 32.

[36] Wiltgen, *The Wine flows into the Tiber* (Chawleigh, Devon, 1979), pp. 37–38.

including Scripture and defined dogmas ('Tradition') is not negotiable, whereas orthopraxis (the received body of 'traditions'), determined as this is by the dynamic of evolution, can and should be changed according to the needs of the times.

Devaluation of the 'non-essential', 'archaic' elements of Judaism was likewise a characteristic of the modern reform movement that arose in the United States during the nineteenth century. For the Liberal Jews,

> Judaism was primarily a universalistic and moral religion. Only the moral law was binding. Ceremonial laws which could be adapted to the views of the modern environment were to be maintained. Other Mosaic and rabbinic laws which regulated diet, priestly purity, and dress could be discarded.[37]

Tradition and Custom

While this updating of religion may seem reasonable and desirable in theory, the constant practice of the Catholic Church in the spheres of liturgy and discipline has been a cautious conservatism in the spirit of the guiding axiom *lex orandi, lex credendi*. The ancient Jews also viewed their *masōreth* as a law, and it is no coincidence that the Classical Latin word *traditio* had been used a legal term (i.e. 'legal delivery of property'). Accordingly, St Thomas Aquinas taught that the disciplinary and liturgical traditions of the Church are actually canonizations of custom, and custom 'has the force of a law, abolishes law, and is the interpreter of law'.[38] The legal character of customs gave them a permanence within the wider Catholic tradition, hence there could be no question of regarding them as easily discardable accidents of Christian life: 'The customs of God's people and the institutions of our ancestors are to be considered as laws. And those who throw contempt upon the customs of the Church ought to be punished as those who disobey the law of God.'[39]

The liturgy of the Eastern Churches is nothing if not the canonization of custom, even though when modern Orthodox theologians speak of 'living tradition', they are aware that its historical forms have grown spontaneously and organically:

> The Orthodox conception of Tradition is not static but dynamic, not a dead acceptance of the past but a living experience of the Holy Spirit in the present. Tradition, while inwardly changeless (for God does not change), is constantly assuming new forms, *which supplement the old without superseding them*.[40] (Emphasis added)

Eastern Orthodoxy makes the same distinction as Latin Catholicism between 'Tradition' (infallible teaching) and 'traditions' (ecclesiastical customs and pious beliefs),[41] but in dealing with the latter, the abolitionist mentality is altogether lacking. In telling contrast, a relativistic attitude to custom prompted Möhler and his Catholic associates at Tübingen to endorse some of the disciplinary and liturgical

---

[37] Yagod, *op. cit.*, cols 1310–11.
[38] *Summa Theologica*, Prima Secundæ, Q. 97, art. 3.
[39] Ibid.
[40] Ware, *op. cit.*, p. 206.
[41] Ibid., p. 205.

reforms advocated by the eighteenth-century Jansenists and Febronians and firmly condemned by the Church in 1794: the abolition of private Masses, of Communion in one kind, of liturgical Latin . . .[42]

New Models of Church

During the Conciliar debates on the liturgy Pope John XXIII hinted at his sympathy with the same abolitionism when he made the ambiguous remark that 'the Christian life is not a collection of ancient customs'.[43] Most if not all the reforms that would follow the Council had been on the agenda of the apostles of *aggiornamento*, and one of their leaders, French Dominican theologian Yves Congar, has done more than anyone else to promote the ecclesiology of Johann Möhler in modern Catholicism.[44] As early as 1935 Fr Congar was asserting that: 'The Church is not *principally* a social and hierarchical organization . . . but a living organism in which all are members and all take part in the life of the whole'[45] (emphasis added).

Now this statement is true in the sense that the mystical concept of the Church, highlighted by Möhler and consonant with Eastern theology ('the Church is a sacramental communion with God in Christ and the Holy Spirit'), founds and transcends the hierarchical reality of the Church in exactly the same way that the law of prayer founds and transcends the law of belief.[46] The primacy is chronological, not qualitative: the Apostles were united in a common faith in the Trinity before they put into shape after the first Pentecost the ecclesial structures implicit in that faith. Moreover, to stress the juridical and hierarchical aspects of the Church at the expense of its mystical reality can and does lead to clericalism. But just as the liturgical tradition needs theology to justify its perpetuation to the human mind, so too does the Mystical Body rely on hierarchy for its external cohesion and perpetuation in the world.

While recognizing in principle the need for balance and consistently excluding any facile dichotomy between an invisible 'church of charity' and a visible 'church

---

[42] Vidler, *op. cit.*, p. 32.

[43] Wiltgen, *op. cit.*, p. 40.

[44] See, for instance, Congar, *La Tradition et les traditions* (Paris, 1960–1963), Vol. 1 *Essai historique*, Vol. 2 *Essai théologique*. Long before the French Dominican took him up, Möhler had become something of a cult figure among German Catholic theologians. Consider, for example, the extravagant encomium that Patricius Schlager contributed to the American *Catholic Encyclopedia* in 1913:

> Möhler . . . had an uncommonly attractive personality. He was an ideal priest, almost perfect in stature and comeliness, deeply pious and of childlike modesty, with a heart full of affection and gentleness, penetrated with the desire for peace in personal intercourse and for the restoration of harmony between the different creeds. He exercised a peculiar fascination over all who approached him, and men of every belief and party confidently turned to him on all manner of questions. He charmed his hearers by his classic diction, and his ripe knowledge. It may be said that he gave new life to the science of theology; also, and this is greater praise, that he reawakened the religious spirit of the age. He was, in the judgment of a Protestant, an epoch-making mind and a brilliant light of the Catholic Church . . . ('Möhler', *CE*, X, p. 431)

[45] 'L'Église n'est pas principalement une organisation sociale hiérarchique . . . mais un organisme vivant où tous sont membres et ont part à la vie du tout'. See Congar's 'La pensée de Möhler et l'ecclésiologie orthodoxe', *Irenikon*, 12 (1935), p. 327.

[46] Kavanagh, *op. cit.*, p. 46.

of law', Congar has tended to stress the former.[47] At the Second Vatican Council he was successful in persuading the framers of the Dogmatic Constitution on the Church (*Lumen Gentium*) to give preference to the biblical definition of the Church as 'the People of God'. In his commentary on this document, Avery Dulles, SJ, remarks:

> This title, solidly founded in Scripture, met a profound desire of the Council to put greater emphasis on the human and communal side of the Church, rather than on the institutional and hierarchical aspects which have sometimes been overstressed in the past for polemical reasons.[48]

The accent in *Lumen Gentium* is on the 'Pilgrim Church', rather than on the Church Militant as a perfect society. In a more recent work, Dulles develops Congar's metaphoric ecclesiology by comparing several distinct but complementary 'models of church', in which the received notion of 'the Church as institution' is put on the same level as 'the Church as mystical communion' (Congar, Hamer), 'the Church as sacrament' (De Lubac), 'the Church as herald' (Barth), or 'the Church as servant' (Teilhard de Chardin, Bonhoeffer).[49] The old 'institutional' model, maintained in principle by Congar, is heavily outnumbered – and marginalized – by a host of mystical ones.

In these new ecclesiologies the apparent parallel with the Byzantine tradition is illusory, for in the East the mystical definition of the Church is in practice well counterbalanced by a healthy respect for the institutional Church and the faithful maintenance of ecclesiastical custom. Indeed Timothy Ware reminds his readers that 'Orthodoxy insists upon the hierarchical structure of the Church, upon the Apostolic Succession, the episcopate, and the priesthood . . .', and observes that the spiritual and mystical doctrine of the Church held by Orthodox does not cause them to neglect its earthly organization; on the contrary they 'have many strict and minute rules, as anyone who reads the Canons can quickly discover'.[50] The

---

[47] Congar admitted in 1976 that

> just as the crisis in the Church is principally due to the impact in the Church of the overall crisis of civilization and society, so the opposition between Left and Right is having its repercussions in the Church. Taking it to an extreme, there would be two Churches; for two conceptions of the faith and the kind of worship that one should render to God would exist – a dogmatic faith, an orthodox faith based on history, a faith of orthopraxis, with a ceremonial, sacerdotal form of worship; and a form of worship related to earthly justice, in the spirit of the prophets. Of course we can't accept such a division.

Hence, for Fr Congar,

> the necessity for a statute of pluralism and the falsity of insisting on a 'partisan' Church: except that she must indeed defend and promote the cause of Man and that, in the choice of analyses or possible options, not all of these are of the same value with regard to the Gospel.
> (*Challenge to the Church: The Case of Archbishop Lefebvre* [London, 1977], p. 64)

[48] Walter M. Abbott, SJ, ed., *The Documents of Vatican II* (New York/Cleveland, 1966), p. 24, n. 27.

[49] Dulles, *Models of the Church* (New York, 1974).

[50] Ware, *op. cit.*, pp. 243–44. According to the ecclesiology of the Orthodox the Church, as the Mystical Body of Christ, is not a 'whole' consisting of parts, but an organic unity of local communities celebrating the same Eucharist. Yet there can be no unity without structure: 'This organism', writes Alexander Schmemann,

> is the Body of Christ and the definition is not merely symbolical but expresses the very nature of the Church. It means that the visible organizational structure of the Church

philosophy of the Eastern Churches may be fundamentally patristic, with roots in Platonic idealism, but the ecclesiastical polity of the Orthodox is as thoroughly realistic and pragmatic as that of the post-Scholastic Western Church. Second in importance of the seven 'chief characteristics of Eastern theology' enumerated by Professor Bratsiotis of the Athens Orthodox Theological Faculty is 'strict union of authority and liberty', the first characteristic being traditionalism itself.[51]

Tradition as Actuality

Congar's practical downgrading of the 'institutional model' of the Church is especially evident in his criticisms of traditionalist opposition to the New Theology and the liturgical reform, for example his booklet *La crise dans l'Église et Mgr Lefebvre* (1976). The thought and emphasis here are unmistakably Möhlerian: 'The Church is tradition, the handing-down of what has been given once and for all: revelation, sacraments and ministry.' However,

> [T]he great river of tradition is wider than a straight canal with cemented parapets. . . . Tradition isn't the past, it isn't old habits kept up by *esprit de corps*. Tradition is actuality, simultaneously handing on, receiving and creating. Tradition is the presence of a principle at every moment of its development. No break can be admitted. The Church never stops innovating, by the grace of the Holy Spirit, but she always takes from the roots and makes use of the sap which comes from them.[52]

The work in which this passage appears is, admittedly, a popularizing one, but as the writing of a theological heavyweight it reads perilously like an antiquarianist rejection of accumulated custom, the very substance of orthopraxis. It is doubtless Fr Congar's vitalist proclivities that account for the dialectical discrepancy between the above statement and his unambiguous affirmation of 1963 that

> the subjective instinct of the faith should always seek expression in the objective setting of the truths, customs, rites and behaviour on which the Church agrees, and in the fellowship in space as well as time which, in its Councils, has always borne witness using such terms as 'This is what the Church believes, this is what she has always believed; it is what we have received from our Fathers and what we have lived by, faithful to their traditions.'[53]

After Vatican II Congar's thinking on tradition was evidently influenced by his own corrective reaction against a Counter-Reformation theology that did not pay sufficient attention to the distinction, observed by the Fathers and the Councils,

---

is the manifestation and realization of the Body of Christ or, in other terms, that this structure is rooted in the Church as the Body of Christ. ('The Idea of Primacy in Orthodox Ecclesiology', pp. 33–34)

[51] The others are: 'stress on the divinity of Christ rather than on His humanity; theosis, deification of man through grace; emphasis on eschatology (the last things); participation of the laity in the life of the Church; a synodal system of government and contempt for civil power'. George A. Maloney, SJ, 'Eastern Theology, History of', *CESH*, III, p. 638.

[52] Congar, *Challenge to the Church*, pp. 48, 57.

[53] Congar, *Tradition and the Life of the Church*, p. 78.

between 'the subjective instinct of the faith' and 'the objective content received from preceding generations'. In criticizing the post-Tridentine refusal to grant autonomy to 'the subjective, mystical instinct of spiritual things' and its overstressing of 'the aspect of "Church" or "Magisterium"', Congar and the New Theologians have themselves overreacted by emphasizing 'active' tradition (i.e. the role of man as the 'subject' of tradition) to the detriment of 'the passive object of a purely mechanical transmission'.[54]

Hence for post-conciliar liturgists the ideal for the public worship of the Church is a so-called 'liturgy rooted in life'. This liturgy, like modern Christology, is in the 'ascending mode': 'It is not the Mystery that must come down to everyday life. It is everyday life that must enter the Mystery', stresses French Redemptorist Pierre Loret, who is nevertheless confident that this can be achieved without secularization.[55] Fr Congar's own acceptance of the secular ethic in modern Catholic worship is reflected in his personal distaste for traditional orthopraxis, something that emerges graphically – and grotesquely – in the very booklet he wrote to conciliate alienated and angry French traditionalists in 1976:

> I loved the Latin Mass, which I celebrated [in the Dominican use] for nearly forty years, but I wouldn't want to go back to it. I recently assisted . . . at a 'St Pius V' Mass on the occasion of the burial of a friend. To be honest, it was intolerable. Those present didn't say a word; they saw nothing and heard almost nothing of what the priest, his back to the people, was doing at the altar.[56]

Yet thirteen years earlier, when Congar's vitalism was still only mental, he could write, in reference to the venerable rite he would one day find 'intolerable', that

> if Tradition in its dogmatic foundation is an interpretation of Scripture continuing that of Christ and the apostles, the liturgy is truly the holy ark containing sacred Tradition at its most intense. It communicates the spirit of Christ as the radiant centre of the whole history of salvation . . . And it does so, not so much by learned instruction as by realizing the mystery of Christ concretely, here and now, by celebrating and almost acting it, returning to it ceaselessly to illuminate it, like the sun which shines on a beautiful landscape successively from different viewpoints and with a varying intensity of light.[57]

In Praise of 'Ascending Worship'

While the spirit of the liturgical revolution undoubtedly owes a great debt to Johann Möhler, the anti-traditional rites of Paul VI derived their actual design from the antiquarianist programme of reform, with its typical idolization of the practices of the early Church. Both currents converged, in fact, in Fr Josef Jungmann's theories on the development of the Roman liturgy. The basic contention of the Tyrolean Jesuit was that the worship of the early Church, unlike its decadent

---

[54] Ibid., pp. 78, 48–49.
[55] Loret, op. cit., p. 130.
[56] Congar, Challenge to the Church, p. 33.
[57] Congar, Tradition and the Life of the Church, p. 132.

medieval development, was in the 'ascending mode', communitarian rather than numinous and hierarchical.

The primitive Eucharist, Jungmann observes, was man-centred in the sense that it was the act of the Christian community giving thanks to God for His blessings by offering to the Father the eucharistic sacrifice of His Son. Although it was essential that the assembly be led by an episcopally ordained priest who alone had the power to consecrate, the Eucharist was first and foremost the joint, corporate act of the whole Christian people, both clerical and lay. For this reason the oldest prayers of the Roman rite were phrased in the first person plural: *offerimus* 'we offer', *te rogamus* 'we beseech Thee', etc.[58] Although the very celebration of the Eucharist made Christ sacramentally present (hence the element of *latria* or adoration), the liturgical action itself was the work of man, initiated by him in obedience to the Lord's command at the Last Supper. Did the Greek word λειτουργία not originally mean 'public work'?

By the early Middle Ages this post-apostolic approach to the Eucharist had been reversed in the churches of Northern and Western Europe, a negative development to Jungmann's way of thinking:

> In the earlier periods of liturgical life we saw an emphasis placed on the Mass as *eucharistia*, as a prayer of thanks from the congregation who were invited to participate by a *Gratias agamus*, and whose gifts, in the course of the Mass, were elevated by the word of the priest into a heavenly sacrificial offering. But now an opposite view was taking precedence in men's minds, swayed as they were especially by the teaching of Isidore of Seville. The Eucharist is the *bona gratia* [act of favour], which God grants us, and which at the climactic moment of the Mass, the consecration, descends to us. . . .
>
> And so, too, the conscious participation of the community in the oblation of Christ [was] lost sight of, and with it that approach of the community towards God to which the Sacrament in its fullness is a summons or invitation. Instead the Mass becomes all the more the mystery of God's coming to man, a mystery one must adoringly wonder at and contemplate from afar.[59]

Liturgy in the 'descending mode' made the role of the sacrificing priest all-important, Jungmann complained. Symptomatic of this 'clericalization' of the liturgy were the plethora of new prayers addressed to God in the first person singular (*Confiteor Deo omnipotenti*, 'I confess to Almighty God', the *Suscipe Sancte Pater* . . .), the continued cultic use of Latin long after it had ceased to be comprehensible to the congregation, the fencing off of the sanctuary from the nave with rails and rood screens in the West and iconostases in the East, the loss of vocal participation of the laity in the rite, and their increasingly infrequent reception of Holy Communion, which they were soon forbidden to touch with their 'profane' fingers.[60]

Jungmann explains how this new 'awe and dread' mentality stemmed in the main from an orthodox reaction to the christological heresies that had plagued the early Church. The Arians denied that Christ was God, while the sophistry of the

---

[58] Jungmann, *op. cit.*, I, pp. 77–78.
[59] Ibid., I, pp. 82, 84.
[60] All features of what Jungmann disparagingly terms 'the Gothic period' in the history of the Roman liturgy. Ibid., pp. 103–27.

Nestorians played down His divinity. Therefore Catholics stressed the unity of the Blessed Trinity, and blurred the older distinctions between the three Persons in their liturgical prayers. In the Gallicano-Roman rite, for instance, prayers addressed to the Father (*Deus qui . . .*) now ended illogically with *Qui vivis et regnas . . .* invoking the Son. Prayers to the Trinity were interspersed through the order of Mass (*Suscipe Sancta Trinitas, Placeat tibi Sancta Trinitas* etc.).[61] The predominant use of the Preface of the Holy Trinity for ordinary Sundays from the 1752 edition of the missal of St Pius V was a continuation of this same trend.

Similarly, since the Pelagians denied original sin and the need for grace, Catholics, in reaction, multiplied prayers emphasizing the sinfulness of the priest offering the sacrifice. Manichaeism, which resurfaced in the East as Bogomilism and in the West as Catharism, despised all that was material in creation, and consequently the priesthood and the liturgy. Catholicism responded with an exultant ritualism, glorying in an aesthetic worship that sanctified through a direct appeal to the human senses.

Whereas Jungmann sees these 'reactions' as so many distortions of the original ethos of Christian eucharistic worship, the intelligent traditionalist accepts most of them as providential and beneficial gains in the organic growth of the liturgy. Just as the Christian cultus had been enhanced by the adoption of compatible elements from Judaism and pagan religions, so too did these corrective responses to the challenges of heresy have a fertilizing and creative effect. They were catalysts of change and promoters of growth rather than agents of decay, unless, like Jungmann, one takes an immobilist view of liturgy.

The logic of Jungmann's thesis is obvious: since Catholic theology was being renewed in the light of early Christian thought, it was the task of the modern Church to restructure its rites in harmony with these new insights. *Lex credendi, lex orandi.* And the need for reform was not merely limited to the Latin Church: Jungmann's judgements on the 'unhealthy' development of the Roman rite in its received gallicanized form amount, in fact, to condemnations of aspects of liturgical growth common to the *whole* Catholic tradition, since the Eastern rites of the Church suffer from identical 'defects'.

Post-conciliar Rome and 'Subjective Tradition'

The convergence of theological vitalism and liturgical antiquarianism in postconciliar Catholicism is frankly admitted by Fr Avery Dulles in his condemnation of Archbishop Lefebvre's 'objectivist authoritarian' concept of tradition: 'Tradition is not so much content as process – a process that is, in its own words, living, creative and community-based. What Lefebvre dismisses as "Modernist influence" can therefore be defended . . . as a rediscovery of an ancient and precious heritage'[62] (emphasis added).

Here is the logical outcome of the modern split of Tradition into 'objective' and 'subjective' aspects: the subordination of the former and the tendency to absolutize the latter. Accordingly, Mgr Lefebvre's great sin, for the author of the Apostolic

---

[61] Ibid., p. 80.
[62] Dulles, *The Reshaping of Catholicism: Current Challenges in the Theology of Church* (San Francisco, 1988), p. 78.

Letter *Ecclesia Dei Adflicta*, signed by Pope John Paul II in July 1988, was the opposite (and traditional) absolutization of 'objective' (and here by implication 'dead') tradition. Ignoring the real causes of Mgr Lefebvre's 'schismatic act' – Rome's unprecedented tampering with traditional orthopraxis and her toleration of doctrinal aberrations – the Apostolic Letter accused him of

> an incomplete and contradictory notion of Tradition. Incomplete, because it does not take sufficiently into account the living character of Tradition, which, as the Second Vatican Council clearly taught, 'comes from the Apostles and progresses in the Church with the help of the Holy Spirit. . . .'

Archbishop Lefebvre's writings will be searched in vain for any passage denying the latter conciliar statement. In reality the condemnation of 1988 was one of several indications that the pontificate of John Paul II was firmly committed to vitalism, the orthodoxy of which the Holy See has not been inclined to question. Early in the pontificate of Paul VI, Fr George Tavard had noted in an article on tradition that Möhler's 'living Church' theory, which 'began to spread widely after the struggle against Modernism (1903–1907) . . . dominates contemporary theology'.[63]

The Idolatry of Meaning

Although some scholars have labelled Möhler a precursor of Modernism,[64] the Church never condemned his writings precisely because, while his emphases are arguably erosive of orthodoxy, he did not formally deny any part of the Catholic dogmatic tradition. Doctrines were not repudiated, but rather given new meaning or 'transsignified'. Now while it may be true that various modern theologians accept, or sympathize with, certain of the propositions catalogued in St Pius X's encyclical *Pascendi Domini Gregis* (1907), it must be conceded that the more authoritative exponents of the 'New Theology' would claim to reject the central tenet of Modernism: its denial of external Revelation.

Fundamentally agnostic and immanentist, Modernism passes judgement on those teachings of the Magisterium that cannot be harmonized with modern philosophy, science and historical criticism. In this system human experience is the only source of religious truth. The New Theology, by contrast, reinterprets the teaching of the Magisterium without repudiating its bases. It formally accepts the traditional dogmas of faith, but tends to relativize them through a subjectivistic exegesis. Thus the historicity of the Resurrection and the reality of transubstantiation are not explicitly denied, but are deemed of less importance than the practical significance of the phenomena for Christians living today.

In this same vein, modern liturgists claiming to be orthodox shift the emphasis from the words of Our Lord at the Last Supper to His action in instituting the

---

[63] George Tavard, AA, 'Tradition', *CESH*, XI, p. 39.
[64] For instance, A. Fonck, 'Möhler et l'école catholique de Tubingue', *Revue des sciences religieuses*, VI (1926), pp. 250–66; 'Möhler', *DTC*, X (1928), p. 2063:

> Möhler s'est fait du christianisme une conception inspirée des théories de Schleiermacher qu'on ne conçoit pas qu'il ait abandonnée, qu'on ne conçoit même pas qu'il ait pu abandonner, tant elle s'accordait avec son tempérament mystique et par là on peut avouer que Möhler a été un précurseur inconscient du modernisme catholique.

Sacrament of Unity. According to Pierre Loret, pre-conciliar preoccupations with form and validity smacked of magic:

> [Christ] did not say "Retell this [in memory of me]", tying us to an exact set of words; he gave us the words "Do this", binding us to the deep meanings of the action he performed. . . .
> Here we see God's 'style' of revealing. God does not send magic formulas down from heaven; what we receive are the responsible testimonies of the disciples freely welcoming God's SPIRIT.[65]

Meaning, not reality, is what matters to the vitalists. (Möhler once colourfully described the faith of the primitive Church as an 'orthodox gnosticism' . . .)[66] The 'orthodoxy' of the vitalists is not a heritage to be protected, but a goal towards which the Church strives. Yet God is a Person, not an abstraction, and Christianity is a faith and a way of life, not a mere ideology. Even granted the duty of the apostolic Church to preach the Gospel in an idiom that the people of each age can readily understand, the Catholic approach to doctrine is necessarily realist. Therefore, to the extent that the New Theology leads to a predominantly subjective approach to doctrine, and to the rejection of cumulative custom, it may well merit the same condemnation as Modernism. Dom Aidan Kavanagh has made the apt observation that 'meaning becomes delusion as it loses its connection to reality and falls under the sway of ideology, cant, and fads'.[67]

Doctrinal and ecclesiological developments which allow divine and absolute realities to be eclipsed by changing human meanings are consequences of the Western subordination of primary theology (the liturgical tradition) to secondary theology (the dogmatic tradition). In recognizing the primacy and centrality of the Christian cult, man's meeting place with God, the faithful of the early Church (like those of the East today) understood the sacred liturgy as the work of the Holy Ghost, an organism with its own dynamic of growth.

The contrasting and fatal error of Western Christians has been to view the sacred liturgy not as the heartfelt and life-giving celebration of their faith, but as one principal means of expounding it. In rudely refashioning the Church's cultus in the same way as they reformulated their crude explanations of divine truths, the Reformers – Protestant, Jansenist and modern Catholic – have usurped the Holy Spirit's creative role in the *opus Dei*, the thing intended to be the very heart and treasury of Christian life. And so the mysterious life-giving cult of God has become the 'meaningful' yet lifeless cult of man, with that narcissistic practice, Mass facing the people, as its emblem.

---

[65] Loret, *op. cit.*, pp. 12, 14.
[66] Rondet, *op. cit.*, pp. 103–04.
[67] Kavanagh, *op. cit.*, p. 5.

14

PAX AMERICANA

And now all doubts and hesitations to the wind, and on with the banner of Americanism, which is the banner of God and humanity. Now realize all the dreams you ever dreamed, and force upon the Curia by the triumph of Americanism that recognition of English-speaking peoples that you know is needed.

MGR DENIS O'CONNELL TO ARCHBISHOP
IRELAND (1898)

In America nothing dies easier than tradition.

RUSSELL BAKER

The Cultural Imperative

Historically the Modernist heresy condemned by Pope Pius X was the application in Catholic theology of the principles of liberal Protestantism. However, one important thing distinguished the Catholic Modernists from contemporary liberal Protestants: their determination to remain in the Catholic Church and to transform it from within. As Mary Louise Cozens relates:

> It would seem simpler, having decided that the Church's creed was untrue, to leave the Church. This these worshippers of the Age refused to do, claiming a right to remain within the visible Church and form therein an esoteric body who, instead of moulding their beliefs to her creed, should mould her creed to their beliefs.[1]

The reason for the reluctance of the early Modernists to leave the Church on conscientious grounds (as Lamennais had done) was cultural. All of the French and Italian turn-of-the-century Modernists were individuals steeped in Catholic civilization. In Latin countries where Catholicism was, or had been, the established faith, the sort of religious individualism typical of England and other Protestant nations was inconceivable. The last thing the Latin Modernists desired was to form a sect cut off from the culture that had shaped them. Paradoxically, their plan to subvert the Church stemmed from two sound Catholic instincts: the need to preserve the unity of the Church and appreciation of the inculturated nature of Catholicism.

[1] M. L. Cozens, *A Handbook of Heresies* (London, 1928), p. 83.

Exactly the same policy has been adopted by those who seek to revolutionize the Church today. Despite their refusal to conform their beliefs and consciences to the teaching of the Magisterium, most apostles of heterodoxy and heteropraxis are determined to remain within the earthly structures of the Church, and in their work of subversion their interests are more cultural than doctrinal. The Neo-Modernist objective is, in fact, to change the *culture* in which Catholicism is professed and lived.

An Inculturated Religion

This concern with culture is all the more significant in that Catholicism is a religion and not a mere philosophy, an ideology, or a set of theological propositions. Its core teachings are set in a distinct way of life including not only prayer and rituals, but also social customs and sentiments, intellectual ideals, artistic activities, and a certain political outlook. In other words, Catholicism is not possible without a Catholic culture.

What is culture? The word is so often used, but one rarely reflects on its real meaning. A good definition has been given by Thomas Day, an American Catholic writer:

> 'Culture', in its original sense, means cultivation of the land. . . . From this image of tilling the soil the meaning of the word expanded to include the breeding of animals, keeping of livestock, the building of dwellings, the establishment of laws, the development of customs, and indeed the whole ordering of society – all the things necessary to keep control over land and nature. People who identify themselves with a particular culture have, in effect, made choices that help them find a sense and an order in the chaos of the universe. Their culture is what they choose to remember and cherish. Culture, then, is a way of life, a system of signs and symbols which people call their own. Individuals communicate with one another through culture's symbols (language, dress, manners, etc.). Christianity and all other religions of the world did not just announce their messages in mathematically neutral formulas; instead, they 'acted out' these messages, they 'translated' them into the signs and symbols of culture.[2]

Under the Roman Empire Christianity was persecuted precisely because, unlike other religions, it did not fit easily into Roman civilization. Christians had strange rites and customs that distinguished them from their fellow citizens and aroused their suspicion. They drew attention to themselves by refusing to worship the emperor as a god. They also condemned the murderous games of the arena, criticized the institution of slavery and abhorred the sexual licence of their pagan contemporaries. The Christian emphasis on charity, compassion and forgiveness struck pagan Romans as cowardly and weak.

---

[2] Thomas Day, *Why Catholics Can't Sing: The Culture of Catholicism and the Triumph of Bad Taste* (New York, 1990), pp. 7–8.

The Danger of Decontextualization

The Reformation tradition beginning in the sixteenth century was not simply a heretical movement, but a reculturation and ultimate exculturation of Christianity. It was an attempt to remove Christian belief and practice from the cultural setting to which it had always belonged and to place it in a different, more secular one. In Western Catholic civilization, religious authority was vested in the Church as guided by the Roman Pope. In the new Protestant culture, religious authority became a function of the state, and the new autonomous churches became government departments. The principle *cujus elector, ejus religio* meant not only that Christians must adopt the religion of their rulers, but that rulers had the right to determine the beliefs and practices of the official religion.

The consequences were legion. In Catholic culture God was publicly worshipped in a sacral language. In Protestantism the liturgy was in the language of the surrounding secular culture. Other vestiges of the past out of harmony with contemporary secular culture – fasts, vestments, celibate clergy, monasticism and so on, soon disappeared. At first, a form of Christian belief, corrupted by heresy, was removed from its Catholic cultural context into a secular one which nevertheless professed a religious outlook. But as these societies became increasingly godless, especially during the twentieth century, the local forms of Protestantism tended to shed what remained of their religious culture. A new religion founded exclusively on the Bible easily became a philosophy based on the desire to accommodate Christian belief to the parameters and dictates of contemporary secular life.

St Pius X, the pope who strove to root out the Modernist heresy, was equally concerned to revitalize Catholic life, and to this end launched his liturgical renewal. During the subsequent pontificates of Benedict XV, Pius XI and Pius XII, the Modernist danger seemed to have passed. Candidates for the priesthood were by now required to swear an anti-Modernist oath, rigid doctrinal orthodoxy was enforced in all Catholic teaching institutions, and theologians deemed unsafe, like Pierre Teilhard de Chardin, were kept in check. However, the cumulative effect of these measures was not to destroy Modernism, but to cause it to mutate and nourish other theological orientations more apt to subsist within the framework of official orthodoxy, Möhlerian vitalism being the principal one.

The American Era

Repressed in Europe, the new ideas – or rather their spirit – would find a more favourable climate in North America. The poisons in question may have been European in origin, but American influence eventually ensured their spread through the Mystical Body. But why *American* influence? The reason is historical. Since Christianity was born in the Roman Empire, the culture indispensable to the Catholic faith in most places took on a strong Graeco-Roman stamp. In the same way the culture of modern Catholicism is being reshaped by that of the dominant world power today: the United States of America. On analysis, the so-called 'spirit of Vatican II' – the triumph of individualism over collectivism as distinct from the orthodox teaching of the Council – reveals itself to be largely an American thing.

In his lucid study of the initial phase of the liturgical revolution, French professor Louis Salleron devotes a whole chapter to the cultural context of the new

Catholicism. What created this changed context, according to Salleron, was the Second World War. 'We are confronted', he writes,

> with the imposing fact that liturgical subversion, which cannot be dissociated from the crisis affecting the Church as a whole, is the direct result of the war and its aftermath. At first this relationship seems strange. What can the fighting between 1940 and 1945 have to do with the way of saying Mass, the disappearance of Gregorian chant, and all the other changes of this kind? And yet the relationship is close, and undeniable.[3]

Professor Salleron goes on to contrast the First World War, a mainly European conflict ending in the victory of a coalition, with the Second World War, which spread over the whole globe and which – even though a coalition was involved – really culminated in the victory of the United States over Nazi Germany and its allies. The Americans' strongest ally in their fight had been Soviet Russia, and so the allied victory of 1945 led to the division of Europe into two spheres of influence, a Russian sphere in the east and an American sphere in the west. 'After their victory Europe's liberators', Salleron continues,

> were also its conquerors. Now every occupation by a victorious army means the importation of the ideas of the occupying nation. This is true even when the occupier is a hated enemy. When Napoleon conquered Europe he was not loved, but he introduced everywhere the ideas of the French Revolution. When the occupier is actually a liberator, people welcome his ideas even more willingly.[4]

Certainly it would be unfair to compare American influence in Western Europe to the political despotism and social slavery introduced by the Soviets into the satellite states of the East. America's intentions towards Europe were undoubtedly benevolent, and American generosity is, after all, proverbial. Europe had nonetheless a high price to pay for its liberation from Nazi tyranny: the loss of its cultural autonomy and, ultimately, of much of its cultural integrity. Indeed:

> A liberated Europe, a Europe saved, was also a conquered Europe. For democratic Europe had not delivered itself from fascist Europe by its own strength. She had been delivered from it by the forces of American democracy and those of Soviet democracy. When, in 1945, Europe professed again the values of democracy, it was the values of American democracy and Russian democracy she was professing.
>
> After the war Europe attempted a recovery on the basis of her own values. And, since her political values had been submerged by those of America and the Soviet Union, she appealed to her deeper, most ancient, safest values: the values of Catholicism. Hence the magnificent efforts of Robert Schuman [in France], of Adenauer [in West Germany], and of De Gasperi [in Italy]. But they could not see their plan through. We must candidly admit that it was a failure.[5]

---

[3] Salleron, *op. cit.*, p. 61.
[4] Ibid., p. 62.
[5] Ibid., p. 63.

Apostles of Democracy

During the critical postwar period when the United States was supervising and financing the reconstruction process, the fundamental principles of American popular democracy were implanted in the culture of Western Europe. Apart from a strong sense of gratitude towards the United States which opened the minds of most Europeans to the American worldview, the fact that the Americans professed belief in Christianity, and the fierce Communist persecution of the Church in Eastern Europe, tightened the emotional bonds between Catholics and their liberators from across the Atlantic.

At the same time, since the *raison d'être* of the American ideology being promoted was the destruction of fascism, and since the United States' allies in this crusade had been the Russian Soviets, the American hegemony paradoxically advanced the spread of Marxism in Western Europe. Americans detested Communism, but they detested fascism more. Indeed, as Louis Salleron points out, American and Soviet ideology had more in common than at first appeared:

> One might have thought that Soviet influence and American influence would partially cancel each other out, so apparently opposed were the U.S.S.R. and the U.S.A. But the opposition is more of a rivalry in the areas of political and economic life. Certainly one cannot lump the two countries together, but basically their philosophies are the same, in that they are forms of democratic humanism. It might be an atheistic humanism in the U.S.S.R., and a deistic humanism in the U.S.A., but centuries earlier Pascal had noted the similarity between atheism and a deism without dogma. In fact between the declared materialism of Soviet atheism and the latent materialism of American deism, there are deep affinities. The common denominator of the religions of the two countries is a marked anthropocentrism which is in radical contrast with the theocentrism of Catholicism.[6]

Here we have the essential problem. American democracy, no less than Communism, is based on the anthropocentric view of life that gained currency during the eighteenth century. While the American ethos admits the existence of God, it does not enjoin any particular beliefs about this deity and His requirements of mankind. Making God a potential irrelevancy is only one step away from denying His existence altogether.

Clipping the Right Wing

Catholicism, by contrast, is naturally theocentric. It was logical, therefore, that after the French Revolution the popes should have preferred conservative governments of the Right, which assigned Christianity a central role in the national culture, to left-wing Liberal and Marxist governments which sought to minimize or destroy the influence of religion in society. The reigning pontiff at the time of the American liberation of Western Europe was Pius XII. This pope was no exception to the traditional Roman preference for conservative governments, all the more so in that his pontificate and the preceding one had seen Communist attempts to

---

[6] Ibid., pp. 66–67.

stamp out the Christian faith in Russia, Spain and Mexico. Whatever the faults of the Fascists, they at least recognized – even if for the wrong reasons – the import-ance of the Catholic tradition. The Lateran Treaty of 1929 with Mussolini had been largely beneficial to the Church. Hitler had come to power in Germany in 1933 with the backing (however unenthusiastic) of the Catholic Centre Party, and Pius XII was culturally a germanophile who surrounded himself with German advisers and servants.

The American liberation of Europe brought to the attention of the world the genocidal atrocities committed by the Nazis against Jews, Slavs, Gypsies and other peoples. World liberal opinion was outraged, and newspaper editorials asked why the Pope, who presumably knew what had been going on in Catholic countries, had made no strong public condemnation of the war crimes of the Germans and their allies. The Vatican's reply, which gave little satisfaction, was that to have made such a condemnation would only have aggravated the sufferings of the victims, and furthermore risked provoking a wholesale persecution of the Church. A Rome compromised with the worst of the Old World would soon have to answer to the most powerful and conscientious nation of the New, one that proudly styled itself 'God's own country'.

During the late 1940s and the 1950s the Vatican relied no less than the rest of Western Europe on American financial support. But in this particular case most of the aid came directly from the coffers of the rich American Catholic Church. Cardinal Francis Spellman, Archbishop of New York, tireless apostle of charity and financial wizard, was instrumental in helping to set the Roman Church on its feet again. Here too, there was a price to pay for the Vatican's dependence on American money: a new openness to American-style democracy and the gradual breaking of the conservative alliances of the prewar period.

The new climate of American-style democracy in Western Europe, and Pius XII's hesitant change of foreign policy, announced a general swing to the Left that emboldened the Modernist elements in the churches of France, Germany, Belgium, Holland and Italy to come out of the woodwork. It was precisely at this time, in the 1950s, that the floodgates of liturgical revolution were unwittingly loosened by the Pope. Then, after the death of Pius XII in 1958, a liberal-minded pope was elected, to the delight of the progressives. John XXIII, as Bishop Angelo Roncalli, had himself been under suspicion of sympathizing with the spirit (though not the tenets) of Modernism during the pontificate of St Pius X.[7]

Pope John was also a close friend of the Benedictine Dom Lambert Beauduin, the pioneer of an ecumenism that put Protestantism on the same footing as Eastern Orthodoxy, and a prophet of the liturgical revolution that would ultimately be forced upon the Church by Pope Paul VI.[8] 'Dom Lambert Beauduin's method is the right one', Cardinal Roncalli had said of the controversial liturgical and ecclesiological theories of the Belgian monk.[9] Significantly, American financial aid to the Vatican reached its peak in the pontificate of John XXIII, which also coincided with the period in office of America's first Catholic president, John F. Kennedy (1960–63).

[7] Peter Hebblethwaite, *John XXIII: Pope of the Council* (London, 1984), pp. 72–75; Didier Bonneterre, *Le movement liturgique de Dom Guéranger à Annibal Bugnini ou le cheval de Troie dans la cité de Dieu* (Escurolles, 1980), p. 40.
[8] Bonneterre, *op. cit.*, pp. 113–14.
[9] Ibid., p. 40.

Affirming the World

Roncalli's main purpose in calling the Second Vatican Council was to consecrate his programme of *aggiornamento*. The Council, held between 1962 and 1965, was essentially pastoral in orientation, and defined no new dogma. Most of the conciliar constitutions were sound, if sometimes less than forthright, statements of the traditional teaching of the Magisterium. But two conciliar documents deeply troubled the conservative Fathers at the Council. *Gaudium et Spes*, the Council's manifesto of *aggiornamento* subtitled 'The Church in the Modern World', seemed rather too impregnated with an uncritical acceptance and even an admiration of much in the contemporary Western world that posed a serious threat to Catholic doctrine, morality and culture. This was evident to Dr Robert McAfee Brown, a Protestant observer at the Council, who warned that

> [t]here is a danger that in the laudable desire to affirm the world, the document may affirm it too uncritically . . . [There is] a temptation throughout the document to assume that the gospel crowns the life of natural man, rather than being, as well, a challenge to, and a judgement upon, that life. The document minimizes the degree to which the gospel is also a scandal and a stumbling-block, by which men can be offended as well as uplifted . . . The making of common cause with others must not be achieved at the price of blunting the uniqueness and distinctiveness of the Christian message.[10]

There were similar deficiencies in the Declaration on Religious Liberty (*Dignitatis Humanæ*), which minimized traditional papal teaching regarding the duty of the state in a predominantly Catholic country to support Catholicism as the true religion, and to limit the public expression and proselytizing activities of all other confessions.[11]

Gaudium et Spes was greeted with great enthusiasm by Americans, Catholic, Protestant and Jewish alike. As for *Dignitatis Humanæ*, it was dubbed at the Council the 'American constitution', and for good reason: its principal author was the American Fr John Courtney Murray. The ambition of this Jesuit theologian had been to impose on the Council the Americanist view of religious liberty, i.e. that all religions have an equal right to be tolerated, and that Catholicism must not have a privileged status where Catholics form the majority of the population. Father Murray and the American bishops who actively supported him in Rome were convinced that their democratic approach to religious ethics, once accepted by the Council, would bring many blessings to the Church.[12] In the past, Christendom had been plagued by the negative legacy of the *Pax Romana*, which had manifested itself as caesaropapism in the East and papal imperialism in the West. The exciting promise of the *Pax Americana* was a new, and better, epoch for Catholicism.

---

[10] Abbott, ed., *op. cit.*, p. 315.

[11] According to many commentators, the Declaration contradicted the earlier teaching of Pius X (*Vehementer Nos*, 1906) and Pius XI (*Quas Primas*, 1925). For traditionalist reservations about these aspects of the Council, see especially Michael Davies, *Pope John's Council, op. cit.*, pp. 67–70, 163–72, 215–16.

[12] The theological problems arising from the Declaration on Religious Liberty are discussed in Michael Davies, *The Second Vatican Council and Religious Liberty* (Long Prairie, Minnesota, 1992).

The Cult of Quantity

The United States, although a predominantly Protestant land, had never had an established religion, and most Americans deemed this its chief glory. By the 1960s the nation's bishops could boast that nowhere in the world had the Catholic faith expanded so prodigiously as in the United States. In Europe the rate of church attendance was dropping drastically, whereas in the United States not only were the bulk of Catholics loyal to the Church, but Protestantism itself was declining and large numbers of Protestants were converting to Catholicism. The rate of conversions was already about 30,000 annually in the 1920s, and in the decade of the 1950s over 1.3 million Americans embraced the Catholic faith.[13] In addition to this, there was an abundant harvest of American vocations to the priesthood and the religious life.

Much the same situation obtained in other English-speaking and mainly Protestant countries: Anglophone Canada, Australia, and New Zealand. All these countries had one thing in common with the United States: the Catholic Church was free to operate in a climate of perfect religious liberty and in regimes that favoured no particular church.[14] At a time when the very survival of Catholicism seemed to hang in the balance in many historically Catholic countries, who could blame the American Catholics from concluding that the principle of religious pluralism was a must for the Church in the modern world?

In the 1960s it was easy to be impressed by the resounding successes of American, or rather, Anglo-Saxon Catholicism. However, in retrospect there was a considerable risk in playing the 'numbers game', in placing quantity before quality. The English-speaking churches certainly were imposing in terms of quantity, but subsequent developments within them, especially the catastrophic falling away from religious practice by the majority of United States, Canadian, Australian and New Zealand Catholics after 1970, suggest that the roots of American-style Catholicism were far from deep and strong. These are the countries today where the Catholic Church is most ravaged by aggressive heterodoxy, secularization and a liturgical anarchy frequently bordering on the sacrilegious.

The Sower and the Seed

While it can hardly be denied that these ills now manifest themselves in other countries, too, there is an important difference to note, one that clearly confirms Christ's parable of the sower and the seed. In Great Britain and Ireland, in southern and eastern Europe, in parts of Latin America and in India, there was on the whole more resistance to the religious revolution, at least until the 1990s. Here the new liturgy of Paul VI may be the norm, but most priests tend to celebrate it with at least a modicum of reverence. Furthermore, many of the popular traditions of pre-conciliar Catholicism – festivals of saints, traditional forms of liturgical singing, Marian devotions, burial customs and prayers for the dead, processions and

---

[13] Francis X. Curran, 'Catholic Church in the United States, Part 3', *CESH*, II, p. 373.
[14] Generally representative was Section 116 of the Commonwealth of Australia Constitution Act of 1900: 'The Commonwealth shall not make any law for establishing any religion, or for imposing any religious observance, or for prohibiting the free exercise of any religion, and no religious test shall be required as a qualification for any office or public trust within the Commonwealth.'

pilgrimages – have remained firmly rooted in the life of the laity. Even in progressive churches like those of France, the Low Countries and Germany there is a strong traditionalist reaction defending and promoting the immemorial rite.

The reason why the seedlings of faith have withered in the soil of the materially prosperous lands of the New World is again the inculturated nature of Catholicism. In the long run, the Faith cannot prosper unless it is enshrined and rooted in an authentically Catholic way of life. American-style Catholicism flourished luxuriantly for a time because, apart from being free to expand in tolerant modern democracies, it was supported by a strong Papacy that upheld doctrinal, moral and liturgical orthodoxy and enforced ecclesiastical discipline.

It is no coincidence that the Catholicism of North America and Australasia used to be remarkable for its ultramontanism: its staunch and enthusiastic obedience to every directive coming from Rome. Other, older Catholic nations were less spontaneous in their obedience wherever local traditions and sentiment clashed with Roman centralism. But when Rome forfeited her effective leadership in the 1960s, the exemplary docility of North American and Australasian Catholics gave way to a disobedience possibly unparalleled in the rest of the world.

Tabula rasa

In the American philosophy man's highest purpose is to assert his 'unalienable right' to 'Life, Liberty, and the pursuit of Happiness' on earth. Eternal life is an optional extra for those who choose to believe in it. Since God, heaven and hell are shrouded in the mists of individual perception, it is the here and now that matters above all. Given the American ascendancy in the world today, it is hardly surprising that the trends and fads of the post-conciliar American Church reflective of this earthbound outlook should now have wider appeal to the Catholics of other lands than the laws and traditions of the official Church.

Moreover, since Catholicism, even Modernist Catholicism, requires a culture in which to thrive, this all-powerful American ascendancy is busily propagating through what remains of the Roman obedience the culture it has now fully embraced: that of modern liberalism. In the post-conciliar era American money still influences papal policy. A case in point was the permission given by the Congregation for Divine Worship and the Sacraments on 15 March 1994 for female altar servers: it was rumoured at the time that the US bishops' conference had applied strong pressure on the Vatican to authorize the innovation.[15] It comes as no surprise that American Catholic progressives should have been pushing for a heteropractic reform of this kind, since the radical feminism that demanded it is in harmony with the secular-democratic ethic to which the missionary *Pax Americana* is fervently committed.

---

[15] When the Vatican finally acceded to the American Episcopal Conference's wishes in this matter, its president, Archbishop William Keeler of Baltimore, publicly stated – two days before the letter authorizing this abuse arrived from Rome – that: 'the decision of the Holy Father to allow the possibility of women and girls assisting at the altar at Mass is a welcome one. . . . I would expect our conference to discuss this matter at its next regular business meeting which is scheduled for November 1994' (*Origins: CNS Documentary Service*, Vol. 23, No. 45 [28 April 1994], p. 779).

At the same time it would be incorrect as well as unjust to view America as the source of all that is wrong in the modern Church. Indeed, today there is a higher rate of religious practice in the United States than in most European countries. In the United States there are also numerous Catholics who strongly deplore the current vocation of American Catholicism as the chief vector of heterodoxy and heteropraxis. But if good American Catholics are still recovering from the shock of this sudden change of direction, it is because, on the eve of the Council, the Catholic Church in the United States seemed to be perfectly orthodox. Few of the faithful were then alerted to the inherent danger in American Catholicism: its subsistence in an alien culture. In considering the United States, one should not forget that this nation was founded by men who rejected the older traditions of Europe and aspired to forge a new world. Beginning with the Pilgrim Fathers, American civilization was built on a *tabula rasa*, a clean slate (or so the pioneers liked to believe). The new white masters of the North American continent were transplanted Europeans, but Europeans with a diminished sense of history. Scorning a past that had persecuted their Puritan forebears in England, they looked enthusiastically to the future, and their real religion was progress, material as well as spiritual.

Brave New Church

Protestant Americans were thus convinced, from their national beginnings, of their messianic role as creators of a new world order, and native Catholics came to be no exception to the psychological norm. Many earnestly believed that Catholicism, combined with American liberalism, freed from its old cultural baggage and pared back to its basic beliefs and principles, would be a great force for the spiritual progress of mankind. As Thomas Day writes of his Catholic compatriots in the 1960s:

> American Catholics justifiably took pride in belonging to the 'one true Church' located in 'the greatest country on earth'. There were other nations, but, according to popular mythology, these countries had inadequate plumbing and were civilized only to the degree to which they had adopted the American Way of Life. If Catholics did things a little differently in other countries, it was because they were backward, or simply wrong.[16]

Historically, the American Catholic Church was the creation of seventeenth-century English immigrants, and eighteenth-century settlers of English, Irish and German stock, immigrants who, because of their religion, were at first unwelcome in a New World proud of its Puritan heritage and its 'modern' culture of rationalism and democracy. For native Anglo-Americans, Catholicism stood for Old World authority and for a traditional way of life viewed as the very antithesis of progress. It appeared for a time that the fate of Catholics in the United States was to live in a ghetto. Then, at the end of the eighteenth century, came a man with the vision and drive to bridge the gap between the Catholic religion and an American culture hostile to it – and needlessly hostile, in his view.

Pope Pius VI named American-born John Carroll the first bishop of the United States in the fatal year 1789. Bishop Carroll, whom Jay P. Dolan describes as 'an

---

[16] Day, *op. cit.*, p. 8.

intellectual heir of the Enlightenment' and whose 'thinking on the nature of the church leaned in the modern direction', attempted what to many minds seemed the impossible at that time: the reconciliation of American civilization and the Catholic faith.[17] A great proponent of the principle of religious liberty, Carroll was also a friend of President George Washington and Thomas Jefferson. In seeking equal rights for American Catholics, the former Jesuit was careful to encourage his flock to participate in the social and political life of their country.

Catholics under Carroll's guidance were at pains to show their loyalty to the Republic, and the Bishop composed special prayers for the government and its Masonic ministers to whom Catholics owed, he said, so many blessings. An indefatigable builder, John Carroll established new parishes and dioceses all over the country, opened schools, attracted teaching orders to America, and founded Georgetown University.[18] The cultivation of the active virtues loomed large in Carroll's teaching, and while he was scrupulously faithful to the discipline of the Church, he favoured the modernization of religious life, looking forward, for instance, to the eventual introduction of an all-vernacular liturgy.[19]

As Archbishop of Baltimore, John Carroll set the tone of American Catholicism: intensely patriotic and accepting of everything in the national culture that did not conflict with doctrine of the Faith. The goal of American Catholics was to be indistinguishable from their neighbours except in their religion, which American liberalism made the private affair of the individual. Jay Dolan notes that Archbishop Carroll's programme of adaptation to the American cultural situation

> clearly pointed in the modernist direction. Though these types of adaptation were more external and would not alter the intrinsic meaning of the church, Carroll did go further and promoted the idea of religious liberty. This touched on the very meaning of the church . . . Carroll celebrated religious liberty not as a pragmatic concession to a religiously pluralist society, but as a human right. This, too, challenged the prevailing Roman Catholic position that error had no rights.[20]

What became the all-consuming Catholic ambition of social acceptance by the Protestant-Masonic establishment would reach its fulfilment two centuries later in the person of President John F. Kennedy. At the time of his rise to power, his jubilant co-religionists overlooked the significant fact that during his presidential campaign the Catholic senator had made a televised speech to a committee of Protestant clergymen in Houston, Texas, solemnly promising that, if elected, he would not allow his religious beliefs, or the Catholic hierarchy, to influence him in the conduct of his office.[21]

---

[17] J. P. Dolan, *The American Catholic Experience: A History from Colonial Times to the Present* (New York, 1985), p. 304.
[18] Annabelle Melville, 'Carroll, John', *CESH*, II, p. 300.
[19] J. Dolan, *op. cit.*, p. 304.
[20] Ibid., p. 305.
[21] Henry James Jr, who knew Kennedy well in the 1940s, recalled of him that

> He found great difficulty in believing most of the tenets of the Catholic faith. Church bored him! He hardly ever went. Religion didn't interest him. He was all for being *au courant*, very much up to date with the things that were going on at the time, but not eternal verities. He wasn't going to drop his religion. He liked the way it made him special, different in a Protestant world. But otherwise it didn't give him the things people need religion for. (Nigel Hamilton, *J.F.K.: Reckless Youth* [London, 1992], p. 357)

How many American and Australian 'Catholics' today does this description fit?

The Great Irish Unculture

The cultural matrix that produced President Kennedy deserves closer examination. Catholics in the United States were a small minority until the massive influx of Irish immigrants in the 1840s. Most of these newcomers were impoverished peasants fleeing famine in Ireland. Speaking their native Gaelic, many of them knew no English at all, and the majority were illiterate. Resented and discriminated against by their neighbours on account of their different religion, language and culture, these Irish immigrants, desperate to improve their lot in life, were highly motivated to become integrated into American society.

Strongly attached to their Catholic faith, and bearing a legacy of hatred of Protestant England, the Irish were not tempted to embrace the majority religion in any form. Instead, they opted to sacrifice their cultural diversity in the interests of social acceptance. Relieved to have left an Ireland where many of them had known only misery, they learned to speak English as quickly as they could, and deliberately omitted to teach their ancestral tongue to their children. The voluntary anglicization of the nineteenth-century Irish was just one further stage in a long process of cultural alienation, since the thread of authentic Irish civilization and its venerable Gaelic literature had already been broken by the Penal Age. Because so few Irish emigrants had any formal education, the secular culture they brought to America consisted solely of Gaelic folk traditions. The rapid loss of these created a vacuum which opened the door to complete assimilation into the Anglo-Saxon civilization of the United States. While the eventual assimilation of all immigrant groups is to be expected, the Irish situation was unique in that it reproduced trends transforming the home country: in this case a cultural suicide perversely driven by a majority of the Catholic clergy.[22]

Recklessly ignoring the Gaelic adage *tír gan teanga, tír gan chroí* ('land without a language, land without a heart'), the Irish clergy wanted to anglicize their people in order to make them ambassadors and missionaries of the Catholic faith in an English-speaking world dominated by Protestantism. As admirable as this goal may have been as a religious objective, it was also criminal, from an anthropological point of view, to deprive a nation of its language and authentic culture in the process. From the long-term consequences of this early Irish experiment in the divorce of identity and culture the wider Catholic Church would have much to suffer. The Irish at home would later regret and attempt – too late as it turned out – to reverse this philistine and impoverishing policy.[23] But in America it found fertile ground and, applied in the religious sphere, laid a sharp axe at the roots of Catholic orthopraxis.

Encouraged to make their Catholic faith rather than Gaeldom the emblem of their ethnicity, the American Irish attempted, in their practice of Catholicism, to appear as inconspicuous, and therefore as Protestant, as possible. For over a hundred years the Irish had been inhibited in the practice of their faith by the repressive

---

[22] De Fréine, *op. cit.*, pp. 71–74.
[23] Since Irish independence the Church has played an active role in the revival of Gaelic, which became a compulsory subject of study in both state and Catholic schools. Nevertheless, by the 1920s the vast majority of Irishmen already had English as their mother tongue, and the nineteenth-century Catholic clergy had been responsible to a large degree for the disastrous language shift which was born of materialism and bred materialism.

legislation enacted by the British government in Ireland. Yet instead of proudly reasserting their religious culture in the free air of America, the immigrants, fearing social ostracism and its economic consequences, clung to the unobtrusive ways of their old penal Catholicism.

Hence in the New World, too, Irish Catholics performed indoors all their religious rites except burials, and shied away from holding religious ceremonies and public liturgical processions. Their priests walked the streets dressed like Protestant ministers in clerical suits. In church the Low Mass, without chanting, was the popular norm, and the hymns sung by Catholics on special occasions were modern, sentimental tunes like those composed by Protestants. And not least importantly, American flags were placed in the sanctuaries of Catholic churches, where they competed visually with the cross.[24]

Hibernian Imperialism

The arrival, mid-century, of German and other continental European immigrants precipitated a crisis in the Irish-dominated American Church. The pattern of cultural conformity eagerly adopted by the Irish was unpalatable to many of the newcomers. In their homelands these latter had not suffered the complete social degradation of the Irish, and so had no inclination to divorce their Catholic faith from their Catholic culture. Thomas Day recalls how 'Many of the Catholic immigrants from the Continent suffered the worst kind of culture shock when they went to their local church and discovered there, not the familiar old folk customs and festivals, but the Immense Irish Silence.'[25]

All over the country priests from Europe set up separate German, Polish, Lithuanian and Italian parishes where sermons were in the language of the immigrants and old-world traditions could be freely practised. Looking on, the Irish American Catholics felt that their own pure faith did not need these 'trappings' which their ancestors, too, had once possessed but did not pass down to them – doubtless for good reason. Thomas Day argues that this attitude was

> an expression of honest cultural preference and it followed logically from a history of the Irish associating religious music with the oppressors. The Catholic Irish farmer, during the years of persecution, heard the sound of the bell and the hymn coming from the Protestant church, but, as far as he was concerned, these things were not beautiful; they were a provocation, a slap in the face. The enthusiasm

---

[24] Meanwhile things were not improving at home in the liturgical sphere. The Belgian Benedictine Dom Bernard Botte writes how, in the interwar period, the liturgical movement

> spread widely in all Catholic countries, except in Ireland. An Irishman who replied to a questionnaire about it said: 'The history of the liturgical movement in Ireland is as simple as that of the snake: there have never been any snakes in Ireland.' In 1915 I attended a funeral in Ireland. I was told it was the only occasion when the Mass was sung. All the clergy of the neighbouring parishes were brought in, and all twenty of them were present to roar out the Requiem Mass. It was appalling. (Botte, *op. cit.*, p. 57)

However, there were apparently also bright spots on the Irish liturgical landscape; see Hemming, *op. cit.*, p. 23.

[25] Day, *op. cit.*, p. 22.

and jubilation of the music only rubbed in the bitter fact of *their* triumph and *his* defeat.[26]

By the second half of the century most of the American bishops were of Irish extraction, and they keenly resented the presence of foreign Catholics stubbornly determined not to fit into New World society. In 1891 Archbishop Gibbons of Baltimore secured the Holy See's rejection of a memorial from German American Catholics asking for better treatment and respect for their cultural diversity.[27] So great was episcopal intolerance of these 'un-American' brethren that a series of schisms took place in the last decade of the century. Ruthenian Uniates were not the only groups of Catholics to seek refuge in other ecclesial communions as a result of Latin persecution. Between 1895 and 1897 hundreds of Polish Catholics in Chicago, Buffalo and Scranton rebelled against their unsympathetic Irish American pastors and formed the Polish National Catholic Church.[28] A similar schismatic church was established by American Lithuanians in 1914.[29]

Practical Catholicism

The American bishops were hostile to non-Irish Catholicism not simply because they deemed it an obstacle to americanization. Particularly abhorrent to many of them was the contemplative proclivities of these other traditions, something that jarred in a Church passionately devoted to the active virtues and somewhat inclined to the materialistic view of prayer as a means to an end. It is no coincidence that the leader of the anti-Uniate bishops in the 1890s was the same Archbishop Ireland who was the central figure in the Americanist crisis that stirred the Holy See to action around the turn of the century.

The xenophobic attitudes of the United States hierarchy of the 1890s reflected their contempt for the culture of the Old World. In their messianic exaltation of the New World, the *tabula rasa*, they proved their filial loyalty to the Pilgrim Fathers. Mgr Denis O'Connell (future Bishop of Richmond, Virginia), saw the Spanish–American War of 1898 as much more than an attempt by the US government to take control of Cuba, Puerto Rico, Guam and the Philippines. For the Irish-born prelate the conflict was a holy crusade. When the war broke out he was in Rome, and he wrote the following to his kindred spirit, Archbishop Ireland:

> For me this is not simply a question of Cuba. If it were, it were no question or a poor question. Then let the 'greasers' eat one another up, and save the lives of our dear boys. But for me it is a question of much more moment: – it is the question of two civilizations. It is the question of all that is old and vile and mean and rotten and cruel and false in Europe against all that is free and noble and open and true and humane in America. When Spain is swept off the seas much of the meanness and narrowness of Europe goes with it to be replaced by the freedom and openness of America. This is God's way of developing the world. And all continental

---

[26] Ibid., p. 21.
[27] Melville, *op. cit.*, p. 370.
[28] Donald Bartoszek, 'Polish National Catholic Church', *CESH*, VIII, pp. 532–33.
[29] Ibid., p. 533.

Europe feels the war is against itself and that is why they are all against us, and Rome more than all because when the prestige of Spain and Italy will have passed away, and when the pivot of the world's political action will no longer be confined within the limits of the continent, then the nonsense of trying to govern the universal Church from a purely European standpoint – and according to exclusively Spanish and Italian methods – will be glaringly evident even to a child . . .[30]

What Catholicism rightly sought in America was, according to the nativists, liberation from the prison of its traditional culture. Archbishop Ireland once declared that 'The religion we need today does not consist in singing beautiful anthems in cathedral choir stalls, vested in cloth of gold, while the nave and aisle are empty of people, and the world outside is dying of spiritual starvation.'[31] Such a statement betrays a bias that has a long history in American Catholicism: the conviction that the traditional Catholic culture in its fullness is at best superfluous to the faith, and at worst a threat to true orthodoxy. Thomas Day makes some interesting revelations about the temper of the pre-conciliar Church in the United States:

I was raised to believe that, on the continent of Europe, Catholicism was almost extinct. The flashy organ playing in French churches or thunderous hymns in the churches of Bavaria . . . were unmistakable signs of decadence. . . . The streamlined American Church was quietly slipping away from these useless, wasteful affectations left over from the past (except in special places, such as seminaries).[32]

Already in the decades preceding Vatican II the spirit of liturgical reform (or, in the American case, liturgical minimalism) was in the air:

The new parishes looked so cheap, so temporary. Two quick Low Masses replaced the big High Mass that used to involve so many youngsters. The boys' choir disappeared years ago. (Catholic parishes in the United States probably got rid of or downgraded more choirs during the 1940s and 1950s than during the puritan purges of the 1960s.) Vespers were discontinued about the same time that the trolley cars were replaced by buses. The efficient Catholic culture of the 1950s had very little room for the kind of religious enthusiasm she had known in her earlier days.[33]

The complement of this contempt for the ecclesiastical culture of the past was, predictably enough, an uncritical admiration of the culture of the surrounding secular society. Thus one is not startled by Archbishop Ireland's conviction that 'An honest ballot and social decorum will do more for God's glory than midnight flagellations or Compostellan pilgrimages.'[34] Another nineteenth-century bishop, John Spalding of Peoria, ignored Pope Pius IX's warnings against modern civilization in the *Syllabus of Errors*, and uninhibitedly extolled 'the marvellous, political,

---

[30] The complete text of this letter, dated 24 May 1898, is quoted in Thomas Timothy McAvoy, *The Great Crisis in American Catholic History, 1895–1900* (Chicago, 1957), pp. 207–10.

[31] H. Daniel-Rops, *A Fight for God 1870–1939*, tr. John Warrington (London/New York, 1966), p. 209.

[32] Day, *op. cit.*, p. 8.

[33] Ibid., p. 16.

[34] Paul Edward Ward, 'Ireland, John', *CESH*, V, p. 540.

social, moral and intellectual achievements which give the nineteenth century its character'. Spalding was a typically American man of action, and once caused a stir by claiming that a concern for learning and philosophy was alien to Christ's ideal of His Church.[35]

This Americanist belief that the traditional cultural setting of Catholicism was not necessary to the Faith itself may be termed 'confessional Catholicism', the diametrical opposite of 'cultural', i.e. traditional Catholicism. In a lecture given in Paris at the invitation of French liberal Catholics in 1892, Archbishop Ireland, dressed provocatively in a clerical suit instead of the episcopal cassock, foreshadowed *aggiornamento* by stating that 'An intimate union of the Church and the age is desirable for both. It is better to study works on social economy than those of Bourdaloue.'[36]

Archbishop Ireland's abhorrence of Uniate priests as well as his 'Roman' imperialism in church government consorted very well with his puritan enthusiasm for progress. There is here an obvious analogy with the combined puritanism and contempt for traditionalists typical of aggressive conservatives and progressives after the Second Vatican Council. In the case of the Americanist archbishop's encounter with Father Alexis Toth, described in Chapter 12, it was as if the married Ruthenian priest, who represented an ancient custom repudiated by the Latin West was (like the Gaelic speakers and Gaelic Leaguers who embarrassed the new anglophile clergy in Mother Ireland) the incarnation of a repressed part of the Archbishop's psyche, an intolerable reminder of things that had been denied, and hence had to be excoriated.

Democratic Catholicism

Potent a model as John Ireland was, the real prophet of the Americanists was the priest Isaac Hecker, a convert from Protestantism, one-time Transcendentalist and ex-Redemptorist. Widely admired for his tireless efforts to reconcile Catholicism and American democracy, Hecker had founded the Missionaries of Saint Paul in 1858. The Paulists were a congregation of priests without vows dedicated to apostolic work among Protestants. Henri Daniel-Rops colourfully writes of Father Hecker:

> A strong personality, whom some regarded as a superman and a saint even during his lifetime, Father Hecker was hostile to book learning, almost impervious to logical argument, but of uncommon energy and generosity. He was, moreover, a mystic, believed himself to be guided directly by the Holy Ghost, and was therefore little inclined to attach much importance to tradition and hierarchical institutions.[37]

---

[35] Daniel-Rops, *op. cit.*, pp. 208–09.

[36] Ibid., p. 210. Louis Bourdaloue was an eminent French Jesuit preacher of the seventeenth century.

[37] Hecker and his circle were accused of semi-Pelagian views by his former collaborator Orestes Brownson and others; the Paulist founder's staunch anti-puritanism and strong belief in the basic goodness of human beings were evidently at the root of confused thinking on original sin. Whatever his theological shortcomings, Fr Hecker was an indefatigable promoter of Catholic doctrine for missionary ends through his publishing and journalistic activities. See David J. O'Brien, *Isaac Hecker: An American Catholic* (New York, 1992), pp. 120, 155, 290.

Displaying certain counter-cultural and quasi-Modernist attitudes which were novel then but are very familiar to us today, the Americanists were vigorously opposed by the tradition-minded exponents of cultural Catholicism, men like Archbishop Michael Corrigan of New York and Bishop Bernard McQuaid of Rochester. These conservatives were outraged when, in 1893, Archbishop Ireland, Archbishop Gibbons of Baltimore, and Bishop John Keane attended the World Parliament of Religions in Chicago and spoke about Catholicism as a religion on an equal footing with others.[38]

Archbishop Ireland was astute enough to recognize the schools as the key to the americanization of the Catholic faithful. Consequently, he opposed segregated parochial schools in which students would imbibe a purely Catholic, i.e. 'Old World' culture. Instead, he proposed that Catholic parents send their children to state schools where provision for the after-hours teaching of religion was made.[39] The conservative Catholics who resisted Ireland's educational policies did so in the belief that state schools were impregnated with the Masonic philosophy of the American government.

Archbishop Gibbons did not share the horror of Freemasonry that was second nature to most Catholics. In the 1880s he energetically defended the Knights of Labour, a secret society set up to protect the rights of workers which had been condemned as Masonic by Mgr Eléazar Taschereau, Bishop of Quebec, and by the Holy Office. Gibbons gave his support to a certain Terence Powderly, a Catholic who had been elected Grand Master Workman of this organization, and he persuaded the Holy Office to lift its ban forbidding membership to American Catholics.[40]

In 1886, on the occasion of his taking possession of the cardinal church of Santa Maria in Trastevere in Rome, Gibbons publicly stated that the success of the Catholic Church in the United States owed everything to the complete separation of Church and state.[41] The underlying principle was, of course, one deplored by the Vatican: when, during the following decade, Pope Leo XIII urged Catholics of France to embrace the French Republic, his advice was for them to infuse Christian principles into the secular government, not to accept it uncritically. Yet this was precisely what the Americanists were doing; and in the process they allowed the secularist principles of American democracy to colour their own Catholicism.

The Catholic schools crisis caused by Archbishop Ireland eventually moved Leo XIII to send a permanent Apostolic Delegation to the United States. The first delegate, Archbishop Francesco Satolli, encountered considerable hostility from an American hierarchy who resented papal surveillance of their 'tried and true' integration policies and their manner of dealing with state and federal governments. In 1892 Satolli reported back to the Pope on the disturbing tendency of the United States' clergy to minimize the differences between Catholicism and Protestantism.[42]

---

[38] Ibid.
[39] Ward, *op. cit.*, pp. 539–40.
[40] William Rohrenbeck, 'Catholic Church in the United States: Part 2', *CESH*, II, p. 369.
[41] Peter Beckman, OSB, 'Gibbons, James', *CESH*, IV, p. 579.
[42] Bro. Thomas Kostka, FSCH, 'Satolli, Francesco', *CESH*, IX, p. 633.

The Phantom Heresy

Three years later, Pope Leo wrote his encyclical *Longinqua Oceani* to the American episcopate in an effort to reconcile its opposed elements and to clarify the Church's teaching on the separation of Church and state. In this letter the Pope stated unambiguously that the American model of the Church fell far short of the Catholic ideal:

> the Church amongst you, unopposed by the Constitution and government of your nation, fettered by no hostile legislation, protected against violence by the common laws and the impartiality of the tribunals, is free to live and act without hindrance. Yet, though all this is true, it would be very erroneous to draw the conclusion that in America is to be sought the type of the most desirable status of the Church, or that it would be universally lawful or expedient for Church and State to be, as in America, dissevered and divorced.[43]

Then, in 1899, responding to the controversy that had flared up in France between partisans of the ideas of Fr Hecker and his conservative detractors, Leo XIII issued a new apostolic letter, *Testem Benevolentiæ*, in which he condemned a whole series of propositions attributable to Isaac Hecker and like-minded American clerics.[44] Americanism, according to the definitions of this letter, consisted of the tendencies to scorn the Church's liturgy in its fullness; to teach the superiority of the natural virtues over the supernatural, of the active over the passive; to question the value of vows and the usefulness of the older, contemplative orders; to frown on spiritual direction and to advocate greater reliance on the direct action of the Holy Ghost in the soul independent of the sacraments. Above all, Pope Leo rejected the Americanist view

> [t]hat in order the more easily to bring over to Catholic doctrine those who dissent from it, the Church ought to adapt herself somewhat to our advanced [American] civilization, and, relaxing her ancient rigour, show some indulgence to modern popular theories and methods.[45]

Cardinal Gibbons, to whom the letter was addressed, had gone to great lengths to prevent its publication. He failed in this endeavour, and when the encyclical appeared, he denied that anyone in the American Church held the condemned views.[46] In the United States Americanism was thereafter dubbed 'the phantom heresy'. Fortunately for Catholicism, the following decades of American church history were dominated by staunchly orthodox prelates like Archbishops Hayes and Spellman of New York, and McIntyre of Los Angeles. But like its more lethal contemporary, Modernism, Americanism hibernated for some sixty years until

[43] § 6. Full text given in Claudia Carlen Ihm, ed., *The Papal Encyclicals* (Beloit, Kansas, 1981), III, p. 364.
[44] The papal text did not target any writing of the now-deceased Fr Hecker but rather ideas put forward in Abbé Félix Klein's preface to Louise de Ravilliax's French translation of Fr Walter Elliott's 1891 biography, *The Life of Father Hecker*, to which Archbishop Ireland had contributed an introduction.
[45] Vincent Holden, CSP, 'Americanism', *CESH*, I, p. 219.
[46] Curran, *op. cit.*, p. 371; Holden, *op. cit.*, p. 220.

the American political and economic domination of Western Europe afforded it an opportunity to reassert itself with a vengeance during the Second Vatican Council.

Indeed in one sense Americanism historically has proved to be far more lethal to the Faith than Modernism. In its early phase Modernism attacked Catholic belief, but those affected by the contagion were mostly intellectuals. Americanism, by contrast, eroded the traditional Catholic culture of the ordinary faithful. The variety of 'liberal' Catholicism pioneered by Fréderic Ozanam, Henri Lacordaire and Albert de Mun in nineteenth-century France (and eventually endorsed in its more orthodox form by Leo XIII) was concerned not with a radical transformation of the Catholic faith itself, but with the pragmatic question of the Church's relationship with modern democratic governments. The democrat Lacordaire and the legitimist Guéranger were equally devoted to immemorial Catholic worship and discipline. It was the peculiar contribution of American liberal Catholicism to introduce the divorce of orthodoxy from orthopraxis that took hold of the liberal Catholic movement in continental Europe and has become the basis of post-conciliar Neo-Modernism.

The perils of Americanism can perhaps best be assessed by its effects on the liturgical tradition, the heart of the Catholic faith. As Thomas Day ruefully admits:

> the majority of Roman Catholic parishes in the United States do not share with the Eastern Rites, the Orthodox churches, and Anglicanism a common understanding of the sung ritual as a symbol of a burning faith. Most Roman Catholic parishes are no longer part of the 'Catholic' liturgical family; maybe they left this family long before the Second Vatican Council.[47]

America's Meltdown

If England was, according to Napoleon, 'a nation of shopkeepers' (*une nation de boutiquiers*), its commerce-loving American offshoot was even more so. The arrival at the White House of John F. Kennedy, son of a stock market investor and importer of spirits, consummated the social 'arrival' of United States Catholics. But the robust faith of this large religious minority, which already had to contend with the assaults of Americanism, was now caught up in the consumer culture revolution, the prelude to economic rationalism. The 1960s saw the largely self-sufficient family units of North America transformed into groups of consumers of factory-made goods, a metamorphosis speeded by the recent advent of television as a potent advertising medium. This economic revolution coincided with liberation movements that inspired the first nationwide generation of prosperous youth to question the conservative ideals of their parents and which added women and minority groups to the ranks of salaried consumers.

The great capitalist counterattack gradually reversed an earlier socialist-inspired reaction to the inhuman abuses of the Industrial Revolution by which the governments of the developed countries implemented policies of interventionism to protect the public from the rapacity of industrialists. But when the postwar 'economic miracle' created by this state regulation of economies collapsed with the

---

[47] Day, *op. cit.*, p. 41.

return to neo-liberalism in the 1980s, the existing respect-based culture fell with it, and a newly unbridled capitalism quickly substituted the horizontalizing 'culture of desire' for vertical social standards. It was characteristic of the new order to adopt compulsory informality as one of its conventions, popularizing – and distorting – the Quaker custom of addressing others by their first names regardless of age or station, and thus sustaining a commercially expedient illusion of social equality.

In promoting a free market economy, the American neo-liberals took full advantage of the recent sexual revolution and liberation ethos to market the products most attractive to the masses: commodities appealing to their baser instincts, such as junk food, cigarettes, alcohol, cosmetics, and vulgar entertainments of all kinds, including rock music and pornography. Illegal trade in mind-altering narcotics accompanied this trend. The abolition of strict censorship and blasphemy laws facilitated the commercial sector's marketing of sexuality and Hollywood's production of films which undermined the Christian faith of the majority of the population. Teenagers with pocket money and part-time jobs were especially targeted, given their future potential as consumers, as were the indulged children of the prosperous.

Traditional morality and religion were the first casualties of this onslaught. In the education system, syllabuses were simplified and 'dumbed down' to accommodate a new generation brought up to be more interested in hedonistic pursuits than in study, and restive of old-fashioned discipline. Meanwhile, in the Catholic Church, the severely pruned Pauline liturgy in flat vernacular translations became the perfect vehicle for making public worship trivial, boring and ultimately meaningless for a population addicted to novel entertainments and intimidated by contemplation and reflection. With strong religious sentiment no longer present to curb human concupiscence, conservative priests found it difficult to guide the spiritual development of their increasingly free-thinking congregations. As the rationalist sociologist R. G. Price has observed of 'America's meltdown':

> The reality in America today is that private industry dominates our culture. The majority of social interactions that people have today are within the context of the marketplace. The profit-driven approach to these interactions is to make all consumers feel as though they are right about everything, and to make them feel good about themselves. The result is that industry, the dominant element of our culture, bows down to the lowest denominator. [. . .]
>
> When soft drink companies produce advertisements that show teenagers hanging out with baggy pants, talking slang, and acting stupid, they claim that 'they are just trying to reach their target market at their level'. This is true, but they are, at the same time, also validating and promoting a type of culture.[48]

Indeed big business soon progressed from influencing cultural and social values to determining them by instituting what the same writer has described as 'the lowest common denominator society':

> Due to profit motive and markets there is no motivation for business to challenge potential customers. Business is not going to tell teenagers to straighten up, tuck

---

[48] R. G. Price, 'Understanding Capitalism Part IV: Capitalism, Culture and Society' (2005), p. 20. At: http://rationalrevolution.net/articles/capitalism_culture.htm.

in your shirt, and get a haircut, because teenagers might not like that, and if they don't like it they won't buy their product, they will go to a competitor. Hence, industry is motivated to tell teenagers to do whatever they want to, and in order to be even more accessible to them they will talk to their target markets on their level. If that level is poor grammar, then so be it. If that level is laziness, then so be it.[49]

Were R. G. Price a Christian, he might have added: 'If that level is apostasy from Christianity, then so be it.' That American Catholicism should come to breathe this poisoned air was a tragedy; that the United States was now the world power made it a catastrophe.

[49] Ibid.

15

THE GREAT HIJACK

It was believed that after the Council there would be a day of sunshine in the history of the Church. There came instead a day of clouds, storm and darkness, of search and uncertainty. Through some fissure the smoke of Satan has entered the Temple of God.

POPE PAUL VI, GENERAL AUDIENCE, 29 JUNE 1972[1]

The reform was the work of arid people: arid, I tell you. You see, I knew them. As for doctrine, I remember how Cardinal Ferdinando Antonelli, of venerated memory, used often to say: 'What are we going to do with liturgists who don't know theology?'

MGR DOMENICO BARTOLUCCI, MAESTRO PERPETUO OF
THE SISTINE CHAPEL (2009)

The Need for Reform

Though often forced to co-exist with governments far less benign than that of the United States, the Catholic Church in Europe showed a remarkable ability to survive and flourish before Vatican II. The post-Tridentine era was distinguished by a superabundance of devotion, sanctity and courage, but it was also, as has been shown, a period in which certain universals of Catholic tradition were perilously narrowed and distorted. Indeed the more closely one examines the shortcomings of the pre-conciliar Church, the harder it becomes to justify the tendency of conservative Catholics to present the doctrinal and liturgical revolution which followed the Council as a thoroughly wicked assault on an ecclesiastical system that had few if any faults.

According to Dr Dietrich von Hildebrand, the psychological deficiencies in the seminaries and religious orders of the Latin Church were among the main causes of the present state of affairs:

There certainly were many abuses of authority in religious orders and seminaries which led to a depersonalization of religious life and sometimes even to a blunting

---

[1] Cardinal Virgilio Noè, Paul VI's chief liturgist, testified (CWNews.com, 16 May 2008; www.catholicculture.org/news/features/index.cfm?recnum=58473) that the pope made this statement in direct reference to the epidemic of abuses that accompanied the implementation of his liturgical reform.

of conscience. By making formal obedience the most important virtue, by blurring the essential difference between moral virtues and mere disciplinary correctness, by overemphasizing things which, because of the *parvitas materiæ*, were trivial, those in authority produced a state of affairs in which the personality of the religious or the seminarian was in danger of being emptied and in which the sense of a hierarchy of values was almost inevitably deadened.[2]

Countless former inmates of Catholic seminaries on the eve of the Council could vouch for the accuracy of this description. In that era of muscular Christianity the religious life was valued less for its beauty than for its 'heroism'. This was a system whose products too often measured their personal virtue and apostolic effectiveness against their ability to behave in as unnatural a manner as possible, as if this were an authentic outer sign of the inner spiritual perfection for which devout Christians strive. A personality-stifling culture of obedience in religious houses could lead on the one hand to inflated egos and delusionism on the part of superiors, and on the other to sycophancy, hypocrisy and cynical careerism on the part of subordinates. At the same time, the deadly combination of personal inadequacy and self-importance in priests fomented clericalism, which in turn engendered anti-clericalism and, worse, to popular hostility to the Church, problems by no means corrected by the Vatican II reforms.

The deficiencies in pre-conciliar seminary training were inherited from the nineteenth century. At a time when Latin had already ceased to be the prime medium of learning in Europe, students for the priesthood were still being taught in this language, though many had difficulty mastering it. Inability to express oneself coherently and intelligently in the classroom because of poor Latin skills inhibited speculation and tended to kill the love of study. Furthermore, since the arts, sciences and knowledge of the secular world were shut out of the seminary for the sake of spirituality, young men were often ordained with little understanding of, or sympathy for, the world in which they would have to minister.

Adrien Dansette has observed of the clergy of this period that they 'were not without some claim to admiration. They were as virtuous as they were intended to be.'[3] But the seminary system inculcated mediocrity, as if this were the natural companion of the virtue of humility, and poorly educated priests were no match for a society addicted to the cult of scientific progress. According to Dansette, French seminary professors were themselves

> often men of mediocre stamp. Many knew hardly more than their own senior pupils. Instead of specializing, they passed freely from one chair to another, restricting themselves to a slavish following of the manuals. Like the rest of the clergy, they had minds rooted in the past. The Revolution was for them the great evil and they systematically avoided considering either the Revolution itself or its consequences. Seminarists who showed any intellectual curiosity, those who were 'unlike the others', were looked upon with disapproval by their superiors. In other words, intellectual mortification with regard to anything new was not only practised, but was looked upon as a virtue.[4]

[2] Dietrich von Hildebrand, *Trojan Horse in the City of God* (Chicago, 1969), p. 30.
[3] Adrien Dansette, *Religious History of Modern France*, II (Freiburg, 1961), p. 7.
[4] Ibid., pp. 6–7.

The sinister 'Quiet Revolution' (*Révolution Tranquille*) that overtook Catholic Quebec in the 1960s and paralysed the local church had its seed bed in a provincial society long dominated socially and politically by priests formed in this very mould.

For the more pious students, seminary life was sweetened by the joys of the liturgical life, but for too many – those who aspired to holy orders for worldly reasons at a time when, unhappily, the priesthood was a prestigious career – the liturgy was a burden, made the worse by the custom of presenting the official prayer of the Church as the chief of the numerous obligations of the dutiful cleric. And for intellectually inclined students, the official straitjacketing of thought was stifling and degrading. In hindsight and in human terms it is not difficult to understand how an 'aliturgical' Catholic who rightly rejected the excesses and distortions of the post-Tridentine regime could automatically repudiate the 'Tridentine' liturgy and culture bound up with it.[5]

The Problem of Abstractionism

A mindset that stressed the abstract and the absolute at the expense of the concrete and the relative was the root cause of clerical indifference to the liturgy. Concern for clarity and precision in doctrine tended to highlight what was black and white, and ignored grey areas: this was the cocksure era in which there was 'a Catholic answer to every question'. In such a milieu the orthodox teaching that error has no rights could be abstracted at the expense of the human beings in whom error is incarnated and who have indisputable rights. The result was a vague misanthropy towards those who lived outside the bounds of strict orthodoxy, the very pharisaicism against which St Augustine warned with his dictum *Interficite errores, diligite errantes* ('Slay errors but love those who err'). Abstractionism made possible such a theological deviation as that of the American Jesuit Leonard Feeney, which the Holy See had to condemn in 1949: the quasi-Calvinistic teaching that denied the reality of baptism of desire by narrowing (and thereby falsifying) the *de fide* teaching on salvation.

The dualism underlying abstractionism was manifested in its negative tendencies to exalt the formal and despise the material, and to concentrate on text and ignore context, both imbalances conducive to the drawing of erroneous conclusions. For example, typical of abstractionist occidentocentrism was the compulsion to judge the Oriental rites on the criteria of Latin sacramental theology, oblivious that while the matter of each sacrament is the same throughout the Church, the form of each could legitimately vary according to rite. Such black-and-white minds had no personal sympathy for or interest in the Eastern Orthodox, who though formally outside the Church were materially Catholic. That most Orthodox believers were not individually culpable of schism or heresy, and the facts that their sacraments

---

[5] As for female religious, there appears to be a direct relationship between the vapid and dissipated behaviour of so many ageing and habitless nuns in English-speaking countries and north-western Europe today and the degree of personality crushing these same women endured in pre-conciliar convents, where routine humiliation – misrepresented as mortification of the spirit – was sometimes seen as the fast track to holiness. What happened to 'liberated' nuns is as good an example as any of one extreme generating its opposite. John Patrick Shanley's 2004 play *Doubt: A Parable* (filmed in 2008) presents with remarkable accuracy the contrast between the over-disciplined existence of American nuns in the early 1960s and the more relaxed and self-indulgent lives of contemporary secular priests.

were valid, that Christ was really present in their Eucharists and that they honoured the Blessed Virgin and Catholic saints could not soften the prejudice of zealots of this kind.[6] With such a closing of minds and hardening of hearts, the hubris of the 'golden age' of modern Catholicism was inviting its nemesis.

After Vatican II the same abstract reasoning would allow 'sedevacantist' ultramontanists to conclude that popes who said or did things to qualify them as possible material heretics were *ipso facto* formal heretics and hence impostors, as if the indefectibility of the Church protected incumbents of the papal office from sin or from error outside the bounds of infallibility, and as if the material sin of unintentional heterodoxy could be judged by ordinary members of the Church, which herself has no authority to impute moral guilt.[7]

High Hopes

Rigidity and aridity, especially when laced with smugness or fanaticism, proved to be a lethal cocktail in the highly ideologized 1950s. Not surprisingly it was the priests and religious, especially those individuals with good reason to resent the shortcomings of the contemporary clerical system, who responded most enthusiastically to Pope John XXIII's announcement, in 1960, of a new general council to 'update' (*aggiornare*) the Catholic Church. This great gathering of the world's bishops around the Chair of Peter promised to bring a second spring to Christianity. Compounding the growing optimism was news of Roncalli's resolution to end the era of Counter-Reformation 'triumphalism' that had reached its apotheosis in the pontificate of his predecessor.

About to end, too, was the 'fortress mentality' of the post-Tridentine 'Church Militant'. Instead of finding foes everywhere, Catholics would now build bridges,

---

[6] The Orthodox Church today has a parallel problem with converts from Catholicism and Protestantism who engage in apologetics, adopting extremist positions which seem motivated more by a personal need to exorcise their own Western past than to make the traditions of Eastern Orthodoxy better known and understood. In a not dissimilar category are Roman-rite Catholics repelled by the Pauline reform who apply to transfer to an Eastern rite to evade their responsibility to fight for tradition in the rite of their baptism, and then airily dismiss Western traditionalists as Christians 'disobedient to their Patriarch'. Authenticity must be safeguarded in the Catholic and independent Eastern Churches as much as in the Latin Church. In any case, since Benedict XVI took the bizarre step of abolishing as 'obsolete' the Roman Pope's historically and ecumenically essential title of 'Patriarch of the West' on 22 March 2006, Latin-rite traditionalists can no longer be properly styled anti-patriarchal.

[7] One of the stock arguments of the sedevacantists is that no pope prior to John XXIII ever made evil laws concerning religion. It suffices to consider the whole Roman tradition of heteropractic legislation against Eastern Christians to expose the baselessness of such a claim. Sedevacantism's contention that a pope can be deposed for heresy stands on more solid ground. In the twelfth century Gratian stated that the pope 'is to be judged by no-one, unless he be caught deviating from the faith' (*nisi deprehendatur a fide devius*, *Decretum*, I, dist. 60, ch. 6); Pope Innocent III conceded that 'it is solely for a sin committed against the faith that I may be judged by the Church' (*propter solum peccatum quod in fide committitur possem ab Ecclesia judicari*, *Sermo II: In Consecratione*, PL 218.656); and Pope Paul IV (1555–1559) declared that a pope who was found to have deviated from the faith before his election (*a fide catholica deviasse*) could be deposed without trial (*Cum ex Apostolatus Officio*, par. 6). The problem faced by those claiming that the Chair of St Peter has been empty since 1958 is to prove that John XXIII and his successors have actually met the requirements for *ipso facto* loss of office by intentionally (and hence culpably) teaching *formal* heresy, as opposed to making objectively heretical statements *unintentionally* as private doctors (as did John XXII in 1331), thereby committing material sin.

becoming the peacemakers of the Beatitudes on a global scale. Solidarity with all mankind would be pursued with a new respect for the individual and his rights and needs. And members of the Church would make a definite commitment to seeking a fruitful *modus vivendi* with the modern world, cheerfully facing contemporary challenges, while of course remaining true to their faith.

Aggiornamento was presented not as a revolution establishing a break with the past, but as a long overdue evolution wholly compatible with Catholic tradition. In such a heady atmosphere those longing to see the sacred liturgy restored to its pride of place in the Latin Church were delighted when the Council placed divine worship at the top of its agenda. *Sacrosanctum Concilium* gave prime importance to the liturgical life, declaring it to be 'the summit toward which the activity of the Church is directed' and 'the fountain from which all her power flows' (1, 10). In another conciliar statement, which drew on Saint Paul and the Apocalypse, the eschatological dimension of the liturgy was fully acknowledged:

> In the earthly liturgy, by way of foretaste, we share in that heavenly liturgy which is celebrated in the holy city of Jerusalem toward which we journey as pilgrims, and in which Christ is sitting at the right hand of God, a minister of the sanctuary and of the true tabernacle; we sing a hymn to the Lord's glory with all the warriors of the heavenly army; venerating the memory of the saints, we hope for some part and fellowship with them; we eagerly await the Saviour, our Lord Jesus Christ, until He, our life, shall appear and we too will appear with Him in glory.[8]

Renewal in the West

Such 'Oriental' (but in fact genuinely Catholic) insights in a Latin document marked a considerable advance, yet it was no sudden about-turn. For seven decades the Western liturgical movement had been striving to replace the old, utilitarian approach to liturgy with the more traditional, cosmic view of it that would eventually be enshrined in the conciliar constitution.

A good deal had been achieved in this international renewal of Catholic worship which refused to ignore the Church's integral Oriental traditions. After the aggressive ultramontanism and liturgical centralism of the pontificate of Pius IX, the reforms of Leo XIII concerning the Eastern Churches had been a salutary corrective to the attitude, hitherto current in West, and expressed by Dom Prosper Guéranger in his *Institutions liturgiques* (1840), that the Oriental rites were, in as much as they differed from the 'perfect' Roman liturgy, structurally imperfect and doctrinally suspect.[9] If Eastern Catholics have no reason to remember the French Benedictine fondly, and his own compatriots might well deplore his campaign against the Neo-Gallican uses, Catholics in general owe him an enormous debt of gratitude, for it was he, more than any other, who inspired new interest in the study and cultivation of the liturgy for its own sake. 'It is in the liturgy that the Spirit who inspired the Scriptures speaks again', wrote Dom Guéranger, for whom the liturgy was 'Tradition itself at its highest degree of power and solemnity.'[10]

---

[8] *Sacrosanctum Concilium*, I, 8.
[9] Guéranger, *op. cit.*, II, pp. 724–40. See especially pp. 724–28, 735–36.
[10] Congar, *Tradition*, p. 125.

True to the Benedictine maxim that Christians 'should prefer nothing to divine worship', the restorer of the Order of Saint Benedict in France devoted his life's work to the liturgical apostolate and strove to make the Roman liturgy loved and appreciated by the Catholic faithful. His masterpiece, *The Liturgical Year*, published between 1841 and 1901, was intended as a popular manual explaining and reflecting on the ceremonies and feasts of the Christian calendar. Influenced by contemporary Romanticism, Guéranger's liturgical ideal was the prayer and worship of the Middle Ages which he reproduced as faithfully as possible in his model Benedictine monastery of Solesmes.

A man of often misplaced zeal, Guéranger has been not unfairly criticized for this 'medieval archaeologism' as well as for his Roman-rite imperialism.[11] However, what proved to be of enduring value in his work was his teaching, in the best traditions of orthodoxy, that the sacred liturgy is, in the first place, 'confession, prayer and praise', and only secondly an instruction.[12] His theocentric approach to divine worship was at the time a necessary corrective to the existing tendency, influenced by eighteenth-century rationalism, to stress the didactic qualities of the Church's cultus.

Restoring All Things in Christ

Although the priorities of his pontificate were pressing doctrinal and social issues, Leo XIII was concerned from time to time with liturgical questions. He took steps, for instance, to remedy the deplorable state of church music in his day, and in 1884 instructed the Congregation of Rites to publish a decree banning the liturgical use of 'operatic and dance music, polkas, waltzes, mazurkas, minuets . . ., quadrilles, galops, dances of Scotland, Poland and Lithuania, erotic popular songs and romances', as well as the playing in church of profane instruments like 'tambourines, bass drums, cymbals, barrel organs and pianos'.[13]

Pope Leo also advanced the work of the liturgical movement by taking vernacular translations of the Roman Missal off the Index of Prohibited Books in 1897.[14] Permission to make all the sacred texts accessible to the ordinary worshipper was a great boost to the cause of liturgical education, and the publication of vernacular missals as substitutes for the old devotional manuals formerly used at Mass became one of the main activities of the Belgian Benedictines of Maredsous and Mont-César. Learned and pastoral reviews aiming to sensitize the clergy to liturgical questions were another Benedictine endeavour.[15]

There were of course many things to correct in the current liturgical outlook. Dom Bernard Botte, whose childhood straddled the turn of the century, recalls how, in the chapel of his old school in Wallonia:

Mass was said by an old, more or less voiceless, priest – even in the first row the only thing you'd hear was a murmur. The group rose for the gospel, but nobody

---

[11] Bouyer, *op. cit.*, pp. 11–15.
[12] Guéranger, *op. cit.*, I, ch. 1.
[13] Gough, *op. cit.*, p. 167.
[14] Jungmann, *op. cit.*, I, p. 161.
[15] For example, *Le Messager des fidèles* (founded 1884), *Revue bénédictine* (1890), *Le Messager de Saint Benoît* (1898).

dreamed of telling us which gospel it was. We didn't even know which saint's feast it was or which deceased persons were being prayed for at the Masses with black vestments.[16]

At his parish church, on the other hand,

There were some sung Masses, but they were a dialogue between the clergy and the cleric-organist. The people remained quiet and passive, doing whatever each one liked, saying the rosary or losing oneself in *The Most Beautiful Prayers of St Alphonsus Liguori* or *The Imitation of Christ*. As for communion, it was distributed before Mass, after Mass, or in the middle of Mass, but never at the moment indicated in the liturgy. . . . Communion appeared to be a private devotion without any special link to the Mass.[17]

From its beginnings, the Belgian liturgical movement, while remaining faithful to Dom Guéranger's theocentric emphasis, was concerned to promote the liturgical life for its immense pastoral value. Hence, after the Liége Eucharistic Conference of 1899 Dom Gérard van Caloen campaigned for the revival of the Communion of the faithful during Mass. This proposal won the strong sympathy of the pastorally minded Mgr Giuseppe Sarto, Bishop of Mantua and later Patriarch of Venice. When Sarto ascended the papal throne as Pius X in 1903, one of his first pontifical acts was to issue the motu proprio *Tra le sollecitudini* which, though primarily intended to restore Gregorian chant and other authentic musical traditions of the Roman rite, was a general endorsement of the Franco-Belgian liturgical movement:

Since our most lively desire is for the true Christian spirit to flourish again in every way and to maintain itself among all the faithful, it is necessary before everything else to attend to the holiness and to the dignity of the temple where the faithful gather precisely to find there that spirit in its primary and indispensable source, that is: active participation in the sacred Mysteries and the public and solemn prayer of the Church.[18]

A number of liturgical reforms, all dictated by pastoral necessity, followed. Five years before he lowered the age for the first reception of Holy Communion St Pius encouraged the frequent Communion of those prepared by prayer, fasting and (where necessary) confession with his decree *Sacra Tridentina Synodus* (1905). Even the Pope's controversial reform of the Roman breviary in 1911 was described by Dom Fernand Cabrol, one of its severest critics, as capable of producing an immediate renewal of the Christian spirit.[19]

The most tireless apostle of the liturgical movement during the pontificate of St Pius X was Dom Lambert Beauduin, then one of the Mont-César Benedictines. At the Catholic Congress of Malines, organized in 1909 by Cardinal Mercier, Beauduin launched a programme of renewal with the following objectives: to

---

[16] Botte, *op. cit.*, p. 2.
[17] Ibid., pp. 2–3.
[18] Quoted in Ellard, *Mass of the Future*, p. 255.
[19] Reid, *op. cit.*, p. 77.

make Catholic piety more liturgical; to publish more translations of the missal so as to foster greater popular interest in the Mass and Sunday Vespers; to promote the Communion of the faithful at Mass; to popularize Gregorian chant; and to encourage members of church choirs to make retreats in centres of liturgical life such as Benedictine monasteries.[20] Beauduin also founded two highly successful journals, *Questions liturgiques et paroissiales* and *Semaines liturgiques*.[21]

In the following decades the liturgical movement took off in France, with the dioceses of Lille, Chartres and Strasbourg and the archdiocese of Paris as its focal points. In Germany the movement's development centred on the Benedictine houses of Maria Laach, Sankt Josef, Ettel and Beuron. The Netherlands, Northern Italy, Catalonia and the United States also responded. The French movement led the world in the cultivation of Gregorian chant, and 1924 saw the foundation of a Gregorian Institute in Paris, while in Italy the Piedmontese composer Don Lorenzo Perosi worked on the restoration of polyphonic and homophonic singing. Belgium established itself as the leading producer of bilingual missals for the laity printed in a wide variety of languages for use all over the world.[22]

On the recommendation of Dom Gaspar Lefebvre and the Franco-Belgian liturgists, in 1922 Pope Pius XI gave permission for the congregation to recite aloud the Latin responses at Low Mass. This reform, authorized merely *ad experimentum*, was seen by some as an improvement on the old 'silent' Mass, even if, given the solemn nature of the Catholic liturgy, it was hardly a substitute for the normative sung Mass, nor was it really traditional in the Latin rites. The 'Dialogue Mass' soon became rooted in the habits of French, Belgian and German Catholics. Due consideration was also given to an appropriate use of the vernacular in the administration of the sacraments, and during the following decades bilingual editions of the Roman ritual were published all over the world.

The achievements of the liturgical movement are impressive. By the 1940s Catholic congregations in many countries were taking a conscious interest in the ceremonies they attended, and participated vocally in them instead of losing themselves in private meditations and devotions. How, then, does one deal with the problematical fact that the apparent result of these initiatives was not a renewal of the Western liturgical heritage, but its vandalization and virtual destruction? *Sacrosanctum Concilium* called for the preservation of Latin and Gregorian chant; they were abolished. The Council said nothing about Mass facing the people, yet this became the norm thereafter, passed off as 'one of the reforms of Vatican II'. In the revision of the Mass rites 'due care was to be taken to preserve their substance' and yet an artificial order of service was devised by a papal committee and subsequently foisted on the entire Roman rite. What had gone wrong?

Attempting the Impossible?

It has been shown how the psychological conditioning of the faithful by post-Tridentine authoritarianism guaranteed popular acceptance of the liturgical revolution. Apart from the unlikelihood that people trained for generations to obey

[20] Bonneterre, *op. cit.*, p. 26.
[21] Ibid.
[22] Ibid., pp. 29–34.

without question every directive of the hierarchy and clergy would rise to defend a time-hallowed orthopraxis that their leaders now scorned, there was now also a cultural gap between them and their own heritage. Why, for instance, would Catholics mourn the loss of liturgical Latin when they had either never studied Latin at school or, when they did, they had been taught the classical idiom and authors without any reference to the distinctive Latin of the Church and its rich literature? Why should those who barely understood a word of Latin object to the celebration of the whole rite of Mass in their own language?

The truth is that against the deeply engrained habits and attitudes of the Counter-Reformation legacy the efforts of the liturgical movement had been largely ineffective, despite its achievements in other areas. Fr Bouyer put his finger on this problem seven years before the Council. Referring to the medieval and baroque devotions that had substituted themselves for the true liturgical life, he wrote:

> We can now see that these novelties were able to take hold of the minds of the faithful so successfully because the liturgy itself had lost its hold upon them. Moreover, their very success made it more difficult to reestablish a true understanding and practice of the liturgy, since these new devotions involved a mentality not only foreign to that of the liturgy but almost irreconcilable with it. *It is when people are no longer in touch with the authentic spirit of the liturgy that such devotions are developed; but once these are in possession, a return to the liturgy is almost impossible.* You cannot at the same time hail Christ as if He were still a little Baby in His cradle, and adore Him as the risen Lord, the Christos-Pneuma. You cannot weep for His Passion as if you did not know that it has already ended in victory, and also exult in the Resurrection. You cannot combine a mysticism centred on Jesus considered as the 'Prisoner of the tabernacle', with celebrating the Eucharist as the saving Mystery by which Christ sets us free from all created limitations to bring us into the divine life. *The more attached to one set of these alternatives, the more you must accept the loss of the other. And thus the way was barred to any possible return to pristine liturgical life.*[23] (Emphasis added)

What was Protestantism, after all, but a religion of pieties that made the Holy Scriptures its principal devotion? Catholicism may be in essence a liturgical religion, but given the instinctive ultramontanism of the modern faithful, the protests of lone traditionalists were bound to be greeted with incomprehension, indignation and derision. Catholics whose religion was actually an amalgam of private piety and obedience to the precepts of the Church (attending Sunday Mass being the first of these) could, and did, adapt themselves to the new rites with a minimum of inconvenience and regret.

The Pauline revolution was launched at precisely the time when its authors had a reasonable certainty of its success. If the new worship accelerated, rather than slowed down, the already rapid dechristianization of Western society, it was in part because the New Theology, in stressing the concepts of Christian maturity and individual responsibility (salutary correctives at the time of the Council), also de-emphasized the concepts of obligation and personal sin. A blunting of Christian consciences was the result.

---

[23] Bouyer, *op. cit.*, p. 248.

The Price of Integrism

Contrary to what many conservative Catholics have been led to believe, the ritual revolution of the 1960s and 70s was hardly a sudden occurrence, the oddly perverse corollary to a perfectly orthodox liturgical movement. In reality the movement had been infiltrated and ultimately hijacked not only by convinced antiquarianists, but by the partisans of 'didacticism', the tendency to make the liturgy a vehicle of instruction and edification to the detriment of its more important contemplative aspect. As for traditionalists, too often they have mistaken this 'subversion' as a conspiracy of Modernists aiming to destroy the Catholic faith by attacking its very heart. It is true that the heterodox liturgical movement sprang up in the wake of the Modernist crisis, but most of its leaders were far from being convinced apostles of heresy. There was a causal link with Modernism, but it was an indirect one; the didacticists' programme of destruction was in fact a by-product of the anti-Modernist campaign of the first three decades of the last century.

The great misfortune of the pontificate of St Pius X was that his providential and necessary condemnation of religious liberalism led to a new climate of repression in the Church, with scholars and teachers subject to surveillance and often individual persecution. Among the victims of this over-cautious reaction, which became known as 'integrism', were such sound Catholic thinkers as Fr Marie-Joseph Lagrange, Albert de Mun, Mgr Batiffol and Mgr Radini-Tedeschi.[24]

As exemplified by the thought of Loisy, Tyrrell and Fogazzaro, Modernism had been a grave deviation in an otherwise laudable attempt to narrow the gap between Catholic orthodoxy and modern civilization. However, when integrism slammed the door shut on free speculation and discussion of those aspects of Catholicism that were subject to adaptation, for example doctrinal exegesis and methods of social action, the mental energies of the Catholic intelligentsia were channelled into other areas more sheltered from the searchings of Vatican censors. One of these safe havens was the liturgical movement.

In Germany many scholars inhibited by Rome's distrust of all philosophical and theological speculation outside the perimeter of Neo-Scholasticism took up liturgiological studies. In a Church which no longer understood the liturgical tradition as primary theology it was 'safe' to subject the sacred rites to rigorous critical analysis. This the Benedictine scholars of the German abbey of Maria Laach did with distinction from the First World War period onwards. Their efforts made notable advances in liturgical science, but there was also a negative side to these achievements.

Dom Ildefons Herwegen and Dom Odo Casel developed a method of analysis that separated the 'subjective' elements of liturgy from its 'objective' core on the analogy of the relationship between the unchanging deposit of faith and its variable exegesis. However, the delicate synthesis of Catholic liturgy was undermined as the integral, outward forms of the ritual tradition were devalued as mere culturally determined expressions of the *mysterium*.[25] In rejecting the 'subjective' ritual legacies of the medieval and baroque periods, the scholars of the Germanic liturgical movement adopted a frankly immobilist position. Having decided that subjectivism had caused the liturgy to become hypertrophied, they advocated an antiquarianist

[24] Daniel-Rops, *op. cit.*, p. 231.
[25] Bouyer, *op. cit.*, pp. 18–19.

model of reform that made the earliest and most 'objective' expression of the liturgical tradition normative for Catholicism.

Towards a Practical Liturgy

The learned monks of Maria Laach found an enthusiastic admirer in Father Pius Parsch, a canon of the Augustinian monastery of Klosterneuburg, near Vienna. Taking the theory of cultural relativity to its logical conclusion, the Austro-Moravian liturgist substituted for the immobilist antiquarianism of the Maria Laach school an evolutionism more in keeping with modern thought. His pragmatic aim was to harmonize the essentials of the eternal liturgy with contemporary cultural forms.

Parsch's principally pastoral concerns were, historically, a development of the didacticism earlier promoted by Dom Lambert Beauduin in his Belgian liturgical apostolate. Dom Jacques Froger recalled in 1948 that

> Dom Lambert Beauduin's work did not only have the effect of giving a new impulse to the movement started by Dom Guéranger; it eventually presented the liturgy under a new light. Dom L. Beauduin's point of view was no longer exactly that of Dom Guéranger, for whom it was contemplative prayer, disinterested lyricism singing its love without any care but to give praise. Although Dom L. Beauduin was aware of this aspect of the liturgy, his interest was the action of the liturgy on souls rather than its sanctifying role. . . . His interest was not the liturgy in itself, but liturgical pastoral work.[26]

This rationalistic tendency in Dom Beauduin, checked by the impeccable orthodoxy of the early Belgian movement, was to take on a heteropractic complexion in Germany, where it blended with antiquarianism – something that had held no interest for Beauduin. By contrast, Fr Parsch, far from rejecting the antiquarianism of the German Benedictines, sought to exploit those aspects of it that were in harmony with a 'functional' approach to liturgical worship. Mass facing the people was a case in point.

Pius Parsch believed that in order for the faithful to take an active part in the sacred rites it was essential not only that they participate vocally, but that they see what the priest was doing at the altar. He accepted uncritically the antiquarianist claim that the *versus populum* position had been the norm in the early Church (an opinion that has since proved highly questionable),[27] and made this practice a hallmark of his liturgical apostolate. The Augustinian canon's description of the first 'popular' liturgy he improvised for a Catholic youth convention in 1922 speaks for itself:

> [When] I heard about a *Missa Recitata* that was going to be celebrated at the students' convention, I resolved to celebrate with my group the first community Mass. This was on Ascension Day, 1922. The day before, I had gathered the group members in the chapel of Saint Gertrude, destined to become the cradle of the

---

[26] Quoted in Bonneterre, *op. cit.*, p. 27.
[27] For the case that Mass facing the people was not the norm in the early Church, see note 64, below.

popular liturgical movement, and I explained to them the ceremonies and meaning of the sung Mass (in those days we called it the 'Liturgical Mass'). But this
exercise caused a parting of the ways, for quite a few Catholics with a subjectivist
mind set decided to leave our group. This sung Mass was still in its embryonic
stage: the Kyrie, Sanctus and Agnus Dei were sung in German; Professor Goller
had composed some simple choral melodies for us. The lessons and prayers were
read by the president. We [the congregation] made an offering and even the kiss
of peace took the form of a handshake. This was no doubt the first celebration of
the Mass in the spirit of popular liturgy in a German-speaking country.[28]

Though Fr Parsch's great interest was the relationship of Sacred Scripture to
divine worship, his programme of reform went far beyond urging the restoration
of the lessons, Gradual and Gospel to their rightful prominence in the Mass of the
Catechumens. Whereas the Church had always viewed the Liturgy of the Word
as the proclamation and, hence, the activation of the Word of God within the
Christian assembly, Parsch went a step further, considering it an immediate revelation of God equal to His sacramental revelation in the Liturgy of the Eucharist.
Such an approach could only upset the traditional balance of the two component
parts of the Catholic Mass, in which the proclamation of the Word had always
been absorbed, as it were, in the greatness of the eucharistic mystery. Indeed in
Parsch's 'biblical worship' the Liturgy of the Word tended to overshadow and
subordinate the Liturgy of the Eucharist. The result was a didactic rather than a
latric (i.e. worship-based) cult.[29]

The German Episcopal Putsch

Pius Parsch's initiative was not an isolated one. Its social context was the
Jugendbewegung or Youth Movement that formed a generation of German
Catholics in the interwar decades. At the youth rallies and camps of the movement
(which included a branch of the *Hitlerjugend* after 1933), the liturgical principles
of Sankt Gertrud became common, if not the norm. Indeed, they proved their
worth in the mid-1930s, when Nazism was inhibiting Catholic social action and
increasingly confining religious activities to church and sacristy.

Denied a voice in contemporary society, the clergy and lay activists of the
Hitlerian era refused to be satisfied with the role of Job embraced by their Eastern
Orthodox counterparts in Soviet Russia. They found a solution to their problem
by using the liturgy, their one free domain, as a forum for the proclamation of the
social gospel suppressed everywhere else. This could be achieved only by making
the most of the didactic dimension of the liturgy and exploring further the possibil-
ities of the 'Parsch method'. An atmosphere of experimentation ensued, the result,
according to Klaus D. Grimm, of 'a communal-socialist perspective according to
which tradition and authority were inherently limiting to the energy and innocence
of nature and of youth intent on building a New World Order'.[30]

---

[28] Pius Parsch, *Le renouveau liturgique au service de la paroisse: sens et portée de la liturgie
populaire* (Mulhouse, 1950), p. 12.
[29] Bonneterre, *op. cit.*, pp. 48–49.
[30] Note in Gamber, *op. cit.*, pp. 43–44, n. 42.

From 1936 the anti-traditional extravagances transforming divine worship throughout Germany, especially in the *Jugendbewegung* milieu, provoked the concern and indignation of conservative churchmen. Even Mgr Johannes Wagner, one of the movement's apologists, later admitted that 'abuses and exaggerations were not lacking in it'.[31] The conservatives were not comforted when the bishops of Germany, at their 1940 Fulda meeting, confirmed Mgr Simon Landesdorfer, the new and progressivist Benedictine Bishop of Passau, in his position as head of the national Liturgisches Referat. Landesdorfer's principal assistants were the Italo-German liturgists Fr Romano Guardini and Fr Josef Jungmann, SJ.[32]

In January 1943 Mgr Conrad Gröber, archbishop of the Swabian city of Freiburg-im-Breisgau, addressed a seventeen-point memorandum to his episcopal colleagues, warning them of the dangers of this now officially endorsed liturgical experimentation.[33] As well as stressing the banquet aspect of the Eucharist at the expense of its sacrificial aspect, the experimenters 'treat the rubrics in the most cavalier fashion, indulging in every eccentricity', complained Archbishop Gröber. These modernistic aspects of the movement were combined with an antiquarianism traceable to the school of Maria Laach and its disciples in the Liturgisches Referat: 'What worries me is that, together with a radical and unjustified criticism of everything that has been held valid until the present and has appeared in the course of history, they demand a practical, audacious and brusque return to the norms of ancient and even very ancient periods, declaring at the same time that the evolution that has occurred since then has been a deviation.'[34]

Another source of concern for Gröber was the reformists' insistence upon the Dialogue Mass and the German Sung Mass.[35] The now popular Dialogue Mass was soon complemented by Rome's authorization of a mainly vernacular Roman ritual and a revival of the eighteenth-century custom of the people's singing the ordinary of the Mass in German while the priest recited it at the altar in Latin.[36] The Archbishop of Freiburg's protest was not against these pastoral reforms in themselves, but against the way in which they were being exploited to undermine

---

[31] Johannes Wagner, 'Le mouvement liturgique en Allemagne', *La Maison-Dieu*, No. 25, 1951. Quoted in Bonneterre, *op. cit.*, p. 50. Wagner would become one of the authors of the New Mass in the 1960s.

[32] 'Italo-German' in both cases because Guardini, though born in Italy, had emigrated with his family to Germany as a child; Jungmann was a native of the South Tyrol, a region of Austria that was ceded to Italy in 1918.

[33] Anti-Catholic writers have vilified this controversial German prelate as pro-Nazi and it is commonly stated that he earned the nickname 'the brown bishop' because of his early support not only of the National Socialists but also of the SS. Among Gröber's mistakes were his widely resented authorization of the Nazi salute in the schools of his archdiocese, a strongly anti-Jewish Good Friday sermon in 1941, and failing to back and defend priests who opposed the regime. Nevertheless, as the criminal character of the Nazi government became more apparent, he turned to public criticism of it, targeting such abominations as the euthanasia programme and the wholesale persecution of German citizens of Jewish background. It would appear that where interwar Germany is concerned, political and liturgical attitudes cannot be equated (except perhaps in the case of declaredly liberal Catholics), witness the pro-Nazi excesses of Theodor Innitzer, Archbishop of Vienna and of Cardinal Adolf Bertram, Archbishop of Breslau, Mgr Gröber's strongest opponents in the liturgical controversy (see below). Innitzer is remembered *inter alia* for personally welcoming the Führer to Austria after the Anschluss, while Bertram ordered the celebration of requiem Masses for the dictator after learning of his suicide.

[34] Bonneterre, *op. cit.*, pp. 61, 60.

[35] Ibid., p. 61.

[36] In the eighteenth-century Catholic Rhineland, Febronian rulers had forced the so-called *Singmesse* on congregations very much attached to the Latin chant. See Gamber, *op. cit.*, p. 18.

Catholic doctrine and orthopraxis: 'the New Liturgists have seen in the Dialogue Mass the expression of their own conceptions about the priesthood of all believers, and a way to insist on the right of laymen to co-offer the sacrifice of the Mass'.[37]

Shortly after the circulation of Mgr Gröber's memorandum, Rome intervened with a letter to the German episcopate, expressing concern about the experimentation and demanding a full report on the situation. In the meantime Cardinal Theodor Innitzer, the Jesuit Archbishop of Vienna, wrote to Mgr Gröber on 24 February, denying that the Germanic liturgical movement posed a threat to orthodoxy, and suggesting that any intervention by the Holy See would stifle the research of theologians and the creativity of liturgists.[38] In April, Cardinal Adolf Bertram sent a memorandum to Pope Pius XII in which he not only strongly defended all the main positions of the German and Austrian reformists but proposed further reforms, including a drastic reduction of the traditional eucharistic fast from midnight, a new Latin translation of the Psalter, the 'enrichment' of the Roman ritual with scriptural passages, and the transfer to the evening of the ceremonies of Maundy Thursday and Good Friday.[39]

In the Vatican's reply to the German bishops, dated 24 December 1943, Cardinal Maglione, Pius XII's Secretary of State, while confirming Rome's approval of the Dialogue Mass and the German Sung Mass, criticized the reported doctrinal deviations of the German liturgical movement.[40] Four years later the encyclical *Mediator Dei* would expressly condemn the modernization and antiquarianism so typical of the German reformists. Nevertheless, and most significantly, the 1943 instruction left the regulation of liturgical matters to the discretion of the German bishops, a remarkably liberal step by the authoritarian Pius XII, but one which, in the current circumstances, left the episcopal patrons of liturgical reform free to act at will.

Across the Rhine

The German reformists had numerous sympathizers in France, mostly members of the Jesuit and Dominican orders. Observing how the Vatican, rigidly conservative and unbending in theological matters, now seemed willing to decentralize itself in the area of discipline, these progressive churchmen quickly understood that the future of radical liturgical reform lay in winning local bishops and, especially, national episcopates over to their cause.

Since the early 1920s Fr Paul Doncœur, SJ, a pioneer of the French Catholic scouting movement, had enjoyed close relations with the leaders of the *Jugendbewegung*

---

[37] Ibid., p. 62.

[38] Ibid., p. 63.

[39] Ibid., p. 64. The Vatican acceded to German demands for a new Latin Psalter by proposing for use (but not imposing) in 1945 the *Novum Psalterium* (*Versio Piana*), which had been translated by the German Jesuit Augustin Bea into classical (rather than ecclesiastical) Latin from the Hebrew Masoretic text. The Franciscans and Carmelites adopted the reform, but most Catholics found the language so stiff and artificial that the beloved old *Versio Gallicana* remained in general use, and was the only edition of the Psalter employed by traditionalists after Vatican II. The Psalter included in the new Roman breviary of 1971 was also a new version from the Hebrew, but this time the translators were careful to keep more closely to the vocabulary and idiom of received ecclesiastical Latin.

[40] Ibid.

in Germany. At Burg Rothenfels, Doncœur became acquainted with the practice of Mass facing the people (promoted there by Fr Guardini)[41] and returned home a convert to the ideal of 'practical' liturgy. Under his direction the chaplains of the French Scouts would increasingly take the sacred mysteries out of their proper setting, celebrating on the road and at youth camps educational *al fresco* Eucharists in which informality and ritual inventiveness were the keynotes.[42] On Easter Sunday 1951, Fr Doncœur gathered a group of Jesuits and laymen for a 'Paschal Mass' in a private house. A large *galette* (flat bread cake) was used and every one of those present 'concelebrated' by breaking off a piece of the bread cake over a cup of wine. Doncœur's confrère, Pierre Teilhard de Chardin, on hearing of this event (possibly invalid and certainly sacrilegious from the Catholic point of view) was amused: evidence, according to Malachi Martin, of the latter's increasing 'insensitivity to traditional pieties and personal devotion to Jesus' which 'could only have been made possible by a collapse of genuine belief'.[43]

Though the Jesuit Doncœur was one of the leading lights of the French liturgical reformists in the two preceding decades, the majority were Dominicans grouped around the leftist Éditions du Cerf, founded in 1932, and inspired by the 'integral humanism' of Jacques Maritain.[44] In the years leading up to the Second World War, Father Augustin Maydieu, OP, had taken his liturgical experiments to Notre Dame cathedral itself, where he celebrated avant-garde Masses facing the people for the progressivist members of Les Amis du Sept.[45] The anti-latric and downright secularizing tendency of these French initiatives was exposed in 1956 by Father Louis Bouyer, who pinpointed as their fundamental flaw the tendency to make the modern environment, and not the Christian parish, the actual arena of worship. The French reformists, Bouyer complained, gave 'precedence to missionary work among modern pagans rather than to the work of helping faithful Christians in the Church to discover their treasures'.[46]

The sacred liturgy is of its very nature an end in itself, as much in a dechristianized society as in a God-fearing one, but in France it was becoming increasingly difficult to maintain this traditional view. The Vatican's condemnation of Action Française in 1926, which dashed the hopes of monarchist Catholics, also vindicated the contention of the triumphant liberals in the clergy that if evangelization was to succeed in the modern situation, it needed to free itself from the shackles of the past. More and more, the received Catholic cultus was seen as one of these 'shackles'. This ferment, according to Louis Bouyer:

[41] Gamber, *op. cit.*, p. 143.
[42] Bonneterre, *op. cit.*, pp. 53–54. Before becoming Pope Paul VI, Mgr Montini attracted the unfavourable attention of conservatives in the Vatican for similar liturgical exploits while prosecretary of state between 1952 and 1954. In his informative but undocumented biography of Mother Pascalina (Josefina Lehnert), Pius XII's housekeeper and secretary, Paul Murphy relates:

> '[His] Holiness [Pacelli] furthermore thought that Mgr Montini did not possess the stature to be Holy Father' she once told Cardinal Spellman. The nun made it clear to the prelate that the Pontiff barely tolerated Montini's sidewalk services, which he conducted for peasants and others in the streets of Italy. The monsignor went about carrying his own portable altar and Mass kit in a large briefcase. . . . Pius considered Montini's public oratory as 'theatrics' that harmed rather than advanced the Holy See's image. (*La Popessa* [New York, 1983], p. 286)

[43] Malachi Martin, *op. cit.*, p. 295.
[44] Bonneterre, *op. cit.*, p. 54.
[45] Ibid., p. 55.
[46] Bouyer, *op. cit.*, p. 67.

could lead, and sometimes led to some neglect of the traditional aspect of the liturgy, and to an interest perhaps not perfectly balanced in making up or re-making the liturgy. The creation and overwhelming success of what have been called 'para-liturgies' are proofs of what we have just been saying. Composed first to be a means of education, a transitional device preparing the way for an understanding of the liturgy itself, these 'para-liturgies' have often become ends in themselves. Some people, that is, have been tempted to find in these para-liturgies, not a means towards taking part in the real liturgy, but rather a 'liturgy of the future' which will more or less replace or refashion the official liturgy itself.[47]

In the French reform movement, even more than in the German one, the sacred liturgy was subordinated to the contemporary *moral* preoccupations of the clergy, and ran the risk of becoming a mere vehicle for the pursuit of social justice. Thus was laid in France one of the foundations of the post-conciliar style of worship.

Around the same time the officially approved Dialogue Mass began to be used as a means of subversion. In 1937 Dom Gaspar Lefebvre of the Belgian Benedictine abbey of Saint-André-lez-Bruges published his prestigious *Missel quotidien et vespéral* in collaboration with the Parisian Societé Liturgique. The introduction to the new missal contained a section on '*La messe dialoguée en français*' which began with the recommendation: 'In order to keep children occupied, without distracting them from the Mass, the following prayers may be said . . .'[48] There followed ten pages of verbose vernacular prayers paraphrasing the liturgical action, to be recited aloud and alternatively by 'one voice' and 'all' while the priest muttered his Low Mass in Latin. The lay commentator (male or female) was to declaim even the Words of Institution at the Consecration. This weird juxtaposition of the Latin Mass and a quasi-presbyterian paraliturgy was the forerunner of the commentated public worship that became a passing fad after Vatican II. Meanwhile, it quickly became clear which of the two competing services commanded the loyalty of modern-minded congregations.

Ecumenism: Anglican-style

Another clerical preoccupation of the heteropractic liturgical movement was ecumenism. This was pioneered during the 1920s, principally by Dom Lambert Beauduin, who had earlier made such a valuable contribution to the renewal of public worship. Active in the Belgian Resistance during the First World War, Dom Beauduin had been forced to flee to Great Britain, where he made lifelong friendships with members of the Anglo-Catholic party in the Church of England.[49] Convinced of the genuine Catholicity of the Anglican Church, ignoring the irrevocable papal ruling *Apostolicæ Curæ* (1896), and turning a blind eye to the Protestant and Latitudinarian elements in Anglicanism, Beauduin was the prime mover of the Malines Conversations sponsored between 1921 and 1926 by his patron, Cardinal Mercier. The Belgian Benedictine's suggestion that, following the

---

[47] Bouyer, *op. cit.*, pp. 67–68.
[48] On p. 65.
[49] One of Beauduin's early contacts was the Rev George Bell, chaplain to Archbishop Davidson of Canterbury, future Bishop of Chichester and a pioneer of the ecumenical movement. Quitslund, *op. cit.*, p. 48.

'absorption' of the 'Catholic' Church of England into the Roman communion, the existing Roman ordinaries resign their sees in favour of the existing Anglican bishops, did not endear him to British Catholics.

Following his return to Belgium after the war, Beauduin made the acquaintance of Mgr Andrej Szeptycki, Greek Catholic metropolitan of Lviv. From contact with the great Ukrainian prelate he developed a keen interest in the liturgical tradition of the Eastern Churches.[50] This led in 1925 to his founding at Amay-sur-Meuse, and with the encouragement of Pope Pius XI, of a 'monastery of union' in which the Roman and Byzantine rites would be celebrated and cultivated side by side.[51] During these years the Belgian apostle of ecumenism made his own the Anglican 'branch theory', according to which the Catholic Church had remained one even after its triple division into Roman, Orthodox and Anglican communions. Since all three sections of the Church were equally Catholic in all essentials, fullness of unity could be achieved simply by the restoration of communion between the Sees of Rome, Constantinople and Canterbury.[52] Beauduin's rash error of placing Anglicanism on the same footing as Eastern Orthodoxy led up a blind alley at Malines, and would have dire consequences, both for its author personally, and for the Catholic Church generally.

Indeed, the Amay-sur-Meuse adventure ended unhappily for Dom Beauduin in 1928, when Pius XI reacted strongly against false ecumenism with his encyclical *Mortalium Animos*. This caused two of the monks to defect to Eastern Orthodoxy, and was a great setback for the prior himself.[53] His plan for Amay had been for it to become a centre for ecumenical activity, whereas the Eastern Congregation intended the monastery to become a linchpin of Rome's long-term plan for the conversion of the Orthodox Russians to Eastern-rite Catholicism. Frustrated by his inability to pursue his ecumenical dream, Beauduin resigned as superior that same year.[54]

Three years later the Belgian ecumenist was called to Rome to account for his views, then exiled for two years to the French monastery of Encalcat in Languedoc and forbidden to have any relations with Amay. Regaining his freedom of movement in 1933, Dom Beauduin was pleasantly surprised to find himself the object of admiration of the Institut Catholique and of the progressivist ordinaries of Chartres, Évreux, Versailles and Paris, who tried unsuccessfully to appoint him secretary general of the French liturgical movement. A subsequent bid to secure Beauduin's services as professor of liturgy at the Institute was also blocked by Rome.[55] Unable to return to Belgium, Beauduin remained in France where, protected by Mgr Martin-Jérôme Izart, Archbishop of Bourges, he set about spreading

[50] Ibid., pp. 100–01.
[51] Ibid., pp. 111–21.
[52] Beauduin also put Lutheranism in the same 'Catholic' category as Anglicanism. His biographer records that when, in July and August of 1925, Archbishop Meletios Metaxakis (the same Orthodox Patriarch of Alexandria who had naïvely recognized the validity of Anglican orders) 'concelebrated' the Eucharist with the Archbishop of Canterbury and the Lutheran Archbishop of Uppsala, 'for Beauduin, these events literally consecrated the fact of [ecumenical] intercommunion, even though it remained a practice reserved for special occasions' (Quitslund, *op. cit.*, p. 99). Beauduin lost interest in the Uniate cause when he learned, at the Unity Week Conference in Brussels in 1925, that the Orthodox considered them an obstacle to reunion with Rome (ibid., p. 127).
[53] Ibid., pp. 141–42.
[54] Ibid., p. 144.
[55] Ibid., p. 190.

his condemned ideas through publications in the liberal Catholic press and in the clerical retreats he was invited to give all over the country.[56]

The jaded visionary was soon throwing all his weight behind the French reformists' 'pastoral' policy of cultivating the sacred liturgy as an instrument of evangelization and social reform. To the existing reform programme he soon added a third point: that of making the liturgy serve the interests of his horizontalizing ecumenism. The intellectual wing of the movement responded well to this new stimulus, but the ecumenical thrust of the liturgical renewal was now in the direction of Protestantism, and not towards the Eastern Orthodoxy with which the Latin West had so much in common and from which it had so much to learn.

Planning the Revolution

Following closely the promising developments in Germany, Dom Beauduin presided over the foundation, on 20 May 1943 (within a month of the Fulda Conference's challenge to the Holy See), of the Centre de Pastorale Liturgique in Paris (CPL). The CPL began under the auspices of Éditions du Cerf, and its principal collaborators were the Dominicans Maydieu, Duployé, Roguet, Chenu, Chéry; the Jesuits Doncœur and Daniélou; the Oratorian Louis Bouyer; Mgr Aimé-Georges Martimort of Toulouse; and the Belgian Benedictines Dom Bernard Capelle and Dom Bernard Botte.

In January 1945 Beauduin penned the editorial of the first issue of *La Maison-Dieu*, official organ of the CPL. His 'Practical Norms for Liturgical Reforms' lamented the current impoverishment of sacred liturgy, describing the contemporary Roman rite as 'mummified'. 'Shouldn't we rather', asked the writer, 'emancipate ourselves prudently from the excessively tight discipline of the present liturgical rules and restore to the sacramental signs and to Christian institutions all their strength and efficacy?'[57] Beauduin was convinced that the only way of doing this was to work, cautiously and gradually, within the system, an approach that had already borne such fruit in Germany:

> We will have to proceed in cooperation with the hierarchy, taking only initiatives that are in conformity with the current liturgical regulations. We must proceed patiently, modestly using what is available to us today and preparing for the future by making people desire and love all the riches contained in the ancient liturgy. We must prepare people's minds, for Rome fears above all scandalizing the faithful. We must proceed methodically . . . and also stress the moral and practical aspects [of the liturgy]: frequent Communion, [reducing] the Eucharistic fast, [changing] the times of Mass: the Church is not afraid to modify her discipline for the good of her children.[58]

But since the Pope himself must authorize and promote the necessary reforms, it was important above all to convert the Holy See to the reformers' ideals:

---

[56] Bonneterre, *op. cit.*, p. 42.
[57] Ibid., p. 70.
[58] Ibid., p. 72. See also Botte, *op. cit.*, pp. 67, 79.

We need to be able to count on sympathies born of conviction and leading to action. . . . The CPL must take the trouble to make its works known and appreciated by the consultors of the Holy Congregation [of Rites], by the members of the Liturgical Academy and so on. . . . If it must never allow itself to anticipate the decisions of competent authorities, it has the right and the duty to make these aware of the desiderata and the wise and properly motivated wishes of the most zealous pastors and of the faithful, in particular the devoted members of Catholic Action.[59]

The German experience had taught them how to exploit the Holy See's willingness to accede to the liturgical requests of bishops, especially when these were presented as pastorally desirable.

While members of the contemporary worker-priest movement took it upon themselves to celebrate in French the audible parts of their over-the-counter Eucharists in urban factories and workshops, like-minded prelates saw the merits of going about the same things the 'correct' way. In November 1944 Mgr Jean-Joseph-Aimé Moussaron, Archbishop of Albi, staged in Castres Cathedral a special, dramatic paraliturgy with actors expressing 'the shame of conquered France'. This was followed by an equally 'special' Mass for which the Archbishop had apparently received permission from Pius XII. A thrilled eyewitness described the function in these words:

Then Mgr Moussaron, Archbishop of Albi, entered, garbed in his purple cassock. In full view of the congregation he was robed in his vestments while a priest explained their meaning. When midnight struck, the archbishop proceeded to the temporary altar and, facing the congregation, began the celebration of Mass. By special dispensation of the pope, this Mass, except for the Canon, was said in French. The effect on the congregation was instant and profound. For many it was as if they were hearing Mass for the first time . . .[60]

The late 1940s saw the formation of study teams and the holding of seminars, workshops, and international liturgical congresses, all working towards these goals. At the Liturgical Congress of St-Flour, held in 1945, the CPL leaders proposed as their first resolution that the practice of celebrating Mass facing the people be promoted as a standard reform.[61] During the next decade the liturgical movement radicalized itself (at times disconcerting members of its right wing like Bouyer and Botte, and even Dom Beauduin himself),[62] and a new generation of reformists emerged to take the lead. Mass facing the people became a mark of 'progress' not only in Germany and France, but also in the United States, where the

[59] Ibid., p. 73.
[60] Ellard, *Mass of the Future*, pp. 154–55. Castres was situated in what was then still a strongly Occitan-speaking region, even if many the inhabitants of the town had already gone over to French. So much for the vernacular principle.
[61] Quitslund, *op. cit.*, p. 208.
[62] See Botte, *op. cit.*, pp. 62–63, 80–81. Dom Beauduin also had a number of incongruous conservative quirks; for instance, he was in favour of maintaining liturgical Latin, 'a major weakness in his liturgical career' according to Professor Quitslund (*op. cit.*, p. 206). This opposition to the vernacular must, however, be seen in the context of the antiquarianist views Beauduin embraced in the latter part of his career.

Archbishop of Kansas City, Edwin O'Hara, was encouraging it as early as 1951,[63] on the basis of a tendentious interpretation of a rubric in the *Ritus servandus* of the Roman missal.[64]

Meanwhile in Europe the Jesuit Cardinal Augustin Bea sponsored a series of 'International Meetings for Liturgical Studies' (Maria Laach 1951, Mont-Sainte-Odile 1952, Lugano 1953, Louvain 1954, Assisi 1956, Montserrat 1958, Munich 1960) which discussed and proposed the shape of the Roman liturgy of the future. The ageing (and reportedly senilescent) Pius XII, quite unaware of the direction the movement was taking, cheered the 1956 Assisi meeting with the following message of encouragement:

> The Liturgical Movement has appeared as a sign of the providential designs of God in our present age, as the movement of the Holy Ghost through His Church to draw men nearer to the mysteries of the faith and the riches of grace that flow from the active participation of the faithful in the liturgical life.[65]

Pope Pius in the meantime had approved a whole range of seemingly harmless and sensible liturgical innovations, to be regulated by the Pontifical Commission for the Reform of the Liturgy set up in 1948, the year after the publication of *Mediator Dei*. Some of these changes purported to restore the Roman rite to its authentic form; for example, the new Office of Holy Week, 1955.[66] Others were moderni-

---

[63] Gerard Ellard, SJ, *The Mass in Transition* (Milwaukee, 1956), pp. 114–15. In a directive of 1951 the Archbishop stated: 'Since we believe that it is very helpful that the people have an occasional opportunity to gaze upon the altar at Mass, the Ordinary lets it be known that for field Masses, and other such occasions when a temporary altar is set up, permission will be readily accorded to have the Mass celebrated *versus populum* . . .' However, that O'Hara soon became an advocate of *versus populum* celebrations inside churches as well is evident from the photograph in Fr Ellard's book showing him doing just this on the feast of Christ the King, 1954.

[64] The rubric in question (5, 3) states:

> If the altar faces the people . . . the celebrant, already facing the congregation, does not turn his back when saying '*Dominus vobiscum*', '*Orate, fratres*', '*Ite, Missa est*', and on imparting the blessing. Instead, he kisses the altar in the centre, extends and rejoins his hands as directed above, and salutes the people or blesses them.

The reference in this ancient directive is to the high altar of St Peter's and of a few other old basilicas in Rome (Sta Maria in Trastevere, San Cesareo in Palazio, San Giorgio in Velabro), which were originally set up facing east so that the priest could celebrate in that position. That the congregation happened to be positioned on the other side of the altar was merely coincidental and circumstantial. 'Facing the people' was never the point of this rare, and Roman, practice. Moreover, since the other clergy took their place behind the celebrant in these 'occidented' basilicas, the priest did not face the whole congregation. The practice of placing high crucifixes and candlesticks virtually obscuring the view of the priest from those in the apse also shows that facing the people was not considered a liturgical principle at all. Since elsewhere in Christendom all churches were at first built with the apse facing east, *versus populum* celebrations were always unknown, and even when this architectural custom lapsed in many countries, the priest continued to stand at the altar with his back to the congregation (i.e. leading them in prayer, hardly 'ignoring' them), which is still the practice of all the separated Eastern Churches and most Uniate communities. There is even strong evidence that in the early centuries the congregation in the apse of these Roman basilicas stood in the aisles facing each other, and not facing the altar. See Gamber, *op. cit.*, pp. 77–89, and Part II, 'Facing the Lord: On the Building of Churches and Facing the East in Prayer', pp. 115–79, and M. Davies, *PPNM*, pp. 389–417.

[65] Bonneterre, *op. cit.*, p. 100.

[66] The new Office of Holy Week restored to their correct times the ceremonies of Maundy Thursday, Good Friday and Holy Saturday which, since the disappearance of afternoon and evening eucharistic celebrations of Mass in the late Middle Ages, had been anomalously performed in the morning. On the less fortunate aspects of this reform, see Bonneterre, *op. cit.*, pp. 109–10;

zations prompted by alleged pastoral needs: the reduction of the eucharistic fast to three hours in 1953, and the simplification of the rubrics of the breviary in 1955. (A parallel reform of the rubrics of the missal would follow in 1960, during the pontificate of John XXIII.) However, a negative feature common to all these reforms was the tendency to abolish absolutely prayers, feasts, octaves and actions of secondary importance instead of making them optional, as is the procedure in the Oriental rites when practical necessities dictate the shortening of services.

Dom Bernard Botte makes a revealing admission about the revolutionary thrust of the liturgical movement when he refers in his memoirs to the refusal of Mgr Michel Andrieu, dean of Strasbourg University's Faculty of Theology, to attend the Mont-Sainte-Odile meeting called by the Liturgical Commission of Strasbourg. This eminent French liturgiologist was, in fact,

> the best historian of the Roman liturgy. His editions of the *Ordines Romani* and the pontificals are admired by all scholars. We would have liked him to come, but a position he had taken was an obstacle: the liturgy could not be reformed; it was a given element of tradition which had to be accepted. He was allergic to the idea that the liturgy could be modified for pastoral goals.[67]

In a remarkably superficial, not to say secular-minded, analysis, Botte attributed such conservatism – sound Christian instinct that it is – to the mere political humour of individuals: 'Politics also influence judgements on liturgical reform. The more to the right you are, the less you like it.'[68]

The Blueprint

There was great excitement in the ranks of the liturgical movement when, in 1960, Pope John XXIII announced that the ecumenical council he was planning would consider a general reform of the Roman liturgy. The following year Dom Adrien Nocent, professor of liturgy at the Collegio Sant'Anselmo in Rome, published with the imprimatur of Belgian Cardinal Suenens his work *L'avenir de la liturgie* ('The Future of the Liturgy'), which gave its readers a concrete idea of the type of rite that, in his view, would issue from the conciliar reforms.[69] Its shape embodied the resolutions of the International Meetings for Liturgical Studies, especially the Lugano conference of 1953.

The 'Mass of Dom Adrien Nocent' is, without a shadow of a doubt, the blueprint of Paul VI's *Novus Ordo Missæ* and of the heteropractic style in which it would be commonly implemented. This Eucharist of the future would be celebrated facing the people, and the altar, restored to the shape of a table, would be covered with a cloth only during celebrations. While the preparatory prayers of the Mass would be simplified, the Liturgy of the Word would be expanded with an extra reading from the Old Testament. The Prayer of the Faithful would be resurrected. After the Creed, recited only on Sundays, would come a drastically shortened Offertory

---

and Daniel L. Dolan, 'John is its Name . . . Pre-Conciliar Liturgical Change', *Roman Catholic* (June 1983), pp. 4–10.

[67] Botte, *op. cit.*, p. 81.
[68] Ibid., p. 66.
[69] Bonneterre, *op. cit.*, pp. 120–21.

with the oblations raised by the priest in silence, as in the primitive Roman rite.[70] The Secret would be recited aloud, the new Eucharistic Prayer would be stripped of its prayers of intercession and most of its signs of the cross and genuflections, and said aloud and in the vernacular, if pastoral needs warranted. The *Pater Noster* would be recited by all, and the Kiss of Peace would take the form of a handshake. A leavened loaf could be used instead of individual hosts, and the Body of Christ would be placed in the hands of standing communicants. The Last Gospel and the Leonine Prayers at the end of Mass would be suppressed.[71]

Meanwhile in Poland the French, German and Belgian reformers of the liturgy had a fellow traveller in Karol Wojtyła, Archbishop of Cracow. During a discussion in 1965 about the need for 'inculturation' he predicted an even more atomized future for the Roman Mass: 'Certainly, we will preserve the basic elements, the bread, the wine, but all else will be changed according to local traditions: words, gestures, colours, vestments, chants, architecture, decor. The problem of liturgical reform is immense.'[72]

Time Bombs

Were such radical changes really ordered by the Council? Since this question has been hotly debated since 1969, one cannot dispense with a close examination of what is at once claimed by progressives as the charter of revolution and by conservatives as the safeguard against such tendencies. On close analysis the Liturgy Constitution reveals itself to be a highly ambiguous document, appearing at times to be upholding a traditional approach to liturgical renewal, and at other times to serve as a basis for more radical restructuring – 'time bombs' to use the expression popularized by Michael Davies.

The preface of *Sacrosanctum Concilium* closed with the recommendation that 'where necessary, the rites be carefully and thoroughly revised in the light of sound tradition'. They should, on the other hand, *'be given new vigour to meet the circumstances and needs of modern times'.*[73] (Arguably subversive clauses like the latter are italicized in the quotations that follow.)

Section II dealt with not only the traditional desideratum of pastoral instruction in liturgical prayer, but also the new (and as it turned out, highly ambiguous) concept of *participatio actuosa* 'zealously active participation', translated into English as 'active participation'.[74] Article 14 stated that

---

[70] One particularly daft piece of rationalism was Nocent's suggestion that the celebrant wash his hands only if they were actually dirty! See Bonneterre, *op. cit.*, p. 123.

[71] Ibid. For more detail on the pre-conciliar liturgical movement, see Alcuin Reid's thoroughgoing study, *The Organic Development of the Liturgy, op. cit.*

[72] Mieczysław Malinski, *Mon ami Karol Wojtyła* (Paris, 1980), p. 220.

[73] *Sacrosanctum Concilium*, Preface, § 4.

[74] In Lewis and Short's *Latin Dictionary* (Oxford, 1969) the adjective *actuosus* is glossed as 'full of activity, very active (with the access[ory] idea of zeal, subjective impulse; diff[erent] from *industrius*, which refers more to the means by which an object is attained' (p. 25). There have been several objections to the inaccurate translation of *actuosa* as merely 'active' (= *industria*), which has since been exploited by modernists to turn divine worship into a superficial and boisterous dialogue between celebrant and congregation. See Michael Davies (*Pope John's Council*, pp. 236–37); Hemming, *op. cit.*, pp. 31–32.

[i]n the restoration and promotion of the sacred liturgy, this full and active par-
ticipation by all the people is the aim to be considered above all else; for it is the
primary and indispensable source from which the faithful are to derive the true
Christian spirit.

Section III was entitled 'The Reform of the Sacred Liturgy', and subsection C
provided 'Norms based upon *the Educative and Pastoral Nature of the Liturgy*':
'33. Although the sacred liturgy is above all things the worship of the divine
Majesty, *it likewise contains abundant instruction for the faithful.*'
  In the revision of the liturgy, the following general norms were to be observed:
'34. *The rites should be distinguished by a noble simplicity; they should be short,*
clear, and unencumbered by useless repetitions;[75] *they should be within the people's*
powers of comprehension, and normally should not require much explanation.'
  Chapter II, 'On the Most Sacred Mystery of the Eucharist', added:

50 *The rite of the Mass is to be revised in such a way that the intrinsic nature and*
purpose of its several parts, as also the connection between them, can be more
clearly manifested, and that devout and active participation by the faithful can
be more easily accomplished.

  For this purpose the rites are to be simplified, while due care is taken to preserve
their substance. *Elements which, with the passage of time, came to be duplicated,*
or were added with but little advantage, are now to be discarded. Where oppor-
tunity allows, other elements which have suffered injury through accidents of
history are now to be restored to the earlier norm of the holy Fathers.

On the question of liturgical language:

36. § 1. Particular law remaining in force, the use of the Latin language is to be
preserved in the Latin rites.

§ 2. *But since the use of the mother tongue, whether in the Mass, the adminis-*
tration of the sacraments, or other parts of the liturgy, may frequently be of great
advantage to the people, the limits of its employment may be extended. This
extension will apply in the first place to the readings and directives, and to some
of the prayers and chants, according to the regulations on this matter to be laid
down separately in subsequent chapters.

§ 3. *It is for the competent territorial ecclesiastical authority . . . to decide*
whether, and to what extent, the vernacular language is to be used according to
these norms . . .

Finally, as for the 'Norms for Adapting the Liturgy to the Genius and Traditions
of Peoples':

38 Provided that the substantial unity of the Roman rite is maintained, *the revi-*
sion of the liturgical books should allow for legitimate variations and adaptations

---

[75] One wonders what would happen to music if some economy-obsessed reformer armed with a
carte blanche to prune were to decree the elimination of 'useless repetitions' in a concerto of
Mozart or in a symphony of Beethoven.

*to different groups, regions and peoples, especially in mission lands. Where oppor-
tune, the same rule applies to the structuring of rites and the devising of rubrics.*

That the italicized clauses above were patient of an uncatholic interpretation
and could later be exploited to unleash a liturgical revolution upon the Latin
Church escaped the overwhelming majority of Council Fathers who signed this
document.

Dom Adrien Nocent had predicted accurately in 1961 that the role of the
Council would be to open the door to liturgical change generally, but to disallow
at the same time further 'legitimate' developments considered inopportune for the
moment for pastoral reasons. When, later, new pastoral needs revealed themselves,
the stop on these innovations would be lifted.[76] In retrospect it is not difficult to
find examples of this subversive strategy in action: innovations not authorized
by the Council which were to become the liturgical norm in its aftermath, from
Mass facing the congregation[77] and Communion in the hand and its distribution
by persons other than priests and deacons to, most recently, the admission of girls
and women to the sanctuary as servers.

Spring Cleaning in Lombardy

The Council Fathers had agreed that 'The practical norms which follow . . . should
be taken as pertaining only to the Roman rite.'[78] Yet the laying down of norms for
'the Latin rites' elsewhere in the Liturgy Constitution brought the Milanese liturgy
directly into the picture.[79] In any case Paul VI, the pope of liturgical reform, had
been Archbishop of Milan from 1947 to 1958, and had a personal interest in seeing
his achievements in the Roman rite extended to that of the great Cisalpine see.[80]

So after the Council the Milanese liturgy, too, was revised, not indeed 'in the
light of sound tradition'[81] but in slavish imitation of the changes then taking place
in the Roman rite. The Ambrosian missal itself was not overhauled until 1976,
seven years after the appearance of the Roman *Novus Ordo Missæ*, but in the
intervening period a number of important ritual changes had been introduced into

---

[76] Bonneterre, *op. cit.*, p. 122.
[77] In spite of all the weight of scholarly evidence to the contrary, the antiquarianist hoax of Mass
facing the people as an 'ancient tradition' would become the main pillar of latter-day Catholic
heteropraxis. No doubt the most absurdly bourgeois justification for it to date is the one given
in Matthews, *Popular Guide*, p. 45:

> On arriving at the altar the priest kisses it and goes straight to his chair where he does
> something he has never done before. He greets the people: says 'hello' in a liturgical way.
> When you think about it, the priest has never acted like a gentleman at the beginning of
> Mass because, without a word to the people (many of whom he probably knows well), he
> turns his back on them and gets on with his own preparation for Mass . . . Now that has
> been put right. The priest has become a gentleman, so he faces the people . . . [In the new
> Entrance Rite t]he priest and his people have been 'introduced'.

The basic difference between a religious ritual and a social function seems sadly to have eluded
the (1970) master of ceremonies at Westminster Cathedral.
[78] *Sacrosanctum Concilium*, Preface, § 3.
[79] Ibid., 36, § 1.
[80] As a native of Brescia in Eastern Lombardy (a city long under Venetian influence), Montini's
home rite was the Roman, not the Milanese.
[81] Ibid., § 4.

the churches of Western Lombardy and the adjoining Swiss Canton Ticino: Mass facing the people, lessons read by laity of both sexes, Communion received standing, and general use of the 'vernacular' (not the genuine vernacular of Ambrosian Catholics – the structurally Gallic Lombard dialect – but Italian, the language favoured by the hierarchy and bourgeoisie of Lombardy and Italian Switzerland). The innovations kept pace with those of the Roman rite, and the late 1980s would see the introduction of Communion in the hand and extraordinary ministers of the Eucharist.

Cardinal Giovanni Colombo, who presided over the revision of the Ambrosian liturgy, wrote in the promulgation decree of the all-Italian *Messale ambrosiano festivo*, issued on Palm Sunday (11 April) 1976, that:

> For its broad renewal our missal has been inspired by scriptural and patristic texts, and especially by the works of the great masters of ancient liturgical prayer like Saint Ambrose and Saint Leo the Great. It has likewise drawn freely on the ancient sacramentary of our own and other rites, not without occasionally accepting the ideas and guidelines of the documents of the Second Vatican Council. Obviously the Pauline missal [= the Mass of Pope Paul VI] could not have been anything but a copious source of inspiration and moreover widely used as a model for reform' (*Copiosa fonte, non solo d'ispirazione ma altresì di larga utilizzazione, non poteva non essere evidentemente il messale paolino*).[82]

Cardinal Colombo's claims of a reform on eclectic antiquarianist principles have no basis in fact as regards the ordinary of the Mass, for it is evident from the new Milanese *ordo* that the chief, and indeed practically the sole source of inspiration has been the Mass of Paul VI. A comparison of the traditional text with that of 1976 reveals a local redaction of the *Novus Ordo Missæ* with occasional concessions to the traditional Ambrosian order. Almost totally destroyed was the Mass of the Catechumens with its Gallican prayers and gestures, its Greek ejaculations and invocation of St Ambrose in the *Confiteor*. In violation of Gallican tradition the Creed was shifted from the end of the Offertory to after the Gospel. A few of the old Offertory prayers survived, but only as alternatives to the Jewish blessings of the Pauline rite. The three new eucharistic prayers of the 1969 *Missale Romanum* compete with the Ambrosian Canon, replete with the mistranslation of *pro multis* as *per tutti* ('for all').[83]

Exhumation in Spain

The text of the Hispanic rite of Toledo fared slightly better than the Milanese, no doubt because here the reform was not undertaken until the 1980s, by which time the traditionalist reaction may well have had some effect on the thinking of the Holy See. Rather than aping the *Novus Ordo Missæ*, the new Mozarabic Mass order was an exercise in pure antiquarianism. But this course of action was all

---

[82] Inos Biffi, ed., *Messale ambrosiano festivo* (Milan, 1976), pp. 4–5.
[83] As a result of the Roman indult of 1984, the traditional Ambrosian Mass was revived and celebrated weekly (before a small congregation) in the Milanese church of San Rocco al Gentilino.

the more deplorable in that the traditional Spanish liturgy, like the Roman, was hybrid in nature.

Between the ninth and the twelfth centuries the classic structure of the Mozarabic rite had absorbed, spontaneously and organically, a large number of euchololologi-cal and ceremonial embellishments of Gallicano-Roman origin. Many of these elements, of great lyrical beauty, were fixed in the service books edited in the thirteenth century.[84] In no way did they distort the clear Spanish lineaments of the liturgy, of which they remained an integral part until the committee of experts entrusted with the revision of this venerable rite between 1982 and 1986 agreed on the need to 'purify it of the unauthentic elements that were obscuring the clarity of its structure'.[85] Accordingly, these 'grave deformations of the structure of the Mass' that adorned the Foremass, the Offertory and the Communion rite were hacked away from the 'restored' Mozarabic *ordo* which the Holy See approved on 17 July 1988.[86]

As might be expected, this pedantic and vandalistic reform was accompanied by the automatic introduction of typically Neo-Roman abuses: exclusive use of the vernacular, *versus populum* celebrations, Communion in the hand, and, in the Canon, the standard false rendering *por todos los hombres* ('for all men') for *pro multis*. The one and only real benefit of the Mozarabic reform was the potential extension of the national liturgy, hitherto restricted to Toledo, to the whole of Spain, subject to the granting of faculties to celebrate.[87]

Mission Accomplished – Nearly

By the 1990s the architects and pioneers of liturgical utilitarianism could con-gratulate themselves on their nearly total success in the Roman rite, and in its Occidental sister liturgies. Nearly total because, though the traditional Roman, Milanese, Mozarabic rites ceased officially to exist, and though the Dominicans, Discalced Carmelites, Premonstratensians, Carthusians and Cistercians had all gleefully forsaken their ritual heritage to embrace the Pauline reform, one Western liturgy, that of the archdiocese of Braga in northern Portugal, had come through the post-conciliar maelstrom unharmed, technically at least. The Metropolitan of Braga, Mgr Francisco Maria da Silva, recommended that this medieval variant of the Roman rite be simply reapproved by the Holy See on 3 October 1972 with-out any substantial alteration (and with the signature of Archbishop Bugnini!).[88] However, this was only because the liturgy in question was practically defunct: the Roman rite – now reformed – was already the norm in the archdiocese.

The disruption of liturgical tradition was thus virtually complete in the Latin Church. But there was an irony: the legacy of the despised pre-conciliar order, which the new worship was designed to extinguish, survived in the reformism so

---

[84] Jordi Pinell, OSB, 'Missale hispano-mozarabicum: Prænotanda', *Notitiæ: Congregatio pro Cultu Divino*, 267 (October 1988), p. 722.

[85] Ibid., p. 670 ('purificado de los elementos no auténticos que oscurecían la nitidez de su estructura').

[86] Ibid., p. 722.

[87] With episcopal permission, the Old Spanish liturgy can now be celebrated all over Spain on feast days of national saints in the Mozarabic calendar, and for the reconsecration of churches and chapels dating from Roman, Visigothic and Mozarabic times. Ibid., p. 725.

[88] *Ordinário da Missa Bracarense*. Braga: Empresa do Diário do Minho, 1972 (Introduction).

strongly endorsed by Rome. And this reformism was merely another manifestation of the puritan spirit distilled, like Protestantism, from the Latin Church's old and dangerous neglect of *theologia prima*.

On the sad outcome of the liturgical movement, Mgr Klaus Gamber has commented:

> Unfortunately, man has a tendency to go from one extreme to another. If, in the past, the emphasis had been on the clergy performing the ritual of liturgical worship and administering the sacraments, now too much emphasis is being given to the congregation actively participating in the liturgy and doing away with many of the essential elements of liturgical cult and ceremony. Because many of these elements have been eliminated and are now in a state of common neglect, they are fading away rapidly. Also, we are now experiencing – and this applies especially to worship in larger group settings – a diminishing sense of solemnity. Solemnity is an integral part of the liturgical ceremony. But we are now breathing the thin air of Calvinistic sterility.[89]

The true object of celebration in the Catholic liturgy is the Mystery of God and its operation throughout human history. What we have today is a cult that amounts to little more than the celebration, now rational, now sentimental, of the Christian (or sub-Christian) belief and morality of our age: *righteous* worship rather than *right* worship. The truth is that the liturgical movement, so promising in its beginnings, failed miserably to make traditional worship once again the living heart of Christianity in the West, something it has never ceased to be in the East. It is a failure to be measured against the fact that none of its leaders, as Mgr Gamber recalls, 'truly understood the liturgy of the Eastern Church'.[90]

---

[89] Gamber, *op. cit.*, p. 5.
[90] Ibid., p. 4. Fr Lawrence Cross has commented on the same note that 'Catholics who know nothing of the Byzantine inheritance are ignorant of a considerable aspect of the Catholic tradition of prayer itself and may run the risk of misconceiving certain essential elements with which they are familiar. In other words, they may get their own faith wrong' ('Some Essential Features of Orthodox Catholic Christianity', in *Ukrainian Settlement in Australia* [Sydney, 1989], p. 100).

16

RUINS IN THE EAST

*Despite the fact that the Roman Church has made efforts to maintain
the Oriental rites, some of its representatives are diligently working
to deprive the Eastern Churches of their own inheritance in different
ways. This is a great sin against the Catholicity of the Church. The
Latin West is in need of a conversion to Catholicism and to the
universality of the heritage of Christ.*

GEEVARGHESE CHEDIATH (1981)

From the beginning the success of the Catholic liturgical movement depended on its
cross-fertilization by an Eastern ritual tradition untouched by the spirit of rationalism. Ultimately, however, this approach was shunned, the movement choosing
instead to follow the peculiarly Western paths to Protestantism and secularism.
The movement's failure was therefore one of ecumenical dimensions, and all the
more regrettable in that the pontificate of Leo XIII (1878–1903) had been a time
of great promise for East–West rapprochement in the Catholic Church.

Towards Inclusion

The unhappy events in India, the United States and elsewhere in the last decades
of the nineteenth century were bringing home to the Vatican the real possibility
that if earlier guarantees to respect the distinct traditions of the Orientals were
not upheld, there would be little to stop more disgruntled Uniates from returning
to their communions of origin. Contemporary Protestant proselytizing among the
dissident Eastern Christians of the Middle East and Kerala, and the forging of
friendly ties between the Anglican and Orthodox Churches, also threatened Rome's
interests in the Oriental domain.

Pope Pius IX had opened a new road to reconciliation with the independent
Eastern Churches by clarifying the Roman teaching on the ancient doctrine that
there is no salvation outside the Church. In his encyclical *Quanto Conficiamur
Mœrore* (1863) the Pope stated that a person who found himself outside the
Catholic Church through no 'guilt of voluntary fault' could not for this reason
alone be damned to eternal punishment. This was necessary in the light of the
restrictive statement in the *Decretum Pro Jacobitis* at the Council of Florence
(1438–1445) that any person who was not joined to the Catholic Church before
death would be damned, 'even if he shed his blood in the name of Christ' and, further, that only for her members 'do the Church's sacraments contribute to salvation

and do fasts, almsgiving and other works of piety and practices of the Christian militia produce eternal rewards'.[1] Since in this context the term 'Catholic Church' could appear to denote a Roman communion that was, as it were, hermetically sealed, it is understandable that these propositions were deeply offensive to members of the dissident Oriental Churches who believed that they had never deviated from the faith of the Apostles.[2] Nevertheless, Pius IX's clarification, without repudiating the *de fide* identification of the institutional Catholic Church with the Roman communion, demonstrated the truth that everyone possessing sanctifying grace has some connection with the Catholic Church, since all grace is ecclesial.

From Uniatism to Unionism

Better times dawned for inter-ecclesial relations with the pontificate of Leo XIII. Disturbed by the damning report that Cardinal Serafino Vannutelli, the Apostolic Delegate in Constantinople, had made about the injustices suffered by Eastern Catholics within the Church, the Pontiff-elect determined to right as many wrongs as possible.[3] The 'first modern Pope' is remembered for the impetus he gave to the Benedictine revival in 1887, when he founded the College of Sant'Anselmo in Rome as an international centre of studies for the venerable order. What is less well known is that one of Leo's plans for Sant'Anselmo was the training of Benedictines in the traditions of the Eastern Churches. Groups of Catholic monks could then be sent to the East and, by their example, promote the reconciliation of the dissidents – not by aggressive conversion tactics, but by prayer and good example within a familiar cultural setting.[4]

In an audience of 1893 Pope Leo told the students of Sant'Anselmo:

> You know how concerned I am for the reconciliation of the Eastern Churches. Well, I count on you to help me bring this about. I have often said to myself: I need Benedictines for this. The Orientals still have a deep respect for them, because they have remained men of prayer and of the liturgy, and their origin goes back so many centuries . . .[5]

A few years earlier the Pope had charged the eminent Belgian Benedictine, Dom Gérard van Caloen, with the task of establishing a 'monastery of union': a house of monks who worshipped in both the Roman and the Byzantine rites. (This project was not in fact realized, but served as the inspiration, three decades later, for Dom

---

[1] Session 11, 14 February 1442.
[2] This revised teaching appeared in the Catechism of Pope Pius X (Q. 29), and was amplified by Pius XII in *Mystici Corporis* (1943, DS 3821) and in 1949 by a decree concerning the errors of Fr Leonard Feeney, SJ, in which the Holy Office confirmed that 'invincible ignorance' of the one true Church was not an impediment to salvation (DS 3870, 3821). The constitution *Lumen Gentium* at Vatican II would develop this doctrine further, and the contentious concept of the Church of Christ *subsisting* in (rather than being conterminous in an absolute sense with) the juridical Catholic Church (I, 8) appears to mean – when interpreted in the light of Tradition – that to the extent that separated Churches have elements of Catholicism within them, these bodies are materially and potentially Catholic while not being formally part of the Church.
[3] Taft, *op. cit.*, p. 424.
[4] Quitslund, *op. cit.*, pp. 94–95.
[5] Ibid., p. 96.

Lambert Beauduin's biritual monastery of Amay). In 1891 Dom Gérard wrote the first of a series of articles in the *Revue Bénédictine* outlining the ideal method of executing the papal project:

> These monks, formed in advance in the liturgy, the language and the customs of the Greeks, will go toward them as brothers, establish themselves there and lead a purely monastic and liturgical life which the Greeks admire so sincerely. It will not be a question of converting them or of proselytizing. They will limit themselves to forming great centres of prayer, of liturgy, and of serious studies. . . .
>
> One can easily imagine what influence such monks and monasteries will soon have and what a powerful balance they will bring to the ideas of unity which are beginning to appear in the Orient. By their life, liturgy, relations, writings and preaching, these monks will dispel little by little the prejudices which still exist against the Roman Church. They will win hearts by abstaining from all irritating polemic. Finally, they will make the Greeks see that the Roman Church does not in the least dream of taking away from them their rites, customs, and ancient and venerable traditions, since she will even go to the point of authorizing Latin monks to adopt them out of love for their separated brothers.[6]

In two apostolic letters of 1894 Pope Leo boldly broke with the Counter-Reformation strategy of assimilationist uniatism and inaugurated in its stead a policy of unionism which demanded that the dissident clergy and laity of the East be treated as members of Churches of apostolic institution whose legacy was highly valued in Catholicism and whose separation from Rome was an unfortunate ill to be remedied, rather than the shameful legacy of culpable schism. In the first encyclical, *Præclara Gratulationis Publicæ* (20 June), the Pope stated, in regard to the desirable reunion of Christendom:

> We cast an affectionate look upon the East, from whence in the beginning came forth the salvation of the world. Yes, and the yearning desire of Our heart bids us conceive and hope that the day is not far distant when the Eastern Churches, so illustrious in their ancient faith and glorious past, will return to the fold they have abandoned. We hope it all the more, that the distance separating them from Us is not great: nay, with some few exceptions, we agree so entirely on other matters that, in defence of the Catholic Faith, we often have recourse to reasons and testimonies borrowed from the teaching, the rites, and customs of the East.

At the same time the letter stressed that the reunion of all Christians 'of Greek or other Oriental rites who are separated from the Catholic Church' could not be based merely on 'a certain kind of agreement in the tenets of belief and an intercourse of fraternal love' but that 'the true union between Christians is that which Jesus Christ, the Author of the Church, instituted and desired, and which consists in a unity of faith and unity of government'.

In *Orientalium Dignitas* (30 November 1894) the Pope solemnly proclaimed the equal dignity of the Eastern and Roman rites, and reconsecrated the Church's liturgical pluralism founded in tradition:

---

[6] Gérard van Caloen, *Revue Bénédictine*, VIII (1891), pp. 117–29, and quoted in Quitslund, *op. cit.*, pp. 95–96.

Nothing else, perhaps, is so breathtakingly effective for illustrating the mark of Catholicity in God's Church than that striking sight of differing forms of ceremonies and noble examples of the tongues of the ancient past – made all the more noble by their use by the Apostles and Fathers – rendering their submission to the Church.

This second encyclical expressly prohibited attempts by Western missionaries to latinize the liturgies and institutions of Eastern Catholics. Unionism required that Oriental Catholics become 'true heralds and peacemakers of holy unity between the Eastern Churches and the Roman Church, which is the centre of unity and love' so that 'our dissident brethren may seek out more readily the embrace of their Mother, the Church'.[7] The existing Eastern Catholic Churches thus needed to delatinize themselves and return integrally to their own traditions in order to attract their dissident counterparts back to full Catholic unity.[8] The final destiny of the Eastern Catholics was not to represent Oriental traditions within the Western Church as a sort of token presence – as beneficial as this presence might be for Latin Christendom – but to return one day to their mother Churches after these themselves had restored communion with Rome.[9]

---

[7] Leo XIII established the term 'dissident brethren' in relation to the non-Catholic Orientals. The term was not merely irenic, but correct, since St Thomas Aquinas had defined schism in active rather than passive terms, and taught that 'Those are properly called "schismatics" who freely and deliberately separate themselves from the Church's unity . . .' (*Summa Theologica*, IIa, IIae, 39, art. *corpus*). Fr Augustine Rock, OP, clarifies this definition, explaining that:

> If separation from the Church is not free and deliberate, it may be error or dissidence, but it is not schism. This is the condition of the Eastern Orthodox Churches, whose prelates and members are separate from Rome but not as a result of malice or guilt. These Churches are known as dissident rather than heretical or schismatical. ('Schism', *CESH*, IX, p. 659)

Consequently, claims that the Orthodox Churches are heretical, made by some Catholics today, are unfounded as well as unjust. Since there has been no dogmatic development in these Churches since their formal separation from Rome, it is extravagant to allege that non-acceptance of dogmas defined since then (the Immaculate Conception, Papal Infallibility, etc.) constitutes rejection of teachings which are, in any case, implicit in the liturgical texts and theology of the dissident Easterners, even if this may be denied by the more hard-line Orthodox theologians. On this question, Edward E. Finn, SJ, writes:

> Some Western writers go so far as to point to heretical teachings which must now be added to the position of schismatic, affirming that the rejection of the universal jurisdictional authority claimed by the Bishop of Rome involves a doctrinal as well as a disciplinary element. Here, however, a caution must be observed, for according to the teaching of the Orthodox Churches, a new definition or declaration of doctrine would involve the convocation of another ecumenical council. Since, in their view, no ecumenical council has been legitimately convoked since Second Nicaea in 787, then no new doctrinal declarations or definitions have occurred since that time. We should distinguish, then, between one who positively and deliberately rejects a doctrine now taught by the Church and, on the other hand, one who has never been called upon to accept such a doctrinal teaching. (*These are My Rites: A Brief History of the Eastern Rites of Christianity* [Collegeville, Minnesota, 1980], p. 69).

See also the statements of Leo Allatius in note 19 to Chapter 12 of the present work.

[8] Peri, *op. cit.*, pp. 384–85.
[9] Cross, *Eastern Christianity*, p. 99.

Leonine and Pian Reforms

That same year the Pope removed the Jesuits from the Greek College, which he now placed under the direction of the Sant'Anselmo Benedictines, who he knew would be more sympathetic to the Byzantine tradition and sensitive to the cultural diversity of the students.[10] These Benedictines were given faculties to celebrate in the Byzantine rite and instructed to restore the standard Greek prayers and customs, eliminating all the latinizations and hybridisms imposed by Jesuit rectors in the past. Discarding the Roman soutane and biretta, the students began at last to wear the clerical dress of their rite: the black *rason* and the *kamēlaukion*.[11] The following year Pope Leo instituted a patriarchate for the Catholic Copts and erected the two Egyptian dioceses of Minya and Thebes. A separate Ruthenian College, endowed by the Austrian emperor Franz Josef, was also opened in Rome in 1894.[12]

Pope Leo's programme of renewal for the Eastern Catholic Churches had been inspired by the publication, in 1894, of a study entitled *L'Orient et Rome: Étude sur l'union*. Its author, Fr Pierre Michel of the White Fathers, had undertaken his research with the encouragement of his provincial, Cardinal Lavigerie, who was convinced that the only way to achieve this goal was to show full respect for the institutions of the Easterners. To this end, sixteen years earlier Lavigerie had founded in Jerusalem the Seminary of Saint Anne, where Melkite candidates for the priesthood could be trained according to the authentic traditions of the Byzantine rite.[13] Around the same time, in 1877, Pope Pius IX had also taken the first of a number of steps to improve conditions in Kerala by replacing the Discalced Carmelite vicars apostolic, so resented by the Malabarese, with non-Carmelite European bishops. But it was Leo XIII who finally granted the Thomas Christians' request for bishops of their own nationality and rite, and in 1896 he appointed three Malabarese vicars apostolic, responsible to the Congregation for the Propagation of the Faith.[14]

Meanwhile in Eritrea, where the prevailing policy of Catholic missionaries was to eschew the problematical Ethiopic liturgy and merely translate the Roman Missal and ritual into Ge'ez, the first prefecture apostolic, erected in 1894, was entrusted to an Italian Capuchin, Fr Michele Da Carbonara, who was firmly opposed to the latinization favoured by the Vincentians. The new prefect did everything possible to promote the revision of the indigenous rite for Catholic use, which was eventually the achievement of the Abyssinian priest Abba Takla Maryam.[15]

In 1908 Cardinal Merry del Val, Pius X's secretary of state, communicated to Fr Aleksei Zerchaninov, administrator of the mission to the Russian Catholics, a papal decree '*to observe the laws of the Greek-Slavonic Rite faithfully and in all their integrity, without any admixture from the Latin rite or any other rite; he must also see that his subjects, clergy and all other Catholics, do the same*'. The

---

[10] The first Benedictine rector of the Greek College was the pope's friend Hildebrand de Hemptinne, former abbot of Maredsous and first rector of Sant'Anselmo, see Quitslund, *op. cit.*, p. 97.
[11] Fortescue, *Uniate Eastern Churches*, p. 159. The *rason* is the ample over-cassock equivalent to the Roman surplice worn by Orthodox priests; the *kamēlaukion* is the brimless cylindrical hat worn by the secular clergy.
[12] Ibid., p. 153.
[13] Ibid., p. 230.
[14] Podipara, *Rise and Decline*, pp. 33–35.
[15] Korolevsky, *op. cit.*, pp. 151–55.

background to this decree were questions raised by the Russian Uniates (then a tiny community partly of Old Believer origin) about whether they should imitate the latinisms then current in the liturgy of the Galicians. The new Pope's directive that Byzantine practices be followed *nec plus, nec minus, nec aliter,* 'no more, no less, no differently', from the contemporary Orthodox norm came to be used thereafter as watchwords by champions of the Catholic Eastern rites.[16]

Universalism Vindicated

Since 1622 the affairs of the Eastern Churches (especially those deprived of patriarchs) had been regulated by the Latin-dominated Propaganda Congregation. However, in 1917 Pope Benedict XV erected a separate Congregation for the Eastern Churches under the presidency of the Vatican secretary of state, Cardinal Pietro Gasparri. The function of the new Oriental Congregation was to supervise the work of delatinizing the Eastern rites begun by Leo XIII. 'The Church of Jesus Christ', wrote Pope Benedict, 'is neither Latin nor Greek nor Slav – she is Catholic; all her sons are equal before her: whether they are Latin, Byzantine, Slav, or of any other nation, all have the same place before the Apostolic Chair.'[17]

By this time the Vatican had strengthened its committment to the new policy. Reforms in the direction of sound tradition were now extended to all the Oriental Churches. Nevertheless, administrative anomalies remained. For instance, when a native hierarchy was fully restored to the Malabarese in 1923, the title of patriarch was withheld from its leader, the Archbishop of Ernakulam.[18] The 'Syro-Malabar' Church was made directly subject to the Oriental Congregation, without any regard for the fact that this section of Christendom had been, until the sixteenth century, an integral part of the East Syrian Church, now represented in Catholicism by the Chaldean Church governed by the Patriarch of Babylon.

The next Roman pontiff, Pius XI, had a keen interest in the Eastern Churches, founding for example an Ethiopian College within the bounds of the Vatican State. He also applauded the reforming endeavours of Maronite Patriarch Anthony Arida, who between 1931 and 1942 directed his scholars to work on a new edition of the sacramentary of their rite, restored along the lines of the authentic West Syrian tradition.[19] And when, in 1934, the Malabarese bishops petitioned the Congregation for approval of a Syriac translation of the Latin pontificals that had been in common use in India, the Pope denied their request, replying that 'Latinism ought not to be encouraged among the Orientals. The Holy See does not wish to latinize, but to catholicize. Half-measures are neither generous nor fruitful. Let a Commission be nominated with the task of revising the most ancient Pontifical.'[20]

An important precedent was thus set, and over the next twenty-five years the Sacred Congregation for the Eastern Churches, in consultation with Indian liturgy

---

[16] St Pius used this Latin phrase in a letter to a prominent laywoman, Mlle Natalia Ushakova, who had solicited the papal opinion on the matter.
[17] Cited by D. Attwater in Nicholas Liesel, *The Eastern Catholic Liturgies: A Study in Words and Pictures* (London/Glasgow, 1960), p. ix.
[18] Podipara, *Rise and Decline*, p. 39.
[19] Murtagh, *Maronite Church*, p. 13.
[20] Podipara, *Rise and Decline*, p. 43.

scholars, worked on the restoration of the Syro-Malabarese missal, sacramentary and calendar. In 1935 the Oriental Congregation finally put an end to the latinizing tendencies of the Abyssinian Catholic Church and ordered a complete restoration of the Ethiopic liturgy. The restored ordinal was ready in 1940 and the completed missal was approved four years later.[21]

Ratti's successor, Pius XII, clarified in his 1944 encyclical *Orientalis Ecclesiæ* the new traditionalist principles of the Holy See. The Pope commanded that respect be shown to Oriental traditions

> whether these be concerned with the sacred liturgy and hierarchical Orders or with other observances of the Christian life, so long as they are in keeping with the true faith and the moral law. Each and every nation of Oriental rite must have its rightful freedom in all that is bound up with its own history and its own genius and character, saving always the truth and integrity of the teaching of Jesus Christ. . . . We would have this to be known and appreciated by all, both by those who were born within the bosom of the Catholic Church, and by those who are wafted towards her, as it were, on the wings of yearning and desire. The latter especially should have full assurance that they will never be forced to abandon their legitimate rites or to exchange their own venerable and traditional customs for Latin rites and customs. All these are to be held in equal esteem and equal honour, for they adorn the common Mother Church with a royal garment of many colours. Indeed this variety of rites and customs, preserving inviolate what is most ancient and most valuable in each, presents no obstacle to a true and genuine unity.[22]

Dragging the Chain

These words echoed the firm reassurance that Leo XIII had offered in 1894 to any of the independent Eastern Churches possibly considering reunion with Rome. On that occasion the Pope made a sanguine yet (as it often turned out) erroneous prediction:

> Nor is their any reason for you to fear . . . that We or any of Our Successors will ever diminish your rights, the privileges of your Patriarchs, or the established ritual of any one of your Churches. It has been and will always be the intent and tradition of the Apostolic See to make a large allowance, in all that is right and good, for the ancient traditions and special customs of every nation. On the contrary, if you re-establish union with Us, you will see how, by God's bounty, the glory and dignity of your Churches will be remarkably increased.[23]

Unhappily, the Popes' new-found enthusiasm for things Eastern was not shared by many bishops of the Latin Church in the twentieth century. Although Leo XIII had instituted the practice of referring to the independent Oriental Churches as 'dissident' in their relationship with Rome, thus removing any suggestion of continuing

---

[21] Korolevsky, *op. cit.*, pp. 161–62.
[22] Sections 26, 27, in Ihm, *op. cit.*, p. 85.
[23] *Praeclara Gratulationis Publicae*, 20 June 1894.

guilt, the pejorative label 'schismatic' remained in the Catholic vocabulary in reference to the estranged half of Christendom. As Lawrence Cross has commented, 'While the Popes of this [the twentieth] century have all been concerned to foster knowledge of Eastern Christianity' for the sake of authenticating and strengthening Catholicity 'as well as for reasons of charity and ecumenism, it seems to me that [Western] Catholics are not really interested. They are largely indifferent at the level of knowledge, and often hostile at the level of practical life.'[24]

The pontificates following that of Leo XIII saw plenty of passive resistance to the papal reform even where there was no open oppression of Eastern-rite Catholics and Orthodox. In the Middle East especially, most Catholic missionaries remained avowed partisans of latinization, whatever the Pope or the Oriental Congregation might say. In 1929, when Dom Lambert Beauduin visited the Jesuit high-school in Cairo, where the sons of wealthy Muslims and Orthodox were sent to be educated, he was appalled to find the Belgian principal boasting of the Society's success in obtaining from Rome a decree permitting Eastern-rite children to make their First Communion in the Roman rite.[25]

In interwar Palestine, where numerous members of the Orthodox, Armenian and Ethiopian clergy were open to the possibility of reconciliation with Rome, the Latin Patriarch of Jerusalem and the Franciscan order resolutely refused to work for reunion. The Latin clergy in general persistently ignored the new legislation from the Oriental Congregation stipulating that converts from Orthodoxy join the equivalent Catholic rite, and continued to encourage the passage of reconciled Easterners to the Roman rite.[26] Centuries of shameless 'poaching' of this kind had in fact brought into existence a sizeable community of indigenous Latin Catholics in the Holy Land.

At Nazareth Fr Stephen Zeitoun, the Greek Catholic parish priest, complained to Dom Lambert and his companion 'of the lack of help offered to the Melkite clergy by the Franciscans who, in comparison, lived in the lap of luxury, often spending money foolishly, at least in the eyes of their poorer brethren'.[27] Even the head of the Melkite Church fared no better in his treatment by the Latins:

When the Latin patriarch learned that the Melkite patriarch planned to visit Transjordan, the former hired a man to hinder any activity on the patriarch's part and to see that he would not be well received. Latin priests generally had little respect for the Melkite patriarch, but the emissary was charged to inform them that they were to refuse the use of their churches and even housing to the Greek Catholic clergy (who had nothing to start with).[28]

---

[24] Cross, 'Some Essential Features', p. 100.
[25] Quitslund, op. cit., p. 155.
[26] Ibid., p. 162.
[27] Ibid., p. 166.
[28] Ibid., p. 162. The story of the Latin Patriarch's (Mgr Luigi Barlassina's) doings leaked out when he refused to pay his agent more than the agreed sum, and the latter revealed everything to the Melkites in Jerusalem and to the authorities in Rome.

Maintaining the Latin Ascendancy

Meanwhile the United States was not the only country where the Latin majority in the hierarchy lorded it over the Eastern-rite bishops. Up until the Second Vatican Council the Latin episcopal majority in India – a clerical network noted for its fervent ultramontanism – excluded the Malabarese and Malankarese eparchies from missionary activity outside Kerala. In addition to this, individual Syrian Christian priests and nuns were accepted to work among Hindus and Muslims in the Latin missions solely on the condition that they adopt the Roman rite for this purpose.[29] The implication of these regulations was clear: conversion of pagans to Catholicism meant baptism into the Roman rite.

During the interwar period the Latin bishops of the United States and Canada resented the foundation, by Roman decree, of Eastern-rite eparchies in various parts of their countries, though they could congratulate themselves on their successful exclusion of married Oriental priests, allegedly a potential source of scandal to Western Catholics. However, the greatest hostility to Eastern Christianity came from the hierarchies of Poland and Croatia, Latin-dominated lands with large Byzantine-rite Catholic or Orthodox minorities. Tellingly symptomatic of the post-Tridentine substitution of exclusive loyalty to a Roman power base for inclusive fidelity to Catholic tradition was the opinion of Mgr Alojs Stepinac, Archbishop of Zagreb, that 'schismatical Orthodoxy' was 'the greatest of evils in Europe, almost greater than Protestantism'.[30]

After the partitions of Poland at the end of the eighteenth century, the Greek Catholic Church was liquidated in several phases and reabsorbed into Orthodoxy in the lands annexed by Tsarist Russia,[31] but it survived and flourished in Galicia and Ruthenia, regions placed under Austro-Hungarian rule. By 1923 the dismantling of the Hapsburg Empire following the First World War had brought this Uniate population into the new Polish and Czechoslovak states.[32] In Ruthenia, now

[29] Mattam, *op. cit.*, p. 118.

[30] Edmond Paris, *Genocide in Satellite Croatia, 1941–1945: A Record of Racial and Religious Persecutions and Massacres* (Chicago, 1961), p. 67.

[31] The Greek Catholics of Belorussia and the adjacent Ukrainian region of Volhynia became citizens of Russia after the Third Partition of Poland (1795), but they were at first left in peace by the Tsarist government thanks to the influence of the local Polish Catholic aristocracy. However, in the 1820s, the Russians encouraged the growth of a pro-Orthodox party among the local Greek Catholic clergy, resulting in the conversion of a number of Uniate parishes to Russian Orthodoxy. These pressures intensified after the failure of the 1830–1831 Polish uprising and finally, at the Synod of Polock in 1839, the union with Rome was dissolved by the turncoat bishop József Siemaszko and the Uniate dioceses were absorbed into the Russian Orthodox Church, against the wishes of most of the faithful. (After this time the eparchy of Cholm, in Russian 'Congress' Poland, was the only Greek Catholic church still tolerated in the Tsarist empire until its brutal liquidation in 1874.) In 1905 the government of Tsar Nicholas II allowed over 200,000 Belorussians to return to the Catholic Church, but only on the condition that they follow the Roman rite of the Poles and Lithuanians. It was not until these communities came under Polish rule after 1918 that a small number of them were able to recover their Byzantine liturgical identity. Some 30,000 other ex-Orthodox subsequently joined them, but this ill-fated Church was again forced to join the Russian Orthodox when western Belorussia was ceded to the Soviet Union after the Second World War. See Nichols, *op. cit.*, pp. 299–300. See also Christopher Zugger, *The Forgotten: Catholics of the Soviet Empire from Lenin through Stalin* (Syracuse, 2001), pp. 85–87.

[32] The Galician Ukrainians, the vast majority of whom were Greek Catholics, declared their independence as the 'Western Ukrainian Republic' on 1 November 1918. Poland's subsequent occupation of the territory was confirmed by the Western Powers in 1923 on the condition, never honoured by the Warsaw government, that the Ukrainians be granted autonomy. This political oppression complicated and embittered Polish–Ukrainian relations under the Second Polish

the eastern extremity of Czechoslovakia, the Greek Catholic Church was left undisturbed, and its position also remained strong in the eastern part of Polish-ruled Galicia. However, in the western eparchies of Cholm and Peremyshl, the Greek Catholic lands of the Ruthenian Lemkos bordered on the *Lebensraum* of the Latin Catholic majority. The Polish government, insecure at the constant threat of Ruthenian secession, conceived the plan of assimilating this exposed section of the inconvenient minority.

In 1934 the Polish hierarchy, needing little persuasion from the national government, petitioned Rome to detach the Lemko deaneries from the Greek Catholic diocese of Peremyshl and place them under an apostolic administrator.[33] This enabled the Latin bishops and clergy to interfere in the affairs of the Uniates and, especially, to take over the property of the Greek Catholic Church. A contemporaneous repression of Uniatism in the neighbouring eparchy of Cholm caused the closure, destruction or conversion to the Roman rite of 150 out of the 383 parish churches of that diocese by 1939.[34]

The collaboration of some Ukrainians with the Nazi army of occupation during the Second World War gave the Polish government a pretext to complete its annihilation of the Greek Catholic Church and culture once the tide had turned in 1945. The anti-Uniate offensive was also in retaliation for the slaughter of over 100,000 ethnic Poles (including clergy) during campaigns of ethnic cleansing conducted by Ukrainian partisans in Volhynia and Eastern Galicia in 1943–1944; in Poland the Greek Catholic Church was accused of having given moral support to the military units in question.[35]

By this time the border of the USSR had been shifted westwards to include Poland's former south-eastern voivodeships of Łuck, Tarnopol, Stanisławów and the eastern parts of Lwów and Lublin. Lemkoland (*Łemkowszczyzna*), however, remained within the reduced Polish state. In 1946 the Warsaw government nationalized all property belonging to its ethnically Ruthenian and Ukrainian citizens, now numbering 1,062,000. The Lemkos were encouraged by both the Polish and Soviet governments to migrate east to the Ukrainian Soviet Socialist Republic, the resultant deportations involving some 700,000 souls. This upheaval was attended by numerous murders of Greek Catholic civilians by the local Polish criminal element.[36]

Practically all the 362,000 Lemkos who remained in Poland fell victim, the following year, to 'Operation Vistula' (*Akcja Wisła*), part of Warsaw's own policy of

---

Republic and would have fatal consequences for countless Polish civilians during the Second World War.

[33] Oleh Wolodymyr Iwanusiw, *Church in Ruins: The Demise of Ukrainian Churches in the Eparchy of Peremyshl* (St Catharine's, 1987), p. 21.

[34] Ibid., p. 14.

[35] Murderous partisan attacks on Polish civilians (in reaction to Polish pogroms against Ukrainians between 1934 and 1938) had been condemned as criminal and anti-national by Metropolitan Andrei Szeptycki, head of the Galician Greek Catholic Church who, himself of mixed Ukrainian and Polish lineage, was appalled and grieved by reciprocal violence between two peoples who had lived together in peace for centuries and had so much in common. See Bohdan Budurowycz, 'Sheptytski and the Ukrainian National Movement after 1914', in Paul Robert Magocsi, ed., *Morality and Reality: The Life and Times of Andrei Sheptytski* (Edmonton, 1989), p. 57; Orest Subtelny, *Ukraine: A History* (Toronto, 1988), pp. 474–75; Tadeusz Piotrowski, *Poland's Holocaust* (Jefferson, North Carolina, 1997), pp. 247ff; and Timothy Snyder, *Causes of Ukrainian-Polish Ethnic Cleansing* (Oxford, 2003), pp. 220–22.

[36] Ibid., pp. 14–16.

ethnic cleansing. Ironically, the Lemkos (some of whom did not identify themselves as Ukrainian in nationality) had played no part in the recent atrocities in Volhynia and Eastern Galicia. Forcibly expelled from their homes and resettled among Poles in the northern and western districts taken from Germany, the Uniates had little opportunity to retain their ancestral rite, and the polonization and latinization desired by the Latin hierarchy ensued in most cases.[37] As Lemkoland was resettled by Poles, 346 (50.2 per cent) of its Greek Catholic churches were demolished or allowed to fall into disrepair, 61 (8.9 per cent) were closed or secularized, 9 (1.3 per cent) were turned into museums, 28 (4 per cent) were given to the Orthodox, and 245 (35.6 per cent) were remodelled as Latin churches after the traditional Byzantine fixtures and artwork had been removed and destroyed.[38]

The Sin of Cain

In the Polish Second Republic the hideous fratricidal conflict between Catholics of both rites in the 1930s and 40s had been the work of political extremists taking advantage of the current chaos to perpetrate crimes in which innocent civilians of the two main nationalities were the usual victims. This ordeal was followed by a Communist takeover in the region which subjected the Polish Roman-rite Church to a regime of persecution but had even more dire consequences for Ukrainian Catholicism.

Few religious groups have been more ill-starred in history than the Greek Catholics. Repressed in Poland, they also had much to suffer at the hands of members of the Orthodox Church, who sanctioned or took advantage of the total liquidation of the Uniate eparchies of Galicia, Ruthenia and Transylvania by the governments of the Soviet Ukraine and of Communist Romania between 1945 and 1949. Compounding the tragedy was the fact that the fate of the Uniates was in part the historical backlash of an even more horrendous persecution that had taken place in Yugoslavia during the war. Here the victims were also Christians of Byzantine rite, but Orthodox rather than Catholic.

Western Catholics impatient with the slowness of the Eastern Orthodox to respond to Latin ecumenical overtures since Vatican II (and, indeed, those rightly indignant at the crimes committed by Bosnian Serbs against their Croat and Muslim neighbours in the mid-1990s) need to inform themselves about the doings of the Catholic-dominated government of Croatia during the Second World War. The Independent State of Croatia, carved out of Axis-occupied Yugoslavia, was established as a satellite of Nazi Germany in 1941 and governed by the Ustasha Party under the leadership of the Zagreb lawyer Ante Pavelić.

The 'free' Croatia over which Pavelić ruled as *Poglavnik* ('Leader') included the Krajina, eastern Slavonia and Bosnia-Herzegovina, with their joint population of 2,200,000 Serbs.[39] Centuries of tribal hostility had made the kindred Croats and Serbs bitter enemies, and for the fanatically ultra-nationalist Poglavnik these subject Serbs were socially offensive for their cultural diversity, due historically

---

[37] Ibid., pp. 16–17.
[38] Ibid., pp. 22, 18.
[39] The Orthodox population of the Krajina were descendants of Vlach peasants settled in this border region by the Turks. They had lost their Romance speech and adopted Serbian ethnicity as well as language.

to religious rather than ethno-linguistic factors. His plans for these people were summed up in the saying, popularized by the Ustasha, that the government would expel a third of the Serbs, convert another third to Catholicism, and kill the rest. This proved to be no empty boast. Unaware of the Ustasha's murderous designs, on Easter Day the young Archbishop Stepinac exultantly announced from the pulpit of his cathedral in Zagreb the establishment of the Independent State of Croatia.[40] Ill-boding, moreover, was the Archbishop's view of his native land not as one of the central units of a Christendom sadly divided by schism, but as the bulwark of Christendom (= Latin Catholicism) itself: *antemurale Christianitatis*.[41]

Within a fortnight of the Zagreb celebrations, Ustasha troops began to massacre Serb Orthodox civilians in the district of Bjelovar.[42] A government decree of 25 April prohibited throughout Croatia the public and private use of the Cyrillic alphabet proper to the Serbs. Other laws obliged Serbian Orthodox citizens to wear a blue armband marked with the letter P (for *Pravoslavac*, 'Orthodox') out of doors, confiscated their motor vehicles, and excluded them, together with Jews and Gypsies, from various public places.[43] In May the Orthodox bishops Kir Platon Sokolović of Banja Luka, Metropolitan Petar Zimonjić of Sarajevo, Kir Sava Trlajić of Plaško and several priests were murdered with revolting barbarity by Ustashi, while Kir Dositej Vasić, Bishop of Zagreb, became insane after being severely beaten and tortured.[44]

Deprived of its spiritual leaders, the Orthodox population of independent Croatia was at the mercy of the Ustasha, who, with their Muslim allies, went on a rampage of torture, mutilation and random slaughter that had claimed over 350,000 Serbian lives by 1944 and which shocked even the Nazis.[45] Among the victims were 171 members of the Orthodox clergy.[46] Meanwhile the Catholic hierarchy, compromised by its initial enthusiastic support of the Pavelić régime, could do little to stop the genocide. Apart from Archbishop Stepinac, the only bishop to speak out publicly was Mgr Alojs Mišić of Mostar, whose pastoral letter of 30 June 1941 protested vehemently against Ustasha crimes.[47] Perhaps the most damning element of this deplorable chapter in the history of Latin Catholicism was the complicity and, in several cases, the direct participation of members of the Franciscan order in the atrocities, especially at the Jasenovac death camp, of which one of the friars was commandant.[48]

---

[40] Paris, *op. cit.*, p. 55. When Stepinac was raised to the episcopate in 1934 (after being a priest for only four years), he was, at age thirty-six, the Catholic Church's youngest bishop. Three years later he became Archbishop of Zagreb.

[41] Ibid., p. 197.

[42] Ibid., pp. 59–60.

[43] Ibid., p. 62.

[44] Ibid., pp. 72–73, 78–79. These martyred bishops were subsequently canonized by the Serbian Orthodox Church.

[45] Trevor Beeson, *Discretion & Valour: Religious Conditions in Russia and Eastern Europe* (London, 1974, 1982), p. 307; Paris, *op. cit.*, p. 59.

[46] Paris lists the names of these murdered priests and bishops, pp. 285–89. Forty-seven Jewish rabbis were also exterminated.

[47] Ibid., pp. 109, 177. Mgr Stepinac admonished the priests of his archdiocese to oppose the government's persecution of Orthodox and Jews and to offer them every assistance. He also made private protests to the Poglavnik, but to little avail, Beeson, *op. cit.*, p. 307.

[48] Paris, *op. cit.*, pp. 135–38; Beeson, *op. cit.*, p. 307. These Franciscans had been something of a law unto themselves under the Turkish occupation (ended by Austria in 1878) when they functioned as secular administrators of the region on behalf of the Ottomans. It was members of the same branch of the Franciscans who would involve themselves in promoting the false apparitions

If Pope Pius XII, who had received Pavelić in private audience on 17 May 1941, chose to remain silent about the genocide in Croatia, Mgr Eugène Tisserand, Prefect of the Congregation for the Eastern Churches, was loud in his denunciations. In 1942 the French cardinal berated Nikola Rušinović, the Poglavnik's legate at the Vatican, with these words:

> If you only knew how the Italian officers stationed along the Adriatic coast speak of you! It is indeed frightful. From their reports, just to imagine that such terrible brutality exists is unthinkable. Murders, fires, crimes of every kind and pillages are the order of the day in these regions. I know for sure that even the Franciscans of Bosnia-Herzegovina took an active part in the attacks against the Orthodox population and the destruction of the churches. I learned from an infallible source that the Franciscans from Bosnia-Herzegovina behaved atrociously. How such acts could be perpetrated by civilized and cultured men, let alone priests, is inconceivable.[49]

The evils being committed by pseudo-nationalist criminals to the horror of decent Croatian Catholics were compounded, in Cardinal Tisserand's view, by what amounted to clerical connivance in the forced conversion to Catholicism of thousands of Orthodox Serbs. Tisserand also indignantly rejected claims by Ustasha representatives at the Vatican that the Serb Orthodox minority in Greater Croatia were in fact 'returning' to the Church of their recent ancestors, supposedly Catholics who had been forced into schism by the Turks.[50] Reminding his visitors that he was very well acquainted with the history of Christianity, the cardinal told them that he did not know of a single instance of Latin Catholics being forced into a mass conversion to Eastern Orthodoxy.[51]

In a decree of 30 June 1941 the Ustasha government had outlawed the Orthodox Church and set the norms by which Serbs could convert to Catholicism. This decree, signed by the Minister of the Interior and the Minister of Justice, declared that while Serb peasants were suitable candidates for conversion, care must be exercised not to issue certificates of conversion to Serb 'priests, shopkeepers, artisans, rich Orthodox peasants and, in general, to Orthodox intellectuals, except in cases where personal integrity can be proved, the government having come to a foregone conclusion that recommendations concerning such categories of people are unacceptable'.[52] The reality was that these groups had been marked out for extermination.[53]

There can be no doubt from the reports of witnesses and of survivors that the vast majority of Serbian requests for admission into the Catholic Church were motivated by fear of persecution or death. Conversion to Catholicism was held out to terrorized Orthodox as a guarantee of freedom from molestation and, often, as a means of releasing family members from the dreaded Ustasha concentration

---

of Međugorje from 1981 – once again, in defiance of a conscientious Bishop of Mostar, this time Mgr Pavao Žanić. Međugorje, too, had been the scene of massacres of Orthodox Serbs in the 1940s.

[49] Paris, *op. cit.*, p. 177.
[50] Ibid., pp. 95, 212.
[51] Ibid., p. 95.
[52] Ibid., p. 89.
[53] The Nazis had targeted equivalent classes of Poles from September 1939.

camps. There is, unfortunately, ample evidence of Catholic priests exploiting this situation to secure mass submissions to Rome. In Bosnia-Herzegovina, where the Ustasha murderers were most active, public refusal to convert was soon inviting the death sentence.

Not that apostasy from Orthodoxy always guaranteed survival. In Croatia itself the 2,000 Serb 'catechumens' of Vrgin Most and Čemernica were taken in trucks to the Orthodox church of Glina where, they were told, their conversion to the true faith would be solemnized. Instead, the Ustashi turned the church into a slaughter house, locking in one group of Serbs after another, then massacring them with axes and knives. Among the victims of 4 August were thirty-seven children under ten years of age. The last group of Serbs were not hacked to death like the others. The church was doused with flammable liquid and the people packed into it were burned alive, together with Father Bogdan Opačić, the Orthodox parish priest of Glina.[54]

Instant Latin Catholics

It was not until 17 November 1941 that the Catholic hierarchy, at its Plenary Conference, issued the statement that 'The Catholic Church will accept only persons who, of their own free choice and without any violent persuasion, are urged on by a deep conviction of Catholic faith and truth, and who are in complete agreement with the canonical conditions upon which the conversions are based.'[55] As for the decree of 30 June, the reply of the Zagreb ordinariate dated 16 July, while criticizing the drawing of arbitrary distinctions between various categories of prospective converts, had nonetheless given its support to another article of the law: that forbidding Orthodox Serbs to convert to the Greek Catholic rite, except in districts where Uniate parishes already existed. Now, since the Greek Catholic Church of Croatia, dating from 1611, was a small one, numbering only some 30,000 faithful of Ukrainian rather than indigenous origin,[56] the measure ensured that the vast majority of converts would embrace the Roman rite, which (except in some Dalmatian dioceses where Old Slavonic had survived) used Latin as its liturgical language.

On 17 July 1941 the Oriental Congregation in Rome took action by addressing to Archbishop Stepinac the following corrective instructions:

> The Holy Congregation for the Eastern Churches desires to point out to Your Excellency that the Roman Catholic priests in Croatia should be instructed by their reverend bishops that they are not to prevent those who are not united (Dissidents) from their natural return to the Eastern rite . . .[57]

Accordingly, the Croatian hierarchy passed a strong resolution at their November conference upholding the religious and civil rights of converts to Greek Catholicism,

---

[54] Ibid., pp. 105–06.
[55] Ibid., p. 144.
[56] The Austro-Hungarian authorities facilitated these migrations from Galicia in the late nineteenth century. There were also Greek Catholics in the Vojvodina region of Serbia, descendants of eighteenth-century settlers from Ruthenia.
[57] Ibid., p. 95.

and forbidding the destruction of Serbian Orthodox churches and chapels.[58] Archbishop Stepinac had agreed with the Oriental Congregation that the passage of Orthodox converts to the Catholic Byzantine rite would be 'the easiest and speediest road toward union', as well as 'the greatest gift which Croatia could bestow upon the Holy See'.[59]

Nevertheless, this measure was little able to curb the exploitation of an earlier ruling of 18 October, forced from the Holy See as a result of protests by the Croatian hierarchy, that the promotion of Greek Catholicism was impracticable (read undesirable):

> Wherever there are already established Greek Catholic parishes, those who are not united should be sent there to become united, if they wish to be so. However, in cases where those who have been separated and are not reunited do not want to or cannot keep up their Oriental rite, they are to be free to join the Latin rites.[60]

The truth is that the rank and file of the Croatian clergy had not the slightest intention of carrying out directives that would cause an expansion of the conveniently small Uniate Church within their territory. As for the Orthodox church buildings they seized, these were normally destroyed in districts where the Serbs formed the majority of the population, and transformed into Latin-rite conventicles wherever Catholics outnumbered Serbs. Conversion of Orthodox churches to Latin use meant the demolition of the icon screen or, where this was impractical, the setting up of a second altar in front of it. Before each service the church was to be ritually cleansed. One directive alone, issued by the diocese of Đakovo in April 1942, authorized the conversion of twenty-two Orthodox churches.[61]

The Ustasha government fell in April 1945. Needless to say, thanks to the methods used to persuade the Orthodox Serbs of Greater Croatia to re-enter the communion of Peter, most if not all of the 250,000 'new Catholics' of satellite Croatia returned to their ancestral obedience as soon as they were free to do so.

Any Catholic who engages in ecumenical activities must contend with the fact that Eastern Christians do not (like some Latins) suffer from short memories, amnesia being a common affliction of those addicted to the intoxicants of power and prestige. Even had the nightmare of the 1940s never occurred, one despairs for the cause of reunion with the independent Oriental Churches when it is remembered that until the papal decree *Tradita Est ab Antiquis* in 1912, Latin Catholics were forbidden to receive Communion in Eastern-rite Churches, whereas (unofficially at least) Uniates were often actively encouraged to participate fully in the services of the Roman rite.

Officially integral units of the Catholic Church, the Eastern-rite communities had in fact spent most of their historical existence confined to an ecclesial ghetto, and subsequent developments in the mid-twentieth century showed that even Vatican goodwill could not correct the prejudices of the past. In Uniatism, voluntary or coerced, the traffic had been one-way from the beginning. Could the

---

[58] Ibid., p. 144.
[59] Report sent by Nikola Rušinović, Pavelić's minister at the Vatican to Mladen Lorković, minister of foreign affairs. Ibid., pp. 174–75.
[60] Ibid., p. 96.
[61] Ibid., pp. 213–14. On the genocide in Croatia see also Michael Phayer, *The Catholic Church and the Holocaust, 1930–1965* (Bloomfield, 2000), pp. 31–40.

Orthodox be blamed for doing precisely what most Western Catholics did: considering the Roman Church and Latin Catholicism one and the same thing?

The American Spanner

The stubborn refusal of the Latin bishops of the United States to treat their Eastern-rite brethren as equals was evidently not mollified by knowledge of the horrific sufferings inflicted on Orthodox inhabitants of South-Eastern Europe by Latin Catholics during the Second World War. In fact since the Minnesota schism, far from repenting of their earlier intolerance, they had stiffened their resolve to assimilate the 'doubtfully Catholic' Easterners by encouraging individuals to convert to the more 'American' Roman rite. When the Code of Eastern Canon Law was revised in 1958, the American hierarchy actually prevailed upon the Holy See to abolish the canon requiring converted members of the Orthodox and Lesser Eastern Churches to retain their ancestral rite as Catholics. This understandably raised a storm of protest from Uniate patriarchs and bishops, who called a general synod in Cairo to express their dissatisfaction with such an abusive reform, but to no avail. The Roman authorities admitted that they had bowed to pressure from the American episcopate but declined to rescind the offending legislation.[62]

Before this major setback, the restoration of the Eastern rites had been making great strides. The difficult task of renewing the East Syrian liturgy of the Malabarese Church was completed by 1955, when the Latin text of the restored rite of Mass was published in Rome. Pope John XXIII approved both the text and rubrics in 1959, and in 1960 the official Syriac edition (*Taksa d-Quddaše*) was ready for implementation in Kerala. A new code of canon law for the Maronites, elaborated between 1949 and 1957, led to the elimination of some latinisms in the Antiochene rite of their Church. Some of the more glaring Western influences in the Byzantine liturgy of the Ukrainians were abolished, for example kneeling for Holy Communion, and the inclusion of the *filioque* was made optional in the liturgical Creed.

When the Second Vatican Council came, it seemed to be strongly supportive of the Oriental Catholic traditions. The conciliar documents included a special decree on the Eastern Churches (*Orientalium Ecclesiarum*) which reiterated all the recent papal teaching to the effect that unity of Catholic faith in no way implied uniformity of rite and custom. The decree also declared that 'the Churches of the East, as much as those of the West, fully enjoy the right, and are in duty bound, to rule themselves'.[63] Moreover, Eastern Catholics were not only guaranteed their right to the free practice of their ancestral traditions ('All Eastern rite members should know and be convinced that they can and should always preserve their lawful liturgical rites and their established way of life'), but the decree banned in principle any artificial reform of the Oriental liturgies, which 'should not be altered except by way of an appropriate organic development'.[64]

Nevertheless, there was a negative side to *Orientalium Ecclesiarum*. When the preparatory schema drafted by the Congregation for the Eastern Churches attempted to reverse the unsatisfactory legislation of 1958 facilitating individual

---

[62] J. Murtagh, SMA, *Churches of the Greek Rite* (Dublin, 1964), p. 30.
[63] *Orientalium Ecclesiarum*, Intro., 5.
[64] Ibid., Intro., 6.

conversions to the Roman rite, Bishop Gerald McDevitt of Philadelphia made a strenuous objection. This American churchman (significantly the ordinary of an area where large numbers of Eastern-rite Catholics resided) protested that it was 'quite surprising, not to say cruel' that the Holy See should want to deny individual Christians the right to choose their rite. The traditionalism of the decree contradicted, in his view, all that the Council was saying about freedom of conscience and pastoral needs.[65] Of the 792 Fathers who voted on the schema, 719 (over 90 per cent) gave qualified support to Bishop McDevitt's reservation whereas only 73 opposed it.

Fully aware that the majority opinion implied a belief in the 'superiority' (or at least the greater desirability in the modern context) of the Roman rite, and fearing the consequences of the offence that the proposed amendment would give to the Eastern Catholics and Orthodox, the Commission on the Eastern Churches overruled it.[66] Nevertheless, a provision for the review of individual petitions for a change of rite was inserted into the text, a loophole large enough to placate the American bishops, who had no intention of following the mind of the Church in this matter. Hence *Orientalium Ecclesiarum*, no less than *Sacrosanctum Concilium*, contained a 'time bomb' which left the door open for Latin ritual proselytism:

> each and every Catholic, as also the baptized members of every non-Catholic Church or community who enters into the fullness of Catholic communion, should everywhere retain his proper rite, cherish it, and observe it to the best of his ability. *This rule does not deny the right whereby persons, communities, or areas may in special cases have recourse to the Apostolic See, which, as the supreme judge of interchurch relations, will directly or through other authorities meet the needs of the occasion in an ecumenical spirit and issue opportune directives, decrees, or rescripts.*[67]

All the statements of the Decree concerning the equal dignity of the Oriental rites, and the guarantees that no Easterner would be forced or persuaded to give up his hereditary rite thus remained relative assurances. The one absolute in Vatican policy was the right of the Holy See to allow, when expediency so counselled, defections from any Eastern tradition, a power that deeply disturbed the patriarchs and bishops of the Churches in question.

The new post-conciliar Code of (Latin) Canon Law promulgated in 1983 contained another snare for Eastern Catholics. In a speech of 1986, Cardinal Myroslav Lubachivskyj, head of the Ukrainian Catholic Church, criticized the clause stating that the parents of a child in a mixed-rite marriage are free to decide in which tradition their offspring will be baptized and raised (in the old code the child followed the father's rite if he was a Catholic, or the mother's, if he was not):

> Here we can be somewhat afraid of the future position of the Eastern rites. Why? Most parents will decide on the Western rite for the child's social benefit. His Catholic friends will be western, his church attendance western, and his education possibly at a church school. So in order that the child feel safe and suffer no

---

[65] Wiltgen, *op. cit.*, pp. 202–03.
[66] Ibid., p. 203.
[67] *Orientalium Ecclesiarum*, Intro., 4.

unpleasantnesses as the parents did, the child will be registered as of Western or Latin rite. I hope I am wrong. I hope this will not happen. But I am afraid for the future.[68]

Life on the Fringe

As for *Orientalium Ecclesiarum*, one of the Eastern Fathers at Vatican II, Coptic metropolitan Isaac Ghattas of Thebes, had questioned the very desirability of a separate decree on the Oriental Churches. His reasoning was that such a decree implied that Eastern Catholic communities were something exceptional in the normal scheme of things. If the Uniates were an integral part of the Catholic Church, he argued, then references to them should be interspersed throughout the whole body of conciliar constitutions and declarations.[69]

Indeed the fact that *Sacrosanctum Concilium* was exclusively concerned with the Latin rites bore out the accuracy of the Coptic leader's point. As the statement of a purportedly ecumenical council, the liturgy constitution was in one respect a bizarre document. If the Council was a gathering of all the bishops of the Catholic Church and if all the Catholic rites were equal in importance and dignity, why should conciliar decisions about divine worship apply to the Western section of the Church alone? The clear implication was that the Oriental rites were exceptions to the Church's liturgical norm, and certainly not important enough to feature in deliberations about so central an aspect of Catholic life. But insulting as it was, this telling marginalization of Oriental Catholicism was also providential, since it spared (in theory at least) most Eastern rites the full measure of the gruesome fate awaiting the Roman liturgy.

What these conciliar gaffes demonstrated was that enlightened Roman reforms had proved, and would continue to prove, largely unsuccessful in emancipating Eastern Catholics from their status as second-class citizens of the Universal Church. As late as 1985, one Malabarese could write, in reference to the Latin hegemony and 'one-rite' movement in India that

> [i]n the course of the centuries the promises of popes, especially since Leo XIII, to respect and foster the rites of the Eastern churches, were more honoured in the breach than in the observance, due to the resistance of the Roman Curia. The recognition in the decree on Ecumenism that the principle present in tradition 'has not always been honoured' is in accord with historical facts. It is about this that Pobedonostsev, a Russian, sarcastically remarked: '*Le Pape passe, la Curie romaine reste*' (The Pope passes, the Roman Curia remains). But after the solemn declaration of the Vatican Council the Curia seems to have relented. It is regrettable that this attitude still persists in India. Vatican II passed, the Curia changed, but the attitude towards the Oriental Churches of India remains. Some Bishops seem to remain with the same inveterate urge for uniformity (and convergence) and consciousness of superiority . . .[70]

---

[68] Chediath/Vellilamthadam, *op. cit.*, p. 94.
[69] Wiltgen, *op. cit.*, p. 202.
[70] Geevarghese Panicker, 'An Analysis of the Present Ecclesial Situation in India', in Vellilamthadam *et al.*, *Ecclesial Identity*, p. 166.

Seating the Patriarchs

The Vatican's manifest refusal to establish as normative in Catholicism the principle that the rite of an individual was not a secondary or arbitrary matter but an existential reality determined by Divine Providence was symbolized at the Council by the seating arrangements made for the Eastern patriarchs. Until the eleventh century the most important dignitaries in the Church after the Roman Pope were the bishops of the patriarchal sees of Constantinople, Antioch, Alexandria and Jerusalem. This fact moved Maximos IV Saigh, Melkite Patriarch of Antioch, to request that Pope John XXIII seat the Eastern patriarchs directly after himself at the coming Council, and not after the cardinals. However, the Patriarch's two letters to the Pope remained unanswered, and so in the first year of the Council his peers had to suffer the same humiliation that had been inflicted on their predecessors at Vatican I. Then, in October 1963, Pope Paul VI directed that the patriarchs be seated *opposite* the Roman cardinals, a compromise that hardly vindicated their just claim to precedence.[71] Finally, to compound the injury, the *Annuario Pontificio* of 1966 returned to the practice of listing the patriarchs (those who were not cardinals) after the Roman cardinals.[72]

In a forthright speech of 14 October 1963, Archbishop Ghattas had expressed his pessimism concerning the willingness of the Latin majority among the bishops to take seriously Rome's official stance on the Oriental traditions and on the cultural imperialism of the past:

> It would seem that for many Council Fathers the Universal Church is the Latin Church, which through a separate schema concedes so-called privileges to a minority group, the Eastern Churches. Many churchmen in the Latin Church look upon the Eastern Churches . . . as ecclesiastical oddities or exotic creations [instead of] as sister Churches which together with the Latin-rite Church make up the Universal Church.[73]

Words destined to fall on deaf ears. Certainly, Vatican attitudes had not changed substantially by the early 1990s, when, after the fall of Communism, the Catholic missionaries who streamed into the former Soviet Union to proselytize among a nominally Orthodox population would have no compunction whatsoever in admitting Russian converts to Catholicism into the *Roman* rite, a serious ecclesial abuse and an insult to the Russian nation which Rome to date has done nothing to reverse and little to halt.[74]

---

[71] Wiltgen, *op. cit.*, pp. 199–202.
[72] Ibid., p. 205.
[73] Ibid., p. 198.
[74] This is an injustice to Russia even if the tendency of the Russian Orthodox Church is to consider Uniatism a greater evil than conversion to Latin Catholicism, an attitude based on political rather than cultural considerations (under the Tsarist regime, Byzantine-rite Catholicism was barely tolerated when not totally outlawed).

The New Latinization

The vandalization of the Western rites under Paul VI was not merely a calamity for the Latin Church. The damage became universal when, inevitably, the forces of iconoclasm and heteropraxis invaded the Eastern Catholic Churches. And this in spite of official guarantees by Rome that the age of tampering with the traditions of Oriental Christians within her communion had ended forever.

When one studies the downgrading of liturgical tradition in a particular Eastern rite it often emerges that the mentality the Orientals in question had already become so profoundly latinized that attempts to return to authentic tradition remained largely intellectual initiatives that could not easily filter down to the popular level. Irreparable harm had been done long ago. According to the Malankarese scholar Geevarghese Chediath, Uniatism

> indicates a psychological behaviour which creates an inferiority complex towards most Oriental ways, and a constant tendency towards Latin ways; it expresses itself in the following way: things Western (Latin) stand for civilization and progress; they enjoy greater influence and prestige; they are more practical and convenient. Uniates want to be different from the Orthodox, in most cases leading to latinization. They give up the basic outlook of the Christian East; introduce Western devotions of a deviated piety; they try to adorn themselves with Western dignities such as Monsignore, etc. A crude juridical outlook on Christian life is the worst effect of Uniatism. Because of their Latin-oriented education they are brainwashed, and consciously or unconsciously will accept the verdict of the 'superior' Western Church. They have the interior feeling that 'the Vatican is always right'.[75]

The worst anti-traditional trends manifested themselves among the Malabarese and the Maronites, historically the most latinized Eastern Catholics. Dr Chediath holds out little hope for true liturgical renewal in these quarters:

> These Eastern-rite Catholics have forgotten that they have a great obligation towards the Latins and the Orthodox; that their vocation is unique. In their desire to be united with the Latin Church, which is genuine and legitimate, they lost sight of their ecclesial identity which is as vital as the communion aspect. Vatican II had to tell the Easterners to be aware of their identity, but even after that they cannot see it because they live in the Latin world of ideas.[76]

In such a state of affairs how could Orthodox observers not conclude that union with Rome meant assimilation?

---

[75] G. Chediath, 'Unity versus Uniformity', in G. Chediath/Vellilamthadam, *op. cit.*, p. 22, n. 14.
[76] Ibid., p. 24.

Chaos in Kerala

Most deplorable of all was the post-conciliar situation in Kerala, where, after Vatican II, a liturgical revolution comparable to the Roman one was visited upon the long-suffering Malabarese faithful. When the traditional East Syrian rite had been officially restored in 1962 most of the Syro-Malabar clergy and laity were enthusiastic about the partial shift to the vernacular, but at a time when latinism was synonymous with a growing openness to modernist trends, they were also lukewarm in their reception of what seemed to many of them an unnecessarily elaborate and deliberately archaic liturgy.[77]

Consequently, the 'new' forms were implemented in a rather curious manner, becoming obligatory only for priests ordained after the date of their introduction: all older priests, bishops included, were free to continue using the former hybrid liturgy and Roman vestments. In fact most of the senior clergy took this option, a clear enough indication to Rome of their anti-traditional outlook. To this major-ity – and to many young priests obliged to return to tradition – the long-awaited ritual reform in their own Church seemed at an opposite pole to the 'renewal' they were then witnessing in the Roman rite. 'Why should our liturgy be a museum piece?' some murmured during the Council years.[78]

Among those most vehement in their opposition to the restored liturgy endorsed by Rome were the Syro-Malabarese hierarchy. An additional factor of this mod-ernistic orientation was the conversion of certain Malabarese clergy to the ideal of 'indianization', the attempt to reconcile Christian worship and theology with Hindu rites and beliefs. This faction made the simplistic (and quite preposterous) claim that the Syrian origins of their liturgy made it as alien to Indian culture as the Latin worship of the first Portuguese missionaries.[79]

Inspired by the minimalistic *Missa Normativa* then being piloted in the Roman rite, a team of Malabarese bishops, priests and laymen went to work on the text and rubrics of the restored *Qurbana* and came up with a practical and all-vernacular 'New Order of Mass' which would supposedly be more suited to modern times and could be celebrated in just forty minutes. The ordinary of the particularly latinized eparchy of Trichur, Bishop George Alapatt, took this *Qurbanakramam* ('Book of the Mass') to Rome in 1968 and presented it to the Prefect of the Oriental Congregation, Mgr Maximilien de Fuerstenberg.

In one of the most irresponsible actions in curial history, the Dutch cardinal approved the text *ad experimentum* for three years without having it examined by competent orientalists, and paid little heed to the subsequent protests that poured in from the tradition-minded minority among the Malabarese clergy.[80] The triumphant progressive hierarchy then actually forbade priests to celebrate the 1962 rite in public, banished Syriac from the public worship of the Church, and

[77] Podipara, *Rise and Decline*, p. 41.
[78] Ibid., p. 40.
[79] See, for instance, the pseudo-historical absurdities advanced throughout Cardinal Joseph Parecattil's book, *Syro-Malabar Liturgy as I See It* (Ernakulam, 1987). Of course East Syrian religious traditions had been acclimatizing in Malabar for over a millennium before the arrival of the Portuguese.
[80] Johannes Madey, 'On the Reform of the Chaldeo-Malabar Liturgy: The Holy See of Rome in Defence of the Oriental Patrimony', *Ostkirchliche Studien*, 33 (Sept. 1984), p. 173; Podipara, *Rise and Decline*, p. 64, n. 3.

allowed only the new modernized Malayalam service books to be printed.[81] And all the while a strangely unvigilant Oriental Congregation declined to intervene, even after the expiry of the three-year experimental term.

The discrepancies between the 'Mini-Mass' and the East Syrian ritual norm were enormous. Apart from restoring the whole Eucharistic order, the liturgical directives of 1955–1962 had recommended such necessary reforms as the substitution of Oriental vestments for Roman ones, the fitting and use of a sanctuary veil before the altar, the reception of Communion standing, sung *Qurbana* as the norm, the replacement of Western-style statues and holy pictures by Eastern icons, signing oneself from the right shoulder to the left, as elsewhere in the East, and so on.[82]

The modernizers ignored all of these prescriptions except that relating to the reception of Holy Communion because it happened to match the current trend in the West. From 1968 onwards most bishops encouraged the celebration of Mass facing the people – an anti-traditional practice in any Catholic liturgy. In their bid to create a liturgy in the worst traditions of post-conciliar Rome, the Keralan reformers exhumed a number of the latinisms of the obsolete pre-1962 rite. The sign of the cross opening the rite, but rightly abolished as a Roman intrusion in the reform of 1962, suddenly reappeared. As well as being removed from its proper place in the Offertory and reinserted after the homily, the Nicene Creed was replaced by the Apostles' Creed (the Old Roman Symbol), a text utterly alien to the Eastern tradition. On the other hand the authentic arrangement of the Canon was retained because it happened to agree with that of the new Roman anaphoras.[83]

As for the general 'modernization' of the *Qurbana*, this may be illustrated by comparing a single prayer from the rite of 1968, the prayer before the *Lakhu Mara*, with the restored one it had replaced, which read as follows:

1962: When the sweet savour of the fragrance of Thy love envelops us, O our Lord and Saviour, and our souls are enlightened by the knowledge of Thy truth, may we be accounted worthy to receive the revelation of Thy beloved Son who is from heaven: and there may we confess Thee and praise Thee unendingly in Thy Church crowned in triumph and full of graces and blessings: for Thou art the Lord and Maker of all, Father, Son and Holy Ghost forever.

In striking contrast, one notes in the trite and telegraphic 1968 version of this prayer the substitution of bold futures for the humble subjunctives, and a new man-centred tone:

1968: For all the helps and graces you have given us, for which we cannot thank you enough, we will praise and glorify you unceasingly, in your triumphant Church forever.

---

[81] Madey,
[82] Podipara, *Rise and Decline*, pp. 44–45.
[83] For the text of the 1968 'Mini-Mass', see *Celebration of the Eucharist according to the Syro-Malabar Rite* (Bangalore: National Biblical Catechetical and Liturgical Centre, 1973).

Cultural Cringe

Throughout the post-conciliar period the other Eastern Catholics were more successful than the Malabarese in maintaining their ritual integrity, though few of them have remained completely untouched by the revolution in the West. Most have, for instance, adopted the derisory one-hour eucharistic fast of the Roman Church. In 1968 the Ukrainians in exile dropped the use of Old Slavonic in the Mass, substituting for it a literary form of the vernacular.[84] The Arabic-speaking Copts greatly restricted the use of Coptic in their eucharistic services, while Arabic became the general medium of the Maronite Mass, only the Words of Institution and a few other prayers remaining in Syriac.

Celebration of Mass facing the people has become the norm in Maronite churches outside the Middle East and in most Chaldean and Syrian Catholic parishes in Iraq, Syria and elsewhere, and this in defiance of a 1996 ruling of the Oriental Congregation forbidding this innovation in all the Eastern rites. The Chaldeans and Syrians abroad now commonly neglect to fit their new churches with sanctuary veils, and, like Armenian Catholics, think nothing of decorating them with Western plaster statues. Melkite churches without iconostases are not unknown today in the diaspora. The adoption first of the clerical suit and finally of secular dress has come to characterize the now rarely bearded Oriental Catholic priests, although in these socially conservative communities female religious have remained generally more faithful to the habit. In the Malabarese Church clerical celibacy remains compulsory, and this Occidental custom has long been imposed on the parish priests of the West Syrian, Coptic, Ethiopic and Malankarese rites, unless they happen to be converts from Orthodoxy.[85] The Eucharist is still administered in one kind only in the Maronite and Armenian rites, while Ukrainians outside Europe no longer give Holy Communion to babies after their baptism, and in some parishes laymen have been commissioned as acolytes to help communicate the faithful.

Recently, however, graver signs of decay have appeared on the Eastern Catholic horizon. In 1995 the Maronite diocese of Australia (headed by a Lebanese Jesuit bishop from Rome) allowed nuns to administer the Holy Eucharist during liturgical functions, and took steps, despite popular opposition, to introduce Communion in the hand and female altar servers. 'Youth Masses' with profane pop music have been a facet of Australian Maronite worship for several years, hardly surprising since local candidates for the priesthood are sent to Latin diocesan seminaries for training. Coptic Catholic churches in Australia are crammed with images and statues in the best traditions of nineteenth-century religious kitsch; not only are examples of beautiful Egyptian iconography absent, but the Holy Liturgy is celebrated mainly in Arabic and facing the people in veilless sanctuaries. In 2007

---

[84] However, for two decades or so the anaphora continued to be recited in Old Slavonic on some major feasts, and some older priests still recited the Divine Office in this language which remained in wider use among the Greek Catholics of Ukraine until independence in 1991. Over the following decade Church Slavonic was generally replaced by Ukrainian even there, as also in the Ukrainian Autocephalous Orthodox Church and in the Kiev Patriarchate Orthodox Church, only the Moscow-Patriarchate Ukrainian Orthodox remaining loyal to the traditional liturgical language. The Ruthenian College in Rome phased Old Slavonic out of the liturgy and office in the mid-1990s. Since the Ukrainian redaction and pronunciation of Church Slavonic had a strong vernacular flavour, the abandonment of this sacral language by both Catholics and Orthodox is particularly lamentable and difficult to justify.

[85] Philippe Delhaye, 'Celibacy, History of', *NCE*, III, p. 371.

the hierarchy of the Ruthenian Catholic Church in the United States imposed a 'Revised Divine Liturgy' using English texts with 'gender-neutral' (i.e. feminist) language, provoking protests and petitions from many of the faithful.

Unfortunately such examples from Australia and North America are generally representative of world trends in those lesser Eastern Catholic Churches which, for most of their history, have lacked a powerful and prestigious non-Catholic counterpart, the existence of which would encourage modern Vatican ecumenists to counsel the offending Uniate leaders against tolerating or fomenting such abuses. Today the members of no Eastern Catholic church are immune from the corruptive influences of the post-conciliar 'renewal', given their long-standing habit of attending Mass in Roman-rite churches wherever their own services are not available, sending their children to mainstream Catholic schools and participating in Latin lay movements and functions of a modernistic nature.[86] Moreover, their leaders' official position that the Pauline liturgy and their own more-or-less traditional rites are qualitatively as well as juridically equal serves only to blunt the traditional instincts of the Eastern laity.

Latinism in the Eastern Catholic Churches is now a two-headed monster, manifesting itself in older, pre-conciliar Western influences, and newer modernistic ones even less in harmony with the spirit of Oriental worship. Even if (bar the cases of the Maronites and certain Malabarese) the damage done here is far less than anywhere in the Western Church, the fact remains that a partial loss of identity has been to date the inevitable result of reconciliation with the See of Rome, all legislation to the contrary notwithstanding. The ecumenical consequences are serious, and drew one Ukrainian priest to comment in 1993:

> the Eastern Catholic Churches in union with Rome are, in their present state, stumbling blocks rather than bridges between Roman Catholics and Orthodox. Latinization, largely our own doing, has gone so far that we are scarcely recognizable as orthodox any more to our Orthodox brothers. Even the most historically informed Orthodox, open to the idea of communion with the see of Rome, looks at us Greek Catholics and says, 'So this is what happens. No, thank you.'[87]

---

[86] One disturbing example of this is the invitation that the Melkite Archbishop of Akka in Galilee, Elias Chacour, issued in March 2007 to the Neocatechumenal Way, an aggressively heteropractic Latin lay organization that has been in frequent conflict with the Vatican, to 'preach the Good News' in Greek Catholic parishes, on the basis of its 'excellent fruits'. See 'Melkite Leader Invites Neocatechumenal Way', *Zenit: The World Seen from Rome*, 5 June 2007 (www.zenit. org/article-19795?l=english).

[87] Article in the *Canadian Review* by 'M.B.', quoted in 'Catholicism – Orthodoxy: Prospects for Reunion?', *AD2000*, June 1994, p. 14.

17

THE ART OF DOUBLE STANDARDS

*Today we might ask: is there a Latin Rite any more? Certainly there is
no awareness of it. To most people the liturgy appears to be something
for the individual congregation to arrange.*

JOSEF CARDINAL RATZINGER (1988)

*The Roman Rite, as reformed by Paul VI in conformity with the
Constitution on the Liturgy of the Second Vatican Council, has now
been received and applied with fruit by the great majority of the
faithful.*

VATICAN SECRETARIAT OF STATE (17 JANUARY 1994)

Double Betrayal

Since the Second Vatican Council the story of the official liturgical reform in the
Roman Church has been, sadly, one of broken promises and double standards.
The foregoing study has assessed the extent to which the work of the Consilium
amounted to a betrayal of the wishes of the Council Fathers, but on the pastoral
level, too, there is a long and shameful record of duplicity. During the Council
years the faithful were promised that the Canon of the Mass would always remain
in Latin and that, with the advent of the vernacular Mass, all-Latin celebrations
would still be frequent. People familiar with the Liturgy Constitution expected that
the Divine Office would become more commonly celebrated in parish churches;
in reality even Sunday Vespers disappeared where they had been habitually sung.
And the document that opened the door to Communion in the hand throughout
the world was the same *Memoriale Domini* in which Paul VI stated that the traditional manner of receiving the Eucharist was the one preferred by the Holy See
and should be preserved.

There can be no doubt that the Church's *de facto* abandonment of liturgical
Latin was one of the end results of Pope Paul's reform, and made a mockery of
his earlier protestation, in the apostolic letter *Sacrificium Laudis* (1966), that the
idea of delatinizing the Western Church 'attacks not only this most fertile spring
of civilization and this most rich treasure of piety, but also the decorum, beauty
and original vigour of prayer and of liturgical singing'. Moreover, the near total
disappearance of Latin from the sanctuaries and seminaries of the West occurred
within only a decade of John XXIII's forthright statement of 1962:

Bishops and superiors-general of religious orders . . . shall be on their guard lest anyone under their jurisdiction, being eager for innovation, write against the use of Latin in the teaching of the higher sacred studies or in the liturgy, or through prejudice make light of the Holy See's will in this regard or interpret it falsely.[1]

Romano Amerio, a Swiss Italian critic of *aggiornamento*, was puzzled by papal inconsistency in the matter when he reported a very strange case of the pot calling the kettle black:

It remains inexplicable how Paul VI, receiving in audience the Mayor of Rome in January 1970, could have reproached the Italian state for abolishing the study of Latin in high schools, an abolition he styled 'an insult to Rome and a self-inflicted attack on Roman civilization'.[2]

The Vernacular Fraud

Such examples, which could be multiplied, concern empty promises by Rome to uphold traditional 'options' within the pluralistic framework of the new liturgy. But the Vatican's ever more frequent application of double standards vitiated even the concessions made to the modernizers, in particular the permission to extend the liturgical use of the vernacular. The Council's aim of providing the countless linguistic groups comprising the Latin Church with a vernacular liturgy was evidently a daunting task. Whereas some languages were fully developed and translations of the liturgical texts already existed, others had no euchological literature, and still others were uncultivated and needed to be standardized before the work of translation could even commence. And how would liturgists proceed in areas of mixed population where several languages were spoken side by side?

What in fact happened in most places was that liturgical Latin was not replaced by the actual vernacular, but by the institutionalized literary language, usually the official language of the state. In Western Europe where languages like Italian, French and German were naturally subdivided into many sharply differing dialects, the vernacular principle logically dictated the production of missals and versions of the Roman ritual in such dialects as Sicilian, Neapolitan, Lombard, Walloon, Norman, Swabian, Bavarian and Low German where these were still commonly spoken, especially since they possessed long-standing literary traditions.

However, this option was not even considered by episcopal conferences whose cultural outlook was altogether bourgeois and anti-traditional. So liturgies in Standard Italian, French and German were thrust upon populations for whom these were in fact second languages. Defenders of local linguistic traditions naturally resented the abolition of neutral Latin (the old partner of the regional dialect in popular piety) and the new willingness of Rome to aid and abet the secular forces of cultural assimilation.

This complicity of the Church was especially culpable in regions where local

---

[1] *Veterum Sapientia*, II, 1, 2. An old but unsubstantiated rumour has it that Pope John was personally not very committed to Latin, and issued this encyclical as a sop to conservatives likely to oppose the planned liturgical reform.

[2] *Iota unum: Studio delle variazioni della Chiesa cattolica nel secolo XX* (Milan/Naples, 1989), p. 515, n. 3.

languages were threatened with eventual extinction because of official discourage-
ment or neglect, for instance in Sardinia, Friuli, Occitania, the Basque Country,
Galicia and Gaelic Ireland. Of the situation in Celtic-speaking Brittany, D. B.
Gregor writes:

> the Catholic religion, unlike the Nonconformist sects of Wales, has a Mass, and
> when the use of Latin in it is waived, the language that floods in is not Breton, but
> French. There was only one Breton bishop in Brittany in 1967, and the bishops
> have even been called 'artful instruments of francization', who refuse to say Mass
> in Breton and see no connection between this attitude and a decrease in the size
> of their congregations.[3]

In the ex-colonial countries of America, Africa and Asia, where large sections of the
population did not even understand the new liturgical medium, the introduction
of Mass in English, Spanish, Portuguese, French and various 'national' (in reality,
neo-colonial) languages (Hindi, Indonesian, Tagalog, Swahili etc.) was as absurd
as it was unfair. All the more so in that the multilingual faithful of the mission
countries had usually been sentimentally attached to Latin. The post-conciliar
Church has thus been playing a negative role as a major collaborator of centralistic governments in the denationalization of ethnolinguistic minorities, behaving
in the exact opposite way to the sixteenth-century apostles of Protestantism and
Counter-Reformation Catholicism, who gave to so many of the oppressed peoples
of Europe vernacular versions of the Scriptures and catechisms that would become
the cornerstones of modern national literatures.

Today, forty years after the abandonment of liturgical Latin, true linguistic
equity in the Roman liturgy thus remains a far-off ideal, with institutionalized
discrimination against whole populations for whom some use of the vernacular in
public worship would be pastorally advantageous and culturally constructive.

The Immemorial Rite Abrogated?

Far more serious than any of these injustices was, however, the conspiracy at the
highest levels of the Church to deprive the Roman-rite clergy and faithful of their
integral liturgical heritage. From the standpoint of canon law, the post-conciliar
apostolic constitution *Missale Romanum* obrogated (replaced) the liturgical legislation of 1570 (*Quo Primum*), but it did not abrogate it in the required manner, i.e.
by explicit mention. Since the 1969 constitution contained no clauses to that effect,
every priest of the Roman rite retained the right, deriving from customary law, to use
the missal of St Pius V, the legal introduction of the new forms notwithstanding.[4]

---

[3] Douglas B. Gregor, *Celtic: A Comparative Study* (Cambridge/New York, 1980), p. 319.
[4] According to the Italian canonist Dr Neri Capponi:

> The Bull *Quo Primum* was the first written legislation in the Roman Rite governing the
> celebration of Mass. Until 1570, the celebration of Mass was governed by what is known
> as customary law *ex consuetudine*. The method of celebrating Mass in a particular country,
> district, or even city was protected or regulated by 'immemorial custom'. . . . As with all the
> other missals in use throughout the Roman Rite, the Roman Missal had been regulated by
> customary law until the written legislation of *Quo Primum*, and it certainly constituted an
> immemorial custom. . . . This raises a further question as to the status of an immemorial

Whatever inhibited him from formally abrogating the immemorial rite, Paul VI was determined to prevent the priests of his patriarchate from celebrating it. This resolution was well communicated to the Vatican bureaucracy and to the episcopal conferences of the world. Soon a number of strategies were put in place to achieve in fact what had not been achieved by law. In the official English translation of *Missale Romanum* one particular sentence, *Ad extremum, ex iis quæ hactenus de novo Missali Romano exposuimus quiddam nunc cogere et efficere placet* ('Finally, from the things which we have been explaining so far it pleases us now to draw a conclusion and make a particular point'),[5] was incorrectly rendered as: 'In conclusion we wish to give the force of law to all that we have set forth concerning the new Roman Missal.' Thus the introduction to the new ordo gave every English-speaking priest to believe that the use of the Pauline rite was compulsory.

The circumstances of this mistranslation, which occurred in many other editions of the missal besides the English, were bizarre. When a French priest well versed in Latin first noticed the same inconsistency in the new French-language missal, he wrote to the Centre National de Pastorale Liturgique for clarification. Fr Pierre Jounel, a member of the papal Consilium, replied that it was the Latin text that was inaccurate, and admitted that 'this casts a very legitimate doubt on the Legislator's intention' to make the new missal obligatory. According to Fr Jounel, the original text had been drawn up in Italian and the mistranslated phrase did, in fact, have the same meaning as the French version (*Pour terminer, nous voulons donner force de loi à tout ce que nous avons exposé plus haut sur le nouveau Missel Romain*). What was now necessary, continued Jounel, was for Pope Paul to dispel all doubt by making an authoritative statement confirming his intention.[6]

If Fr Jounel is to be taken at his word, the faceless Roman latinist charged with translating the Italian preamble into the official language of the Church deliberately altered the import of the Italian words which Pope Paul apparently made his own. Was this done – providentially – to save the immemorial rite from abrogation? We shall probably never know, but the fact is that the Pope appended his signature to the Latin text which, however flawed, remains the official one.

The shady circumstances in which the new missal made its appearance in the Roman rite set the tone for the whole reform. There was trouble from the first, the Latin Church splitting in two over the acquiescence of most clergy and laity and the refusal of a passionate and articulate minority to accept an untraditional liturgical reform. Because of the time needed to prepare vernacular translations of the New Order of Mass – the possibility that Latin might persist anywhere as the normal liturgical medium being now generally excluded – the date for its obligatory use throughout the Roman rite was deferred to 28 November 1971.

Since there was considerable doubt as to whether the bull *Quo Primum* was

---

custom if the written law that had come to regulate it should lapse . . . It is our view that it *would* revert to its original status of an immemorial custom, and be protected by customary law, *unless* the legislator abrogated it by special mention. . . . We conclude that at least by virtue of established custom all celebrants should be free to use the Missal of St Pius V, and all the faithful to take part in it. (Michael Davies and Neri Capponi, 'The Legal Status of the Tridentine Mass', *The Latin Mass*, Vol. 3, No. 3 [May/June 1994], pp. 30–33)

[5] The 'particular point' (*quiddam*, lit. 'a certain thing') then presented in the text is that just as the missal of St Pius V had been presented 'as an instrument of liturgical unity and as a witness to the purity of worship in the Church', it was Pope Paul's hope that the new missal, while providing for legitimate local adaptations, would 'bear witness to and affirm the common unity of all'.

[6] Salleron, *op. cit.*, pp. 99–100. See also Davies, *Pope Paul's New Mass*, pp. 51–52, 554.

automatically abrogated by the promulgation of *Missale Romanum*, continuing requests for clarification from various episcopal conferences in 1972 and 1973 led the Congregation for Divine Worship to publish a notification on 28 October 1974 confirming the allegedly compulsory nature of the reform. This document, signed by Cardinal Knox and Archbishop Bugnini, contained the claim, shamelessly *ultra vires*, that the traditional liturgy could no longer be celebrated under 'any pretext of custom, even immemorial custom'. Bishops could grant dispensations for elderly or infirm priests to celebrate the old rite of Mass in private, but in no circumstances were they to allow the use of the Pian missal in celebrations with a congregation of any size present.

All over the world the traditional liturgy disappeared from Roman-rite churches, with only three exceptions: the Brazilian diocese of Campos, where the local ordinary, Mgr Antônio de Castro Mayer, encouraged the continued celebration of the missal of 1570 alongside the new one; England and Wales, where the indult obtained by Cardinal Heenan from Paul VI on 5 November 1971 had allowed the old Mass to survive (albeit with severe restrictions); and in Communist China where, because of forced isolation, the schismatic Patriotic Church and some priests of the underground Papalist movement had maintained the pre-conciliar liturgy.[7] Elsewhere, the small groups of Latin Catholics who insisted on its celebration were treated by the hierarchy as pariahs and schismatics and forced to hold services in rented secular buildings and private residences. Pastors who refused to implement the liturgical reforms were hounded from their parishes by their bishops, with the full approval of Rome.[8]

Drawing the Battle Lines

Late in 1974 Rome ordered an 'apostolic visitation' of the seminary that retired French Archbishop Marcel Lefebvre had founded in 1970 at Écône in Canton Valais, Switzerland, for the training of priests exclusively committed to the traditional liturgy.[9] Reacting to comments by the two apostolic visitors who made no secret of their personal disbelief in an immutable truth and in the bodily resurrection of Christ, the Archbishop made a declaration on 21 November disavowing 'the Rome of Neo-Modernist and Neo-Protestant tendencies which became clearly manifest

---

[7] Underground priests in contact with the Catholic clergy of Hong Kong were more inclined to switch to the new Pauline rites celebrated in Chinese, as a sign of loyalty to the Holy See, though their more isolated confrères have apparently continued to say the old Mass to the present day. In the early 1990s some clergy of the Patriotic Association began to adopt the new Chinese missal and today its use is widespread, though until recently eastward-position celebrations and Communion received reverently and on the tongue remained the norm. In Shanghai churches, at least, the traditional Latin Mass continues to be celebrated for older people alongside the new (Information courtesy of Dr Richard Rigby). In Enver Hoxha's Albania, another zone of isolation where the public and private practice of religion had been banned by government decree in 1967, the few priests not in captivity who were able to celebrate Mass secretly did so according to the old missal. Since the fall of the Stalinist regime in Albania in 1992, the vernacular *Novus Ordo* has invaded that country, too.

[8] For a typical example, see the autobiography of the French Canadian traditionalist Fr Yves Normandin, *Un curé dans la rue* (Quebec, 1976), published in English as *Pastor out in the Cold* (Quebec, 1978).

[9] The two visitors were Belgians: Bishop Albert Descamps, a biblical scholar and former rector of Louvain University, and Mgr Guillaume Onclin, a canon lawyer.

during the Second Vatican Council and, after the Council, in all the reforms that issued from it'. This statement also contained the strongest condemnation to date of the liturgical reform by any Catholic prelate:

> The *lex orandi* [law of prayer] cannot be profoundly modified without also modifying the *lex credendi* [law of belief]. To the new Mass correspond a new Catechism, new priesthood, new seminaries, new universities, a Charismatic Pentecostal Church – all things that are opposed to orthodoxy and the Magisterium as they have always been.
>
> This reform, the fruit of liberalism and modernism, is completely and utterly poisoned; it starts from heresy and ends with heresy. It is accordingly impossible for any aware and faithful Catholic to adopt this reform and to submit to it in any way whatever.[10]

When the Declaration was published in the Parisian journal *Itinéraires* in January the following year the post-conciliar establishment was outraged. Later in 1975 a commission of cardinals, on orders from Paul VI, began proceedings against the Archbishop which led to his suspension *a divinis* on 22 July 1976, a penalty which he ignored. Regarding the role of the Pope in the Church, Lefebvre made the apt observation that

> [t]he Catholic Church is a Mystic Reality which exists not only in space, on the surface of the earth, but also in time and in eternity. In order for the Pope to represent the Church and be the image of Her, he must not only be united to Her in space, but also in time, the Church being essentially a living tradition.[11]

After the death of Pope Paul on 6 August 1978 and the one-month pontificate of John Paul I (Luciano Albini), Mgr Lefebvre was received in private audience by Pope John Paul II on 18 November 1978.[12] While the new Pontiff disagreed with the Archbishop's stand, he was anxious to promote peace in the Church and to undo as much as possible of the damage done during the Montinian era. Archbishop Lefebvre's principled resistance won from John Paul II a series of increasingly generous concessions to disaffected traditionalist Catholics. On 3 April 1980 the Pope published the Instruction on the Eucharist *Inæstimabile Donum*, which listed and denounced many of the abuses that had become common in the reformed Roman liturgy. The Instruction also stated that the wish of members of the faithful to worship 'according to the old Latin forms' must be respected. Four years later, the indult of 3 October 1984 (*Quattuor Abhinc Annos*) authorized local bishops to provide celebrations of the old rite of Mass for those requesting it.

There is no reason to doubt that John Paul II was in good faith in believing that the continued use of the immemorial rite was strictly speaking illegal and hence the object of an indult. In any case, two years later he resolved to clarify the matter, and secretly convened a commission of nine Cardinals (Ratzinger, Mayer, Oddi, Stickler, Tomko, Gantin, Innocenti, Palazzini and Casaroli) to ascertain the juridical status of the missal of St Pius V. This commission ruled that the traditional

---

[10] M. Davies, *Apologia*, I, pp. 37–40.
[11] Interview to *Le Figaro*, 4 August 1976.
[12] An account of this historic meeting is given in M. Davies, *Apologia*, II, pp. 255–68.

liturgy had never in fact been officially abrogated.[13] The obvious implication of the 1986 ruling – that no bishop ever possessed the right to forbid any Latin-rite priest from celebrating the 'Tridentine' Mass, and that 'recalcitrant' clerics had been unjustly persecuted – did little to regain for the Holy See the full confidence of the small but fast-growing traditionalist element in the Church.[14]

Showdown at Écône

In reality little changed, in spite of this compromising Vatican admission and the new legislation. On the contrary, the hierarchy's repudiation of Latin-rite traditionalists – now including a generation of conscientious objectors born after 1969 – remained as determined as before. When, on 14 June 1987, Mgr Lefebvre met Cardinal Ratzinger in Rome to inform him of his intention of consecrating a number of bishops to carry on his work (he was now 82 years of age), the Vatican panicked and initiated negotiations to regularize his position and that of the priests he had ordained. These talks dragged on over the following year but eventually came to nothing, partly because of the ill will of certain members of the episcopate and the Curia, and also because of Mgr Lefebvre's ever-waning confidence in the Pope's will and ability to restore Catholic tradition.[15]

After months of soul searching, the Archbishop finally rejected the protocol of 5 May 1988 which proposed to reinsert his Priestly Fraternity of St Pius X into the mainstream of the Church and to allow him to consecrate one bishop for the continuation of his work. His ordination of four bishops at Écône on 30 June 1988 moved the Vatican to declare, two days later, that Mgr Lefebvre, his co-consecrator Mgr Castro Mayer, and the four new bishops had incurred the penalty of excommunication *latæ sententiæ*.[16]

Some of the Archbishop's priests and followers subsequently made their peace with Rome and established the Priestly Fraternity of Saint Peter. The new clerical society was canonically erected on 18 October that year, and set up its headquarters at Wigratzbad, West Germany. Nevertheless, the majority of Lefebvrist priests

---

[13] Cardinal Silvio Oddi made the public announcement in August 1988 that: 'It needs to be said that the Mass of St. Pius V has in fact never been officially abrogated'. See Coralie Graham, 'Every Roman Catholic Priest Can Now Legally Celebrate the Tridentine Mass', *The Fatima Crusader*, XXIX (1990), pp. 26–27.

[14] That the bull of St Pius V remained in force after 1969 had already been argued by Fr Raymond Dulac, *La Bulle Quo primum tempore* (Paris, 1972), as well as by Count Neri Capponi in *Some Juridical Considerations on the Reform of the Liturgy, op. cit.*

[15] The dispute centred around Rome's plan to place the Society of St Pius X under the jurisdiction of a Roman Commission composed of five members appointed by Rome and only two appointed by Écône; the Holy See's refusal to grant the Society more than one bishop and delaying tactics concerning the consecration of the latter; suggestions that churches of the Society should offer the *Novus Ordo* as well as the traditional Mass; and the demand that Mgr Lefebvre apologize to the pope for 'the injustice he had done to the Holy See'. At no point during the negotiations did the pope make any attempt to confer personally with Mgr Lefebvre. For Écône's view of this affair, see Schmidberger, *op. cit.*; for a contrary view as expressed by a member of the new Fraternity of St Peter, see Engelbert Recktenwald, *The 30th June in the Light of the Faith: On the Problem of the Episcopal Consecrations performed by Archbishop Marcel Lefebvre* (Canberra, 1989).

[16] The four new bishops were: Bernard Tissier de Mallerais (French), Richard Williamson (English), Alfonso de Galarreta (Spanish-Argentinian) and Bernard Fellay (Swiss). The Notification of the excommunication was signed by Bernardin Cardinal Gantin.

remained loyal to their founder. At the same time, larger numbers of tradition-conscious Catholics not associated with the Archbishop began to demand from their pastors and bishops the right of access to the traditional liturgy.

The Ecclesia Dei Commission

The Apostolic Letter *Ecclesia Dei Adflicta* of 2 July 1988 announced the setting up of the Ecclesia Dei Commission

> whose task it will be to collaborate with the bishops, with the Departments of the Roman Curia and with the circles [of the faithful] concerned, for the purpose of facilitating full ecclesial communion of priests, seminarians, religious communities or individuals until now linked in various ways to the Fraternity founded by Mgr Lefebvre, who may wish to remain united to the Successor of Peter in the Catholic Church while preserving their spiritual and liturgical traditions, in the light of the Protocol signed on 5 May last by Cardinal Ratzinger and Mgr Lefebvre.[17]

In his motu proprio the Pope also requested that bishops recognize the 'rightful aspirations' of 'all who seek . . . the use of the Roman Missal according to the 1962 edition' (i.e. not only ex-Lefebvrists) and therefore make for them a 'wide and generous' provision of the necessary liturgical facilities.[18]

The pontifical commission, headed by German archbishop Paul Augustin Mayer, authorized the granting of *celebrets* for all priests (even those ordained according to the new rite) who sought permission to use the traditional liturgy, a permission quite superfluous from the juridical point of view. The episcopate of the Latin Church continued nonetheless to oppose and impede these papal initiatives to such an extent that the followers of Archbishop Lefebvre could feel justified in their decision to break materially with the 'Conciliar Church'.

On 16 May 1989, a secret summit took place in Rome between six prelates hostile to the traditionalist movement: Vatican secretary of state Cardinal Casaroli, the prefect of the Sacred Congregation for Divine Worship Cardinal Martínez-Sómalo and the presidents of the French, Swiss, German and English and Welsh episcopal conferences (Cardinal Decourtray, Bishop Candolfi, Bishop Lehmann and Cardinal Hume). After its meeting, this pressure group actually prevailed upon the Pope to shelve his proposed plan of lifting all remaining restrictions upon the public use of the pre-conciliar rite.[19]

No less disedifying than episcopal ill treatment of Roman-rite traditionalists has been the double dealing of the Ecclesia Dei Commission since July 1991, when Cardinal Mayer was replaced as prefect by Cardinal Antonio Innocenti, one of the nine prelates appointed to investigate the juridical status of the traditional liturgy in 1986.[20] The new Cardinal President, who had been making it increasingly

---

[17] *Ecclesia Dei Adflicta*, 6. a.
[18] Ibid., 6. c.
[19] E. M. de Saventhem, 'Red Light for Roman Celebrets?', *Christian Order*, April 1990, pp. 210–11.
[20] Innocenti, no friend of the traditionalist movement, had been secretary of the Sacred Congregation for the Sacraments and Divine Worship, set up by Paul VI on 31 July 1975, with the iconoclastically inclined Australian cardinal James Knox as its prefect. He had also been rector of

difficult for priests to obtain *celebrets*, informed Bishop Dermot O'Sullivan of Kerry that the concessions were intended not for the general faithful, who were allegedly obliged to accept the new rite, but for former followers of Archbishop Lefebvre.[21]

Volte-face

That Pope John Paul II had in the meantime gone back on his promises of 1984 and 1988 was revealed in his response to the memorandum submitted to him by Dr Eric de Saventhem, president of the International Federation *Una Voce*.[22] This was given in the letter which Archbishop Giovanni Battista Re, of the Vatican Secretariat of State, addressed to Dr de Saventhem on 17 January 1994:

> First of all, it should be observed that the Roman Rite, as reformed by Paul VI in conformity with the Constitution on the Liturgy of the Second Vatican Council, has now been received and applied with fruit by the great majority of the faithful.
>
> By the motu proprio *Ecclesia Dei*, the use of the Roman missal approved in 1962 has been conceded on certain conditions. The various arrangements made since 1984 had as their aim to facilitate the ecclesial life of a certain number of the faithful without, however, making the earlier liturgical forms permanent. The general law remains that the Rite renewed since the Council should be used, while the use of the previous Rite rests on privileges which must keep the character of exceptions. . . .
>
> . . . the prime duty of all the faithful is to deepen the rich meaning that the current liturgy contains, in a spirit of faith and obedience to the Magisterium, while

Mater Ecclesiæ Seminary in Rome, opened by John Paul II on 15 October 1986 to facilitate the 'normalization' of ex-seminarians of Écône. The experiment was a failure (mainly because of the rector's refusal to allow the students frequent access to the traditional liturgy), and the institution was closed in 1989.

[21] Antoni Milan, 'Stonewalled at the Vatican', *Ecclesia Dei Newsletter* (Canberra, Winter 1994), p. 6. The Commission has subsequently returned to its original position, and a ruling of 5 September 1995 admitted that 'the Motu Proprio does not speak of any restrictions, including age limits, on those who aspire to worship according to the liturgical books of 1962. Neither does it state that only those who had previous experience of the Latin liturgical tradition could have such an aspiration.'

[22] John Paul II's indifference to liturgical questions (and, indeed, his apparent inability to see the traditionalist position as anything other than nostalgia and temperamental conservatism) was the logical outcome of his liberal relativism. At the Second Vatican Council Cardinal Wojtyła had been a strong supporter of the principle of inculturation, and in the late 1960s, as Archbishop of Cracow, he caused unfavourable comment by encouraging undignified 'youth Masses' with pop music, and supported the building of the new Le Corbusier-style church of Our Lady Queen of Poland ('Arka Pana') at Nowa Huta, a great monument to popular faith, certainly, but also spectacularly hideous and irremediably anti-liturgical in design. Wojtyła's aliturgical nature has been put down to a defective formation in an underground seminary during the Second World War, where formal training in liturgical principle and practice was of necessity minimal. To this may be added his well-known thespian proclivities, hardly inimical to post-conciliar liturgical improvisation and 'creativity'. John Paul II on occasion presided at or celebrated Mass according to various Oriental rites and was always happy to take part in ecumenical services with Protestants and Jews, but throughout his twenty-seven-year pontificate he consistently refused to celebrate the Mass of his ordination.

avoiding any tension that could damage ecclesial communion. The Holy Father expresses the wish that your Association should contribute to this end.[23]

This message, purporting to come from the Pope himself, could only be seen as legitimizing the new policy of the Ecclesia Dei Commission, which informed a group of United States traditionalists in December 1993 that the papal concession was a 'grace', not a 'law'. Hence there was 'no question in the strict sense of a bishop's having to obey the provisions of the motu proprio', and no appeal against the decision of a bishop to forbid the old rites was possible.[24] As one Australian writer was moved to comment:

> Rather than a redress of grievances, the Una Voce petition has elicited a Vatican demonstration that it is prepared to let the Ecclesia Dei decree, a piece of sovereign legislation by the Pontiff, be treated in the same way as his previous clearly stated policy on altar girls: to be eviscerated by administrative action.[25]

The reference to female altar servers, a sinister aberration from the iconic perspective of traditional Catholicism, is apposite in view of the Vatican's pathetic pleading that this innovation has no symbolic connection with the concept of women priests, discussion of which John Paul II ordered to cease with his apostolic letter *Ordinatio sacerdotalis* of 22 May 1994.[26]

By the mid-1990s it was apparent that the liturgical reform with which Pope John Paul wished Western traditionalists to reconcile themselves was not a closed one, but an ongoing revolution far exceeding the official ritual norms. The situation had reached the point where it was impossible for any conservative Catholic to insist on strict conformity to the official post-conciliar rites when the Pope himself now enthusiastically participated in public ceremonies at which not only the basic rubrics of the Pauline liturgy were flouted, but where serious abuses such as female altar servers and liturgical dancing were admitted.[27]

---

[23] Published in the *Una Voce* newsletter (Rome, January–May 1994), p. 13.

[24] Milan, *op. cit.*, p. 7.

[25] Gary Scarrabelotti, 'Una Voce Petition . . . "Received without fruit"', *Ecclesia Dei Newsletter* (Canberra, Winter 1994), p. 19.

[26] Vatican spokesman Dr Joaquín Navarro-Valls in March 1994 made the astounding claim that the question of female 'acolytes' had no connection with the debate about the ordination of woman, and that the heteropractic ruling of the Congregation for Divine Worship and the Sacraments was 'the result of an interpretation of existing church law [a reference to female lectors and extraordinary ministers of the Eucharist] and not a major innovation of the Church' [!] ('Worship and Sacraments Congregation: Use of Female Altar Servers Allowed', *Origins: CNS Documentary Service*, Vol. 23, No. 45 [28 April 1994], p. 779).

[27] The first such occurrence was in Sydney, Australia, at the public Mass celebrated by John Paul II before a huge outdoor congregation on 18 January 1995 for the beatification of Mary MacKillop (Mother Mary of the Cross). The 'liturgy' of that day, including the plan to have women (Sisters of St Joseph in mufti) serving the Mass, had been approved in advance by the Vatican, and there was certainly no evidence from the televised coverage that the pope was in any way uncomfortable with – let alone disapproving of – the relentlessly heteropractic proceedings over which he presided. One might well suppose, however, that the *beata* in question – a humble woman who valued traditional piety – would have been horrified by the liturgical travesty performed in her name.

When Right is Wrong and Wrong is Right

John Paul II's new wholehearted endorsement of the Western liturgical revolution contrasted glaringly with his condemnation of the exact same revolt against tradition in the Malabarese Church. Incredibly, the Holy See had come to censure the agitation of Latin traditionalists while it applauded the identical defence of an ancient patrimony in the Syro-Malabarese rite: it vindicated the Pauline liturgy and blocked the restoration of the old rite in the West, at the same time as it condemned the Malabarese 'Mini-Mass' of 1968 and imposed in its place the immemorial Edessene rite in the East.

This particular case of Roman double standards is so astounding that the story bears telling in some detail. The 'updating' of the Syro-Malabar rite in the late 1960s, described in Chapter 16, was attended by a growing exodus of clergy and laity (especially those living outside Kerala) to the Roman rite. Between 1935 and 1976 Rome granted dispensations to some 2,000 Malabarese priests and 8,000 nuns to convert to the Roman rite, and in the 1960s the 7,000 Keralan male and female religious working in other parts of India had all been obliged to abandon their ancestral rite as the precondition of undertaking missionary work.[28] The real cause for concern was the willingness with which the priests and nuns in question had forsaken their liturgical heritage. Clearly, local traditionalists argued, the semi-Latin worship introduced into their Church was working towards the total destruction of its unique identity.

In the meantime a well-organized opposition to the modernizing reform had taken shape in the inland archdiocese of Changanacherry. Several graduates of the Oriental Theological School at the St Thomas Apostolic Seminary in Kottayam, passionately devoted to their culture, had obtained doctorates in sacred liturgy and had been consecrated bishops. At meetings of the Syro-Malabarese Episcopal Conference this traditionally minded minority made frequent protests against the liturgical revolution.[29] However, their agitation had little impact locally, since the Conference president and metropolitan of Ernakulam, Cardinal Joseph Parecattil, was the moral leader of the latinizers and modernizers as well as a champion of 'indianization'.

Nevertheless, at this time one of the historic injustices committed against the Malabarese worked providentially to the advantage of the traditionalists. After the Indian Church was illicitly removed from the authority of the Chaldean Patriarch at the end of the sixteenth century and subjected to the rule of Latin hierarchs, common justice should have dictated either the restoration of juridical ties with the Chaldean Church, or the institution of a Malabarese patriarchate. Neither reform ever took place, but since the 'acephalous' Syro-Malabarese Church remained dependent on the Roman Curia, members of the traditionalist opposition were now able to go over the heads of their hierarchy and appeal to the Holy See for help.

By the late 1970s the Oriental Congregation had recovered its erstwhile commitment to tradition, and during their *ad limina* visit to Rome in 1980 the Malabarese bishops were advised that the liturgical question had to be settled once and for

---

[28] Podipara, *Rise and Decline*, p. 47; Podipara, 'Malabar Rite', p. 94. Both the Malabarese and Malankarese Churches have since been allowed by Rome to establish their own Indian missions outside Kerala. Nevertheless, the conversion of Syrian-rite missionaries to Latin Catholicism remains very common.

[29] Madey, *op. cit.*, p. 173.

all. To this end the episcopate was asked to reflect on its ritual patrimony in the light of the earlier (pre-conciliar) Roman directives, and then submit a new order of Mass for eventual approval.[30]

The liturgical committee subsequently set up in Kerala by Cardinal Parecattil was predictably top-heavy with anti-traditionalists who, in 1981, presented the Oriental Congregation with a draft little better than that of 1968. Fortunately, the secretary of the Congregation at this time was the Ukrainian liturgist, Archbishop Myroslav Marusyn, and the negative findings of the commission that examined the draft were strongly endorsed by the new prefect, Polish cardinal Władysław Rubin.[31]

And so, fifteen years after the appearance of the 'Mini-Mass', Rome finally took effective action. On 1 March 1983 Cardinal Parecattil and the other Keralan eparchs were officially notified of the Congregation's rejection of their schema, and the episcopate was requested to submit to Rome by 15 September of the same year a fresh draft of the order of *Qurbana* taking full stock of the criticisms contained in an enclosed instruction entitled *Observations on 'The Order of the Holy Mass of the Syro-Malabar Church 1981'*.[32]

The Malabarese 'Novus Ordo' Condemned

In this document the entire 1981 schema was excoriated as 'a superficial modern westernization based on some of the worst aspects of current Western liturgical practice'.[33] Indeed the innovations and gimmicks of the new rite were 'foreign to any Eastern liturgical tradition'. The censors further complained of

a 'reductionist' tendency to limit and reduce and westernize as much as possible, with little awareness of the nature of ritual activity as understood from the viewpoint of cultural anthropology – that is, one sees hardly any awareness of what an extremely delicate thing it is to touch in any way the established ritual patterns of a tradition.[34]

Perusing Section C of the Vatican instruction, one is struck by the pertinence of its criticisms of the Malabarese 'Mini-Mass' to the new Latin *ordo* of Paul VI which the Holy See continues to enforce as the liturgical norm in the Roman rite. Thus Rome selectively condemns the pseudo-primitive practice of Mass facing the people, stating that 'the priest stands *in medio sanctuarii* facing East (*not* towards the congregation)'.[35] It deplores – but only for the Malabarese rite – the placing and use of 'a table in front of the altar'. As for the announcement of the 'intention' or 'theme' of a particular celebration,

this contemporary Western fad has no basis either in Indian culture or in a proper understanding of the liturgy in any tradition. All liturgy has but one theme, Jesus

---

[30] Ibid., p. 174.
[31] Ibid., p. 175.
[32] Ibid. The entire text of this instruction is printed in Madey, *op. cit.*, pp. 177–99.
[33] Ibid., A. 1: b.
[34] Ibid., A. 1: f.
[35] Ibid., C. 1: b.

Christ dead and risen for our salvation; and the intentions of every Eucharist, including the particular intentions of the local community, are expressed in the liturgical texts themselves at the proper time.[36]

Nor did the Commission mince its words on the question of 'liturgical creativity' in the Syro-Malabarese rite:

Spontaneous prayers are not to be admitted. This Western experiment has opened the door to mediocrity and banality. Very few people have the talent for spontaneous public prayer . . . Furthermore, in public, ritual worship (as distinct from private prayer) there is little room for spontaneity in composition and form. Indeed, such 'spontaneity' is actually not that of the people of God, but of individual celebrants, who often impose their particular ideas and piety on a captive audience. Spontaneity in liturgy is found in the movements of hearts as they respond to grace, not in the liberty of individual priests to impose their personal piety on the common prayer of all.[37]

The 1983 instruction condemned as 'a false principle both historically and liturgically' the idea that 'all liturgical prayers should be said aloud so that everyone can hear them'. For

some prayers are specifically designed to be said during singing or processions or other activities of the people, or are apologies *pro clero*. Just as the clergy do not have to sing everything the people chant, so too the people do not have to hear all the prayers. Indeed to recite all prayers aloud interrupts the proper flow of the liturgical structure.[38]

Similarly, 'silent periods of reflection cannot be allowed to interrupt the liturgy: they have no place in Eastern usage'.[39]

Most interesting were occasional admissions of defects in the new liturgical theology of the Latin Church. Regarding the offertory procession,

even Western liturgists have come to see that the excessive solemnization of the preparation and transfer of gifts was based, in part, on a pseudo-theology according to which the 'offertory' is the laity's liturgy, and the 'eucharistic offering' is the priest's.[40]

As regards the typically Western and rationalist concern to eliminate the dramatic anticipation involved in referring to the unconsecrated elements as Christ's 'Body' and 'Blood' *before* the Anaphora (canon), the Roman instruction claimed that such innovations 'not only depart from the original text, but manifest a total incomprehension of the nature of Christian liturgical language, which is symbolic and often proleptic, and not ontological, pedantic literalism'.[41]

[36] Ibid., C. 1: c.
[37] Ibid., C. 7: b.
[38] Ibid., C. 9: a.
[39] Ibid., C. 23: d.
[40] Ibid., pp. 187–88.
[41] Ibid., p. 191.

The Modernizers Resist

The recommendations of the 1983 instruction amounted in fact to an order for the reinstatement of the service books of 1955–1962. The apparent defeat of the innovators coincided with Cardinal Parecattil's resignation from his see early in 1984. Nevertheless, Parecattil's equally anti-traditional auxiliary bishop and the Eparch of Mananthavady had already written to Rome explaining that the hierarchy found it impossible to accept the directives contained in the instruction, and, as a delaying tactic, requested further clarification. This attempt to sabotage the restoration was countered by a petition to the Holy See from the six traditionalist bishops of Kerala, led by Mar Joseph Powathil, Archbishop of Changanacherry.[42]

The Oriental Congregation agreed with the latter that there was no excuse for any further delay in implementing the norms. Shortly before his death in 1987, Cardinal Parecattil wrote a book criticizing the restoration with the pedestrian argument that 'the Roman rite has, because of its thorough and radical reform, become relevant and meaningful to the people of today. To deny such a privilege to the Syro-Malabar and other Oriental rites would be tantamount to discrimination . . .'[43] The retired metropolitan also made the astonishing claim that 'the changes introduced in the Roman liturgy after the Vatican Council have not disturbed the faith of any member of that rite'.[44]

Unfortunately the episcopal majority, led by Parecattil's successor in Ernakulam from 1984, Cardinal Anthony Padiyara, immediately set about trying to reverse, or at least undermine, the new legislation. They were not, moreover, deterred from their resolve by the intervention of Pope John Paul II, who in February 1986 personally inaugurated the return to tradition by celebrating the *Raza* or solemn *Qurbana* on the occasion of the beatification of a Malabarese priest and nun in Kottayam. Indeed, the reform party were emboldened by the support they received from the new Prefect of the Oriental Congregation, Cardinal Simon Lourdusamy, a Latin-rite Indian who sympathized with their views.

The traditionalists were appalled when, on 5 May 1988, the Congregation issued new liturgical instructions making the restored sections of the *Qurbana* optional subject to the discretion of local bishops, who could once again permit innovations. In thus capitulating to pressure, the Holy See was authorizing a virtual return to the 'simplified' (i.e. mutilated) 1968 form of the Mass, and this meant that the *Qurbana* in its solemn and pontifical forms (i.e. the integral rite) need no longer be celebrated by anyone opposed to it. Furthermore, priests were again given the option of celebrating the Mass of the Catechumens facing the people instead of in the eastward position.[45]

Cardinal Lourdusamy claimed that he had acted from pastoral motives since the sudden reversion to traditional forms had allegedly disconcerted the majority of Malabarese faithful. 'The document of the Congregation for Oriental Churches dated May 5, 1988 and addressed to the Malabar bishops shows that not even Rome takes its decisions and its "final judgements" seriously', complained the Kerala journal *Christian Orient*.[46] In spite of this setback, the traditionalist bishops

[42] Ibid., pp. 175–76.
[43] Parecattil, *Syro-Malabar Liturgy as I see It*, p. 76.
[44] Ibid., p. 134.
[45] Gianni Valente, 'The Restless Sons of St. Thomas', *30 Days* (September–October 1990), p. 26.
[46] Ibid.

(dubbed 'Lefebvrists' by the opposition) carried on their struggle, and in their dioceses a new generation strongly devoted to the ritual customs of their ancestors has since grown up. By contrast, in the latinized eparchies where priests maintain and promote with impunity the liturgical abuses of 1968 and its aftermath (including wholesale 'indianization'), the forces of auto-demolition are in full swing.

Slamming the Stable Door

It is surely not cynical to conclude that Roman action in favour of tradition in Kerala was facilitated by the facts that the Malabarese Church is a small and marginal one and that the abusive post-conciliar reform was known to have been the work of misguided Malabarese clerics rather than a blunder of the Holy See. Here, Rome could attempt to restore justice and peace without any loss of face. Indeed it seems inconceivable, humanly speaking, that the Vatican could accept the logic of its Indian intervention and admit that the whole Pauline reform had been a catastrophic mistake. On the other hand, how can Rome claim, without denying the Catholicity of the East Syrian liturgy and the essential oneness of the Catholic liturgical tradition, that what applies in Kerala does not apply elsewhere in the Church? It can hardly be doubted that the Malabarese episode has seriously compromised the credibility and moral authority of the Holy See in ritual matters.

Few prelates of the Latin Church, even among the handful who actively encouraged the use of the old liturgy in the 1990s, dared to condemn in the Roman rite what had been roundly and unhesitatingly condemned in that of the Syro-Malabarese. The closest any came to this were vague expressions of regret about liturgical abuses (something for which, they implied, the official rites themselves could not possibly be responsible), an old strategy employed since the very first traditionalist protests during the pontificate of Paul VI.

Notable exceptions to this suspicious reticence were Cardinals Ratzinger, Oddi, Mayer and Stickler, all of whom publicly celebrated Mass in the traditional rite after 1988. In 1992 Cardinal Ratzinger, as prefect of the Congregation for the Doctrine of the Faith, wrote that

> we need a new beginning born from the depths of the liturgy, as it was intended by the liturgical movement when it was at the apex of its true nature, when it concerned itself not with inventing texts, actions and forms, but with rediscovering the living core, penetrating the very tissue of its own substance. The liturgical form, however, in its concrete realization, has moved ever farther from its beginning. The result has not been renewal but devastation.[47]

On the other hand the Cardinal was anxious to distance himself as much from the 'extreme' of conscientious traditionalism as from the liturgical anarchy of the updaters. There was little point, he argued, in 'the conservation of ritual forms whose grandeur is always stirring but which, when pushed to extremes, manifests an obstinate isolationism and ultimately leaves nothing but sadness'.[48]

[47] Quoted from Cardinal Ratzinger's introduction to the French version of Gamber, *op. cit.*: *La réforme liturgique en question* (Le Barroux, 1992).
[48] Ibid.

Ratzinger rejected in principle the Pauline rites because of their artificial nature: 'After the Council . . . instead of liturgy as the fruit of development came fabricated liturgy. We abandoned the organic, living process of growth and development over centuries, with a fabrication, a banal on-the-spot product.'[49] However, this apparent belief in the organic growth of the liturgy contradicted, however, his tendency towards rationalistic antiquarianism revealed, for instance, in his stance on such matters as Communion in the hand. When, in an interview with a German journalist published in 2002, he was asked whether this practice should be continued, he frankly stated: 'I wouldn't want to be fussy about that. It was done in the early Church. A reverent manner of receiving Communion in the hand is in itself a perfectly *reasonable* way to receive Communion' (emphasis added).[50]

While excluding a simple return to the pre-conciliar forms of worship, and advocating in rather nebulous terms 'a reform of the reform',[51] the Cardinal was nevertheless unable to say how else the authentic liturgical tradition could possibly be restored. It seemed that he dared not accept the logic of his own thesis, which is that the present official rites must be abolished if the Latin Church is to recover her true nature.

Condemning the Pauline reform while obstinately refusing to call for its abolition also typified Cardinal Augustin Mayer, former prefect of the Ecclesia Dei Commission. Mayer ventured to admit, in relation to the conciliar ban on unnecessary change, that

[o]ne cannot say that this number 23 of *Sacrosanctum Concilium* was considered adequately in that second phase [of the reform]. One cannot really say that the Consilium followed that principle. Some have said that now, instead of having a *gewordene Liturgie*, we have a *gemachte Liturgie*, instead of a liturgy that developed, we have a liturgy that was made. It was done on the [committee] table. . . . Generally liturgy grows through the life of the Church which is especially her prayer. Now they sit down and write it.[52]

The general orientation and aims of the reformers were, in the Benedictine cardinal's view, essentially misguided:

It seems to me that in the selection of the pericopes [of Scriptural passages], there was an exegetical approach rather than a liturgical approach in the choices made. Liturgy always is a serving of and adoration of God. The exegetical point of view can be different. The *Novus Ordo* has a strongly didactic element. We have to admit that the liturgy has also this purpose, but to put it first is wrong. First, is

---

[49] Ibid.

[50] Ratzinger, *God in the World: A Conversation with Peter Seewald* (San Francisco, 2002), p. 410.

[51] See, for instance, Ratzinger, *The Ratzinger Report: An Exclusive Interview on the State of the Church, with Vittorio Messori* (San Francisco, 1985), chapter 9, 'Liturgy: Between Old and New', pp. 119–34. Cardinal Ratzinger told Mr John Travis, the Vatican reporter for the *Catholic News Service*, that he 'agrees with theological arguments for returning the altar to its pre-Second Vatican Council position, in which the priest celebrated Mass with his back to the congregation', but believed, at the same time, that it would be impracticable to reverse the innovation for the present at least, in the interests of 'liturgical peace'.

[52] John Zuhlsdorf, 'Thirtieth Anniversary of Sacrosanctum Concilium, December 4, 1993: Interview of Cardinal Augustin Mayer to Father John T. Zuhlsdorf in Rome', *Sacred Music*, Vol. 121, No. 2 (Summer 1994), p. 17.

the cultic [element], understood correctly of course. We have to concede that the didactic intention often dominates today. But the first important aspect remains adoration, *latria*.

So, in some ways in that second phase the Consilium went beyond what it was intended to do. And perhaps they gave too much freedom, too many options.[53]

In view of the state of Latin Catholic worship today, this last affirmation of Cardinal Mayer's is a considerable understatement.

By contrast, Cardinal Hyacinthe Thiandoum, Archbishop Lefebvre's former pupil and successor at Dakar, was much more forthright in his criticisms: 'The Mass, which is the climax of the liturgy, cannot be left at the mercy and the will of a few people. I hope . . . it will be decided to issue a new Order of Mass. It is intolerable that such confusion is allowed to reign.'[54]

As for Cardinal Oddi, in an interview of 1990 he went so far as to aver, in reference to the late Cardinal Giacomo Lercaro (and with a strange silence about Paul VI, the principal culprit), that

[t]he application of post-conciliar liturgical reform was pernicious. I believe the person most responsible was an Italian cardinal who had the initial task of seeing that the reform was applied. In my judgement he was to blame for the suppression of the Latin Mass against the Council's wishes. It was a crime for which history will never forgive the Church.[55]

Logically, the solution to the problem identified by Cardinals Thiandoum and Oddi could be nothing less than the restoration to the new rites of all the prayers and ceremonies excised in 1969, the exclusion of the non-traditional elements and options added, and the repairing of the structural damage, especially in the sequence of set liturgical actions. This was the only plausible 'reform of the reform'.

Saving Face

Yet a full return to tradition was quite out of the question for Cardinal Mayer, who evinced no great aversion to the *Novus Ordo*, at least in its official form. Faced with the stubborn survival of what Michael Davies styled 'the Mass that will not die',[56] the Cardinal's response was to quote the current party line:

I must say that, according to the mind of the motu proprio, *Ecclesia Dei*, use of that missal [of 1962] should really be more freely given to those who reverently desire it. But we cannot think that the 1962 missal will become again the missal of the whole [sic] Church. We must try to keep the *Novus Ordo* in its real, given form and not go beyond. Those who follow the 1962 missal, on the other hand, shouldn't think that the Church can be 'saved' only with the 1962 missal.

They should avoid being polemical and try positively to develop and share with others the transcendent value of the liturgy, the adoration value of the liturgy,

---

[53] Ibid.
[54] Interview to *30 Days*, 8 September 1992.
[55] Tommaso Paci, 'Confessions of a Cardinal', *30 Days*, Year 3, Number 10 (December 1990), pp. 64–65.
[56] See M. Davies, *The Tridentine Mass: The Mass That Will Not Die* (St Paul, Minnesota, 1990).

the mystery value of the liturgy. They should reveal these values to others without attacking those who participate in the Mass according to the *Novus Ordo*, sincerely acknowledging, as they are asked to do, the doctrinal and juridical value of the new missal.[57]

The point, however, is not validity or legality, but authenticity. Ultimately it is truth that is at stake. If, as Cardinal Mayer earlier claimed, the *Novus Ordo* is an untraditional, committee-made liturgy, there could be only two reasons why conscientious Catholics should refrain from demanding its abolition: integral orthodoxy must be sacrificed in every instance to a spurious unity based on the toleration of heteropraxis and even material heresy; and church leaders must never be criticized or embarrassed, however badly they fail the faithful.

This frankly political approach to the tending of Christ's flock was evidenced in 1971 when a group of prominent French laymen appealed to Cardinal Joseph Lefebvre[58] to have the equivocal translation of *consubstantialem Patri* in the Creed as *de même nature que le Père* ('of the same nature of the Father') replaced by the more orthodox *consubstantiel au Père* ('consubstantial with the Father'). In Catholic theology the point was hardly a trifling one, but the Cardinal responded with characteristic defensiveness:

> when a group of people goes so far as to collect signatures in great numbers in order to present the Episcopate with a petition, in a bid to move the bishops to declare themselves in a public statement, it all looks very much like a challenge to the hierarchy's doctrinal rectitude. All the more so in that all through the Council certain journals incessantly suggested that certain bishops were promoting error. Now if the Episcopate intervenes, it will appear to be giving in and to be taking up a partisan stance. It will lose some of its authority and will no longer have any ability to convince those whom they would like to cure of their slipping into error.[59]

The attitude of the Latin hierarchy, as Professor Louis Salleron later remarked, was, and continues to be: 'Better to let error thrive than to lose face.'[60] The Index of Prohibited Books may have been abolished in 1966, but clericalism and mind control have remained alive and well in the Roman Church, allowing Cardinal Šeper to slam the door shut on traditionalist debate with his peremptory statement of 1978 that 'A Catholic, in fact, may not cast doubt on the conformity with the doctrine of the faith of a sacramental rite promulgated by the Supreme Pastor.'[61] This might be true in a strict legal sense but the problem, which obviously went over the head of the Prefect of the revamped Holy Office, concerned the *lex orandi*, which had never been subject to the Vicar of Christ's charism of infallibility.

Saint Thomas Aquinas saw things very differently when he wrote, echoing Gratian and St Nicholas I: 'It is absurd, and a detestable shame, that we should suffer those traditions to be changed that we have received from the fathers of old.'[62]

---

[57] Zuhlsdorf, *op. cit.*, p. 18.
[58] A cousin – and opponent – of Archbishop Marcel Lefebvre.
[59] Salleron, *op. cit.*, p. 28.
[60] Ibid., p. 29.
[61] Letter to Archbishop Lefebvre, quoted in M. Davies, *Apologia*, II, p. 107.
[62] *Summa Theologica*, I-II, Q. 96, A.4.

18

THE REIGN OF CONFUSION

Clarity and straightforwardness seem to me to be central to Scripture and to Catholic Tradition as a whole. Unfathomable as God and His ways may be, they are never murky or at war with themselves. The Lord told Moses on Mount Sinai that His name was 'I am'. He always 'is what He is', and His teachings eternally 'are what they are'. . . . The worst pontificates in history do not 'see and hear'. They 'are not what they are'. They do not carry out in practice what they seem to teach in theory, and when, occasionally, they do combine theory and practice, they do not do so after the model of Him who spoke 'as one having authority'. The worst pontificate in history would institutionalize and encourage murkiness. And it is exactly this that the pontificate of John Paul II appears to do.

JOHN C. RAO (2004)

Should we not also think of how much Christ suffers in His own Church? How often is the holy sacrament of His presence abused, how often must He enter empty and evil hearts? How often do we celebrate only ourselves, without even realizing that He is there!

BENEDICT XVI, VIA CRUCIS REFLECTIONS (2005)

Keeping the Customer Satisfied

Human intelligence has been defined as the ability to make distinctions, and wisdom as the ability to distinguish the important, the unimportant and the grey areas in between. It is arguable that ever since the Latin Church ditched as its basis for thought the realist philosophy of St Thomas Aquinas – arid perhaps but conducive to crystal-clear reasoning – a cloud of confusion has descended upon Catholics already contaminated by what C. S. Lewis called 'the poison of subjectivism'. At the beginning of the twenty-first century the only certainty is doubt, including and especially doubt about the truths of religion and the value of traditions. Throughout the developed world the conscientious application in Catholicism of the principles of theological liberalism has not only spread doctrinal and moral confusion, but has weakened the psychological resistance of the faithful to economic liberalism and its evil fruits in the social and cultural domains.

The response of most of the clergy and religious to the secularization of Catholic life in the 1970s was craven: to capitulate to the new reality and adapt themselves to the mood of society. Increasingly, they abandoned their role as teachers of the ignorant and admonishers of fellow sinners, and became reluctant to inform consciences. Instead, a great number imitated the captains of industry in treating their congregations as 'customers' and offering them the commodity they craved: 'affirmation'. In the new milieu of moral relativism the only sin was to be 'judgemental' and 'controlling' (i.e. to apply the principles of Christian morality to human behaviour) and the same Catholics who exercised the consumer's 'right to choose' in the marketplace, purchasing products that made them 'feel good', came to view the clergy as persons whose sole function was to 'affirm' them in their 'life choices'.[1]

In the pastoral domain the results of this new orientation were plain to see: never mentioning in sermons the existence of sin, purgatory and hell, holding general absolution services instead of exhorting the faithful to periodical private confession, leaving uncorrected growing disbelief in the Real Presence, administering the Eucharist to unrepentant public sinners and pro-abortion politicians, agreeing to christen babies with secular names (and often ridiculous ones degrading to a Christian), and declining to intervene when people chatted in church and irresponsible parents allowed noisy infants and undisciplined children to disrupt services, making it impossible for other people to pray.[2] Priests aligned with the Vatican II 'renewal' would good-naturedly conduct weddings with piped pop music and other vulgarities and compliantly preside at crematoria. Conforming to neo-liberalism's law of compulsory familiarity, the clergy began taking the liberty of addressing everyone by his or her Christian name and eschewing titles, those of the laity at least. They themselves liked to be known and addressed (with or without the 'Father', according to their ideological orientation) by the pet forms of their baptismal names in the style of contemporary politicians.

---

[1] In First World communities where most Catholics no longer see the point of going to church this affable salesmanlike priest has often given way to the reality-embittered clerical curmudgeon who welcomes only modernist fellow travellers among the laity and who bans hand-held candles on Holy Saturday lest wax drip onto the expensive wall-to-wall carpet of the grounded spaceship he euphemistically calls his church.

[2] A true sign of the times, this problem is by no means restricted to the *Novus Ordo*. One of the many crosses traditional Western Catholics must bear today is the ghettoization of the immemorial liturgy. Deprived of a normal parochial structure and ethos, Latin Mass centres fatally attract a lunatic fringe, including fanatical young couples of bohemian temperament and a robust sense of entitlement who are given to losing themselves in pious meditation at Mass while their offspring tyrannize the congregation with noise and fidgeting that is not occasional but constant. The simultaneous presence of responsible parents who charitably refrain from bringing babies to church services and whose older children are impeccably behaved is cold comfort, given that in any duel between silence and noise the latter is always the victor. The inability of the younger generation of priests to serve the faithful with effective leadership and impose order tactfully in such situations is truly woeful, and indicates that instruction on how to confront the modern problem of congregational indiscipline is not part of current seminary training. One can only wonder about the values of today's would-be traditional priests when needless disturbances that would not be tolerated in any secular theatre, cinema or lecture hall are apparently welcome in buildings where God the Son is sacramentally present. It must be admitted, however, that inappropriate church architecture utterly inconducive to recollection and reverence (interiors that look and feel like gymnasia or cosy living rooms, for instance) has exacerbated the problem, actually encouraging misbehaviour in church. See Michael S. Rose, *Ugly as Sin: Why They Changed our Churches from Sacred Spaces to Meeting Places and How We Can Change Them Back Again* (Manchester, New Hampshire, 2001).

The Nice Shepherd

There was, in sum, a general avoidance of anything that could put off or drive away secular-minded people who might become regular customers of a Church whose 'clientele' was already dramatically shrinking, an inversion of the older, sometimes confronting, apostolic method. American Catholic writer Leon Podles quotes a study published by the National Conference of [United States] Catholic Bishops which admits that priests and seminarians are now generally 'unassertive, . . . and have a high need for abasement (i.e. want to give in and avoid conflict)'.[3] One might add on a cynical note that the monetary contributions of parishioners have continued to be a powerful incentive to priests never to give offence by taking seriously their duty to uphold Christian standards and, more importantly, to admonish and correct whenever necessary for the sake of saving souls.

Foremost among the disconcertingly numerous scandals of the post-conciliar Church is a Catholic clergy with a constitutional inability to feel and express indignation and righteous anger in the face of sin and sacrilege in the moral and ritual spheres. Their refusal to show solidarity with ordinary people outraged by evil revealed its profoundly unchristian character when the epidemic of sexual abuse among the clergy became common knowledge in the 1990s and bred public hostility to priests and bishops inured by a false concept of meekness to think that as Christians they ought never to feel the emotions of hatred and anger. According to Dr Podles,

> They secretly suspect that Jesus was being un-Christian in His attitude to the scribes and the Pharisees when He was angry at them, that He was un-Christian when He drove the moneychangers out of the temple or declared that millstones (not vacations in treatment centres) were the way to treat child abusers.[4]

The same writer recognizes the fact (glaringly obvious in the age of mass media) that this defect extends to the highest levels of the Catholic hierarchy, and attributes it to the age-old tendency of the Roman Curia to substitute diplomacy for moral rectitude:

> Diplomats rule in the Vatican, and diplomats dislike confrontation, anger and hatred, because such emotions make diplomacy difficult. The Vatican has appointed the bishops [who have tolerated and protected clerical criminals]; the bishops have trained the clergy. Therefore, hatred of iniquity has been felt to be something that did not fit into the Christian life. . . . Sorrow at evil without anger is a fault, a fault that the Catholic bishops have repeatedly fallen into in their handling of sexual abuse and that the late pope [John Paul II] fell into when he tolerated the bishops' faults. Until just anger is directed at the bishops, until bishops (including the Pope) feel just anger at their fellow bishops who have disgraced and failed their office, the state of sin in the Church continues.[5]

---

[3] Leon Podles, 'Unhappy Fault', *Touchstone* (Vol. 22/6, July/August 2009), p. 3 (internet version: www.touchstonemag.com/archives/article.php?id=22-06-012-v).
[4] Ibid., p. 1.
[5] Ibid., p. 3.

If post-conciliar priests manifested at the parish level a moral spinelessness that would have appalled their predecessors, at the diocesan level the new liberal bishops inaugurated a regime of pluralism in which all groups claiming the name Catholic were allowed to practise whatever traditional cult or outlandish aberration appealed to their individualism. Thus the practitioners of 'charismatic' hystericism and proponents of perpetual eucharistic adoration could both count on the warm support of their friendly local ordinary. Immigrant Muslims, Hindus and Buddhists seeking to use church premises for their worship would also be graciously accommodated.

The only exception to this historic openness to all humanity was made for Catholics who requested the traditional Latin Mass. In the two decades following the Council it was standard procedure for bishops to persecute and isolate traditionalists, as much because Rome encouraged them in this bullying as from the general belief that these troublemakers were numerically insignificant as church 'customers'. By the 1990s, however, it had become clear that these annoying groups were increasing in number in many countries, especially the United States, largely because so many young people disgusted by the liturgical impostures provided in their parishes were attracted to the old rite. Most of this growing cohort of converts were of middle-class background and wage earners. It can thus be no coincidence that the Vatican's counter-historical move to 'free' the traditional Mass materialized when it did, rather than earlier.

A Unique Pontificate

Pope John Paul II, no less than his bishops and priests, deemed it his duty to pander to the mood of an age. Ever charming to visitors and faces in crowds, his frequent tours abroad and the mass rallies that his papal liturgies everywhere became made him the darling of the media, who elevated him to superstardom. He delighted in modernity and loved youth concerts, instituting in 1985 'World Youth Day', an event which quickly evolved into an amalgam of the worst aspects of contemporary 'junk culture', replete with the deafening rock music which his successor would recognize as 'the work of Satan'.[6] At these tawdry 'Catholic Woodstocks' the Pope publicly joked and danced with young people already worked up by the two dehumanizing devices of crowding and loud electronic noise.[7] The Vatican propaganda machine described the shabbily dressed participants as 'pilgrims' despite the fact that the main purpose of the gatherings was not to pray at the shrine of any saint, but to pay rowdy homage to a living man presented to them as a rock star. In any case by the time of the 2002 World Youth Day held in Toronto most of the assembled youth did not appear to be very deeply interested in Christianity and few, by all accounts, returned to the regular and conscientious practice of their faith once the big party was over.[8]

---

[6] Statement made in 2007. Pope Benedict also cancelled the annual pop concerts that John Paul II had held every Advent (!) at the Vatican for twelve years.

[7] Many people are unaware that the use of these two means of obtaining mass assent was an invention of the Nazis, first used at the Nuremberg rallies.

[8] Any reader inclined to find exaggeration here should view two significant videos of scenes from the world tours of John Paul II available on the internet. The first (www.youtube.com/watch?v=TIoelyZ5qvQ) provides footage from 2 October 1979 of the pope's

Throughout the world John Paul II enthusiastically participated in liturgies in which pagan rites were mingled with secular vulgarities, all in the interest of 'inculturation' and 'respect for peoples'.[9] Wherever he went, he accommodated himself to every conceivable liturgical abuse that was presented to him as 'local custom'. Paying tribute to the *Zeitgeist* he contradicted the teaching of the Scriptures and of the Magisterium by condemning the death penalty as 'cruel and unnecessary', thereby displaying, like the modern liberal judiciary, more sympathy for the worst of criminals than for their victims.[10] In endorsing the conciliar ecumenical movement and attending inter-faith prayer meetings where the true and false religions were placed on an equal footing, he gave the impression that other faiths were valid paths to salvation.

The Pontiff gave fulsome praise and support to two cult-like ultramontanistic organizations, the Legion of Christ (*La Legión de Cristo*) and the Neocatechumenal Way (*El Camino Neocatecumenal*), both symptomatic of a deep-seated malaise in Hispanic Catholicism, the first of them embroiled in scandal and the second notorious for doctrinal deviations and liturgical abuses of the grossest kind. He consistently refused to take appropriate action against clergy found guilty of heinous sexual crimes against children, thus alienating from Catholicism large numbers of those directly or indirectly affected by these breathtaking betrayals of trust. From the late 1980s the Pope satisfied what he imagined was a popular hunger for new saints by canonizing by the score each year *beati* whose causes had been conducted without a devil's advocate (*promotor fidei*) since 1983 and with only one miracle required instead of the standard two (or in some cases) three.[11]

None of these criticisms should be taken to imply that John Paul II acted in bad faith; on the contrary, and incredible as it might seem, there is every indication that he believed he was doing right. Nevertheless, seeing that he was the most prayed-for individual on earth, and the beneficiary of the special graces reserved for the Vicar of Christ, that he could have strayed so far from path of prudence trodden by his predecessors is astounding to say the least.

Conservative Catholics might well be disturbed by the ambiguity of certain actions and utterances of the late Pope, but as loyal supporters of the pluralist order they could hardly murmur about a pontiff who nonetheless balanced these novelties with strong and unequivocal restatements of Catholic dogma on such questions as contraception, abortion, euthanasia and the ordination of women. That underneath all the mortifying extravagances and showmanship there was a true successor of Peter was clear from John Paul's gift to the Church of a new catechism (1992) which, whatever its exegetical shortcomings, presented the principal

---

extraordinary behaviour at New York's Madison Square Garden. The other (www.youtube.com/watch?v=NPNomC8ON08) was filmed at the World Youth Day at Toronto in 2002. Also noteworthy are the comments made at a press conference on 24 September 1999 by Irish rock star 'Bono' (Paul David Hewson) after sharing a stage with the pope: 'He's one of the great showmen of the twentieth century. I told him this and he picked up my wraparound shades [sunglasses] and put them on. He's great; such grace and humanity! The first funky Pontiff' (www.mtv.com/news/articles/1429354/19990924/geldof_bob.jhtml).

[9] See, for example, Abbé Daniel Le Roux, *Pierre, m'aimes-tu?* (Escurolles, 1988); English tr. *Peter, Lovest Thou Me?* (Yarra Junction Vic., 1989).

[10] Homily in St Louis, Missouri on 27 January 1999.

[11] As a result of John Paul II's apostolic constitution *Divinus Perfectionis Magister* there were 482 canonizations (and more than 1,300 beatifications) by the end of his pontificate, as opposed to only 98 canonizations during all of the twentieth century before his election.

tenets of faith and was certainly free of error.[12] Thus, contrary to appearances, the indefectibility of the Church remained unimpaired even if certain serious-minded Catholics, shocked and demoralized by the antics of the 'People's Pope', were unable to make the leap of faith required to accept such a man as a true Vicar of Christ.

Custodian or Compromiser of the Faith?

For the majority of traditionalists, however, the case was not so clear-cut. John Paul II's pantheon of religions at Assisi in 1988 had been one of several events that convinced Archbishop Marcel Lefebvre that a state of emergency existed in the Church and impelled him to consecrate a line of orthodox bishops to perpetuate the traditional faith which post-conciliar Rome professed in theory but allowed to be subverted in practice.

In the remaining years of his pontificate Wojtyła did nothing to convince alarmed Catholics that he was any closer to recognizing the obvious relationship between the programme of heteropraxis over which he willingly presided and its disastrous effects on the life of the Church, a catastrophe which he paradoxically acknowledged and deplored. On the contrary, there is abundant evidence that the force which blinded his intellect was the actor's ego that propelled him into so much undignified and compromising public behaviour, a problem aggravated by a somewhat worldly predilection for frequent travel and tours. It is possible, too, that euphoria from the Pope's success in helping to bring about the fall of Communism in Europe blinded him to the contemporary failure of the post-conciliar 'renewal' to which he was so firmly committed as head of the Church.

What was by far the most scandalous of John Paul II's 'philanthropic' gestures occurred on 1 June 1999. At the end of an audience at the Vatican with an Iraqi delegation, he bowed to a copy of the Koran presented to him by an imam, and kissed it. This 'sign of respect' would have been regarded by orthodox Christians of any other age as an act of apostasy, since Islam's holy book explicitly denies the divinity of Christ.[13] However, the papal action was justified by Vatican apologists as a prodigious 'act of charity', the reverencing of the Koran allegedly showing John Paul's profound esteem for those fellow human beings who hold it sacred, as if charity towards non-Christians were more important than the Pope's duty to witness to the truth and to confirm Christians in their faith. The thousands of early Christian martyrs who preferred gruesome deaths to offering a few grains of incense before images of deified Roman emperors evidently had a vastly different 'faith vision'.

Symbolic actions such as these have great significance, especially when coming

---

[12] A useful compendium of the doctrinal controversies of this pontificate from a traditionalist standpoint is Christopher A. Ferrara and Thomas E. Woods, *The Great Façade: Vatican II and the Regime of Novelty in the Roman Catholic Church*, St Paul, Minnesota, 2002

[13] Surah V (*Al-Mā'idah*), 72–73. *Fides – Vatican News Service of the Congregation for the Evangelization of Peoples*, 4 June 1999. On this occasion the Chaldean Catholic Patriarch, Raphael I Bidawid, introduced to the pope the imam of the Khadum mosque and an Iraqi banker. The photo of John Paul II kissing the Koran was afterwards shown repeatedly on Iraqi television. Similarly, on 26 March of the following year at Wadi al-Kharrar, the site of Christ's baptism in Jordan, John Paul prayed: 'May St John the Baptist protect Islam'. Full text at: www.vatican.va/holy_father/john_paul_ii/travels/documents/hf_jp-ii_spe_20000321_wadi-al-kharrar_en.html.

from the Vicar of Christ. Not surprisingly, many thinking Catholics pondered the connection between this unconventional and often shocking behaviour and the official teaching of the Church. Writing during the last pontificate, Fr Johannes Dörmann noted that

> [t]he crucial problem for today's believing Catholic is: The Pope views this 'new, more broad-minded perspective' of the truly 'Catholic universality' of the faith, which Vatican II gave to the 'Church of the future', merely as a deeper, more complete grasp of the old faith. A Catholic can choose either to view the new perspective as the Pope does, or to admit that a break with tradition has indeed occurred, and what is more, that a substantially new faith has indeed arisen. The question is whether he should disregard all doctrinal concerns, and simply accompany the Pope on his pilgrimage to the 'mystical mountain' in Assisi, or whether he should shudder at the thought of it.[14]

Santo subito!

In the tense days following the death of John Paul II at the beginning of April 2005, Josef Ratzinger, now President of the College of Cardinals, gave every indication that he wholeheartedly supported the status quo, especially when he informed the congregation at the globally televised funeral: 'We can be sure that our beloved Pope is standing today at the window of the Father's house, that he sees us and blesses us. Yes, bless us, Holy Father.'[15] For sober Catholics such a statement of certainty seemed a scandalous act of presumption on the part of a theologian who knew, far better than his listeners, that the salvation of no baptized Christian over the age of reason can be taken for granted until the Church has formally beatified him after a long and thorough investigation.[16] When the requiem Mass was repeatedly interrupted by loutish shouts of *santo subito!* ('Make him a saint immediately!') from young men bussed in for the purpose from Poland, the Cardinal paused and smiled benignly from the other side of the *versus populum* altar. This positive reaction only confirmed in the minds of the uncritical majority

---

[14] Johannes Dörmann, *Pope John Paul II's Theological Journey to the Prayer Meeting of Religions in Assisi* (Kansas City, 1994–1998), I, p. 36.

[15] *Possiamo essere sicuri che il nostro amato Papa sta adesso alla finestra della casa del Padre, ci vede e ci benedice. Sì, ci benedica, Santo Padre.* Traditionalist misgivings were not allayed when, at the same funeral liturgy, Ratzinger took the liberty of giving Holy Communion to a Protestant, Brother Roger Schutz of the Taizé Community in France.

[16] The Council of Trent, in its Decree on Justification, stated that

> No-one, moreover, so long as he lives this mortal life ought in regard to the sacred mystery of predestination so far presume as to state with absolute certainty that he is among the number of the predestined as if it were true that the one justified cannot sin any more, or if he does sin, that he ought to promise himself an assured repentance. For, except by special revelation, it cannot be known whom God has chosen to Himself. (Ch. 12)

'If anyone shall say that he will for certain with an absolute and infallible certainty have that great gift of perseverance even to the end, unless he shall have learnt this by a special revelation let him be anathema' (Can. 16). Cardinal Ratzinger would therefore have been justified in making this statement only if he had received a special revelation (or if John Paul II had communicated his having received the same revelation himself). Moreover, if the Cardinal had indeed been privileged with such a singular revelation, it would have been appropriate for him to make this known in the context of his declaration.

of faithful the idea that the soul of Karol Wojtyła was *a priori* exempt from even the possibility of purification or punishment in the next life, and that he needed no prayers for the salvation of his soul.[17]

In reality there was nothing elitist about this instantaneous beatification: it could hardly be misinterpreted as a special privilege for the Pope, since John Paul II himself had encouraged belief in a qualified *apokatastasis pantōn* or universal salvation. In its full expression this contentious doctrine, which contradicts Christ's teaching on the reality of hell (Matt. 7.13; 25.41), denies the efficacy of divine justice and the necessity of grace. It was condemned in 543 by the Synod of Constantinople and anathematized a decade later by the Fifth Ecumenical Council.[18] Wandering from the approach of orthodox theology, Wojtyła on occasion failed to make a practical distinction between God's will to save all men and the fact that individuals, exercising their own free will, can reject salvation. Following his favourite theologian, Hans Urs von Balthasar, he expressed the view that while perdition is a possibility, it cannot be known for certain whether anyone at all has been eternally damned, and he optimistically inferred from this that universal love as well as faith in Christ's redemption of humanity should move us to hope that hell is indeed empty.[19]

Von Balthasar had actually promoted universal salvation as a 'hope' (which, he argued, Christians have a right and even a duty to nurture) and not as a doctrine. But less subtle minds among the Catholic clergy and faithful, accustomed to clearer formulations of doctrine, quickly progressed to the practical corollary of this dangerous *theologoumenon*: that the virtual certainty of salvation for all makes it no longer necessary to pray daily, perform acts of penance, struggle continually to amend one's life or intercede for the dead. As for those who consciously promoted this 'hope', a greater injustice and failure in charity towards the faithful, living and dead, can scarcely be imagined.

In the liturgical sphere it was this doctrinal aberration that turned Catholic funerals into 'celebrations of the life' of individuals judged by all present to be already in heavenly glory. In reality such 'feel good' delusions about salvation for all, regardless of the faith and deeds of individuals, mask what is a profound

---

[17] On 13 May 2005 the new Pope, Benedict XVI, announced that John Paul II would be put on the 'fast track' to canonization and that the mandatory waiting period of five years before the opening of the cause would be waived. Needless to say, if the present Pontiff or any successor were to proceed with such an ill-advised plan, attempting to raise to sainthood an individual whose policies and conduct caused such scandal and spiritual suffering to the faithful, the existing gulf between the Vatican and the conscientious traditionalist minority would widen irreparably and convince not a few that the arguments of sedevacantists were right all along. Particularly outrageous (and telling) was the statement of Cardinal Stanisław Dziwisz, Archbishop of Cracow (and former personal secretary of the late Pope), that Wojtyła should be beatified as early as April 2010 because 'the world demands it' (*La Stampa*, 18 April 2009). As one Vatican official commented on the same occasion, this indecent haste to raise to the altars a man whose life had not been adequately investigated amounted to beatifying not a person but a personality. Sainthood transsignified?

[18] Apocatastasis had been taught by Origen, Clement of Alexandria and St Gregory of Nyssa.

[19] Note, for example, the statement 'Eternal damnation remains a possibility, but we are not granted, without special divine revelation, knowledge of *whether* or which human beings may be effectively involved [*se e quali esseri umani vi siano effettivamente coinvolti*]' (General Audience of 28 July 1999) and his reference to Christ as 'the everlasting, invincible guarantee of *universal* salvation' (Message to the Abbess General of the Order of the Most Holy Saviour of St Bridget, 21 September 2002) (emphasis added). For the source of this orientation, see Hans Urs von Balthasar, *Dare We Hope 'That All Men Be Saved'? (With a Short Discourse on Hell)*, Fort Collins, 1988.

affront to the natural and God-given sense of justice in human beings. Moreover, it is particularly shocking that a Polish pope, who had personally known survivors of Nazi death camps and the Stalinist gulags, could have entertained the notion that the unrepentant monsters responsible for such hells on earth were destined for the same reward in heaven as their innocent victims.

After the Council the erroneous literal idea of universal salvation, tailor-made for the modern hedonist age, was symbolically enshrined at the heart of the post-conciliar liturgy, at least in the authorized vernacular versions of the *Missale Romanum*. Here the Latin words *pro multis*, 'for many', part of the institution narrative used for the consecration of the wine in the Canon, have been widely mistranslated, with the consent of Rome, as 'for all (men)' (or *per tutti* in Italian, *por todos* in Spanish, *für alle* in German, *za wszystkich* in Polish and so on).[20] However, in the view of some theologians this tampering with the most sacred part of the Mass text and the use of a tendentious translation previously prohibited by the Church has compromised the validity of those vernacular celebrations that include it.[21] Furthermore, the dismay caused by this innovation has led to the popular belief among traditional Catholics that the New Mass is both heretical and invalid as well as unauthentic, one further negative and divisive result of the liturgical reform.

One Step Forward, Two Steps Back?

His disconcerting eulogy of John Paul II notwithstanding, in the pre-conclave homily which he delivered a week later at the *Missa pro eligendo Romano Pontifice* Cardinal Ratzinger surprised orthodox Catholics who by now thought they had good reason to expect the worst from him. This time the congregation heard a grimly realistic appraisal of the 'dictatorship of relativism' in a Church 'thrown from one extreme to the other: from Marxism to liberalism, even to libertinism; from collectivism to radical individualism; from atheism to a vague religious mysticism; from agnosticism to syncretism, and so forth'.[22] In fact, long before being elected pope Ratzinger had complained about those who had erected the Second Vatican Council into a kind of gnostic 'super-dogma', when 'the truth is that this particular Council defined no dogma at all, and deliberately chose to remain on a modest level, as a merely pastoral council'.[23]

By the end of the year the replacement of the 'hermeneutic of rupture' by the 'hermeneutic of continuity' had emerged as the declared mission of Benedict's pontificate.[24] This aroused the ire of liberal Catholics and invited the enmity of the same mass media who had lionized John Paul II. The new Pope wanted to

---

[20] The French translation (strangely enough, given the modernistic bent of the post-conciliar French hierachy) is accurate (*pour la multitude*), as is the Hungarian *sokakért*, the Swedish *för de många*, the Norwegian *for de mange*, and the Mandarin *wèi . . . zhòngrén*. The vernacular Mass rites containing the mistranslation include those in Portuguese (*por todos*), Catalan (*per tots els homes*), Dutch (*voor alle mensen*), Slovak (*za všetkých*), Croatian (*za sve ljude*), Irish (*ar son an chine dhaonna*, 'for the human race'), Breton (*evit an dud*, 'for the people'), Maltese (*ghall-bnedmin kollha*), Indonesian (*bagi semua orang*) and Tetum (*tan ema tomak*).

[21] See M. Davies, *Pope Paul's New Mass*, pp. 623–30.

[22] www.vatican.va/gpII/documents/homily-card-ratzinger_20050408_en.html (full English text).

[23] Address to the Bishops of Chile, 13 July 1988.

[24] Address to the Roman Curia, 22 December 2005.

reassure troubled orthodox Catholics that the Church's perennial Magisterium had not undergone any fundamental change as a result of Vatican II, a claim which sedevacantists and some traditionalists would greet with scepticism. Nevertheless Christopher Ferrara, the same American lawyer who had exposed in detail the doctrinal aberrations of the post-conciliar clerical establishment, found it possible to concur with Benedict XVI to the extent of stating:

> I [am not] aware of a single papal pronouncement since the death of Pius XII that requires Catholics to believe even one doctrine opposed to the perennial Magisterium, much less an indeterminate number of then. True, Paul VI and John Paul II approved, tolerated and even encouraged unprecedented ecclesial innovations which – by permission or omission only and not by any mandate imposed on the universal Church – departed from the Church's traditional liturgy, evangelical approach and condemnation of error. But these changes, however harmful their effects, lie in the pastoral rather than the doctrinal realm; they involve prudential judgments, not binding pronouncements on matters of faith and morals. . . . The idea that Vatican II or the conciliar Popes have imposed new doctrines which contradict previous Church teaching is a myth promoted by neo-Modernists, not by the Magisterium.[25]

The doctrinal problems might indeed be solvable, but in the equally important realm of praxis, traditional Catholics could hardly let down their guard in this pontificate, given the inconsistent and often self-contradictory behaviour of the new Pope. On the one hand, despite his apparent agreement with John Paul II's views on salvation, Pope Benedict XVI decreed on 17 November 2006 that the tendentious mistranslation of *pro multis* as 'for all' be discontinued in all vernacular Mass texts throughout the world within a period of two years.[26] On the other hand he would continue to take part in ecumenical activities, praying in Protestant churches, synagogues and mosques. He also maintained and attended the World Youth Day jamborees of his predecessor (attempting, not very successfully, to curb their excesses), and he lauded and commended Pope John Paul at every turn as a paragon of Catholic faith. Moreover, for all his positive statements about the traditional Roman liturgy and his criticisms of the new, since ascending the papal throne Benedict XVI to date has never publicly used the immemorial rite of Mass. According to Fr Federico Lombardi, SJ, current director of the Vatican Press Office, the Pope habitually concelebrates his daily Mass in his private chapel in the eastward position but according to the Pauline missal and in Italian, not even in Latin.[27]

Summorum Pontificum

Pope Benedict's courageous determination to free the immemorial Roman liturgy from its marginalization by the worldwide episcopate was characterized by a

---

[25] C. Ferrara, 'The Society of St. Pius X and Vatican II', the *Remnant* website (www.remnant-newspaper.com/), 3 March 2009, p. 3.

[26] At the time of writing (three years after the announcement) the change has still not been made mandatory by Rome, an indication, perhaps, of the priorities of the present pontificate.

[27] 'Vatican spokesman: Pope concelebrates daily Mass using current missal', *Catholic News Service*, 17 July 2007, www.catholicnews.com/data/stories/cns/0704072.htm.

similar complexity in regard to the underlying motives and principles. There is every indication that at the beginning of his pontificate the Pope was painfully aware that the vast majority of baptized Catholics, at least those in First World countries, no longer practised their faith and that huge numbers had defected to other religions, especially in Latin America and the United States. The bishops of the Church shared this awareness but, unlike the Pope, most of these men animated and guided by the 'spirit of Vatican II' chose to remain in denial about a cata-strophic situation which they themselves had helped to create by their indifference to orthodoxy. Rather like the Irish Free State's valiant but abortive rehabilitation of Gaelic as the national language of Ireland when it had already reached the verge of extinction and Ireland had become irreversibly anglicized, Benedict's belated gesture in favour of the authentic Roman rite came at a time when the corruptive effects of the Pauline revolution and widespread ignorance of the true liturgical heritage of Latin Catholicism ensured that there would be relatively little demand for its return.[28] This fact would embolden liberal bishops in their opposition to any attempt at restoration, however modest.

In 2007 Benedict XVI chose 7 July, the feast of Sts Cyril and Methodius, to issue his motu proprio *Summorum Pontificum* with an accompanying letter to the episcopate. Henceforth any Catholic priest could celebrate according to the tradi-tional Roman Missal without episcopal permission, and direct appeals to Rome were invited wherever local ordinaries attempted to prevent the exercise of this right.[29] The new documentation stated that 'the Roman Missal promulgated by

---

[28] As already noted, John Paul II, moved by a spirit of equitable pluralism rather than any impulse to return to tradition, had wished to free the immemorial rite completely after 1988 but lacked the determination to follow through when faced with the staunch opposition of his powerful secretaries of state (Agostino Casaroli and Angelo Sodano), the prefects of the Vatican dicasteries and the bishops of France, Germany and England and Wales. After the Roman Synod on the Eucharist in October 2005 Archbishop Piero Marini, papal master of ceremonies in the previous pontificate and former personal secretary of Fr Annibale Bugnini, and Francis Arinze, prefect of the Congregation for Divine Worship, were particularly aggressive in trying to deter Benedict XVI from issuing his motu proprio. In early 2007 Arinze, a Nigerian convert from animism, was reportedly demanding that the new pontiff raise the number of required worshippers to 100 for any authorized celebration of the old Mass. Apparently the Pope, close to exasperation, told the Cardinal to hold his peace, retorting, 'In a few years' time we will be lucky to have that many people attending the new Mass!' Reported by Mgr Bernard Fellay on 16 May 2007; see www. youtube.com/watch?v=WieXocVu1hg.

[29] Apostolic Letter *Summorum Pontificum*, 7 July 2007, art. 2, 7. Episcopal obstructionism ensued in many countries, particular in Italian dioceses, uninhibited by the proximity of Rome. On the hostility to the immemorial liturgy of Mgr Giuseppe Mani, Archbishop of Cagliari, a reporter for the French association Paix Liturgique commented two years later:

> The example of the [Sardinian] parishes of Mandas and Gesico is characteristic of the almost systematic persecutions undergone by priests who freely decide to apply with generosity Benedict XVI's *Summorum Pontificum*. Certainly, if it is possible to point to some improvements here and there, the fact is that in the majority of cases new traditional celebrations are put into effect directly by episcopal curias – as per the indult of 1988 – and remain under episcopal control. When parish priests decide on their own initiative to put into practice the motu proprio of 2007, in most cases a real witchhunt is unleashed. (See blog.messainlatino.it, 22 July 2009.)

Significantly, Mgr Mani, a mainland Italian, is equally ill-disposed to the use of the Sardinian language in the new liturgy.

As Mgr Fellay has incisively commented, whereas the *Ecclesia Dei* decree of 1988 suggested that the old liturgy was prohibited but now could be allowed, *Summorum Pontificum* has reversed this, so that what has always been allowed can now be prohibited if a bishop can prove a lack of demand or need.

St. Pius V . . . must be given due honour for its venerable and ancient usage' and that 'this Missal was never juridically abrogated and, consequently, in principle, was always permitted'.[30] The text of the letter to the bishops reveals its author's anxiety to restore continuity with the past, since 'What earlier generations held as sacred, remains sacred and great for us too, and it cannot be all of a sudden entirely forbidden or even considered harmful (par. 11).' And given the *de facto* schism in the post-conciliar Latin Church today it seemed appropriate to add that

> at critical moments when divisions were coming about, not enough was done by the Church's leaders to maintain or regain reconciliation and unity. One has the impression that omissions on the part of the Church have had their share of blame for the fact that these divisions were able to harden (par. 10).

Nevertheless the truth, suppressed in both documents, is that Paul VI not only strove hard to abolish the traditional rite but actively oppressed those who defended its use, especially Archbishop Marcel Lefebvre. Ratzinger himself had shown little sympathy for the beleaguered Archbishop during the pontificate of John Paul II, and as head of the Holy Office he was responsible for the documentation announcing the excommunications of 1988. Most lamentable, however, is the absence from the July letter of even the hint of an apology to afflicted traditional Catholics for the spiritual misery they had suffered from forty years of papal misrule. The only sympathy the Pope expresses is for conformist Catholics who, like himself, have been 'caused deep pain' by 'hard-to-bear' 'arbitrary deformations' (par. 6) of a reformed rite which, whether by design or by accident, has weakened the faith of the Church and fostered the most appalling abuses.

Ratzinger's disdain of those who question the integrity of Vatican II and the post-conciliar orientation was still obvious in 2007. Two decades earlier he had gone so far as to aver, in reference to 'integralist groups in which the desire for piety, for the sense of the mystery, is finding satisfaction' that 'we cannot resist them too firmly' because 'without a doubt, they represent a sectarian zealotry that is the antithesis of Catholicity'.[31] To these 'zealots' it could easily appear that the new Pope's esteem for the immemorial Roman liturgy (never publicly expressed before the 1980s) was primarily cultural and aesthetic, and that he remained ambivalent about the theology and ecclesiology that had been the natural context of this mode of worship.

Liturgical Realpolitik

Transparent in the motu proprio is the pontiff's realization of a fact particularly galling to the episcopate: that while attachment to the new liturgy is largely a characteristic of the ageing 'hippie generation' and their parents, most of the Latin Catholics demanding the restoration of their ritual heritage today are younger

---

[30] Apostolic Letter *Summorum Pontificum*, 7 July 2007, § 1; *Letter of his Holiness Benedict XVI to the Bishops on the Occasion of the Publication of the Apostolic Letter 'motu proprio data' Summorum Pontificum on the Use of the Roman Liturgy prior to the Reform of 1970*, 7 July 2007, par. 6.
[31] Joseph Ratzinger, *Principles of Catholic Theology: Building Stones for a Fundamental Theology* (San Francisco, 1989), p. 389.

people born after 1969. Pope Benedict accordingly admitted that it was impossible not to encourage once again a liturgical form which appeals not simply to
a few nostalgics of the older generations, for, as 'has clearly been demonstrated
. . . young persons too have discovered [it] . . ., felt its attraction and found in it
a form of encounter with the Mystery of the Most Holy Eucharist, particularly
suited to them (par. 7)'.

Unfortunately the compromise proposed in *Summorum Pontificum*, the plan
of establishing the traditional liturgy as the so-called 'extraordinary form' to exist
alongside the 'ordinary form', i.e. the heteropractic Pauline liturgy, could hardly
restore the full confidence of Catholics who regard the latter in its usual 'pastoral'
applications as an historic aberration, a fount of abuses and a threat to orthodoxy.
Moreover, in view of the spectacular omissions and deficiencies of the Pauline
Mass rite, which presents to any impartial observer the image of a religion quite
removed from pre-conciliar Catholicism, traditionalists could only be amazed by
the papal claim that 'It is not appropriate to speak of these two versions of the
Roman missal as if they were 'two Rites'. Rather, it is a matter of a twofold use of
one and the same rite (par. 5).' That a liturgical concoction of the 1960s should
be styled the 'ordinary' worship of the Roman Church could only be offensive to
traditionalist sentiment, as was the Pope's statement that

> [n]eedless to say, in order to experience full communion, the priests of the com-
> munities adhering to the former usage cannot, as a matter of principle, exclude
> celebrating according to the new books. The total exclusion of the new rite would
> not in fact be consistent with the recognition of its value and holiness (par. 11).

In view of the enormous pressures weighing on the Pope and the undisguised hostility of most bishops to his plans, it is likely that Benedict's solution of biritualism
was dictated more by *Realpolitik* than by his own true feelings. In fact he had for
some time wanted to engineer a natural convergence of the two systems of worship,
a sort of higher synthesis or 'reform of the reform', in which the so-called 'ordinary rite' would become more stable, orderly and open to absorbing the ethos and
trappings of the old. Thus when the *Novus Ordo* finally metamorphosed into what
was essentially a restored immemorial rite, the scandal of the liturgical revolution
would be over and the papal face would have been saved. Only four years earlier,
Cardinal Ratzinger had argued along these very lines in a letter to Dr Heinz-Lothar
Barth, a German philologist:

> I believe, however, that in the long term the Roman Church must have again a
> single Roman rite. The existence of two official rites is for bishops and priests
> simply too difficult to 'manage' in practice. The Roman rite of the future should
> be a single rite, celebrated in Latin or in the vernacular, but standing completely
> in the tradition of the rite that has been handed down. It could take up some new
> elements which have proved their worth, like new feasts, some new prefaces in
> the Mass, an expanded lectionary – more choice than earlier, but not too much,
> an *oratio fidelium*, i.e. a fixed litany of intercession following the *Oremus* before
> the offertory where it had its place earlier.[32]

---

[32] Letter dated 23 June 2003. The original German text will be found in full at 'Brief an Dr. Barth',
www.wolfganglindemann.net/html/brief_an_dr_bath.html. In 2007 there were reports that Pope

Praying for the Jews

Traditionalists antagonistic to Ratzinger's pontificate were soon afforded an opportunity to say 'we told you so' to more conciliatory fellow travellers. On 6 February 2008, a mere seven months after the issuing of *Summorum Pontificum*, the *Osservatore Romano* announced that Benedict XVI would be revising the text of the Good Friday collect for the Jews in the 1962 Roman Missal and that the new prayer would become mandatory for traditional-rite communities from the coming Holy Week. Bowing to pressure from Jewish lobby groups instigated by Catholic ecumenists and led by the Grand Rabbis of Israel, the Pope had resolved to remove all allegedly 'anti-Semitic' language from this eighth petition of the Great Intercessions, prayers of great antiquity dating back in part to the third century.[33] The text used liturgically since 1962 omitted the words italicized below:

> Let us pray also for the *faithless* (*perfidis*) Jews: that our God and Lord would remove the veil from their hearts: that they also may acknowledge our Lord Jesus Christ.
>
> Almighty and everlasting God, who drivest not away from Thy mercy even *the Jewish faithlessness* (*judaicam perfidiam*) [1962: even the Jews]: hear our prayers that we offer for the blindness of that people: that acknowledging the light of Thy truth, which is Christ, they may be rescued from their darkness.

Since the 1920s there had been agitation for the reform or removal of this prayer, but contrary to common belief, it was initiated not by Jews, but by Catholic clerics. In 1926 the priestly association Opus Sacerdotale Amici Israël was founded in Rome to combat a recrudescence of anti-semitism among Catholics; it had eighteen cardinals and numerous bishops as founding members. The initial aim of this group was to obtain a revision of the *Oratio pro Judæis*, which they considered potentially inflammatory, given that it omitted the customary genuflection for reflective prayer in the middle (traditionally explained as a pious Christian reaction to Jews bending the knee to mock the crucified Christ) and that the Latin words *perfidus*, 'faithless', and *perfidia*, 'faithlessness', had the secondary pejorative meaning of 'treacherous, perfidious'.

Pius XI, who was on cordial terms with the Chief Rabbi of Milan, was apparently favourable to the request and directed the Congregation of Rites to look into the matter. However, the Curia reacted negatively on the sound principle of the sacrosanctity of prayer formulas consecrated by many centuries of use, and Cardinal Rafael Merry del Val, secretary of the Holy Office, is said to have commented: 'If we begin with one liturgical reform we'll never stop' (*Se si inizia con una riforma liturgica non ci si ferma più*).[34] Acting on this advice, the Pope rejected the proposal on the same orthopractic grounds and two years later disbanded the

---

Benedict sought to put an end to Mass facing the people, to do away with the second and third eucharistic prayers and to restore the traditional Offertory prayers, at least as an option. These proposals have so far come to nothing.

[33] In the eighth century the Great Intercessions now prayed on Good Friday were still only part of the Spy Wednesday liturgy in Holy Week, which demonstrates that this element of the liturgy conforms to the law of organic development. See Thomas P. Gilmartin, 'Good Friday', CE, VI, p. 643.

[34] Emma Fattorini, *Pio XI, Hitler e Mussolini: la solitudine di un papa* (Milan, 2007), pp. 116–17.

association, not, however, without ordering the Holy Office to issue the following statement: 'Just as it reproves all hatreds and all animosities among peoples, so the Holy See greatly condemns hatred against a people once chosen by God, that hatred that today commonly goes by the name of anti-semitism.'[35]

The lobbying was resumed by judeophile clergy after the Second World War and in 1955 Pius XII decided to insert the usual *Amen* of assent and the kneeling ceremony into the collect (to match the other Great Intercessions)[36] on the not implausible ground that their omission had been a concession to popular anti-semitism in some past age and that the customary justification of the two omissions was spurious (the Gospels in fact making no reference to any Jews kneeling mockingly before the Cross).[37] John XXIII took the reform a step further. In St Peter's Basilica on Good Friday 1959 he actually interrupted the celebrant singing the eighth intercession after hearing the epithet *perfidis* and directed the master of ceremonies to have the collect sung again without the contentious words.[38] He thereafter arranged for them to be dropped from the collect at every Good Friday service which he personally attended, and these omissions were incorporated into the 1962 edition of the missal and thus generalized in the Roman rite.

A certain deviant strand of ecumenism that came to prevail after Vatican II denied Catholic teaching on the Church's duty to convert all mankind, not excluding the Jewish people, to Christianity.[39] Hence, on the subjectivistic grounds of the alleged continuing validity for the Jews (but not for others) of the Old Covenant, the post-conciliar liturgical reformers in 1970 replaced the centuries-old prayer with an entirely new 'anti-supersessionist' collect which implied that Judaism was an alternative path to eternal salvation:

> Let us pray for the Jewish people, the first to hear the word of God, that they may continue to grow in the love of his name in faithfulness to his covenant.
>
> Almighty and eternal God, long ago you gave your promise to Abraham and his posterity. Listen to your church as we pray that the people you made your own may arrive at the fullness of redemption.

'That the language of this prayer is as insipid and uninspiring as we have come to expect from the reformed liturgy is the least of its problems', Christopher Ferrara and Thomas Woods have commented.[40] In this instance the *lex orandi* was made to conform with a novel *lex credendi* which no pre-conciliar pope would have recognized as Christian, let alone Catholic. Nor would have St Teresa Benedicta of the Cross (Edith Stein), the philosopher Carmelite nun and Jewish convert who perished at Auschwitz in 1942 and whose testament stated: 'I beg the Lord

---

[35] Soppressione 'Amici di Israele', 25 March 1928, in *Acta Apostolicae Sedis*, XX (1928), p. 103.
[36] The revised rubric occurred in new text published in the *Osservatore Romano* on 27 November 1955.
[37] This had been argued by a Russian Jewish writer, Solomon Lurie, in his book *Anti-Semitism in the Ancient World* (Petrograd, 1922), p. 7. Two of the evangelists (Matt. 27.39, Mk 15.29) mention people (presumably Jews) who were present 'wagging their heads'; according to the same narratives (Matt. 27.29, Mk 15.19) it was members of the Roman guard who had knelt mockingly before the Lord when He was crowned with thorns.
[38] Phayer, *op. cit.*, p. 209.
[39] The conversion of any person to Catholicism must be the free and serene choice of the individual in question, and must, to be licit, exclude any form of physical, mental or social coercion.
[40] C. Ferrara and T. Woods, *op. cit.*, p. 205.

to take my life and my death . . . as an act of atonement for the unbelief of the Jewish people.'

At it Again

Though the 1962 textual changes to the eighth intercession could be criticized on grounds of praxis, such minor alterations to the prayer can hardly be compared with what Benedict XVI did for political reasons when, imitating the reformers of 1970, he composed an entirely new prayer to replace the traditional one in the so-called 'extraordinary rite':

> Let us also pray for the Jews: that our Lord and God may enlighten their hearts, that they acknowledge Jesus Christ as the Saviour of all men.
>
> Almighty and eternal God, who wants that all men be saved and attain the knowledge of the truth, propitiously grant that as the fulness of the Gentiles enters Thy Church, all Israel be saved.

For the Pope to take such action was tantamount to agreeing that the traditional collect as revised by John XXIII was intrinsically anti-Jewish. Unfortunately for this position, the same charge of anti-semitism would have to be levelled at the New Testament as well, since the passage in the prayer referring to the veil over Jewish hearts (and indeed the thought underlying the text) is derived from the second epistle that Saint Paul wrote, as a convert from Judaism, to the Corinthians.[41] It was this biblical imagery that had inspired the custom of veiling images in churches on the eve of Passion Sunday, not only to retell the cautionary tale of the historic defection of the Jews but, more importantly, to remind the faithful of their own personal betrayal of Christ through sin.

What Benedict XVI was eliminating was thus not some base anti-Jewish barb fossilized in a dark-age rite but a pastorally important allegory of apostolic origin and a prayer motivated by a desire for the eternal welfare of the entire Jewish people. For believing Jews of the twenty-first century the wording of the prayer was certainly a stumbling block, but then so indeed is Jesus Christ, whom the liturgy was created to proclaim. It is a most unpleasant duty for any Catholic to indicate to another human being the falsity of some tenet of that person's cherished faith, but in Catholicism the solemn command to love all mankind and reverence for the truth cannot be separated.

The results of the Pope's effort recall the tale of the Man, the Boy and the Donkey. Jewish polemicists (many of them secular Jews) and their Catholic allies accustomed to rejecting supersessionism as an official teaching of the Church were furious because the new collect mentioned the need for Jews to accept Christ as their Messiah. Some theological conservatives worried that the reference to the salvation of Israel contemporaneous with the full conversion of the Gentiles was eschatological (as indeed has been suggested by the progressivist Cardinal Kasper) and

---

[41] 2 Cor. 3.14-16. The scriptural passage was even more emphatic: 'But their minds were hardened; for to this day, when they read the old covenant, that same veil remains unlifted, because only through Christ is it taken away. Yes, to this day whenever Moses is read a veil lies over their hearts; but when a man turns to the Lord the veil is removed.'

referred to the Jews' accepting Christ at the end of time, not at any point in history.[42]

Traditionalists, for their part, were appalled that the Pontiff should have tampered so directly and arbitrarily with an ancient prayer, following the heteropractic Paul VI in subordinating the law of prayer to the law of belief. Apart from anything else, Benedict's action could not even be given the dubious justification of having been necessary for pastoral reasons, given the political nature of the decision in question. What made this recrudescence of papal inconsistency and the resultant obfuscation worse was that the innovation itself stood condemned by a forthright statement which the Pope himself, as Cardinal Ratzinger, had made in 2000:

> After the Second Vatican Council, the impression arose that the pope really could do anything in liturgical matters, especially if he were acting on the mandate of an ecumenical council. Eventually, the idea of the givenness of the liturgy, the fact that one cannot do with it what one will, faded from the public consciousness of the West. In fact, the First Vatican Council in no way defined the pope as an absolute monarch. On the contrary, it presented him as the guarantor of obedience to the revealed Word. The pope's authority is bound to the Tradition of faith, and that also applies to the liturgy. It is not 'manufactured' by the authorities. Even the pope can only be a humble servant of its lawful development and abiding integrity and identity . . . The authority of the pope is not unlimited; it is at the service of Sacred Tradition.[43]

The 2008 innovation was consequently seen as the thin end of the wedge for future arbitrary changes to the official rite, whether dictated by political correctness or by some hazy agenda for the gradual merger of the authentic liturgy and the counterfeit one through a process of deconstructing both.

Derailment or Sabotage?

Whereas John Paul II had been written up by his media-savvy admirers as the most dynamic and original pope of all time, his successor was immediately stereotyped as conservative and staid – hardly a perceptive assessment of a churchman so deeply involved in the new order. Nevertheless, Benedict XVI has not ceased to unsettle a torpid Church with his ability to surprise. No event has so far shaken the new pontificate more than the worldwide reaction to Benedict's decree of 21 January 2009 lifting the excommunications incurred in 1988 by the four bishops consecrated by Archbishop Lefebvre.

The furore that followed was based in part on the media's misinterpretation of the action taken by the pope, whereby they supposed that the removal of the ecclesiastical penalties as a necessary prelude to talks with the Society of St Pius X constituted a full reinstatement of the four bishops within the hierarchy of the mainstream Church. The matter was complicated a few days later when it came to light that one of the four, the Englishman Richard Williamson, had given an

---

[42] John Vennari, 'The New Good Friday Prayer', *Catholic Family News*, 13 February 2008, pp. 4–5. Posted at www.cfnews.org/goodfriday.htm.
[43] Josef Ratzinger, *The Spirit of the Liturgy*, tr. John Saward (San Francisco, 2000), pp. 165–66.

interview the previous November to Swedish television in which he expressed in clinical terms his doubts about the existence of gas chambers in Nazi extermination camps and minimized the numbers of innocent Jewish civilians murdered there, in the face of the compelling evidence to the contrary available for over half a century.

In view of the extent and enormity of Nazi crimes, Christians all over the world – and not only liberals who place righteous grief over the Jewish genocide on the level of an article of faith – were naturally horrified. There was also much speculation about the Bishop's motive for making such astoundingly insensitive statements. No amount of conservative Catholic indignation at the simultaneously anti-Catholic and pro-Jewish orientation of Western secular humanism since the 1960s moreover justified what appeared to be a retaliatory falsification of historical facts. Catholic liberals seized with glee at what they thought would be a lethal weapon against the traditionalist cause, which could now be tarred by association with the odious brush of anti-semitism.

The uproar escalated as certain ill-informed journalists leapt to the conclusion that the new German pope (who had been unaware of Williamson's attitudes and statements) was himself an anti-Semite and that he was validating racial hatred within the Church. That the entire affair was in reality a red herring – albeit a most sinister one – was borne out by subsequent unequivocal statements by both the Vatican and Écône repudiating the Bishop's actions.[44] The consensus was that Williamson's private views on a matter of secular history had no bearing on the dogmas of the Catholic Church, that they were in no way representative of the thinking of ordinary Catholics, whether progressive or conservative, and that Christ's commands to love one's neighbour as oneself and to seek and revere the truth admit of no exceptions whatsoever.

In the meantime the Society of St Pius X, grateful for the Pope's gesture and hopeful of initiating a process of reconciliation, distanced itself from Bishop Williamson's statements. Its Swiss head, Mgr Bernard Fellay, echoed Pope Benedict's condemnation of Williamson's public remarks as grossly offensive to the feelings of people scarred or haunted by memories of the war crimes in question.[45] However, what the Society was less inclined to admit was that it had, from its inception, been a haven for embittered supporters of anti-republican groups, some of whom had judeophobic proclivities; people who, by the 1970s, were isolated within Western European society.[46] Archbishop Lefebvre, like most conservative French Catholics

---

[44] See Richard Owen and Ruth Gledhill (5 February 2009), 'Pope Insists Bishop Richard Williamson Must Renounce Holocaust Denial', www.timesonline.co.uk/tol/comment/faith/article5663726. ece; Nicole Winfield (27 January 2009), 'Forgiveness Sought for Holocaust-Denying Bishop', *ABC News*, http://abcnews.go.com/International/wireStory?id=6740933.

[45] See 'Statement of the SSPX General Superior Bernard Fellay regarding the Bishop Williamson Interview', http://stlouiscatholic.blogspot.com/2009/01/bishop-fellay.html. In a letter to the Pope, Williamson begged forgiveness for the trouble he had caused but did not retract his remarks. Consequently, he was silenced by the Fraternity and relieved of his regular duties.

[46] The monarchist cause, though far from incompatible with Catholicism, turned septic (consider the Dreyfus affair) after the death of the Count of Chambord (Henry V) in 1883 and as a result of Leo XIII's urging of French Catholics to rally to the Third Republic (a strange policy given that the Vatican refused to recognize the contemporary Kingdom of Italy). While the political creed of right-wing clergy and seminarians at Écône did not determine the Society's agenda, it was a potent influence on some members, and served to create a certain ultra-monarchist element responsible for driving away a significant number of good priests. That other members of the Fraternity managed to pursue their difficult apostolate in the midst of a fanatical subculture

a product of the Right, had more than once compromised his heroic work for the preservation of orthodoxy by making ingenuous recommendations of authoritarian governments run by Catholics of which he had little personal knowledge. These included the regimes of Jorge Videla in Argentina and Augusto Pinochet in Chile, and it caused him serious embarrassment when their criminal nature was revealed to him.[47]

The Archbishop's powers of discernment, as founder of the Priestly Fraternity, are moreover brought into further question by the rapid rise through its ranks of converts whose demeanour and utterances have frequently demonstrated how little they had absorbed of the Catholicity outside of which no priest can effectively carry out his pastoral mission. Some of his convert priests became well known for a particular form of heteropraxis betraying an underlying unorthodox individualism: making quasi-authoritative public statements on matters that interested them personally but had little or nothing to do with the Catholic faith.

Yet if certain members of this priestly fraternity do manifest a narrow dogmatism and an anti-intellectual and clericalist mentality fully to be expected of a movement strongly attached, for want of any surer anchor, to the pre-conciliar culture, such shortcomings are more than compensated for by these men's witness to eternal truths in an age of unprecedented confusion. The deplorable 'Williamson affair', for all the misunderstanding, bad blood and embarrassment it caused, has served at least to jolt a complacent Society of St Pius X into vigilance against reactionary internal elements which, seeking to revive discredited former alliances between Catholicism and fascism, constitute a grave hindrance to the continuation of the mission entrusted to it by its founder, which is the preaching of divine love and the salvation of souls.

An admirably balanced evaluation of the role of Marcel Lefebvre in recent Catholic history was made by the German writer Martin Mosebach in the wake of the Williamson affair:

> But why was Archbishop Lefebvre the only bishop in the entire world who uncompromisingly rejected this attack against the liturgy and thus against the Church? With this 'no' to a process of decomposition so highly dangerous to the Church, Lefebvre entered ecclesiastical history. What gave him the strength was the milieu, only found in France, of a Catholic laity which had acquired its world view in the struggle against aggressive republican secularism. This was the tragedy of Lefebvre and his movement: they rescued the ancient liturgy but linked it to the struggle of political parties in recent French history. The only refuge that the traditional liturgy had found threatened to become its prison. Pope Benedict has now freed it from this prison with his Motu Proprio and has given it back with its universal claim to the entire Church. Must he not, however, have felt a sense of obligation to the SSPX; that, for all its faults, it had become an instrument for preserving the Holy of Holies of the Church in a time of crisis? Whether the SSPX succeeds in

on one hand and in the face of mainstream Church hostility on the other, is all the more remarkable.

[47] Homily of the public Mass in Lille, 29 June 1976, and in clarifications at the press conference of the following 15 September, see M. Davies, *Apologia*, I, pp. 264–66. It is certain in any case that the Archbishop was no supporter of methods of government he knew to be tyrannical or murderous, his own father René, a member of the French Resistance hunted by the Gestapo, having perished in the Nazi concentration camp at Sonnenburg.

finding a place in the multiplicity of the present day Church remains to be seen. Its historic mission, in any case, has been concluded.[48]

Syllabus and Counter-syllabus

That the media-trammelled Society of St Pius X has now played out its part in the struggle for Catholic tradition is, however, unlikely. While Pope Benedict XVI sincerely wishes to restore some measure of orthopraxis to the Church, he remains a right-of-centre liberal committed to Vatican II both as a monument and as a charter for reform. A note of the Vatican Secretariat of State dated 4 February 2009 stated bluntly that 'For a future recognition of the Fraternity of St Pius X, the full recognition of the Second Vatican Council and of the Magisterium of Popes John XXIII, Paul VI, John Paul I, John Paul II and of the same Benedict XVI is an indispensable condition.' To the average post-conciliar ideologue the aim of rallying the Lefebvrists and their supporters to Vatican II is contradictory, while many traditionalist dissenters remain to be convinced that the Council and its aftermath can be shown to be in full harmony with Tradition. The fact that the Pope, when speaking in March 2009 about the formation of seminarians, admitted the need for 'a correct reading of the texts of the Second Vatican Council, interpreted in the light of all the Church's doctrinal heritage' was proof that the conciliar texts themselves lacked the unequivocal nature of the documents issued by the Papacy over the past few centuries, clarity being a quality to be expected of an institution founded to teach the truth.[49]

The new climate of religious liberalism has in fact clouded and complicated all understanding of doctrine ever since the promulgation of the ambiguity-ridden constitutions of Vatican II. In this milieu traditional Catholics find themselves unable to accept those policies of the post-conciliar Papacy which appear to have been condemned in the *Syllabus of Errors* of Pius IX, the anti-Americanist rulings of Leo XIII and the anti-Modernist encyclicals of Pius X. The challenges of finding a way forward are moreover bedevilled by the fact that among those who constantly appeal to Vatican II there is wide disagreement about the significance of several aspects of the Council.

The most problematic of the contested conciliar teachings is a form of ecumenism that appears to promote religious indifferentism by rejecting the unique claims of the Roman Church. Another stumbling block is the new social policy endorsing *in principle* the strict separation of Church and state, and religious liberty, i.e. the freedom of individuals to choose their own religion without any obligation to inform their consciences. Given the perceptible results of these innovations, Cardinal Ratzinger's claim that the conciliar document *Gaudium et Spes* and the texts on religious liberty and world religions were 'a revision of the Syllabus of Pius IX, a kind of countersyllabus', could only deepen the misgivings of traditionalists.[50] Christopher Ferrara and Thomas Woods noted in 2002 that:

Abandoning all pretense of deference to the perennial Magisterium, certain

---

[48] 'Der Papst und die Piusbrüder', *Der Spiegel*, 10 February 2009.
[49] *Catholic News Service*, 16 March 2009.
[50] Ratzinger, *Principles of Catholic Theology*, p. 381.

neo-Catholics [= conservatives] and neo-modernists alike now seek to relegate the Syllabus to the dustbin of history. Yet history has demonstrated that the very errors Blessed Pius IX condemned have led to the total collapse of the moral order in the secularized, pluralist regimes that are enslaved by them, as well as a loss of faith and discipline in the Church, in which many of the condemned propositions are now considered received wisdom by a thoroughly liberalized clergy and laity.[51]

Methodologies which relativize the Church's past dogmatic statements as 'substantial anchorages' suitable for one age but not necessarily for another are for traditional Catholics a daunting obstacle to doctrinal consensus, since the new approach seems to cast doubt on the dogmatic status of every received teaching. The freeing of the traditional liturgy may have been the indispensable first step to the healing of the present *de facto* breach in communion, but the underlying questions concerning the *lex credendi* must be resolved before full and effective unity can possibly be restored.

The Enlightenment's Last Stand?

One of the liberals most disconcerted by Pope Benedict's outreach to the Society of St Pius X was the Archbishop of Clermont, Hippolyte Simon. At the end of an open letter published in *La Croix* on 29 January 2009 in which he expressed his solidarity with outraged liberals, the French prelate made what reads like a Freudian slip in an allusion to the parable of the Prodigal Son. Instead of likening traditional Catholics (those who according to liberal mythology had abandoned the Church) to the wayward brother who was welcomed home, Mgr Simon actually compared them to the elder son who in the parable symbolizes loyalty and stability:

> I'd like to say something to the Catholic faithful who, not without reason, may have the feeling of having been betrayed, not say treated with contempt in this affair: meditate on the parable of the Prodigal Son, and try to apply it. If the elder son, who at first refused to go into the feast, says that he wants to enter, are you going to refuse him? Please have enough confidence in yourselves, and in the Spirit who guides the Church and who also guided the Vatican II Council, to realize that the mere presence of this elder son will not be able to spoil the feast. Give these new arrivals a little time to get used to the light of the Assembly in which you stand.[52]

On the 14 July following the publication of the 2007 motu proprio, Mgr Simon had written an article in which he gloated that the Pope, by declaring the essential unity of the two rites, had cut the legs from under the Lefebvrist argument that the Pauline reform was a real break with tradition. He thought thus to have demolished the entire position of the supposedly light-shy traditionalists:

> So when I read, more or less everywhere, that the Pope is conceding everything

---

[51] C. Ferrara and T. Woods, *op. cit.*, p. 285.
[52] www.la-croix.com/documents/doc.jsp?docId=236708&rubId=47602.

to the fundamentalists and demanding nothing in return, I must beg to differ. He is giving in to them completely in what concerns the ritual forms, but he is demolishing their basic argument. All of Mgr Lefebvre's argumentation rested on a supposed substantial difference between the rite of Pius V and the rite of Paul VI. Now, Benedict reaffirms, it makes no sense to speak of two rites. One could, if hard pushed, justify a resistance to the Council if one thought, in good conscience, that there existed a substantial difference between the two rites. But how can one legitimize this resistance and, what is more, a schism on the mere basis of a difference of forms?

In reality, no bilateral discussions about the liturgy had taken place to prove anything of the sort to anyone, and the Pope, in giving his opinion as a legislator, was not thereby making an infallible definition. The vice-president of the French episcopal conference was not only begging the question but resorting to the old liberal ploy of making an out-of-character ultramontanist appeal to the obedient suspension of thought in order to promote (or, by 2009, to save) an institutionalized revolution. The taunt with which he concluded his article suggested a greater loyalty to modern liberalism than to the pre-conciliar Catholic law of belief exemplied by Pius IX, continuity with which Pope Benedict now has the unenviable task of demonstrating to those in doubt:

It was nonetheless surprising to hear the disciples [of Archbishop Lefebvre] begging the Pope to liberalize the Latin Mass, without realizing that their 'master' had fought all his life to maintain the Syllabus of Pius IX, which condemned in fact all forms of liberalism. But do they know anyway what the Syllabus was really about and what needless dramas it justified?[53]

The task awaiting traditionalists, Mgr Simon continued, was to 'renounce the Syllabus', i.e. to embrace *aggiornamento* in the way that clerics like himself interpreted and applied it. This for him was the heart of the matter. But given the intransigence of both parties, it is difficult to imagine that the work of reconciliation will be plain sailing for anybody, especially since the liberals who now control most of the Church's dioceses remain determined to impose their heterodoxy as the new Catholic orthodoxy and to stigmatize traditional orthodoxy as heresy.

'Heresy' and 'obedience' were words rarely on liberal Catholic lips until the confronting pontificate of Benedict XVI. There have been few more eloquent announcements of the neo-modernists' last stand than the 'fundamental question' which Alois Kothgasser, Archbishop of Salzburg, publicly asked the Church in 2009, also in the wake of the lifting of the 1988 excommunications:

Should the Catholic Church reduce herself to a cult, which only a few, but law-abiding, members practise, or should the Catholic Church of Jesus Christ leave room for diversity, be open and influence society from the inside? . . . Whoever rejects the Second Vatican Council does not stand on the same ground as the Catholic Church. In fact, such people have shut themselves out of the Catholic Church. Insofar as the rejection of statements of the Second Vatican Council are

---

[53] 'Pourquoi j'obéis au pape', *Le Monde*, 14 July 2007; www.lemonde.fr/cgi-bin/ACHATS/acheter. cgi?offre=ARCHIVES&type_item=ART_ARCH_30J&.

obstinately pursued, it seems to me to be not just a question of schism, but of heresy, since there is a selective use of the dogmatic tradition, accepting some elements and rejecting others.[54]

Given the stunning departures from dogmatic orthodoxy now rife in German-speaking dioceses, this might be seen as another instance of the pot calling the kettle black. In any case what the good Austrian Archbishop – who on 16 October 2004 celebrated diversity by donning a red nose during a 'clown Mass' in Salzburg Cathedral[55] – really understands by the now chameleonic expression 'Vatican II' is anyone's guess.

Sins of the Fathers

Musing about the near-hysterical reaction of the German and Austrian hierarchies to the Pope's move towards reconciliation with traditionalists, one English-speaking internet blogger quipped at the time: 'There's nothing like a guilty conscience.' The persistent 'problem of Vatican II' is at its deepest level psychological, inseparable from the mentality of the generation of Josef Ratzinger, Catholics born between the two world wars. Benedict XVI's peers in age are scarred by childhood memories of the Second World War and its horrors, and burdened by the sins of their parents and by the guilt that descended upon European society in the aftermath of that cataclysm. These feelings of blameworthiness were particularly acute in the former Nazi and fascist states but also powerful in those Allied nations that did not do enough before or during the conflict to prevent the escalation of racism into an unprecedented orgy of bloodshed and genocide that eventually claimed some fifty million European lives.

In the 'economic miracle' decades a characteristic reaction to this mass guilt complex was to make common cause with socialism and liberalism, those political creeds most opposed to the right-wing authoritarian governments responsible for these great evils. But the fatal error of the general 'left turn' that animated the Second Vatican Council was that in trading in rightist ideologies that had exploited and discredited Christianity for more 'people friendly' political creeds, they were overlooking the fact that the leftist ideologies, no less than fascism, place the source of authority in man, not in God. The problem here is that the secularist order with which the 'spirit of Vatican II' has allied itself to varying degrees is fundamentally opposed to the social reign of Christ the King, i.e. the right of the Church to intervene in the social order for the defence of faith and morals, taught by Pius XI in his 1925 encyclical *Quas Primas*.

Typifying his 'penitent' generation, a young Fr Ratzinger attended sessions of the Vatican Council defiantly dressed in a business suit and tie, in symbolic deference to the new anthropocentric order in tune with which the rejuvenated Church would absolve herself of the sin of complicity with the pre-war dictatorships. One wonders, then, whether the dark force that drove the would-be assassins of the

---

[54] 'Bei Gott und den Menschen bleiben! Ein Interview mit Erzbischof Alois Kothgasser zur Lage der Kirche', *Erzdiözese Salzburg* (website of the archdiocese of Salzburg), 10 February 2009. www.kirchen.net/portal/page.asp?id=13622.

[55] See the *Kreuz.net Katolische Nachrichten* web article (3 December 2004), 'Lachen bis das Lachen vergeht: Der Hochlustigste Erzbischof von Salzburg', www.kreuz.net/article.237.html.

traditional liturgy was unleashed by the Second Vatican Council after all, or rather by the Second World War. In the twenty-first century the legacy of that hellish conflict and its mark on the survivors continue to haunt the Catholic Church.

Surely one of the most bizarre phenomena of Catholic life today is the refusal of liberal bishops of this interwar generation to recognize the most obvious consequence of their Council's *Declaration on Religious Liberty*: the connection between the disappearance of national governments constitutionally conformed to the moral teaching of the Church and the practical impossibility, in First World and many other countries, of raising Christian families. Nowadays even the most devout parents are destined to face the heartbreak of seeing the sons and daughters they have carefully nurtured in the Faith resolutely refusing to practise their religion soon after they reach adolescence. Such is the power of the surrounding secular culture whose ubiquitous mass media brainwash the young and the spiritually weak by glamorizing sin and ignoring Christianity when they are not blaspheming and mocking it.

True to a fallible human nature that makes it immensely difficult for those who make unwise decisions with baneful consequences to face reality and admit their responsibility, the Ratzinger generation marches to the grave protesting that the Council was a success because of predicted 'fruits of Vatican II' which show no sign of materializing. Thus the Peter in the complex personality of Benedict XVI attempts to release the traditional liturgy from quarantine while the Simon within proclaims his solidarity with the revolution.

The historic theological confrontation issuing from the Pope's lifting of the excommunications of the Lefebvrist bishops nevertheless promises to reveal the extent to which the positions of the current Papacy and that of traditionalists can be reconciled and shown to rest on differences of language and theological method rather than on objective differences of belief.[56] If this meeting of minds has a positive outcome, the wider Church will benefit immeasurably. The time might then be approaching when the immemorial *lex orandi* and the *lex credendi* associated with the Second Vatican Council will be harmonized and the current crisis of authority will be, mercifully, just a bitter memory.

---

[56] Talks between Vatican officials and theologians of the Society of St Pius X began on 26 October 2009.

19

FELIX CULPA?

We can at least pray to the Blessed Virgin that when he becomes aware of the enormous difficulties he will meet in the exercise of his power as Pope, he will reconsider his stance and perhaps conclude that he must return to Tradition.

ARCHBISHOP MARCEL LEFEBVRE, AFTER HIS AUDIENCE
WITH POPE JOHN PAUL II IN 1978

Have the holy fear of God ever before your eyes, and have confidence that He will in mercy turn all to the best.

MARY TUDOR, SHORTLY BEFORE HER DEATH (1558)

Orthodoxy or Obedience?

One of the fundamentals of Catholicism is the teaching that the Universal Church of Christ is the sum of orthodox churches throughout the world in communion with the Bishop of Rome. From the beginning this unity has rested on a delicate balance, and history shows that despite the Lord's promise of indefectibility, His 'seamless robe' has been torn whenever these two Catholic principles of orthodoxy and universality have been neglected or impugned. Dissidence has resulted not only when groups of Christians have, for various reasons, refused communion with the Successor of St Peter but also, as the events of the past fifty years have shown, when the Vicar of Christ has jeopardized the integrity of the Catholic faith by straying down the path of heteropraxis.

The unexpected outcome of the Second Vatican Council has been the quite unprecedented situation of a Papacy fully committed to policies which have proved their destructive nature and their sinister consequences in the religious sphere. Hence many traditional Latin Catholics today, for whom avoiding the new liturgy is a matter of conscience and not merely a cultural preference are, like Eastern Christians in the past, faced with the invidious choice between visible communion with a heteropractic Supreme Pontiff and fidelity to integral orthodoxy in a state of material or formal dissidence. Except in cases where groups of 'sedevacantist' Catholics repudiate the present Pope both in practice and in theory, there can, however, be no question of deliberate (and therefore sinful) schism on the part of those clergy and faithful who, while recognizing the supreme authority of the Pope and wishing to be united with him, are compelled by their consciences to dissent from teachings that appear to contradict the pre-conciliar Magisterium, and consider it necessary not to obey recent papal laws that are manifestly contrary to orthopraxis.[1]

The analogy of the Orthodox Churches is particularly germane to the case of Latin-rite traditionalists today, in that the half-hearted patching up exercise leading up to the excommunication of Archbishop Lefebvre in 1988, and the Latin hierarchy's failure fully to honour promises subsequently made by John Paul II and Benedict XVI, both recall the circumstances of the Council of Florence and its aftermath, the age of Uniatism.

The Vocation of Exclusion

Riven by *de facto* schism, the Roman Church today is grotesquely similar to the Anglican Church it formerly disdained for its division into irreconcilable factions. However, it is the schism not of radical traditionalists in imperfect communion with a heteropractic pope and hierarchy, but of the more numerous Catholic clergy and laity in good canonical standing who are not only heteropraxists but material and even formal heretics. As for the Catholic majority – the doctrinally orthodox Christians who remain in visible communion with the Pope – insofar as they accept the post-conciliar liturgy they share with the heterodox the tendency to stress the visible unity of the Mystical Body at the expense of its traditional integrity. The obverse of their concern for canonical regularity is their relative indifference to the need for authenticity. This attitude also characterizes to some extent those traditionalists who accepted the deal of 1988, reflected in the following opinion that the root error of Lefebvrists

> lies in thinking that the faith and sacraments alone are the criteria for belonging to the Catholic Church, forgetting about the bond with hierarchy. Look what happened in 1054 when the Church of Constantinople broke away from Rome. The eastern Churches have remained totally faithful to the faith and the sacraments but they are no longer Catholic. By breaking the bond of dependence on Peter, they became schismatic. And although the Lefebvrists sincerely protest that they ever caused a schism at all, they are schismatic in practice.[2]

---

[1] The technically non-schismatic character of traditionalist dissidence has, in fact, been recognized by an otherwise hostile Vatican in a serious of declarations since 1993, when (on 28 June) the Congregation for the Doctrine of the Faith declared invalid the excommunication of six parishioners of a chapel of the Society of St Pius X by the extreme leftist Bishop of Hawaii, Joseph Ferrario, on 1 May 1991. On 23 May 2008 Mgr Camille Perl, the Vice-President of the Ecclesia Dei Commission, admitted in a letter to Mr Brian Mershon, an American traditionalist, that 'it is true that participation in the Mass at chapels of the Society of St. Pius X does not of itself constitute "formal adherence to the schism" (cf. Ecclesia Dei 5, c)' while warning (naturally without reference to Rome's own commitment to heteropraxis) that 'such adherence can come about over a period of time as one slowly imbibes a schismatic mentality which separates itself from the teaching of the Supreme Pontiff and the entire Catholic Church'.

[2] Dom Gérard Calvet, quoted in Stefano Paci, 'The Middle Ages Today', *30 Days*, 6 (1994), p. 32. It is interesting to note that Dom Gérard's questionable equation of dissidence and schism follows an Augustinian ecclesiology which considers schism more serious than heresy, whence modern Rome's toleration of heterodox and heteropractic 'Catholics' today, contrasting scandalously with her shabby treatment of traditionalists. By contrast, the Eastern Orthodox (and not a few Western traditionalists) prefer to follow the Latin Father St Optatus of Milevis († c. 387) in his contention that whereas heretics are outside the Church, schismatics (and dissidents even more) 'still have the Church for their Mother: though they stray from her and break her peace, they take

Now it is not true that mainstream traditionalists underestimate the necessity of the bond with the hierarchy, even if the current emergency situation prevents their harmonizing theory and practice. 'Uniate' traditionalists who make statements such as the above are obliged by their political stance to acknowledge the normative status in Catholicism of the artificial rites of Paul VI, and are not free to condemn as loudly as they should the current heteropraxis tolerated when not endorsed by the Vatican. They are also compelled to make the pretence of being in visible communion with a majority in whose worship – if they are true to their convictions – they cannot take part with a serene conscience.

While members of the 'pure' traditionalist camp who manifest their conscientious objection to the liturgical revolution may be accused, on the other hand, of dissidence (for which not they themselves, but the post-Pacellian Papacy is ultimately responsible), the point is that in the emergency situation that now obtains in the Church such Christians feel morally obliged to place orthodoxy before canonical regularity.[3] While dissident Eastern Orthodox and dissident Latin Catholic believers would differ greatly on their definitions of doctrinal orthodoxy, they are (whether they like it or not) at one in their basic stance, which proclaims that effective communion with the Petrine See cannot be restored until the Vatican repents of its deviations from tradition and restores fully the union of Catholic faith and practice.

Plus ça change . . .

In this connexion the new openness to the East inaugurated by the Second Vatican Council is reassuring, since it implies a theoretical break with the rigid institutionalism of the late Middle Ages and the Counter Reformation. The associated rationalist outlook not only widened and hardened the schism of East and West, but has proved to be a constant factor of heteropraxis within the Roman communion itself. Formerly thought to be the guarantee of orthodoxy, institutionalism's juridical model of the Church has now revealed its radically subversive nature, since it is, according to Avery Dulles, SJ, a 'view that defines the Church primarily in terms of its visible structures, especially the rights and powers of its officers'.

---

with them the faith and sacraments which they received from her hands' (see Nichols, *op. cit.*, p. 8). In the end, the view one takes on this question depends on whether one deems fidelity to the truth or the law of charity more important: admittedly a difficult and odious choice.

[3] Traditionalists are arguably not acting in a schismatic manner when, for example, they refuse the ministrations of a local bishop willing to perform confirmations or ordinations in the old rite but who at the same time declines to take action against the promoters of heresy and heteropraxis in his diocese: *salus animarum suprema lex*. Nor is the charge that congregations under the care of the Society of St Pius X are in the same position as the French Jansenists and (orthodox and orthopractic) Anglo-Catholics who prayed liturgically for the Pope and their local Protestant bishop but acted in complete independence of both. The Jansenists were heretics, and the Anglo-Catholics willingly adhered to an ecclesial body that was not schismatical and orthodox, but schismatical and heretical. The four bishops ordained by Mgr Lefebvre in 1988 have not claimed local jurisdiction, and their sole reason for existence is to guarantee sacramental security in an emergency situation where the faithful have good reason to doubt the integral orthodoxy of the present Latin hierarchy. Without a doubt, these bishops would be establishing a schismatic church if they set up rival jurisdictions. Even then, however, the fundamental question would remain: what is the relationship to the Catholic faith of the ages of the post-conciliar popes and hierarchy? If there is indeed a schism, and if the role of the Roman Pope is to preside in love and vigilance over the united *orthodox* dioceses of the world, who is in schism from the Church of Christ? The question is vertiginous.

According to the same ecclesiologist it is imperative to separate the institutional reality of the Catholic Church from the questionable ideal of institutionalism:

> Throughout its history, from the very earliest years, Christianity has always had an institutional side. It has had recognized ministers, accepted confessional formulas, and prescribed forms of public worship. All this is fitting and proper. It does not necessarily imply institutionalism. By institutionalism we mean a system in which the institutional element is treated as primary. From the point of view of this author, institutionalism is a deformation of the true nature of the Church – a deformation that has unfortunately affected the Church at certain periods of its history, and one that remains in every age a real danger to the institutional Church.[4]

However, the partisans of *aggiornamento* (among them the author of the above-quoted passage) who reacted against an ecclesiology in which the role of the laity was merely 'to pray, pay and obey' were too personally tainted by their milieu to abandon in practice what they rejected in theory. Far from disappearing, institutionalism survived the Vatican Council and facilitated the establishment of heteropraxis in the pontificate of Paul VI. What, after all, was the Pauline reform but a legalistic and arrogant clerical revolt against the liturgical and disciplinary traditions held sacred by the Latin Catholic faithful? *Plus ça change, plus c'est la même chose*: institutionalism, metamorphosed through *aggiornamento*, still flourishes in the Roman communion today, whereas the authentic Roman liturgy, the living heart of the Church, is in practice all but repudiated. *Aggiornamento* with the big guns of institutionalism behind it has not only alienated orthopractic Latin Catholics from their lawful patriarch and pope, but ironically (considering the ecumenical aspirations of Paul VI and his successors) has widened the gulf separating Catholics and Orthodox. The Orthodox and other independent Eastern Churches may have survived without a head, but mainstream Catholicism today has banished its heart.

The Genie Out of the Bottle

While the new climate in the pontificate of Benedict XVI is somewhat more propitious for the *metanoia* indispensable for a return to normality, it still seems unlikely that good Catholics' prayers for the Pope's return to the fullness of tradition will be answered during the present pontificate. Given that it is in the nature of establishments and their supporting bureaucracies to perpetuate themselves, only some extraordinary intervention in the present order will give the Church a holy pope who will restore true orthodoxy by reversing the heteropractic laws of the past three pontificates, correcting current errors in teaching, and righting the wrongs that have weakened, divided and demoralized the faithful since the Second Vatican Council.

Even if such an event were to occur in the foreseeable future, it is necessary to face the grim fact that the destruction of authentic Catholic life since the 1960s has been so profound and far-reaching that it would require a major miracle to return the unchurched millions of the First World and in Latin America to the

---

[4] Dulles, *Models for the Church*, p. 35.

religion of their baptism. The survival of the Church until the end of time may be implicit in her constitution, but just as Christianity, already debilitated by heresy and schism, receded disastrously from its original centre in the Middle East and in North Africa before the advance of Islam, it seems destined – despite its imposing real estate – to shrink to very modest proportions in the one-time homelands and expansion zones of Latin Catholicism.

Today the formerly 'white regions' of Western Europe (the north-west of France, Flanders, the southern Netherlands, the north of Portugal and Spain, North-Eastern Italy, Upper Austria and so on) are populated by new generations as indifferent or antagonistic to the authority and orthopraxis of the Catholic Church as the inhabitants of traditional 'red regions' like north-central France, Wallonia, the south of Portugal and Spain, Emilia-Romagna, Lower Austria etc. Even in those few European states where an ancient loyalty to the Church survives somewhat more strongly (Ireland, Malta, Slovakia, Poland), the Catholicism in question is the diluted variety based on the Pauline liturgy and generally typical of the expanding churches of Africa and Asia. In Latin America, meanwhile, the pace of erosion through aggressive Protestant proselytism is truly alarming, as the example of Nicaragua shows.[5]

Traditional Catholics in areas strafed by the forty-year 'spirit of Vatican II' may be praying for a resurgence of the faith they hold dear, but history teaches how slim are the chances of success for any restoration after any religious culture has been effectively dismantled and a new one installed in its place. During the medieval *Reconquista* in southern Europe, the Albigensian Crusade and later the Counter Reformation, when whole populations already strongly affected by Islam, Catharism or Protestantism were forcibly reintegrated into the Catholic family, the results were far from satisfactory, as can be seen from the quality of faith and practice in former 'zones of apostasy' like the Algarve, Andalusia, southern Occitania, Sicily, Bohemia and eastern Hungary. The abortive Counter Reformation in England, cut short by the death of Queen Mary I after only five years on the throne, provides a particularly vivid illustration of the huge obstacles facing those striving to restore order and revive piety after a thoroughgoing religious revolution.

Satan's Wedge

The tragedy of Mary Tudor's reign (1553–1558) was written into its triumphant opening. When Mary ascended the throne a large majority of Englishmen welcomed the return to Catholicism. Most ordinary citizens had keenly resented the malicious and violent attack on traditional religion unleashed by the government of the boy king Edward VI (1547–1553), whose education, for which his schismatic and dubiously orthodox father Henry VIII was responsible, had included a large dose of Protestant indoctrination of the most extreme kind. However, the energetic work of Catholic restoration undertaken by the new regime and by Mary's bishops – mostly penitent schismatics deprived after her father's reign – in the end proved

---

[5] In Nicaragua Catholics formed an estimated 92 per cent of the population in 1974; the 2005 census revealed that the figure for Catholics had dropped to 58.5 per cent, while 24.2 per cent of Nicaraguans were now Protestant, and 15.7 per cent professed no religion. Similar trends are observable throughout Latin America.

no match for the demons of materialism and cynicism that had taken possession of a politically canny and ambitious minority of the population. Those demons entered the soul of England on the fatal March day in 1536 when Henry VIII, determined to replenish the royal coffers and increase the splendour of his court, agreed to the planned destruction of what had been in better times the heart of the English Church: the 825 abbeys, monasteries and convents of the realm.

Queen Mary's parliament had agreed to the reversion to Catholicism on the condition that the church lands and wealth plundered and sold off by the Crown remain in the hands of the grasping nobility and the class of nouveaux-riches created by the great despoliation. It was among the latter, materially comfortable and socially progressive sectors that Protestant sympathies were liveliest, and it was they who saw to it that most of the 250 or more men and women executed by civil law for the treasonous crime of heresy from 1555 to 1558 were scapegoats from the unmoneyed classes: fanatical Anabaptists (despised by mainstream Protestants as much as by Catholics), uneducated artisans and other unfortunate victims of engineered civil unrest.

The bodies of Mary's martyrs were less fuel for the fires of Smithfield than for the flames of propaganda exploited by the apologists of the coming Protestant ascendancy to discredit forever the authentic religious heritage of England and to defame a benevolent and saintly monarch. The Marian restoration proceeded against the stark background of wrecked abbeys, vandalized shrines, gutted churches, widespread delinquency, a ruined economy and a whole generation confused about, when not ignorant of, the faith of their fathers. If it required a strenuous effort to herd such straying sheep back into the Catholic fold, it was ominously easy to groom this nation, under Elizabeth I and her successors, to lead the quest for a modern civilization founded on select 'liberties' ultimately including many in conflict with the gentle yoke of Christ.[6]

Man's impatience with sacred traditions during periods of social instability is Satan's wedge, a truth unhappily overlooked in the 1960s by the small band of clerics who took it upon themselves to eviscerate the central treasure and life force of the Latin Church.

Ecumenical Impasse

It is remarkable that when Catholic ecumenists interested in the independent Eastern Churches enter into dialogue with fellow Christians whom they know to be profoundly traditional (and 'fundamentalist' from the standpoint of Western modernism) they characteristically gloss over and even conceal the momentous changes in Catholicism that have made reunion much less possible than it was on the eve of the Council. The all-important fact that the official Latin Catholic Church has all but abandoned its traditional orthopraxis, chiefly embodied in the

---

[6] It may be technically true that the sudden wreck of the extraordinarily successful Marian restoration was due to the Queen's premature death, and that Catholicism would have remained the majority religion in England had she been succeeded by a Catholic. Nevertheless, Elizabeth Tudor would have faced much stiffer opposition to her new religious regime from the upper classes if the effects of the recently-reversed Protestant revolution had not been so profound. On England's short-lived Counter Reformation see Eamon Duffy, *Fires of Faith: Catholic England under Mary Tudor* (New Haven/London, 2009).

immemorial liturgy, rarely if ever features as a topic of discussion in ecumenical encounters, precisely because if the Orthodox, understanding as they do the link between worship and belief, realized the extent of current Latin heteropraxis they would retreat in horror from all 'fraternal' dialogue, as many instinctively do without even a full knowledge of the facts. The struggle to restore the immemorial liturgy to the Latin Church can thus be seen to have a significant, if so far largely ignored, ecumenical dimension.

Fifty years of dialogue between the Catholic and Orthodox Churches have made no difference to the fundamental conviction of the right-believing members of both bodies that *their* Church is exclusively the true Church of Christ to which all dissident Christians must return. After decades of the tendentious use of the term 'Sister Church' to imply that the Roman and the Orthodox Churches are merely two branches of the one Catholic Church, Rome has clarified her official position that the Church of Christ is substantially the Roman communion, while the majority of Orthodox continue to believe that Catholics need to 'come home' to Orthodoxy.[7] Thus, the new climate of polite relations notwithstanding, the impasse of 1054 remains, even though some Orthodox theologians attribute to traditional Catholics a 'material Orthodoxy' parallel to the material Catholicism that open-minded Catholics recognize in Eastern Orthodoxy.[8]

The reality of formal separation has not been changed by such initiatives as the Catholic–Orthodox Balamand Declaration of 1993, which, while making many true and noble statements, committed the fatal error of affirming, with disregard for the official teaching of both Churches, that 'in the search for re-establishing unity there is no question of *conversion* of people from one Church to the other in order to ensure their salvation' (point 15). For this reason the Declaration has been fiercely attacked by both Orthodox and Catholic traditionalists, as well as by members of the Uniate Churches, whose very reason for existence the signatories implicitly brought into question.

Meanwhile the two principal obstacles to the progress of rapprochement are, first, on the Orthodox side, a widespread and often visceral hostility to Catholicism

---

[7] The Congregation for the Doctrine of the Faith issued in 2000 a *Note on the Expression 'Sister Churches'* approved by John Paul II in his Audience of 9 June and according to which the use of this term in relation to churches not in union with Rome is theologically incorrect.

[8] Nicholas Zernov explains that ecumenically minded Orthodox have in all historical periods regarded Catholics not as Christians cut off from the Church and her life of grace, but 'as disobedient members of the Church still subjected to its jurisdiction'. According to this inclusive view of membership of the Orthodox Church,

all Christians baptized in the name of the Holy Trinity are members of the One Catholic Church and are regenerated by the grace of the Holy Spirit. Their affiliation with the Church, however, differs considerably, for owing to the state of schism many of them belong to the communities which only imperfectly introduce their members to the riches of the Eucharistic Life. Because the federation of Byzantine Churches has preserved better than any other communion the harmony of the Apostolic tradition, it can therefore be regarded as the Mother Church of Christendom, occupying the central position among its diverse confessions. The present treatment of the heterodox is consistent with this view of the Orthodox role in the contemporary world. Those Christians who belong to the Churches which stand closer to the Byzantine federation by their doctrine and organization are received into the fellowship of the Orthodox Church through the sacrament of Confession. Those who come from the Protestant bodies, who renounced the apostolic ministry, are received through Chrismation. Those who were not baptized in the name of the Holy Trinity, through Baptism. ('The Challenge of the West', in A. J. Philippou, ed., *Orthodoxy, Life & Freedom* [Oxford, 1973], pp. 112–13) which in no way matches the general openness among Catholics towards reunion with the Orthodox. This is reflected in the writings of Orthodox scholars who contend that Western speculative theology and Eastern empirical theology are not complementary, but mutually contradictory and emblematic of distinct religions. Moreover, whereas many Catholics feel a natural cultural and spiritual affinity with Eastern Orthodoxy, most Orthodox seem indifferent and incurious in regard to Catholicism and are strangely oblivious of the liturgical revolution that has transformed the lives of Western Christians since the 1960s.

In other words there is a serious attitudinal obstacle which the Orthodox will attribute to the virtue of faith, but which Catholics tend to see as a failure in charity, evidence of bad faith on the part of the Orthodox hierarchy, and a predominantly emotional and time-collapsing approach to religious history diametrically opposed to (but every bit as bad as) Western hyperrationalism. With indifference or hostility predominating on the Orthodox side and unrealistic aims linked to dubious theological novelties characterizing so many Catholic ecumenists, hopes of a rapid healing of the thousand-year schism now seem remoter than ever.[9]

This leads to the conclusion that it is futile to think and talk of reunion until both Churches set their respective houses in order, until the spirit of schism disappears in the East and the cancer of heteropraxis is eradicated in the West. And Latin heteropraxis, as the foregoing study has attempted to demonstrate, is not merely an internal Western problem, but affects Catholicity itself, as Rome's generally dismal record in relation to the Eastern Catholic Churches makes abundantly clear. The fact that neither of these ancient evils seems ready to relinquish its hold on Christians suggests that the lively ecumenical hopes of the 1960s were really delusions and that what is most needed today is prayer and penance, not pipe dreams and parleys.

Light from the East

Fortunately, there have recently appeared among certain outward-looking Orthodox leaders signs of appreciating the enormity of the domestic crisis in the Roman Church, even if most Catholic bishops still prefer to bury their heads in the sand. One of those alert Orthodox minds that have awoken to the danger of contamination from contact with post-conciliar Latin abuses is the present Patriarch of the Russian Church. In 2000, while still Metropolitan of Smolensk and Kaliningrad, Archbishop Kirill Gundiayev made some interesting observations in a British documentary on the Russian Orthodox Church. 'Tradition', he told his interviewer,

> has great significance, both spiritual traditions and cultural traditions. And so the question arises whether we can change traditions to satisfy the demands of various

[9] The question of reunion has now been further complicated by Benedict XVI's baffling decision on 1 March 2006 to abolish the ancient papal title of 'Patriarch of the West', first adopted by the Graeco-Palestinian pope Theodore I in 642, on the questionable grounds that this attribute of the Pope is of Eastern rather than Roman origin. Since Oriental ecclesiology considers the Catholic Church to be a union of patriarchates (rather than the union of an essential and normative Roman church connected to a group of relatively unimportant satellite patriarchates in the East), it is difficult to see how this new reform will not become an ecumenical obstacle and reinforce Latin imperialist tendencies.

groups of radically inclined people without considering the cost of such reforms. Can you or anyone else tell me that as a result of modernization (адаптация, i.e. *aggiornamento*) there has been a strengthening of Christianity in the Western world? Can you say that as a result of modernization there are more believers, that your churches are fuller, that the role of the Church has become more active, visible and necessary for people? Have more people been going to Catholic churches since Vatican II? Have more people started going to Anglican churches since they began ordaining women? Unless you can give me convincing statistics to reflect on, I shall continue to think that all these drastic reforms have done nothing to strengthen church life in Western society.[10]

A few weeks after the publication of *Summorum Pontificum* in 2007 the then Russian Orthodox Patriarch Alexei II applauded as 'a positive fact' the recent papal decree guaranteeing more freedom to celebrate the traditional Roman liturgy. 'We strongly adhere to tradition', the Patriarch commented. 'Without being faithful to her liturgy, the Russian Orthodox Church would have failed to survive persecutions in the 1920s and 1930s.' He also suggested that the Pope's decision might contribute to establishing closer links with the Orthodox churches.[11]

One month before his enthronement on 1 February 2009, while still patriarchal locum tenens, Metropolitan Kirill made it clear that he strongly opposed modernizing reforms in the Church, and stated his belief that none of the 145 other nominees for the patriarchal office had reform aspirations. Twice in the past Russia had learned

> the necessity of careful attitudes towards traditions, especially church traditions. The first lesson we learned was the ecclesial split of the Old Believers. Our second lesson was the notorious [Communist-directed modernistic] innovations of the 1920s. Both processes caused agitation and divided people, but neither of them reached the goals set by the reformers. Church reforms cannot attain their goals unless they are rooted in people's lives. Our Church is strong because of its ability to preserve both belief and a flawless moral paradigm from one generation to another. The Church is conservative by nature since it maintains the faith of the Apostles. If we wish to pass on the Faith from one generation to another for centuries, belief must remain intact. Any reform damaging belief, traditions and values is called heresy.[12]

After Benedict XVI's lifting of the 1988 excommunications the same month, Fr Alexandre Siniakov, a Paris-based Russian Orthodox priest and seminary rector engaged in ecumenical work, stated in a similar vein:

> We can only rejoice that positive steps have been taken to restore eucharistic communion between the bishops of the Fraternity of St Pius X and Pope Benedict XVI. . . . I was astonished to note an absence of solidarity among certain Catholics in relation to the Pope's decision. . . . It seems to us that the Pope does not want to stand in contrast to the pre-Vatican II tradition and he wishes to leave in peace the

[10] Derek Bailey (writer and director), *The Great Spiritual Revival of the Russian Orthodox Church*, IBP Films Distribution Ltd., 2000.
[11] 'Alexy II praises letter on 1962 missal', *Zenit*, 29 August 2007, www.zenit.org/article-20364?l=english.
[12] 29 December 2008. Reported by *Interfax* website (www.interfax-religion.com).

faithful attached to it rather than to exercise force on them. From our perspective (liturgical) reforms, even those issuing from councils, cannot be imposed on the faithful, without the clear consensus of the people of God who receive them in an integral way. This would do violence to Christ's body. The Russian Church has known a schism for liturgical reasons: after the Council of 1666–67. That was the schism of the Old Believers. The reforms were much less significant than those influenced by the Second Vatican Council. But excommunications were issued at the time and the schism endured ever since.[13]

Neo-imperialism on the Fringe

It is sadly symptomatic of a one-sided traditionalism on the part of Latin Catholics that this Russian Orthodox sympathy for the Society of St Pius X is not generally reciprocated by members of that body. While their defence of the immemorial Roman liturgy has won them deserved admiration, it is also true that most Lefebvrists retain many of the anti-Oriental attitudes inherited from pre-conciliar Latin imperialism which popes since Leo XIII have striven in vain to eradicate.

Already accustomed to welcoming to its exclusively Roman-rite chapels Lebanese Catholics who then effectively abandon their hereditary Maronite and Melkite rites,[14] the Society has gone so far as to accept members of these Eastern Churches as candidates for the Roman-rite priesthood in disregard of cultural realities and without permission from the Oriental ordinaries of these individuals. As if this were not enough, the Lefebvrist bishops recently took the highly questionable step of interfering in an internal dispute of the Ukrainian Greek Catholic Church.

In the 1990s the Fraternity began giving encouragement to a small schismatic group in Galicia which displayed many of the worst aspects of old-fashioned Uniatism. The organization in question, the Priestly Society of St Josaphat Kuncevych, was hostile to ecumenical dialogue with the Orthodox and anachronistically committed to latinized forms of the Byzantine liturgy established by the 1720 Synod of Zamość but which had been duly phased out by the Ukrainian hierarchy since the 1930s in obedience to the entire series of legitimate papal directives for delatinization since 1894. (The only positive elements of this sect's liturgical agenda appear to be the preservation of Old Slavonic as a liturgical language and the reversal of recent truncations of the rite.)[15]

The group's founder, Fr Vasyl' Kovpák, was declared excommunicate by Cardinal Ljubomyr Huzar in 2004 and an appeal lodged in Rome was rejected in 2007. In the meantime, on 22 November 2006, the Lefebvrist bishop Richard Williamson had travelled to Warsaw and illicitly ordained *in the Roman rite* two priests and seven deacons for the schism. Subsequent ordinations were also performed by Bishop Bernard Tissier de Mallerais in defiance of Eastern Catholic canon law and without consideration of the rights and institutions of the Ukrainian Greek

---

[13] 22 February 2009. Reported by the *Eucharistie Miséricordieuse* website, http://eucharistiemis-ericor.free.fr/index.php?page=2202096_orthodoxes.

[14] Admittedly diaspora Maronites have often to cope with heteropraxis in their churches, but there is no similar excuse for the Melkites, whose churches generally maintain traditional worship.

[15] See Arnaud Sélégny, SPPX, 'The Society of St Josaphat: Who? What? Where? How? Why?, *The Angelus* (March 2008), pp. 1–2. For an internal perspective, see Vasyl' Kovpak, *Peresliduvana Tradycija* [Переслідувана Традиція, 'Persecuted Tradition'] (Kiev, 2003).

Catholic Church, which can scarcely be written off as a hotbed of modernism, some disquieting modern trends and imprudent relaxations notwithstanding. That these latest attacks on the *opus Dei* should have been carried out by the very organization that has spearheaded the fight for the immemorial liturgy of the Latin Church and should have appreciated the need to respect authentic Catholic rites merely illustrates how entrenched are heteropractic attitudes among Latin Catholics, even those who see themselves as leading defenders of tradition.[16]

In Defence of the Lex Orandi

While the Latin West remains in a state of liturgical confusion because of widespread misunderstanding (even among the staunchest defenders of tradition) of the true relationship between theology and the sacred liturgy, the Eastern Orthodox Church today is distinguished by a crystalline clarity in its vision of the synergy of the *lex orandi* and the *lex credendi*. Late in 2008 Bishop Hilarion Alfeyev, Eparch of Vienna and Austria, remarked:

> Another divorce which needs to be mentioned is that between liturgy and theology. For an Orthodox theologian, liturgical texts are not simply the works of outstanding theologians and poets, but also the fruits of the prayerful experience of those who have attained sanctity and theosis. The theological authority of liturgical texts is, in my opinion, higher than that of the works of the Fathers of the Church, for not everything in the works of the latter is of equal theological value and not everything has been accepted by the fullness of the Church. Liturgical texts, on the contrary, have been accepted by the whole Church as a 'rule of faith' (*kanon pisteos*), for they have been read and sung everywhere in Orthodox churches over many centuries . . .
>
> The *lex credendi* grows out of the *lex orandi*, and dogmas are considered divinely revealed because they are born in the life of prayer and revealed to the Church through its divine services. Thus, if there are divergences in the understanding of a dogma between a certain theological authority and liturgical texts, I would be inclined to give preference to the latter. And if a textbook of dogmatic theology contains views different from those found in liturgical texts, it is the textbook, not the liturgical texts, that need correction.[17]

What prompted these observations was an event in the Roman Church already mentioned: Benedict XVI's politically motivated correction of the centuries-old oration for the Jews in the Good Friday liturgy. It augurs badly for the current leadership of the Catholic Church when a pope violates the laws of orthopraxis after publicly vindicating them and it takes a representative of the Eastern Orthodox Church to point out the ecumenically problematic inconsistency. According to Bishop Alfeyev:

---

[16] It is particularly mortifying that the Fraternity should have pursued a course of action so hurtful to the Ukrainian Catholic clergy and faithful, given that Ukrainian churches have been welcoming havens for liturgically homeless Latin traditionalists all over the world since the 1970s. *Nil homine terra pejus ingrato creat.*

[17] Lecture on 'Theological Education in the 21st Century' at Wycliffe College, University of Toronto, 22 October 2008, at: http://en.hilarion.orthodoxia.org/6_20.

Even more inadmissible, from my point of view, is the correction of liturgical texts in line with contemporary norms. Relatively recently the Roman Catholic Church decided to remove the so-called 'anti-semitic' texts from the service of Good Friday. Several members of the Orthodox Church have [also] begun to propagate the idea of revising Orthodox services in order to bring them closer to contemporary standards of political correctness . . . [on the alleged grounds that] it was Pontius Pilate and the Roman administration who are chiefly responsible for Jesus' condemnation and crucifixion.

This is just one of innumerable examples of how a distortion of the *lex credendi* inevitably leads to 'corrections' in the *lex orandi*, and vice versa.[18]

Ἰχθὺς ἐκ τῆς κεφαλῆς ὄζειν ἄρχεται

Half a century ago the spectacle of non-Catholic clergy explaining to Catholics forgotten truths of their faith would have been inconceivable. The crisis in the Catholic Church today is not a crisis of the grass roots but of the head. The clergy, not the laity, have been the motor of the revolution that has brought the Bride of Christ to her knees before the world. But Catholicism, unlike Islam, is a religion with a priesthood, and nothing will change for the better without a thorough-going reform of those who minister at its altars and lead its congregations. There is indeed no greater threat to the Church than from men who are attracted to the priesthood more by the dangerous glamour of power than by the awesome call to self-sacrifice.

In an authentic reform of the Church there would have to be a consensus that any man who is not profoundly God-fearing and distinguished by an ardent love of the immemorial liturgy of his own ancestral rite, heightened by a sincere love of humanity (*philanthropia*), simply should not be ordained to the diaconate or the priesthood, whatever his commitment to doctrinal orthodoxy or to works of

---

[18] The Bishop goes on to explain that

> [t]he main theme of all four Gospels is the conflict between Christ and the Jews, who in the end demanded the death penalty for Jesus. There was no conflict between Christ and the Roman administration, the latter being involved only because the Jews did not have the right to carry out a death penalty. It seems that all of this is so obvious that it does not need any explanation. This is exactly how the ancient Church understood the Gospel story, and this is the understanding that is reflected in liturgical texts. However, contemporary rules of 'political correctness' demand another interpretation in order to bring not only the Church's services, but also the Christian faith itself in line with modern trends.

It is noteworthy that apart from the modernist movement in the Orthodox Church to which Bishop Hilarion alludes, there has also been an antiquarianist one led by Protopresbyter Alexander Schmemann, who praised the Pauline liturgical reform and was given to remarks such as the following:

> the irony of our present situation is that while some Western Christians come to Orthodoxy in order to salvage the *rite* they cherish (Book of Common Prayer, Tridentine Mass, etc.) from liturgical reforms they abhor, some of these reforms, at least *in abstracto*, are closer to the structures and the spirit of the early Western Rite and thus to the Orthodox liturgical tradition, than the later rites – those precisely that the Orthodox Church is supposed to 'sanction' and to 'adopt'. ('Some Reflexions upon a Case Study', *St. Vladimir's Theological Quarterly*, Vol. 24, No. 4 [1980], p. 269)

Schmemann's claim that the *Novus Ordo Missæ*, compared with the Mass of Pius V, is closer in structure and spirit to the Byzantine liturgy is quite remarkable.

charity and no matter how impressive his moral integrity, intellectual capacity, administrative ability or charisma. Love of the traditional liturgy cannot, however, be the sole prerequisite for the priestly life and, conversely, those whose attraction to the *opus Dei* is primarily aesthetic or cultural and who are relatively indifferent to the doctrinal and apostolic mission of the Church, or have vicious inclinations would need to be disabused of any illusions of a sacerdotal calling.

Moreover, if the Church is to recover her true self, men preparing to receive Holy Orders will need constantly to reflect on the significance of the liturgical custom of laying out a priest's corpse with his head pointing to the altar rather than with his feet in that direction as at the funeral of a layman. For on the last day, each priest will stand *versus populum* to face those he was commissioned humbly to serve on earth, who will testify to his deeds, after which he shall turn around, *versus ad Orientem*, to hear the Sun of Righteousness render His final judgement. And priests with episcopal ambitions will need to reflect deeply and often on the saying, attributed variously to St Athanasius, St Jerome and St John Chrysostom, that 'the floor of hell is paved with the skulls of bishops'.

Ex Malo Bonum

Four decades ago the same Council that empowered the well-meaning vandals of the liturgy also solemnly committed all Catholics to the pursuit of the Christian unity for which Our Lord prayed at the first Eucharist. It may be true that traditional Latin Catholics have to date been hostile to ecumenism of any kind owing to their general diffidence towards the *aggiornamento* policies of Paul VI and his successors. Yet neither the vagaries and distortions of certain theologians, nor the fact that post-conciliar ecumenism has been weighted in favour of the utopian and futile attempt to achieve reunion with Protestants, should blind traditionalists to the justness and merits of the call to heal the scandalous divisions separating Catholics from those closest to them in faith and praxis. Hence, far from being a petty domestic dispute within the modern Western Church, present-day traditionalist dissidence reveals its providential role in the history of Catholicism, since it has brought into clearer relief the real cause of the centuries-old division between the Eastern Churches and Rome, a conflict arising from culture rather than from faith.

From a human perspective the complete recovery of orthodoxy and orthopraxis in Catholic life may seem at present an impossible dream, yet Christ's promise that the gates of hell will not prevail against His Church gives faithful Catholics every reason for hope. For when Peter, incumbent of the First See, finally repents of the faults of Simon that led to our present chastisement, the worst wound ever inflicted on the Mystical Body shall at last begin to heal. Only when this comes to pass can Catholics begin to hope that estranged Eastern Christians, whose unswerving fidelity to the *opus Dei* has been a beacon of light to the darkening West, will rise to the challenge of forgiveness and find the courage to unfold the fullness of the faith they jealously guard. From such an embrace of reconciliation – the fruit of a war-weary Christendom's resolve to fulfil the prayer of the Good Shepherd – will dawn the day of light and grace when the venerable Churches of the East will become wholly catholic again, united to a renewed Roman Church that is authentically orthodox.

BIBLIOGRAPHY

A. Documents and Reference Works

Abbott, Walter M., SJ, ed., *The Documents of Vatican II*. New York/Cleveland: Chapman, 1966.

Adam, Antoine, ed., *Blaise Pascal: lettres écrites à un provincial*. Paris: Flammarion, 1981.

Aquinas, Thomas. *S. Thomæ Aquinatis O.P. doctoris angelici et omnium scholarum catholicarum patronis Summa Theologica accuratissime emendata ac annotationibus illustrata a quibusdam scholæ S. Thomæ discipulis (= ST)*. Paris: Lethielleux, 1887. Five vols.

Attwater, Donald, ed., *The Catholic Encyclopaedic Dictionary*. London: Cassell, 1931.

Biffi, Inos, ed., *Messale ambrosiano festivo*. Milan: Marietti, 1976.

Cabrera Delgado y Silveira, Antonio. *Ordo missæ pontificalis ritu hispano mozarabico peragendæ: Esquema general, rúbricas, notas e introducciones*. Toledo: private edition, 1975.

Catechism of the Catholic Church. Vatican City: Libreria Editrice Vaticana, 1994.

Catholic Encyclopedia (= CE). New York: Universal Knowledge Foundation, 1907–1914. Fifteen vols.

Catholic Encyclopedia for School and Home (= CESH). New York: McGraw-Hill, 1965. Twelve vols.

Catholic One Year Bible: Arranged in 365 Daily Readings. Wheaton, Illinois: Tyndale House, 1978.

Celebration of the Eucharist according to the Syro-Malabar Rite. Bangalore: National Biblical Catechestical and Liturgical Centre, 1973.

Christian Worship: Encyclical Letter (Mediator Dei) of His Holiness Pius XII by Divine Providence Pope to his Venerable Brethren the Patriarchs, Primates, Archbishops, Bishops and other Ordinaries at Peace and in Communion with the Apostolic See on the Sacred Liturgy. London: Catholic Truth Society, 1947; repr. 1967.

Davies, J. G., ed., *A Dictionary of Liturgy & Worship*. London: SCM Press, 1972.

Denzinger, Heinrich Joseph. *Enchiridion Symbolorum et Definitionum, quæ de rebus fidei et morum a Conciliis Œcumenicis et Summis Pontificibus emanerunt*. Würzburg, 1865; 10th edn, Clemens Bannwart, SJ, 1910; 32nd edn, Adolf Schönmetzer, ed., Freiburg im Breisgau: Herder, 1963.

Dictionnaire d'histoire et de géographie ecclésiastiques (= DHGE). Paris: Letouzey et Ané, 1912–.

Dictionnaire de théologie catholique: contenant l'exposé de la théologie catholique (= DTC). Paris: Letouzey et Ané, 1903–1950.

Eicher, Peter, ed., *Dictionnaire de théologie*. Paris: Éditions du Cerf, 1988.

Feyerabend, Karl. *Hebrew Dictionary to the Old Testament*. Berlin: Langenscheidt, n.d.

Flannery, Austin. *Vatican Council II: The Conciliar and Post-Conciliar Documents*. Dublin: Dominican Publications, 1987.

General Instruction on the Roman Missal (Principles and Rubrics). Tr. Clifford Howell, SJ. London: Catholic Truth Society, 1973.

Hardon, John A., S.J. *Modern Catholic Dictionary*. New York: Doubleday, 1980.

Hickey, J. S., O.Cist. *Summula Philosophiæ Scholasticæ in Usum Adolescentium*. Dublin: M. G. Gill, 1919; repr. 1923.

Ihm, Claudia Carlen, ed., *The Papal Encyclicals 1740–1981*. Five vols. Beloit, Kansas: McGrath Publishing, 1981.

Lewis, Charlton T. and Short, Charles. *A Latin Dictionary founded on Andrews' Edition of Freund's Latin Dictionary*. Oxford: Clarendon Press, 1969.

Luther, Martin. *Table Talk [Dris Martini Lutheri colloquia mensalia, 1569]*. Tr. William Hazlitt. Philadelphia: Lutheran Publication Society, 1873.

McHugh, John A., OP, and Callan, Charles, OP, tr., *Catechism of the Council of Trent for Parish Priests, Issued by Order of Pope Pius V*. New York, 1923; repr. Rizal: Sinag-Tala, 1974.

Mansi, Giovan Domenico. *Sacrorum Conciliorum nova et amplissima collectio*. Thirty-one vols. Florence/Venice: 1758–1798; Graz: Akademische Druck- und Verlagsanstalt, 1960–1961.

Migne, Jacques-Paul. *Patrologia Latina*. Paris: Garnier, 1844–1855.

Misa en rito hispano-mozárabe: ordinario de la misa. Toledo: Instituto de Estudios Visigótico-Mozárabes, 1993.

New Catholic Encyclopedia (= NCE). New York: McGraw-Hill, 1967. Twelve vols.

Payne Smith, J., ed., *A Compendious Syriac Dictionary founded upon the Thesaurus Syriacus of R. Payne Smith, D.D.* Oxford, 1903; repr. Winona Lake, Indiana: Eisenbrauns, 1998.

Rahner, Karl and Vorgrimler, Herbert. *Kleines theologisches Wörterbuch*. Freiburg: Herder, 1965; *Concise Theological Dictionary*, tr. Richard Strachan. London: Burns & Oates, 1966.

Quasten, Johannes. *Patrology*. Four vols. Utrecht/Antwerp: Spectrum, 1950; repr. 1963.

Salaverri, Joaquín, SJ. *Sacræ Theologiæ Summa*. 2nd edn. Madrid: Biblioteca de Autores Cristianos, 1952.

Simpson, D. P., ed., *Cassell's New Latin Dictionary*. New York: Funk & Wagnalls, 1959.

Soter, Michael. *The Divine Liturgy according to St John Chrysostom in Albanian and English, Parallel Texts*. Boston: Albanian Orthodox Church in America, 1988.

The Teachings of Pope Paul VI, 1969. Vatican City: Libreria Editrice Vaticana, London: Geoffrey Chapman, 1970.

Tonneau, Raymond and Devreese, Robert. *Les homélies catéchétiques de Théodore de Mopsueste*. Rome: Biblioteca Apostolica Vaticana, 1949.

Wehr, Hans. *A Dictionary of Modern Written Arabic*. 3rd edn. Ithaca, New York: Spoken Language Services, 1976.

B. *Liturgiological, Theological, Historical and Polemical*

Acton, Lord (John). *Lectures on Modern History*. London, 1905; repr. with an introduction by Hugh Trevor-Roper. London/Glasgow: Collins-Fontana, 1960.

Adam, Adolf. *Die Messe in neuer Gestalt*. Würzburg: Seeborge-Verlag Echter, 1974.

——*Das Kirchenjahr mitfeiern: Seine Geschichte und seine Bedeutung nach der Liturgieerneuerung*. Freiburg im Breisgau: Verlag Herder, 1979. Tr. Matthew J. O'Connell. *The Liturgical Year: Its History and its Meaning after the Reform of the Liturgy*. New York: Pueblo, 1981.

Adam, Antoine, ed., *Blaise Pascal: lettres écrites à un provincial*. Paris: Flammarion, 1981.

Adam, Karl. *Das Wesen des Katholizismus*. Düsseldorf: Schwann. Tr. Justin McCann, 1933; repr. *The Spirit of Catholicism*. Steubenville: Franciscan University Press, 1996.

Amerio, Romano. *Iota unum: studio delle variazioni della Chiesa cattolica nel secolo XX*. Milan/Naples: Riccardo Ricciardi, 1989.

Attwater, Donald. *Christian Churches of the East*. Milwaukee: Bruce Publishing, 1961–1962. Two vols.

Aubert, Roger. *Le pontificat de Pie IX*. Paris: Bloud & Gay, 1952.

——'Guidi (Filippo Maria)'. *DHGE*, XXII, cols 791–92.

Bainton, Roland H. *Here I Stand: A Life of Martin Luther*. New York: New American Library, 1950.

Baldwin, Monica. *I Leap over the Wall*. London: Hamish Hamilton, 1951.

Bartoszek, Donald. 'Polish National Catholic Church'. *CESH*, VIII, pp. 532–53.

Batiffol, Pierre. *L'Église naissante et le catholicisme*. Paris: Gabalda, 1927.

Beckman, Peter, OSB. 'Gibbons, James'. *CESH*, IV, pp. 579–81.

Beeson, Trevor. *Discretion & Valour: Religious Conditions in Russia and Eastern Europe*. London: Collins, 1974, 1982.

Benoît, Paul, OSB. *La vie des clercs dans les siècles passés: études sur la vie commune et les autres institutions de la perfection au sein du clergé depuis Jésus-Christ jusqu'à nos jours*. Paris: P. Féron-Vrau, 1915.

Billington, James H. *The Icon and the Axe: An Interpretative History of Russian Culture*. New York: Vintage, 1976.

Boehmer, Heinrich. *Les Jésuites*. Paris: Armand Colin, 1910.

Bolton, Charles A. *Church Reform in 18th Century Italy (The Synod of Pistoia, 1786)*. The Hague: Martinus Nijhoff, 1969.

Bonneterre, Didier. *Le movement liturgique de Dom Guéranger à Annibal Bugnini ou le cheval de Troie dans la cité de Dieu*. Escurolles: Fideliter, 1980.

Botte, Bernard, OSB. *From Silence to Participation*. Tr. John Sullivan. Washington, DC: Pastoral Press, 1988.

Bourgeois, C., SJ. 'Chez les paysans de la Podlachie et du nord de la Pologne: mai 1924–décembre 1925'. *Études (Revue bimensuelle publiée par des Pères de la Compagnie de Jésus)*, 191 (1927), pp. 580–88.

Bourke, D. Francis, CM. *St Justin De Jacobis, Hero of Ethiopia*. Rockhampton: Record Printing, 1975.

Bouyer, Louis. *Life and Liturgy*. London: Sheed & Ward, 1956.

Bride, André. 'Rite'. *DTC*, XIII (1937), cols 2738–44.

Bugnini, Annibale. *The Reform of the Liturgy 1948–1975*. Tr. Matthew J. O'Connell. Collegeville, Minnesota: Liturgical Press, 1990.

Capponi, Neri. 'Alcune considerazioni giuridiche in materia di riforma liturgica'. *Archivio Giuridico*, CXC, fasc. 2 (1976), pp. 147–73; Engl. tr. *Some Juridical Considerations on the Reform of the Liturgy*. Una Voce Scotland, 1979.

——"La nevrosi dell'Occidente". Unpublished article. Florence, 1991.

Čekada, Anthony. *The Problems with the Prayers of the Modern Mass*. Rockford, Illinois: Tan Books, 1991.

——*The Ottaviani Intervention: Short Critical Study of the New Order of Mass by Alfredo Cardinal Ottaviani – Antonio Cardinal Bacci – A Group of Roman Theologians*. Rockford, Illinois: Tan Books, 1992.

Chadwick, Henry. *The Early Church*. Harmondsworth: Penguin, 1967.

Chadwick, Owen. *The Reformation*. Harmondsworth: Penguin, 1964.

Chatbèrt, Ramon, ed., *Letras de Joan Bodon a Enric Mouly*. Naucelle: Societat dels Amics de Joan Bodon, 1986.

Chediath, Geevarghese and Vellilamthadam, Thomas, eds, *Ecumenism in Danger*. Kottayam: Denha Services, 1986.

Ciszek, Walter J., SJ, with Daniel L. Flaherty, SJ. *With God in Russia*. New York: Image, 1966.

Coffey, David. 'The Church as Community'. In *Gospel in Word and Action (Faith and Culture No. 17)*. Catholic Institute of Sydney, 1990, pp. 44–55.

Congar, Yves. 'La pensée de Möhler et l'ecclésiologie orthodoxe', *Irenikon*, 12 (1935), pp. 321–29.

——*Lay People in the Church*, tr. D. Attwater. Paramus: Newman, 1956.

——*La Tradition et les traditions*. Paris: Fayard, 1960–1963. Two vols.

——*La tradition et la vie de l'Église*. Paris: Fayard, 1963. English tr. *Tradition and the Life of the Church*. London: Burns & Oates, 1964.

——*Challenge to the Church: The Case of Archbishop Lefebvre*. London: Collins, 1977.

Conway, Fr Bertrand. *The Question Box*. New York: Paulist Press, 1929.

Corrie, George Elwes, ed., *Sermons by Hugh Latimer, Sometime Bishop of Worcester, Martyr, 1555*. Cambridge, UK: Cambridge University Press, 1844; rpt. Whitefish, Montana: Kessinger Publishing, 2007.

Cozens, Mary Louise. *A Handbook of Heresies*. London/New York: Sheed & Ward, 1928.

Crichton, James D. *Liturgical Changes: The Background*. London: Catholic Truth Society, 1975.

Cross, Lawrence. *Eastern Christianity: The Byzantine Tradition*. Sydney: E. J. Dwyer, 1988.

——'Some Essential Features of Orthodox Catholic Christianity'. In *Ukrainian Settlement in Australia*. Sydney: School of Modern Languages, Macquarie University, 1989, pp. 94–104.

Crouan, Denis. *La liturgie confisquée: lettre ouverte aux évêques et tous ceux qui trahissent la liturgie conciliaire* (Paris: Pierre Téqui, 1997); Tr. Mark Sebanc. *The Liturgy Betrayed*. San Francisco: Ignatius Press, 2000.Curran, Francis X. 'Catholic Church in the United States, Part 3'. *CESH*, II. pp. 372–81.

Daniel-Rops, Henri. *A Fight for God 1870–1939*. (Vol. 9 of *History of the Church of Christ*). Tr. John Warrington. London: J. M. Dent & Sons/New York: E. P. Dutton, 1966.

Dansette, Adrien. *Religious History of Modern France*. Two vols. Freiburg: Herder, Edinburgh/London: Nelson, 1961.

Davies, Michael. *Cranmer's Godly Order: The Destruction of Catholicism through Liturgical Change*. Chawleigh, Devon: Augustine Publishing Company, 1976; 2nd ed. Fort Collins, CO: Roman Catholic Books, 1995.

——*Pope John's Council: Part Two of Liturgical Revolution*. Chawleigh, Devon: Augustine Publishing Company, 1977.

——*The New Mass*. Chawleigh, Devon: Augustine Publishing Company, 1977.

——*The Tridentine Mass*. Chawleigh, Devon: Augustine Publishing Company, 1977.

——*The Roman Rite Destroyed*. Chawleigh, Devon: Augustine Publishing Company, 1978.

——*Apologia pro Marcel Lefebvre*. Dickinson, Texas: Angelus Press, 1979, 1983, 1988. Three vols.

——*The Order of Melchisedech: A Defence of the Catholic Priesthood*. Harrison, New York: Roman Catholic Books, 1979, 1993.

——*Pope Paul's New Mass: Part Three of Liturgical Revolution* (= *PPNM*). Dickinson, Texas: Angelus Press, 1980.

——*The Tridentine Mass: The Mass That Will Not Die*. St Paul, Minnesota: Remnant, 1990.

——*The Second Vatican Council and Religious Liberty*. Long Prairie, Minnesota: Neumann Press, 1992.

——*On Communion in the Hand and Similar Frauds*. St Paul, Minnesota: The Remnant Press, n.d.

Davies, Michael and Capponi, Neri. 'The Legal Status of the Tridentine Mass'. *The Latin Mass*, Vol. 3, No. 3 (May/June 1994), pp. 30–33.

Davis, R[alph] H. C. *A History of Medieval Europe from Constantine to Saint Louis*. London: Longman, 1957; repr. 1970.

Day, Thomas. *Why Catholics Can't Sing: The Culture of Catholicism and the Triumph of Bad Taste*. New York: Crossroad, 1990.

De Clerck, Paul. '"Lex orandi, lex credendi": sens originel et avatars historiques d'un adage équivoque'. *Questions liturgiques*, 59 (1978), pp. 193–212.

De Fréine, Seán. *The Great Silence: The Study of a Relationship between Language and Nationality*. Dublin/Cork: Mercer, 1965.

Delhaye, Philippe. 'Celibacy, History of'. *NCE*, III, pp. 369–74.

Denis, Henri. *Des sacrements et des hommes dix ans après Vatican II*. Lyons: Chalet, 1975.

Dolan, Daniel L. 'John is its Name . . . Pre-Conciliar Liturgical Change'. *Roman Catholic* (June 1983), pp. 4–10.

Dolan, Jay P. *The American Catholic Experience: A History from Colonial Times to the Present*. New York: Doubleday, 1985.

Dörmann, Johannes. *Pope John Paul II's Theological Journey to the Prayer Meeting of Religions in Assisi*. Four vols. Kansas City: Angelus Press, 1994–1998.

Douglas, Mary. 'The Contempt of Ritual'. *Blackfriars*, Part 1/49 (June 1968), pp. 475–82; Part 2/49 (July 1968), pp. 528–35.

Duchesne, Louis. *The Churches Separated from Rome*. London: Kegan Paul, Trench, Trübner, 1907.

Duffy, Eamon. *The Stripping of the Altars: Traditional Religion in England c. 1400–c. 1580*. New Haven/London: Yale University Press, 1992.

——*Fires of Faith: Catholic England under Mary Tudor*. New Haven/London: Yale University Press, 2009.

Dulac, Raymond. *La Bulle Quo primum tempore*. Paris: Itinéraires, 1972.

Dulles, Avery, SJ. *Models of the Church*. New York: Image/Doubleday, 1974.

——*The Reshaping of Catholicism: Current Challenges in the Theology of Church*. San Francisco: Harper & Row, 1988.

——'The Filioque: What is at Stake?' *Concordia Theological Quarterly* (January/April 1995), pp. 31–47.

Dures, Alan. *English Catholicism 1558–1642: Continuity and Change*. Harlow, Essex: Longman, 1983.

Durkheim, Émile. *Le suicide*. 1897, repr. Paris: Presses Universitaires de France, 1960.

Dvornik, Francis. 'Byzantium and the Roman Primacy', *The American Catholic Review*, 1961, pp. 289–312.

——*Byzantine Missions among the Slavs: SS. Constantine-Cyril and Methodius*. New Brunswick/New Jersey: Rutgers University Press, 1970.

——'Eastern Schism', *NCE*, V, pp. 21–25.

Dwyer, John C. *Church History: Twenty Centuries of Catholic Christianity*. New York: Paulist Press, 1985.

El-Hayek, Elias. 'Maronite Rite'. *NCE*, IX, pp. 245–53.

Ellard, Gerard, SJ. *The Mass of the Future*. Milwaukee: Bruce Publishing, 1948.

——*The Mass in Transition*. Milwaukee: Bruce Publishing, 1956.

Eppstein, John. *Has the Catholic Church Gone Mad?* London: Tom Stacey, 1971.

Erickson, Carolly. *Bloody Mary*. New York: St Martin's Griffin, 1978.

Fanning, William H. W. 'Baptism'. *CE*, III, pp. 258–74.

Fattorini, Emma. *Pio XI, Hitler e Mussolini: la solitudine di un papa*. Milan: Einaudi, 2007.

Fears, J. Rufus, ed., *Selected Writings of Lord Acton*. Three vols. Indianapolis: Liberty Classics, 1988.

Ferrara, Christopher A. and Woods, Thomas E. *The Great Façade: Vatican II and the Regime of Novelty in the Roman Catholic Church*. St Paul, Minnesota: Remnant, 2002.

Festugière, Maurice, OSB. 'La liturgie catholique: essai de synthèse'. *Revue de Philosophie*, I (1913), pp. 692–886.

Fichtner, Joseph, OSC. 'Tradition (Theological)'. *NCE*, XIV, pp. 225–28.

Finn, Edward E., SJ. *These are My Rites: A Brief History of the Eastern Rites of Christianity*. Collegeville, Minnesota: Liturgical Press, 1980.

Florovsky, Georges. 'The Elements of Liturgy'. In Constantin G. Patelos, ed., *The Orthodox Church in the Ecumenical Movement: Documents and Statements 1902–1975*. Geneva: World Council of Churches, 1978, pp. 172–82.

Fogarty, Gerald P., SJ. *The Vatican and the Americanist Crisis: Denis J. O'Connell, American Agent in Rome, 1885–1903*. Rome: Università Editrice, 1974.

Foley, Albert, SJ. 'Slavery'. *CESH*, X, pp. 149–53.

Fonck, A. 'Möhler et l'école catholique de Tubingue'. *Revue des sciences religieuses*, VI (1926), pp. 250–66.

——'Möhler, Jean-Adam'. *DTC*, X–2 (1928), cols. 2063–4.

Fortescue, Adrian. *The Mass: A Study of the Roman Liturgy*. London: Longmans, Green, 1912.

——*The Lesser Eastern Churches*. London: Catholic Truth Society, 1913.

——*Uniate Eastern Churches: The Byzantine Rite in Italy, Sicily, Syria and Egypt*. London: Burns, Oates & Washbourne, 1923.

Gamber, Klaus. *La réforme liturgique en question*. Le Barroux: Éditions Sainte-Madeleine, 1992.

——*The Reform of the Roman Liturgy: Its Problems and Background*. San Juan Capistrano, California: Una Voce, 1993.

Geanakoplos, Deno John. *Byzantine East and Latin West: Two Worlds of Christendom in Middle Ages and Renaissance*. New York: Harper & Row, 1966.

Gelineau, Joseph, SJ. *Demain la liturgie: essai sur l'évolution des assemblées chrétiennes*. Paris: Éditions du Cerf, 1976.

Gianpietro, Nicola, OFM.Cap. *Il Card. Ferdinando Antonelli e gli sviluppi della riforma liturgica dal 1948 al 1970*. Rome: Studia Anselmiana, 1998.

Gilmartin, Thomas P. 'Good Friday'. *CE*, VI, pp. 643–45.

Gough, Austin. *Paris and Rome: The Gallican Church and the Ultramontane Campaign 1848–1853*. Oxford: Clarendon Press, 1986.

Granfield, Patrick. 'The Possibility of Limitation'. In Gerard Mannion, Richard Gaillardetz, Jan Kerkhofs and Kenneth Wilson, eds, *Readings in Church Authority: Gifts and Challenges for Contemporary Catholicism*. Aldershot: Ashgate, 2003.

Gregor, Douglas B. *Celtic: A Comparative Study*. Cambridge/New York: Oleander Press, 1980.

Guéranger, Prosper, OSB. *Institutions liturgiques*. Three vols. Le Mans: Fleuriot/Paris: Débécourt, 1840–1851.

Guibert, Joseph de, SJ. *The Jesuits – Their Spiritual Doctrine and Practice: A Historical Study*. St Louis: Institute of Jesuit Sources, 1972.

Hales, E. E. Y. *Pio Nono: A Study in European Politics and Religion in the Nineteenth Century*. London: Eyre & Spottiswoode, 1956.

Hamilton, Nigel. *J.F.K.: Reckless Youth*. London: Arrow, 1992.

Hardon, John A., SJ. 'Mixed Marriages: A Theological Analysis'. *Église et Théologie*, I (1970), pp. 229–60.

Hebblethwaite, Peter. *John XXIII: Pope of the Council*. London: Geoffrey Chapman, 1984.

Heer, Friedrich. *The Medieval World: Europe 1100–1350*. (*Mittelalter*, 1961.) Tr. Janet Sondheimer. New York/Scarborough: New American Library, 1961.

Hemming, Laurence Paul. *Worship as a Revelation: The Past, Present and Future of Catholic Liturgy*. London/New York: Burns & Oates, 2008.

Hinka, John-Paul. *Religion and Nationality in Western Ukraine: The Greek Catholic Church and the Ruthenian National Movement in Galicia, 1867–1900*. Montreal: McGill-Queens University Press, 1999.

Holden, Vincent, CSP. 'Americanism'. *CESH*, I, pp. 218–20.

Hughes, Philip. *A Popular History of the Catholic Church*. London: Burns & Oates, 1939.

——*A History of the Church*. III. London: Sheed & Ward, 1947.

Hull, Geoffrey. 'The Vernacular Fraud'. *Catholic* (Yarra Junction, Vic.), Vol. 2, No. 6 (June 1983), pp. 1, 9–10.

——'The Proto-History of the Roman Liturgical Reform'. *Christian Order*, Vol. 32, No. 11 (November 1991), pp. 548–68.

——'Reflections on "Ascension Sunday" 1992'. *AD 2000* (August 1992), pp. 6–7.

——'Liturgical Revolution and Counter-Revolution in Kerala'. *Ecclesia Dei News* (Canberra). No. 6 (Winter 1992), pp. 4–12.

——*The Malta Language Question: A Case Study in Cultural Imperialism*. Valletta: Said International, 1993.

——'Anglican "Uniates" in the Traditional Catholic Revival'. *Ecclesia Dei Newsletter* (Canberra), Vol. 1, No. 11 (1994), pp. 8–9.

——'Sacred and Vernacular Languages in Catholic Worship'. In Mark Garner, ed., *Tongues of Angels and Men*. Melbourne: River Seine Publications, 1994, pp. 46–51.

Hutchings, Arthur. *Mozart: The Man*. London: Thames & Hudson, 1976.

Iwanusiw, Oleh Wolodymyr. *Church in Ruins: The Demise of Ukrainian Churches in the Eparchy of Peremyshl*. Shevchenko Scientific Society Ukrainian Studies, Vol. 56. St Catharine's: Religious Association of Ukrainian Catholics of Canada, 1987.

Jorgenson, James. 'Father Alexis Toth and the Transition of the Greek Catholic Community in Minneapolis to the Russian Orthodox Church'. *St Vladimir's Theological Quarterly*, 32 (1988), pp. 119–37.

Judin, Aleksej and Protopopov, Grigorij. *Cattolici in Russia e Ucraina*. Rome: La Casa di Matriona, 1992.

Jungmann, Joseph A., SJ. *The Mass of the Roman Rite: Its Origins and Development* (*Missarum Sollemnia*). Two vols. Tr. Francis A. Brunner, CSSR. 1950; repr. Westminster, Maryland: Christian Classics, 1986.

Kaftandjian, Joseph. 'Armenian Rite'. *NCE*, I, pp. 834–37.

Kavanagh, Aidan. *On Liturgical Theology: The Hale Memorial Lectures of Seabury-Western Theological Seminary 1981*. New York: Pueblo, 1984.

Kenny, J. P., SJ. *Roman Catholicism, Christianity and Anonymous Christianity – The Role of the Christian Today* (*Theology Today* No. 44). Hales Corners, Wisconsin: Clergy Book Service, 1973.

Khouri-Sarkis, Gabriel. 'Syrian Rite'. *NCE*, XIII, pp. 899–905.

Kilmartin, Edward, SJ. *Christian Liturgy: Theology and Practice*. Two vols. Kansas City: Sheed & Ward, 1988.

King, Archdale A. *Liturgies of the Primatial Sees*. London: Longmans, Green, 1957.

Knowles, David and Obolensky, Dimitri. *The Middle Ages* (*The Christian Centuries* Vol. 2). London: Darton, Longman & Todd, 1969.

Kocik, Thomas M. *The Reform of the Reform? A Liturgical Debate: Reform or Return*. San Francisco: Ignatius Press, 2003.

Korolevsky, Cyril. *Living Languages in Catholic Worship: An Historical Inquiry*. Tr. Donald Attwater. London: Longmans, Green & Co, 1957.

Kostka, Thomas, FSCH. 'Satolli, Francesco'. *CESH*, IX, pp. 632–33.

Krailsheimer, Alban J., ed., *Pascal: Pensées*. Harmondsworth: Penguin, 1966.

Laisney, François. *Archbishop Lefebvre and the Vatican 1987–1988*. Dickinson, Texas: Angelus Press, 1989.

Le Roux, Abbé Daniel, *Pierre, m'aimes-tu?* Escurolles: Éditions Fideliter, 1988; English tr. *Peter, Lovest Thou Me?* Yarra Junction, Vic.: Instauratio Press, 1989.

Le Roy Ladurie, Emmanuel. *Le territoire de l'historien*. Paris: Gallimard, 1973.

Lefebvre, Marcel. *Un évêque parle: écrits et allocutions 1963–1973*. Jarzé: D. Morin, 1974.

——*La messe de toujours: le trésor caché*. Étampes: Éditions Clovis, 2005.

Lehmann, Karl. 'Gottesdienst als Ausdruck des Glaubens: Plaidoyer für ein neues Gespräch zwischen Liturgiewissenschaft und dogmatischer Theologie'. *Liturgisches Jahrbuch*, 30 (1980), pp. 197–214.

Liesel, Nicholas. *The Eastern Catholic Liturgies: A Study in Words and Pictures*. London/ Glasgow: Sands, 1960.

Likoudis, James and Whitehead, Kenneth D. *The Pope, the Council and the Mass: Answers to the Questions the 'Traditionalists' are Asking*. W. Hanover, Massachusetts: Christopher, 1981.

Loret, Pierre, CSSR. *The Story of the Mass: From the Last Supper to the Present Day*. Missouri: Liguori Publications, 1982.

Lurie, Solomon. *Антисемитизм в древнем мире* [*Anti-Semitism in the Ancient World*]. Petrograd: Byloe, 1922.

McAvoy, Thomas Timothy. *The Great Crisis in American Catholic History: 1895–1900*. Chicago: Henry Regnery, 1957.

——*The Americanist Heresy in Roman Catholicism, 1895–1900*. Indiana: Notre Dame, 1963.

Madey, Johannes. 'On the Reform of the Chaldeo-Malabar Liturgy: The Holy See of Rome in Defence of the Oriental Patrimony'. *Ostkirchliche Studien*, 33 (September 1984), pp. 172–99.

Magocsi, Paul Robert, ed., *Morality and Reality: The Life and Times of Andrei Sheptytski*. Edmonton: Institute of Ukrainian Studies, 1989.

Mahoney, Leonard. 'St Nicholas I'. *CESH*, VII, pp. 626–27.

Malinski, Mieczysław. *Mon ami Karol Wojtyła*. Paris: Centurion, 1980.

Maloney, George A., SJ. 'Eastern Theology, History of'. *CESH*, III, pp. 637–43.

——'Malankar Rite, Liturgy of'. *NCE*, IX, p. 106.

Marbach, Joseph F. 'Eastern Catholics, United States'. *CESH*, III, pp. 625–30.

Martimort, Aimé-Georges. 'Mais qu'est-ce que la messe de S. Pie V?' *La Croix*, 26 August 1976.

Martin, Malachi. *The Jesuits: The Society of Jesus and the Betrayal of the Roman Catholic Church*. New York: Linden Press, 1987.

Martin, Marie-Madeleine. *Le latin immortel*. Chiré-en-Montreuil: Diffusion de la Pensée Française, 1971.

Mattam, Abraham. 'Missionary Consciousness of the Thomas Christians'. In Thomas Vellilamthadam *et al.*, eds, *Ecclesial Identity of the Thomas Christians*. Kottayam: Oriental Institute Publications, 1985, pp. 105–22.

Matthews, Edward. *A Popular Guide to the New Mass*. Southend-on-Sea/Melbourne: Sacred Heart Publications, 1970.

Mazza, Enrico. *Le odierne preghiere eucaristiche*. Bologna: Edizioni Dehoniane, 1984. Tr. *The Eucharistic Prayers of the Roman Rite*. Collegeville, Minnesota: Liturgical Press, 1986.

Melville, Annabelle. 'Carroll, John'. *CESH*, II, pp. 299–302.

Meyendorff, John, Schmemann, Alexander, Afanassieff, Nicholas and Koulomzine, Nicholas. *The Primacy of Peter in the Orthodox Church*. Leighton Buzzard: Faith Press, 1963. 2nd edn 1973.

Mitchell, Peter. *The Jesuits: A History*. London: Macdonald, 1980.

Möhler, Johann Adam, tr. J. B. Robertson. *Symbolism or Exposition of the Doctrinal Differences between Catholics and Protestants as Evidenced by their Symbolic Writings*. 2nd edn. Two vols. London: Catholic Publishing & Bookselling Company, 1834.

Mohrmann, Christine. *Liturgical Latin: Its Origin and Character*. Washington, DC: Catholic University of America Press, 1957.

Mosebach, Martin. *The Heresy of Formlessness: The Roman Liturgy and its Enemy*. San Francisco: Ignatius Press, 2006.

Murphy, Arthur. 'Dictatus Papæ'. *CESH*, III, pp. 496–97.

Murphy, Paul I. with Arlington, R. Rene. *La Popessa*. New York: Warner Books, 1983.

Murtagh, J., SMA. *Churches of the Greek Rite*. Dublin: Catholic Truth Society of Ireland, 1964.

——*The Maronite Church*. Dublin: Catholic Truth Society of Ireland, 1965.

Navatel, Jean-Joseph, SJ. 'L'Apostolat liturgique et la pieté personnelle'. *Études*, 137 (1913), pp. 449–78.

Nemec, Ludvik. 'Michael Cerularius'. *CESH*, VII, pp. 135–39.

Nichols, Aidan, OP. *Rome and the Eastern Churches: A Study in Schism*. Edinburgh: T&T Clark, 1992.

Nienaltowski, Henry Raphael, OFM.Cap. *Johann Adam Möhler's Theory of Doctrinal Development: Its Genesis and Formulation*. Washington, DC: Catholic University of America Press, 1959.

——'Möhler, Johann Adam'. *NCE*, IX, pp. 1004–05.

Normandin, Yves. *Pastor out in the Cold*. Quebec: St Raphael's Publications, 1978.

O'Brien, David J. *Isaac Hecker: An American Catholic*. New York: Paulist Press, 1992.

O'Connor, Desmond, SJ. *What's Wrong with the Catholic Church Today?* Melbourne: Australian Catholic Truth Society Publications, 1975.

O'Rourke, Kevin, OP. 'Cardinals, Sacred College of'. *CESH*, II, pp. 274–77.

Örsy, Ladislas. 'Conciliarism (Theological Aspect)'. *NCE*, IV, pp. 111–13.

Oury, Guy, OSB. *La messe de St Pie V à Paul VI*. Solesmes: Abbaye Saint-Pierre, 1975.

Paci, Stefano. 'The Middle Ages Today'. *30 Days*, 6 (1994), pp. 28–34.

Panicker, Geevarghese. 'An Analysis of the Present Ecclesial Situation in India'. In Thomas Vellilamthadam *et al.*, eds, *Ecclesial Identity of the Thomas Christians*. Kottayam: Oriental Institute Publications, 1985, pp. 145–75.

Parecattil, Joseph. *Syro-Malabar Liturgy as I See It*. Ernakulam: n.p., 1987.

Paris, Edmond. *Genocide in Satellite Croatia: A Record of Racial and Religious Persecutions and Massacres*. Tr. Lois Perkins. Chicago: American Institute for Balkan Affairs, 1961.

Parsch, Pius. *Le renouveau liturgique au service de la paroisse: sens et portée de la liturgie populaire*. Mulhouse: Salvator/Casterman, 1950.

Parsons, John. 'The History of the Synod of Pistoia'. Paper read to the Campion Fellowship Conference. Sydney, 1982.

Pathikulangara, Varghese. 'Liturgy and Theology in Eastern Christian Tradition'. In Thomas Vellilanthadam *et al.*, eds, *Ecclesial Identity of the Thomas Christians*. Kottayam: Oriental Institute Publications, 1985.

——*Church in India*. Kottayam: Denha Services, 1986.

Peri, Vittorio. *Lo scambio fraterno tra le chiese: Componenti storiche della comunione*. Vatican City: Libreria Editrice Vaticana, 1993.

Peters, Edward, ed., *Christian Society and the Crusades 1198–1229: Sources in Translation, including the Capture of Damietta by Oliver Paderborn translated with notes by John J. Gavigan*. Philadelphia: University of Philadelphia Press, 1971.

Phayer, Michael. *The Catholic Church and the Holocaust, 1930–1965*. Bloomfield: Indiana University Press, 2000.

Philippou, Angelos J. ed., *Orthodoxy: Life & Freedom: Essays in Honour of Archbishop Iakovos*. Oxford: Studion, 1973.

Pinell, Jordi, OSB. 'Missale hispano-mozarabicum: Praenotanda'. *Notitiæ: Congregatio pro Cultu Divino*, 267 (October 1988), pp. 670–727.

Piotrowski, Tadeusz. *Poland's Holocaust*. Jefferson, North Carolina: McFarland, 1997.

Podipara, Placid, CMI. 'Malabar Rite'. *NCE*, IX, pp. 92–96.

——*The Rise and Decline of the Indian Church of the Thomas Christians*. Kottayam: Oriental Institute for Religious Studies, 1979.

——*The Latin Rite Christians of Malabar*. Kottayam: Denha Services, 1986.

Poisson, Henri. *L'Abbé Jean-Marie Perrot, fondateur du Bleun-Brug*. Rennes: Plihon, 1955.

Price, R. G. 'Understanding Capitalism Part IV: Capitalism, Culture and Society'. 2005. At: http://rationalrevolution.net/articles/capitalism_culture.htm.

Protopopov, Grigorij. 'La Chiesa greco-cattolica ucraina: origine e caratteristiche'. In A. Judin and G. Protopopov, *Cattolici in Russia e Ucraina*. Rome: La Casa di Matriona, 1992, pp. 141–56.

Quitslund, Sonya A. *Beauduin: A Prophet Vindicated*. New York: Newman, 1973.

Rabban, Raphael. 'Chaldean Rite'. *NCE*, III, pp. 427–30.

Raffard de Brienne, Daniel. *Lex orandi – la nouvelle messe et la foi*. Vouillé: Chiré-en-Montreuil, 1983.

Rao, John C. *Removing the Blindfold: Nineteenth-Century Catholics and the Myth of Modern Freedom*. St Paul, Minnesota: Remnant, 1999.

Rassinier, Paul. *L'Opération vicaire: le rôle de Pie XII devant l'histoire*. Internet: Éditions de l'AAARGH, 2002.

Ratzinger, Josef. *Theologische Prinzipienlehre: Bausteine zur Fundamentaltheologie*. Munich: Wevel, 1982. Tr. Sister Mary Frances McCarthy, SND. *Principles of Catholic Theology: Building Stones for a Fundamental Theology*. San Francisco: Ignatius Press, 1989.

——*The Ratzinger Report: An Exclusive Interview on the State of the Church, with Vittorio Messori*. San Francisco: Ignatius Press, 1985.

——*Der Geist der Liturgie: Eine Einführung*. Freiburg: Herder, 2000. Tr. John Saward. *The Spirit of the Liturgy*. San Francisco: Ignatius Press, 2000.

——*Gott und die Welt: Glauben und Leben in unserer Zeit: Ein Gespräch mit Peter Seewald*. Munich: Deutsche Verlags-Anstalt, 2000. Tr. Henry Taylor. *God in the World: A Conversation with Peter Seewald*. San Francisco: Ignatius Press, 2002.

Ratzinger, Josef and Bertone, Tarcisio. 'The Primacy of the Successor of Peter in the Mystery of the Church: Reflections of the Congregation for the Doctrine of the Faith'. *Osservatore Romano*, 18 November 1998, pp. 5–6.

Recktenwald, Engelbert. *The 30th June in the Light of the Faith: On the Problem of the Episcopal Consecrations performed by Archbishop Marcel Lefebvre*. Canberra: Ecclesia Dei Society, 1989.

Reid, Alcuin, OSB. *The Organic Development of the Liturgy: The Principles of Liturgical Reform and their Relation to the Twentieth Century Liturgical Movement Prior to the Second Vatican Council*. Farnborough: Saint Michael's Abbey Press, 2004.

Reilly, Bernard. 'St Hormisdas'. *CESH*, V, pp. 283–84.

Renié, R. 'Le nouvel Ordo Missae serait-il héretique?' *Chevalier: Supplément à Magistère-Information des Chevaliers de Notre Dame*, Nos 24–25 (1974–1975), pp. 11–15, and No. 26 (1975), pp. 5–10.

Rey, Sir Charles Fernand. 'Abyssinia'. *Encyclopedia Britannica*, I (1961), pp. 65–73.

Robeck, Nesta de. *St Clare of Assisi*. Milwaukee: Bruce Publishing, 1951.

Rock, Augustine, OP. 'Schism'. *CESH*, IX, p. 659.

Rohrenbeck, William. 'Catholic Church in United States: Part II'. *CESH*, II, pp. 360–71.

Roman Theologians Take a Look at the New Order of the Mass (*Breve esame critico del Novus Ordo Missæ*). Tr. Mary Ambrose. Edinburgh: Una Voce in Scotland, n.d.

Rommen, Heinrich A. 'Avignon Papacy'. *CESH*, I, pp. 516–19.

Rondet, Henri, SJ. *Do Dogmas Change?* London: Burns & Oates, 1961.

Rose, Michael S. *Ugly as Sin: Why they Changed our Churches from Sacred Spaces to Meeting Places and How We Can Change Them Back Again*. Manchester, New Hampshire: Sophia Institute Press, 2001.

Runciman, Steven. *A History of the Crusades. Volume I: The First Crusade and the Foundation of the Kingdom of Jerusalem*. Cambridge, UK: Cambridge University Press, 1951.

——*The Eastern Schism*. Oxford: Oxford University Press, 1955.

Salleron, Louis. *La nouvelle messe*. Paris: Nouvelles Éditions Latines, 1970; 2nd ed. 1981.

Sayers, Dorothy L., tr. *The Comedy of Dante Alighieri the Florentine. Cantica 1 Hell* (*L'Inferno*). Harmondsworth: Penguin, 1949.

Scarisbrick, John J. *The Reformation and the English People*. Oxford: Basil Blackwell, 1984.

Schatz, Klaus. *Papal Primacy: From Its Origins to the Present*. Collegeville, Minnesota: Liturgical Press, 1996.

Schlager, Patricius. 'Möhler, Johann Adam'. *CE*, X, pp. 430–32.

Schmemann, Alexander. 'The Idea of Primacy in Orthodox Ecclesiology'. In J. Meyendorff, A. Schmemann, N. Afanassieff and N. Koulomzine. *The Primacy of Peter in the Orthodox Church*. Leighton Buzzard: Faith Press, 1963, pp. 30–56.

——'Theology and Liturgical Tradition'. In Massey Shepherd, ed., *Worship in Scripture and Tradition*. New York: Oxford University Press, 1963, pp. 165–78.

——'Some Reflexions upon a Case Study'. *St. Vladimir's Theological Quarterly*, Vol. 24, No. 4 (1980), pp. 266–69.

Schmidberger, Franz. *The Episcopal Consecrations of 30 June 1988*. London: Society of St Pius X, 1989.

Senyk, Sophia. 'The Ukrainian Church and Latinization'. *Orientalia Christiana Periodica*, 56 (1990), pp. 165–87.

Setton, Kenneth M., ed., *A History of the Crusades*. Philadelphia: University of Pennsylvania Press, 1955.

Sheppard, Lancelot. *The Mass in the West*. London: Burns & Oates, 1962.

——ed., *The New Liturgy*. London: Longman & Todd, 1970.

Simon, Konstantin, SJ. 'Alexis Toth and the Beginnings of the Orthodox Movement among the Ruthenians in America (1891)'. *Orientalia Christiana Periodica*, 54 (1988), pp. 387–428.

Smith, Jeremiah J., OFM.Conv. 'Filioque Controversy'. *CESH*, IV, pp. 291–93.

Snyder, Timothy. *Causes of Ukrainian-Polish Ethnic Cleansing*. Oxford: Oxford University Press, 2003.

Southern, Richard W. *Western Society and the Church in the Middle Ages*. Harmondsworth: Penguin, 1970.

Stasiewski, Bernhard. 'Papal Hopes for Unification: The Independent Eastern Churches'. In Hubert Jedin, ed., *History of the Church, Vol. IX: The Church in the Industrial Age*. New York: Crossroad, 1981, pp. 335–80.

Steiger, Joseph, SJ. 'Causes majeures'. *DTC*, II, cols 2039–40.

Stenhouse, Paul, MSC, 'Why Do We? – Receive Communion in the Hand, Standing?' *Annals Australia* (March 1986), pp. 9–10.

Subtelny, Orest. *Ukraine: A History*. Toronto: University of Toronto Press, 1988.

Sullivan, John F. *The Externals of the Catholic Church: A Handbook of Catholic Usage*. London: Longmans, 1955.

Taft, Robert J., SJ. 'Between East and West: The Eastern Catholic ("Uniate") Churches'. In Sheridan Gilley and Brian Stanley, eds, *The Cambridge History of Christianity: World Christianities c. 1815–c. 1914* (Volume 8). Cambridge, UK: The University Press, 2006, pp. 412–25.

Tautu, Louis Aloys. 'Rumanian Rite'. *NCE*, XII, pp. 718–21.

Tavard, George, AA. 'Tradition'. *CESH*, XI, pp. 37–40.

Thurston, Herbert, SJ. *Lent and Holy Week Chapters on Catholic Observance and Ritual*. London: Longmans, Green, 1914.

Tierney, Brian. 'Conciliarism, History of'. *NCE*, III, pp. 109–11.

Tourn, Giorgio. *I valdesi: La singolare vicenda di un popolo-chiesa*. Turin: Claudiana, 1977, 1993.

Trame, Richard E., SJ. 'Inquisition, The'. *CESH*, V, pp. 475–81.

Turek, Miroslav. 'Easter Controversy'. *CESH*, III, pp. 621–22.

Ullmann, Walter. 'Conciliarism', *CESH*, III, pp. 105–11.

Vacandard, Elphège Florent. 'Carême (Jeûne du)'. *DTC*, II, Part 2, cols 1724–50.

Vagaggini, Cipriano, OSB. 'Il nuovo Ordo Missae e l'ortodossia'. *Rivista del Clero Italiano*, 50 (1969), pp. 688–99.

——(tr. L. J. Doyle and W. A. Jurgens). *Theological Dimensions of the Liturgy*. Collegeville: Minnesota: Liturgical Press, 1976.

Vellilamthadam, Thomas, Koikakudy, Joseph, Koodapuzha, Xavier and Vellanickai, Mathew, eds, *Ecclesial Identity of the Thomas Christians*. Kottayam: Oriental Institute Publications, 1985.

Vidler, Alec R. *The Church in an Age of Revolution: 1789 to the Present Day*. Harmondsworth: Penguin, 1961.

Vogels, Heinz-Jürgen. *Celibacy – Gift or Law? A Critical Investigation*. Tr. G. A. Kon. Tunbridge Wells: Burns & Oates, 1992.

Von Balthasar, Hans Urs. *Dare We Hope 'That All Men Be Saved'? (With a Short Discourse on Hell)*. Fort Collins: Ignatius Press, 1988.

Von Euw, Charles. 'Malabar Rite, Liturgy of'. *NCE*, IX, pp. 96–97.

Von Hildebrand, Dietrich. *Trojan Horse in the City of God*. Chicago: Franciscan Herald Press, 1969.

Voss, Gerhard. 'Johann Adam Möhler and the Development of Dogma'. *Theological Studies*, IV (1943), pp. 428–35.

Wagner, Johannes. 'Le mouvement liturgique en Allemagne'. *La Maison-Dieu*, No. 25. Paris: Cerf, 1951.

Walker, Leslie J. 'Voluntarism'. *CE*, XV, pp. 505–06.

Ward, Paul Edward. 'Ireland, John'. *CESH*, V, pp. 538–41.

Ware, Timothy (Archimandrite Kallistos). *The Orthodox Church*. Harmondsworth: Penguin, 1963.

Wathen, James F., OSJ. *The Great Sacrilege*. Rockford, Illinois: Tan, 1971.

Weber, Eugen. *Peasants into Frenchmen: The Modernization of Rural France 1870–1914*. London: Chatto & Windus, 1979.

Why the Tridentine Mass? (Pamphlets on the Liturgy No. 2) New York: Una Voce, n.d.

Wiltgen, Ralph. *The Rhine Flows into the Tiber: A History of Vatican II*. Chawleigh, Devon: Augustine Publishing Company, 1979.

Wybrew, Hugh. 'The Byzantine Liturgy from the Apostolic Constitutions to the Present Day'. In Cheslyn Jones, Geoffrey Wainwright and Edward Yarnold, SJ, *The Study of Liturgy*. London: SPCK, 1978, pp. 208–19.

——*The Orthodox Liturgy: The Development of the Eucharistic Liturgy in the Byzantine Rite*. Crestwood, New York: St Vladimir's Seminary Press, 1989.

Yagod, Rabbi Leon. 'Tradition'. *Encyclopedia Judaica*, XV, cols 1307–11.

Yannaras, Christos. 'Orthodoxy and the West'. In A. J. Philippou, ed., *Orthodoxy: Life & Freedom*. Oxford: Studion, 1973, pp. 130–47.

Yeo, Margaret. *A Prince of Pastors: St Charles Borromeo*. London: Catholic Book Club, 1938.

Zernov, Nicholas. *Eastern Christendom: A Study of the Origin and Development of the Eastern Orthodox Church*. London: Weidenfeld & Nicholson, 1961.

——'The Challenge of the West'. In A. J. Philippou, ed., *Orthodoxy, Life & Freedom*. Oxford: Studion, 1973, pp. 105–15.

Zugger, Christopher. *The Forgotten: Catholics of the Soviet Empire from Lenin through Stalin*. Syracuse: Syracuse University Press, 2001.

Zuhlsdorf, John. 'Thirtieth Anniversary of Sacrosanctum Concilium, December 4, 1993: Interview of Cardinal Augustin Mayer to Father John T. Zuhlsdorf in Rome'. *Sacred Music*, Vol. 121, No. 2 (Summer 1994), pp. 17–20.

INDEX